MARTHA STEWART LIVING

Annual Recipes

2003

MARTHA STEWART LIVING

Annual Recipes

2003

from the editors of **MARTHA STEWART LIVING**

Originally published in book form by Martha Stewart Living Omnimedia, Inc. in 2002.
Published simultaneously by Oxmoor House, Inc.
These recipes were previously published by Martha Stewart Living Omnimedia, Inc.

Printed in the United States of America.

Library of Congress Catalog Card Number: 2002113946

ISBN 0-8487-2541-7
ISSN 1541-9541

Acknowledgments

It took the collaboration of many individuals to create this book. Thank you to our food department's editorial director, Susan Spungen, and food editor Frances Boswell, for leading a team of wonderful, creative cooks, and to recipes editor Evelyn Battaglia, for her diligence in making sure every recipe is written just so. Thank you to Ellen Morrissey and Christine Moller of the books department, for overseeing the creation of this book from start to finish, and to Debra Puchalla, Christiane Angeli, and Marc Bailes, for their keen attention to detail. Thanks to Jill Groeber, Alanna Jacobs, and James Dunlinson, for developing and directing the new design of this book, and to the production team of Duane Stapp and Matthew Landfield. A very special thank you to the food department, for their tireless development of wonderful recipes, notably Susan Sugarman, Jennifer Aaronson, Tara Bench, Samantha Connell, Yolanda Florez, Amanda Graff, Amy Gropp Forbes, Aida Ibarra, Heidi Johannsen, Anna Kovel, Wendy Kromer, Judith Lockhart, Claire Perez, Gertrude Porter, Mark Ski, and for the support of Caroline Cleary, Elizabeth Durels, and Najean Lee. And thanks to everyone who contributed their time and energy to the creation of this book, among them Roger Astudillo, Brian Baytosh, Douglas Brenner, Dora Braschi Cardinale, Peter Colen, Loren Cunniff, Allison Fishman, Amanda Genge, Angela Gubler, Irie Greco, Eric Hutton, Jennifer Jarett, Johanna Kletter, Kelly Kochendorfer, Katherine Lagomarsino, Vanessa Lenz, Amy Marcus, Stacie McCormick, Jim McKeever, Elizabeth Parson, Melissa Perry, Meg Peterson, Eric A. Pike, George D. Planding, Romy Pokorny, Margaret Roach, Nikki Rooker, Nicole Slavin, Curtis Smith, Lauren Podlach Stanich, Ellen Tarlin, Mory Thomas, Gael Towey, Laura Trace, Joyce Sangirardi, Sara Tucker, Beverly Utt, Alison Vanek, and Bunny Wong, and to everyone at Oxmoor House, Spectragraphics, and R. R. Donnelley and Sons. Finally, thank you to Martha, for inspiring us to develop delicious recipes and menus using the freshest ingredients, all year long.

Contents

WINTER

JANUARY

Starters **15**

Salads **18**

Main Courses **19**

Side Dishes **24**

Desserts **25**

Drinks **32**

FEBRUARY

Starters **35**

Salads **37**

Main Courses **38**

Side Dishes **40**

Desserts **40**

Drinks **50**

MARCH

Starters **53**

Salads **57**

Main Courses **58**

Side Dishes **61**

Desserts **62**

Miscellaneous **64**

SPRING

APRIL

Starters **93**

Salads **97**

Main Courses **98**

Sandwiches **100**

Side Dishes **105**

Desserts **107**

Drinks **114**

Miscellaneous **114**

MAY

Breakfast **117**

Starters **117**

Salads **121**

Main Courses **122**

Side Dishes **126**

Desserts **128**

Drinks **134**

JUNE

Drinks **137**

Starters **137**

Salads **141**

Main Courses **142**

Side Dishes **146**

Muffins **147**

Desserts **149**

SUMMER

JULY

Starters **181**

Salads **184**

Main Courses **189**

Side Dishes **191**

Desserts **193**

Drinks **201**

Miscellaneous **202**

AUGUST

Breakfast **207**

Starters **208**

Salads **209**

Main Courses **211**

Side Dishes **212**

Desserts **213**

Drinks **214**

Miscellaneous **214**

SEPTEMBER

Starters **217**

Salads **218**

Main Courses **218**

Side Dishes **222**

Desserts **222**

Miscellaneous **224**

AUTUMN

OCTOBER

Starters **253**

Salads **254**

Main Courses **255**

Side Dishes **260**

Desserts **263**

Drinks **267**

Miscellaneous **268**

NOVEMBER

Starters **271**

Salads **272**

Main Courses **273**

Side Dishes **275**

Desserts **281**

Miscellaneous **285**

DECEMBER

Starters **289**

Salads **292**

Main Courses **294**

Side Dishes **296**

Desserts **301**

Truffles **310**

Drinks **312**

MENUS **339**

SOURCES **342**

DIRECTORY **344**

INDEX **346**

PHOTOGRAPHY CREDITS **365**

CONVERSION CHART **366**

Introduction

Another fun and exciting year of cooking has passed, and so our second volume of collected recipes is bound for posterity. The members of the MARTHA STEWART LIVING food department work tirelessly each year to create delicious, original, and innovative recipes. I am proud of the work we do, and I take satisfaction, as I hope you do, in having all of the year's recipes in one place.

I am excited to tell you about a few changes in this year's volume. The book is now arranged by seasons, with color photography following each, so the color sections are now longer and even more delicious to look at. To make it easy to find recipes you recall from the magazine, we kept the recipes from each month together within the seasons, but have ordered them in a new way. They are now arranged roughly in the order that they would be eaten: breakfast recipes first, followed by starters, salads, main courses, and desserts. We think you'll find that this makes the book even easier and more enjoyable to use.

Along with a comprehensive index for reference, we have included a new section called "Menus," in which we list the menus from Entertaining stories and What to Have for Dinner columns, making it easy to find out what dishes we served together. We hope you enjoy the changes we've made, and that you find this book easy to use, fun to flip through, and pleasurable to cook from.

SUSAN SPUNGEN
Editorial Director, Food

Winter

TENDER POT ROAST WITH ROASTED POTATOES
RUBY RED GRAPEFRUIT IN MOSCATO
SPICY CLAMS WITH SPAGHETTI
HEARTY CHILI FOR A CROWD

January

STARTERS

15 baked oysters with spinach and champagne beurre blanc

15 cream of belgian endive soup

16 eggplant kuku

16 fresh-herb kuku

17 moules poulette (broiled mussels with mushrooms, lemon, and cream)

17 pommes frites

18 shrimp summer rolls

SALADS

18 cold sesame noodle salad

19 green and white salad

19 greens with orange vinaigrette and toasted sesame seeds

MAIN COURSES

19 braised lamb stew (fresh-herb khoresh)

20 chicken and dumplings

20 chicken cacciatore

21 chicken tortilla soup

22 chili con carne

23 cock-a-leekie

23 grilled soy-lime chicken breasts

23 striped sea bass with blood oranges and olives

24 winter vegetable chicken stew

SIDE DISHES

24 baked potato slices

24 baked saffron rice

25 brown-sugar cornbread

DESSERTS

25 belgian chocolate birthday cake

27 cereal-cube castle

27 chocolate mousse with banana purée and grated coconut

27 chocolate whole-wheat biscuit cake

28 inside-out german chocolate torte

28 persian almond brittle

29 raspberry-filled layer cake

30 vanilla crêpes

31 white sheet cake

DRINKS

32 spiced lemonade

baked oysters with spinach and champagne beurre blanc

MAKES 2 DOZEN

2 to 3 cups rock or coarse salt, for baking sheet

2 dozen oysters, shucked, liquor and bottom shells reserved separately

1 cup heavy cream

1 cup dry Champagne or sparkling wine

3 large shallots, minced (about ½ cup)

¼ cup white-wine vinegar

1¼ cups (2½ sticks) chilled unsalted butter, cut into pieces

Coarse salt and freshly ground white pepper

1 pound fresh spinach, stems removed, or 2 10-ounce packages frozen, thawed

Snipped fresh chives, for garnish

1 Pour salt onto a rimmed baking sheet. Nestle oyster shells in the salt; set aside.

2 Bring cream to a simmer in a small saucepan; cook until reduced by half. Remove from heat.

3 Meanwhile, bring Champagne, shallots, and vinegar to a simmer in another small saucepan. Cook until liquid is almost evaporated. Add reduced cream, and cook 1 minute.

4 Remove pan from heat, and whisk in the butter, one piece at a time, adding each just before the previous one has melted completely. (The sauce should not get hot enough to liquefy; it should be the consistency of thin hollandaise.) Stir in ½ cup oyster liquor, and season with salt and white pepper. Keep warm.

5 If using fresh spinach, rinse it thoroughly several times, and place in a large saucepan with just the water that clings to the leaves. Cover the pan, and cook spinach until bright green and just tender, about 2 minutes. Drain well, and roughly chop. (Squeeze excess moisture from thawed frozen spinach; do not cook.)

6 Heat broiler with rack 5 inches from heat. Divide spinach equally among the shells. Top with a shucked oyster. Spoon enough sauce to cover each oyster, about 1 tablespoon per shell. Broil until sauce bubbles and edges of oysters start to curl, about 1 minute. Remove from oven. Garnish with chives, and serve.

from Celebrating Wedding Anniversaries

cream of belgian endive soup

SERVES 8 TO 10 | PHOTO ON PAGE 70

2 leeks, white and light-green parts only

8 heads Belgian endive, plus more leaves for garnish

2 Russet potatoes

3 tablespoons unsalted butter

½ cup dry white wine

5 cups homemade or low-sodium canned chicken or vegetable stock

1 cup heavy cream

1½ teaspoons coarse salt

¼ teaspoon freshly ground white pepper

Pinch of freshly grated nutmeg

1 Cut leeks in half lengthwise, and thinly slice crosswise. Place in a bowl with cold water to remove grit; drain leeks, and set aside.

2 Cut each head of endive in half lengthwise, and cut out and discard the cores. Thinly slice crosswise; set aside.

3 Peel potatoes, and cut into ½-inch pieces. Set aside in a bowl of cold water to prevent discoloration.

4 Heat butter in a saucepan over medium heat. Add leeks; cook until they start to soften, about 3 minutes. Drain potatoes well; add to pot along with sliced endive. Cook until vegetables begin to soften, about 10 minutes; do not let brown.

5 Add wine and stock, and bring to a gentle simmer. Cook until vegetables are very tender, about 1 hour. Cool slightly.

6 Working in batches, purée soup in a blender (be careful not to fill more than halfway as hot liquid expands when blended), or pass it through a food mill. Transfer to a clean saucepan; stir in cream. Bring to a simmer; remove from heat. Add salt, pepper, and nutmeg. Garnish with endive.

from A Winter Dinner Party With Friends

eggplant kuku

MAKES ONE 9-INCH ROUND | **PHOTO ON PAGE 69**

Kuku is a Persian egg dish similar to a frittata.

- 2 large or 9 Japanese eggplants
  (about 3 pounds total)
- 1½ teaspoons coarse salt, plus more for sprinkling
- 4 tablespoons extra-virgin olive oil, plus more for brushing
- 2 large onions, thinly sliced
- 6 garlic cloves, thinly sliced
- 5 large eggs
- ¼ cup chopped fresh flat-leaf parsley, plus sprigs for garnish
- ¼ teaspoon ground saffron, dissolved in 1 tablespoon hot water
  Juice of 1 lime (about 2 tablespoons)
- 1 teaspoon baking powder
- 2 tablespoons all-purpose flour
- ¼ teaspoon freshly ground pepper

1 Peel eggplants, reserving four long strips of peel to garnish top of kuku; cut flesh lengthwise into 1-inch-thick slices. Place slices on baking sheets lined with paper towels, and sprinkle generously with salt. Turn slices, and sprinkle other side with salt. Let sit 20 minutes. Rinse with cold water, and pat dry with paper towels.

2 Heat broiler. Place eggplant slices on baking sheets; brush both sides with olive oil. Broil about 6 inches from heat until golden brown on both sides, 6 to 8 minutes per side. Transfer to a large bowl, and mash with a fork; set aside.

3 Heat 2 tablespoons oil in a large skillet over medium heat. Add the onions and garlic; cook, stirring occasionally, until onions are tender and golden brown, 10 to 12 minutes. Add to bowl with mashed eggplant.

4 Reduce oven heat to 350°F. In a medium bowl, combine eggs, parsley, saffron water, lime juice, baking powder, flour, salt, and pepper. Whisk until thoroughly combined. Add to eggplant mixture, and mix thoroughly with a fork.

5 Coat bottom and sides of a 9-inch springform pan with 1 tablespoon oil. Place pan on a baking sheet, and place in the oven 5 minutes to heat the oil. Pour eggplant mixture into pan, and place the reserved eggplant peel across the top. Bake 30 minutes. Remove from oven, and drizzle remaining tablespoon oil over the top. Return to oven, and continue baking until golden on top, about 20 minutes more.

6 Transfer pan to a wire rack to cool slightly before unmolding. Arrange reserved eggplant strips in an "x" on top, and place a few sprigs of parsley in the center. Cut in wedges; serve warm or at room temperature.

from A Winter Dinner Party With Friends

fresh-herb kuku

MAKES ONE 9-INCH SQUARE | **PHOTO ON PAGE 69**

- 10 large eggs
- 2 tablespoons all-purpose flour
- 2 teaspoons baking powder
- 2 teaspoons coarse salt
- 1½ teaspoons freshly ground pepper
- 1 teaspoon ground cinnamon
- 1 teaspoon ground cumin
- ½ teaspoon ground cardamom
- 4 garlic cloves, minced
- 2 cups finely chopped chives or scallions
- 2 cups finely chopped fresh flat-leaf parsley
- 2 cups finely chopped fresh cilantro
- 2 cups chopped fresh dill
- 1 tablespoon dried fenugreek (optional)
- 6 tablespoons extra-virgin olive oil
  Labne or other thick plain yogurt, for serving (optional)

1 Preheat oven to 350°F. Combine eggs, flour, baking powder, salt, pepper, cinnamon, cumin, and cardamom in a medium bowl. Whisk until combined. Add garlic, chives, parsley, cilantro, dill, fenugreek if desired, and 2 tablespoons olive oil. Whisk thoroughly to combine.

2 Coat bottom and sides of a 9-inch square nonstick metal baking pan with 2 tablespoons oil. Place in the oven 5 minutes to heat the oil. Pour egg mixture into pan; bake 30 minutes. Remove from oven, and pour remaining 2 tablespoons oil over the top. Return to oven, and continue baking until golden on top, about 10 minutes more.

3 Transfer pan to a wire rack to cool slightly before unmolding. Invert onto a serving platter, and cut into pieces. Serve hot or at room temperature with yogurt, if desired.

from A Winter Dinner Party With Friends

moules poulette (broiled mussels with mushrooms, lemon, and cream)

MAKES ABOUT 3 DOZEN | PHOTOS ON PAGES 68-69

- 2 cups dry white wine
- 2 pounds large mussels, scrubbed and debearded
- 2 tablespoons unsalted butter, softened
- 1 tablespoon all-purpose flour
- 1 cup thinly sliced mushrooms, such as shiitake or oyster (3 ounces)
- ½ cup heavy cream
- Juice of 1 lemon (about 2 tablespoons)
- 1 teaspoon coarse salt
- ¼ teaspoon freshly ground pepper
- ½ cup freshly grated Gruyère cheese (1 ounce)

1 Bring wine to a simmer in a large skillet over high heat. Add mussels, and cook, stirring frequently, until they have opened, up to about 5 minutes. Transfer mussels as they open to a bowl to cool. Discard any mussels that did not open or that have broken shells. Strain cooking liquid through a fine sieve into a glass measuring cup, reserving 1 cup liquid and discarding any grit.

2 Using a paring knife, open each mussel, discarding the empty half shell. Loosen each mussel from shell, and arrange mussels in shells on an ovenproof platter or rimmed baking sheet. Cover with plastic wrap; refrigerate while making sauce.

3 In a small dish, mash 1 tablespoon butter with the flour until smooth; set aside. Melt remaining tablespoon butter in a small saucepan over medium heat. Add mushrooms, and cook until tender, about 4 minutes. Add reserved cup mussel liquid, and bring to a boil. Whisk in the butter-and-flour mixture until combined. Whisk in the cream, lemon juice, salt, and pepper. Reduce heat; simmer until liquid is reduced by two-thirds and thickened. Remove from heat, and keep warm.

4 Heat broiler with rack 3 to 4 inches from heat. Remove mussels from refrigerator, and spoon sauce over each one until well coated. Sprinkle with grated cheese, and broil until golden brown, 3 to 4 minutes. Serve immediately.

from A Winter Dinner Party With Friends

pommes frites

SERVES 8 TO 10 | PHOTO ON PAGE 69

A deep-fryer works best, but you can also use a saucepan. It should hold at least five quarts, so the oil won't bubble over.

- 8 russet potatoes
- Vegetable oil, for frying
- Coarse salt
- Homemade Mayonnaise (recipe follows)

1 Peel potatoes, if desired; cut into ½-inch-thick matchsticks. Place in a bowl of cold water; let soak 10 minutes. Remove potatoes from water; dry well with paper towels. In a large saucepan, heat oil to 325°F on a deep-fry thermometer.

2 Working in batches, carefully lower potatoes into oil; blanch 2 minutes. Transfer to paper-towel–lined baking sheets to drain; let cool completely.

3 Raise oil temperature to 375°F. Preheat oven to 250°F. Lower potatoes into oil in batches; fry until golden, about 3 minutes. Drain well on paper towels; place on a rimmed baking sheet. Sprinkle with salt; keep warm in oven while frying remaining potatoes. Serve immediately with mayonnaise.

from A Winter Dinner Party With Friends

homemade mayonnaise

MAKES ABOUT 1 CUP

- ½ cup light olive oil
- ½ cup canola oil
- 1 large egg
- Pinch of dry mustard
- ¼ teaspoon coarse salt
- 1 tablespoon freshly squeezed lemon juice

1 Combine olive oil and canola oil in a glass measuring cup. Place egg, mustard, and salt in the bowl of a food processor fitted with the plastic blade. Blend until mixture is foamy and pale, about 1½ minutes.

2 With the machine running, add the oil, drop by drop, through the feed tube, until the mixture starts to thicken (about ¼ cup oil); do not stop the machine at this point or the mayonnaise may not come together. Add the remaining oil in a slow, steady stream. When all the oil has been incorporated, slowly add the lemon juice. The mayonnaise can be kept, refrigerated in an airtight container, up to 3 days.

NOTE: Raw eggs should not be used in food prepared for pregnant women, babies, young children, the elderly, or anyone whose health is compromised.

shrimp summer rolls

MAKES 8

1 pound (about 30) small shrimp, peeled and deveined

8 nine-inch round rice papers

8 large red-leaf lettuce leaves, cut in half lengthwise

1 carrot, cut into matchsticks

1 small daikon radish, peeled and cut into matchsticks

1 red bell pepper, seeds and ribs removed,
   cut into matchsticks

1 bunch fresh chives, ends trimmed

¼ cup tightly packed fresh mint leaves

   Soy Dipping Sauce (optional; recipe follows)

1 Bring a large pot of water to a boil; reduce to a simmer. Add shrimp; poach until pink and opaque, about 2 minutes. Transfer to a plate, and slice in half lengthwise. Set aside.

2 Fill a bowl large enough to hold the rice paper with hot water. Dampen a clean kitchen towel with water; spread it out on a clean surface. Dip one sheet of rice paper in the hot water 5 seconds; transfer to dampened towel, and smooth out (wrapper will still feel hard but will soften as it sits).

3 Place four shrimp halves cut side up in a row 2 inches from bottom edge of wrapper. Place two pieces of lettuce over shrimp. Top with more shrimp halves and some carrot, daikon, pepper, chives, and mint.

4 Fold bottom edge of rice paper over filling. Roll tightly into a cylinder so shrimp halves are enclosed (they will show through rice paper).

5 Place finished roll on a plate; cover with a damp paper towel. Continue filling and rolling until all ingredients are used. Serve with dipping sauce, if desired.

from Celebrating Wedding Anniversaries

soy dipping sauce

MAKES ABOUT 1 CUP

½ cup soy sauce

½ cup rice vinegar

2 tablespoons thinly sliced scallions

Combine ingredients in a small dish, and serve.

SALADS

cold sesame noodle salad

SERVES 4

Udon is a thick Japanese noodle similar in size to linguine; it can be found in Asian markets and some supermarkets. The salad can also be garnished with enoki mushrooms and fresh bean sprouts.

2 large garlic cloves, minced

1 tablespoon grated fresh ginger

2 tablespoons dark sesame oil

¼ cup soy sauce

¼ cup rice vinegar

½ cup smooth peanut butter

1 tablespoon Asian chili paste (optional)

2 scallions, thinly sliced, plus more for garnish

2 tablespoons toasted sesame seeds, plus more for garnish

2 tablespoons finely chopped fresh cilantro,
   plus more for garnish

1 teaspoon coarse salt

1 12-ounce package udon noodles or linguine

1 Combine garlic, ginger, sesame oil, soy sauce, vinegar, peanut butter, chili paste if desired, scallions, sesame seeds, cilantro, and salt in a medium bowl. Whisk until thoroughly combined; set aside.

2 Bring a large pot of water to a boil. Add the noodles, and cook until al dente according to package instructions, about 8 minutes. Drain in a colander, and rinse with cold water to stop the cooking.

3 Transfer noodles to a serving bowl, pour dressing over, and toss to coat well. Sprinkle with remaining scallions, sesame seeds, and cilantro. Serve.

from Celebrating Wedding Anniversaries

green and white salad

SERVES 4

2 teaspoons white-wine vinegar

½ teaspoon Dijon mustard

¼ cup extra-virgin olive oil

Coarse salt and freshly ground pepper

1 head endive, trimmed and sliced crosswise ½ inch thick

6 ounces frisée, torn into bite-size pieces

1 stalk celery, sliced ⅛ inch thick

1 tablespoon chopped fresh tarragon

½ bunch fresh chives, cut into 1-inch lengths (about ¼ cup)

1 Make vinaigrette: In a small bowl, whisk together the vinegar and mustard. Gradually whisk in olive oil in a slow, steady stream until emulsified. Season with salt and pepper.

2 In a serving bowl, combine the endive, frisée, celery, tarragon, and chives. Drizzle the dressing over the salad; toss well to combine. Serve.

from What to Have for Dinner

greens with orange vinaigrette and toasted sesame seeds

SERVES 12 | PHOTO ON PAGE 76

Add a little avocado to this salad for a delicious variation. Toasting whole cumin seeds before grinding them is the best way to bring out their distinctive flavor.

¼ cup sesame seeds

1 teaspoon cumin seeds

⅔ cup freshly squeezed orange juice

3 tablespoons red-wine vinegar

1 teaspoon coarse salt

1 teaspoon sugar

½ cup extra-virgin olive oil

Freshly ground pepper

1½ to 2 pounds crisp lettuces (such as romaine, radicchio, and frisée), cleaned and finely sliced or torn into bite-size pieces (20 to 24 cups)

1 In a small dry skillet over medium heat, toast the sesame seeds, shaking the skillet until the seeds are fragrant, 2 to 3 minutes; set aside to cool. Repeat to toast the cumin seeds, and then grind in a clean spice or coffee grinder or with a mortar and pestle until fine.

2 Make vinaigrette: In a medium bowl, whisk together the orange juice, vinegar, salt, and sugar. Gradually whisk in olive oil in a slow, steady stream until emulsified. Whisk in the ground cumin, and season with pepper to taste.

3 Drizzle salad with dressing, and sprinkle with sesame seeds.

from Chili for a Crowd

MAIN COURSES

braised lamb stew (fresh-herb khoresh)

SERVES 8 TO 10 | PHOTO ON PAGE 70

¼ cup plus 2 tablespoons extra-virgin olive oil

4 pounds boneless leg of lamb, cut into 1-inch cubes

4 onions, thinly sliced (about 1½ pounds)

4 garlic cloves, thinly sliced

1 tablespoon coarse salt

2 teaspoons freshly ground pepper

2 teaspoons ground turmeric

½ teaspoon ground saffron, dissolved in 1 tablespoon hot water

6 whole dried Persian limes, pierced with a knife (optional)

1 cup dried kidney beans

4 cups water

6 cups finely chopped fresh flat-leaf parsley

2 cups finely chopped garlic chives or scallions

2 cups finely chopped fresh coriander

1 teaspoon ground fenugreek (optional)

4 tablespoons dried Persian lime powder or ½ cup freshly squeezed lime juice

1 Heat ¼ cup olive oil in a medium stockpot over medium heat. Add lamb, onions, and garlic. Cook, stirring occasionally, until meat is no longer pink and onions are softened, about 20 minutes. Add salt, pepper, turmeric, saffron water, Persian limes if desired, and kidney beans; cook a few minutes more. Add the water; bring to a boil, cover, and simmer over low heat, stirring occasionally.

2 Meanwhile, heat a large nonstick skillet over medium-low heat. Add parsley, garlic chives, coriander, and fenugreek if desired. Cook, stirring frequently, until herbs are wilted, about 10 minutes. Add remaining 2 tablespoons oil, and cook, stirring constantly, until herbs are very fragrant, about 10 minutes more.

3 Add herb mixture and lime powder or juice to lamb mixture. Cover pot; continue simmering until meat and beans

are tender, about 2½ hours. Remove lid, and continue cooking until beans are very tender and stew has thickened slightly. Adjust seasoning as desired, and serve hot.

from A Winter Dinner Party With Friends

chicken and dumplings

SERVES 6

If you want to make the dish in advance, prepare chicken and sauce through step two. Let cool completely, then cover and refrigerate overnight. Rewarm gently before proceeding.

FOR THE CHICKEN:

- 1 pound boneless and skinless chicken thighs (5 to 6)
- 1 pound boneless and skinless chicken breast halves (about 3)

  Fine sea salt or coarse salt

  Freshly ground pepper
- 1 tablespoon unsalted butter
- 1 large onion, finely chopped
- 1 14½-ounce can low-sodium chicken broth, skimmed of fat
- 1½ teaspoons finely chopped fresh thyme
- 2 tablespoons cornstarch
- 2 tablespoons all-purpose flour
- 2 cups low-fat (1 percent) milk
- 3 carrots, sliced on the diagonal ¼ inch thick
- ½ pound green beans, trimmed and cut into 1-inch pieces

FOR THE DUMPLINGS:

- 1 cup all-purpose flour
- ½ cup yellow cornmeal
- 2 teaspoons baking powder
- ¼ teaspoon fine sea salt
- 2 tablespoons chilled unsalted butter, cut into small pieces
- ⅔ cup low-fat (1 percent) milk

1 Sprinkle chicken with salt and pepper. Heat a 6-quart skillet or Dutch oven over medium heat; add thighs. Cook, turning once, until nicely browned on both sides and cooked through, 8 to 10 minutes. Transfer to a plate. Repeat with breasts; cut breasts crosswise into thirds.

2 Melt butter in skillet, and add onion; cover, and cook, stirring occasionally, until softened, about 6 minutes. Stir in broth and thyme; bring to a boil. Combine cornstarch and flour in a bowl; gradually whisk in milk, and then whisk milk mixture into broth. Boil, whisking constantly, until thickened, about 5 minutes. Return chicken to skillet; remove from heat.

3 Bring a medium saucepan of water to a boil; add salt. Add carrots and green beans; cook until crisp-tender, about 5 minutes. Drain in a colander, then rinse with cold water to stop cooking. Stir into chicken mixture.

4 Prepare dumplings: In a medium bowl, whisk together flour, cornmeal, baking powder, and salt. Add butter; using your fingers, combine until mixture is the texture of coarse meal. Pour in milk; stir with a fork until dough comes together. Return chicken mixture to a simmer, and drop dough by the tablespoon on stew. Cover; cook 15 minutes without lifting lid. (The dumplings will puff up.) Serve hot.

PER SERVING: 442 CALORIES, 12 G FAT, 126 MG CHOLESTEROL, 42 G CARBOHYDRATE, 810 MG SODIUM, 40 G PROTEIN, 4 G FIBER

from Fit to Eat: Chicken Soups and Stews

chicken cacciatore

SERVES 6

This stew can be made up to two days ahead and stored in the refrigerator. Gently reheat before serving.

- 1½ chickens (about 3 pounds each), cut into 12 pieces
- 1 tablespoon extra-virgin olive oil
- 1½ pounds cremini or white mushrooms, quartered
- 2 large onions, sliced ¼ inch thick
- 2 large bell peppers (preferably 1 red and 1 green), seeds and ribs removed, sliced ¼ inch thick
- 4 garlic cloves, smashed
- ½ cup dry red wine
- 1 28-ounce can crushed Italian tomatoes
- 1 14½-ounce can low-sodium chicken broth, skimmed of fat

  Coarse salt
- ¾ pound linguine
- ¼ cup chopped fresh basil or flat-leaf parsley, for garnish (optional)

1 Reserve chicken wings for another use. Remove skin from chicken; halve breasts crosswise (you will have six pieces of dark meat and six pieces of light meat).

2 Heat a deep 10-inch skillet or 6-quart Dutch oven over medium heat. Add half the chicken pieces; cook until browned on both sides, about 8 minutes, turning once. Transfer to a plate. Repeat with remaining chicken.

3 In same skillet, heat ½ tablespoon olive oil. Add mushrooms; cook on medium-high, stirring occasionally, until softened and browned, about 7 minutes. Transfer to a bowl.

4 Add remaining ½ tablespoon oil to skillet; add onions, peppers, and garlic; cook on medium-high, stirring occasionally, until onions are golden, about 4 minutes. Pour in wine; bring to a boil. Cook until almost evaporated, about 3 minutes. Add tomatoes and broth; return chicken to pan. Simmer over low heat, turning occasionally, until meat is tender and sauce is thickened, about 1 hour. Stir in mushrooms. Bring a large pot of water to a boil; add salt. Cook linguine until al dente according to package directions. Drain; serve topped with chicken and sauce. Garnish with basil or parsley, if desired.

PER SERVING: 599 CALORIES, 9 G FAT, 151 MG CHOLESTEROL, 61 G CARBOHYDRATE, 573 MG SODIUM, 59 G PROTEIN, 6 G FIBER

from Fit to Eat: Chicken Soups and Stews

chicken tortilla soup

SERVES 6 | PHOTO ON PAGE 70

Steps one and two can be completed one day ahead; refrigerate until ready to serve.

1¼ **pounds boneless and skinless chicken breast halves (3 to 4 pieces)**

2 **cups fresh cilantro plus 2 tablespoons finely chopped leaves**

2 **14½-ounce cans low-sodium chicken broth, skimmed of fat**

3 **cups water**

1½ **tablespoons corn oil**

4 **plum tomatoes**

2 **small onions, halved lengthwise (unpeeled)**

4 **garlic cloves (unpeeled)**

½ **teaspoon coarse salt**

1¼ **cups fresh or frozen corn kernels**

¾ **cup cooked or canned chickpeas, drained and rinsed**

5 **corn tortillas (5½-inch diameter), cut into ¼-inch-wide strips**

½ **small avocado**

2 **tablespoons freshly squeezed lime juice**

1 **tablespoon minced and seeded jalapeño**

3 **tablespoons reduced-fat sour cream**

1 In a large saucepan, combine chicken, cilantro sprigs, broth, and the water. Bring to a boil; reduce heat, and simmer gently until chicken is just cooked through, about 10 minutes. Transfer chicken to a plate; let cool. Cut into ½-inch dice. Strain broth through a fine sieve lined with several layers of cheesecloth into a medium bowl. Wipe out saucepan.

2 Heat ½ tablespoon oil in a cast-iron skillet over medium-high heat. Add three tomatoes, onions, and garlic; cover and cook, turning occasionally, until skins are nicely charred, about 10 minutes. Remove from heat. When vegetables are cool enough to handle, remove skins, stems, and cores; discard. Place tomatoes, onions, and garlic in a blender with ½ cup reserved broth; blend until smooth. Scrape mixture into saucepan; cook, stirring frequently, over medium heat until thickened and darker, about 6 minutes. Stir in remaining broth, ¼ teaspoon salt, corn, chickpeas, and chicken. Remove from heat.

3 Preheat oven to 375°F. Place tortilla strips on a rimmed baking sheet; toss with remaining tablespoon oil and ⅛ teaspoon salt. Bake until golden and crisp, about 12 minutes, turning once or twice. Let cool.

4 Finely dice avocado; gently rinse with cold water. Place in a bowl. Finely dice remaining tomato, and add to avocado with lime juice, jalapeño, chopped cilantro, and remaining ⅛ teaspoon salt. Rewarm soup; ladle into bowls. Garnish with avocado mixture, sour cream, and tortilla strips.

PER SERVING: 307 CALORIES, 9 G FAT, 54 MG CHOLESTEROL, 32 G CARBOHYDRATE, 724 MG SODIUM, 27 G PROTEIN, 5 G FIBER

from Fit to Eat: Chicken Soups and Stews

chili con carne

SERVES 12 | **PHOTO ON PAGE 76**

This recipe uses two varieties of whole dried peppers: the citrusy ancho and the sweet, dusky mulato. Both stand safely on the cool side of medium-hot. Control the heat by increasing or decreasing the number of chiles; be sure to have good ventilation over the stove when pan-roasting them. If you have two large cast-iron skillets, save some time by using both at once. If you like, serve this deep, dark chili with traditional garnishes, such as shredded extra-sharp cheddar and Monterey Jack cheeses, sour cream, and chopped cilantro, in addition to the guacamole.

- 1 **pound dried pinto beans, soaked according to package directions**
- ¼ **cup plus 3 tablespoons corn oil**
- 3½ **pounds plum tomatoes (about 18)**
- 2½ **pounds yellow onions (about 7), stem ends trimmed, quartered lengthwise (unpeeled)**
- 10 **garlic cloves (unpeeled)**
- 4 **mulato chiles**
- 3 **ancho chiles**
- 1 **14½-ounce can low-sodium beef broth**
- 1 **cup water**
- 5 **pounds ground round or ground chuck**
- 1 **tablespoon coarse salt**
- 2 **ounces Mexican or semisweet chocolate, chopped**
- ½ **teaspoon freshly ground pepper**
  Chunky Guacamole (recipe follows)

1 Drain and rinse the soaked beans, and place in a large saucepan with water to cover by 2 inches. Bring to a boil, cover, and reduce heat. Simmer gently until beans are tender, about 1½ hours. (You can prepare beans up to 2 days ahead; let cool, cover, and refrigerate in cooking liquid.)

2 Heat 2 tablespoons oil in a 12-inch cast-iron skillet over medium heat; add tomatoes, and cook, turning occasionally, until skins begin to char, about 5 minutes. Cover pan, reduce heat to medium-low, and continue to cook, turning, until tomatoes have softened, 7 to 8 minutes more. Transfer to a large bowl. When cool enough to handle, peel and core tomatoes. Place tomato flesh in a clean bowl; set aside.

3 While tomatoes cool, place two-thirds onions in same skillet with 2 tablespoons oil. Cover, and cook over medium heat, turning occasionally, until nicely charred and softened, 12 to 15 minutes. Transfer to a bowl to cool. Repeat with garlic cloves, remaining onion, and another tablespoon oil. When cool enough to handle, peel garlic and onion, cutting off and discarding roots and peels and adding flesh to bowl with

tomato. Working in batches, transfer vegetables and any accumulated juices to the jar of a blender, and process until nearly smooth. Set aside in a large bowl.

4 Tear chiles in half, discarding stems and seeds. In the same skillet over medium heat, toast chiles in remaining 2 tablespoons oil, turning with tongs, until smoky, about 3 minutes. Transfer to the blender. Bring broth and water to a boil in a small saucepan; pour over chiles, and let stand until chiles are pliable, about 5 minutes. Purée until smooth; stir into tomato mixture.

5 In a 7-quart Dutch oven over medium heat, cook a third of the meat, breaking it up with a spoon and stirring occasionally until nicely browned, about 8 minutes. While first third of meat is cooking, brown another third in the skillet; add to the first in the Dutch oven. Stir tomato mixture into meat in Dutch oven. Brown remaining beef in same skillet; add to Dutch oven. Drain cooked beans; add them to Dutch oven along with salt.

6 Bring chili to a boil; reduce heat, cover, and simmer gently, stirring occasionally, until meat is tender and sauce is thick, about 1½ hours. Remove from heat; stir in chocolate, and season with pepper. Serve with guacamole.

from Chili for a Crowd

chunky guacamole

MAKES 6 CUPS

Serve this lively dip with tortilla chips or on top of chili. If you want to make it a day ahead, be sure to press plastic wrap directly on the surface of the guacamole.

- 6 **ripe Hass avocados**
- ¼ **cup freshly squeezed lime juice**
- ¼ **cup freshly squeezed lemon juice**
- 4 **plum tomatoes, finely chopped**
- 1 **medium onion, finely chopped**
- 1 **jalapeño chile, minced (with seeds, if desired)**
- 3 **garlic cloves, minced**
- 1¼ **teaspoons coarse salt**
- ½ **teaspoon freshly ground pepper, or to taste**

Halve avocados, and remove pits. Score flesh into cubes with a small sharp knife, and scrape into a bowl. Stir in lime juice, lemon juice, tomatoes, onion, chile, and garlic. Add salt and pepper, and serve.

cock-a-leekie

SERVES 6

If you make this soup up to one day ahead, you may need to add a bit of water or stock when reheating.

- 1¼ pounds skinless chicken thighs (on the bone; 4 pieces)
- 1¼ pounds skinless chicken breast halves (on the bone; 3 pieces)
- 4 14½-ounce cans low-sodium chicken broth, skimmed of fat
- 2 cups dry white wine or water
- 2 large stalks celery, halved crosswise
- 1 large carrot
- 2 large garlic cloves
- 6 leeks, white and light-green parts, halved lengthwise and thinly sliced crosswise
- 12 pitted prunes, quartered (⅔ cup packed)
- ½ cup barley
- ½ cup finely chopped fresh flat-leaf parsley

1   Heat a 6-quart skillet or Dutch oven on medium-high. Add thighs; cook until browned on both sides, turning once, about 8 minutes. Transfer to a bowl. Repeat with breasts.

2   In same skillet, add broth, wine, celery, carrot, and garlic. Bring to a boil; using a wooden spoon, scrape any browned bits from bottom. Return chicken to skillet, reduce heat, and simmer, skimming surface as needed, 1 hour. Transfer chicken to a plate; let cool. Transfer vegetables to another plate; set aside.

3   Add leeks, prunes, and barley to broth in skillet. Bring to a boil; reduce heat, and simmer until thick, about 40 minutes. Once chicken has cooled, shred meat. Finely chop carrot and celery. Stir chicken, vegetables, and parsley into soup; heat through, and serve.

PER SERVING: 416 CALORIES, 5 G FAT, 132 MG CHOLESTEROL, 32 G CARBOHYDRATE, 754 MG SODIUM, 43 G PROTEIN, 5 G FIBER

from Fit to Eat: Chicken Soups and Stews

grilled soy-lime chicken breasts

SERVES 4

- ¼ cup freshly squeezed lime juice (about 2 limes)
- ¼ cup soy sauce
- ¼ cup extra-virgin olive oil
- 4 boneless and skinless chicken breasts
- 1 head Boston lettuce, leaves separated
- 1 bunch fresh mint
- 1 bunch fresh cilantro

1   Whisk together lime juice, soy sauce, and oil in a small bowl. Place chicken breasts on a work surface between two layers of waxed paper or plastic wrap. Using the smooth side of a meat mallet, pound the chicken breasts until all the pieces are an even ½-inch thickness.

2   Place chicken breasts in a resealable plastic bag or glass dish. Pour marinade into bag or over chicken in dish. Refrigerate, covered, at least 3 hours or overnight.

3   Heat a grill or grill pan. Remove chicken from marinade, letting excess drip off. Grill chicken until browned and cooked through, about 3 minutes per side. Shred or slice chicken, and serve with lettuce leaves and herbs on the side.

from Celebrating Wedding Anniversaries

striped sea bass with blood oranges and olives

SERVES 4 | **PHOTO ON PAGE 71**

- 6 blood or navel oranges
- 4 fillets striped sea bass (about 6 ounces each)
  Coarse salt and freshly ground pepper
- 1 tablespoon canola oil
- 6 tablespoons chilled unsalted butter
- 2 shallots, cut into ¼-inch pieces
- 1 ounce small pitted green olives, cut into quarters

1   Squeeze three to four oranges to make 1 cup juice; set aside. Using a sharp paring knife, remove the peel and pith of the remaining oranges, following the shape of the fruit. Cut between membranes to remove whole segments, and set aside in a small bowl.

2   Score skin side of fish, and sprinkle with salt and pepper. Heat oil in a medium skillet over medium-high heat. Add fish, skin side up; cook until golden brown, about 3 minutes. Turn fish; reduce heat to medium, and continue to cook until fish is

opaque and completely cooked through, about 3 minutes. Transfer fish to a serving dish; keep warm.

3 While fish is cooking, melt 1 tablespoon butter in a small saucepan over medium heat. Add shallots, and cook, stirring frequently, until golden, about 5 minutes. Add reserved orange juice, and bring to a simmer. Cook until juice has reduced by half, about 5 minutes. Remove from heat, and whisk in the remaining 5 tablespoons butter, 1 tablespoon at a time. Stir in reserved orange segments and the olives. Pour sauce over the fish, and serve immediately.

from What to Have for Dinner

winter vegetable chicken stew

SERVES 6

12 ounces boneless and skinless chicken thighs (about 4 pieces)

 1 pound boneless and skinless chicken breast halves (about 3 pieces)

 ½ teaspoon coarse salt

 ⅛ teaspoon freshly ground pepper

 4 carrots, cut into ¾-inch pieces

 3 large stalks celery, cut into ¾-inch pieces

 2 medium parsnips (6 ounces), peeled, cut into ¾-inch pieces

 4 small onions, quartered lengthwise with roots intact

 3 cups water

 1 14½-ounce can low-sodium chicken broth, skimmed of fat

 1 tablespoon fresh rosemary leaves or 1 teaspoon dried

 ½ pound wide egg noodles

 ¼ cup finely chopped fresh flat-leaf parsley

 1 tablespoon unsalted butter

 4 garlic cloves, thinly sliced

 1 bunch (1½ pounds) Swiss chard, leaves and stems coarsely chopped

 2 ounces Parmesan cheese, shaved

1 Cut chicken into 1-inch pieces; season with salt and pepper. Heat a 6-quart skillet or Dutch oven over medium heat. Add half the chicken; cook, turning occasionally, until browned, about 7 minutes. Transfer to a large bowl. Repeat with remaining chicken; set aside.

2 Place carrots, celery, parsnips, and onions in the skillet. Add the water, broth, and rosemary; scrape browned bits from the bottom with a wooden spoon. Cover, and bring to a simmer over low heat. Cook, stirring occasionally, until vegetables are barely tender, about 10 minutes.

3 Cook noodles until al dente according to package instructions; drain. Stir noodles, parsley, reserved chicken, and any accumulated juices in the bowl into skillet. Cook on low until chicken is heated through, 1 to 2 minutes. Remove from heat; keep warm.

4 Meanwhile, melt butter in a large nonstick skillet over medium-high heat. Add garlic; stir until golden, about 1 minute. Add chard; cook, turning occasionally, until tender, about 5 minutes. Divide chard among six bowls. Ladle soup on top; serve with shaved Parmesan cheese.

PER SERVING: 481 CALORIES, 11 G FAT, 142 MG CHOLESTEROL, 55 G CARBOHYDRATE, 724 MG SODIUM, 41 G PROTEIN, 6 G FIBER

from Fit to Eat: Chicken Soups and Stews

SIDE DISHES

baked potato slices

SERVES 4 | PHOTO ON PAGE 70

A Japanese or French mandoline is great for slicing vegetables uniformly—anywhere from very thin to thick—and takes much less time than slicing with a knife.

1½ pounds Yukon gold potatoes, peeled and very thinly sliced

 2 tablespoons olive oil, plus more for pan

 2 teaspoons fresh thyme leaves
   Coarse salt and freshly ground pepper

1 Preheat oven to 400°F with a rack in the center. In a medium bowl, combine the potatoes, oil, and thyme. Season with salt and pepper, and toss until well coated.

2 Generously brush a large rimmed baking sheet with oil, and arrange potatoes in a single layer, overlapping the slices slightly. Bake until potatoes are golden brown and crisp in spots, about 30 minutes.

from What to Have for Dinner

baked saffron rice

SERVES 8 TO 10 | PHOTO ON PAGE 70

 3 cups basmati rice

5½ cups water

 1 tablespoon coarse salt

 4 tablespoons extra-virgin olive oil

 ¼ teaspoon ground saffron, dissolved in 2 tablespoons hot water

1 Rinse rice well; drain in colander. Place in a deep non-stick saucepan or rice cooker with the water and salt. Bring to a boil over high heat; reduce to a simmer. Cook, uncovered, until all liquid is absorbed, 15 to 20 minutes.

2 Drizzle oil over top of rice; stir gently with a wooden spoon. Gently press rice into an even layer. Reduce heat to medium-low. Place a clean dish towel over top of pan; cover firmly, wrapping sides of towel around top of lid to prevent steam from escaping. Cook over medium-low heat for 50 to 60 minutes. Gently pull rice away from side of pan with a spatula—there should be a nice golden crust.

3 Remove from heat; remove lid, and drizzle saffron water over the rice. Cover immediately, and let cool 5 minutes.

4 Remove lid; invert carefully onto a serving plate. Serve warm, cut into wedges.

from A Winter Dinner Party With Friends

brown-sugar cornbread

MAKES TWO 9-BY-4¼-INCH LOAVES | PHOTO ON PAGE 76

1 cup (2 sticks) unsalted butter, plus more for pans
2⅔ cups yellow cornmeal
2 cups all-purpose flour
2 tablespoons plus 1½ teaspoons baking powder
1 teaspoon salt
⅔ cup packed dark-brown sugar
2 cups milk
4 large eggs, lightly beaten

1 Preheat oven to 350°F. Butter two 9-by-4½-inch loaf pans, and set aside.

2 In a large bowl, whisk together the cornmeal, flour, baking powder, and salt; set aside.

3 Heat the butter and brown sugar in a small saucepan over medium-low heat, just until melted, and whisk until smooth. Remove from heat; whisk in milk and then eggs. Pour into cornmeal mixture, stir until blended, and divide evenly among prepared pans, smoothing tops with a rubber spatula.

4 Bake in the middle of the oven until loaves are golden and a cake tester inserted in the centers comes out clean, about 30 minutes. Turn the loaves out onto wire racks, and let cool. Serve warm or at room temperature.

from Chili for a Crowd

DESSERTS

belgian chocolate birthday cake

SERVES 10 | PHOTO ON PAGE 87

You can bake the cake up to three days ahead; wrap well, and keep at room temperature.

4 ounces hazelnuts
13⅓ tablespoons unsalted butter (1⅔ sticks), softened, plus more for pan
⅔ cup Dutch-process cocoa powder, plus more for pan
6 tablespoons granulated sugar
1⅔ cups all-purpose flour
1½ teaspoons baking soda
¼ teaspoon salt
⅔ cup boiling water
1¾ cups packed dark-brown sugar
4 large eggs, at room temperature
1⅓ cups buttermilk, at room temperature
2½ teaspoons pure vanilla extract
Ganache Glaze (page 26)
Candied Hazelnuts and Chocolate Curls (page 26)

1 Preheat oven to 350°F. Spread nuts in a single layer on a rimmed baking sheet. Bake until fragrant and toasted, about 12 minutes. Transfer to a clean kitchen towel; rub to loosen skins. Butter a 9-by-3-inch springform pan; dust with cocoa, and tap out any excess.

2 In the bowl of a food processor, grind nuts with granulated sugar until fine but not pasty. Transfer to a large bowl; stir in the flour, baking soda, and salt.

3 In a medium heat-proof bowl, whisk together cocoa and boiling water until smooth. (Mixture will thicken as it cools.)

4 In the bowl of an electric mixer fitted with the paddle attachment, cream butter and brown sugar on high speed until light and fluffy, 3 to 4 minutes. Beat in eggs, one at a time, until well blended.

5 Stir buttermilk and vanilla into cocoa mixture. Mixing on low, add half the flour mixture to butter mixture until well blended; pour in cocoa mixture, and add remaining flour mixture, mixing just until incorporated. Scrape batter into prepared pan; smooth top. Bake 60 to 70 minutes, or until a cake tester inserted in the center comes out clean. Remove from oven; let cool in pan for 10 minutes. Remove from pan, and cool completely. Place cooled cake on a 9-inch cardboard round.

6 Place half the ganache in a bowl set in an ice bath; whip with a balloon whisk until pale and spreadable, removing bowl from ice bath and returning it as needed.

7 Spread the whipped ganache smoothly on top and sides of cake; chill the cake in the refrigerator. Gently stir remaining ganache every 5 minutes until thickened and cool but still pourable.

8 Place cake (still on cardboard round) on a wire rack over a rimmed baking sheet lined with waxed or parchment paper. Using a small ladle, pour ganache over top of cake, moving the ladle in a circular fashion and letting the ganache run down the sides. Scrape up excess, if desired, and reserve for another use. Let cake stand at room temperature until set. Garnish with candied nuts and chocolate curls.

from A Winter Dinner Party With Friends

ganache glaze
MAKES ABOUT 4 CUPS

This ganache will thicken as it sits. If using for the Inside-Out German Chocolate Torte and the Belgian Chocolate Birthday Cake, it should be pourable but thick enough to coat the cakes.

1 **pound bittersweet or semisweet chocolate, very finely chopped**
2½ **cups heavy cream**

Place chocolate in a large heat-proof bowl. Bring cream in a small saucepan to a boil over medium-high heat; pour over chopped chocolate. Let stand 10 minutes. Use a rubber spatula to gently stir chocolate and cream until well combined. Let stand at room temperature, stirring occasionally, until cooled and just thickened, 30 to 60 minutes, depending on the temperature of the room.

candied hazelnuts and chocolate curls
GARNISHES ONE 9-INCH CAKE

Make curls up to three days ahead and store at room temperature in an airtight container layered with parchment. Store nuts in a resealable plastic bag until ready to use, up to one week.

2 **cups hazelnuts**
1 **cup granulated sugar**
2 **tablespoons water**
1 **pound bittersweet chocolate, very finely chopped**
¼ **cup unsweetened cocoa**

1 Preheat oven to 350°F. Spread nuts in a single layer on a rimmed baking sheet. Bake until fragrant and toasted, about 12 minutes. Transfer to a clean kitchen towel; rub to loosen skins. Bring sugar and the water to a boil in a medium-size heavy skillet. Stir with a fork over medium-high heat until dissolved; let boil 3 minutes more without stirring. Add nuts to pan; stir with a wooden spoon until caramel seizes around nuts. Transfer to a parchment-lined baking sheet; let cool.

2 Once nuts are cool, place half the bittersweet chocolate in a large heat-proof bowl. Set over a pan of simmering water; stir until chocolate is melted and hot. Add remaining chocolate to bowl; remove bowl from pan of water, and let stand about 5 minutes. Stir until smooth.

3 Pour half the chocolate onto an inverted baking sheet; spread with a bench scraper until ⅛ inch thick or slightly thinner (chocolate should be opaque on surface). Let stand until just tacky. Holding scraper at a 45-degree angle, scrape chocolate off surface, forming curls.

4 While curls set, add candied nuts to remaining chocolate in bowl, and stir until coated. Spread nuts on a parchment-lined baking sheet, and let stand until set. Sift cocoa powder on top of dried nuts, and toss to coat.

cereal-cube castle

MAKES 16 TWO-INCH CEREAL BLOCKS

You can use any puffed cereal for this recipe.

5 tablespoons unsalted butter

7 cups mini marshmallows

½ teaspoon salt

5 cups puffed cereal

Nonstick cooking spray

1 Combine butter, marshmallows, and salt in a large saucepan. Cook over medium-low heat, stirring frequently, until smooth. Turn off heat, and add cereal. Stir into the marshmallow mixture until thoroughly combined, scraping all the mixture from bottom of pan.

2 Coat an 8-by-3-inch square professional baking pan with cooking spray. Cut out an 8-by-20-inch sheet of waxed paper. Set it in pan, with excess extending from two sides. Coat with nonstick spray. Spoon in mixture; coat palms of hands with cooking spray, and press firmly into pan, making sure that there are as few air pockets as possible. Be sure to press into corners of pan. Let cool.

3 Remove mixture from pan by lifting the overhanging waxed paper. Using a serrated knife, cut into 2-inch cubes. Stack cubes, as desired, to form a castle.

from Birthday Cakes

chocolate mousse with banana purée and grated coconut

SERVES 8 TO 10

4 large ripe bananas (about 2 pounds)

1 cup Champagne or sparkling wine

1 cup sugar

9 ounces semisweet chocolate, finely chopped

3 large eggs

2 cups chilled heavy cream

½ cup grated fresh or shredded sweetened coconut, for garnish

1 Peel bananas, and cut into large pieces. Place in a saucepan with Champagne and ¼ cup sugar. Bring to a boil; reduce to a gentle simmer. Cook, partially covered, until very soft, 10 to 15 minutes. Transfer to the bowl of a food processor fitted with the metal blade; blend until smooth. Set aside to cool. Transfer to a bowl, and cover with plastic wrap; chill until ready to serve, up to 6 hours.

2 Place the chocolate in a medium heat-proof bowl set over a pan of simmering water. Stir until melted; set aside.

3 Place eggs and remaining ¾ cup sugar in another large heat-proof bowl; whisk until combined. Place over simmering water; whisk until warm. Remove bowl from heat, and whisk until the mixture is pale and thick. Whisk in the melted chocolate.

4 Place cream in a mixing bowl, and whisk until stiff peaks form. Fold cream into chocolate mixture.

5 Place about 2 tablespoons banana purée in each individual serving dish; top with a dollop (about ½ cup) of chocolate mousse. Refrigerate, covered with plastic wrap, until ready to serve, up to 4 hours. Garnish with coconut.

from A Winter Dinner Party With Friends

chocolate whole-wheat biscuit cake

SERVES 4

½ cup (1 stick) unsalted butter, plus more for pan

4 ounces semisweet chocolate, finely chopped

1 large egg

¼ cup superfine sugar

1½ teaspoons water

1½ teaspoons rum (optional)

1 8½-ounce box whole-wheat biscuit cookies, such as wheatmeal biscuits or Carr's Wheatolo English Biscuits, coarsely crumbled

2 ounces (about ½ cup) walnuts, coarsely chopped

2 ounces (about ⅓ cup packed) dried sour cherries, coarsely chopped

½ cup heavy cream, whipped (for serving; optional)

1 Lightly butter an 8-inch springform pan; set aside. In a medium heat-proof bowl, combine chocolate and the butter. Set bowl over a pan of simmering water. Stir mixture occasionally until melted and smooth, about 3 minutes. Remove bowl from pan; set aside.

2 In another medium heat-proof bowl, whisk together egg, sugar, and the water. Set over the pan of simmering water; whisk until pale, fluffy, and thick, 3 to 4 minutes. Remove bowl from pan; whisk in chocolate mixture and the rum, if desired. Let cool 5 minutes, stirring occasionally.

3 Fold the crumbled cookies and half the walnuts and cherries into chocolate mixture. Pour into prepared pan; smooth top with a rubber spatula. Sprinkle remaining nuts and cherries on top. Cover with plastic wrap; chill until set, about 1 hour. Serve with whipped cream, if desired.

from What to Have for Dinner

inside-out german chocolate torte

MAKES ONE 9-INCH TORTE

The chocolate glaze takes time to cool; have it ready before assembling the torte.

- 10 tablespoons (1¼ sticks) unsalted butter, plus more for pans
- 7 ounces bittersweet chocolate, finely chopped
- 1¼ cups all-purpose flour
- ¼ teaspoon salt
- 1 cup sugar
- 2 large eggs
- 2 teaspoons pure vanilla extract
    Coconut-Pecan Filling (recipe follows)
    Ganache Glaze (page 26)

1 Preheat oven to 350°F. Butter two 9-inch springform pans. Line the bottoms with parchment paper, and butter the paper; set aside. Place chocolate and butter in a medium heat-proof bowl set over a pan of simmering water. Stir occasionally until melted; set aside.

2 Into a medium bowl, sift together flour and salt; set aside. Place sugar and eggs in the bowl of an electric mixer fitted with the paddle attachment, and beat until fluffy and combined, 3 to 5 minutes. Add vanilla and chocolate mixture, and stir to combine. Add flour mixture, and stir to combine. Divide batter between prepared pans, using an offset spatula to distribute batter evenly and smooth the layers. Bake until the center is set when touched with your finger, about 20 minutes. Transfer pans to a wire rack to cool completely before unmolding.

3 Place one layer on a 9-inch cardboard cake round. Spread filling over the layer, and invert the second layer on top, leaving the smooth side up. Press gently on top layer to evenly distribute filling to edges. Using an offset spatula, smooth filling flush with sides of cake. Refrigerate until ready to glaze.

4 Carefully transfer torte from cardboard round to a wire rack set over a rimmed baking sheet. Pour enough ganache glaze over cake to fully coat, shaking sheet gently to help spread ganache if necessary. Let sit 15 to 20 minutes. The excess ganache on the sheet may be melted and strained through a fine sieve back into glaze. Pour remaining glaze over torte, allowing excess to drip down sides. If top is not smooth, gently shake pan or run an offset spatula quickly over surface. Let set at least 30 minutes. Before serving, carefully slide the cake onto a serving platter.

from Birthday Cakes

coconut-pecan filling

MAKES ABOUT 2 CUPS, ENOUGH FOR ONE 9-INCH TORTE

- 1 14-ounce can sweetened condensed milk
- 10 tablespoons (1¼ sticks) unsalted butter
- 1 teaspoon pure vanilla extract
- 4 large egg yolks
- 2 cups sweetened shredded coconut
- 1½ cups finely chopped pecans

1 Place milk, butter, and vanilla in a medium saucepan, and cook over medium-low heat, stirring occasionally, until melted and combined.

2 Whisk egg yolks in a medium bowl; whisking constantly, add some of the hot milk mixture until combined. Whisk the mixture back into the saucepan, and cook, stirring constantly with a wooden spoon, until slightly thickened, about 5 minutes.

3 Remove from heat, and stir in coconut and pecans. Cool completely, and refrigerate in an airtight container until ready to use, up to 2 days.

persian almond brittle

MAKES 2 DOZEN PIECES

- ½ teaspoon ground saffron
- 2 tablespoons rose water or plain water
- 1 cup sugar
- 3 tablespoons honey
- 4 tablespoons vegetable oil
- 6 ounces slivered almonds
- 4 tablespoons finely chopped pistachios

1 Line a baking sheet with parchment paper. Dissolve saffron in rose water; set aside. Fill a bowl with ice water; set aside.

2 Place sugar, honey, and oil in a medium-size heavy saucepan over high heat, and stir constantly until sugar is melted.

3 Stir in the almonds, and cook, stirring constantly, until the mixture has thickened and is golden, about 2 minutes.

4 Add the saffron water, and cook, stirring constantly, until the mixture is golden brown. Drop a spoonful of the mixture into the ice water. If it hardens immediately, the mixture is ready. Reduce heat to the lowest setting.

5 Quickly drop mixture by the tablespoon onto the parchment paper at 1-inch intervals. Sprinkle immediately with the chopped pistachios. Cool completely before serving. Store in an airtight container at room temperature.

from A Winter Dinner Party With Friends

raspberry-filled layer cake

MAKES ONE 8-INCH 4-LAYER CAKE

The fluffy exterior of this cake conceals a delicious pink filling, made simply by combining some of the frosting with raspberry jam. Cake layers can be baked up to two weeks in advance and stored in the freezer; wrap well in plastic.

¾ cup (1½ sticks) unsalted butter, softened, plus more for pans and wire racks

3 cups sifted cake flour (not self-rising), plus more for pans

4 teaspoons baking powder

½ teaspoon salt

1½ cups sugar

1 cup milk

1 tablespoon pure vanilla extract

4 large egg whites

Seven Minute Frosting (recipe follows)

1 cup raspberry jam

1 Preheat oven to 350°F. Butter two 8-inch professional round cake pans, line the bottoms with parchment paper, and butter the parchment. Dust pans with flour, and tap out any excess; set aside.

2 Sift together the cake flour, baking powder, and salt into a medium bowl, and set aside. In the bowl of an electric mixer fitted with the paddle attachment, cream the butter until pale. Add the sugar to the butter in a steady stream; continue beating until light and fluffy, about 3 minutes. Reduce speed to low, and add flour mixture in three batches, alternating with the milk and vanilla and starting and finishing with the flour; be careful not to overmix. Set batter aside.

3 In a medium metal bowl or clean bowl of an electric mixer, whisk egg whites just until stiff peaks form. Fold one third of the egg whites into the batter until just combined. Fold in remaining whites in two batches. Divide batter between prepared pans, and smooth tops with an offset spatula. Bake until a cake tester inserted near the center comes out clean and the cake springs back when pressed lightly in the center, about 30 minutes. Transfer pans to wire racks; let cool 15 minutes. Loosen the sides with a small offset spatula or paring knife, and invert onto greased wire racks. To prevent the layers from splitting, invert again so that the tops are up. Let cool completely before assembling cake or storing.

4 If cakes are not level, use a serrated knife to trim tops off. Carefully slice each cake horizontally into two equal layers. (You will have four layers.) Place a third of the frosting in a bowl, and fold in raspberry jam.

5 To assemble, place one layer on an 8-inch cardboard cake round. Spread ¼-inch layer of raspberry frosting on top. Repeat with remaining layers and raspberry frosting, placing the final layer, unfrosted, bottom side up. Lightly coat top and sides of cake with a thin layer of white frosting to seal in crumbs. Finish with a smooth layer of remaining white frosting. Serve immediately, or keep refrigerated until ready to serve, up to 2 days.

from Birthday Cakes

seven minute frosting

MAKES ABOUT 2 QUARTS

1¾ cups sugar

2 tablespoons light corn syrup

¼ cup water

6 large egg whites

1 In a small heavy saucepan, combine 1½ cups sugar, corn syrup, and the water. Place over medium heat, stirring occasionally, until the sugar has dissolved, about 4 minutes. Test by rubbing between your fingers. Raise heat, and bring to a boil without stirring. Boil until a candy thermometer registers 230°F (depending on the humidity, this can take anywhere from 4 to 10 minutes), occasionally washing down sides of pan with a pastry brush dipped in cold water to prevent sugar crystals from forming.

2 Meanwhile, in the bowl of an electric mixer fitted with the whisk attachment, beat egg whites on medium speed until soft peaks form, about 2½ minutes. With the motor running, gradually add the remaining ¼ cup sugar. Remove the syrup from the heat when the temperature reaches 230°F (it will keep rising after pan is removed from heat). With the mixer on medium-low speed, pour the syrup in a steady stream down the side of the mixing bowl to avoid splattering.

3 Continue beating the frosting on medium speed until it is cool, about 7 minutes. (It should be thick and shiny.) Use immediately.

vanilla crêpes

MAKES ABOUT 2 DOZEN | **PHOTOS ON PAGES 65-66**

Set out a stack of crêpes—some flavored with vanilla and rum, others with chocolate—along with bowls of fillings and sauces. Let everyone choose his or her own combinations. In addition to the four recipes that follow, we set out bowls of mixed berries, sliced peaches, and whipped cream. To make chocolate crêpes, substitute ¼ cup sifted cocoa powder for ½ cup flour.

1½ cups milk

2 tablespoons pure vanilla extract

1 tablespoon rum, brandy, or other liqueur (optional)

3 large egg yolks

2 tablespoons sugar

1 teaspoon salt

1½ cups sifted all-purpose flour

5 tablespoons melted butter

Vegetable oil, for brushing pan

Hot Fudge Sauce (recipe follows)

Lemon Curd (recipe follows)

Ricotta-Mascarpone Crêpe Filling (page 31)

Sautéed Pineapple Crêpe Filling (page 31)

1 Place milk, vanilla, and rum if desired in the jar of a blender. Add yolks, sugar, salt, flour, and butter. Blend on high speed 30 seconds. Scrape sides of blender; blend 30 seconds more. Transfer batter to an airtight container; refrigerate at least 2 hours or overnight. Brush a 6½- to 7-inch crêpe pan or non-stick skillet with oil. Heat on medium until just starting to smoke. Remove pan from heat; quickly pour 2 tablespoons batter into middle of pan.

2 Quickly (in 2 to 3 seconds) tilt pan in all directions so the batter covers entire bottom in a thin layer. Return pan to heat for about 1 minute. Jerk pan sharply back and forth to loosen.

3 Lift edges with a spatula; if underside is golden brown, turn by using two spatulas or by flipping crêpe with a toss of the pan.

4 Cook about 30 seconds more, or until brown in spots. Slide crêpe onto a plate. Grease pan again with oil, heat to just smoking, and repeat process with remaining batter. To keep warm, cover with an ovenproof dish in a 200°F oven. Crêpes can be made up to 1 day in advance; reheat, covered with foil, in a 300°F oven.

from Dessert of the Month

hot fudge sauce

MAKES ABOUT 2 CUPS

We served this rich sauce with chocolate crêpes filled with fresh strawberries and blackberries and topped with a dollop of whipped cream.

1 cup heavy cream

⅓ cup light corn syrup, plus more as needed

12 ounces bittersweet chocolate, finely chopped

Combine heavy cream and corn syrup in a small saucepan; stir to combine, and bring to a boil over medium-high heat. Remove from heat, and add chocolate. Whisk until the chocolate is melted. If necessary, adjust consistency with additional corn syrup. Serve hot.

lemon curd

MAKES 1½ CUPS

This curd can be prepared several days in advance and stored in the refrigerator.

3 large egg yolks

Grated zest of 1 lemon

¼ cup freshly squeezed lemon juice (about 2 lemons)

6 tablespoons sugar

4 tablespoons chilled unsalted butter, cut into pieces

1 Combine yolks, lemon zest, lemon juice, and sugar in a small saucepan; whisk to combine. Set over medium heat, and stir constantly with a wooden spoon, making sure to stir sides and bottom of pan. Cook until mixture is thick enough to coat the back of the spoon, 5 to 7 minutes.

2 Remove saucepan from heat. Add butter, one piece at a time, stirring with the wooden spoon until mixture is smooth.

3 Transfer mixture to a medium bowl. Place a sheet of plastic wrap directly on surface to prevent a skin from forming; wrap tightly. Let cool; refrigerate until firm, at least 1 hour. Store, refrigerated in an airtight container, up to 2 days.

ricotta-mascarpone crêpe filling

MAKES ABOUT 2 CUPS

8 ounces fresh ricotta cheese

8 ounces mascarpone cheese

¼ cup confectioners' sugar

Whisk together cheeses and sugar in a medium bowl. Store, refrigerated in an airtight container, up to 2 days.

sautéed pineapple crêpe filling

MAKES ABOUT 2 CUPS

1 pineapple

4 tablespoons unsalted butter

¼ cup packed light-brown sugar

1 Peel pineapple; cut into quarters lengthwise. Cut out and discard core; cut each quarter in half lengthwise. Cut each piece crosswise into ¼-inch-thick slices.

2 Heat butter in a large skillet over medium heat. Add pineapple; toss to coat with butter. Sprinkle with brown sugar; toss to coat. Cook, stirring occasionally, until pineapple is lightly browned, about 8 minutes. Transfer to a bowl; keep warm until ready to serve.

white sheet cake

MAKE 1 TWELVE-BY-SEVENTEEN-INCH LAYER

The cake ingredients are enough to make one layer; you will need to bake two to assemble the cake. The cake layers can be baked up to two weeks in advance and stored, wrapped well in plastic, in the freezer.

18 tablespoons (2¼ sticks) unsalted butter, softened, plus more for pan and wire rack

4½ cups sifted cake flour (not self-rising), plus more for pan

2 tablespoons baking powder

¾ teaspoon salt

2¼ cups sugar

1½ cups milk

1½ tablespoons pure vanilla extract

7 large egg whites

White Confectioners' Sugar Icing (page 32)

6 ounces semisweet chocolate, finely chopped

1 Preheat oven to 350°F. Butter a 17-by-12-inch baking pan; line bottom with parchment paper, and butter paper. Dust pan with flour, and tap out excess; set aside.

2 Sift together the flour, baking powder, and salt into a medium bowl, and set aside. In the bowl of an electric mixer fitted with the paddle attachment, cream the butter until it is pale. With the motor running, add the sugar in a steady stream; continue beating until light and fluffy, about 3 minutes. Reduce speed to low, and add flour mixture in three batches, alternating with the milk and vanilla and starting and ending with the flour; be careful not to overmix. Set batter aside.

3 In a medium metal bowl or clean bowl of an electric mixer, whisk egg whites just until stiff peaks form. Fold a third of the egg whites into the batter until combined. Fold in remaining whites in two batches. Pour batter into prepared pan, and smooth top with a metal spatula. Bake until a cake tester inserted near the center comes out clean and the cake springs back when pressed lightly in the center, about 30 minutes. Transfer pan to a wire rack; let cool 15 minutes before unmolding. Loosen the sides with a small metal spatula or paring knife, and invert onto a greased wire rack. To prevent the layer from splitting, invert again so that the top side is up.

4 While this layer cools, repeat steps with a second batch of ingredients for a second cake layer. Cool completely before assembling cake or storing.

5 To assemble, trim tops of each layer so they are flat. Place one layer of cake on serving platter. Measure out 1 cup of the icing for coloring; set aside. Spread ¼-inch layer of the icing

on top, and cover with second cake layer. Frost top and sides of cake, using remaining untinted icing. Chill cake until ready to decorate, up to 1 day.

6 Place chocolate in a medium heat-proof bowl set over a pan of simmering water; stir, using a rubber spatula, until melted. Remove bowl from pan, and let cool about 15 minutes, until no longer warm but still liquid. Roll a parchment triangle into a tight cone. Fill halfway with melted chocolate. Avoid overfilling, because it will be more difficult to pipe decorations. Roll down the top of the cone as you would a tube of toothpaste. Remove cake from refrigerator; using sharp kitchen shears, cut a very small hole in tip of filled cone. Pipe desired decoration with chocolate; let stand 10 minutes, until set. If desired, color remaining cup of icing and pipe designs on cake.

from Birthday Cakes

white confectioners' sugar icing
MAKES ENOUGH FOR 2 TWELVE-BY-SEVENTEEN-INCH LAYERS

1½ cups (3 sticks) unsalted butter, softened

3 one-pound boxes confectioners' sugar

¾ teaspoon salt

3 tablespoons pure vanilla extract

¾ cup milk, plus more as needed

In the bowl of an electric mixer fitted with the paddle attachment, cream butter and sugar until combined. Add salt, vanilla, and milk, and beat until smooth and creamy. If icing seems too thick, add another tablespoon of milk. Use immediately, or refrigerate, covered with plastic wrap, up to 2 days. Before frosting cake, bring to room temperature and beat until creamy.

spiced lemonade
MAKES ABOUT 3 QUARTS

9 cups water

1 cup freshly squeezed lemon juice

2 cups freshly squeezed orange juice

2 cups sugar

1 tablespoon pure vanilla extract

⅛ teaspoon ground clove

Combine all ingredients in a 4-quart saucepan. Simmer over medium-low heat, stirring, until sugar is dissolved and mixture is heated through. Serve immediately, or refrigerate and reheat before serving.

from Good Things

February

STARTERS

35 gougères

36 pea bisque with shrimp and tarragon

36 roasted-garlic hummus

37 warm red-lentil dal with pita chips

SALADS

37 arugula salad with french lentils, smoked chicken, and roasted peppers

MAIN COURSES

38 black-eyed peas with escarole, potatoes, and turkey sausage

38 crisp mustard-glazed chicken breasts

39 pot roast

39 pot roast ragu

SIDE DISHES

40 braised potatoes

40 winter greens and bacon

DESSERTS

40 bananas foster

41 chocolate caramel tart

42 chocolate cream pie

43 chocolate fudge

43 chocolate gelato

44 chocolate sandwich cookies

44 chocolate spice cake

45 cream puffs

46 éclairs

47 frozen chocolate malted

47 mocha steamed puddings

48 molten chocolate cakes with earl grey ice cream

49 profiteroles

50 vanilla pudding

DRINKS

50 spiced rose lassi

gougères

MAKES 12 ½ DOZEN

A gougère is pastry made from pâte à choux flavored with Gruyère cheese.

Pâte à Choux (recipe follows)

4 ounces Gruyère cheese, finely grated, plus more for sprinkling

1 teaspoon salt

½ teaspoon freshly ground pepper

¼ teaspoon nutmeg

1 large egg beaten with 1 tablespoon water, for egg wash

Oil, for plastic wrap

1 Preheat oven to 425°F with a rack in the center. Line two unrimmed baking sheets with parchment paper or Silpat baking mats.

2 Make pâte à choux batter; add cheese, salt, pepper, and nutmeg at the end. (If too stiff, add teaspoonfuls of water until the proper consistency is reached.) Fill a pastry bag fitted with a large round tip (we used an Ateco #804); pipe ¾-inch rounds that are about ½ inch high (about the size of gum-drops) onto baking sheets at 2-inch intervals. Use your finger to gently coat entire top with egg wash, being careful not to let wash drip onto the surrounding baking sheet (it will inhibit rising). Sprinkle with grated cheese.

3 Cover one baking sheet with lightly oiled plastic wrap, and place in the refrigerator. Transfer the other to the oven. Bake 10 minutes; reduce oven heat to 350°F. Bake 15 minutes more, until golden brown. Turn off oven; prop door open slightly to let steam escape. Let gougères dry in the oven until crisp, about 10 minutes. Transfer to a wire rack. Raise heat back to 425°F. Repeat process for remaining batch. Serve warm.

from Pâte à Choux

pâte à choux

This basic dough is used to make several pastries.

1 cup water

½ cup (1 stick) unsalted butter

1 teaspoon sugar

½ teaspoon salt

1 cup all-purpose flour

4 large eggs, plus 1 lightly beaten

1 Combine the water, butter, sugar, and salt in a medium saucepan over medium-high heat. Bring to a boil, and immediately remove from heat. Stir in flour, and return to heat. (This mixture is called a panade.) Dry the panade by stirring constantly for 4 minutes. It is ready when it pulls away from the sides and a film forms on the bottom of the pan.

2 Transfer panade to the bowl of an electric mixer fitted with the paddle attachment, and beat on low speed, about 2 minutes, until slightly cooled. Add 4 eggs, one at a time, on medium speed, letting each one incorporate completely before adding the next. Test the batter by touching it with your finger and lifting to form a string. If a string does not form, add the last egg a little at a time until the batter is smooth and shiny. If you have added all the eggs and the batter still doesn't form a string, add water 1 teaspoon at a time until it does.

3 The batter may be used immediately or stored in an air-tight container in the refrigerator for up to 2 days. If using chilled, stir to soften before filling piping bag.

pea bisque with shrimp and tarragon

SERVES 6 | **PHOTO ON PAGE 80**

- ½ pound green split peas, picked over and rinsed
- 2 8-ounce bottles clam juice
- 6 cups water, plus more for soaking
- 1 onion, chopped
- 1 10-ounce package frozen baby peas, thawed
- 1 pound medium shrimp, peeled, deveined, and halved lengthwise
- 3 garlic cloves, minced
- 4½ teaspoons lemon zest, finely grated
- 1 teaspoon hot paprika
- ¼ teaspoon coarse salt
- 1 tablespoon unsalted butter
- 1 tablespoon freshly squeezed lemon juice
- 1 tablespoon finely chopped fresh tarragon

1 Place split peas in a large bowl with enough water to cover by 2 inches; let stand 6 hours or overnight.

2 Drain split peas, and transfer to a large stockpot. Add clam juice, the water, and onion; bring to a boil, reduce heat, and simmer, stirring occasionally, until peas are soft but not mushy, 35 to 40 minutes.

3 Stir in baby peas, and simmer 5 minutes; let cool slightly. Place in the bowl of a food processor, working in batches if necessary so as not to fill more than halfway; purée until smooth. Press through a fine sieve into a large saucepan, and keep warm over low heat.

4 In a large bowl, stir together shrimp, garlic, lemon zest, paprika, and salt. Melt butter in a nonstick medium skillet over medium-high heat. Add shrimp, and cook, stirring, until they begin to turn pink and opaque. Add lemon juice, and stir for 1 minute more. Remove from heat, and stir in tarragon.

5 Ladle bisque into six soup bowls, and place a mound of shrimp in the center of each serving.

PER SERVING: 310 CALORIES, 4 G FAT, 120 MG CHOLESTEROL, 38 G CARBOHYDRATE, 577 MG SODIUM, 30 G PROTEIN, 14 G FIBER

from Fit to Eat: Lentils and Peas

roasted-garlic hummus

SERVES 6

Hummus is traditionally enriched with copious amounts of olive oil and tahini (sesame paste). In this version the amount of fat is drastically reduced; be sure to use high-quality olive oil and tahini for the best flavor.

- 3 large garlic cloves, unpeeled
- 1 teaspoon plus 1 tablespoon extra-virgin olive oil
- 1 19-ounce can chickpeas, drained and rinsed
- ¼ cup freshly squeezed lemon juice
- 3 tablespoons tahini
- 3 tablespoons water
- 1 teaspoon coarse salt
- ¼ teaspoon cayenne pepper
- ¼ cup fresh minced chives
  Assorted crudités, for serving

1 Preheat oven to 400°F. Place garlic cloves on a small piece of foil, and lightly drizzle with 1 teaspoon oil. Seal foil to form a pouch, and roast garlic in oven until soft, about 20 minutes. Remove garlic from oven, and let cool slightly; peel, and transfer to the bowl of a food processor fitted with the metal blade. Add the chickpeas, and process until finely chopped.

2 Add lemon juice, tahini, water, salt, cayenne pepper, and remaining tablespoon oil, and process until mixture is light and fluffy but not entirely smooth, about 2 minutes. Stir in chives, and transfer to a serving bowl. Serve with assorted crudités.

PER SERVING: 153 CALORIES, 7 G FAT, 0 MG CHOLESTEROL, 19 G CARBOHYDRATE, 538 MG SODIUM, 5 G PROTEIN, 4 G FIBER

from Fit to Eat: Lentils and Peas

warm red-lentil dal with pita chips

SERVES 6

Serve this dal as a dip with pita chips or as a side dish with grilled meats or fish.

- ½ pound red lentils (about 1¼ cups), picked over and rinsed
- 1 14½-ounce can low-sodium chicken broth, or homemade, skimmed of fat
- 1 cup water
- ½ teaspoon turmeric
- 2 tablespoons unsalted butter
- 4 garlic cloves, minced
- 1¼ teaspoons cumin seeds
- ½ teaspoon crushed red-pepper flakes
- 1 large tomato, seeded and finely chopped
- ¼ cup fresh mint, finely chopped
- ½ teaspoon coarse salt

1 In a medium saucepan, combine lentils, broth, water, and turmeric. Bring to a boil; reduce heat, and simmer, stirring occasionally, until lentils are tender, about 20 minutes.

2 Meanwhile, melt butter in a small saucepan; add garlic, cumin seeds, and crushed red pepper. Cook, stirring, until fragrant, about 3 minutes. Remove from heat.

3 Remove lentils from heat, and stir in garlic mixture, tomato, mint, and salt. Serve warm.

PER SERVING: 189 CALORIES, 5 G FAT, 11 MG CHOLESTEROL, 25 G CARBOHYDRATE, 291 MG SODIUM, 12 G PROTEIN, 3 G FIBER

from Fit to Eat: Lentils and Peas

arugula salad with french lentils, smoked chicken, and roasted peppers

SERVES 6

The lentils can be made up to a day in advance and the salad assembled at the last minute. Poached or grilled chicken breast produce equally appetizing results.

- ½ pound French green lentils, picked over and rinsed
- 1 14½-ounce can low-sodium chicken broth, or homemade, skimmed of fat
- 1 cup water
- 4 sprigs thyme, plus ½ tablespoon fresh thyme leaves
- 2 red bell peppers
- 1½ teaspoons plus 2 tablespoons extra-virgin olive oil
- 1 tablespoon red-wine vinegar
- 1 tablespoon balsamic vinegar
- ½ teaspoon coarse salt, plus more for seasoning
- 6 ounces baby arugula (about 6 cups)
- 6 ounces smoked skinless and boneless chicken breast, cut into matchsticks
- Freshly ground black pepper

1 In a medium saucepan, combine lentils, broth, water, and thyme sprigs. Bring to a boil; reduce heat to medium-low, and simmer, uncovered, until lentils are tender, about 20 minutes. Drain, and transfer to a bowl; let cool.

2 While lentils are cooking, roast red peppers over a gas flame or under the broiler, turning occasionally, until blackened. Place in a medium bowl; cover with plastic wrap, and let stand until cool. Peel and seed peppers, and cut into ½-inch-thick slices. Place strips in a small saucepan with 1½ teaspoons oil; cover, and cook gently over low heat, stirring occasionally, until very tender, about 10 minutes. Remove from heat, and let cool.

3 In a large bowl, whisk together vinegars, salt, thyme leaves, and remaining 2 tablespoons oil until blended. Pour half the dressing over lentils, and toss to coat. Add arugula, chicken, and pepper strips to remaining dressing, and toss. Season both salads with salt and pepper. Arrange a mound of lentils on each of six salad plates; form a well in the center, and fill with arugula mixture.

PER SERVING: 250 CALORIES, 9 G FAT, 15 MG CHOLESTEROL, 26 G CARBOHYDRATE, 560 MG SODIUM, 17 G PROTEIN, 3 G FIBER

from Fit to Eat: Lentils and Peas

black-eyed peas with escarole, potatoes, and turkey sausage

SERVES 6 | **PHOTO ON PAGE 80**

The black-eyed peas need to soak for at least six hours, so plan accordingly. Look for turkey sausage made with all-white meat.

½ pound black-eyed peas (1¼ cups), picked over and rinsed

1 large onion, finely chopped

2 14½-ounce cans low-sodium chicken broth, or homemade, skimmed of fat

2 cups water

1 pound white or red new potatoes

2 pounds turkey sausage

1½ tablespoons unsalted butter

3 garlic cloves, minced

1¼ pounds escarole, trimmed and coarsely chopped

¼ teaspoon coarse salt

Freshly ground pepper

1 Place the peas in a large stockpot, and add enough water to cover by 2 inches. Soak for at least 6 hours or overnight. Drain and rinse, and return to the pot. Add the onion, broth, and water; bring to a boil, reduce heat, and simmer until peas are tender, about 30 minutes.

2 Meanwhile, place potatoes in a medium saucepan; add enough cold water to cover by 1 inch. Simmer until potatoes are tender, about 25 minutes. Drain and let cool, and cut into quarters.

3 In a grill pan or under a broiler, cook the sausage, turning occasionally, until browned and cooked through, 12 to 15 minutes. Remove from heat; cut into 2-inch pieces.

4 Melt butter in a large nonstick skillet over medium heat. Add garlic, and cook until golden. Add escarole; cook, stirring occasionally, until tender, 8 to 10 minutes.

5 Add potatoes and escarole to peas, and return to a simmer over medium heat. Remove from heat. Divide among six shallow soup bowls, and arrange sausage pieces on top. Add salt, and season with pepper.

PER SERVING: 389 CALORIES, 6 G FAT, 68 MG CHOLESTEROL, 38 G CARBOHYDRATE, 435 MG SODIUM, 48 G PROTEIN, 13 G FIBER

from What to Have for Dinner

crisp mustard-glazed chicken breasts

SERVES 4 | **PHOTO ON PAGE 80**

4 boneless chicken breasts, skin on

2 tablespoons olive oil, plus more for coating breasts

Coarse salt and freshly ground pepper

2 tablespoons unsalted butter, softened, plus 2 tablespoons melted

2½ tablespoons Dijon mustard

¾ cup coarse breadcrumbs

2 tablespoons chopped fresh thyme, plus more for garnish

¾ cup homemade or low-sodium canned chicken stock

½ cup heavy cream

1 Preheat oven to 375°F. Rub chicken breasts lightly with oil, and season with salt and pepper.

2 In a small bowl, combine 2 tablespoons softened butter with the mustard; reserve 2 teaspoons for the sauce. Mix remaining 2 tablespoons melted butter with breadcrumbs and thyme in a separate bowl, and season with salt and pepper.

3 In a large skillet, heat the oil over medium-high heat. Sear chicken, skin side down, until crisp, about 5 minutes. Remove from heat. Smear with mustard mixture, and sprinkle with breadcrumb mixture. Turn skin side up, and repeat with mustard and breadcrumb mixture.

4 Transfer skillet to oven, and roast until chicken is cooked through and golden brown, 15 to 20 minutes. Transfer chicken to a serving platter.

5 To same skillet, add stock and cream; cook over medium heat, stirring with a wooden spoon until creamy and reduced to about ¾ cup, about 3 minutes. Remove from heat, and stir in reserved 2 teaspoons mustard mixture. Strain sauce through a fine sieve, and serve with chicken. Garnish with thyme.

from What to Have for Dinner

pot roast

SERVES 6 TO 8

Inexpensive cuts of meat, such as chuck and rump roasts, work best in this recipe, as higher-grade meats will dry out. When shopping, tell the butcher you are making pot roast, and he will guide you to an appropriate piece of meat. Also ask him to tie the roast; this will keep it from falling apart as it softens. You can replace some of the potatoes with turnips, if you like. Use leftovers to make Pot Roast Ragu (recipe follows), or, for a French dip, warm the sliced pot roast in beef stock, and pile it onto crusty bread with a little horseradish mayonnaise.

5 large russet potatoes, peeled and quartered

5 tablespoons extra-virgin olive oil

3 teaspoons coarse salt,
   plus more for seasoning

¾ teaspoon freshly ground pepper, plus more for seasoning

5 sprigs flat-leaf parsley

5 sprigs thyme

1 dried bay leaf

1 tablespoon all-purpose flour

½ teaspoon paprika

½ teaspoon ground allspice

1 beef rump roast (3¼ to 3½ pounds)

4 medium leeks, white and light-green parts,
   cut into 1-inch half moons, washed well and drained

3 garlic cloves, thinly sliced

1 cup dry red wine

6 cups homemade or low-sodium canned beef stock

2 tablespoons tomato paste

6 large carrots

1 Preheat oven to 400°F. Place potatoes in a large roasting pan, and toss with 3 tablespoons oil. Sprinkle with 2 teaspoons salt and ¼ teaspoon pepper. Roast until golden brown and crisp, 30 to 40 minutes. Remove from oven; set aside. Reduce oven temperature to 350°F.

2 Make bouquet garni: Lay parsley, thyme, and bay leaf on a piece of cheesecloth. Bundle and tie with kitchen twine; set aside.

3 Combine flour, remaining teaspoon salt and ½ teaspoon pepper, paprika, and allspice in a small bowl. Place beef on a work surface, and pat dry with paper towels. Sprinkle flour mixture over meat, and pat to coat well.

4 Heat remaining 2 tablespoons oil in a large (7-quart) Dutch oven over medium heat until hot but not smoking. Sear on all sides until golden brown, about 2 minutes per side. Transfer to a plate; set aside.

5 Reduce heat to medium-low. Add leeks and garlic; cook, stirring occasionally, until leeks are just softened, about 3 minutes. Add wine; deglaze pan, scraping any browned bits from the bottom with a wooden spoon. Bring to a boil; cook until most of the wine has evaporated. Add beef stock, tomato paste, bouquet garni, and reserved roast. Cover, and place in oven 30 minutes. Turn the roast, and continue cooking 30 minutes more.

6 Add carrots; cover, and return to oven for 1½ hours, turning the roast every 30 minutes.

7 Place roasted potatoes in pan, submerging them halfway in the liquid (this leaves the vegetables tender and crisp). Return to oven, uncovered, 30 minutes more to let some of the liquid evaporate. Season with salt and pepper, if desired.

8 Transfer meat to a cutting board; let rest 5 minutes. Discard string, and slice meat on the bias. Serve with vegetables and sauce on the side.

from Pot Roast 101

pot roast ragu

SERVES 4 | PHOTO ON PAGE 81

This recipe can be doubled, depending on how much pot roast and vegetables are left over. Cooled completely, it can be frozen for up to one month.

2 tablespoons extra-virgin olive oil

1 medium shallot, finely chopped

2 garlic cloves, minced

½ cup dry red wine

2 cups combined finely chopped leftover pot roast
   and vegetables

½ cup leftover gravy or homemade or low-sodium
   canned beef stock

1 28-ounce can whole plum tomatoes,
   roughly chopped, with juice

1 teaspoon chopped fresh thyme

1 teaspoon coarse salt

¼ teaspoon freshly ground pepper

Cooked pappardelle or other pasta

Freshly grated Parmesan cheese, for garnish

Crushed red-pepper flakes, for garnish (optional)

1 Heat oil in a large skillet over medium heat. Add shallot and garlic, and cook until softened, about 3 minutes. Add wine, and cook until most of the liquid has evaporated.

2 Add chopped pot roast and vegetables, gravy or beef stock, tomatoes, and thyme. Bring to a boil, and reduce to a

simmer. Cover; cook 30 minutes, until flavors blend and sauce thickens slightly. Stir in the salt and pepper.

3 Serve hot over cooked pasta, garnished with grated Parmesan cheese and red-pepper flakes, if desired.

from Pot Roast 101

SIDE DISHES

braised potatoes

SERVES 4

We used a combination of fingerling and tiny new potatoes, but this dish would be just as delicious with quartered or halved new potatoes.

3 tablespoons extra-virgin olive oil

1 tablespoon unsalted butter

1 medium onion, thinly sliced

1½ pounds fingerling and very small new white potatoes

6 small shallots

2 to 3 sprigs rosemary, plus 1 tablespoon roughly chopped leaves for garnish

Coarse salt and freshly ground pepper

1 cup homemade or low-sodium canned chicken stock

1 Preheat oven to 375°F. Heat the oil and butter over medium-low heat in a large ovenproof skillet. Add onion, and cook until very soft, about 15 minutes. Stir in the potatoes and shallots and half the rosemary sprigs; season with salt and pepper. Raise heat to medium-high, and cook until potatoes begin to brown, about 10 minutes. Remove from heat, and add remaining rosemary sprigs and the stock.

2 Cover skillet, and transfer to oven; cook until potatoes are fork-tender, about 10 minutes (timing will vary with size of potatoes). Uncover, and cook until liquid is reduced, about 20 minutes. Remove from oven; sprinkle with chopped rosemary. Serve warm.

from What to Have for Dinner

winter greens and bacon

SERVES 4

Any combination of kale, chard, or mustard or collard greens works well in this recipe.

4 slices thick-cut bacon, cut into ½-inch strips

1 pound kale, ribs removed, leaves torn into 2-inch pieces

1 bunch Swiss chard, ribs removed, leaves torn into 2-inch pieces

¾ cup water

2 teaspoons cider vinegar

Coarse salt and freshly ground pepper

1 In a large skillet over medium heat, cook bacon until browned, about 5 minutes. Transfer to a paper-towel–lined plate with a slotted spoon, and set aside. Pour off all but 2 tablespoons rendered fat.

2 Add greens and the water to skillet, and bring to a boil. Cover, reduce heat, and simmer until greens are wilted and almost all the water has evaporated, about 8 minutes.

3 Remove from heat. Stir in vinegar, and season with salt and pepper. Toss in bacon. Serve warm.

from What to Have for Dinner

DESSERTS

bananas foster

SERVES 4

Our home-style version of this fancy restaurant treat—traditionally prepared and set aflame at tableside—is finished in a skillet in a matter of minutes. If you cannot find banana liqueur, you may substitute one-quarter cup of water.

1 pint vanilla ice cream

4 large bananas

¼ cup banana liqueur

½ cup dark rum

6 tablespoons unsalted butter

¼ cup packed light-brown sugar

½ teaspoon ground cinnamon

1 Line a small rimmed baking sheet (one that will fit in your freezer) with parchment paper, and place in the freezer until chilled, about 10 minutes. Quickly scoop ice cream into 12 small balls; place on prepared baking sheet. Return to freezer until firm and ready to serve, at least 1 hour and up to 1 day ahead (cover with plastic wrap once firm for longer storage).

2 When ready to serve, peel bananas and quarter them, cutting lengthwise and then crosswise; set aside. Pour banana liqueur and rum into separate glass measuring cups; set aside.

3 Heat 3 tablespoons butter in a large skillet over medium heat. Sprinkle sugar and cinnamon over butter, and cook until dissolved. Remove from heat, and carefully stir in liqueur. Add bananas, flat side down; return pan to heat. Cook until bananas are softened and lightly browned on the bottom. Remove from heat, and add rum. Return to heat, and cook until rum is heated, about 10 seconds. If using a gas stove, carefully tip the pan away from you until the vapors from the rum ignite. (Alternatively, light the rum with a long match.) When flames have subsided, remove pan from heat, and gently stir in remaining 3 tablespoons butter.

4 Place 3 scoops of ice cream in each of four serving bowls. Spoon the banana mixture and sauce over each. Serve immediately.

from Dessert of the Month

chocolate caramel tart

MAKES 1 NINE-INCH TART | **PHOTO ON PAGE 88**

Chocolate Pâte Sucrée (recipe follows)
1 cup chopped pecans
1 cup sugar
¼ teaspoon salt
¼ cup water
1½ cups heavy cream
2 tablespoons unsalted butter, room temperature
1 teaspoon pure vanilla extract
6 ounces bittersweet chocolate, finely chopped
Cocoa, for dusting (optional)
Caramel-Dipped Pecans (optional; page 42)

1 Preheat oven to 350°F. Roll pâte sucrée ⅛ inch thick, and fit into a 9-inch fluted tart pan with a removable bottom. Prick bottom of tart all over with a fork. Refrigerate the shell 30 minutes.

2 Spread pecans in a single layer on a rimmed baking sheet, and toast in oven until slightly darkened and fragrant, about 10 minutes. Remove from oven; set aside.

3 Line tart shell with parchment paper, pressing into edges, and cover with dried beans or pie weights. Place on a baking sheet; bake 20 minutes. Remove paper and beans, and continue baking until crust is golden, about 10 minutes. Transfer to a wire rack to cool completely.

4 Make the caramel by placing sugar, salt, and the water in a small saucepan. Bring mixture to a boil over medium-high heat; wash down sides of the pan with a pastry brush dipped in water to prevent crystals from forming. Cook, gently swirling pan (do not stir), until caramel is a rich amber color. Remove from heat, and add ½ cup cream, butter, and vanilla; stir until smooth. Pour mixture into chocolate tart shell.

5 Sprinkle the toasted pecans over the caramel, and place in the refrigerator.

6 Place chocolate in a medium heat-proof bowl. Bring remaining cup of cream to a boil in a small saucepan; pour over chocolate. Let sit 5 minutes; stir until completely smooth. Pour over caramel and nuts; return tart to refrigerator to chill for at least 1 hour.

7 To serve, dust top of tart with cocoa powder, and garnish with caramel-dipped pecans, if desired.

from Chocolate Desserts

chocolate pâte sucrée

MAKES ENOUGH FOR 1 NINE-INCH TART

1¼ cups all-purpose flour, plus more for work surface
2 tablespoons unsweetened cocoa powder
⅓ cup sugar
½ teaspoon salt
6 tablespoons unsalted butter, chilled, cut into pieces
3 large egg yolks
½ teaspoon pure vanilla extract

1 Place the flour, cocoa, sugar, and salt in the bowl of a food processor fitted with the metal blade, and pulse several times to combine. Add butter, and pulse until mixture resembles coarse meal, about 10 seconds. Add egg yolks and vanilla; process just until mixture comes together to form a dough, no more than 30 seconds.

2 Turn dough out onto a lightly floured surface, and flatten into a disk. Cover with plastic wrap; refrigerate 30 minutes or until ready to use.

caramel-dipped pecans

MAKES 24

To produce interesting curves in the caramel drops, stand the skewers upright in floral foam or a heavy container while the caramel sets. If the caramel hardens before all the pecans have been dipped, rewarm it over low heat. A foolproof way to clean the caramel from the pan is to bring it to a boil with a bit of added water.

24 pecan halves

3 cups sugar

¾ cup water

1 teaspoon cream of tartar

1 Gently insert an 8-inch wooden skewer into each pecan half. Set aside.

2 Prepare an ice bath, and set aside. Combine sugar, water, and cream of tartar in a medium saucepan, and bring to a boil over medium-high heat; wash down sides of pan with a pastry brush dipped in water to prevent sugar crystals from forming. Cook, gently swirling pan (do not stir), until caramel is a rich amber color. Plunge pan in ice bath 5 seconds to stop the cooking.

3 Let caramel stand until slightly thickened, about 15 minutes. (To test: Dip a wooden spoon into the caramel, and lift it several inches above pan; if a drip slowly forms and then hardens, the caramel is ready.) When caramel is ready, dip pecans, then lift up and rotate slightly to fully coat. Hold skewer over the pan to let the drip lengthen and harden, about 1 minute. If necessary, use a pair of scissors to cut the drip from the caramel remaining in the pan. Place skewers on an inverted baking sheet lined with waxed paper, and allow the caramel to completely harden, about 5 minutes. Gently remove skewers just before serving.

chocolate cream pie

MAKES 1 EIGHT-INCH PIE

For the smoothest, glossiest peaks, be careful not to overbeat the egg whites.

1 12-ounce box chocolate wafers

7 tablespoons unsalted butter, melted

½ cup milk

1 teaspoon unflavored gelatin

1 cup heavy cream

¾ cup plus 2 tablespoons sugar

8 ounces milk chocolate, finely chopped

1 teaspoon pure vanilla extract

4 large egg whites

1 Place the chocolate wafers in the bowl of a food processor fitted with the metal blade, and pulse until finely ground. Transfer to a mixing bowl. Add melted butter, and stir until well combined. Press into an 8-inch springform pan, evenly coating bottom and half the sides. Cover pan with plastic wrap, and place in the refrigerator to chill 30 minutes.

2 Pour milk into a small bowl. Sprinkle gelatin over the milk, and let soften 5 minutes. Place cream and 2 tablespoons sugar in a small saucepan, and bring to a boil, stirring to dissolve sugar. Add gelatin mixture, and stir to combine. Remove from heat. Add chocolate and vanilla; cover, and let stand 3 minutes. Stir until thoroughly combined.

3 Pass mixture through a fine sieve into prepared cookie crust; leave behind any undissolved chocolate to prevent filling from becoming grainy. Transfer filled crust to refrigerator 6 hours or overnight.

4 Place the egg whites and remaining ¾ cup sugar in the heat-proof bowl of an electric mixer, and place over a pan of barely simmering water. Stir constantly until whites are warm to the touch and sugar is dissolved, about 3 minutes. Attach bowl to mixer; using the whisk attachment, beat on medium until soft peaks form, about 3 minutes. Raise speed to high, and beat until stiff and glossy but not dry, about 1½ minutes.

5 Remove pie from refrigerator. Using a rubber spatula, drop meringue on top, lifting to create tall peaks. Use a kitchen blowtorch to brown top of meringue peaks, or place under a broiler, watching carefully since it will brown very quickly.

6 Chill the pie in the refrigerator, and serve cold. The pie will keep in the refrigerator up to 2 days, stored in an airtight container.

from Chocolate Desserts

chocolate fudge

MAKES 25 PIECES

The marshmallow cream in this recipe imparts a very smooth and delicate consistency. Be sure to cut while still soft, before it has had time to set. We find that the flavor and texture of the fudge improves after a few days' rest in the refrigerator.

½ cup heavy cream

2 tablespoons cardamom pods, crushed (optional)

5 ounces bittersweet chocolate

2 ounces unsweetened chocolate

⅓ cup marshmallow cream

1 teaspoon pure vanilla extract

1½ cups sugar

½ cup sweetened condensed milk

⅓ cup water

4 tablespoons unsalted butter, cut into pieces

Cocoa powder, for garnish (optional)

1 Line an 8-inch square baking dish with aluminum foil, smoothing surfaces as much as possible.

2 Place the heavy cream and the cardamom, if using, in a small saucepan, and bring to a boil. Remove from heat, and let steep 15 minutes.

3 Place the bittersweet chocolate, unsweetened chocolate, marshmallow cream, and vanilla extract in a large heat-proof bowl.

4 Strain the heavy cream through a fine sieve into a 3-quart saucepan, discarding cardamom. Add the sugar, condensed milk, water, and butter. Stir over medium-low heat until sugar has dissolved. Wash down sides of pan with a pastry brush dipped in water to prevent sugar crystals from forming. Raise heat to high, and bring to a boil. Attach a candy thermometer to the pan, and reduce heat to medium-high. Stir slowly with a wooden spoon until candy thermometer reads 232°F.

5 Remove pan from heat, and pour boiling mixture over chocolate mixture in bowl; do not scrape pan. Stir vigorously with a wooden spoon until mixture is well combined and glossy. Pour into prepared pan, and smooth the top with a small offset spatula. Allow the fudge to set in refrigerator until firm, about 2 hours.

6 Cut fudge into 1¼-inch rounds using a cookie cutter. Alternatively, you may cut into squares with a sharp knife. If desired, cut a small heart stencil out of parchment or waxed paper. Place stencil over a piece of fudge, and lightly sift cocoa powder over. Remove stencil, and repeat with remaining fudge. Store fudge in an airtight container in refrigerator up to 1 month.

from Chocolate Desserts

chocolate gelato

MAKES 1½ QUARTS

Use the best-quality chocolate you can find.

3 cups whole milk

1½ cups heavy cream

⅓ cup unsweetened cocoa powder

8 large egg yolks

⅓ cup sugar

6 ounces bittersweet chocolate, finely chopped

Chocolate Bowls (recipe follows)

1 Prepare an ice bath; set aside. In a large saucepan, bring milk, cream, and cocoa to a simmer over medium-low heat. Combine the egg yolks and sugar in the bowl of an electric mixer fitted with the whisk attachment; beat on medium speed until pale yellow and very thick, 3 to 5 minutes.

2 Add half the milk mixture to the yolk mixture, and whisk until blended. Stir mixture back into remaining milk mixture. Add the chocolate, and cook over low heat, stirring constantly with a wooden spoon, until mixture is thick enough to coat the back of the spoon.

3 Pass mixture through a very fine sieve into a large mixing bowl. Set the bowl in the ice bath, and chill completely, stirring occasionally. Freeze in an ice-cream maker, according to manufacturer's instructions, until gelato just holds its shape. Transfer to a metal loaf pan, cover with plastic wrap, and freeze until firm, at least 2 hours. Serve scoops of gelato in chocolate bowls.

from Chocolate Desserts

chocolate bowls

MAKES 8

Unmold these bowls one or two at a time, leaving the rest refrigerated while you work. Use care when deflating the balloons to prevent the bowls from cracking.

10 ounces dark chocolate, finely chopped

1 Blow up eight small balloons (about 4 to 5 inches in diameter when fully inflated). Line a baking sheet with parchment paper; set aside.

2 Place half the chocolate in a heat-proof bowl set over a pan of simmering water; stir until completely melted. Remove from heat, and stir in remaining 5 ounces chocolate until thoroughly smooth.

3 Spoon ½ teaspoon melted chocolate onto prepared pan to form a small disk. Dip balloon into bowl of melted chocolate,

coating about a third of balloon. Place dipped end on chocolate disk. Repeat with remaining balloons and chocolate. Transfer pan to refrigerator to set, about 30 minutes.

4 To release air from balloons, pinch the balloon just under the knot, and cut a small hole in the surface between fingers and knot. Very gradually release air; if air is released too quickly, the bowls may break. Carefully peel deflated balloons from chocolate bowls, and patch any holes with remaining chocolate. Return bowls to refrigerator until ready to serve.

chocolate sandwich cookies

MAKES 3 DOZEN | **PHOTO ON PAGE 82**

1¾ cups all-purpose flour, plus more for work surface
¼ cup unsweetened cocoa powder
½ teaspoon baking powder
¼ teaspoon salt
8 tablespoons (1 stick) unsalted butter
1 cup sugar
1 large egg
1 teaspoon pure vanilla extract
½ cup heavy cream
12 ounces white chocolate, finely chopped

1 In a large bowl, sift together flour, cocoa, baking powder, and salt. Set aside.

2 In the bowl of an electric mixer fitted with the paddle attachment, cream the butter and sugar until light and smooth. Beat in egg and vanilla.

3 Add the flour mixture, and mix on low speed until combined. Divide the dough in half, and wrap each portion in plastic; chill in the refrigerator 1 hour.

4 Preheat oven to 325°F. On a lightly floured surface, roll out dough to ⅛ inch thick. Using a cookie cutter, cut into 1½-inch squares. Transfer to parchment-paper–lined baking sheets, and refrigerate until firm, about 30 minutes. Gather any scraps, wrap in plastic, and chill 30 minutes before rerolling and cutting into squares. Bake until edges just begin to brown, about 12 minutes. Transfer to wire racks to cool.

5 Make ganache: Bring cream to a boil in a small saucepan. Remove from heat, and add 9 ounces white chocolate. Let stand, covered, 5 minutes. Transfer to a medium bowl, and stir until completely smooth. Place in the refrigerator, and

chill until thick enough to spread, about 1 hour, stirring every 10 minutes. Use an offset spatula to spread ganache on half the cookies; top with remaining cookies.

6 Melt remaining 3 ounces chocolate in a small heat-proof bowl set over a pan of simmering water. Make a small cone of parchment paper, or fit a small pastry bag with a coupler and an Ateco #2 round tip. Fill, and decorate as desired.

from Chocolate Desserts

chocolate spice cake

MAKES 1 EIGHT-INCH BUNDT CAKE | **PHOTO ON PAGE 82**

While this cake tastes best the same day it is made, it can be stored in an airtight container at room temperature for up to two days. To keep the frosting rich and glossy, do not refrigerate the finished cake.

1 cup (2 sticks) unsalted butter, room temperature, plus more for pan
1 cup all-purpose flour, plus more for pan
1 tablespoon grated fresh ginger
¼ cup water
½ cup dried cranberries
¼ cup golden raisins
¼ cup unsweetened cocoa powder
¾ teaspoon baking powder
¼ teaspoon baking soda
¼ teaspoon salt
1 tablespoon ground ginger
1 cup sugar
2 large eggs
1 teaspoon pure vanilla extract
¾ cup sour cream
Chocolate Fudge Frosting (recipe follows)

1 Preheat oven to 350°F. Butter and flour a 6-cup Bundt pan, and set aside. Place the grated ginger, the water, cranberries, and raisins in a small saucepan, and bring to a boil. Reduce to a simmer, and cook until liquid has evaporated, about 5 minutes. Set aside to cool.

2 In a medium bowl, sift together flour, cocoa, baking powder, baking soda, salt, and ground ginger. Place the butter and sugar in the bowl of an electric mixer fitted with the paddle attachment; beat on medium-high speed until light and fluffy, 2 to 3 minutes. Add the eggs one at a time, beating well after each addition. Scrape down sides of bowl as needed. Stir in vanilla. Add the flour mixture and sour cream in alternating small batches, starting and ending with the flour mixture; beat just until combined. Fold in dried fruit mixture.

3 Pour batter into prepared pan, and bake 40 to 50 minutes or until a cake tester inserted into center comes out clean. Transfer to a wire rack, and let cake cool in the pan 30 minutes. Invert cake onto wire rack; let cool completely.

4 Place cake on a cake plate or serving platter, and tuck waxed-paper strips under the edges of the cake to keep the plate clean. Using a small offset or rubber spatula, spread a thick coating of chocolate fudge frosting over cake. Remove waxed paper before serving.

from Chocolate Desserts

chocolate fudge frosting

MAKES 3 CUPS

If not using immediately, store in an airtight container at room temperature for up to two days. The frosting should not be refrigerated, or it will lose its lovely sheen.

12 ounces semisweet chocolate chips
1¾ cups heavy cream
3 tablespoons unsalted butter, room temperature
1 tablespoon corn syrup

1 Prepare an ice bath; set aside. Place chocolate chips in the bowl of a food processor fitted with the metal blade; pulse until roughly chopped.

2 Combine cream, butter, and corn syrup in a small saucepan. Bring to a boil over medium heat, stirring constantly until butter is melted.

3 With the motor running, pour cream mixture through the feed tube of the food processor; process until completely smooth, about 2 minutes. Transfer frosting to a bowl set over the ice bath. Stir every 10 minutes, until frosting is thick and spreadable, about 1½ hours.

cream puffs

MAKES 90

For variety, garnish some puffs with confectioners' sugar and ice the rest.

   All-purpose flour, for cookie cutter
   Pâte à Choux (page 35)
1 egg mixed with 1 tablespoon water, for egg wash
   Crystal sanding sugar (optional)
   Chopped nuts (optional)
   Oil, for plastic wrap
¾ cup heavy cream
   Pastry Cream Filling (page 46)
   Confectioners' sugar, for dusting
   Silver dragées, for decorating (optional)

FOR PINK ICING:

2 cups confectioners' sugar, sifted
1 tablespoon unsalted butter, melted
3 tablespoons plus 1 teaspoon water
   Pink food coloring

1 Preheat oven to 425°F with rack in center. Line two unrimmed baking sheets with parchment paper or Silpat baking mats. Dip 1-inch round cookie cutter into flour and mark spaces for piping pâte à choux dough on baking sheets at 2-inch intervals.

2 Fill a pastry bag fitted with a coupler or ½-inch (Ateco #806) tip with pâte à choux batter. Pipe 1-inch rounds onto baking sheets at 2-inch intervals. Using fingers, rub egg wash over entire tops, and flatten tips, being careful not to let it drip onto surrounding baking sheet (it will inhibit rising). Sprinkle with crystal sanding sugar or chopped nuts, if desired.

3 Cover one sheet with lightly oiled plastic wrap, and place in refrigerator. Transfer the other to the oven. Bake 10 minutes; reduce oven heat to 350°F. Bake 15 to 20 minutes more, or until puffs are golden brown. Transfer to a wire rack to let cool slightly. Raise oven temperature back to 425°F, and repeat process for remaining batch.

4 Whip heavy cream to stiff peaks in a small bowl. Stir pastry cream filling to soften. Add whipped cream to pastry cream filling in two batches; stir to combine after each. Fill

a pastry bag fitted with a coupler and large round tip (Ateco #230). Insert tip into the underside of each cream puff, and fill. Cool completely before dusting with confectioners' sugar or applying icing.

5   Make icing: combine sugar, butter, and water in a medium bowl. Stir until smooth. Add the food coloring a little at a time until desired color is reached. Dip the tops of cooled cream puffs into icing; let excess drip off before turning over. Let set a few minutes; decorate with a dragée, if desired. Serve, or store up to 2 hours in an airtight container in the refrigerator.

from Pâte à Choux

pastry cream filling

MAKES 4 CUPS

6   large egg yolks
1   large whole egg
¾   cup plus 2 tablespoons sugar
3   tablespoons cornstarch
3   tablespoons all-purpose flour
3   cups milk
3   tablespoons unsalted butter
2   teaspoons pure vanilla extract

1   Set aside a rimmed baking sheet for cooling pastry cream. In a medium bowl, combine egg yolks, egg, and 2 table-spoons sugar. Add cornstarch and flour; whisk until smooth and pale yellow. Set aside.

2   In a medium saucepan, combine milk and remaining ¾ cup sugar. Stir over medium-high heat until milk begins to steam. Whisking constantly, add half the hot milk to egg-yolk mixture. Stir until smooth; return mixture to remaining hot milk in the pan. Bring mixture to a boil, whisking rapidly to prevent scorching. Remove from heat, and stir in butter and vanilla. Immediately transfer pastry cream filling to baking sheet, and spread into a thin layer with a large rubber spatula. Cover entire surface with plastic wrap, and transfer to the refrigerator until chilled, about 15 minutes. Use immediately, or store up to 3 days in an airtight container in the refrigerator.

éclairs

MAKES 30

You can use either of the glazes below; each is enough to glaze thirty éclairs. Glazed éclairs can be stored in an airtight container in the refrigerator up to one day.

Pâte à Choux (page 35)
Oil, for plastic wrap
Pastry Cream Filling (recipe above)

FOR CHOCOLATE GLAZE:

¼   cup water
¼   cup light corn syrup
½   cup granulated sugar
4½   ounces semisweet chocolate, finely chopped

FOR COFFEE GLAZE:

2   cups sifted confectioners' sugar
1   tablespoon unsalted butter, melted
3   tablespoons hot brewed coffee

1   Preheat oven to 425°F with rack in center. Line two unrimmed baking sheets with parchment paper or Silpat baking mats.

2   Fill a pastry bag fitted with a ½-inch (Ateco #806) tip with pâte à choux; pipe oblong shapes, about 3½ inches long and 1 inch wide, onto prepared baking sheets at 2-inch inter-vals. Gently run a fork dipped in water along tops, making straight lines to ensure even rising.

3   Cover one sheet with lightly oiled plastic wrap, and place in refrigerator. Transfer the other to the oven. Bake 10 min-utes; reduce oven heat to 350°F. Bake 25 to 30 minutes more, or until golden brown. Turn off oven; prop door open slightly to let steam escape. Let éclairs dry in oven about 15 minutes or until centers are damp but no wet dough remains (test by cutting into the center of one). Transfer to a wire rack to cool slightly. Raise heat back to 425°F, and repeat process for remaining batch. If serving immediately, fill while still warm so they can take more cream. If filling at a later time, insert a skewer into one end, and move it around to expand opening for cream; set aside.

4   In a medium bowl, stir pastry cream filling to soften. Fill a pastry bag fitted with a coupler and large round tip (Ateco #230) with pastry cream. Insert tip into one end of each éclair; fill. Serve, or glaze as follows.

5   For chocolate glaze, combine water, corn syrup, and sugar in a small saucepan. Stir over medium-high heat until sugar is dissolved. Bring mixture to a boil, washing down sides of pan with a pastry brush dipped in water to prevent crystals

from forming. Once at a boil, remove from heat; add chocolate. Let stand 2 minutes; stir gently until smooth. Dip top of each éclair into glaze; let excess drip off before turning over. Transfer to a wire rack to allow glaze to set.

6 For coffee glaze, combine sugar, butter, and coffee in a medium bowl; whisk thoroughly until sugar has dissolved and mixture is smooth. Dip top of each éclair into glaze; let excess drip off before turning over. Transfer to a wire rack to allow glaze to set.

from Pâte à Choux

frozen chocolate malted
MAKES TWO 1½-CUP SERVINGS

This dessert was inspired by the Frozen Hot Chocolate at Serendipity 3, a restaurant in New York City.

1¼ cups heavy cream
¼ cup milk
7 tablespoons sugar
6 tablespoons unsweetened cocoa powder
1 tablespoon malted-milk powder
3 cups ice cubes
   Chocolate shavings, for garnish (optional)

1 Whip ½ cup cream until soft peaks form, and set aside.

2 Place the milk, remaining ¾ cup cream, sugar, cocoa, and malted-milk powder in the jar of a blender, and blend until smooth and frothy.

3 With the motor running, add ice cubes, a few at a time, until the mixture is thick and smooth. Pour the mixture into tall glasses, and top with whipped cream and chocolate shavings, if desired.

from Chocolate Desserts

mocha steamed puddings
MAKES 4 | **PHOTO ON PAGE 83**

We found that when making these steamed puddings, whisking instead of folding the egg whites into the melted chocolate mixture produced the creamiest texture.

½ cup sugar
2 tablespoons all-purpose flour
1 teaspoon cocoa powder
1 teaspoon instant espresso powder
3 ounces bittersweet chocolate, finely chopped
2 tablespoons unsalted butter, softened
¾ cup milk, scalded
1 teaspoon pure vanilla extract
2 large eggs, separated
½ cup heavy cream
   Espresso Crème Anglaise (page 48)

1 Preheat oven to 325°F. Combine 6 tablespoons sugar with the flour, cocoa, and espresso powder in a large bowl; whisk to combine.

2 Melt chocolate and butter in a medium heat-proof bowl set over a pan of simmering water. Remove from heat; stir in scalded milk and vanilla. Whisk chocolate mixture into flour mixture until well combined.

3 Beat egg yolks until pale and very thick, 2 to 3 minutes. Gradually pour into chocolate mixture, whisking constantly.

4 Whisk egg whites until frothy. Add remaining 2 tablespoons sugar, and whisk until stiff peaks form. Whisk egg whites into chocolate mixture.

5 Place four 1-cup ramekins or ovenproof cups in a roasting pan, and fill each with batter. Pour boiling water into pan so that it comes halfway up the sides of the baking cups. Bake 45 to 50 minutes, or until tops begin to crack. Remove roasting pan from oven, and transfer baking cups to a wire rack to cool slightly.

6 Just before serving, whip the heavy cream until soft peaks form. Serve the steamed puddings warm, topped with espresso crème anglaise and whipped cream.

from Chocolate Desserts

espresso crème anglaise

MAKES 1½ CUPS

This sauce will add an elegant note to most anything chocolate, from airy brownies to a dense chocolate torte. Store any unused sauce in an airtight container in the refrigerator for up to two days.

4 large egg yolks
¼ cup sugar
1 cup milk
¾ cup heavy cream
1 teaspoon instant espresso powder

1   Prepare an ice bath, and set aside. Combine the egg yolks and sugar in the bowl of an electric mixer fitted with the whisk attachment, and beat until mixture is pale yellow and very thick, 3 to 5 minutes.

2   Place the milk, cream, and espresso powder in a small saucepan, and bring to a boil over medium-high heat. Remove from heat, and gradually pour half the milk mixture into the egg-yolk mixture, whisking constantly. Return the mixture to saucepan.

3   Cook over medium-low heat, whisking constantly, until the mixture is thick enough to coat the back of a spoon. Strain the crème anglaise through a fine sieve into a small bowl set in the ice bath; let cool completely, stirring frequently. Serve chilled. If not using immediately, store in an airtight container in the refrigerator until ready to use.

molten chocolate cakes with earl grey ice cream

MAKES 6 | PHOTO ON PAGE 82

Since the batter needs to be frozen before baking, these cakes are perfect to store in the freezer for those unexpected moments when you need a quick dessert. The frozen chocolate truffle imbedded in the batter melts in the oven to produce a liquid core. Using semisweet chocolate in the truffles is essential; if bittersweet is used, the centers of the cakes will not ooze. Make the chocolate curls by shaving a block of chocolate with a vegetable peeler.

6 tablespoons unsalted butter, room temperature, plus more for ring molds
12 ounces semisweet chocolate
5 large eggs, separated
10 tablespoons sugar
½ teaspoon pure vanilla extract
6 Chocolate Truffles (recipe follows)
Earl Grey Ice Cream (recipe follows)
Chocolate curls, for garnish (optional)

1   Butter six 2½-by-2¾-inch ring molds. Place on a rimmed baking sheet lined with parchment paper, and set aside.

2   Place chocolate and butter in a medium heat-proof bowl set over a pan of simmering water, and heat until melted. Stir to combine.

3   Combine egg yolks and 6 tablespoons sugar in a large bowl, and whisk until mixture is pale yellow and thick, 3 to 5 minutes. Stir in vanilla extract. Add chocolate mixture to egg-yolk mixture, and stir to combine.

4   Place egg whites in the bowl of an electric mixer fitted with the whisk attachment, and beat until frothy. Add remaining 4 tablespoons sugar, and whisk until stiff peaks form. Fold egg-white mixture into chocolate mixture.

5   Spoon about ¼ cup batter into each ring, and place a truffle in the center of each. Spoon remaining batter over the truffles, and place in the freezer to set, at least 1 hour.

6   Preheat oven to 350°F. Transfer baking sheet with filled ring molds to oven, and bake until sides are set but center is still soft, 20 to 25 minutes. Using a thin spatula, carefully transfer the cakes (still in the ring molds) to a serving plate. Lift and remove the ring molds. Serve warm with Earl Grey ice cream, and garnish with chocolate curls, if desired.

from Chocolate Desserts

chocolate truffles

MAKES 6

4 ounces semisweet chocolate, finely chopped
¾ cup heavy cream

Place chocolate in a medium heat-proof bowl. Bring cream to a boil in a small saucepan, and pour over chocolate. Let sit 5 minutes; stir until thoroughly combined. Place mixture in the freezer until set, about 45 minutes, stirring every 15 minutes. Divide mixture into six equal parts, and roll each into a ball. Cover truffles with plastic wrap; freeze until ready to use.

earl grey ice cream

MAKES ABOUT 5 CUPS

Two tablespoons of loose tea leaves may be substituted for the tea bags in this recipe. If you use loose tea, you will need to strain the tea mixture before combining it with the egg yolks.

8 large egg yolks
½ cup sugar
2 cups milk
2 cups heavy cream
4 Earl Grey tea bags

1 Prepare an ice bath, and set aside. In the bowl of an electric mixer fitted with the whisk attachment, beat egg yolks and sugar until pale yellow and very thick, 3 to 5 minutes.

2 Place milk, cream, and tea bags in a medium saucepan, and bring to a boil. Remove from heat; cover, and let steep 10 minutes. Remove tea bags, and return mixture to a boil. Gradually pour half the milk mixture into the egg-yolk mixture, whisking constantly. Return mixture to the saucepan.

3 Cook mixture over medium-low heat, whisking constantly, until thick enough to coat the back of a spoon. Strain through a fine sieve into a bowl set in the ice bath, and chill completely. Freeze in an ice-cream maker, according to manufacturer's instructions, until the ice cream just holds its shape. Transfer ice cream to a metal loaf pan; cover with plastic wrap, and freeze until firm, at least 2 hours.

profiteroles

MAKES 26 | **PHOTO ON PAGE 82**

Garnish with delicate curls made by shaving a block of chocolate with a vegetable peeler.

Pâte à Choux (page 35)
1 egg mixed with 1 tablespoon water, for egg wash
  Oil, for plastic wrap
2½ pints ice cream
10 ounces semisweet chocolate, finely chopped
½ cup heavy cream
2 tablespoons corn syrup

1 Preheat oven to 425°F with a rack in the center. Line two unrimmed baking sheets with parchment paper or Silpat baking mats.

2 Fill a pastry bag fitted with a coupler or ½-inch (Ateco #806) tip with pâte à choux batter. Pipe 2-inch rounds that are about 1 inch high onto prepared baking sheets at 2-inch intervals.

3 Using your finger, gently rub egg wash over entire tops, and flatten the tips, being careful not to let egg wash drip down onto sheet (it will inhibit rising). Cover one sheet with lightly oiled plastic wrap, and place in refrigerator. Transfer the other to the oven. Bake for 10 minutes; reduce oven heat to 350°F. Bake until puffs are golden brown, 15 to 20 minutes more. Turn off oven, and prop door open slightly to let steam escape. Let profiteroles dry out in the oven about 15 minutes, or until centers are slightly damp but no wet dough remains (test by cutting into the center of one). Transfer to a wire rack to cool completely. Raise oven heat back to 425°F, and repeat process for remaining batch.

4 Scoop out 26 balls of ice cream; place on a parchment-lined baking sheet. Place in freezer to harden, 20 minutes.

5 Make chocolate sauce: Place chocolate in a bowl. Combine cream and corn syrup in a small saucepan; bring to a boil. Pour over chocolate; let sit 5 minutes, and stir to combine. Let cool slightly before serving, or store in refrigerator up to 1 week; before serving, gently reheat over low heat.

6 Cut each profiterole in half horizontally, and fill with a scoop of ice cream. Place two profiteroles on each plate, and spoon warm chocolate sauce on top.

from Pâte à Choux

vanilla pudding

SERVES 4 | **PHOTO ON PAGE 85**

This pudding can be made up to one day before serving and allowed to chill, covered, in the refrigerator.

- 2 tablespoons plus 2 teaspoons cornstarch
- ½ cup sugar
  Pinch of salt
- 2 large eggs
- 2 cups milk
- 1 vanilla bean, split and scraped
- 1 tablespoon unsalted butter, cut into small pieces
- 2 teaspoons pure vanilla extract
- 1 ounce milk chocolate shavings, for garnish (optional)

1 Prepare an ice bath; set aside. In a small bowl, combine cornstarch, 2 tablespoons sugar, and salt. Whisk eggs in a separate bowl until smooth; whisk in cornstarch mixture.

2 Combine milk, remaining sugar, and vanilla-bean scrapings in a medium saucepan. Bring to a boil over medium-high heat. Slowly pour half the milk mixture into egg mixture, whisking constantly.

3 Return mixture to saucepan set over medium-high heat. Bring to a boil, whisking constantly, until thickened, about 2 minutes. Remove pan from heat, and transfer mixture to a medium heat-proof bowl.

4 Whisk in butter and vanilla extract. Set bowl in ice bath, stirring occasionally, until chilled. Serve pudding with chocolate shavings on top, if desired.

from What to Have for Dinner

spiced rose lassi

MAKES 2

Our version of this chilled yogurt drink from India, pronounced "LAH-see," is refreshing anytime but especially as a mouth-cooling accompaniment to spicy food.

- 1½ cups yogurt
- ¼ cup water
- 3 tablespoons sugar
- 2 teaspoons rose water, plus more to taste
- ¼ teaspoon ground cardamom
  Pinch of ground cinnamon
  Pesticide-free rose petals, for garnish (optional)

Place yogurt, the water, sugar, rose water, and spices in the jar of a blender. Blend on high speed until smooth and frothy. Serve cold, garnished with rose petals, if desired.

from Good Things

March

STARTERS

53 artichoke bruschetta

53 cold soba noodles with basil flowers

53 marinated goat cheese with oregano

53 pan-fried scallops on caramelized fennel

54 pistou soup

55 roasted cherry tomatoes, baked buffalo mozzarella, and eggplant

55 tomato essence and timbales of pressed tomatoes

SALADS

57 salad of crisp squid, asparagus, and tangerines

57 tomato and bean salad with garlic-chive blossoms

MAIN COURSES

58 boneless pork chops and roasted yam fries

58 confit of wild salmon on cucumber salad with horseradish sauce

59 cornflake-crusted chicken with red cabbage slaw and rutabaga potatoes

59 fish and chips

60 roast best end of highgrove lamb and fava beans with mint and marjoram

60 spaghetti with clams

61 veal scallopini milanese

SIDE DISHES

61 fricassée of wild mushrooms

61 sautéed chicory

DESSERTS

62 grapefruit in moscato

62 melon and berries steeped in red wine, sauternes, basil, and mint

62 peach tartes tatin

63 rice pudding tarts with blood oranges

64 thyme-roasted figs over brioche pain perdu

MISCELLANEOUS

64 flower sugar

64 pickled garlic

64 rose petal jelly

artichoke bruschetta

SERVES 4 | **PHOTO ON PAGE 78**

Frozen artichoke hearts may be used in place of marinated. You will need to thaw them slightly before sautéeing with the garlic; also, increase the cooking time by three to four minutes to ensure proper browning.

2 garlic cloves

4 slices rustic bread, each about ¾ inch thick

2 tablespoons extra-virgin olive oil, plus more for drizzling

1 12-ounce jar marinated artichoke hearts, drained

½ cup fresh ricotta cheese

Coarse salt and freshly ground pepper

Shaved Parmesan cheese, for garnish

1   Thinly slice 1 garlic clove, and set aside. Gently crush remaining clove, and rub over one side of each bread slice. Brush both sides of bread with 1 tablespoon oil. Toast slices on a grill or in a skillet over medium-high heat until golden and crisp on both sides. Transfer to a serving platter, and set aside.

2   Heat remaining tablespoon oil in a medium skillet over medium-high heat. Add reserved garlic and the artichoke hearts. Sauté until golden, 3 to 4 minutes. Set aside.

3   Season ricotta with salt and pepper; spread about 2 table-spoons on each slice of bread. Top with sautéed garlic and artichokes. Season again with salt and pepper. Garnish with shaved Parmesan cheese, and drizzle with oil.

from What to Have for Dinner

cold soba noodles with basil flowers

SERVES 4 | **PHOTO ON PAGE 72**

Tatsoi have small dark leaves and crunchy stalks; we use the leaves in this salad. Chopped spinach would work just as well.

3 tablespoons soy sauce

2 tablespoons mirin

2 teaspoons toasted sesame oil

2 teaspoons freshly squeezed lime juice

1 teaspoon fresh ginger, grated

9 ounces soba noodles

½ cup Thai basil leaves and flowers, plus more flowers for garnish

½ cup tatsoi leaves

1   Combine soy sauce, mirin, sesame oil, lime juice, and ginger in a small bowl; whisk to combine. Set aside.

2   Bring a large pot of water to a boil. Cook noodles until al dente, 8 to 10 minutes. Transfer to a colander; run under cold water to stop cooking. Drain well.

3   In a large bowl, combine noodles, basil, tatsoi, and reserved dressing. Toss to combine. Garnish with basil flowers.

from Herb Flowers

marinated goat cheese with oregano

SERVES 4 TO 6

5 goat-cheese buttons

¼ cup oregano flowers and leaves

1 garlic clove

1 teaspoon whole black peppercorns

1 cup extra-virgin olive oil

Combine goat cheese, oregano, garlic, and peppercorns in a jar. Add oil. Store, refrigerated, up to 5 days.

from Herb Flowers

pan-fried scallops on caramelized fennel

SERVES 4 | **PHOTO ON PAGE 75**

2 pounds fennel bulbs (about 2 medium)

1 garlic clove, finely chopped

2 shallots, finely chopped

2 dried bay leaves

Zest of 1 orange

½ teaspoon ground cardamom

8 tablespoons olive oil

1 tablespoon coarse salt

Pinch of freshly ground white pepper

2 teaspoons light-brown sugar

1 14½-ounce can low-sodium chicken broth, or homemade

1 sprig thyme

¾ cup water

8 large scallops (about 14 ounces), muscles removed

⅓ cup fresh flat-leaf parsley, packed

2 tablespoons freshly squeezed lemon juice

2 tablespoons toasted pine nuts, for garnish

Shaved truffle, for garnish (optional)

1   Preheat oven to 325°F. Trim feathery tops from fennel bulbs, and discard. Trim stem pieces and outer leaves from

bulbs; clean, and reserve 2 cups (about 8 ounces) of these trimmings for the purée. Slice each bulb through the root into four ½-inch-thick strips.

2 In a small roasting pan, combine garlic, 1 shallot, 1 bay leaf, orange zest, ¼ teaspoon cardamom, 3 tablespoons oil, ½ teaspoon salt, pepper, 1 teaspoon brown sugar, and chicken broth. Add fennel slices, and gently toss to coat. Cover roasting pan with foil, and roast until fennel is tender and most of liquid has evaporated, about 45 minutes. Remove from oven, and transfer fennel to a plate to cool.

3 Coarsely chop reserved fennel trimmings. In a medium saucepan, heat 1 tablespoon oil over medium-high heat. Add trimmings, remaining shallot, bay leaf, ¼ teaspoon cardamom, and thyme. Cook, stirring occasionally, until trimmings soften, about 4 minutes.

4 Add the water, ½ teaspoon salt, and ½ teaspoon brown sugar; bring to a boil. Reduce heat; cover pan, and simmer until trimmings are soft when pierced with a fork, about 20 minutes. Discard bay leaf and thyme; transfer mixture to the bowl of a food processor fitted with the metal blade. Purée, adding 2 tablespoons oil through the feed tube with the motor running. Set aside.

5 In a large nonstick skillet over medium-high heat, sauté reserved fennel slices until golden brown, 2 to 3 minutes on each side. Transfer to a plate, and set aside. In same pan, heat remaining 2 tablespoons olive oil. Add scallops, and sprinkle with 1 teaspoon salt; sauté until brown on first side, about 4 minutes. Turn, sprinkle with remaining teaspoon salt, and add parsley. Sauté until other side is brown, about 2 minutes. Remove from heat; add lemon juice to pan. Toss scallops and parsley in pan juices.

6 To serve, place two ¼-cup dollops of fennel purée on each plate; top each dollop with a fennel slice and scallop. Garnish with wilted parsley leaves, toasted pine nuts, and shaved truffle, if desired.

from From the Garden to the Table

pistou soup

SERVES 4 | **PHOTO ON PAGE 75**

This wholesome French stew, similar to Italian minestrone, gets its name and distinctive flavor from pistou, a paste made with crushed basil, garlic, and olive oil. In this recipe, it is embellished with toasted pine nuts, as in pesto.

FOR THE PISTOU:

1 cup basil leaves, packed

1 tablespoon toasted pine nuts

1 garlic clove

½ teaspoon coarse salt

¼ teaspoon freshly ground pepper

½ cup olive oil

FOR THE CROUTONS:

12 baguette slices (about 1 inch thick)

½ cup freshly grated Parmesan cheese

FOR THE SOUP:

3 sprigs thyme

3 sprigs flat-leaf parsley

1 dried bay leaf

1½ tablespoons plus ¼ cup olive oil

1 medium onion, finely chopped

2 garlic cloves

1½ pounds fresh fava beans, shelled (8 ounces)

6 cups water, plus more for cooking pasta

2½ teaspoons coarse salt

3 ounces dry rigatoni or other pasta

1 medium carrot, peeled and sliced into ⅛-inch rounds

1 stalk celery, sliced ¼ inch thick

2 small leeks, white and light-green parts, cut crosswise into ¼-inch half moons, washed well and drained

½ small fennel bulb, cut into ¼-inch pieces

½ teaspoon freshly ground pepper

⅔ cup fresh or frozen peas

½ medium zucchini, cut into ¼-inch pieces

Freshly grated Parmesan cheese, for garnish

1 Make pistou: In the bowl of a food processor fitted with the metal blade, combine basil, pine nuts, garlic clove, salt, and pepper. Pulse a few times to combine; with machine running, add oil until mixture is smooth, 1 to 2 minutes. Transfer to a bowl; set aside.

2 Make croutons: Heat broiler. Place baguette slices on a baking sheet, and sprinkle each slice with some of the

Parmesan cheese. Place under broiler, and broil until cheese begins to brown, about 2 minutes. Remove from oven; set aside.

3   Make soup: Bundle thyme, parsley, and bay leaf with kitchen twine to make a bouquet garni. In a 6-quart stockpot, heat 1½ tablespoons oil over medium heat. Add half the onion, the bouquet garni, and the garlic cloves; sauté until onion begins to soften, about 4 minutes. Add shelled fava beans; cook 2 minutes more. Add 2 cups water and ½ teaspoon salt. Reduce heat to low; cover, and simmer gently 30 to 40 minutes. Transfer beans and cooking liquid to a heatproof bowl; discard garlic and bouquet garni.

4   While beans are cooking, bring a medium saucepan of water to a boil; add pasta and 1 teaspoon salt. Cook until al dente according to package instructions. Drain in a colander, and set aside.

5   In the same saucepan used to cook the beans, heat remaining ¼ cup oil over medium-high heat. Add remaining onion with the carrot, celery, leeks, and fennel; sauté 2 minutes. Add remaining 4 cups water, teaspoon salt, and pepper; cook 5 minutes more. Add peas, zucchini, reserved beans and cooking liquid, and pasta. Bring to a boil, and immediately remove from heat to preserve bright color of vegetables.

6   To serve, ladle soup into four shallow bowls, and top each with a few croutons. Drizzle 2 tablespoons pistou into each bowl; garnish with Parmesan cheese.

from From the Garden to the Table

roasted cherry tomatoes, baked buffalo mozzarella, and eggplant

SERVES 4 | PHOTO ON PAGE 75

¾ cup extra-virgin olive oil

10 fresh basil leaves, finely chopped

½ garlic clove, finely sliced

½ teaspoon coarse salt

¼ teaspoon freshly ground pepper

1 ball buffalo or other fresh mozzarella (about 1 pound), quartered (not sliced)

2 Japanese or small eggplants

1 tablespoon white-wine vinegar

3 tablespoons water

1½ teaspoons sugar

1½ pounds vine-ripened cherry tomatoes on four individual vines

½ ounce Parmesan cheese, freshly grated (about 4 tablespoons)

Balsamic vinegar, for serving

1   In a medium shallow bowl, combine ¼ cup oil with the basil, garlic, salt, and pepper. Add the mozzarella, and toss to coat. Cover bowl with plastic wrap, and marinate 2 hours in the refrigerator.

2   Slice each eggplant into eight wedges by cutting in half lengthwise and cutting each half into quarters; transfer to a medium bowl. In a separate bowl, whisk together vinegar, the water, sugar, and remaining ½ cup olive oil. Pour over eggplant, and turn to coat; cover, and place in refrigerator 1 hour.

3   Heat broiler. Remove eggplant from marinade, and shake off excess liquid. Place on a baking sheet, and broil until crisp and browned, about 10 minutes, turning once. Transfer to paper towels to drain.

4   With tomatoes still on the vine, place on one end of a rimmed baking sheet. Remove mozzarella from marinade; place on baking sheet beside tomatoes. Drizzle tomatoes with marinade, and sprinkle mozzarella and tomatoes with Parmesan cheese. Broil until tomatoes burst and mozzarella has melted, about 6 minutes.

5   To serve, transfer tomatoes and mozzarella to a serving platter, and place eggplant spears on the side. Drizzle lightly with balsamic vinegar.

from From the Garden to the Table

tomato essence and timbales of pressed tomatoes

SERVES 4

This recipe can be prepared over several days. After puréeing the marinated tomatoes, allow them to drain overnight; store extracted juices in the refrigerator for up to one day.

FOR THE TOMATO ESSENCE:

2¼ pounds vine-ripened cherry or other ripe, flavorful tomatoes, halved

½ stalk celery, coarsely chopped

1½ teaspoons finely chopped shallot

½ cup chopped fennel (about ¼ bulb)

¾ teaspoon chopped fresh thyme leaves

¼ teaspoon chopped fresh tarragon

4 tablespoons chopped fresh basil

1 garlic clove

1 tablespoon coarse salt

Pinch of cayenne pepper

2 drops Worcestershire sauce

2 drops hot-pepper sauce, such as Tabasco

FOR THE TIMBALES:

4 large tomatoes (about 2 pounds)

½ garlic clove, minced

2 tablespoons chopped fresh basil, plus whole leaves, freshly sliced, for garnish

¾ teaspoon coarse salt

¼ teaspoon freshly ground pepper

4 teaspoons balsamic vinegar

1 tablespoon water

1 teaspoon sherry vinegar

1½ teaspoons sugar

½ medium zucchini

½ Japanese or small eggplant

1 tablespoon olive oil, plus more for drizzling

Tomato Sorbet (recipe follows)

1 Make the tomato essence: Combine all ingredients in a large bowl; cover, and marinate at room temperature 4 hours.

2 Transfer to the bowl of a food processor; pulse to combine, about 5 seconds (do not overblend). Drape two 14-inch squares of cheesecloth over a deep bowl or stockpot, and transfer mixture to the cheesecloth. Tie ends together tightly, and suspend over bowl to catch juices, preferably overnight. Transfer juices to an airtight container, and store in refrigerator until needed, up to 1 day. Discard contents in cheesecloth.

3 Make the timbales: Bring a medium saucepan of water to a boil over high heat. Score an X in the bottom of each large tomato; place in boiling water 10 seconds. Remove with a slotted spoon, and let cool slightly. Peel tomatoes, discarding skins. Using a paring knife, gently cut outer flesh away from core into four petal-shape pieces, following the shape of the fruit and cutting from top to bottom. You should have a total of sixteen petals; set aside.

4 Remove and discard seeds from core of tomatoes, and finely chop remaining flesh. Combine chopped tomatoes in a small bowl with garlic, chopped basil, ¼ teaspoon salt, ⅛ teaspoon pepper, and balsamic vinegar; set aside. Using a 2-inch round cutter, cut out eight circles from eight petals, and place one each in the bottom of four sterilized 4-ounce jelly jars, prettiest side down. Set aside remaining four circles. Finely chop the scraps, and add to the marinating mixture.

5 Use two of the remaining petals to line sides of each jar, overlapping slightly to cover. Place 4 to 5 tablespoons chopped tomato mixture in each jar to fill, and place one of the reserved circles on top. Press down lid; screw on ring lid. Place in refrigerator 1 hour or overnight.

6 In a small bowl, whisk water, sherry vinegar, sugar, and remaining ½ teaspoon salt and ⅛ teaspoon pepper. Set aside.

7 Cut off ends of zucchini and eggplant. Use a paring knife to slice lengthwise into ¼-inch-thick strips; cut each strip into 1-inch squares. In a medium sauté pan, heat oil over medium heat. Add eggplant skin side down; cook 30 seconds. Add zucchini skin side down, and cook 1 minute on each side. Pour sherry-vinegar mixture into pan, and remove from heat.

8 Remove jars from refrigerator; run the tip of a paring knife around the inside of each jar to loosen, and unmold. Place a timbale in the center of each of four chilled bowls. Surround with eggplant and zucchini. Ladle tomato essence around bowl; drizzle with olive oil. Place a scoop of sorbet on each timbale, and garnish with basil. Serve immediately.

from From the Garden to the Table

tomato sorbet

SERVES 4

We used this tart sorbet in Tomato Essence and Timbale of Pressed Tomatoes, but it would be equally delicious as a palate cleanser between courses.

2 tablespoons olive oil

½ cup finely chopped onion

Grated zest of 1 orange

2 sprigs thyme, leaves coarsely chopped

1¼ pounds vine-ripened cherry or other ripe, flavorful tomatoes, halved

1 teaspoon salt

2 tablespoons sugar

⅛ teaspoon cayenne pepper

1 Heat oil in a medium sauté pan over low heat. Add onion, zest, and thyme; sauté until onion is soft, 8 to 10 minutes.

2 Add 8 ounces tomatoes (just under half) along with the salt, sugar, and cayenne. Cook until liquid has evaporated and tomato mixture thickens to a paste, about 10 minutes.

3 Remove from heat, and add remaining 12 ounces tomatoes. Transfer mixture to the jar of a blender, working in batches, if necessary, so as not to fill more than halfway; purée until smooth. Pass through a fine sieve into a large bowl. Chill strained mixture over an ice bath or in the refrigerator. Transfer to an ice-cream maker, and freeze according to manufacturer's directions. Store in freezer until ready to use, up to 1 week.

salad of crisp squid, asparagus, and tangerines

SERVES 4 | **PHOTO ON PAGE 73**

- 2 tablespoons extra-virgin olive oil
- ¾ cup plain breadcrumbs
- ½ teaspoon dried oregano, crumbled
- ½ teaspoon dried thyme, crumbled
- ½ teaspoon coarse salt, plus more for cooking water
- ¼ teaspoon freshly ground pepper
- 2 pounds squid, cleaned and cut into ¼-inch-thick rings
- 1 pound medium asparagus, trimmed
- 1 teaspoon red-wine vinegar
- 1 tablespoon freshly squeezed tangerine juice
- 8 cups (about 8 ounces) mixed salad greens
- 1 medium red onion, thinly sliced into rings
- 2 tangerines, peel and pith removed, cut into whole segments

1 Preheat oven to 450°F. Brush two large baking sheets with 1½ teaspoons oil each. Set aside.

2 In a medium bowl, combine breadcrumbs, oregano, thyme, ¼ teaspoon salt, and ⅛ teaspoon pepper. Rinse and drain squid (do not dry); add to breadcrumb mixture, and toss to coat well. Arrange squid in a single layer on prepared baking sheets. Transfer to oven; cook until golden and crisp underneath, about 10 minutes. Remove from oven; let stand 5 minutes, and loosen with a metal spatula.

3 Meanwhile, bring a pot of water to a boil; add salt. Place asparagus in water until crisp-tender, about 4 minutes. Transfer to a colander; rinse with cold water to stop cooking, and drain well. Slice diagonally into ¼-inch lengths.

4 In a large bowl, whisk together vinegar, tangerine juice, and remaining tablespoon oil. Add asparagus, greens, onion, and tangerines; season with remaining ¼ teaspoon salt and ⅛ teaspoon pepper. Arrange on a platter, layered with squid.

PER SERVING: 433 CALORIES, 12 G FAT, 528 MG CHOLESTEROL, 3 G CARBOHYDRATE, 529 MG SODIUM, 45 G PROTEIN, 7 G FIBER

from Fit to Eat: Oven Frying

tomato and bean salad with garlic-chive blossoms

SERVES 4

We used orange cherry tomatoes and yellow pear tomatoes, but any ripe tomatoes will work.

- 1 small shallot, minced
- 1 tablespoon red-wine vinegar
- 2 tablespoons garlic chives, finely chopped
- 6 tablespoons extra-virgin olive oil
- 1 teaspoon coarse salt, plus more for seasoning
- 12 ounces green beans, trimmed and halved
- 24 ounces mixed cherry and pear tomatoes, halved
- ¼ cup garlic-chive blossoms
  Freshly ground pepper

1 Prepare vinaigrette: Combine shallot, vinegar, and garlic chives in a small bowl; let macerate 10 minutes. Add oil slowly, whisking until emulsified. Set aside.

2 Prepare an ice bath; set aside. Bring a medium saucepan of water to a boil; add 1 teaspoon salt. Add green beans; cook until bright green, about 2 minutes. Transfer to ice bath to stop cooking. Drain in a colander, and pat dry with paper towels.

3 Combine green beans, tomatoes, and garlic-chive blossoms in a large bowl. Add vinaigrette, and toss to combine. Season with salt and pepper.

from Herb Flowers

boneless pork chops and roasted yam fries

SERVES 4 | **PHOTO ON PAGE 78**

2 medium yams (about 14 ounces), peeled

1 tablespoon packed dark-brown sugar

1½ tablespoons extra-virgin olive oil

½ teaspoon coarse salt

½ teaspoon freshly ground pepper

2 slices whole-wheat bread, finely ground in food processor to make breadcrumbs

½ teaspoon dried oregano

4 four-ounce boneless pork-loin medallions (¾ inch thick), trimmed

2 bunches (about 20 ounces) baby spinach, cleaned, with water clinging to leaves

Lime wedges, for serving

1 Preheat oven to 450°F with racks in upper and lower thirds.

2 Cut each yam lengthwise into six spears. Place on a baking sheet, and toss with brown sugar, 1 tablespoon oil, and ¼ teaspoon each salt and pepper. Place on lower rack of oven, and roast 15 minutes. Remove from oven, and turn each spear with a metal spatula. Return to lower rack until well browned, about 15 minutes. Remove from oven, and keep warm until ready to serve.

3 After returning yams to oven, combine breadcrumbs, oregano, and remaining ¼ teaspoon each salt and pepper in a shallow bowl. Dredge pork medallions one at a time in breadcrumbs, turning to coat completely. Transfer to a plate while repeating with remaining medallions.

4 Coat a cast-iron or ovenproof skillet with remaining ½ tablespoon oil. Add pork medallions, and transfer to upper rack of oven. Cook 6 minutes; turn and cook until pork is browned and firm to the touch, about 6 minutes more. Transfer to a cutting board.

5 While pork and potatoes are cooking, place wet spinach leaves in a large saucepan over high heat. Cover, and steam, stirring occasionally, until wilted, about 3 minutes. Remove from heat.

6 Slice pork on the bias, and place on serving plate with yams, steamed spinach, and lime wedges.

PER SERVING: 416 CALORIES, 17 G FAT, 67 MG CHOLESTEROL, 40 G CARBOHYDRATE, 565 MG SODIUM, 28 G PROTEIN, 7 G FIBER

from Fit to Eat: Oven Frying

confit of wild salmon on cucumber salad with horseradish sauce

SERVES 4 | **PHOTO ON PAGE 75**

2 cups plus 2 tablespoons olive oil

3½ tablespoons finely grated lemon zest (6 to 7 lemons)

3 tablespoons prepared horseradish

3 tablespoons sour cream

3½ teaspoons coarse salt

¼ teaspoon plus a pinch of granulated sugar

Pinch of cayenne pepper

4 tablespoons fresh dill, chopped

1½ teaspoons light-brown sugar

½ teaspoon freshly ground white pepper

1 boneless and skinless salmon fillet (½ pound), cut into 4 equal portions

1 medium cucumber (about 8 ounces), peeled, cut in half lengthwise, and seeds removed

1 tablespoon white-wine vinegar

¾ cup (about 3 ounces) cauliflower florets

2 cups water

1 cup (about 2 ounces) baby greens, such as arugula or mizuna

½ ounce (about 1 tablespoon) salmon roe, for garnish (optional)

1 In a small saucepan over medium heat, combine 2 cups oil and 2 tablespoons lemon zest. Heat until a deep-fry thermometer registers 120°F. Remove from heat, and let flavors infuse 30 minutes. The oil can be kept at room temperature, covered, up to 24 hours.

2 Make horseradish sauce: In a small bowl, mix together horseradish, sour cream, ¼ teaspoon salt, ¼ teaspoon sugar, and cayenne. Pass through a fine sieve into another small bowl, and transfer to the refrigerator until needed.

3 Combine 3 tablespoons chopped dill, remaining 1½ tablespoons lemon zest, 1½ teaspoons salt, the brown sugar, and white pepper. Rub the mixture evenly over the salmon; place in a shallow bowl, and cover. Place in the refrigerator, and let marinate 1 hour.

4 Use a mandoline or sharp knife to thinly slice cucumber lengthwise into thin ribbons. Transfer to a small bowl, and sprinkle 1½ teaspoons salt evenly over cucumbers. Let sit 25 minutes. Pat dry with paper towels, and set aside.

5 Make the vinaigrette: In a small bowl, whisk together vinegar, remaining 2 tablespoons olive oil, ¼ teaspoon salt, and pinch of granulated sugar. Set aside.

6 Make salmon confit: Strain the reserved oil infusion through a fine-mesh sieve into a medium saucepan, and discard lemon zest. Clip a deep-fry thermometer to the side of the pan, and heat oil until it reaches 120°F. Remove salmon from refrigerator, and wipe off herbs with a paper towel. Place salmon in the hot oil, and poach 25 minutes, adjusting heat if necessary to maintain a constant temperature of 120°F. Using a slotted spatula, transfer salmon to a paper-towel–lined plate to drain. Set aside.

7 While salmon is cooking, place cauliflower florets in a small heat-proof bowl. Bring the water to a boil in a small saucepan, and pour over florets. Let sit 1 minute, and drain in a colander. Set aside. Toss baby greens with 2 tablespoons reserved vinaigrette.

8 To serve, place cucumber ribbons in a mound in the center of each of four plates. Place a piece of salmon on top of the cucumbers, and top with a small dollop of salmon roe, if desired. Arrange cauliflower and baby greens on the side, and drizzle plates with horseradish sauce and remaining vinaigrette; garnish with remaining tablespoon dill.

from From the Garden to the Table

cornflake-crusted chicken with red cabbage slaw and rutabaga potatoes

SERVES 4 | **PHOTO ON PAGE 78**

1 large russet potato (about 8 ounces), peeled and cut into 1-inch cubes

½ medium rutabaga, peeled and cut into ¾-inch cubes

1 teaspoon coarse salt, plus more for cooking water

2 tablespoons plus ½ cup low-fat (1 percent) milk

¾ teaspoon freshly ground pepper

½ small red cabbage, cored and very thinly sliced

1 carrot, coarsely grated

2 tablespoons minced fresh chives

2 teaspoons distilled white vinegar

½ teaspoon sugar

4 5-ounce boneless and skinless chicken breast halves, trimmed

1 tablespoon cornstarch

2 large egg whites, lightly beaten

2 cups unsweetened cornflakes, chopped (not ground) in food processor or crushed with a rolling pin

2 tablespoons extra-virgin olive oil

1 Place potato and rutabaga in a medium saucepan with enough water to cover by 1 inch. Bring to a boil; add salt, and reduce heat. Simmer until vegetables are tender, about 25 minutes. Drain, and force through a food mill or potato ricer back into saucepan. Stir in 2 tablespoons milk and ¼ teaspoon each salt and pepper. Set aside; keep warm, or reheat just before serving.

2 Meanwhile, combine cabbage, carrot, chives, vinegar, sugar, ¼ teaspoon each salt and pepper, and remaining ½ cup milk. Toss well, and set aside.

3 Preheat oven to 450°F. Place chicken in a medium bowl; sprinkle with cornstarch and remaining ½ teaspoon salt and ¼ teaspoon pepper. Dip chicken in egg whites, and dredge in cornflakes, turning to completely coat. Heat a 12-inch cast-iron skillet over medium-high heat; add oil, swirling the pan to coat evenly. Add chicken, and cook until crisp and golden underneath, 1 to 2 minutes. Turn chicken; transfer to oven, and cook until chicken is firm to the touch and cooked through, about 7 minutes. Transfer to cutting board; slice diagonally into thin strips.

4 Place a mound of slaw on each serving plate, and top with chicken. Serve rutabaga-potato mixture on the side.

PER SERVING: 304 CALORIES, 2 G FAT, 82 MG CHOLESTEROL, 31 G CARBOHYDRATE, 672 MG SODIUM, 38 G PROTEIN, 3 G FIBER

from Fit to Eat: Oven Frying

fish and chips

SERVES 4

2 large russet potatoes (about 1 pound), scrubbed

2 tablespoons extra-virgin olive oil

½ teaspoon coarse salt

½ teaspoon freshly ground pepper

4 six-ounce Chilean sea bass or cod fillets (about 1 inch thick), skin removed

⅓ cup low-fat buttermilk

½ cup yellow cornmeal

¼ teaspoon paprika

Lemon wedges, for serving

Malt vinegar, for serving

1 Preheat oven to 450°F with racks in upper and lower thirds.

2 Cut potatoes lengthwise into ¼-inch-thick strips. Rinse well in a large bowl of cold water, and pat dry with a kitchen towel. Transfer to a large baking sheet. Drizzle with 1 tablespoon oil, and sprinkle with ¼ teaspoon each salt and pepper; toss well. Arrange strips in an even layer on the sheet. Bake on lower rack until golden and crisp, about 30 minutes, turning halfway through.

3 Meanwhile, place fish fillets in a large bowl. Add buttermilk, and gently turn fish to coat. In another shallow bowl, combine cornmeal, paprika, and remaining ¼ teaspoon each salt and pepper. Dredge fillets in cornmeal mixture one at a time, turning to completely coat. Transfer to a plate while repeating with remaining fillets.

4 Heat a 12-inch cast-iron skillet over medium-high heat. Add remaining tablespoon oil; swirl to coat. Add fillets, being careful not to overcrowd pan. Cook until crust is crisp, about 1 minute; turn with a spatula. Transfer skillet to upper rack of oven, and cook until fillets are firm but beginning to flake when pressed in the center, about 8 minutes. Transfer to plates, and serve with potatoes. Serve lemon wedges and malt vinegar on the side.

PER SERVING: 366 CALORIES, 11 G FAT, 72 MG CHOLESTEROL, 30 G CARBOHYDRATE, 506 MG SODIUM, 36 G PROTEIN, 2 G FIBER

from Fit to Eat: Oven Frying

roast best end of highgrove lamb and fava beans with mint and marjoram

SERVES 4 | **PHOTO ON PAGE 74**

Have your butcher french the rack of lamb for you by removing the meat from the end of the bones. Serve this with Fricassée of Wild Mushrooms (page 61).

½ cup breadcrumbs

1 teaspoon plus 2 tablespoons Dijon mustard

6 tablespoons chopped fresh flat-leaf parsley

2 sprigs thyme, leaves finely chopped

½ teaspoon finely chopped fresh rosemary

2½ tablespoons extra-virgin olive oil

2 teaspoons coarse salt

1 teaspoon freshly ground pepper

1 rack of lamb (8 rib bones), frenched

2 tablespoons finely chopped shallots

4½ pounds fresh fava beans (1½ pounds shelled)

1 tablespoon finely chopped fresh mint

1 teaspoon finely chopped fresh marjoram

2 teaspoons freshly squeezed lemon juice

1 Combine breadcrumbs, 1 teaspoon mustard, parsley, thyme, rosemary, and 1 tablespoon oil in a small bowl. Mix well with a fork; stir in ½ teaspoon salt and ¼ teaspoon pepper. Set aside.

2 Preheat oven to 375°F. In a large skillet, heat remaining 1½ tablespoons oil over medium-high heat. Sprinkle lamb with 1 teaspoon salt and ½ teaspoon pepper; place in pan, and sear on all sides, 4 to 5 minutes total, reducing heat if oil begins to smoke. Transfer lamb to a small roasting pan, reserving oil in skillet.

3 Brush lamb with remaining 2 tablespoons mustard; press breadcrumb mixture on all sides until completely covered. Roast in oven 35 to 40 minutes, or until a meat thermometer inserted into thickest part without touching bone registers 155°F. Remove from oven; let rest 5 minutes before serving.

4 While lamb is cooking, heat reserved oil in skillet over medium heat. Add shallots, and sauté until they begin to soften, about 30 seconds. Add fava beans and remaining ½ teaspoon salt and ¼ teaspoon pepper. Cover; cook until beans are tender, about 3 minutes.

5 Just before serving, stir in mint, marjoram, and lemon juice. Serve bean mixture as a bed for the lamb on a serving platter.

from From the Garden to the Table

spaghetti with clams

SERVES 4 | **PHOTO ON PAGE 79**

Coarse salt

1 pound spaghetti

2 tablespoons olive oil

2 garlic cloves, minced

1 small dried chile pepper, crumbled, or pinch of crushed red-pepper flakes

1½ pounds littleneck clams, scrubbed

1 cup dry white wine

2 tablespoons coarsely chopped fresh flat-leaf parsley, plus whole leaves for garnish

Juice of 1 lemon

3 tablespoons unsalted butter

Freshly ground black pepper

1 Bring a large pot of water to a boil; salt generously. Add spaghetti, and cook until slightly underdone, about 7 minutes. Drain pasta, reserving 1 cup of cooking liquid. Set aside.

2 Meanwhile, heat oil in a large skillet over medium heat. Add garlic and chile pepper; cook until garlic is golden, about 2 minutes. Add clams and white wine, and raise heat to high. Bring to a boil; cover, and cook, shaking occasionally, 2 to 3 minutes, until clams open (discard any that don't open). Stir in parsley. Transfer to a bowl; set aside.

3 Return skillet to medium-high heat. Add reserved pasta water and lemon juice; reduce until slightly thickened, about 2 minutes. Remove from heat; whisk in butter. Add clam mixture and spaghetti. Cook over medium-low heat until heated through, 2 to 3 minutes. Season with salt and pepper; garnish with parsley.

from What to Have for Dinner

veal scallopini milanese

SERVES 4 | PHOTO ON PAGE 78

- 1 small spaghetti squash (about 4 pounds), halved lengthwise
- ½ cup plain breadcrumbs
- ¼ cup finely grated Parmesan cheese
- ¼ teaspoon freshly ground pepper
- 1 pound veal scallopini, pounded thin
- 1½ teaspoons plus 1 tablespoon extra-virgin olive oil
- 1 garlic clove, halved
- 1 tablespoon freshly squeezed lemon juice
- ¼ teaspoon coarse salt
- 1 cup grape or cherry tomatoes, halved
- 3 ounces sunflower sprouts (2 cups packed)
- 2 ounces pea shoots (3 cups packed)

1 Preheat oven to 400°F. Place squash cut side down in a baking dish; add ¼ inch water. Cover with foil, and bake in oven until fork-tender, about 1 hour. Scoop out and discard seeds. Scrape strands from the flesh with a fork. Transfer to a bowl; cover with foil to keep warm.

2 Heat broiler. In a shallow bowl, combine breadcrumbs, Parmesan, and ⅛ teaspoon pepper. Place veal in another bowl, and coat with 1½ teaspoons oil. Dredge veal in breadcrumb mixture; turn to coat well. Transfer to a baking sheet.

3 Rub inside of a large salad bowl with garlic. Add lemon juice, salt, and remaining tablespoon oil. Add tomatoes, sprouts, and shoots to bowl; toss, and set aside.

4 Place veal about 5 inches under broiler, and cook until golden and browned in spots, 2 to 3 minutes, rotating every minute. Turn veal; cook 2 to 3 minutes more. Transfer to serving plates. Toss sprout mixture with remaining ⅛ teaspoon pepper. Serve on top of veal, with spaghetti squash on the side.

PER SERVING: 443 CALORIES, 14 G FAT, 171 MG CHOLESTEROL, 27 G CARBOHYDRATE, 344 MG SODIUM, 50 G PROTEIN, 6 G FIBER

from Fit to Eat: Oven Frying

SIDE DISHES

fricassée of wild mushrooms

SERVES 4

- 14 ounces chanterelle mushrooms, tough ends of stems removed
- 7 ounces blue-foot or oyster mushrooms, tough ends of stems removed
- 2 ounces black trumpet mushrooms
- 5 tablespoons unsalted butter
- 1 garlic clove, minced
- 1 medium shallot, finely chopped
  Coarse salt and freshly ground pepper
- 1 teaspoon freshly squeezed lemon juice
- ⅓ cup dry white wine
- 6 tablespoons roughly chopped fresh flat-leaf parsley
- 3 tablespoons finely chopped fresh chives
- 3 tablespoons chopped fresh chervil

1 Rinse chanterelles quickly with cold water in a colander (do not soak), and dry thoroughly on paper towels. Wipe the other mushrooms with a damp paper towel, or if necessary, rinse with cold water and dry well on paper towels.

2 In a large sauté pan, melt 3 tablespoons butter over medium heat. Add garlic and shallot; cook until shallot begins to soften, about 1 minute. Add blue-foot mushrooms; cook, stirring often, until mushrooms wilt, about 4 minutes. Season with salt, pepper, and lemon juice.

3 Add white wine, and cook until fully evaporated, 1 to 2 minutes. Add chanterelle and trumpet mushrooms, parsley, chives, chervil, and remaining 2 tablespoons butter; cook until mushrooms wilt, 1 to 2 minutes. Serve immediately.

from From the Garden to the Table

sautéed chicory

SERVES 4

- 2 tablespoons extra-virgin olive oil
- 2 anchovy fillets, coarsely chopped (optional)
- 1 head radicchio (about 10 ounces), trimmed and sliced into ½-inch pieces
- 1 bunch chicory (about 1½ pounds), trimmed and roughly chopped
  Coarse salt and freshly ground pepper
  Balsamic vinegar, for drizzling

Heat oil in a large skillet over medium-high heat. Add anchovies, if desired, and cook 1 minute. Add radicchio and chicory; sauté until slightly wilted, 1 to 2 minutes. Season with salt and pepper. Transfer to serving platter, and drizzle with balsamic vinegar.

from What to Have for Dinner

DESSERTS

---

grapefruit in moscato

SERVES 4

1 **ruby red grapefruit, chilled**

4 **sugar cubes**

1 **750-ml bottle Moscato d'Asti or other sparkling wine**

Cut the top end off the grapefruit, and remove the peel and pith with a sharp paring knife, following the shape of the fruit. Carefully carve out segments from between membranes. Place several grapefruit segments and 1 sugar cube in each of four Champagne flutes or serving glasses, and fill with Moscato. Serve immediately.

from What to Have for Dinner

melon and berries steeped in red wine, sauternes, basil, and mint

SERVES 4 | **PHOTO ON PAGE 86**

The steeping liquid needs to chill for at least four hours, so plan accordingly.

1 **tablespoon roughly chopped basil (about 6 large leaves)**

1½ **tablespoons coarsely chopped fresh mint (about 12 large leaves), plus whole sprigs for garnish**

1 **cup Sauternes or other dessert wine**

½ **cup Cabernet Sauvignon or other dry red wine**

4 **tablespoons sugar**

1 **vanilla bean, split lengthwise**

½ **Charentais or other melon such as cantaloupe, honeydew, or Crenshaw, scooped into 12 balls**

8 **ounces strawberries, hulled and quartered**

¼ **cup blackberries**

6 **ounces raspberries (½-pint container)**

½ **cup chilled rosé Champagne or sparkling wine**

Fresh currants, for garnish (optional)

1 Prepare an ice bath; set aside. Tie basil and mint in a small square of cheesecloth. In a small saucepan, combine Sauternes, red wine, sugar, vanilla bean, and mint-basil bundle. Bring mixture to a boil, stirring to dissolve sugar. Remove from heat; transfer pan to ice bath. Chill until luke-

warm. Add melon, strawberries, and blackberries; transfer to a large bowl. Cover; place in refrigerator 4 to 6 hours.

2 To serve, remove the vanilla bean. Stir in the raspberries. Divide the mixture among four bowls. Drizzle about 2 tablespoons Champagne over each bowl, and garnish with currants, if desired, and mint.

from From the Garden to the Table

peach tartes tatin

MAKES 4

The peaches may be baked and stored in the refrigerator up to six hours in advance.

FOR THE TARTS:

6 **ripe yellow peaches (about 2 pounds)**

Unsalted butter, for pans

Sugar, for pans

All-purpose flour, for work surface

8 **ounces store-bought or homemade puff pastry**

¼ **cup pistachios or sugared almonds, for garnish (optional)**

FOR THE CARAMEL SAUCE:

¾ **cup sugar**

3 **tablespoons unsalted butter**

2 **tablespoons water**

1 **cup heavy cream**

1 Make the tarts: Preheat oven to 375°F. Bring a medium saucepan of water to a boil. Blanch peaches in boiling water 15 to 20 seconds; remove with a slotted spoon. Use a paring knife to peel and cut peaches in half. Remove pits, and reserve four peach halves. Quarter remaining peach halves.

2 Butter four 5-inch tart pans with removable bottoms; dust with sugar. Arrange eight peach segments around edge of each pan, and place a reserved peach half cut side up in the center. Loosely wrap bottoms of pans with foil; place on a baking sheet. Bake until peaches are tender and sugar and juices start to caramelize, about 30 minutes. Transfer to a wire rack to cool 10 minutes.

3 Cover tart pans with a layer of plastic wrap, and place another baking sheet on top to gently flatten peaches. Place filled cans or other weights on top of the baking sheet, and transfer to the refrigerator to chill at least 1 hour.

4 Raise oven temperature to 400°F, and butter a rimmed baking sheet. On a lightly floured surface, roll out puff pastry to ⅛ inch thick, and cut out four 5½-inch circles. Place rounds on prepared baking sheet, and place in freezer 10 minutes. Remove from freezer, and place another baking

sheet, buttered on the bottom, on top of the pastry rounds. Bake until golden brown and crisp, about 30 minutes. Transfer to a wire rack to cool.

5   Make the caramel sauce: Heat sugar, butter, and the water in a small saucepan until sugar dissolves; wash down sides of pan with a pastry brush dipped in water to prevent crystals from forming. Cook over medium-high heat, gently swirling pan occasionally (do not stir), until caramel is a medium amber color, 6 to 8 minutes. Remove from heat, and slowly add heavy cream, stirring to combine. Be careful when adding cream to the caramel, as it will bubble vigorously. Set aside.

6   Remove tarts from refrigerator, and place a pastry crust on top of each. Invert onto serving plates; pour about 3 tablespoons caramel sauce over each. Garnish with pistachios or sugared almonds, if desired. Serve immediately.

from From the Garden to the Table

rice pudding tarts with blood oranges

MAKES 6 FOUR-INCH TARTS | **PHOTOS ON PAGE 84**

Keep in mind that rice pudding will continue to thicken even after cooking. This dessert can be served warm or at room temperature.

All-purpose flour, for work surface
Pâte Sucrée (recipe follows)
4   blood oranges
1   cup Arborio rice
4   cups milk
½   vanilla bean, split lengthwise and scraped
Pinch of salt
½   cup sugar
1   cup heavy cream
2   large egg yolks

1   Preheat oven to 400°F. Place six 4-inch tart rings on a baking sheet lined with a Silpat baking mat or parchment paper. Set aside.

2   On a lightly floured surface, roll out pâte sucrée to ⅛ inch thick. Cut out six 6-inch circles of dough with a sharp paring knife, using an overturned 6-inch bowl as a guide if necessary. Press dough into tart rings; trim excess with a sharp knife. Prick bottom of tart shells all over with a fork. Transfer to the freezer until firm, about 15 minutes.

3   Cut out six 6-inch parchment-paper circles, and line rings; fill with pie weights or dried beans. Bake until the edges begin to brown, about 20 minutes. Remove from oven, and carefully remove parchment and beans. Return to oven, and continue baking until golden brown all over, about 10 minutes

more. Transfer to a wire rack to cool completely. Carefully remove tart shells from tart rings, and set aside.

4   Grate the zest of one orange, and set aside. Cut the ends off all four oranges, and remove the peel and pith with a paring knife, following the curve of the fruit. Working over a bowl to catch the juices, slice between sections to remove whole segments, leaving membranes intact. Transfer to a separate bowl, and set aside. Squeeze the membranes to extract as much juice as possible; reserve ¼ cup juice. Discard membranes.

5   Bring a medium saucepan of water to a boil. Add rice, and blanch 2 minutes. Drain well, and return to saucepan. Add milk, zest, vanilla bean and scrapings, salt, and sugar; cook at a gentle simmer over medium heat, stirring occasionally, until rice is tender and most of the liquid has been absorbed, 30 to 35 minutes. Remove from heat, and discard vanilla bean.

6   In a large bowl, whisk together heavy cream, yolks, and reserved ¼ cup orange juice. Gradually whisk in rice mixture, and return to saucepan. Place pan over medium-low heat; cook, stirring constantly, until mixture boils and thickens, about 10 minutes. Remove from heat, and let stand 5 minutes. Pour filling into baked tart shells. Arrange orange segments in a floral pattern over rice pudding, and serve immediately.

from Dessert of the Month

pâte sucrée

MAKES 6 FOUR-INCH ROUND TART SHELLS

2½   cups all-purpose flour
3   tablespoons sugar
1   cup (2 sticks) chilled unsalted butter, cut into pieces
2   large egg yolks
¼   cup ice water

1   Place flour and sugar in the bowl of a food processor fitted with the metal blade, and pulse for a few seconds to combine. Add butter, and process until mixture resembles coarse meal, about 20 seconds. In a small bowl, lightly beat egg yolks and ice water until combined. Pour egg mixture through the feed tube in a slow, steady stream, with the machine running. Process just until dough holds together, no more than 30 seconds.

2   Turn dough out onto a clean work surface. Divide into two equal pieces, and place each on a sheet of plastic wrap. Flatten into disks. Wrap, and refrigerate at least 1 hour or overnight.

thyme-roasted figs over brioche pain perdu

SERVES 4 | **PHOTO ON PAGE 67**

10 to 12 ripe figs (about 12 ounces)

2 to 3 tablespoons thyme-flower honey

4 sprigs thyme, plus more for garnish

¼ cup water, plus more as needed

6 large eggs

¾ cup heavy cream

1 teaspoon ground cinnamon

6 slices (¾ inch) day-old brioche

1½ tablespoons unsalted butter

½ cup crème fraîche

2 tablespoons thyme flowers, for garnish

1 Preheat oven to 300°F. Combine figs, honey, thyme, and water in a small ovenproof skillet. Bring to a simmer over medium-high heat. Transfer to oven; cook until figs have softened, about 40 minutes, basting occasionally with the cooking liquid. Remove pan from heat, and set aside.

2 Combine eggs, cream, and cinnamon in a medium bowl; whisk to combine. Dip brioche in egg mixture, and place on a plate. Heat butter in a large nonstick skillet over medium heat. Cook brioche until golden, about 1 minute on each side. Transfer to a serving platter. Serve with roasted figs and cooking liquid. Top with crème fraîche, and garnish with fresh thyme sprigs and flowers.

from Herb Flowers

....

MISCELLANEOUS

....

flower sugar

MAKES ½ CUP

This sugar will give baked goods such as shortbread and pound cake new flavor; it is also perfect in a steaming cup of tea.

½ cup sugar

2 tablespoons fennel flowers or hyssop flowers

Place the sugar and herb flowers in a mortar, and grind with a pestle (alternatively, you can place them in a bowl and use a wooden spoon for mashing). The mixture will keep, stored in an airtight container, for up to 1 month.

from Herb Flowers

pickled garlic

MAKES 1 QUART

This pickling process works overnight. The peeled garlic cloves can be tossed in salads or spread on bread.

6 heads garlic

4 cups white-wine vinegar

4 tablespoons sugar

1 teaspoon whole black peppercorns

4 whole cloves

2 small dried chile peppers

1 dried bay leaf

Zest of 1 lemon

1 Trim garlic heads, leaving stem intact and peeling off all but one layer of papery skin. Set aside.

2 Combine vinegar, sugar, peppercorns, cloves, peppers, bay leaf, and lemon zest in a medium saucepan. Bring to a boil over high heat; boil 2 minutes more. Add garlic; boil 4 minutes. Remove from heat; cover, and let sit overnight in refrigerator. Garlic may be canned, placed in a sterilized jar, or stored in the refrigerator in an airtight container up to 1 month.

from Good Things

rose petal jelly

MAKES 3¼ CUPS

This sweet floral jelly is lovely on buttered bread. Make it with roses you grow yourself to be sure they're chemical free.

2 cups water

3 cups unsprayed pink rose petals, thicker tissue at base of petals removed

2½ cups sugar

¼ cup freshly squeezed lemon juice

3 ounces liquid pectin (available in most supermarkets)

1 tablespoon rose water

1 Bring the water to a boil in a medium saucepan; remove from heat. Add petals; cover, and steep 30 minutes. Strain liquid into a clean saucepan. Discard petals.

2 Add sugar and lemon juice to pan. Bring mixture to a boil, stirring, over medium-high heat. Boil 2 minutes; add pectin, and boil 2 minutes more (for firmer jelly, boil up to 2 minutes more). Remove from heat, and add rose water. Pour into sterilized jars, and let cool completely. Jelly can be canned or stored in an airtight container in refrigerator up to 6 months.

from Good Things

VANILLA CREPES | **PAGE 30**

CREPES HOW-TO

1 Brush a crêpe pan or nonstick skillet with oil. Heat on medium until just starting to smoke. Quickly pour 2 tablespoons crêpe batter into pan.

2 Tilt pan in all directions so the batter covers entire bottom in a thin layer. Return pan to heat for 1 minute; jerk pan back and forth to loosen crêpe.

3 When the underside is golden brown, turn crêpe by using two spatulas or by flipping with a toss of the pan. Cook until both sides are brown in spots.

CHOCOLATE CREPES | **PAGE 30**

THYME-ROASTED FIGS OVER BRIOCHE PAIN PERDU │ **PAGE 64**

MOULES POULETTE | PAGE 17

POMMES FRITES WITH HOMEMADE MAYONNAISE | **PAGE 17**

MOULES POULETTE | **PAGE 17**

EGGPLANT KUKU | **PAGE 16**

FRESH-HERB KUKU | **PAGE 16**

BRAISED LAMB STEW | PAGE 19

BAKED SAFFRON RICE | PAGE 24

CREAM OF BELGIAN ENDIVE SOUP | PAGE 15

BAKED POTATO SLICES | PAGE 24

CHICKEN TORTILLA SOUP | PAGE 21

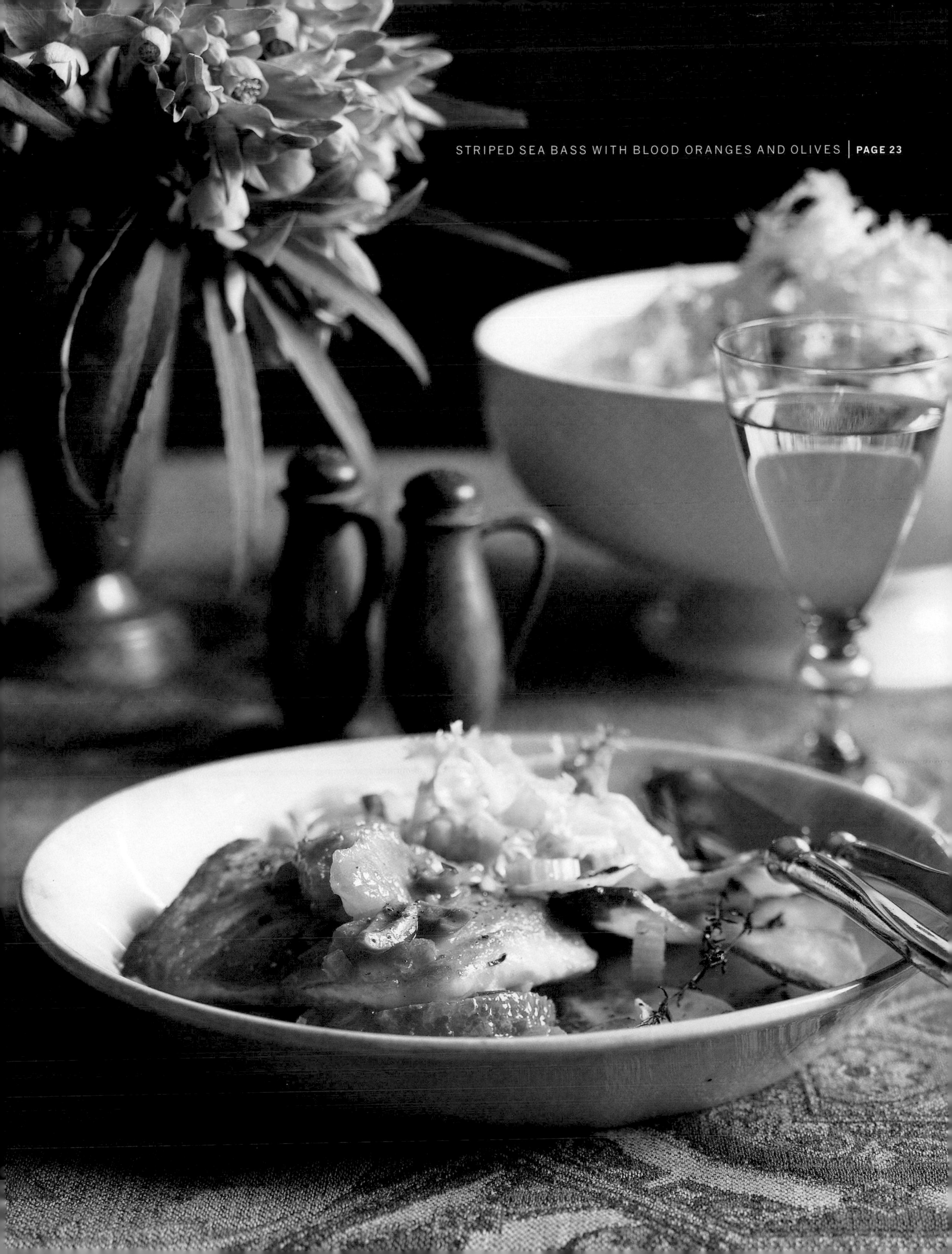

STRIPED SEA BASS WITH BLOOD ORANGES AND OLIVES | PAGE 23

COLD SOBA NOODLES WITH BASIL FLOWERS | PAGE 53

SALAD OF CRISP SQUID, ASPARAGUS, AND TANGERINES | **PAGE 57**

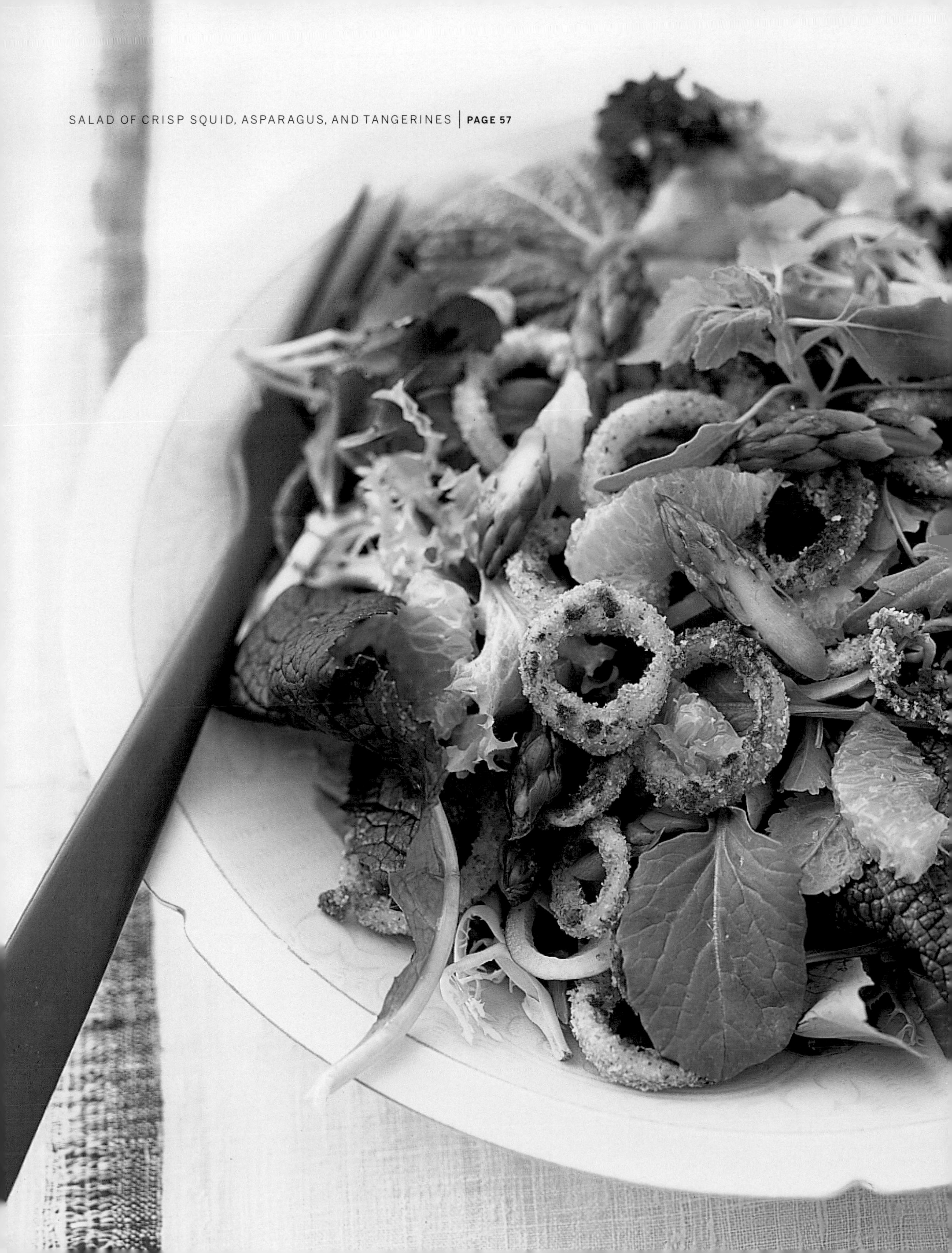

ROAST BEST END OF HIGHGROVE LAMB AND FAVA BEANS WITH MINT AND MARJORAM | **PAGE 60**

PAN-FRIED SCALLOPS ON CARAMELIZED FENNEL | **PAGE 53**

ROASTED CHERRY TOMATOES, BAKED BUFFALO
MOZZARELLA, AND EGGPLANT | **PAGE 55**

PISTOU SOUP | **PAGE 54**

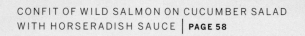

CONFIT OF WILD SALMON ON CUCUMBER SALAD
WITH HORSERADISH SAUCE | **PAGE 58**

CHILI CON CARNE | **PAGE 22**

BROWN-SUGAR CORNBREAD | **PAGE 25**

GREENS WITH ORANGE VINAIGRETTE
AND TOASTED SESAME SEEDS | **PAGE 19**

CHUNKY GUACAMOLE | **PAGE 22**

ARTICHOKE BRUSCHETTA | **PAGE 53**

VEAL SCALLOPINI MILANESE | **PAGE 61**

CORNFLAKE-CRUSTED CHICKEN WITH RED CABBAGE
SLAW AND RUTABAGA POTATOES | **PAGE 59**

BONELESS PORK CHOPS AND ROASTED YAM FRIES | **PAGE 58**

SPAGHETTI WITH CLAMS | **PAGE 60**

BLACK-EYED PEAS WITH ESCAROLE, POTATOES, AND TURKEY SAUSAGE | PAGE 38

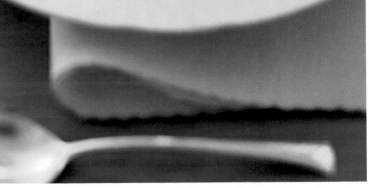

FRENCH DIP (MADE FROM LEFTOVER POT ROAST) | PAGE 39

CRISP MUSTARD-GLAZED CHICKEN BREASTS | PAGE 38

PEA BISQUE WITH SHRIMP AND TARRAGON | PAGE 36

POT ROAST RAGU | **PAGE 39**

MOLTEN CHOCOLATE CAKE WITH
EARL GREY ICE CREAM | **PAGE 48**

CHOCOLATE SANDWICH COOKIES | **PAGE 44**

PROFITEROLES | **PAGE 49**

CHOCOLATE SPICE CAKE | **PAGE 44**

MOCHA STEAMED PUDDINGS | **PAGE 47**

RICE PUDDING TARTS HOW-TO

1 Add sugar to a pot of blanched Arborio rice, along with milk, blood orange zest, vanilla bean and scrapings, salt, and sugar. Cook mixture at a gentle simmer until rice is tender.

2 Pour filling into baked tart shells.

3 Arrange several blood orange segments in a rose pattern over each rice pudding tartlet.

VANILLA PUDDING | **PAGE 50**

MELON AND BERRIES STEEPED IN RED WINE, SAUTERNES, BASIL, AND MINT | **PAGE 62**

BELGIAN CHOCOLATE BIRTHDAY CAKE WITH CANDIED
HAZELNUTS AND CHOCOLATE CURLS | **PAGE 25**

CHOCOLATE CARAMEL TART | **PAGE 41**

Spring

LEMON SEMIFREDDO CAKE

PEA SOUP WITH VIDALIA ONIONS

TEMPTING STACKS OF TEA SANDWICHES

LEG OF LAMB PRIMER

April

STARTERS

93 asparagus timbale

93 avocado with grapefruit and sweet-onion salsa

94 brie and apple custard tart

95 fluke sashimi with baby greens

95 fried roasted-garlic custard

96 miso soup with tofu and kale

96 radish butter on toasted baguette

96 spring pea soup with smoked bacon

SALADS

97 asian steak salad with spicy vinaigrette

98 jícama and orange salad with citrus-cumin vinaigrette

MAIN COURSES

98 broccoli with orecchiette

99 long island duckling two ways

100 roasted chicken and jerusalem artichokes

SANDWICHES

100 almond-crusted curry chicken salad tea sandwiches

101 bacon-and-egg salad tea sandwiches

101 caramelized onion and roast beef tea sandwiches

101 egg-yolk butter and asparagus tea sandwiches

102 grated vegetables with herb cream cheese tea sandwiches

102 lemon-caper butter and smoked salmon tea sandwiches

103 mozzarella, prosciutto, and pesto butter tea sandwiches

103 roquefort butter and red pear tea sandwiches

103 sautéed-mushroom butter and bacon tea sandwiches

104 shrimp salad tea sandwiches

104 smoked duck and chutney butter tea sandwiches

104 southwest black bean, smoked turkey, and avocado tea sandwiches

105 sweet onion sandwiches

SIDE DISHES

105 baked stuffed sweet onions

105 braised sweet onions

106 glazed baby turnips and cipollini onions

106 herbed couscous

106 soft polenta with fresh herbs

107 white asparagus with hollandaise sauce

(continued on next page)

(continued from previous page)

DESSERTS

107 baked camembert with fresh fruit

108 chocolate and mint parfaits

109 chocolate pots de crème

109 crème brûlée

110 flan

110 grapefruit tart

111 lamingtons

112 mango-lime granita

112 maple pudding

113 raspberry floating islands

113 walnut shortbread

DRINKS

114 blueberry breakfast shake

MISCELLANEOUS

114 caramelized sweet onions

asparagus timbale

SERVES 6 TO 8

You will need a metal brioche pan that measures eight inches across the top and three and a half inches at the base. Be sure to fit the plastic wrap into the curves, smoothing it as much as possible before filling with custard.

1 teaspoon coarse salt, plus more for cooking water

10 ounces medium asparagus, tough ends trimmed

½ cup thawed frozen spinach (about 4 ounces)

1 tablespoon unsalted butter

½ cup chopped onion

1 small garlic clove, chopped

5 large eggs

⅛ teaspoon freshly ground pepper

¼ teaspoon freshly ground nutmeg

1 cup heavy cream

½ cup mâche or field greens, for garnish (optional)

1 Preheat oven to 325°F. Line a 9-by-13-inch baking pan with a kitchen towel. Line brioche pan with plastic wrap.

2 Prepare an ice bath; set aside. Bring a medium pot of water to a boil; generously add salt. Add asparagus, and cook just until tender and bright green, 1 to 2 minutes. Using a slotted spoon, transfer asparagus to the ice bath to stop cooking. Drain, and set aside. Add spinach to boiling water, and cook 4 minutes. Transfer to a colander to drain; set aside.

3 In a small skillet, melt butter over medium-low heat. Add onion and garlic; sauté, stirring frequently, until onion is softened and just starting to color, 6 to 8 minutes. Remove from heat.

4 Bring a large pot of water to a boil. Cut asparagus spears in half crosswise. Slice bottom ends in half lengthwise, and cut crosswise into thin half-moons; set aside. In the bowl of a food processor fitted with the metal blade, combine asparagus tops, reserved spinach, and onion mixture. Process until very smooth, about 5 minutes, stopping to scrape down the sides as necessary. Transfer to a large bowl. Add eggs, 1 teaspoon salt, pepper, and nutmeg; whisk to combine. Set aside.

5 In a small saucepan over medium heat, heat cream until bubbles form around the edges and it starts to steam, about 2 minutes. Remove from heat. Whisking constantly, slowly add cream to egg mixture. Stir in reserved sliced asparagus. Pour custard into lined brioche pan, and place in lined baking pan. Carefully pour the boiling water into baking pan until it reaches halfway up sides of brioche pan.

6 Bake until center is firm when gently touched with your finger, about 65 minutes. Transfer brioche pan to a wire rack; let cool 5 minutes. Carefully invert onto serving platter, and gently lift pan to remove. Slice timbale into wedges; serve garnished with greens, if desired.

from Custard

avocado with grapefruit and sweet-onion salsa

SERVES 4

Cut avocados just before serving to keep them from discoloring.

2 pink grapefruits

¼ cup finely chopped sweet onion

2 tablespoons chopped fresh cilantro

Coarse salt

2 avocados, halved lengthwise, pitted and peeled

1 Cut off both ends of grapefruits; using a sharp paring knife, remove the peel, pith, and outer membranes, following the curve of the fruit. Working over a bowl to catch the juices, use the knife to carefully slice between sections of each grapefruit to detach segments from membranes; reserve juice. Slice each grapefruit segment into small pieces. Set aside.

2 Place onion in a small bowl. Squeeze remaining juice from grapefruit membranes over onions, and let stand 20 minutes to soften. Pour off and discard juice, and add grapefruit segments and cilantro. Add enough reserved grapefruit juice to moisten. Season with salt. To serve, place 3 to 4 tablespoons salsa on each of the avocado halves.

from Sweet Onions

brie and apple custard tart

MAKES 1 NINE-INCH TART

1 tablespoon olive oil

2 Granny Smith apples, peeled and cored,
each cut into 6 wedges

6 ounces very ripe Brie cheese, room temperature

1 large whole egg

2 large egg yolks

1 cup half-and-half

2 teaspoons coarsely chopped fresh thyme leaves
Salt and freshly ground pepper

1 prebaked Pâte Brisée Tart Shell (recipe follows)

1 Preheat oven to 325°F. Place a medium skillet over medium-high heat. When hot, add the oil. Add apples; cook until browned on all sides, 2 to 3 minutes total. Remove from heat, and set aside.

2 Discard rind from Brie; place Brie in the bowl of a food processor fitted with the plastic blade, and process 15 seconds. Add egg and the yolks one at a time; process after each until well combined. Add ¼ cup half-and-half, and process until smooth. Transfer mixture to a large bowl; slowly stir in remaining ¾ cup half-and-half until smooth and combined. Stir in thyme, and season with salt and pepper.

3 Place tart shell on a baking sheet. Arrange reserved apples around the bottom of the tart shell. Pour custard over apples. Place pan in oven; bake until custard is just set when gently touched with your finger, about 35 minutes. Transfer to a wire rack to cool slightly. Serve warm or at room temperature.

from Custard

pâte brisée tart shells

MAKES 2 NINE-INCH TART SHELLS

The remaining dough can be stored in the freezer for up to three weeks.

2½ cups all-purpose flour, plus more for work surface

1 teaspoon salt

1 teaspoon sugar

1 cup (2 sticks) chilled unsalted butter, cut into small pieces

5 tablespoons ice water

1 Place flour, salt, and sugar in the bowl of a food processor fitted with the metal blade; pulse to combine. Add butter; process until mixture resembles coarse meal, about 20 seconds. Slowly add the ice water through the feed tube with machine running, just until the dough comes together, no more than 30 seconds. Turn out onto a clean work surface. Divide in half, and flatten into disks. Wrap in plastic; refrigerate at least 1 hour or overnight.

2 Place a 9-by-2-inch tart ring on a baking sheet lined with parchment paper; set aside. Preheat oven to 400°F. Remove one disk from refrigerator, and place on a lightly floured work surface. Roll dough into an 11-inch round. Carefully place over the tart ring with dough extending up slightly over the sides. Prick the bottom of dough all over with a fork. Transfer sheet with tart ring to the freezer until firm, about 15 minutes.

3 Remove from freezer, and line shell with enough parchment paper to extend above the sides by about 1 inch. Fill with dried beans or pie weights; bake 20 minutes. Remove from oven, and carefully remove parchment paper and beans. Return to oven, and bake until crust is golden all over, 10 to 12 minutes. Transfer to a wire rack to cool slightly before filling.

fluke sashimi with baby greens

SERVES 4

Fluke is another name for summer flounder; halibut, sole, or cod can also be used. When making sashimi, be sure to buy only the freshest fish possible from a reliable source.

1 8-ounce boneless and skinless fluke fillet

1 teaspoon plus 2 tablespoons extra-virgin olive oil

Coarse sea salt and freshly ground white pepper

4 ounces baby greens

½ cup mixed fresh mint and cilantro leaves, packed, plus 1 tablespoon coarsely chopped, for garnish

Juice of 2 limes (about ¼ cup)

Toasted rustic bread slices, for serving

1 Place four salad plates in the refrigerator until well chilled, about 30 minutes. Using a sharp knife, slice fish fillet crosswise into very thin strips (about ⅛ inch thick). Arrange on the chilled plates, and cover tightly with plastic wrap. Return plates to the refrigerator for 30 minutes.

2 Remove plates from the refrigerator, and unwrap. Drizzle 1 teaspoon olive oil over fish, and evenly coat with a pastry brush. Season with salt and pepper.

3 Mix greens with mint and cilantro, and drizzle with remaining 2 tablespoons olive oil and half the lime juice. Season with salt and pepper, and mound salad mixture in the center of each of the plates over the fish. Sprinkle with remaining lime juice. Garnish with chopped herbs, and serve with toasted bread.

from Spring Harvest Lunch

fried roasted-garlic custard

SERVES 8 TO 10

1 tablespoon olive oil, plus more for pan and plastic wrap

2 heads garlic

3 cups milk

1 sprig rosemary

2 sprigs thyme

1 small shallot, peeled and coarsely chopped

5 whole black peppercorns

Coarse salt

1½ sticks (¾ cup) unsalted butter

½ cup plus 1 tablespoon all-purpose flour

6 large egg yolks

2 large whole eggs

1 cup breadcrumbs

2½ cups vegetable oil

Mixed baby greens, for garnish

1 Preheat oven to 400°F. Brush a 9-inch square baking pan with olive oil, and line with enough plastic wrap to extend over the sides by about 2 inches. Brush plastic wrap with oil, and set pan aside.

2 Slice off just enough from the stem end of garlic heads to expose the tips of the cloves. Place on a piece of aluminum foil; drizzle with the olive oil, and enclose in the foil. Transfer to the oven, and roast until cloves are very soft, about 1 hour. Remove from oven, and set aside until cool.

3 Separate garlic cloves, and gently squeeze flesh into a medium saucepan. Use a fork to mash garlic until smooth. Whisk in milk; add rosemary, thyme, shallot, peppercorns, and salt. Bring to a boil over medium-high heat. Reduce heat, and simmer 10 minutes. Cover, and remove from heat; let stand 10 minutes. Pass through a fine sieve into a medium bowl, pressing to extract as much liquid as possible. Set aside, and discard solids.

4 Melt butter in a small saucepan over medium-low heat. Add flour; cook, stirring constantly, about 5 minutes. Slowly whisk in milk mixture until smooth; continue whisking until mixture has thickened and whisk leaves clear marks, about 10 minutes. Whisk in yolks, one at a time; continue whisking until very thick and whisk leaves even deeper marks, 8 to 10 minutes. Remove from heat.

5 Pour mixture into prepared pan, and smooth surface with an offset spatula. Cover with plastic wrap; refrigerate until firm, about 5 hours or overnight.

6 Preheat oven to 200°F. Remove pan from refrigerator; use the plastic wrap lining to lift custard out of pan. Place on a clean work surface, and cut into 1½-by-1-inch rectangles with a sharp knife. In a medium bowl, lightly beat whole eggs. Place breadcrumbs in a separate shallow bowl. Heat vegetable oil in a large heavy skillet over medium-low heat until a deep-fry thermometer registers 365°F.

7 Working in batches, dip custard pieces into the eggs and then into the breadcrumbs, turning to completely coat each piece. Carefully place custard in the hot oil, and fry until golden on both sides, 1 to 2 minutes per side. Remove with a slotted spatula, and drain on paper towels; season with salt while still hot. Transfer to a baking sheet in a warm oven. Repeat with remaining custard. Serve warm, garnished with mixed greens.

from Custard

miso soup with tofu and kale

SERVES 4 | **PHOTO ON PAGE 166**

This soup is brimming with soy, an excellent source of protein as well as antioxidants. Kale, a cruciferous vegetable, is high in vitamins A and C, folic acid, calcium, and iron.

5 cups water or unsalted vegetable broth

2 scallions, white and light-green parts only, thinly sliced

2 teaspoons grated fresh ginger

1 garlic clove, thinly sliced

3 tablespoons light-colored miso

2 teaspoons low-sodium soy sauce

3 ounces kale, trimmed and shredded

6 ounces firm tofu, drained, cut into ½-inch cubes

1 Bring the water or broth to a boil in a medium saucepan over medium-high heat. Add scallions, ginger, and garlic. Reduce heat; cover, and simmer 10 minutes.

2 Add miso, and stir to dissolve. Add soy sauce, kale, and tofu; return to a simmer, and continue cooking until kale is tender, about 5 minutes. Serve immediately.

PER SERVING: 82 CALORIES, 3 G FAT, 0 MG CHOLESTEROL, 8 G CARBOHYDRATE, 797 MG SODIUM, 8 G PROTEIN, 1 G FIBER

from Fit to Eat: Antioxidants

radish butter on toasted baguette

SERVES 4

The radish butter would be equally delicious with brown bread or spread on crisp spears of Belgian endive for a light hors d'oeuvre. Radishes can be soaked in cold water for several hours for added crispness.

8 medium radishes (about 1 bunch), cleaned, root ends trimmed

6 tablespoons unsalted butter, room temperature

1 8-ounce baguette

Coarse salt and freshly ground pepper

1 Preheat oven to 375°F. Grate the radishes on the large holes of a box grater; place on paper towels, and squeeze out any excess liquid. Combine the radishes and the butter in a small bowl, and mix well.

2 Slice baguette in half lengthwise, and place in oven; toast until crisp and browned. Remove from oven, and let cool slightly. Spread radish mixture on toasted baguette; season with salt and pepper. Slice each half into four pieces, and serve.

from What to Have for Dinner

spring pea soup with smoked bacon

SERVES 6 TO 8

3 tablespoons unsalted butter

4 ounces smoked slab bacon

½ cup cipollini onions, peeled and chopped

½ cup dry white wine, preferably Riesling

1 garlic clove, peeled and minced

3 cups homemade or low-sodium canned chicken stock

1½ cups water

1 small sprig rosemary

4½ cups fresh shelled or frozen peas, thawed

Coarse salt and freshly ground pepper

Small croutons, for garnish (optional)

Flowering pea shoots, for garnish (optional)

1 Prepare a large ice bath; set aside. Melt 1 tablespoon butter in a medium saucepan over medium heat. Add bacon and onions; cook until onions are softened, about 8 minutes. Add wine and garlic, and cook until almost all wine has evaporated. Add chicken stock, the water, and rosemary; bring to a boil, and simmer 20 minutes over medium-low heat. Strain liquid through a fine sieve. Discard bacon.

2 Return liquid to pan. Stir in 4 cups peas, and cook until tender and bright green, about 2 minutes. Transfer peas with a slotted spoon to a metal bowl set in the ice bath to stop cooking. Reserve cooking liquid. Set aside ½ cup peas.

3 Place remaining peas in the jar of a blender in two batches; add 1 tablespoon butter and about ¼ cup reserved cooking liquid to each batch. Blend thoroughly, and pour purée into a large saucepan. Add more cooking liquid until soup is desired consistency. Season with salt and pepper.

4 Reheat gently over low heat; continue simmering 3 to 5 minutes more, adding more cooking liquid as needed. (You should end up using almost all cooking liquid.) Serve in shallow soup bowls, and garnish with reserved whole peas, as well as croutons and flowering pea shoots, if desired.

from Spring Harvest Lunch

SALADS

asian steak salad with spicy vinaigrette

SERVES 4 | PHOTO ON PAGE 158

In this nutritious salad, papaya, red bell pepper, and cabbage provide vitamins A and C, while carrots contribute large amounts of beta-carotene. Cilantro and mint supply flavonoids, and peanuts add vitamin E and selenium, all potent antioxidants.

FOR THE MARINADE:

Juice and grated zest of 1 lime

1 tablespoon grated fresh ginger

1 garlic clove, minced

1 scallion, white and light-green parts only, sliced into ¼-inch rounds

FOR THE SALAD:

12 ounces flank steak

Freshly ground black pepper

1 red bell pepper, ribs and seeds removed, julienned

2 carrots, julienned

1 head Napa cabbage, tough outer leaves removed, julienned

1 papaya, peeled, seeds removed, cut into 2-inch pieces

¼ cup packed fresh cilantro leaves

¼ cup packed fresh mint leaves

1 cup bean sprouts (optional)

Spicy Vinaigrette (recipe follows)

2 tablespoons chopped toasted peanuts, for garnish

1 Prepare the marinade: Place lime juice and zest, ginger, garlic, and scallion in a small bowl, and whisk to combine. Place steak in a shallow dish; cover with marinade, turning to completely coat. Transfer to the refrigerator; marinate 1 hour.

2 Remove steak from the refrigerator 30 minutes before cooking; let sit at room temperature. Heat a grill or grill pan over medium-high heat. Remove steak from marinade, and season with black pepper. Sear steak until browned on the outside and cooked to desired doneness inside, 5 to 6 minutes on each side for medium-rare. Transfer steak to a cutting board; let cool slightly, and thinly slice on the bias.

3 In a large bowl, combine red bell pepper, carrots, cabbage, papaya, cilantro, mint, and bean sprouts, if using. Drizzle with the vinaigrette, and toss well to combine. Arrange vegetables and steak on four serving plates. Garnish each serving with 1½ teaspoons chopped peanuts.

PER SERVING: 323 CALORIES, 19 G FAT, 44 MG CHOLESTEROL, 20 G CARBOHYDRATE, 245 MG SODIUM, 21 G PROTEIN, 5 G FIBER

from Fit to Eat: Antioxidants

spicy vinaigrette

MAKES ½ CUP

Sesame oil is a good source of vitamin E.

Juice and grated zest of 2 limes

2 tablespoons sesame oil

2 tablespoons water

2 tablespoons rice-wine vinegar

1½ tablespoons grated fresh ginger

1 garlic clove, minced

1 teaspoon crumbled dried chile pepper or crushed red-pepper flakes

¼ teaspoon coarse salt

Place all of the ingredients in a small bowl, and whisk to combine thoroughly.

PER SERVING: 68 CALORIES, 7 G FAT, 0 MG CHOLESTEROL, 2 G CARBOHYDRATE, 121 MG SODIUM, 0 G PROTEIN, 0 G FIBER

jícama and orange salad with citrus-cumin vinaigrette

SERVES 4

Oranges are an excellent source of vitamin C. For maximum health benefits, cut or juice them just before serving. Vitamins A and C and iron are also provided by spinach.

2 oranges

1 jícama (about 1½ pounds), peeled and julienned

3 ounces baby spinach, rinsed

Citrus-Cumin Vinaigrette (recipe follows)

Using a sharp knife, cut both ends off the oranges, and remove the peel and pith. Slice the peeled fruit crosswise into ¼-inch rounds, and remove any seeds. Transfer slices to a large bowl, and combine with jícama and spinach. Toss with the vinaigrette, and serve immediately.

PER SERVING: 144 CALORIES, 4 G FAT, 0 MG CHOLESTEROL, 27 G CARBOHYDRATE, 55 MG SODIUM, 3 G PROTEIN, 7 G FIBER

from Fit to Eat: Antioxidants

citrus-cumin vinaigrette

MAKES ¾ CUP

Cumin seeds contain vitamin E as well as flavonoids, both powerful antioxidants.

1 teaspoon cumin seeds

½ cup freshly squeezed orange juice

2 tablespoons freshly squeezed lemon juice

1 tablespoon extra-virgin olive oil

1 tablespoon honey

2 teaspoons Dijon mustard

Freshly ground pepper

Pinch of coarse salt

1 Toast cumin seeds in a small skillet over medium-high heat until fragrant, about 2 minutes. Remove from heat; cool slightly. Transfer to a spice grinder, and process until finely ground.

2 Combine all ingredients in the jar of a blender; blend until smooth. Store, covered, in the refrigerator up to 3 days.

PER SERVING: 66 CALORIES, 4 G FAT, 0 MG CHOLESTEROL, 9 G CARBOHYDRATE, 34 MG SODIUM, 1 G PROTEIN, 0 G FIBER

MAIN COURSES

broccoli with orecchiette

SERVES 4 | PHOTO ON PAGE 164

Broccoli, a cruciferous vegetable, contains significant amounts of vitamins A and C, as well as calcium, iron, and riboflavin.

8 ounces orecchiette (ear-shaped pasta)

1 tablespoon extra-virgin olive oil

2 garlic cloves, minced

1 bunch (about 1½ pounds) broccoli, stalks peeled and trimmed, stalks and florets roughly chopped

1 teaspoon coarse salt

Freshly ground pepper

2 tablespoons freshly grated Pecorino Romano cheese

1 Bring a large stockpot of water to a boil. Add pasta, and cook until al dente, stirring occasionally to keep the pasta from sticking, about 8 minutes. Transfer to a colander to drain, reserving ½ cup cooking liquid. Set pasta aside.

2 Heat 1 teaspoon oil in a large skillet over medium heat. Add garlic; sauté until golden, stirring to avoid burning, about 2 minutes. Add broccoli and reserved cooking liquid; cook, stirring, until broccoli is tender and bright green, about 3 minutes. Add the salt, and season with pepper. Remove from heat.

3 Add reserved pasta to pan, and toss well to coat. Divide among four serving bowls; drizzle each with ½ teaspoon oil, and garnish each serving with 1½ teaspoons grated cheese.

PER SERVING: 284 CALORIES, 5 G FAT, 4 MG CHOLESTEROL, 49 G CARBOHYDRATE, 801 MG SODIUM, 12 G PROTEIN, 5 G FIBER

from Fit to Eat: Antioxidants

long island duckling two ways

SERVES 6 TO 8

In this sophisticated presentation, the tender duck breasts are pan-roasted and served over a hearty stew made by braising the duck legs in red wine. Ask your butcher to separate the legs (with thighs intact) and whole breasts (with rib bones), and to chop the rest (backbone and wings) for the stock.

2 medium Long Island ducks (4 to 5 pounds each), cut into serving pieces

1 tablespoon grapeseed oil

1 750-ml bottle dry red wine

2 cups homemade or low-sodium canned chicken stock

Zest of 1 lemon

Zest of 1 orange

½ teaspoon whole black peppercorns

2 garlic cloves, crushed

Coarse salt and freshly ground pepper

2 medium carrots, cut into ⅓-inch pieces

2 celery stalks, cut into ⅓-inch pieces

2 leeks, white and pale-green parts only, cut into ⅓-inch pieces and washed

1 medium onion, cut into ⅓-inch pieces

1   Preheat oven to 450°F. Prepare the breasts: Split each duck breast in half with a sharp knife. Place a large heavy skillet over high heat, and add the grapeseed oil. When oil begins to smoke, place the breasts skin side down in the pan. Reduce heat to medium-low. Sauté until breasts are golden brown and nicely crisp on both sides, about 15 minutes total. This process will render most of the fat, which should be poured off as needed while cooking. Reserve 3 tablespoons rendered fat, and set aside. Transfer breasts to a cutting board, and let cool slightly. Remove the rib bones from the breasts; chop the bones, and combine with the other bones provided by your butcher. Set aside the breasts until they are ready to be finished in the oven (step 6). Breasts can be stored, covered, in the refrigerator up to 1 day if not proceeding immediately.

2   Make the stock: In a large ovenproof skillet or Dutch oven, heat 1 tablespoon reserved duck fat over medium heat. Add all of the bones, and transfer pan to oven. Roast until bones are golden brown, about 1 hour. Remove from oven, and pour off excess fat. Return pan to stove, and place over high heat. Add 1 cup red wine; deglaze pan, stirring up any browned bits with a wooden spoon. Continue cooking until almost all wine has evaporated. Add chicken stock and enough water to cover the bones. Add lemon and orange zests, peppercorns, and garlic. Bring to a boil; reduce heat to medium-low, and simmer gently for 1 hour. Pour through a fine sieve into a large bowl; discard bones, and reserve stock.

3   Braise the legs: Reduce oven temperature to 225°F. Heat 1 tablespoon reserved duck fat in a large deep-sided oven-proof skillet over medium heat. Season legs with salt and pepper, and place skin side down in the hot pan. Sear until underside is golden brown, about 6 minutes; turn, and sear until other side is golden brown, about 2 minutes. Drain off excess fat; add remaining red wine and half of reserved duck stock (the legs should be almost covered with liquid). Bring to a boil over high heat; transfer to oven. Braise, uncovered, until legs are fully cooked and tender, about 45 minutes.

4   Remove pan from oven, and transfer legs to a cutting board; set aside. Place pan over medium-high heat, and reduce braising liquid by half (until about 2 cups remain). Meanwhile, heat remaining tablespoon duck fat in a large saucepan, and add diced vegetables. Cook over medium heat until vegetables are softened, about 5 minutes. Add the reduced liquid and remaining reserved duck stock, and bring to a boil. Reduce heat, and simmer 15 minutes.

5   Meanwhile, remove leg meat from bones, and coarsely chop. Discard bones, and add chopped meat to the simmering stock mixture. Continue to simmer 15 minutes more. Remove from heat; season with salt and pepper, and set aside. The stew can be prepared up to this point and refrigerated up to a day ahead; reheat in oven while finishing the breasts.

6   When ready to serve: Raise oven temperature to 450°F. Place a large ovenproof skillet over medium-high heat. When pan is hot, add reserved breasts skin side down. Transfer pan to oven, and roast 6 to 7 minutes; turn, and cook 2 minutes more, or until a meat thermometer registers 125°F for medium-rare. Transfer breasts to a cutting board, and let rest 5 to 10 minutes. Slice each breast crosswise into six or seven pieces, and serve over the stew.

from Spring Harvest Lunch

roasted chicken and jerusalem artichokes

SERVES 4 | **PHOTO ON PAGE 167**

Jerusalem artichokes are also called sunchokes.

1 chicken (about 3 pounds), cut into serving pieces
  Coarse salt and freshly ground pepper
3 tablespoons olive oil
1 lemon, plus more grated zest for garnish
6 large garlic cloves
1 pound small Jerusalem artichokes, peeled
8 large shallots, halved
2 tablespoons fresh thyme leaves, plus more for garnish
1 cup dry white wine
1 cup green olives, pitted

1 Preheat oven to 500°F. Season chicken with salt and pepper, and rub with 1 tablespoon oil. Place chicken in a shallow roasting pan; set aside. Zest the lemon into long strips, and squeeze juice from lemon into a small bowl. Set juice aside.

2 In a medium bowl, combine lemon zest, garlic, artichokes, shallots, and thyme. Add remaining 2 tablespoons oil; season with salt and pepper. Toss to coat, and arrange in pan around chicken. Roast until chicken is golden brown, about 40 minutes.

3 Remove from oven. Add reserved lemon juice, wine, and olives; stir up any browned bits on the bottom of roasting pan with a wooden spoon. Return to oven, and continue cooking until liquid has thickened slightly, 10 to 15 minutes. Remove from oven, and transfer to serving plates. Garnish with grated lemon zest and thyme leaves.

from What to Have for Dinner

almond-crusted curry chicken salad tea sandwiches

MAKES 2 DOZEN | **PHOTO ON PAGE 160**

1 cup sliced blanched almonds
1 whole skinless and boneless chicken breast (about 10 ounces)
1 teaspoon coarse salt
1 small onion, unpeeled and quartered
4 whole black peppercorns
5 cups water
1½ cups mayonnaise
2 teaspoons curry powder
2 tablespoons mango chutney
¾ teaspoon white-wine vinegar
3 tablespoons unsweetened shredded coconut, toasted
½ cup (1 stick) unsalted butter, room temperature
24 thin slices white bread

1 Preheat oven to 350°F. Spread almonds on a baking sheet, and toast until fragrant and golden, 5 to 7 minutes. Transfer to a bowl to cool, and gently crush. Set aside.

2 In a medium saucepan, combine chicken, salt, onion, peppercorns, and the water. Bring to a boil over medium-high heat; reduce heat to a bare simmer, and cook until chicken is cooked through, about 20 minutes. Transfer chicken to a plate to cool; reserve stock for another use.

3 When chicken is cool enough to handle, shred the meat and chop into small pieces. Return to plate; cover, and place in refrigerator until ready to use.

4 In a small bowl, combine mayonnaise, curry powder, chutney, vinegar, and toasted coconut; stir to combine. Reserve ½ cup curry mayonnaise, and stir remaining mayonnaise into chicken. Thinly spread butter on two slices of bread; cover one slice with a thin layer of chicken salad, and top with other bread slice. Set aside. Repeat with remaining ingredients.

5 Stack several sandwiches; use a serrated knife to trim crusts and cut into two rectangles. Arrange sandwiches in a single row on the serving tray; they should rest on one long edge with the short ends standing upright. Spread a dab of reserved curry mayonnaise on short ends, and gently pat on almonds. Serve immediately. (Do not cover with damp paper towels or the almonds will become soft.)

from Tea Sandwiches

bacon-and-egg salad
tea sandwiches

MAKES 3 DOZEN | **PHOTOS ON PAGES 160-161**

  6 large hard-boiled eggs, peeled and finely chopped
  ½ cup mayonnaise
2½ teaspoons Dijon mustard
  ¼ teaspoon cayenne pepper
  6 slices bacon (about 5 ounces), cooked and coarsely chopped
  ½ teaspoon hot-pepper sauce, such as Tabasco
      Coarse salt and freshly ground black pepper
  5 tablespoons unsalted butter, room temperature
 18 thin slices white bread
  ¼ cup finely chopped chives

1 Place chopped eggs in a medium bowl. Add mayonnaise, mustard, cayenne, and bacon; stir to combine. Add hot-pepper sauce, and season with salt and pepper.

2 Thinly spread butter on two slices of bread; cover first slice with egg salad, and top with second slice. Use a serrated knife to trim crusts, and cut into four squares. Dip one edge in chopped chives. Repeat with remaining ingredients. Cover with damp paper towels until ready to serve. Place on a serving platter with chive-side up.

from Tea Sandwiches

caramelized onion and roast beef
tea sandwiches

MAKES 3 DOZEN | **PHOTOS ON PAGES 160-161**

  1 tablespoon unsalted butter
  1 tablespoon olive oil
  4 large Vidalia onions (about 3 pounds), cut into ½-inch dice
  4 tablespoons prepared horseradish
  8 ounces cream cheese, room temperature
      Coarse salt and freshly ground pepper
 18 thin slices wheat bread
  8 ounces roast beef, thinly sliced

1 In a large skillet, heat butter and oil over medium heat. Add onions, and stir to coat; cook, stirring occasionally, until they begin to soften, about 10 minutes. Reduce heat to medium-low; continue cooking, stirring every 20 minutes, until onions are amber colored and completely caramelized, just over 1 hour. Remove from heat, and transfer to a bowl to cool.

2 In a small bowl, mix horseradish and cream cheese; season with salt and pepper. Spread two slices of bread with a thin layer of horseradish cream cheese. Layer first slice with onions and roast beef, and top with the second bread slice. Use a serrated knife to trim crusts, and cut into four small squares. Repeat with remaining ingredients. Cover with damp paper towels until ready to serve.

from Tea Sandwiches

egg-yolk butter and asparagus
tea sandwiches

MAKES 2 DOZEN | **PHOTO ON PAGE 160**

  4 large hard-boiled eggs
  ¼ cup mayonnaise
  2 tablespoons unsalted butter, room temperature
  1 teaspoon Dijon mustard
  ½ teaspoon white-wine vinegar
      Coarse salt
  1 bunch (about 1 pound) asparagus, tough ends removed
 16 slices thin white bread

1 Peel eggs and remove yolks; reserve whites for another use. With a wooden spoon, mash yolks in a small bowl. Add mayonnaise, butter, mustard, and vinegar, and season with salt; stir until smooth. Cover, and refrigerate yolk butter until ready to use.

2 Prepare an ice bath; set aside. Fill a large skillet with 1 inch of water, and bring to a boil over high heat. Add a dash of salt

and asparagus, and blanch until just tender and bright green, 2 to 3 minutes. Place asparagus in ice bath to chill completely. Transfer to paper towels to drain, and set aside.

3 Spread egg-yolk butter on two slices of bread. Cover first slice with asparagus; top with the second slice. Gently trim crusts with a serrated knife. Cut into three rectangles (about 1 by 3 inches). Repeat with remaining ingredients. Cover with a damp paper towel until ready to serve.

from Tea Sandwiches

grated vegetables with herb cream cheese tea sandwiches

MAKES 4 DOZEN | **PHOTOS ON PAGES 160-161**

8 ounces cream cheese, room temperature

¼ cup fresh flat-leaf parsley, finely chopped

1 tablespoon plus 1½ teaspoons finely chopped fresh oregano

1 teaspoon finely chopped fresh rosemary

2 teaspoons finely chopped fresh thyme

Coarse salt and freshly ground pepper

1 bunch red radishes, cleaned and trimmed

3 medium carrots

1 English cucumber, peeled

48 thin slices wheat bread

1 In a medium bowl, combine cream cheese, parsley, oregano, rosemary, and thyme; stir well. Season with salt and pepper, and set aside. Grate radishes, carrots, and cucumber into separate bowls.

2 Spread a thin layer of herb cream cheese on two slices of bread. Cover first slice with an even layer of one of the grated vegetables (use only one in each), and top with the second slice. Use a serrated knife to trim crusts, and cut into two triangles. Repeat with remaining ingredients. Cover with damp paper towels until ready to serve.

from Tea Sandwiches

lemon-caper butter and smoked salmon tea sandwiches

MAKES 2 DOZEN | **PHOTO ON PAGE 160**

¾ cup (1½ sticks) unsalted butter, room temperature

1 teaspoon freshly squeezed lemon juice

Grated zest of 1 lemon

6 tablespoons capers

Coarse salt

24 thin slices black or pumpernickel bread

14 ounces smoked salmon, thinly sliced

1 large bunch fresh dill, cleaned and trimmed, tough stems removed

1 In the bowl of a food processor fitted with the metal blade, combine butter, lemon juice, zest, and capers, and season with salt. Pulse until combined and most of the capers are broken up, about 15 seconds.

2 Spread a thin layer of caper butter on two slices of bread. Layer first slice with salmon and dill sprigs, and top with the second slice. Use a serrated knife to trim crusts, and cut into two triangles. Repeat with remaining ingredients. Cover with damp paper towels until ready to serve.

from Tea Sandwiches

mozzarella, prosciutto, and pesto butter tea sandwiches

MAKES 2 DOZEN | **PHOTOS ON PAGES 160-161**

To make perfectly round sandwiches, cut each of the layers separately with the same biscuit cutter. Ask your butcher to slice the prosciutto more thickly than usual so it can be cut easily without tearing; you will need one round for each sandwich.

- 6 tablespoons unsalted butter, room temperature
- ¾ cup packed fresh basil (about 2 ounces), rinsed well and dried
- ½ garlic clove
- 3 tablespoons finely grated Parmesan cheese
- 1 tablespoon pine nuts
- 8 ounces sliced prosciutto
- 1 pound fresh mozzarella cheese
- 2 loaves rustic bread (about 2 pounds), cut into 48 ¼-inch slices

1 Combine butter, basil, garlic, Parmesan, and pine nuts in the bowl of a food processor fitted with the metal blade; process until well blended. Set aside. Lay prosciutto slices flat on a piece of plastic wrap, and cover with another piece. Place in freezer 10 minutes.

2 Remove prosciutto from freezer; use a 2¼-inch round cutter to cut into 24 rounds. Slice mozzarella ⅛ inch thick, and cut into 24 rounds. Cut bread using the same cutter, being sure to remove all the crust.

3 Spread a thin layer of pesto butter on two bread rounds. Layer first round with a slice each of mozzarella and prosciutto; top with the second bread round. Repeat with remaining ingredients. Cover with damp paper towels until ready to serve.

from Tea Sandwiches

roquefort butter and red pear tea sandwiches

MAKES 2 DOZEN | **PHOTO ON PAGE 160**

The red skins of the pears are a colorful accent to these simple tea sandwiches. Use the Roquefort butter in other combinations such as with watercress or thinly sliced tomato.

- Juice of 1 lemon
- 2 tablespoons water
- 1 red pear, cored and very thinly sliced
- 4 ounces Roquefort cheese, crumbled
- ½ cup (1 stick) unsalted butter, room temperature
- ⅛ teaspoon freshly ground pepper
- 16 thin slices white bread or brioche

1 Combine lemon juice and the water in a small bowl; immerse sliced pears until ready to use to prevent discoloration. Blot dry with paper towels before using.

2 In a medium bowl, gently stir Roquefort into butter, leaving small bits of cheese. Be careful not to overmix, or the butter will turn blue. Add pepper.

3 Spread a thin layer of Roquefort butter on two slices of bread. Line first slice with pears, overlapping slightly, and top with the second bread slice. Use a serrated knife to trim crusts, and cut into three rectangles (about 1 by 3 inches). Repeat with remaining ingredients. Cover with damp paper towels until ready to serve.

from Tea Sandwiches

sautéed-mushroom butter and bacon tea sandwiches

MAKES 2 DOZEN | **PHOTOS ON PAGES 160-161**

- 1 cup (2 sticks) unsalted butter, room temperature
- 1 tablespoon olive oil
- 1 pound shiitake mushrooms, cleaned, tough ends of stems removed, diced
- Coarse salt and freshly ground pepper
- ¼ cup Madeira or sherry
- 24 thin slices wheat bread
- 1½ pounds bacon (about 24 slices), cooked
- 1 bunch arugula, cleaned and trimmed

1 In a large skillet over medium heat, heat 2 tablespoons butter and the oil. Add mushrooms, and season with salt and pepper; sauté until mushrooms begin to soften and juices evaporate, about 8 minutes. Add Madeira, and remove from heat; deglaze pan, stirring up any browned bits with a wooden

spoon until liquid has evaporated. Let cool, and place in the bowl of a food processor fitted with the metal blade. Add remaining butter; pulse until mushrooms are finely chopped, about 1 minute.

2 Thinly spread two slices of bread with mushroom butter; cover first slice with a single layer each of bacon and arugula, and top with the second bread slice. Use a serrated knife to trim crusts, and cut into two triangles. Cover with damp paper towels until ready to serve.

from Tea Sandwiches

shrimp salad tea sandwiches

MAKES 4 DOZEN | PHOTO ON PAGE 160

Using sprouts in these flavorful sandwiches will add color and crunch.

- 1 cup cooked medium shrimp (about 8 ounces), finely chopped
- 1½ tablespoons finely chopped fresh flat-leaf parsley
- 2 teaspoons freshly squeezed lemon juice
-     Finely grated zest of 2 lemons
- 1 teaspoon Worcestershire sauce
- ⅓ cup mayonnaise
-     Coarse salt and freshly ground pepper
- ½ cup (1 stick) unsalted butter, room temperature
- 24 thin slices white bread
- 3 ounces sprouts (optional)

1 In a medium bowl, combine shrimp, parsley, lemon juice, zest, Worcestershire, and mayonnaise. Stir to thoroughly combine; season with salt and pepper.

2 Thinly spread butter on two bread slices. Cover first with shrimp salad and sprouts, if using; top with the second bread slice. Use a serrated knife to trim crusts, and cut into two triangles; cut in half again to make four small triangles. Repeat with remaining ingredients. Cover with damp paper towels until ready to serve.

from Tea Sandwiches

smoked duck and chutney butter tea sandwiches

MAKES 2 DOZEN | PHOTO ON PAGE 160

- 1 cup (2 sticks) unsalted butter, room temperature
- 6 tablespoons peach or apricot chutney
- 24 thin slices black or pumpernickel bread
- 1 pound smoked duck breasts, trimmed of fat, very thinly sliced
- 1 bunch watercress, cleaned and trimmed

1 In the bowl of a food processor fitted with the plastic blade, combine butter and chutney; pulse to combine.

2 Thinly spread chutney butter on two bread slices. Cover first slice with thin layers of duck and watercress; top with the second slice. Use a serrated knife to trim crusts, and cut into two triangles. Repeat with remaining ingredients. Cover with damp paper towels until ready to serve.

from Tea Sandwiches

southwest black bean, smoked turkey, and avocado tea sandwiches

MAKES 2 DOZEN | PHOTO ON PAGE 160

- 1 15½-ounce can black beans, drained
- 3 tablespoons coarsely chopped onion
- ½ jalapeño pepper, seeded and chopped
- ½ garlic clove, coarsely chopped
- ⅛ teaspoon crushed red-pepper flakes or jalapeño seeds
- ½ teaspoon coarse salt
- ¼ teaspoon freshly ground black pepper
- 3 tablespoons coarsely chopped fresh cilantro
- 1 avocado
-     Juice of 1 lime
- 24 thin slices white bread
- 9 ounces smoked turkey, thinly sliced

1 In the bowl of a food processor fitted with the metal blade, combine beans, onion, jalapeño, garlic, red-pepper flakes, salt, and pepper. Pulse until smooth and thick; add water 1 tablespoon at a time, if necessary, to reach spreadable consistency. Transfer to a medium bowl, and stir in cilantro.

2 Peel, pit, and thinly slice avocado. Gently toss avocado with lime juice to prevent discoloration.

3 Spread black-bean mixture on two slices of bread; layer first slice with smoked turkey and tossed avocado, and top with the second slice. Using a serrated knife, trim crusts, and cut into two triangles. Repeat with remaining ingredients. Cover with damp paper towels until ready to serve.

from Tea Sandwiches

sweet onion sandwiches

MAKES 4

½ cup mayonnaise

2 tablespoons coarsely chopped fresh flat-leaf parsley

¼ teaspoon coarse salt

Freshly ground pepper

4 large rustic rolls, sliced in half

12 ounces smoked Gouda cheese, thinly sliced

1 small sweet onion, thinly sliced

1 bunch arugula, washed and drained

In a small bowl, combine mayonnaise and parsley. Season with salt and pepper. Spread 1 tablespoon mayonnaise mixture on each of the halved rolls. Place Gouda on four halves, and top with sliced onion and arugula. Top with remaining halves.

from Sweet Onions

SIDE DISHES

baked stuffed sweet onions

MAKES 4

4 sweet onions

½ teaspoon coarse salt, plus more for cooking water

2 tablespoons olive oil

6 ounces (about 9) cremini mushrooms, washed, trimmed, and cut into ½-inch pieces

4 ounces Virginia ham, cut into ¼-inch pieces

¼ teaspoon freshly ground pepper

3 tablespoons Madeira or sherry

¼ cup chopped fresh flat-leaf parsley

1 cup (about 2 ounces) grated Gruyère cheese

1 Preheat oven to 400°F. Slice ½ inch from the top of each onion, and discard. Slice just enough from the root end so that onions stand upright. Using a melon baller, hollow out the insides, leaving a ⅓-inch- to ½-inch-thick shell. Set aside. Finely chop removed parts, and set aside 1 cup. Discard remaining onion or reserve for another use.

2 Bring a large pot of water to a boil; add salt. Gently submerge onion shells, and boil 5 minutes. Remove with a slotted spoon; transfer to a wire rack to dry.

3 Make the stuffing: Heat 1 tablespoon oil in a large sauté pan over medium heat. Add reserved chopped onions, and cook until translucent, about 8 minutes. Add mushrooms, ham, salt, and pepper; cook until mixture is browned, about 5 minutes. Add Madeira; deglaze pan, stirring with a wooden spoon to loosen any browned bits on bottom. Transfer to a small mixing bowl; let cool slightly, 2 to 3 minutes. Add parsley and Gruyère, and stir to combine.

4 Fill reserved onion shells with stuffing. Place in a small roasting pan; drizzle with remaining tablespoon oil. Cover with aluminum foil. Bake until tender, about 50 minutes; remove foil after 40 minutes to brown stuffing. Remove from oven, and serve.

from Sweet Onions

braised sweet onions

SERVES 4

2 sweet onions

3 tablespoons olive oil

Coarse salt and freshly ground pepper

1 cup homemade or low-sodium canned chicken stock

3 sprigs thyme

3 sprigs rosemary

1 Preheat oven to 350°F. Trim root end of onions, and cut onions in half; cut each half into three wedges. Heat olive oil in a 10-inch cast-iron skillet over medium heat. Add onion wedges, and season with salt and pepper; sauté until golden brown, about 5 minutes on each side.

2 Add chicken stock, thyme, and rosemary; transfer pan to oven. Cook, basting onions periodically with the cooking liquid, until onions are tender and stock has reduced and thickened, 55 to 60 minutes. Remove from oven, and serve.

from Sweet Onions

glazed baby turnips and cipollini onions

SERVES 6 TO 8

To peel cipollini onions, immerse them in boiling water for a few minutes, and remove with a slotted spoon. Allow them to cool slightly, and then slip off the skins.

1 tablespoon unsalted butter

1 teaspoon sugar

Coarse salt and freshly ground pepper

3 to 3½ pounds (about 8 or 9 bunches) baby turnips, peeled and trimmed

3 8-ounce bags cipollini onions, peeled and trimmed

½ cup water

Fresh herbs, such as thyme, marjoram, or rosemary, for garnish

1 Melt butter in a large saucepan over medium-low heat. Add sugar; season with salt and pepper. Cook until butter starts to brown, about 1 minute. Add turnips and onions, swirling pan to coat evenly. Add the water; cover, and cook until almost all water has evaporated and vegetables are glazed, about 20 minutes.

2 Remove the cover, and continue cooking until all of the liquid has evaporated and the vegetables are caramelized, 3 to 5 minutes. Season with salt and pepper. Transfer to a large platter, and garnish with fresh herbs.

from Spring Harvest Lunch

herbed couscous

SERVES 4

1½ tablespoons unsalted butter

2 shallots, minced

¾ teaspoon ground cumin

1 teaspoon crushed fennel seeds

1 cup couscous

1 14½-ounce can low-sodium chicken broth, or homemade

1 teaspoon coarse salt

3 tablespoons finely chopped fresh flat-leaf parsley

1 tablespoon finely chopped fresh sage

2 teaspoons finely chopped fresh marjoram

Melt butter in a medium saucepan over medium heat. Add shallots, cumin, and fennel seeds; cook, stirring frequently, until shallots are translucent, about 2 minutes. Add couscous, chicken broth, and salt. Cover; reduce heat to low, and simmer until liquid is absorbed, about 5 minutes. Remove from heat, and stir in parsley, sage, and marjoram. Serve hot.

from What to Have for Dinner

soft polenta with fresh herbs

SERVES 6 TO 8

3 cups homemade or low-sodium canned chicken stock

3 cups water

5 tablespoons unsalted butter

1 sprig thyme

1 sprig rosemary

1½ cups polenta

Coarse salt and freshly ground pepper

2 cups milk

2 tablespoons minced mixed fresh herbs (such as parsley, chives, chervil, or tarragon)

1 Bring chicken stock and the water to a boil in a large saucepan over medium-high heat. Add 4 tablespoons butter, and stir until melted. Add thyme and rosemary; remove from heat, and let steep 10 minutes. Remove and discard herbs.

2 Return cooking liquid to a boil over medium-high heat. Stirring constantly, gradually add polenta in a steady stream. Season with salt and pepper, and reduce heat to medium-low. Cook, adding milk ¼ cup at a time and stirring until completely absorbed after each addition, until polenta mixture is soft and creamy, 40 to 50 minutes. Stir in remaining tablespoon butter and minced herbs. Serve immediately.

from Spring Harvest Lunch

white asparagus with hollandaise sauce

SERVES 6 TO 8 | **PHOTO ON PAGE 163**

White asparagus spears are generally thicker than their green counterparts, so be sure to trim the tough ends of the stalk and cook until they are perfectly crisp-tender.

6 **quarts water**

3 **tablespoons coarse salt**

3 **to 4 bunches (3 to 4 pounds) white asparagus, peeled and tough ends of stalks trimmed by 1 inch**

Hollandaise Sauce (recipe follows)

Bring the water to a boil in a large stockpot, and add the salt. Place asparagus spears in the water; cook just until tender, about 5 minutes. Gently transfer to a colander to drain, being careful not to damage the tips. Blot dry with paper towels, and arrange on a large serving platter. Serve warm with hollandaise sauce.

from Spring Harvest Lunch

hollandaise sauce

MAKES 3 CUPS

Clarifying the butter is a foolproof way to achieve perfect hollandaise sauce.

2 **cups (4 sticks) unsalted butter**

6 **large egg yolks**

⅓ **cup dry white wine**

2 **tablespoons water**

2 **teaspoons freshly squeezed lemon juice**

Coarse salt

Cayenne pepper (optional)

1 Clarify the butter: Slowly melt butter in a small saucepan over medium heat; skim off surface foam. Pour clear layer of butter into a large glass measuring cup, leaving behind the milky residue in the bottom of the pan, which can be discarded. Let butter cool until it is lukewarm.

2 Meanwhile, place egg yolks and wine in a heat-proof bowl set over a pan of simmering water. Whisk vigorously until mixture is very pale and whisk leaves a trail, 3 to 4 minutes. Remove bowl from heat; continue whisking until mixture is lukewarm, about 30 seconds.

3 Whisking constantly, add butter to the egg mixture a drop at a time at first and gradually increasing to a steady stream. When fully incorporated, stir in the water and lemon juice, and season with salt and cayenne pepper, if desired. Serve immediately, or keep warm over a pan of simmering water removed from heat.

DESSERTS

baked camembert with fresh fruit

SERVES 4

Camembert should be very soft when gently pressed in the center. Baking the cheese in its box makes for an unusual presentation and easy cleanup. Buy only wooden containers, and remove any plastic before baking. If the sides of the box are not stapled together, secure them with kitchen twine.

1 **8-ounce round Camembert cheese in wooden container**

2 **apples, cut into wedges**

2 **firm but ripe pears, cut into wedges**

Assorted crackers, for serving

Preheat oven to 375°F. Remove and discard box lid and paper wrapper from cheese. Return unwrapped cheese to box; place in oven. Bake until heated through and very soft, about 20 minutes. Place box with cheese on a serving platter, if desired, or scoop out and place on four serving plates. Serve immediately with fruit and crackers.

from What to Have for Dinner

chocolate and mint parfaits

MAKES 8

These parfaits freeze well for up to one month. The preparation can be spread over the course of one or several days; the chocolate mixture needs to freeze at least five hours before using, and the parfaits another five hours before serving.

FOR THE CHOCOLATE MIXTURE:

3 ounces bittersweet chocolate, finely chopped

½ cup plus ⅓ cup heavy cream

1 large egg yolk

1 large whole egg

¼ cup sugar

1 tablespoon light corn syrup

2 tablespoons water

FOR THE MINT MIXTURE:

1 bunch (3¼ ounces) fresh mint leaves and stems

½ cup sugar

2 tablespoons light corn syrup

3 teaspoons dried mint

2 tablespoons water

4 large egg yolks

1 large whole egg

2 cups heavy cream

Chocolate Sauce, for garnish (recipe follows)

Sugared mint leaves, for garnish (optional)

1 Make the chocolate mixture: Place chocolate in a medium heat-proof bowl. Heat ½ cup heavy cream in a small saucepan, and pour over chocolate. Let stand 10 minutes, then stir until completely melted and smooth. Set aside.

2 Place egg yolk and egg in the bowl of an electric mixer fitted with the whisk attachment, and beat until light and frothy, about 2 minutes. Set aside.

3 Place sugar, corn syrup, and the water in a small saucepan. Heat, without stirring, over medium heat, until a candy thermometer registers 245ºF. Wash down sides of pan with a pastry brush dipped in water to prevent crystals from forming. With mixer on low, slowly pour sugar mixture into eggs; beat until room temperature, about 2 minutes.

4 In another bowl, whip remaining ⅓ cup cream to soft peaks. Fold into egg mixture; fold in chocolate mixture. Fill eight 3-ounce plastic cups one-third full. Place in freezer until firm, 4 to 5 hours. Unmold onto a baking sheet lined with waxed paper; cover with plastic wrap, and return to freezer for at least 1 hour.

5 Make the mint mixture: Prepare an ice bath, and set aside. Bring a large pot of water to a boil; quickly blanch fresh mint 1 minute. Transfer to ice bath to stop cooking and preserve bright color; let cool completely. Remove from ice bath, and place on paper towels; gently squeeze to extract excess water.

6 Combine sugar, corn syrup, dried mint, and the water in a small heavy saucepan. Heat, without stirring, over medium heat, until a candy thermometer registers 245ºF, washing down sides of pan with a pastry brush dipped in water to prevent crystals from forming. Remove from heat; let cool.

7 Add blanched fresh mint; transfer to the jar of a blender. Blend until mixture is a smooth paste, about 3 minutes. Strain through a fine sieve back into saucepan. Place over medium heat, and gently reheat 2 to 4 minutes. Place egg yolks and egg in the bowl of an electric mixer fitted with the whisk attachment, and beat until light and frothy, about 4 minutes. With mixer on low speed, slowly pour sugar mixture into eggs; continue mixing until room temperature, about 5 minutes.

8 In another clean bowl, whip cream to soft peaks; fold into egg mixture with a rubber spatula. Fill eight 6-ounce ramekins or custard cups halfway, and place frozen chocolate mixture in the center of each. Level with remaining mint parfait mixture. Cover with plastic wrap, and place in freezer until completely set, 5 to 6 hours. Store in freezer up to 1 month.

9 To serve, unmold parfaits onto serving plates, and garnish with chocolate sauce and sugared mint leaves, if desired.

from Spring Harvest Lunch

chocolate sauce

MAKES ABOUT 1 CUP

This sauce can be made up to one week ahead and stored in the refrigerator until ready to use. Gently reheat over a pan of simmering water before serving.

4 ounces bittersweet chocolate, finely chopped

½ cup plus 2 tablespoons heavy cream

Place chocolate in a large heat-proof bowl. Bring the cream to a boil over medium-high heat; pour over chocolate. Let stand 10 minutes; stir with a rubber spatula until melted and combined. Serve hot.

chocolate pots de crème

MAKES 8 FIVE-OUNCE OR 10 FOUR-OUNCE SERVINGS

1¼ cups heavy cream

6 ounces semisweet chocolate, finely chopped

1¼ cups half-and-half

⅓ cup sugar

3 large whole eggs

5 large egg yolks

2 teaspoons pure vanilla extract

Whipped cream, for garnish (optional)

Cocoa powder, for garnish (optional)

Chocolate curls, for garnish (optional)

1 Preheat oven to 325°F. Place eight 5-ounce or ten 4-ounce ramekins or custard cups in a large baking pan lined with a kitchen towel. Bring a large pot of water to a boil; keep hot until ready to use.

2 Bring cream to a boil in a small saucepan over medium-high heat; remove from heat. Add chocolate, and let stand 5 minutes; whisk slowly until melted and combined. Transfer to a large mixing bowl, and set aside.

3 In a small saucepan, heat half-and-half with sugar over medium heat until mixture begins to bubble around the edges and to steam, about 3 minutes. Whisk into chocolate mixture until smooth. In another large mixing bowl, lightly beat eggs with yolks and vanilla until smooth. Slowly whisk in chocolate mixture.

4 Pour custard into ramekins. Carefully pour the boiling water into pan until it reaches halfway up sides of ramekins. Bake until just set in center when gently touched with your finger, 25 to 30 minutes. Transfer ramekins to a wire rack to cool slightly. Serve warm (or cover with plastic wrap, and place in refrigerator to chill completely, 6 hours or overnight). Garnish with whipped cream, cocoa powder, or chocolate curls, if desired.

from Custard

crème brûlée

MAKES 4 SIX-OUNCE SERVINGS

To produce the delightful hard surface that crackles when tapped with a spoon, you will need to brown the sugared tops of the custards with a small kitchen blowtorch, available at most specialty gourmet stores.

2 cups heavy cream

½ vanilla bean, split and scraped

½ cup sugar, plus 6 tablespoons for sprinkling

5 large egg yolks

1 Preheat oven to 325°F. Place four shallow oval 6-ounce ramekins in a large baking pan lined with a kitchen towel. Bring a large pot of water to a boil, and keep hot until ready to use.

2 In a small saucepan, heat cream, vanilla bean, and scrapings over medium heat until bubbles form around the edges and mixture starts to steam, about 6 minutes. Turn off heat.

3 In a large bowl, whisk together ½ cup sugar and the egg yolks until combined. Whisking constantly, slowly add hot cream mixture. Strain mixture through a fine sieve into a clean bowl; skim off any surface foam with a spoon.

4 Pour custard into ramekins. Carefully pour the boiling water into baking pan until it reaches halfway up sides of ramekins. Bake until custard is just set in the center when gently touched with your finger, about 35 minutes. Transfer ramekins to a wire rack to cool. Cover with plastic wrap, and place in refrigerator to chill completely, 2 to 3 hours or overnight.

5 Transfer to freezer 45 minutes before serving. Remove from freezer, and sprinkle 1½ tablespoons sugar over entire surface of each. Using a kitchen torch, pass the flame in a circular motion 1 to 2 inches above the surface of each until the sugar bubbles, turns amber, and forms a smooth surface. Serve immediately.

from Custard

flan

MAKES 8 FOUR-OUNCE SERVINGS | **PHOTO ON PAGE 175**

You can also make one large flan; bake custard in an eight-inch round cake pan set in a water bath for the same amount of time. For best results, make flan a day ahead to let the caramel form a slightly liquefied layer.

1½ cups sugar

¼ cup water

3 cups milk

3 large egg yolks

4 large whole eggs

1 teaspoon pure vanilla extract

1 Preheat oven to 325°F. Prepare an ice bath, and set aside. Place eight 4-ounce ramekins in two baking pans lined with kitchen towels. Bring a large pot of water to a boil; keep hot until ready to use.

2 Meanwhile, in a small saucepan, heat ¾ cup sugar with the water over medium heat; cook until sugar has dissolved, about 5 minutes. Swirl pan occasionally, but do not stir. Wash down sides of pan with a pastry brush dipped in water to prevent crystals from forming. Increase heat to medium-high; continue cooking until caramel is amber, about 8 minutes, gently swirling pan to color evenly.

3 Remove from heat, and immerse bottom of pan in the ice bath for 3 seconds to stop cooking. Dry bottom of pan. Working quickly, divide caramel evenly among ramekins (about 1 tablespoon in each); swirl to coat the bottoms evenly. Set aside.

4 In a small saucepan, heat milk over medium heat just until bubbles form around the edges and milk starts to steam, 5 to 6 minutes. Turn off heat.

5 In a large bowl, whisk together yolks, eggs, and remaining ¾ cup sugar until combined. Slowly add hot milk, whisking constantly. Pour mixture through a fine sieve into a clean bowl; skim off surface foam with a spoon. Stir in vanilla, and pour custard into ramekins, dividing evenly among them. Carefully pour the boiling water into the baking pan until it reaches halfway up sides of ramekins.

6 Bake until custard is just set in the center when gently touched with your finger, 30 to 35 minutes. Remove from oven; transfer to a wire rack to cool completely. Cover with plastic wrap, and place in the refrigerator to chill, at least 6 hours or overnight. To unmold, run a sharp knife around edges, and place a serving plate upside down over the top of each ramekin; invert, and gently lift ramekin to remove. Serve.

from Custard

grapefruit tart

GOOD - BETTER CHILLED

MAKES 1 NINE-INCH TART | **PHOTO ON PAGE 175**

3 large ruby red or pink grapefruits

⅔ cup sugar

3 large whole eggs

2 large egg yolks

¾ cup heavy cream

1 prebaked Pâte Sucrée Tart Shell, still in tart pan (recipe follows)

Confectioners' sugar, for dusting

1 Preheat oven to ~~300°~~ 325° F. Squeeze juice from 1 grapefruit into a large measuring cup, and set aside. You should have ¾ cup. Cut off both ends of remaining 2 grapefruits; using a sharp paring knife, remove the peel, pith, and outer membranes, following the curve of the fruit. Working over a bowl to catch the juices, use the knife to carefully slice between the sections of each grapefruit to detach the segments from the membranes. Cover with plastic wrap, and set side.

2 In a large bowl, whisk together sugar, eggs, and yolks. Slowly whisk in cream and reserved grapefruit juice until combined and smooth. Pour through a fine sieve into a medium bowl; discard solids. Skim off surface foam with a spoon.

3 Pour custard mixture into tart shell. Place in oven, and bake until the center is set when gently touched with your finger, about 40 minutes. Transfer to a wire rack to cool completely. The tart can be refrigerated at this point up to 1 day.

4 To serve, hold a plate or bottom of tart pan over custard (do not touch); dust edges of crust with confectioners' sugar. Slice into wedges; serve with reserved grapefruit segments.

from Custard

pâte sucrée tart shells

MAKES 2 NINE-INCH TART SHELLS

You can freeze the dough for up to three weeks. The tart shells can be baked a day in advance and kept uncovered at room temperature before being filled.

2½ cups all-purpose flour, plus more for work surface
 4 tablespoons sugar
 1 teaspoon salt
 1 cup (2 sticks) chilled unsalted butter, cut into small pieces
 2 large egg yolks, plus 1 lightly beaten
 ¼ cup ice water

1 In the bowl of a food processor fitted with the metal blade, combine flour, sugar, and salt; pulse to combine. Add butter, and process until mixture resembles coarse meal, about 20 seconds. Beat 2 egg yolks and the ice water together in a small bowl. Add to flour mixture, and pulse until dough just comes together when pinched, 10 to 15 seconds. Divide dough in half, and flatten into two disks. Wrap well with plastic, and refrigerate at least 1 hour or overnight.

2 Preheat oven to 400°F. Remove one disk from refrigerator, and place on a lightly floured work surface. Roll dough into a 10½-inch round. Carefully lift and place over a 9-inch tart pan with a removable bottom; fit dough into sides and bottom of pan. Trim excess dough with a paring knife. Prick the bottom of the shell all over with a fork. Place in the freezer until firm, about 15 minutes. Repeat with second disk.

3 Remove from freezer. Line with parchment paper extending over sides by 1 inch. Fill with dried beans or pie weights, and place on a baking sheet. Bake 20 minutes. Remove from oven; remove parchment and beans, and immediately brush with remaining yolk. Return to oven; bake until golden brown, 10 to 12 minutes. Transfer to a wire rack to cool.

lamingtons

MAKES 24 | **PHOTO ON PAGE 171**

These petits fours are perennial best sellers at Australian bake sales and are the preferred accompaniment to afternoon tea. The cakes should be made a day in advance and chilled or frozen before icing.

1 cup (2 sticks) unsalted butter, room temperature, plus more for pans
2⅔ cups cake flour (not self-rising), plus more for pans
 2 cups sugar
 2 teaspoons pure vanilla extract
 4 large eggs
 2 teaspoons baking powder
 ¼ teaspoon salt
 1 cup milk
 ⅔ cup strawberry jam
 1 pound shredded sweetened coconut
   Chocolate Icing (page 112)

1 Preheat oven to 325°F. Butter two 9-by-13-inch baking pans; line bottoms with parchment; butter parchment. Dust with flour; tap out excess; set pans aside. In the bowl of an electric mixer fitted with the paddle attachment, cream together butter and sugar until light and fluffy, about 3 minutes. Add vanilla and eggs, one at a time; beat until incorporated.

2 In a medium bowl, sift together flour, baking powder, and salt; add to egg mixture in three additions, alternating with the milk and beginning and ending with the flour mixture.

3 Divide batter between prepared pans. Place in oven; bake until a cake tester inserted into centers comes out clean, about 30 minutes. Cool slightly on wire racks. Turn out cakes onto racks; cool completely.

4 Spread one of the cooled cakes with jam; place other cake on top. Using a serrated knife, trim edges of sandwiched cakes; cut into 24 two-inch squares.

5 Place coconut in a medium bowl; set aside. Place the bowl of chocolate icing over a saucepan filled with 2 inches of gently simmering water. Place a jam-filled cake square in bowl of chocolate icing; using forks to turn the square, coat all sides.

6 Allow excess icing to drip off; transfer square to bowl of coconut. Using clean forks to turn square, coat it with coconut. Transfer coated square to wire rack to stand until coating has set, about 15 minutes. Continue until all squares have been coated. Lamingtons can be kept in an airtight container at room temperature for up to 2 days.

from Dessert of the Month

chocolate icing

COATS 24 LAMINGTONS

To ensure that the icing stays at the proper spreading consistency while the cakes are prepared, the bowl must sit over a pan of barely simmering water.

1 cup milk

4 tablespoons unsalted butter

1 tablespoon pure vanilla extract

8 cups confectioners' sugar, sifted

1 cup cocoa powder, sifted

Place the milk and butter in a small saucepan over medium heat, and heat until butter is melted. Transfer to a medium heat-proof bowl; add the vanilla extract, confectioners' sugar, and cocoa powder. Stir until combined.

mango-lime granita

SERVES 4

Mangoes contain vitamins A and C. Whisking the granita as it freezes ensures that it reaches the proper consistency.

3 cups chopped ripe mango (about 3 mangoes)

1 cup water

Juice of 2 limes (about ¼ cup)

2 tablespoons sugar

1 Place chopped mango in the bowl of a food processor fitted with the metal blade, and process until smooth. Transfer to a medium bowl. Add the water, lime juice, and sugar; stir to dissolve.

2 Pour mixture into a 9-by-5-inch deep-sided metal pan, and place in the freezer until nearly set, about 3 hours, whisking mixture every hour. Remove from freezer, and scrape surface with the tines of a fork until it is the texture of shaved ice. Return to freezer until ready to serve. Granita can be stored in an airtight container in the freezer up to 2 weeks.

PER SERVING: 108 CALORIES, 0 G FAT, 0 MG CHOLESTEROL, 28 G CARBOHYDRATE, 4 MG SODIUM, 1 G PROTEIN, 1 G FIBER

from Fit to Eat: Antioxidants

maple pudding

SERVES 6

Walnut Shortbread (page 113) makes a delicious accompaniment to this custard.

6 tablespoons cornstarch

6 large egg yolks

1 cup pure maple syrup

3 cups milk

2 tablespoons unsalted butter

½ cup heavy cream (optional)

1 tablespoon walnut-flavored liqueur, such as Nocello (optional)

1 In a large mixing bowl, whisk together cornstarch, egg yolks, and maple syrup until smooth and combined. Set aside.

2 In a medium saucepan, heat milk over medium-high heat just until it comes to a boil, 5 to 6 minutes. Slowly whisk milk into the egg mixture until smooth and combined. Strain mixture through a fine sieve back into the saucepan.

3 Place saucepan over medium-low heat. Bring the mixture to a boil, stirring constantly with a wooden spoon; be sure to scrape the corners and across the bottom of the pan. Continue cooking until mixture is very thick and the spoon leaves a trail when stirring, about 12 minutes. (If mixture begins to form clumps on the bottom, remove from heat and whisk vigorously.) Remove from heat, and stir in butter until combined.

4 Transfer to a medium bowl, and gently press plastic wrap directly onto surface of custard. Refrigerate until well chilled, at least 6 hours and up to 2 days.

5 If desired, combine heavy cream and Nocello in a small bowl, and whip until soft peaks form. Divide custard among six serving dishes, and top each with a dollop of Nocello cream.

from Custard

raspberry floating islands

SERVES 6 | **PHOTO ON PAGE 173**

Since raspberry seeds are small enough to pass through the finest mesh strainer, you may need to strain the raspberry purée several times.

- 2 **half-pints fresh raspberries**
- 2 **tablespoons plus ¾ cup granulated sugar**
- 1 **quart milk**
- 6 **large egg whites**
- **Pinch cream of tartar**
- ½ **teaspoon pure vanilla extract**
- **Crème Anglaise (recipe follows)**
- **Confectioners' sugar, for dusting**

1 Make the raspberry purée: Place 1 half-pint raspberries in a small skillet over medium heat; add 2 tablespoons sugar. Cook, stirring occasionally, until sugar is dissolved and raspberries start to break down, about 2 minutes. Remove from heat. Pass through a fine sieve into a small bowl, pressing down to extract as much pulp as possible. Set purée aside to cool.

2 In a high-sided 10-inch skillet, bring milk to a boil. Reduce heat to a gentle simmer while you make the meringue.

3 Make the meringue: In a heat-proof bowl of an electric mixer, combine remaining ¾ cup granulated sugar with egg whites and cream of tartar. Place over a pan of simmering water; whisk constantly until sugar is dissolved and mixture is warm to the touch, 1 to 2 minutes.

4 Transfer bowl to the mixer fitted with the whisk attachment. Beat on low speed, gradually increasing to high speed until glossy peaks form, 5 to 7 minutes. Add vanilla, and mix to combine. Transfer meringue to a large bowl, and spread out with a large spoon or spatula. Drizzle 1 to 2 tablespoons raspberry purée on top; run a knife back and forth to streak.

5 Make the floating islands: Working in batches, use two soup spoons to scoop meringue ¼ cup at a time into simmering milk. Do not overcrowd skillet. Poach until firm, about 2 minutes per side. Remove with a slotted spoon, and transfer to paper towels to drain. Repeat, skimming surface skin from milk between batches.

6 Divide the crème anglaise among six soup bowls. Place two meringue islands on top of each. Garnish with the remaining half-pint raspberries, raspberry purée, and a dusting of confectioners' sugar.

from Custard

crème anglaise

MAKES ABOUT 2 CUPS

Stirring the mixture constantly with a heat-proof silicone spatula or straight-edged wooden spoon while heating will ensure a smooth sauce. Be sure to scrape the corners and across the entire bottom of the pan to avoid scorching.

- 2 **cups milk**
- ½ **cup sugar**
- 5 **large egg yolks**
- 1 **teaspoon pure vanilla extract**

1 Prepare an ice bath, and set aside. In a small saucepan, heat the milk over medium-high heat just until bubbles form around the edges and the milk starts to steam, about 4 minutes. Turn off heat.

2 In a medium bowl, whisk together the sugar and egg yolks until pale and thick, about 2 minutes. Slowly add the hot milk, whisking constantly. Strain mixture through a fine sieve back into the pan.

3 Place pan over medium-low heat; cook, stirring constantly with a wooden spoon, until custard is thick enough to coat the back of the spoon and leaves a clean mark when you run your finger across the spoon, 10 to 12 minutes. Stir in vanilla, and transfer to a clean bowl. Place in ice bath to chill, stirring occasionally. Serve, or store in an airtight container in the refrigerator up to 3 days.

walnut shortbread

MAKES 3 DOZEN

Reroll the scraps and continue making cookies until all the dough has been used. Shortbread can be stored in an airtight container at room temperature for up to one week.

- 2 **cups all-purpose flour, plus more for work surface**
- ¼ **teaspoon salt**
- 1 **cup (2 sticks) unsalted butter, room temperature**
- ½ **cup granulated sugar**
- ½ **cup finely ground walnuts (2 ounces), plus 36 halves for the tops**
- 1 **teaspoon pure vanilla extract**
- **Sanding sugar, for decorating (optional)**

1 Line two baking sheets with parchment paper. Sift together flour and salt in a small bowl; set aside.

2 Place butter and granulated sugar in the bowl of an electric mixer fitted with the paddle attachment. Beat on medium speed until light and fluffy, 3 to 5 minutes. Add ground walnuts and vanilla, and beat to combine. Add flour mixture;

beat on low speed, periodically scraping down sides, until flour is just incorporated and dough sticks together when pinched. Form dough into flattened disk; wrap well in plastic, and refrigerate until firm, at least 1 hour or overnight.

3 Preheat oven to 325°F. Place parchment paper on work surface, and lightly dust with flour. Roll dough to ¼ inch thick. Cut out cookies with 2½-inch cookie cutter; place 1 inch apart on lined baking sheets. Transfer to freezer until firm, about 15 minutes.

4 Remove from freezer. Roll edges in sanding sugar, if desired. Gently press a walnut half into each cookie. Bake, rotating halfway through, until firm and lightly golden, about 25 minutes. Transfer to a wire rack to cool completely.

from Custard

DRINKS

blueberry breakfast shake

MAKES 2 EIGHT-OUNCE SERVINGS | **PHOTO ON PAGE 155**

In this refreshing smoothie, yogurt provides protein as well as calcium and B vitamins. Blueberries rank third as a natural source of antioxidants after prunes and raisins.

½ cup blueberries, picked over and rinsed

½ cup low-fat vanilla yogurt

½ cup skim milk

2 tablespoons honey

5 ice cubes

Place all ingredients in the jar of a blender, and process until smooth. Serve immediately in tall glasses.

PER SERVING: 155 CALORIES, 1 G FAT, 4 MG CHOLESTEROL, 33 G CARBOHYDRATE, 72 MG SODIUM, 5 G PROTEIN, 1 G FIBER

from Fit to Eat: Antioxidants

MISCELLANEOUS

caramelized sweet onions

MAKES 1½ CUPS

To ensure proper caramelization, don't salt the onions until after they have finished cooking.

4 tablespoons unsalted butter

6 sweet onions, peeled and cut into ¼-inch rounds

½ teaspoon coarse salt

¼ teaspoon freshly ground pepper

Melt butter in a large skillet over medium heat. Add onions; cook, stirring occasionally, until all juices have evaporated, about 20 minutes. Reduce heat to medium-low, and cook, stirring occasionally, until onions are very tender and golden brown, 1 to 1½ hours. Add salt and pepper, and serve.

from Sweet Onions

May

BREAKFAST

117 coddled eggs with fines herbes

STARTERS

117 bouchées

119 cheese straws

119 chilled fennel and leek soup

120 mexican fiesta soup with roasted tomatillo and cilantro pesto

120 mini corn cakes with goat cheese and pepper jelly

121 vol-au-vents

SALADS

121 rice salad with lemon, dill, and red onion

MAIN COURSES

122 arugula risotto

122 braised lamb shanks with tomato and fennel

123 butterflied leg of lamb with lemon and garlic marinade

123 grilled trout with oregano

124 herb-stuffed chicken breasts

124 mint and pistachio stuffed leg of lamb

125 roasted whole leg of lamb with fresh herb rub

125 seared salmon with creamy leek sauce

126 seared shrimp with lemon and garlic

SIDE DISHES

126 flageolets

126 mango and tomato salsa

127 polenta

127 simple steamed thick asparagus

127 sugar snap peas with toasted almonds

127 toasted couscous tabbouleh

DESSERTS

128 breton butter cake

128 butterflies

129 chocolate turnovers

129 cream horns

130 fresh-raspberry gelatin and whipped cream

130 lemon semifreddo cake

131 napoleon

132 palmiers

133 pithiviers

133 raspberry tart

134 sacristains

134 tarte tatin

DRINKS

134 peach tea punch

coddled eggs with fines herbes

SERVES 4 | **PHOTO ON PAGE 156**

The easiest way to coddle eggs is to place them in egg coddlers, special containers with tight-fitting lids, but you can also use ramekins or custard cups covered tightly with foil. Fines herbes is a combination of chopped fresh herbs, most often those below but sometimes including others such as marjoram or savory.

1 slice whole-wheat bread, trimmed of crusts and cut into ¼-inch cubes, for garnish

Freshly ground pepper

1 tablespoon finely chopped fresh chives

2 tablespoons finely chopped fresh chervil

1 tablespoon finely chopped fresh tarragon

1 tablespoon finely chopped fresh flat-leaf parsley

4 large whole eggs

4 large egg whites

1 tablespoon plus 1 teaspoon heavy cream

1 teaspoon coarse salt

Nonstick cooking spray

1 Preheat oven to 350°F. Lightly coat four egg coddlers with cooking spray, and set aside. Lightly coat a rimmed baking sheet with cooking spray. Place bread cubes on prepared baking sheet; sprinkle with pepper. Bake until golden and crisp on all sides, turning once during cooking, about 7 minutes. Remove from oven; set aside.

2 Line bottom of a large saucepan with a clean kitchen towel, and fill with enough water to come just below rim of egg coddlers. Place pan over medium-high heat; bring water to a boil. Combine herbs in a small bowl, and mix well. Place 2 teaspoons mixed herbs in the bottom of each coddler; to each, add 1 whole egg and 1 egg white, and drizzle with 1 teaspoon heavy cream. Add ¼ teaspoon salt to each, and season with pepper. Screw lids on tightly.

3 Using tongs, carefully place egg coddlers in the boiling water. Reduce heat to medium, and simmer 6 minutes. Turn off heat; cover pan, and let stand 4 to 5 minutes. Remove coddlers from pan, and remove lids. Serve eggs in the coddlers. Top each with a few croutons, and garnish with remaining mixed herbs.

PER SERVING: 127 CALORIES, 7 G FAT, 219 MG CHOLESTEROL, 4 G CARBOHYDRATE, 628 MG SODIUM, 11 G PROTEIN, 0 G FIBER

from Fit to Eat: Cooking with Herbs

bouchées

MAKES 2 DOZEN

Basically a miniature version of vol-au-vents (page 121), bouchées make lovely hors d'oeuvres. Since they are so small, it's easier to pipe rather than spoon in the filling; use a parchment-paper piping cone or pastry bag. Some nice filling combinations are crème fraîche and caviar with fresh dill, or smoked salmon with cream cheese and fresh chives.

All-purpose flour, for work surface

1 pound Puff Pastry dough (page 118)

1 large egg yolk

1 tablespoon heavy cream

1 Lightly flour a clean work surface. Using a rolling pin, gently roll out dough until it is about ¼ inch thick. Using a 1½-inch round cookie cutter, cut out 48 rounds. Using a 1-inch round cookie cutter, cut out centers from 24 rounds to form rings. Discard centers.

2 In a small bowl, whisk together egg yolk and cream for the egg wash. Using a pastry brush, moisten tops of rounds and rings with egg wash, being careful not to let any drip down over the cut edges. Lay one ring on top of each round; place on an ungreased baking sheet. Cover with plastic, and place in refrigerator 1 hour.

3 Preheat oven to 425°F. Transfer baking sheet to the oven, and bake until bouchées are puffed and golden on the outside, about 8 minutes. Reduce heat to 350°F; continue baking 8 to 10 minutes more to let insides cook through.

4 Transfer bouchées to a wire rack. While still warm, cut out centers of tops using a paring knife; set aside. Remove and discard inside dough; let shells cool completely. Pipe in desired filling. Replace tops, and serve.

from Puff Pastry

puff pastry

MAKES ABOUT 2½ POUNDS

Puff pastry is not complicated to make; it just cannot be rushed. If at any point in the rolling process the dough becomes too soft or elastic, return it to the refrigerator to rest for at least thirty minutes. The dough can be made in advance through the fourth turn and stored overnight in the refrigerator or for up to one month in the freezer before continuing. You can also freeze the finished dough for several months before using.

FOR THE DOUGH PACKAGE:

3 cups all-purpose flour, plus more for work surface

¾ cup cake flour (not self-rising)

1½ teaspoons salt

4 tablespoons unsalted butter, cut into ½-inch pieces, well chilled

1¼ cups cold water

FOR THE BUTTER PACKAGE:

1 tablespoon all-purpose flour

1¾ cups (3½ sticks) unsalted butter, well chilled

1 Make the dough package: In a large mixing bowl, combine both flours with the salt. Scatter butter pieces over the flour mixture; using your fingers or a pastry cutter, incorporate butter until mixture resembles coarse meal.

2 Form a well in center of mixture, and pour the water into the well. Using your hands, gradually draw the flour mixture over the water, covering and gathering until mixture is well blended and begins to come together. Gently knead mixture in the bowl just until it comes together to form a dough, about 15 seconds. Pat dough into a rough ball, and turn out onto a piece of plastic wrap. Wrap tightly, and place in refrigerator to chill 1 hour.

3 Make the butter package: Sprinkle half the flour on a sheet of waxed or parchment paper. Place uncut sticks of butter on top, and sprinkle with remaining flour. Top with another sheet of paper; using a rolling pin, pound butter to soften and flatten to about ½ inch. Remove top sheet of paper, and fold butter package in half onto itself. Replace top sheet of paper, and pound again until butter is about ½ inch thick. Repeat process two or three times, or until butter becomes quite pliable. Using your hands, shape butter package into a 6-inch square. Wrap well in plastic, and place in refrigerator until it is chilled but not hardened, no more than 10 minutes.

4 Assemble and roll the dough: Remove dough package from refrigerator, and place on a lightly floured work surface. Using a rolling pin, gently roll out dough into a 9-inch round. Remove butter package from refrigerator, and place it in the center of the dough round. Using a paring knife or bench scraper, lightly score the dough to outline the butter square; remove butter, and set it aside. Starting from each side of the center square, gently roll out dough with the rolling pin, forming four flaps, each 4 to 5 inches long; do not touch the raised square in the center of the dough. Replace butter package on the center square. Fold flaps of dough over the butter package so that it is completely enclosed. Press with your hands to seal.

5 Using the rolling pin, press down on the dough at regular intervals, repeating and covering the entire surface area, until it is about 1 inch thick.

6 Gently roll out the dough into a large rectangle, about 9 by 20 inches, with one of the short sides closest to you. Be careful not to press too hard around the edges, and keep the corners even as you roll out the dough by squaring them with the side of the rolling pin or your hands. Brush off any excess flour. Starting at the near end, fold the rectangle in thirds as you would a business letter; this completes the first single turn. Wrap in plastic; place in refrigerator 45 to 60 minutes.

7 Remove dough from refrigerator, and repeat process in step 6, giving it five more single turns. Always start with the flap opening on the right as if it were a book. Mark the dough with your knuckle each time you complete a turn to help you keep track. Chill 1 hour between each turn. After the sixth and final turn, wrap dough in plastic; refrigerate at least 4 hours or overnight before using.

cheese straws

MAKES ABOUT 2 DOZEN

When twisting the straws into shape, don't worry if you lose up to three tablespoons of cheese; plenty will remain inside, and you can sprinkle any lost over the outside.

All-purpose flour, for work surface

1½ **pounds Puff Pastry dough (page 118)**

1 **large egg, lightly beaten**

¼ **teaspoon salt**

⅛ **teaspoon cayenne pepper**

4 **ounces Parmesan cheese, coarsely grated (about 1½ cups)**

1 On a lightly floured work surface, using a rolling pin, gently roll pastry dough into a 14-inch square ⅛ inch thick. Be careful not to press too hard on the edges. Using a pastry brush, dust off excess flour; brush some of the beaten egg over lower half of dough until it is well moistened.

2 In a small bowl, mix together salt and cayenne. Sprinkle half the salt mixture over egg-washed portion of dough. Sprinkle half the grated cheese over the same half; fold the uncovered dough over the cheese-covered section. Gently press all over the dough with your fingers to seal the halves together.

3 Brush top of dough with beaten egg to moisten; sprinkle remaining salt mixture and cheese evenly over the top.

4 Using a pastry wheel or sharp knife, trim edges, and cut dough into ½-inch strips. Twist strips into spiraled straws, and lay 1 inch apart on three ungreased baking sheets. To prevent straws from straightening out again, gently press both ends to adhere them to the baking sheet. Cover with plastic wrap; place in refrigerator 1 hour.

5 Preheat oven to 425°F. Transfer baking sheets to oven, and bake 15 minutes. Reduce oven heat to 350°F; continue baking until straws are golden brown and cooked all the way through, about 5 minutes. Remove from oven; using a thin spatula, immediately transfer straws to a wire rack to cool completely before serving.

from Puff Pastry

chilled fennel and leek soup

MAKES 4½ QUARTS

This soup tastes best when it is served very cold, so for optimal results, prepare it a day ahead and let it chill overnight, covered, in the refrigerator.

6 **medium leeks (about 1¼ pounds), white and light-green parts only, thinly sliced**

½ **cup (1 stick) unsalted butter**

1 **large yellow onion, finely chopped**

1 **teaspoon fennel seeds**

Coarse salt and freshly ground pepper

2 **garlic cloves, minced**

3 **medium fennel bulbs (about 2 pounds), trimmed and roughly chopped**

8 **cups homemade or low-sodium canned chicken stock**

4 **cups cold water**

2 **tablespoons Pernod (optional)**

Chervil sprigs, for garnish

1 Place leeks in a large bowl of cold water; stir, and let stand 5 minutes to allow dirt and sand to settle to the bottom. You may need to repeat several times, changing the water each time. Transfer to paper towels to drain.

2 Melt butter in a large saucepan over medium-low heat. Add onion and fennel seeds; season with salt and pepper. Cook, stirring occasionally, until onion is softened and translucent, about 10 minutes. Add garlic; cook until fragrant but not brown, about 2 minutes.

3 Add leeks and fennel to pan, and cook until vegetables are tender, about 10 minutes. Add chicken stock and the water, and bring to a boil; reduce heat, and simmer 20 minutes more.

4 Remove from heat, and let cool slightly. Working in several batches, transfer soup to the jar of a blender, being careful not to fill more than halfway and to cover lid with a kitchen towel. Purée until smooth; let cool. Transfer to an airtight container, and place in the refrigerator to chill completely, at least 4 hours or overnight.

5 To serve, stir in Pernod, if using, and season with salt and pepper. Ladle into soup bowls, and garnish with chervil.

from A Mother's Day Album

mexican fiesta soup with roasted tomatillo and cilantro pesto

SERVES 4

Cilantro's pungent fragrance partners well with fruity tomatillos in a lively pesto. The mixture offsets the spiciness of the cumin and jalapeño in this delectable soup.

4 tomatillos, husks removed and rinsed

⅔ cup packed fresh cilantro leaves, rinsed well

2 garlic cloves, minced

2 tablespoons freshly squeezed lime juice

1 small white onion, finely chopped

1 jalapeño, finely chopped, plus more sliced for garnish (optional)

½ teaspoon ground cumin

1 28-ounce can whole peeled tomatoes (about 8 tomatoes), drained and crushed

3 ears corn, quartered

4 cups homemade or low-sodium canned chicken stock, skimmed of fat

Freshly ground pepper

½ ripe avocado, peeled, pitted, and cut into ¼-inch-thick slices

Nonstick cooking spray

1 Preheat oven to 375°F. Place tomatillos on a small rimmed baking sheet. Roast in oven, turning once midway through, until they are softened and slightly charred, about 25 minutes. Remove from oven; let cool slightly. Transfer to the bowl of a food processor fitted with the metal blade; add cilantro, 1 garlic clove, and lime juice. Process until smooth and combined.

2 Lightly coat the bottom of a large nonstick saucepan with cooking spray. Add onion, remaining garlic clove, and chopped jalapeño; cook, stirring occasionally, over medium heat until onion is softened, about 7 minutes. Add cumin, tomatoes, corn, and chicken stock. Bring liquid to a boil; reduce heat, and simmer until vegetables are tender, 12 to 15 minutes.

3 Remove from heat; stir in 3 tablespoons reserved tomatillo pesto, and season with pepper. Add sliced avocado. Ladle into serving bowls; garnish with jalapeño slices, if desired. Serve with remaining tomatillo pesto.

PER SERVING: 230 CALORIES, 6 G FAT, 3 MG CHOLESTEROL, 41 G CARBOHYDRATE, 717 MG SODIUM, 9 G PROTEIN, 7 G FIBER

from Fit to Eat: Cooking with Herbs

mini corn cakes with goat cheese and pepper jelly

MAKES 3½ DOZEN

An old-fashioned cast-iron skillet with shallow round indentations is ideal for making uniform corn cakes. Since these pans can be rather hard to find, you can use a regular cast-iron skillet and achieve equally lovely, if less uniform, results. Pepper jelly adds subtle heat and a bit of sweetness. Look for it at farmer's markets and in gourmet shops.

1½ cups all-purpose flour

¼ cup sugar

½ cup yellow cornmeal

1 tablespoon baking powder

½ teaspoon salt

1¼ cups milk

2 large eggs, room temperature

⅓ cup vegetable oil, plus more for pan

3 tablespoons unsalted butter, melted

1 15¼-ounce can corn kernels, drained

8 ounce log fresh goat cheese, thinly sliced

1 cup pepper jelly

1 Whisk together flour, sugar, cornmeal, baking powder, and salt in a medium bowl. In a separate bowl, whisk together milk, eggs, oil, and butter until smooth and combined. Add milk mixture to flour mixture, and stir just until batter is combined; fold in corn kernels.

2 Heat a cast-iron skillet over medium heat, and rub with enough oil to coat surface. Working in batches, drop batter by the tablespoon into the skillet to make 2-inch cakes. Cook until undersides are golden brown, 45 to 60 seconds; turn over, and continue cooking until the other sides are browned and the cakes are heated through, about 1 minute. Transfer to a baking sheet. To serve, top each cake with a slice of goat cheese and some pepper jelly.

from A Mother's Day Album

vol-au-vents

MAKES 4

These pastries make a stunning first course when filled with a seafood stew, soft scrambled eggs, or creamed mushrooms. For best results, use a vol-au-vent cutter, although round cookie cutters can also be used.

All-purpose flour, for work surface
1 **pound Puff Pastry dough (page 118)**
1 **large egg yolk**
1 **tablespoon heavy cream**

1 Lightly flour a clean work surface. Using a rolling pin, gently roll out dough until it is about ¼ inch thick. Using a 4-inch vol-au-vent cutter, cut out four vol-au-vents. Cut out centers from half the vol-au-vents with a 2½-inch round cookie cutter to form rings.

2 In a small bowl, whisk together egg yolk and cream. Using a pastry brush, moisten top of each vol-au-vent with egg wash, being careful not to let any drip down over the cut edges. (Or moisten each ring and round with egg wash; lay one ring on top of each round, lining up outside edges.) Place vol-au-vents on an ungreased baking sheet. Cover with plastic wrap; place in refrigerator 1 hour.

3 Preheat oven to 425°F. Transfer baking sheet to the oven, and bake until vol-au-vents are puffed and golden on the outside, about 12 minutes. Reduce heat to 350°F; continue baking 10 to 12 minutes to let insides cook through.

4 Transfer vol-au-vents to a wire rack. While still warm, cut out center of tops with a paring knife; set aside. Remove and discard inside dough, and let shells cool completely. Spoon or pipe in desired filling. Replace tops, and serve.

from Puff Pastry

rice salad with lemon, dill, and red onion

SERVES 4

¾ **teaspoon coarse salt, plus more for cooking water**
1 **cup white long-grain rice**
½ **small red onion, finely chopped (about ⅓ cup)**
3 **tablespoons red-wine vinegar**
3 **tablespoons freshly squeezed lemon juice (1 lemon)**
2 **tablespoons plus 1½ teaspoons extra-virgin olive oil**
1½ **teaspoons finely chopped garlic**
¼ **teaspoon freshly ground pepper**
3 **tablespoons roughly chopped fresh dill**
Grated zest of 1 lemon

1 Bring a medium saucepan three-quarters full of water to a boil; add salt. Stir in rice, and return water to a boil. Reduce heat to a simmer; cook uncovered until rice is tender, about 14 minutes. Drain rice in a sieve, and transfer to a medium bowl.

2 Meanwhile, mix together red onion and vinegar in a small bowl. Let sit 5 minutes; strain onion in a sieve, discarding vinegar. Place lemon juice, oil, garlic, ¾ teaspoon salt, and the pepper in another small bowl, and whisk to combine.

3 Drizzle lemon juice mixture over hot rice. Add reserved onion, dill, and lemon zest; toss to combine. Serve.

from What to Have for Dinner

arugula risotto

SERVES 12

Since this recipe makes a large quantity of risotto, be sure to use a wide shallow saucepan or skillet to let the rice cook evenly.

3 to 3½ quarts (12 to 14 cups) homemade or low-sodium canned chicken stock (6 14½-ounce cans)

¼ cup extra-virgin olive oil

8 shallots, minced

3 cups Arborio or Carnaroli rice

1½ cups dry white wine

½ cup (1 stick) unsalted butter

1½ cups freshly grated Parmigiano-Reggiano cheese, plus more for serving

¼ cup plus 2 tablespoons Arugula Purée (recipe follows)
Coarse salt and freshly ground pepper
Arugula flowers, for garnish (optional)

1 Bring chicken stock to a simmer in a large stockpot over medium heat; cover, and keep at a steady simmer until ready to use. At the same time, heat oil in a large heavy-bottom saucepan over medium heat. Add shallots; cook, stirring occasionally, until shallots are softened and translucent, about 10 minutes. Add rice, and cook, stirring constantly, until rice is thoroughly coated and makes a clicking noise, 3 to 4 minutes. Add wine; cook, stirring constantly, until wine is completely absorbed.

2 Using a ladle, add about 1½ cups hot stock to the rice; cook, stirring constantly with a wooden spoon, until most of liquid has been absorbed and mixture is just thick enough to leave a clear trail behind the spoon. Add another ¾ cup hot stock to rice; cook, stirring constantly, until most of liquid is absorbed.

3 Continue adding stock ¾ cup at a time, stirring constantly after each addition, until the rice is mostly translucent but still opaque in the center, a total of 20 to 25 minutes. As rice nears doneness, watch carefully, and gradually reduce the amount of added liquid to make sure the mixture does not overcook; it will continue to thicken after it is removed from heat. The final mixture should be thick enough to suspend the rice in liquid the consistency of heavy cream.

4 Remove from heat. Stir in butter, cheese, and arugula purée; season with salt and pepper. To serve, mound risotto in the center of shallow serving bowls, and sprinkle with additional cheese. Garnish with arugula flowers, if desired.

from A Mother's Day Album

arugula purée

MAKES ½ CUP

This verdant purée is also delicious tossed with pasta or drizzled over boiled potatoes like a pesto. It can be stored in an airtight container for up to five days in the refrigerator.

2½ teaspoons plus ¼ teaspoon coarse salt

1 bunch arugula (about 3½ ounces), stems removed

⅓ cup extra-virgin olive oil

⅛ teaspoon freshly ground pepper

1 Prepare an ice bath; set aside. Bring a medium saucepan of water to a boil, and add 2½ teaspoons salt and arugula. As soon as the water returns to a boil, remove from heat. Using a slotted spoon, transfer arugula to the ice bath to stop cooking. Working in batches, transfer arugula to paper towels; let drain, squeezing out as much excess water as possible.

2 Transfer arugula to the jar of a blender. Add oil, remaining ¼ teaspoon salt, and pepper; purée until mixture is smooth and resembles a thick pesto with a small amount of unincorporated oil on the surface. Before using, stir gently to combine.

braised lamb shanks with tomato and fennel

SERVES 4

Serve with Polenta (page 127).

4 lamb shanks (about 1½ pounds each), trimmed
Coarse salt and freshly ground pepper

½ cup all-purpose flour

4 tablespoons extra-virgin olive oil

2 tablespoons unsalted butter

2 onions, sliced ¼ inch thick

1 large leek, white and light-green parts only, sliced into ¼-inch half moons and washed well

4 garlic cloves, thinly sliced

1 cup dry red wine

2 cups homemade or low-sodium canned chicken stock

1 28-ounce can peeled whole plum tomatoes, drained

2 tablespoons tomato paste

1 tablespoon fresh thyme leaves

2 dried bay leaves

2 fennel bulbs, sliced ¼ inch thick

1 Preheat oven to 375°F. Season lamb all over with salt and pepper. Place flour in a shallow bowl. Dredge lamb in flour, turning to coat evenly; shake off excess. Heat oil and butter

in an 8-quart Dutch oven or skillet over medium heat. Working in two batches, cook until shanks are well browned, about 5 minutes per side. Transfer shanks to a large plate; drain off all but 2 tablespoons fat from the skillet.

2 Return skillet to medium heat; add onions and leek, and sauté until they are lightly browned, about 6 minutes. Add garlic; cook 4 minutes more. Add red wine; deglaze pan by scraping up any browned bits from the bottom with a wooden spoon. Return shanks to skillet, and add chicken stock, tomatoes, tomato paste, thyme, and bay leaves. Bring to a boil; cover, and place in oven. Braise 2 hours; add fennel, and cook 30 minutes more.

3 Using a slotted spatula, transfer shanks and vegetables to a large bowl. Cover; set aside. Using a ladle, skim fat from surface of cooking liquid; cook over medium heat until liquid is thickened, 5 to 7 minutes. Return shanks and vegetables to pan; cook until heated through. Remove from heat, and season with salt and pepper.

from Leg of Lamb Primer

butterflied leg of lamb with lemon and garlic marinade

SERVES 6

You may want to secure the lamb with metal or wooden skewers that are at least twelve inches long. If you use wooden ones, be sure to soak them thoroughly in water to prevent them from scorching on the grill.

1 **leg of lamb (about 6 pounds), trimmed of excess fat and butterflied**
2 **lemons, plus more cut into wedges for garnish**
½ **cup extra-virgin olive oil**
¼ **cup roughly chopped fresh oregano, plus more for garnish**
2 **garlic cloves, finely chopped**
   Coarse salt and freshly ground pepper
   Grilled red onion slices, for garnish

1 Place lamb on a clean work surface, and cover with plastic wrap. Using a mallet, pound lamb to 1 inch thick. Transfer to a large shallow bowl, and set aside.

2 Zest and juice both lemons, and combine in a small bowl. Add oil, oregano, and garlic; whisk to combine. Pour lemon mixture over lamb, and rub with your hands to coat evenly and thoroughly. Cover bowl with plastic wrap, and place in the refrigerator; let marinate at least 6 hours or overnight, turning occasionally. Remove from refrigerator 1 hour before serving, and let come to room temperature.

3 Heat grill or grill pan. Remove lamb from marinade, and place on a large baking sheet; season all over with salt and pepper. Using four long skewers, secure lamb on each side, with two skewers at the short ends and the other two running lengthwise, each 2 to 3 inches from the edge of the lamb. Transfer to grill or grill pan, and cook over medium-high heat until lamb is browned on the outside and still slightly pink on the inside, 7 to 9 minutes on each side for medium rare. Transfer to a platter, and let rest 10 minutes.

4 When ready to serve, remove skewers, and thinly slice lamb against the grain. Garnish with lemon wedges, oregano, and slices of grilled red onion.

from Leg of Lamb Primer

grilled trout with oregano

SERVES 4 | **PHOTO ON PAGE 163**

Pungent oregano balances the richness of the trout; the acidity of the lemons binds everything together. We like the briny flavor that sea salt gives to this easy-to-prepare dish, but coarse salt works equally well.

4 **whole trout (about 12 ounces each), cleaned and scaled**
1 **teaspoon sea salt**
   Freshly ground pepper
1 **lemon, sliced into 8 rounds, plus 1 lemon cut into wedges for garnish**
1 **large bunch fresh oregano**
4 **teaspoons extra-virgin olive oil**
   Nonstick cooking spray

1 Lightly coat grill or broiler pan with cooking spray; heat grill or broiler. Sprinkle exterior and cavity of each fish with ¼ teaspoon salt, and season with pepper. Place two lemon rounds and a few oregano sprigs in cavity of each fish.

2 Spray fish with cooking spray; place on grill or under broiler. Cook until golden and firm, about 4 minutes on each side. Transfer to a serving platter; drizzle each fish with 1 teaspoon oil. Garnish with lemon wedges and remaining oregano.

PER SERVING: 278 CALORIES, 14 G FAT, 100 MG CHOLESTEROL, 1 G CARBOHYDRATE, 626 MG SODIUM, 36 G PROTEIN, 0 G FIBER

from Fit to Eat: Cooking with Herbs

herb-stuffed chicken breasts

SERVES 4 | PHOTO ON PAGE 169

- 1 tablespoon extra-virgin olive oil
- 4 leeks, white and light-green parts only, washed well and sliced into ¼-inch rounds
- 1 tablespoon finely chopped fresh rosemary
- 1 tablespoon plus 1 teaspoon fresh thyme leaves
- 1 teaspoon coarse salt
- 1 teaspoon freshly ground pepper
- 2 whole boneless and skinless chicken breasts (about 1⅓ pounds), halved
- 2 slices whole-wheat bread
- 4 teaspoons Dijon mustard
- 1 cup homemade or low-sodium canned chicken stock, skimmed of fat

1 Preheat oven to 350°F. In a large ovenproof skillet, heat 1 teaspoon oil over medium heat. Add leeks, and cook 4 minutes. Add 2 teaspoons each rosemary and thyme; cook 1 minute more. Season with ¼ teaspoon salt and ½ teaspoon pepper. Transfer to a medium bowl; let cool.

2 Using a sharp knife, carve a pocket in the center of each chicken breast by inserting the tip into the thickest part and cutting an opening (leaving about 1 inch uncut on each side), being careful not to cut all the way through the breast. Place 2 tablespoons leek mixture in each pocket. Heat 1 teaspoon oil in the skillet over medium-high heat. Add chicken breasts, and sauté until golden, about 3 minutes on each side. Remove from heat, and transfer to a clean work surface.

3 Place bread in the bowl of a food processor fitted with the metal blade; process until fine crumbs form. Transfer to a small bowl. Add remaining teaspoon rosemary, 1 teaspoon thyme, ¾ teaspoon salt, and ½ teaspoon pepper. Spread 1 teaspoon mustard over one side of each chicken breast; cover with 3 tablespoons herbed breadcrumbs, pressing gently to adhere. Drizzle remaining teaspoon oil over all.

4 Return chicken to the skillet, and transfer to the oven; roast chicken until it is golden and cooked through, about 15 minutes. Remove from oven; transfer chicken to a serving dish, and cover loosely with foil while you make the sauce. Place skillet over medium heat, and add chicken stock; deglaze pan, stirring to loosen any browned bits from bottom with a wooden spoon. Continue cooking until stock is reduced by half, about 3 minutes. Remove from heat; add remaining teaspoon thyme. Serve sauce with the chicken.

PER SERVING: 296 CALORIES, 7 G FAT, 86 MG CHOLESTEROL, 20 G CARBOHYDRATE, 807 MG SODIUM, 37 G PROTEIN, 2 G FIBER

from Fit to Eat: Cooking with Herbs

mint and pistachio stuffed leg of lamb

SERVES 6 TO 8 | PHOTO ON PAGE 165

Serve with Flageolets (page 126) and sautéed Swiss chard.

- 2 cups loosely packed fresh mint leaves
- 2 cups loosely packed fresh flat-leaf parsley leaves
- 1 cup unsalted roasted pistachio nuts
- 2 garlic cloves
- 1 tablespoon plus 1½ teaspoons freshly squeezed lemon juice
- ½ cup plus 1 tablespoon extra-virgin olive oil
- Coarse salt and freshly ground pepper
- 1 leg of lamb (6 to 7 pounds), trimmed of excess fat and butterflied (about 2 inches thick)
- 1 cup homemade or low-sodium canned chicken stock

1 Preheat oven to 350°F. Place mint, parsley, pistachios, garlic, and lemon juice in the bowl of a food processor fitted with the metal blade. Pulse to combine. With machine running, add ½ cup olive oil through the feed tube; process until smooth and combined. Season with salt and pepper.

2 Lay lamb flat on a clean work surface. Spread mint mixture evenly over lamb, leaving a 1-inch border all around. Starting at the narrow end, roll lamb into a tight log; tie well with kitchen twine.

3 Heat remaining tablespoon olive oil in a cast-iron or ovenproof skillet over medium heat. Place lamb in skillet, and cook until browned on all sides, 7 to 10 minutes. Place skillet in oven; roast until a meat thermometer registers 140°F when inserted near center of meat, avoiding stuffing, about 1 hour 10 minutes. Transfer lamb to a platter or cutting board, and let rest 15 minutes.

4 Meanwhile, make sauce: Pour off fat from skillet, and place over medium-high heat. Add stock, and deglaze pan by scraping up any browned bits from the bottom with a wooden spoon. Simmer until liquid is slightly thickened, about 5 minutes. Remove from heat, and serve with stuffed lamb.

from Leg of Lamb Primer

roasted whole leg of lamb with fresh herb rub

SERVES 8

- 1 leg of lamb (6 to 7 pounds), trimmed
  Coarse salt and freshly ground pepper
- 2 garlic cloves, thinly sliced
- 2 tablespoons plus 2 teaspoons Dijon mustard
- 2 tablespoons chopped fresh thyme, plus 1 bunch for pan and garnish
- 1 tablespoon chopped fresh rosemary, plus 1 bunch for pan and garnish
- 2 tablespoons extra-virgin olive oil
- 2 onions, quartered
- 4 carrots
- 4 stalks celery
- 6 new potatoes, halved if large
- 2 tablespoons all-purpose flour
- 2 tablespoons unsalted butter, softened
- ½ cup dry red wine
- 1 cup homemade or low-sodium canned beef stock
  Mint Jelly (optional; recipe follows)

1 Preheat oven to 500°F. Season lamb all over with salt and pepper. Make 1-inch slits all over; place a sliver of garlic in each. Rub 2 tablespoons mustard over lamb; coat evenly with thyme and rosemary, patting gently.

2 Rub oil over bottom of roasting pan; cover with herb sprigs. Place lamb on top. Roast 20 minutes; reduce heat to 375°F. Add onions, carrots, celery, and potatoes; season with salt and pepper. Roast until a meat thermometer inserted near center, avoiding bone, reads 140°F, about 70 minutes. Transfer lamb and vegetables to a platter; let rest 20 minutes.

3 Meanwhile, make sauce: Knead flour and butter together. Pour off fat from roasting pan; place pan over medium heat. Add wine; reduce by half. Add remaining 2 teaspoons mustard and stock; stir, and reduce slightly. Strain into a small saucepan; simmer. Add butter mixture in small pieces, whisking constantly. Remove from heat; season with salt and pepper. Garnish platter with herbs, and serve the sauce on the side, along with mint jelly, if desired.

from Leg of Lamb Primer

mint jelly

MAKES ABOUT 2 CUPS

- 2 cups firmly packed fresh mint
- 2 cups water
- 3 tablespoons freshly squeezed lemon juice (1 lemon)
- 3½ cups sugar
- 3 ounces liquid pectin
- 2 drops green food coloring

1 Blend mint and the water in the jar of a blender until mint is finely chopped. Transfer to a small saucepan; bring to a boil. Remove from heat; let steep 45 minutes. Strain mixture through a fine sieve into a small bowl; reserve liquid (you should have 1¾ to 2 cups). Discard mint.

2 Return liquid to saucepan; add lemon juice and sugar. Bring to a boil, stirring until sugar is dissolved; cook 1 minute. Add pectin, and return to a boil; cook 1 minute. Remove from heat; stir in food coloring. Skim surface. Transfer to a large airtight container; let cool completely. Cover; let chill overnight in refrigerator. Store in refrigerator up to 5 days.

seared salmon with creamy leek sauce

SERVES 4

- 3 tablespoons unsalted butter
- 3 medium leeks, white and light-green parts only, sliced into ½-inch rounds and washed well (about 1½ cups)
- ⅓ cup dry white wine
- ⅓ cup heavy cream
- 3 tablespoons finely chopped fresh chives
  Coarse salt and freshly ground pepper
- ¼ cup low-sodium canned chicken broth or water
- 1 tablespoon olive oil
- 4 salmon fillets (about 6 ounces each)
  Arugula, washed well and dried, for garnish
  Lemon wedges, for garnish

1 Melt butter in a medium skillet set over medium-low heat. Add leeks; sauté, stirring occasionally, 5 minutes. Add wine, and simmer until leeks are very tender, about 4 minutes. Add cream and 2 tablespoons chives; return to a simmer. Season with salt and pepper. Reserve half; transfer remaining mixture to the jar of a blender. Add chicken broth, and purée until leek sauce is smooth.

2 Meanwhile, heat oil in a large sauté pan over medium heat. Season fillets with salt and pepper; place skin side down in

pan. Cook until skin side is well browned, about 5 minutes. Turn over, and sauté just until fish is cooked through, 3 to 6 minutes more; it should still be slightly pink in the center. Transfer to a platter.

3 Serve the salmon with the leek sauce. Garnish with reserved leek mixture, remaining tablespoon chives, arugula, and lemon wedges.

from What to Have for Dinner

seared shrimp with lemon and garlic

SERVES 12 *make sure Shrimp is dry*

This dish is delicious served piping hot or at room temperature.

4 **lemons**
4 **pounds large shrimp, peeled, deveined, and rinsed**
3 **garlic cloves, minced**
½ **cup extra-virgin olive oil**
1½ **teaspoons coarse salt**
¼ **teaspoon freshly ground pepper**

1 Finely grate zest of three lemons. Juice all four lemons; strain juice, and set aside. Place shrimp in a large bowl; add lemon zest, garlic, and ¼ cup olive oil; toss well to coat evenly. Add salt and pepper.

2 Heat a large sauté pan over medium heat. Add 1 tablespoon oil, and heat until hot but not smoking. Working in batches, arrange a single layer of shrimp in pan, being careful not to overcrowd pan. Cook until underside is golden brown, 45 to 60 seconds. Turn over, and continue cooking until other side is golden brown and shrimp is cooked through, about 1 minute. Transfer to a large serving platter. Deglaze pan with 1 to 2 tablespoons reserved lemon juice, stirring up any browned bits from the bottom with a wooden spoon, and pour over shrimp. Cover loosely with foil while repeating process with remaining batches, adding 1 tablespoon oil each time.

from A Mother's Day Album

flageolets

MAKES 2 CUPS

The flageolet, a pale-green kidney bean, is prevalent in French cooking. Its delicate flavor is well suited to simple preparations and is particularly good with lamb. We served flageolets with Mint and Pistachio Stuffed Leg of Lamb (page 124).

1½ **cups dried flageolet beans, sorted and rinsed well**
8 **cups water, plus more for soaking**
1 **sprig rosemary**
1 **dried bay leaf**
¼ **cup extra-virgin olive oil**
Coarse salt and freshly ground pepper

1 Place beans in a large stockpot. Cover with cold water by 2 inches; let soak overnight in the refrigerator.

2 Transfer beans to a colander to drain. Return beans to stockpot; cover with the water. Add rosemary and bay leaf. Bring to a boil; reduce heat, and simmer, covered, until beans are tender, about 1 hour 10 minutes. Transfer to a serving bowl; discard herbs. Gently toss with the oil, and season with salt and pepper. Serve.

from Leg of Lamb Primer

mango and tomato salsa

MAKES 1 QUART

This salsa should be prepared at least a few hours in advance. It can be stored in an airtight container in the refrigerator for up to three days. Serve at room temperature with Seared Shrimp with Lemon and Garlic (recipe above).

½ **red onion, cut into ¼-inch pieces**
2 **ripe mangoes, peeled, pitted, and cut into ¼-inch pieces**
2 **ripe tomatoes, cut into ½-inch pieces**
1 **jalapeño pepper, seeds and ribs removed, minced**
2 **tablespoons plus 1½ teaspoons freshly squeezed lemon juice**
2 **tablespoons freshly squeezed lime juice**
½ **teaspoon coarse salt**
¼ **teaspoon freshly ground pepper**
½ **cup loosely packed fresh cilantro leaves, coarsely chopped**

Combine onion, mangoes, tomatoes, jalapeño, lemon juice, lime juice, salt, and pepper in a small bowl. Toss well to coat evenly, and let stand, covered, at least 2 to 3 hours at room temperature. Stir in cilantro just before serving.

from A Mother's Day Album

polenta

MAKES 2¼ CUPS

We served the polenta with Braised Lamb Shanks with Tomato and Fennel (page 122), but it is equally delicious with chicken, veal, or pork, or as part of a vegetarian meal with a green salad.

4 cups cold water

1 teaspoon coarse salt

1 cup polenta

2 tablespoons unsalted butter

Bring the water to a boil in a medium saucepan; add the salt. Stirring constantly, slowly add polenta, letting the grains pass through your fingers in a steady stream. Reduce heat; simmer, stirring constantly, until polenta is tender but not mushy, 30 to 35 minutes. Remove from heat, and stir in butter. Serve hot.

from Leg of Lamb Primer

simple steamed thick asparagus

SERVES 12

Don't be tempted to undercook the asparagus; the stalks should be tender and bend slightly when held in the center.

2 bundles thick asparagus (about 2 pounds)

2 tablespoons extra-virgin olive oil

Coarse salt and freshly ground pepper

1 Trim and peel the tough ends of the asparagus stalks. Fill a large sauté pan with ½ inch cold water, and bring to a boil over high heat.

2 Place asparagus in sauté pan, working in batches if necessary, and cover tightly with a lid or foil. Let steam until asparagus is tender and slightly limp, 3 to 4 minutes. Transfer to a serving platter; drizzle with olive oil, and season with salt and pepper. Serve hot or at room temperature.

from A Mother's Day Album

sugar snap peas with toasted almonds

SERVES 4

½ cup whole almonds (about 2½ ounces)

3 tablespoons unsalted butter

1 pound fresh sugar snap peas, ends trimmed

3 tablespoons freshly squeezed lemon juice (1 lemon)

½ teaspoon coarse salt

¼ teaspoon freshly ground pepper

1 Preheat oven to 400°F. Spread almonds in a single layer on a rimmed baking sheet; toast in oven until golden and fragrant, 8 to 10 minutes. Remove from oven; let cool completely. Transfer half the almonds to a cutting board, and chop coarsely. Place remaining half in the bowl of a food processor fitted with the metal blade; process until almonds are finely chopped, 15 to 20 seconds. Add coarsely chopped almonds, and stir to combine.

2 Melt butter in a large skillet over medium heat. Add peas, lemon juice, salt, and pepper; stir until all ingredients are well combined and heated through, about 2 minutes. Sprinkle with almonds, and toss to coat. Transfer to a serving bowl, and serve.

from What to Have for Dinner

toasted couscous tabbouleh

SERVES 4 | PHOTO ON PAGE 166

Toasting couscous in the pan before adding water imparts a nuttiness that complements the flavors of mint and parsley.

1 red onion, cut into ¼-inch pieces

2 cups water, plus more for soaking

8 ounces Israeli couscous

1½ teaspoons coarse salt

¼ cup roughly chopped fresh flat-leaf parsley

¼ cup roughly chopped fresh mint

2 teaspoons extra-virgin olive oil

2 teaspoons freshly squeezed lemon juice

Lemon wedges, for garnish

Nonstick cooking spray

1 Place onion in a small bowl, and cover with water. Let soak 30 minutes; transfer to paper towels, and drain.

2 Lightly coat a medium saucepan with cooking spray, and place over medium heat. Add couscous; cook, stirring constantly, 1 minute. Add the water, and bring to a boil. Add 1 teaspoon salt; cook until all water has been absorbed and

couscous is al dente, about 8 minutes. Remove from heat; let cool completely.

3 In a large bowl, combine couscous, reserved onion, parsley, mint, oil, and lemon juice; toss to combine. Add remaining ½ teaspoon salt. Serve, garnished with lemon wedges.

PER SERVING: 253 CALORIES, 3 G FAT, 0 MG CHOLESTEROL, 48 G CARBOHYDRATE, 718 MG SODIUM, 8 G PROTEIN, 4 G FIBER

from Fit to Eat: Cooking with Herbs

DESSERTS

breton butter cake

MAKES 1 NINE-INCH CAKE | **PHOTO ON PAGE 170**

1 cup (2 sticks) unsalted butter, room temperature, plus more for pan
1 cup sugar
1 tablespoon pure vanilla extract
6 large egg yolks
2¾ cups all-purpose flour
¼ teaspoon salt
1 large whole egg, lightly beaten
   Strawberry Compote (recipe follows)

1 Preheat oven to 350°F. Cream butter and sugar in the bowl of an electric mixer fitted with the paddle attachment until light and fluffy. Beat in vanilla and yolks one at a time, beating well after each addition. Add flour and salt; beat just until combined. Do not overmix.

2 Transfer batter to a buttered 9-inch tart pan with a removable bottom; using a small offset spatula, spread batter and smooth top. (If necessary, chill batter 10 minutes before smoothing.) Place pan in refrigerator 15 minutes.

3 Remove pan from refrigerator. Brush top with beaten egg, and mark a crisscross pattern with a fork. Brush again with egg. Bake until cake is deep golden brown and edges pull away from sides of pan, about 50 minutes.

4 Transfer to a wire rack to cool slightly. Remove cake from pan, and slice while still warm. Serve with strawberry compote.

from Dessert of the Month

strawberry compote

MAKES ABOUT 3 CUPS

1½ pounds strawberries, hulled and each cut lengthwise into six segments
2 tablespoons Grand Marnier
1 tablespoon finely grated orange zest
1½ cups freshly squeezed orange juice, strained

1 Combine berries, Grand Marnier, and zest in a small bowl. Toss; let stand 30 minutes.

2 Bring juice to a boil in a small saucepan over medium heat; reduce heat, and simmer until liquid is reduced to ¼ cup, about 20 minutes. Remove from heat; let cool. Pour over strawberries, and toss to combine.

butterflies

MAKES 3 DOZEN

1 cup sugar
1½ pounds Puff Pastry dough (page 118)
1 large egg white, lightly beaten

1 Sprinkle half the sugar on a clean work surface. Place dough on top, and sprinkle with remaining sugar. Using a rolling pin, roll out dough into a 12-by-16-inch rectangle ⅛ inch thick. Using a pastry wheel or sharp knife, trim edges, and cut rectangle into four 4-by-12-inch strips.

2 Using a pastry brush, apply beaten egg white in a lengthwise stripe down the center of three strips, avoiding edges; stack the strips, one on top of the other, and lay the remaining unwashed strip on top. Using a narrow rolling pin or wooden cake dowel, gently press down in the center to seal the layers and mark the dough; fold the stacked dough in half at the indentation. Wrap in plastic; place in refrigerator 1 hour.

3 Remove dough from refrigerator. Using a sharp knife, cut crosswise into ¼-inch slices. Unfold layers of each slice, and twist each once in middle. Arrange butterflies on an ungreased baking sheet with the ends curving down like an inverted V. Cover with plastic wrap; return to refrigerator 1 hour.

4 Preheat oven to 400°F. Remove sheet from refrigerator. Bake until butterflies are crisp and golden brown, about 19 minutes. Remove from oven; using a spatula, immediately transfer butterflies to a wire rack to cool completely before serving.

from Puff Pastry

chocolate turnovers

MAKES 9

These turnovers are a variation on the classic pain au chocolat. For maximum flavor, look for the best-quality chocolate, such as Callebaut, Valrhona, or Scharffen Berger.

All-purpose flour, for work surface
1 pound 6 ounces **Puff Pastry dough (page 118)**
1 **large egg yolk**
1 **tablespoon heavy cream**
2¼ ounces **semisweet chocolate, cut into 9 equal pieces**

1 Preheat oven to 400°F. On a lightly floured work surface, roll out pastry dough into a 12-inch square about ⅛ inch thick with a rolling pin. Brush off excess flour. Using a pastry wheel or sharp knife, trim edges and cut square into nine 3½-inch squares. Place squares on an ungreased baking sheet.

2 In a small bowl, whisk together egg yolk and cream for the egg wash. Using a pastry brush, moisten two adjacent edges of each square with some of the egg wash. Place a piece of chocolate just below center of each square; fold down un-washed edges over chocolate to form a triangle, completely enclosing chocolate. Using your fingers, gently but firmly press pastry edges together to seal. Cover with plastic wrap; place in refrigerator 30 minutes.

3 Remove turnovers from refrigerator, and brush tops liberally with remaining egg wash. Bake until turnovers are puffed and golden brown all over, 25 to 30 minutes. Remove from oven; using a spatula, immediately transfer turnovers to a wire rack to cool completely before serving.

from Puff Pastry

cream horns

MAKES 1 DOZEN

You'll need twelve cream-horn molds to make these horns. For a delicious alternative, add almond extract, raspberry purée, or mini chocolate chips to the whipped cream.

All-purpose flour, for work surface
1 pound **Puff Pastry dough (page 118)**
1 **large egg, lightly beaten**
½ **cup granulated sugar**
½ **cup heavy cream**
2 **tablespoons confectioners' sugar**
½ **teaspoon pure vanilla extract**

1 On a lightly floured work surface, roll out pastry dough into a 12-by-18-inch rectangle. Brush off excess flour. Using a pastry wheel or sharp knife, trim edges and cut dough lengthwise into twelve ¾-inch-wide strips.

2 Lay one of the strips flat on a clean work surface; using a pastry brush, moisten top with beaten egg. Starting at pointed end of a cream-horn mold, wrap strip, with the egg-washed side up, around it in a spiral fashion, with each spiral overlapping slightly. Tuck or press loose end into last spiral; place tucked side down on an ungreased baking sheet. Repeat with remaining strips. Wrap in plastic; place in refrigerator 1 hour.

3 Preheat oven to 425°F. Remove dough from refrigerator; brush again with beaten egg. Spread granulated sugar in a shallow pan; dip one side of each horn in sugar to coat. Return each, sugar side up, to baking sheet.

4 Bake until horns are golden brown and puffed, about 12 minutes; reduce oven heat to 350°F. Remove from oven; using a kitchen towel, carefully remove molds from horns. Return horns to baking sheet, and continue baking until insides are lightly golden brown, 8 to 10 minutes more. Remove from oven; immediately transfer horns to a wire rack to cool completely. Horns can be prepared up to this point and stored in an airtight container at room temperature up to 3 days before filling and serving.

5 When ready to serve, place cream in the bowl of an electric mixer fitted with the whisk attachment. Beat on medium speed until soft peaks form. Sift in confectioners' sugar, and add vanilla; continue beating until stiff peaks form. Transfer whipped cream to a pastry bag; pipe cream into horns. Serve immediately.

from Puff Pastry

fresh-raspberry gelatin and whipped cream

SERVES 4

¾ cup water

¾ cup sugar

½ bunch fresh mint leaves (about ½ cup)

½ cup white grape juice

1 tablespoon freshly squeezed lime juice

1½ teaspoons unflavored gelatin (½ envelope)

1 6-ounce container fresh raspberries, rinsed

½ cup heavy cream

1 tablespoon confectioners' sugar

1 In a medium saucepan over high heat, bring the water, sugar, and mint to a boil. Reduce heat to medium; simmer 2 minutes, swirling pan to dissolve sugar. Strain mixture through a fine sieve into a small bowl; discard mint.

2 Combine grape juice, lime juice, and gelatin in a medium heat-proof bowl set over a pan of simmering water, and stir until gelatin is dissolved. Remove bowl from heat; add mint mixture and berries, stirring with a wooden spoon to break some berries into pieces. Divide mixture among four 6-ounce ramekins. Cover with plastic; refrigerate until firm, at least 4 hours and up to 2 days.

3 Just before serving, place heavy cream in bowl of an electric mixer fitted with whisk attachment; beat on medium speed until soft peaks form, 3 to 4 minutes. Add confectioners' sugar, and continue beating until soft peaks return, 1 to 2 minutes. To serve, spoon a dollop of whipped cream onto each serving.

from What to Have for Dinner

lemon semifreddo cake

MAKES 2 FOUR-BY-EIGHT-INCH CAKES

For perfectly smooth slices, cut the layered cake with a hot serrated knife. Cake can be wrapped well in plastic and stored in the freezer for up to three weeks.

Vanilla Sheet Cake (recipe follows)

9 large egg yolks, room temperature

1 cup plus 1 tablespoon granulated sugar

5 tablespoons confectioners' sugar

½ cup dry white wine

½ cup plus 1 teaspoon freshly squeezed lemon juice

Finely grated zest of 2 lemons

½ cup cold water

5 large egg whites

2 cups heavy cream

3 tablespoons light rum

1 Line bottoms and sides of two 5-by-9-inch loaf pans with parchment paper or plastic wrap with at least 2 inches extending over both long sides; set aside. Using a serrated knife, trim all edges of vanilla sheet cake by 1 inch so it measures 8 by 12 inches. Slice cake widthwise, through the top, into three rectangular pieces, each 4 by 8 inches. Split each piece in half, slicing horizontally through the crumb. You should have six 4-by-8-inch layers. Set aside.

2 Make the semifreddo: In a large heat-proof bowl set over a pan of simmering water, whisk together the egg yolks, ½ cup granulated sugar, and 2 tablespoons confectioners' sugar until smooth.

3 Add wine, ½ cup lemon juice, and lemon zest; cook, stirring constantly with a wooden spoon and scraping across the bottom to prevent mixture from sticking to bowl, until mixture is thick enough to coat the back of the spoon, 6 to 7 minutes. Remove from heat, and let cool to room temperature, or place bowl in an ice bath, stirring occasionally, to expedite chilling.

4 When custard has cooled, combine the water, ½ cup granulated sugar, and remaining teaspoon lemon juice in a small saucepan. Bring mixture to a simmer over medium heat. Cook until slightly thickened and mixture registers 240°F on a candy thermometer, about 8 minutes; wash down sides of pan with a pastry brush dipped in water to prevent crystals from forming. Remove from heat. Let syrup cool 2 to 3 minutes.

5 Meanwhile, in the bowl of an electric mixer fitted with the whisk attachment, beat egg whites and remaining tablespoon granulated sugar on medium-high speed until stiff but not dry peaks form. With mixer still running, slowly drizzle syrup into egg whites; continue beating until meringue has cooled slightly and the bowl is cool to the touch.

6 In another large mixing bowl, whip cream with remaining 3 tablespoons confectioners' sugar until soft peaks form. Fold whipped cream into cooled lemon mixture; fold in egg white mixture until very smooth. Place rum in a small bowl.

7 Fit one of the cake layers in the bottom of each prepared loaf pan. Using a pastry brush, lightly moisten top of cake with rum. Using an offset spatula, evenly spread 1½ cups lemon filling over each. Repeat process, making two more layers of cake, rum, and filling. Wrap cakes in plastic; place in freezer at least 5 hours or overnight.

8 Just before serving, remove pans from freezer. Run a hot knife around edges of cakes. Using overhanging parchment or plastic wrap, lift cakes out of pans. Remove the parchment or plastic, and slice into servings.

from A Mother's Day Album

vanilla sheet cake

MAKES 1 NINE-BY-THIRTEEN-INCH SHEET CAKE

Because there is no butter in the sponge cake, it will remain soft when frozen as part of the Lemon Semifreddo Cake.

1 cup all-purpose flour
Pinch of salt
½ teaspoon baking powder
4 large eggs, separated
1 cup sugar
3 tablespoons boiling water
1 vanilla bean, split and scraped

1 Preheat oven to 350°F. Line a 9-by-13-inch baking pan with parchment paper, and set aside. Sift together flour, salt, and baking powder in a medium bowl; set aside.

2 In the bowl of an electric mixer fitted with the whisk attachment, beat together egg yolks and sugar on medium-low speed until light and fluffy. Beat in the water and vanilla bean scrapings. Add flour mixture in three batches, scraping down sides of bowl with a rubber spatula as needed, just until flour mixture is incorporated after each addition.

3 In another mixing bowl, beat egg whites until stiff but not dry peaks form; whisk one quarter into batter to lighten. Fold in remaining egg whites, and pour batter into prepared pan. Bake until cake springs back when gently pressed in the center, 15 to 20 minutes. Transfer to a wire rack to cool completely.

napoleon

SERVES 6 | **PHOTO ON PAGE 176**

A perfectly layered napoleon is a showstopping dessert; slicing it, however, can be a tricky matter. Don't be discouraged if yours doesn't cut neatly into serving pieces; even if it's slightly flattened and oozing pastry cream, each bite will still be delicious. To pipe the white chocolate, you'll need a piping cone made from parchment paper.

All-purpose flour, for work surface
1¾ **pounds Puff Pastry dough (page 118)**
⅓ **cup heavy cream**
2½ **ounces semisweet chocolate, coarsely chopped (about ⅓ cup)**
½ **teaspoon corn syrup**
¼ **ounce white chocolate, coarsely chopped (about 1 tablespoon)**
Pastry Cream (page 132)

1 Make puff pastry strips: Lightly flour a clean work surface. Using a rolling pin, gently roll out dough into a 16-by-18-inch rectangle about ⅛ inch thick, being careful not to press too hard around the edges. Using a pastry wheel or sharp knife, cut rectangle crosswise into thirds, with each strip 6 by 16 inches. Transfer to a baking sheet; prick the dough all over with a fork. Cover with plastic wrap; place in refrigerator 1 hour.

2 Preheat oven to 425°F. Transfer baking sheet to oven; bake until strips are puffed and golden all over, about 14 minutes. Set a baking sheet directly on pastry strips, and continue baking until pastry is cooked through and well browned, about 6 minutes. Remove top baking sheet; bake 4 minutes more. Transfer to a wire rack to cool completely. Using a serrated knife, trim each to 4¼ by 12 inches.

3 Make the glaze: In a small saucepan, bring heavy cream just to a boil. Place semisweet chocolate in a bowl, and pour hot cream over chocolate; whisk until chocolate is melted and mixture is combined. Whisk in corn syrup. Strain through a fine mesh sieve into a clean bowl.

4 Place white chocolate in a medium heat-proof bowl set over a pan of simmering water. Whisk until chocolate is melted; remove from heat. Let cool.

5 Using an offset spatula, spread semisweet chocolate glaze over one side of the flattest puff pastry strip, making sure to coat entire surface. Place white chocolate in a piping cone; pipe thin lines ¾ inch apart across width of chocolate-coated strip. To create the distinctive flourish, gently drag the tip of a paring knife or a skewer lengthwise through both coatings, in lines perpendicular to the white chocolate lines. Begin at one of the short ends, and make each line ¾ inch apart. Alternate the direction each time.

6 Place one of the unglazed puff pastry strips on a serving tray. Spread half the pastry cream over the top, leaving a ½-inch border all around. Top with remaining unglazed pastry strip; press down gently, and repeat with remaining pastry cream. Top with glazed pastry strip. Transfer to refrigerator, and chill 30 minutes uncovered. Using a long serrated knife, cut into six pieces, and serve.

from Puff Pastry

pastry cream

MAKES ABOUT 4 CUPS

Be sure to make the pastry cream on the same day you plan to use it; otherwise it might become thin and runny.

- ¼ **cup plus 1 tablespoon cornstarch**
- ¼ **cup plus 1 tablespoon all-purpose flour**
- 1 **cup sugar**
- ½ **teaspoon salt**
- 3 **large eggs**
- 4 **cups milk**
- 2 **tablespoons chilled unsalted butter, cut into small pieces**
- 1½ **teaspoons pure vanilla extract**

1 Prepare an ice bath, and set aside. In a medium bowl, combine cornstarch, flour, ½ cup sugar, and salt; stir to mix. In another medium bowl, whisk eggs until smooth. Add flour mixture to egg mixture, and whisk to combine.

2 In a medium saucepan, combine milk and remaining ½ cup sugar. Bring mixture to a boil over medium-high heat, stirring until sugar is dissolved. Remove from heat; whisking constantly, slowly pour into egg mixture.

3 Transfer mixture to a clean saucepan set over medium-high heat. Bring to a boil, whisking constantly, until thickened, about 3 minutes.

4 Transfer mixture to a large heat-proof bowl. Whisk in butter and vanilla; set bowl in ice bath, stirring occasionally, until completely chilled, 10 to 12 minutes. Cover with plastic wrap, pressing it directly on surface of pastry cream to prevent a skin from forming. Place in refrigerator until ready to use.

palmiers

MAKES ABOUT 2½ DOZEN

Once the palmiers are in the oven, watch them closely—they can go from a perfect dark golden brown to burnt in seconds.

- ¾ **cup sugar**
- 14 **ounces Puff Pastry dough (page 118)**

1 Sprinkle half the sugar on a clean work surface. Place dough on top, and sprinkle evenly with remaining sugar.

2 Using a rolling pin, gently roll out dough into a 9½-by-15-inch rectangle ⅛ inch thick, being careful not to press too hard around the edges. Continually coat both sides with sugar.

3 Position dough so that one of the long sides is closest to you. Using your fingers, roll dough lengthwise into a long cylinder, as tightly as possible without stretching it, as you would a roll of wrapping paper, stopping when you reach the middle. Repeat the same rolling procedure with the other long side until you have two tight cylinders that meet in the middle. Wrap tightly in plastic; place in refrigerator at least 1 hour.

4 Unwrap dough; using a sharp knife, cut dough crosswise into ⅜-inch-thick slices. Place palmiers on an ungreased baking sheet, and firmly flatten with the palm of your hand. Cover with plastic wrap; place in refrigerator 1 hour.

5 Preheat oven to 425°F. Place palmiers in oven, and bake 5 minutes. Reduce oven heat to 400°F; continue baking until pastry is golden brown and well caramelized, about 10 minutes. Remove from oven; using a thin spatula, immediately transfer palmiers to a wire rack to cool completely. Serve shiny side up.

from Puff Pastry

pithiviers

MAKES 1 NINE-INCH TART

This classic tart, essentially a frangipane filling enclosed between two layers of puff pastry, is named for the French town in which it was created. We recommend using an insulated baking sheet instead of a regular one to prevent the bottom from getting too browned during baking.

⅔ cup whole blanched almonds

½ cup sugar

3 large egg yolks

3 tablespoons chilled unsalted butter, cut into ½-inch pieces

2 tablespoons light rum

All-purpose flour, for work surface

1 pound Puff Pastry dough (page 118)

1 tablespoon heavy cream

1 Make the frangipane: In the bowl of a food processor fitted with the metal blade, process almonds and sugar until very fine crumbs form. With the machine running, add 2 egg yolks, butter, and rum; continue processing until mixture is smooth and combined.

2 On a lightly floured work surface, roll out pastry dough into a rectangle at least 9¼ by 18½ inches and about ⅛ inch thick. Using a 9-inch round cake pan as a guide, cut out two 9-inch rounds with a pastry wheel or sharp knife.

3 In a small bowl, whisk together remaining egg yolk and cream for the egg wash. Place one pastry round on a baking sheet, and spread almond mixture on top, leaving a 1-inch border all around; brush border with egg wash. Using an aspic or cookie cutter, cut a ½-inch hole in the center of remaining round; place on top of other round, pressing lightly around filling to seal edges together. Place in refrigerator 1 hour.

4 Preheat oven to 425°F. Remove tart from refrigerator; using a small paring knife, score the top by making curved lines from the center to the edge like a pinwheel. Brush top of tart with egg wash, being careful not to let any excess drip down over cut edge of dough, as it will inhibit proper rising. Return to refrigerator to chill again, if needed.

5 Place baking sheet in oven, and bake tart 30 minutes. Reduce heat to 375°F; loosely cover tart with aluminum foil, and continue cooking 30 minutes more.

6 Transfer to a wire rack, and let cool 20 minutes. Remove tart from pan by sliding it onto a serving platter. Serve warm or at room temperature, cut into wedges.

from Puff Pastry

raspberry tart

SERVES 6 TO 8 | PHOTO ON PAGE 171

The tart shell can be made up to one day in advance; avoid filling it until an hour or two before you are ready to serve it in order to keep the shell as crisp and flaky as possible.

All-purpose flour, for work surface

1 pound Puff Pastry dough (page 118)

1 large egg, lightly beaten

1⅓ cups Pastry Cream (page 132)

½ cup heavy cream

2 6-ounce containers fresh raspberries, rinsed and dried

Confectioners' sugar, for dusting

1 Lightly flour a clean work surface. Using a rolling pin, gently roll out dough into a 9-by-18 inch rectangle about ⅛ inch thick, being careful not to press too hard around the edges. Using a pastry wheel or sharp paring knife, trim edges, and cut out four 1-inch strips, two from one of the short ends and one from each of the long sides. Set aside. The resulting rectangle should be about 6 by 15 inches. Transfer dough to a baking sheet.

2 Prick the dough all over with a fork. Using a pastry brush, moisten dough with beaten egg, being careful not to let any drip down over the cut edges as it will inhibit rising.

3 Lay reserved 1-inch strips on top of the edges of the large rectangle, positioning them to line up exactly with the outside edge; this will be the raised border that will encase the filling. Trim strips to fit, overlapping them at the corners; brush egg wash underneath each of the four overlapping corners to seal them together. Brush tops of strips with egg wash, being careful not to let any drip down the sides. Cover with plastic wrap, and place in refrigerator to chill 1 hour.

4 Preheat oven to 400°F. Transfer tart shell to oven, and bake until well browned and puffed all over, about 15 minutes. Remove from oven; using a balled-up clean kitchen towel, press down on the center, leaving the borders puffy. Return to oven; bake 5 minutes more. Transfer to a wire rack to cool. Press down on center again, if needed.

5 When tart shell is completely cooled, place pastry cream in a medium bowl. In a separate mixing bowl, whip heavy cream until soft peaks form; fold into pastry cream. Using a small offset spatula, spread cream mixture over bottom of tart shell. Arrange raspberries neatly in rows on top of cream mixture to cover bottom of tart. Dust with confectioners' sugar; cut into strips, and serve.

from Puff Pastry

sacristains

MAKES 2 DOZEN

These are basically sweet versions of the savory Cheese Straws (page 119).

½ cup sugar

¾ pound Puff Pastry dough (page 118)

1 Sprinkle half the sugar on a clean work surface. Place dough on top; sprinkle remaining sugar over dough. Using a rolling pin, gently roll out dough into an 8-by-12-inch rectangle about ⅛ inch thick. Be careful not to press too hard around the edges. Using a pastry wheel or sharp paring knife, trim edges and cut rectangle along the short side into twenty four ½-inch-thick 8-inch-long strips. Twist strips into spiraled straws, and lay 1 inch apart on two ungreased baking sheets. Cover with plastic wrap; place in refrigerator 1 hour.

2 Preheat oven to 400°F. Transfer sheet to oven, and bake until sugar is well caramelized and straws are cooked all the way through, about 16 minutes. Remove from oven; using a spatula, immediately transfer straws to a wire rack to cool completely before serving.

from Puff Pastry

tarte tatin

MAKES 1 TEN-INCH TART

This tart is best served the day it is made; otherwise, the puff pastry crust loses some of its crispness. To achieve the wonderful caramelized surface that defines this rustic tart, you will need to use a cast-iron skillet.

All-purpose flour, for work surface

1 pound Puff Pastry dough (page 118)

3½ pounds Granny Smith apples (about 7), peeled and cored, each cut into eight wedges

Juice of 1 lemon (about 3 tablespoons)

6 tablespoons unsalted butter

1 cup sugar

1 Lightly flour a clean work surface. Using a rolling pin, gently roll out dough into an 11-inch round about ⅛ inch thick, being careful not to press too hard around the edge. Transfer to a baking sheet; cover with plastic wrap. Place in refrigerator at least 1 hour.

2 In a large bowl, toss apple wedges with lemon juice. Heat a 9-inch cast-iron skillet over medium heat; melt butter in pan, and sprinkle sugar in an even layer on top. Remove from heat; arrange apple wedges around bottom of pan in a circular pattern, starting from the edge and working toward the center. Since this layer of apples will be the top of the tart, once inverted, it should be arranged attractively. Once bottom of pan is covered with apples, lay remaining wedges on top, distributing them evenly throughout pan.

3 Place pan over medium-low heat; cook until apples start to soften and their juices are thickened and bubbling, about 30 minutes. Remove from heat. Let cool about 10 minutes.

4 Preheat oven to 425°F. Place pastry round over apples, and press around the edge of pan to fully enclose. Bake until pastry is puffed and golden brown all over and apples are well caramelized, 35 to 40 minutes. If during this time the pastry is browning too much, cover it loosely with aluminum foil.

5 Transfer pan to a wire rack; let tart cool slightly, about 1 hour. When ready to turn out, place pan over medium heat to loosen caramel and apples from the bottom, about 3 minutes. Remove from heat; run a sharp knife around the edge, and carefully invert tart onto a large serving plate. Allow pan to sit for 1 minute on top of tart after inverting to allow the apples to completely loosen. Gently lift off pan; replace any apples that may have stuck. Cut into wedges, and serve.

from Puff Pastry

- -

DRINKS

- -

peach tea punch

MAKES 2½ QUARTS

Almost any type of fruit nectar can be substituted for peach for equally delectable results. We especially like the exotic flavor of mango or guava.

3 tea bags

6 cups boiling water

4 cups peach nectar

1 bunch mint, trimmed and rinsed well

2 lemons, washed and thinly sliced

Ice cubes, for serving

1 Brew tea bags in the boiling water to make a strong tea. Discard tea bags, and place tea in refrigerator until chilled.

2 Combine tea with peach nectar in a large serving bowl or pitcher. Add mint and lemon slices; let stand about 1 hour in the refrigerator to allow the flavors to infuse. Add ice cubes, and serve immediately.

from A Mother's Day Album

June

DRINKS

137 lingonberry punch

STARTERS

137 blinis with caviar and cucumber-dill dressing

138 garden and snap pea soup with vidalia onions

138 karjalan potato pies with egg butter

139 pea pancakes with sour cream and bacon

139 pickled herring canapes

140 rye sourdough bread

140 warm goat cheese with wasabi-pea crust, peas, and greens

SALADS

141 arugula and cannellini salad with olive vinaigrette

141 cucumber salad

141 garden tomato salad

141 pita-bread salad with cucumber, mint, and feta

MAIN COURSES

142 braised chicken with olives, carrots, and chickpeas

142 finnish fish chowder

143 fish stew

144 hot-smoked salmon steaks with morel sauce

144 linguine with two-olive tapenade

145 pasta with peas, crab, and basil

145 risotto with peas, marjoram, and asiago

146 salt-and-pepper shrimp with aïoli

SIDE DISHES

146 baby red potatoes with cilantro

146 mashed potatoes and peas

147 quick braised artichokes

147 swiss chard with olives

MUFFINS

147 breakfast muffins

148 cinnamon-sugar mini muffins

148 corn muffins

149 health muffins

DESSERTS

149 cherry clafoutis

150 cloudberry cake

150 coffee ice cream affogato

150 espresso granita

151 fruit granita

151 fruit sherbet

152 sorbets, assorted

lingonberry punch

SERVES 20 TO 25

Tiny, tart lingonberries are widely available in Scandinavia and are also grown in small amounts in the United States. Check your local farmer's markets. Since they are part of the cranberry family, you can also make this refreshing drink with frozen cranberries and their juice.

2 cups fresh lingonberries

1 liter good-quality vodka, chilled

2 gallons lingonberry juice, chilled

1 Place lingonberries in a resealable plastic storage bag, and place in the freezer until they are completely frozen and solid, at least 2 hours.

2 Combine vodka and lingonberry juice in a large punch bowl or divide among several large pitchers; add frozen berries. Serve immediately.

from Midsummer Night Dinner in Minnesota

blinis with caviar and cucumber-dill dressing

MAKES 54

A sourdough starter gives the blinis their tangy flavor. They are delicious served with sour cream, smoked salmon, capers, and finely diced red onion.

4 cups milk

10 large eggs

2 teaspoons salt

2 cups Rye Sourdough Starter (recipe follows)

4 cups all-purpose flour

1 cup rye flour

3 tablespoons unsalted butter, room temperature

3½ cups salmon roe

Cucumber-Dill Dressing (recipe follows)

1 In a large bowl, whisk together milk, eggs, and salt. Add sourdough starter and flours, and whisk until mixture is well combined. Cover with a kitchen towel, and let stand 1 hour.

2 Heat a griddle or large cast-iron skillet over medium heat. Brush bottom of pan with ½ teaspoon butter. Working in batches, ladle about ¼ cup batter (enough to make 4-inch blinis) onto griddle, being careful not to overcrowd; cook

until bubbles form on the surface and underside is golden brown, about 1 minute. Turn blinis over, and cook until underside is golden brown, about 1 minute. Transfer to a large oven-proof plate or baking sheet, and place in a warm oven. Repeat with remaining batches, adding ½ teaspoon butter to pan before each. Serve hot, with salmon roe and cucumber-dill dressing on the side.

from Midsummer Night Dinner in Minnesota

rye sourdough starter

MAKES 3¼ CUPS

Once it is fermented, the dough can be stored in the refrigerator indefinitely as long as it is replenished every two weeks by adding equal parts flour and water. You can use two cups starter instead of one package active yeast in most recipes.

1 teaspoon active dry yeast

1 cup warm water

2 cups buttermilk, room temperature

2 tablespoons sugar

1¾ cups rye flour

1 In a large mixing bowl, combine yeast and the water; let stand until yeast is dissolved and bubbles form on the surface, about 5 minutes.

2 Stir in buttermilk, sugar, and 1½ cups flour. Cover with a clean kitchen towel, and let stand in a warm place 24 hours. Whisk in remaining ¼ cup flour until it is well combined. Set aside, covered, at room temperature another 24 hours before using or storing in a jar or airtight container.

cucumber-dill dressing

MAKES 6 CUPS

2 cucumbers, seeded and cut into ¼-inch pieces

2 cups mayonnaise

2 cups sour cream

1 small onion, finely chopped

1 large garlic clove, finely chopped

¼ cup finely chopped fresh dill

1 teaspoon freshly ground pepper

½ cup white vinegar

Combine all ingredients in a large bowl. Cover with plastic wrap, and place in refrigerator until dressing is well chilled.

garden and snap pea soup with vidalia onions

SERVES 8 | **PHOTO ON PAGE 159**

We like this soup best when served hot, but it is also delightfully refreshing well chilled.

2 tablespoons unsalted butter

2 Vidalia or other sweet onions, roughly chopped

Coarse salt and freshly ground pepper

6 cups homemade or low-sodium canned chicken stock, plus more for thinning

1¼ pounds sugar snap peas, ends trimmed and strings removed (about 1¼ cups)

1¾ pounds fresh garden peas, shelled (1¾ cups) or frozen

½ cup heavy cream

1 Prepare an ice bath, and set aside. Melt the butter in a medium saucepan over medium-low heat. Add onions, and season with salt and pepper. Cook, stirring frequently, until onions are soft and translucent, about 8 minutes.

2 Add stock; bring to a boil. Reserve about ¼ cup each snap and garden peas. Add remaining snap peas to saucepan, and return stock to a boil. Add remaining garden peas; cook until all peas are tender, about 4 minutes. Transfer pan to ice bath. Stir until mixture is cool.

3 Working in batches, transfer mixture to the jar of a blender; process until smooth. Return to saucepan, and set over medium heat. Stir in cream, and adjust consistency with more stock, if needed. Season with salt and pepper.

4 Meanwhile, prepare a small ice bath, and bring a small saucepan of water to a boil. Add reserved snap peas and garden peas. Blanch until they are just tender, 2 to 3 minutes. Using a slotted spoon, transfer to ice bath; drain in a colander. Cut snap peas into small pieces.

5 To serve, divide soup among soup bowls, and garnish each serving with blanched mixed peas.

from Peas

karjalan potato pies with egg butter

MAKES 28

These traditional pies can be baked up to one day in advance and stored, covered with plastic wrap, in the refrigerator; reheat them in the oven just before serving.

12 large russet potatoes, peeled and cut into 2-inch pieces

1 large onion, finely chopped

1½ cups (3 sticks) unsalted butter, melted

1½ cups heavy cream

4 teaspoons coarse salt, plus more for seasoning

Freshly ground pepper

5 cups rye flour

3 cups all-purpose flour, plus more for work surface

2½ to 3 cups cold water

Egg Butter (recipe follows)

1 Place potatoes in a large saucepan, and cover with cold water. Bring water to a boil over high heat; reduce to a simmer, and cook until potatoes are tender when pierced with a fork, about 15 minutes. Transfer to a colander, and drain. While still hot, pass the potatoes through a ricer or food mill into a large bowl.

2 Add onion, 1 cup butter, and cream to mashed potatoes, and stir well to combine. Season with salt and pepper. Set aside until mixture is cool.

3 Preheat oven to 400°F. Meanwhile, in another large bowl, combine flours and 4 teaspoons salt. Gradually add the cold water until mixture just comes together to form a dough; it should not be sticky. Turn out onto a lightly floured work surface; knead until dough is smooth and elastic. Roll out dough to ¼ inch thick. Using a 3½-inch biscuit cutter, cut dough into rounds; cover loosely with plastic wrap to keep them from drying out while you work. Reroll and cut dough scraps until you have 28 rounds.

4 Roll out each round into a wafer-thin oval shape, about 7 inches long and 4½ inches wide, using more flour if dough feels sticky. Spoon ½ cup potato mixture onto center of each oval. Keeping most of it mounded in the center, spread some of the filling out toward the edge in every direction, leaving a 1-inch border all around. Fold uncovered border up over filling, leaving the center exposed. The pies should be slightly boat-shaped. Using your fingers, gently press edges of dough to adhere to filling.

5 Arrange pies on parchment-paper–lined baking sheets. Bake until filling is golden brown and puffed and dough has formed a crisp shell, about 30 minutes. Remove from oven, and immediately brush with remaining ½ cup butter. Serve hot with egg butter on the side.

from Midsummer Night Dinner in Minnesota

egg butter

MAKES 2½ CUPS

This simple combination of hard-boiled eggs, butter, and fresh herbs is a common condiment in Finnish cooking. We used parsley; dill or tarragon would taste just as good.

6 large eggs

1 cup (2 sticks) unsalted butter, softened

1 cup loosely packed fresh flat-leaf parsley leaves, coarsely chopped

Coarse salt and freshly ground pepper

1 Place eggs in a medium saucepan, and cover with water. Bring water to a boil over medium-high heat; turn off heat, cover, and let stand 13 minutes. Remove with a slotted spoon, and place in cold water until they are cool. Peel eggs, and cut into small pieces.

2 In a large bowl, combine eggs with butter and parsley. Season with salt and pepper. Use immediately, or cover with plastic wrap, and store in refrigerator up to 3 days. Bring to room temperature before serving.

pea pancakes with sour cream and bacon

MAKES 16

The batter can be prepared up to an hour in advance and kept covered in the refrigerator.

1 cup all-purpose flour

½ teaspoon baking powder

1 tablespoon plus 1 teaspoon coarse salt

1¾ pounds fresh garden peas, shelled (1¾ cups) or frozen

½ cup heavy cream

2 tablespoons unsalted butter, melted

2 large eggs, room temperature

¼ pound bacon, cut into ½-inch pieces

½ cup sour cream

1 Prepare an ice bath; set aside. In a small bowl, whisk together flour and baking powder, and set aside. Bring a medium saucepan of water to a boil. Add 1 tablespoon salt and the peas. Return water to a boil; cook 1 minute. Drain in a colander; transfer peas to the ice bath to stop cooking and preserve their color. Drain, and pat dry with paper towels.

2 Transfer ⅔ cup peas to the jar of a blender. Add cream, butter, and remaining teaspoon salt; blend until mixture is smooth and combined. Add eggs, and process a few seconds more, just until they are fully combined. Fold pea mixture into flour mixture, and fold in remaining whole peas; set aside.

3 Heat a medium sauté pan over medium heat. Add bacon, and cook until fat is rendered and bacon is golden and crisp, about 5 minutes. Using a slotted spatula, transfer bacon to a paper-towel–lined plate; let drain. Pour off all but 2 teaspoons rendered fat from pan into a heat-proof bowl, and set aside.

4 Return pan to medium heat. Working in batches, drop heaping tablespoons of pea batter into pan, being careful not to overcrowd. Cook until underside is golden, about 2 minutes. Turn pancakes over, and cook until other side is golden and pancakes are cooked through, about 2 minutes more. Transfer to a large plate. Repeat with remaining batter, adding reserved fat as needed between batches.

5 Place pancakes on a large serving tray or individual plates. Top each pancake with a dollop of sour cream, and sprinkle with bacon. Serve immediately.

from Peas

pickled herring canapes

SERVES 4

This recipe can be easily multiplied to feed a crowd. If dill flowers are unavailable, you can use freshly snipped dill sprigs.

1 large egg

4 tablespoons unsalted butter, room temperature

4 slices brown bread

4 pickled herring fillets

½ small white onion, diced

Fresh dill flowers, for garnish (optional)

1 Place egg in a small saucepan; cover with cold water, and bring just to a boil. Reduce heat to a gentle simmer, and cook 5 minutes. Remove from heat, and let stand 3 minutes. Pour off hot water, and hold egg under cold running water to stop cooking. Peel and coarsely chop.

2 Spread 1 tablespoon butter on one side of each slice of bread. Slice herring fillets into 1-inch-wide pieces, and arrange on buttered side of bread. Sprinkle egg and onion on top of and around herring pieces. Garnish with dill flowers, if desired. Serve immediately.

from Midsummer Night Dinner in Minnesota

rye sourdough bread

MAKES 1 TEN- TO TWELVE-INCH ROUND LOAF

This bread will stay fresh for several days when stored in a bread box or an airtight container at room temperature. We made it with dry yeast, but if you like, you can substitute the yeast with two cups Rye Sourdough Starter (page 137). Omit the first step, combine buttermilk with starter, and proceed.

1 envelope active dry yeast (¼ ounce)

½ cup warm water

4 cups buttermilk

9 to 10 cups rye flour, plus more for work surface, baking sheet, and hands

4 teaspoons salt

Canola or vegetable oil, for bowl

1 In a large mixing bowl, combine yeast and the warm water; let stand until yeast is dissolved and mixture is frothy, about 5 minutes.

2 Heat buttermilk in a small saucepan over medium heat until it is warm to the touch, and add to yeast mixture. Using a wooden spoon, gradually stir 3 cups flour into yeast mixture until it is combined but mixture is still soupy. Cover with a kitchen towel; let stand in a warm place 8 to 12 hours.

3 Add 1 cup flour to mixture; let stand, covered, 12 hours.

4 Add 5 cups flour and the salt, and stir until mixture just comes together. Turn out onto a well-floured work surface, and knead 5 minutes, adding more flour as necessary; the dough will be very sticky. Place in a lightly oiled bowl, and cover with plastic wrap. Let rise until it is doubled, about 2 hours.

5 Preheat oven to 350°F. Line a baking sheet with parchment paper, and lightly dust parchment with flour. Using floured hands, punch down dough and turn out onto a lightly floured work surface. Form into a large round loaf. Place on prepared baking sheet, and cover with a damp kitchen towel; let rise until dough is doubled and beginning to crack on the surface, 45 to 60 minutes.

6 Bake until loaf is nicely golden and makes a hollow sound when tapped on the bottom, about 60 minutes. Transfer to a wire rack to cool before serving.

from Midsummer Night Dinner in Minnesota

warm goat cheese with wasabi-pea crust, peas, and greens

SERVES 6 | **PHOTO ON PAGE 163**

Wasabi peas are a popular cocktail snack. In this recipe, they are ground and used to encrust goat cheese buttons, providing an innovative alternative to breadcrumbs. For best results, slice goat cheese with a piece of thread.

2 cups wasabi peas

1 12-ounce log firm fresh goat cheese

¾ cup extra-virgin olive oil

½ tablespoon wasabi paste

3 tablespoons rice vinegar

1 tablespoon mayonnaise

Pinch of sugar

Coarse salt

5 ounces sugar snap peas, ends trimmed and string removed (about 1½ cups)

5 ounces snow peas, trimmed (about 1½ cups)

6 ounces pea shoots

1 Place 1½ cups wasabi peas in the bowl of a food processor fitted with the metal blade. Process until a coarse powder forms; transfer to a large plate.

2 Slice the goat cheese log into six 1-inch-thick disks. Pour ½ cup olive oil on a small plate. Place the disks, one at a time, in the oil, turning to completely coat. Dredge in ground wasabi powder, turning to coat all sides, and shake off excess. Transfer to a baking sheet; cover with plastic wrap. Refrigerate at least 1 hour.

3 Preheat oven to 425°F. Prepare an ice bath, and set aside. In a small bowl, whisk together wasabi paste and vinegar. Whisk in mayonnaise, sugar, and remaining ¼ cup oil until mixture is smooth. Season with salt; set aside.

4 Bring a medium saucepan of water to a boil, and generously add salt. Add sugar snap and snow peas; blanch until they are tender and bright green, about 2 minutes. Drain in a colander; transfer peas to the ice bath to stop cooking and preserve their color. Drain; pat dry with paper towels.

5 Remove coated goat cheese disks from refrigerator. Place in oven; bake until disks are soft and hot in the center, about 7 minutes. Remove from oven.

6 Combine blanched peas, pea shoots, and remaining ½ cup wasabi peas in a large bowl. Season with salt, and drizzle with wasabi-paste dressing. Toss well to lightly coat, and divide among six salad plates. Place one goat cheese disk on each plate, and serve immediately.

from Peas

arugula and cannellini salad with olive vinaigrette

SERVES 4

This colorful salad can also be served family-style in a large bowl; toss the arugula in the vinaigrette along with the beans and tomatoes, and let everyone help themselves. Niçoise olives have an appealing nuttiness that complements peppery arugula.

½ cup pitted oil-cured olives, such as Niçoise (about 36)

¼ cup water

1 garlic clove

½ cup packed fresh basil leaves

2 teaspoons sherry vinegar

½ teaspoon ground cumin

1 15½-ounce can cannellini beans, drained and rinsed

1½ cups pear, grape, or cherry tomatoes, halved

½ red onion, thinly sliced

1 bunch arugula (about 6 ounces), trimmed and washed

1 Make vinaigrette: Combine olives and the water in the bowl of a food processor fitted with the metal blade. Process until olives are finely chopped. Add garlic, basil, vinegar, and cumin; process until mixture is smooth and combined, stopping to scrape down sides of bowl with a rubber spatula as needed.

2 In a medium bowl, combine beans, tomatoes, and red onion, and toss gently. Pour vinaigrette over bean mixture, and toss well to coat. To serve, divide arugula leaves among four plates, and mound bean mixture on top.

PER SERVING: 210 CALORIES, 13 G FAT, 0 MG CHOLESTEROL, 18 G CARBOHYDRATE, 442 MG SODIUM, 5 G PROTEIN, 5 G FIBER

from Fit to Eat: Cooking with Olives

cucumber salad

SERVES 20 TO 25

16 cucumbers, peeled and sliced ¼ inch thick

2 cups white-wine vinegar

1 large bunch fresh dill, roughly chopped

2 tablespoons coarse salt

3 tablespoons sugar

Combine all ingredients in a large bowl; stir until sugar and salt have dissolved and cucumbers are evenly coated. Cover with plastic wrap, and place in refrigerator at least 1 hour and up to 3 days before serving.

from Midsummer Night Dinner in Minnesota

garden tomato salad

SERVES 20 TO 25

To prevent bruising, snip basil with sharp kitchen scissors rather than cutting it with a knife. You may use any combination of tomatoes; cut cherry tomatoes in half.

11 pounds (about 33) ripe tomatoes, cut into 1-inch pieces

2 red onions, halved lengthwise and thinly sliced into half moons

1 cup extra-virgin olive oil

1 tablespoon coarse salt

2 teaspoons freshly ground pepper

1 bunch fresh basil leaves, washed well

Combine tomatoes and onions in a large serving bowl. Drizzle with the olive oil, and sprinkle with the salt and pepper. Cover with plastic wrap; let stand at room temperature at least 1 hour to allow flavors to develop. Snip basil, and toss into salad just before serving.

from Midsummer Night Dinner in Minnesota

pita-bread salad with cucumber, mint, and feta

SERVES 4 | PHOTO ON PAGE 157

2 regular pita breads, cut into 1-inch squares

3 tablespoons white-wine vinegar

¼ cup extra-virgin olive oil

Coarse salt

3 stalks celery, cut into ½-inch pieces

1 cucumber, peeled, seeded, and cut into ½-inch pieces

1 bunch fresh mint leaves, thinly sliced

½ bunch watercress, trimmed

6 ounces feta cheese, crumbled (about 1½ cups)

Freshly ground pepper

1 Preheat oven to 350°F. Spread pita squares in a single layer on a rimmed baking sheet, and bake until they are nicely crisp, about 20 minutes. Remove from oven. In a small bowl, whisk together vinegar and oil; season with salt.

2 In a medium salad bowl, combine toasted pita bread, celery, and cucumber; add vinegar mixture, and toss well to combine. Just before serving, add mint and watercress; gently toss again. Sprinkle feta cheese over the top, and season with pepper.

from What to Have for Dinner

braised chicken with olives, carrots, and chickpeas

SERVES 4

Serve this stewlike chicken dish over couscous or mashed potatoes, or with a crusty baguette to soak up the flavorful broth. We used Cerignola olives from Italy; they are firm enough to hold up to slow-cooking methods like braising.

1 tablespoon olive oil

4 whole chicken legs, skinned and cut into thighs and drumsticks (about 2½ pounds)

1 yellow onion, cut into ½-inch pieces

3 carrots, cut into ½-inch pieces

2 garlic cloves, minced

1 1½-inch piece fresh ginger, finely chopped (about 2 tablespoons)

1 cup low-sodium canned chicken broth, skimmed of fat

1 cup water

1 cup dry white wine

4 sprigs thyme

⅓ cup raisins

½ cup pitted and roughly chopped large green olives, such as Cerignola (about 6)

¾ cup canned chickpeas, drained and rinsed

1 Preheat oven to 350°F. In a large ovenproof skillet or Dutch oven, heat oil over medium heat. Place chicken pieces in skillet, being careful not to overcrowd the pan. Sauté until chicken is nicely crisped and browned on both sides, about 5 minutes per side. Transfer chicken to a large plate, and set aside.

2 Reduce heat to medium-low; to the same skillet, add onion, carrots, garlic, and ginger. Sauté, stirring frequently, until onion is soft and translucent, about 5 minutes. Add chicken broth, the water, and wine; bring to a boil, and deglaze pan by scraping up any browned bits from the bottom with a wooden spoon. Return chicken to skillet, and add thyme. Bring liquid back to a boil; cover, and transfer to the oven. Braise 45 minutes.

3 Remove skillet from oven, and stir in raisins, olives, and chickpeas. Return to oven; continue braising, uncovered, 20 minutes more. Remove from oven, and discard thyme. Serve hot.

PER SERVING: 406 CALORIES, 14 G FAT, 139 MG CHOLESTEROL, 26 G CARBOHYDRATE, 868 MG SODIUM, 36 G PROTEIN, 5 G FIBER

from Fit to Eat: Cooking with Olives

finnish fish chowder

SERVES 20 TO 25

This soup is traditionally prepared in giant iron pots set over an outdoor fire. If you are cooking for ten to twelve people, reduce the amount of each ingredient by half. We used perch, but any firm-fleshed white fish such as cod or red snapper works just as well.

¾ cup (1½ sticks) unsalted butter

3 large onions, cut into ¾-inch pieces

Fish Stock (recipe follows)

2 tablespoons whole black peppercorns

1 tablespoon allspice

10 large carrots, cut into ¾-inch pieces

9 large russet potatoes, peeled and cut into ¾-inch pieces

3 tablespoons coarse salt, plus more for seasoning

4½ pounds skinless perch fillets, cut into bite-size pieces

4 cups heavy cream

2 large bunches dill, thick stems removed, coarsely chopped

3 bunches chives, cut into ½-inch pieces

Freshly ground pepper

1 Melt ¼ cup butter in a 16-quart stockpot over medium heat. Add onions; cook, stirring occasionally, until they are soft and translucent, about 15 minutes.

2 Add fish stock to pot. Place peppercorns and allspice on a small piece of cheesecloth, and tie into a pouch with kitchen twine. Add spice sachet to pot, tying one end of twine to handle of pot for easy removal. Raise heat, and bring stock to a boil. Add carrots and potatoes, and return to a boil. Reduce heat, and simmer until vegetables are tender, about 25 minutes more. Stir in 3 tablespoons salt.

3 Add fish pieces to pot. Simmer until fish is cooked through and opaque, about 3 minutes.

4 Stir in remaining ½ cup butter and heavy cream. Continue cooking until soup is heated through, but do not allow it to boil, as it will separate. Remove spice sachet. Stir in dill and chives, and season with salt and pepper.

from Midsummer Night Dinner in Minnesota

fish stock

MAKES 5 QUARTS

Have your fishmonger remove the gills from the fish heads and cut the bones to fit in a sixteen-quart stockpot; wash both heads and bones well in cold water before using. While it is best used the day it is made, this flavorful stock can be stored in an airtight container in the freezer for up to three months.

2 dried bay leaves

3 to 5 sprigs fresh flat-leaf parsley

3 to 5 sprigs thyme

3 to 5 sprigs tarragon

3 to 5 sprigs dill

1 tablespoon fennel seeds

1 tablespoon whole black peppercorns

4 tablespoons unsalted butter

2 large leeks, white and pale-green parts only, quartered lengthwise and sliced ½ inch thick, washed well

1 large Spanish onion, cut into 1-inch pieces

1 pound white mushrooms, quartered

2 carrots, cut into 1-inch pieces

2 celery stalks, cut into 1-inch pieces

1 fennel bulb, trimmed and cut into 1-inch pieces

7 pounds heads and bones of nonoily fish, such as sole, flounder, or bass

3 cups dry white wine

1 Make a bouquet garni by tying bay leaves, parsley, thyme, tarragon, dill, fennel seeds, and peppercorns in a piece of cheesecloth; set aside.

2 Melt butter in a 16-quart stockpot over medium-high heat. Add leeks, onion, mushrooms, carrots, celery, and fennel; cook until vegetables are tender, 8 to 10 minutes. Raise heat to high; add fish heads and bones, wine, bouquet garni, and enough water to just cover the bones (about 4½ quarts). Bring mixture to a boil; reduce heat to medium-low, and simmer 25 minutes. Skim foam from surface with a large spoon, as needed.

3 Prepare an ice bath. Remove stockpot from heat, and strain stock, in batches if necessary, through a fine sieve into a large heat-proof bowl set in ice bath; let cool slightly before using.

fish stew

SERVES 4

Although we used steamer clams, smaller varieties such as cockles or littleneck can be used for a more refined stew. Spanish empeltre olives are slightly sweet and very succulent. Picholine olives work just as well.

1 tablespoon olive oil

1 yellow onion, sliced ¼ inch thick

⅓ cup pitted small brown olives, such as empeltre (about 40)

2 garlic cloves, minced

1 jalapeño pepper, thinly sliced into rounds

1 tablespoon freshly squeezed lime juice

2 tablespoons roughly chopped fresh oregano

½ teaspoon finely grated orange zest

½ cup dry white wine

1 tomato, cut into ½-inch wedges

1 8-ounce bottle clam juice

1 cup water

1 cup low-sodium canned chicken broth

½ pound skinless red snapper fillet, cut into 2-inch pieces

8 large clams, cleaned and scrubbed (about 14 ounces)

¼ pound (about 8) bay scallops, muscle removed

3 tablespoons roughly chopped fresh flat-leaf parsley, for garnish

1 In a large saucepan, heat the oil over medium-high heat. Add the onion, and sauté, stirring frequently, until it is lightly golden, 2 to 3 minutes.

2 Add olives, garlic, jalapeño, lime juice, oregano, and orange zest; cook 1 minute. Add wine; continue cooking until it is reduced by half, 1½ to 2 minutes.

3 Add tomato, clam juice, the water, and chicken broth; bring to a boil. Reduce heat to medium, and add seafood. Cover, and simmer until snapper and scallops are opaque and clams have opened, about 12 minutes. (Discard any clams that have not opened.) Serve hot, ladled into soup bowls. Garnish with parsley.

PER SERVING: 240 CALORIES, 8 G FAT, 44 MG CHOLESTEROL, 12 G CARBOHYDRATE, 987 MG SODIUM, 24 G PROTEIN, 1 G FIBER

from Fit to Eat: Cooking with Olives

hot-smoked salmon steaks with morel sauce

SERVES 20

Hot-smoking relies on the heat of the smoke to cook the fish. A home charcoal grill can easily be converted into a smoker; the trick is to build a hot fire and add soaked wood chips to extinguish the flames while the chips continue to smolder. It is the smoldering chips that produce the fragrant smoke. Since this recipe is designed to serve twenty people, you may need to work in batches, depending on the size of your grill, rebuilding the fire in between. You could easily halve or quarter the recipe for fewer guests. Other types of wood chips, such as hickory or mesquite, could also be used.

- 4 pounds apple-wood chips
- 4 cups sugar
- 20 salmon steaks (about 6 ounces each)
  Coarse salt
  Morel Sauce (recipe follows)

1 Place wood chips in a large container. Fill with water, and add the sugar; let stand until the chips are soaked through, at least 1 hour.

2 Meanwhile, place salmon steaks on baking sheets, and generously season both sides with salt. Cover with plastic wrap, and place in refrigerator 1 hour.

3 Build a hot fire in a charcoal grill. When coals are hot, drain wood chips, and evenly distribute them over the coals. This should extinguish the flames and produce a fragrant smoke.

4 Place salmon steaks on grill, being careful not to over-crowd. Cover grill, keeping vents slightly open during smoking process. Smoke salmon steaks until they are heated through but still bright pink in the center, 20 to 30 minutes. The cooking time may vary depending on the heat of the smoke and the desired doneness of the salmon. Be careful of the built-up smoke when removing cover from grill.

5 Transfer salmon to a large serving platter, and serve hot with morel sauce.

from Midsummer Night Dinner in Minnesota

morel sauce

MAKES 2 QUARTS

Cremini or chanterelle mushrooms can be substituted for morels, or you may use a combination of the two. Brush all grit from the spongy caps before using. If necessary, soak them briefly in cold water, and drain on paper towels.

- ¾ cup (1½ sticks) unsalted butter
- 2 cups finely chopped yellow onions (2 medium onions)
- 4 garlic cloves, minced
- 4 pounds fresh morels, coarsely chopped
  Coarse salt and freshly ground pepper
- 1½ cups dry white wine
- 1 cup homemade or low-sodium canned chicken stock
- 3 cups heavy cream
- ½ cup fresh dill, coarsely chopped

1 Melt ¼ cup butter in a large skillet over medium heat. Add onions and garlic; sauté until onions are soft and translucent, about 10 minutes. Transfer to a bowl, and set aside.

2 In the same skillet, melt remaining ½ cup butter over medium heat. Add morels, and season with salt and pepper. Sauté until morels are soft and their released juices have reduced so they just cover bottom of pan, about 20 minutes.

3 Return onion mixture to skillet. Add wine, and cook until reduced by half, about 7 minutes. Add chicken stock and cream; cook, stirring occasionally, until liquid is bubbling and starts to thicken, 18 to 20 minutes. Season with salt and pepper. Remove from heat, and stir in dill just before serving.

linguine with two-olive tapenade

SERVES 4 | PHOTO ON PAGE 166

The tapenade can also be served as a dip for crudités or a zesty sauce for grilled fish. For best results, choose olives with distinctive flavors, such as those suggested below.

- ½ pound linguine
- ⅓ cup pitted brine-cured olives, such as Kalamata (about 16)
- ⅓ cup pitted ripe green olives, such as Picholine (about 18)
  Finely grated zest of 1 lemon
- 2 garlic cloves
- 2 tablespoons plus ⅓ cup roughly chopped fresh flat-leaf parsley, plus whole sprigs for garnish
- ½ teaspoon freshly ground black pepper
- ¼ teaspoon crushed red-pepper flakes
- 1 6-ounce can tuna packed in water, drained
- 1½ cups cherry tomatoes, quartered

1 Bring a large pot of water to a boil. Add linguine; cook according to package instructions, stirring occasionally, until al dente. Drain in a colander, reserving ¼ cup cooking water.

2 Make tapenade: In the bowl of a food processor fitted with the metal blade, combine olives, lemon zest, garlic, 2 tablespoons parsley, black pepper, and red-pepper flakes. Process until mixture is finely chopped and combined.

3 Transfer linguine to a large serving bowl, and toss with reserved cooking water. Add tapenade, tuna, tomatoes, and remaining ⅓ cup chopped parsley; toss well to coat. Serve immediately, garnished with parsley sprigs.

PER SERVING: 365 CALORIES, 9 G FAT, 13 MG CHOLESTEROL, 51 G CARBOHYDRATE, 912 MG SODIUM, 19 G PROTEIN, 5 G FIBER

from Fit to Eat: Cooking with Olives

pasta with peas, crab, and basil

SERVES 6 TO 8 | PHOTO ON PAGE 166

Chopping the peas slightly before cooking them keeps them from rolling off the pasta as you eat.

Coarse salt
1 **pound pappardelle**
4 **tablespoons unsalted butter**
2 **shallots, minced**
2 **pounds fresh garden peas, shelled and roughly chopped (2 cups) or frozen**
Freshly ground pepper
1 **pound lump crabmeat, rinsed and picked over**
1 **cup heavy cream**
¼ **cup loosely packed fresh basil leaves, roughly chopped, plus more for garnish**

1 Bring a large saucepan of water to a boil, and generously add salt. Stir in pasta; cook according to package instructions until al dente. Drain in a colander.

2 Meanwhile, melt the butter in a large sauté pan over medium heat. Add the shallots, and cook until translucent and fragrant, about 2 minutes. Add the peas, and season with salt and pepper; cook until peas are tender and bright green, 4 to 5 minutes. Add the crab, and continue cooking, stirring constantly, until heated through, about 1 minute more. Add the pasta, and stir to combine.

3 Stir in cream and basil, and cook until just heated through. Remove from heat; season with salt and pepper. Divide among plates, and garnish with basil. Serve immediately.

from Peas

risotto with peas, marjoram, and asiago

SERVES 4 | PHOTO ON PAGE 162

Perfect risotto is easy to make; the key is to be sure the stock is fully incorporated after each addition and to avoid overcooking the rice. Risotto will continue to thicken slightly when removed from heat. If you prefer, you may use Parmesan instead of Asiago cheese in this recipe.

6 to 8 **cups homemade or low-sodium canned chicken stock**
3 **tablespoons extra-virgin olive oil**
2 **shallots, minced**
1 **cup Arborio or Carnaroli rice**
½ **cup dry white wine**
1½ **pounds fresh garden peas, shelled (1½ cups) or frozen**
3 **tablespoons unsalted butter**
1 **cup freshly grated Asiago cheese (about 4 ounces)**
1 **tablespoon coarsely chopped fresh marjoram leaves, plus several sprigs for garnish**
Coarse salt and freshly ground pepper

1 Bring chicken stock to a boil in a medium saucepan over medium heat; reduce heat, and keep at a low simmer.

2 Meanwhile, heat oil in a large heavy-bottom saucepan over medium heat. Add shallots, and cook, stirring frequently, until softened and translucent, about 4 minutes. Add rice; cook, stirring frequently, until it is thoroughly coated and slightly fragrant, 3 to 4 minutes. Add wine, and cook, stirring constantly, until completely absorbed.

3 Using a ladle, add ¾ cup hot stock to rice mixture; stir constantly with a wooden spoon until mixture is thick enough to leave a clear wake behind the spoon.

4 Continue adding stock ¾ cup at a time, stirring constantly, a total of 18 to 20 minutes; after 12 minutes of cooking, stir in peas. As rice nears doneness, watch carefully to make sure it doesn't overcook, and add smaller amounts of stock (you may not need to use all of the stock). The final mixture should be thick enough to suspend the rice in liquid that is the consistency of heavy cream. The rice should be al dente but no longer crunchy, and the peas tender and bright green.

5 Remove from heat. Stir in butter, cheese, and chopped marjoram, and season with salt and pepper. Serve immediately, garnished with marjoram sprigs.

from Peas

salt-and-pepper shrimp with aïoli

SERVES 4 | PHOTO ON PAGE 168

Serve the shrimp in their shells, and let your guests peel them. Although the shrimp are cooked in salt, most of it is discarded with the shells.

2 garlic cloves

3 large egg yolks

½ teaspoon Dijon mustard

Coarse salt

¼ cup canola oil

Juice of 1 lemon

½ cup extra-virgin olive oil

1½ pounds (24 to 30) large shrimp, in their shells

Freshly ground pepper

1 Make aïoli: Pulse garlic in the bowl of a food processor until finely chopped. Add egg yolks and mustard, and season with salt; process until mixture is blended. With machine running, add half the canola oil, a few drops at a time, until mixture is emulsified. Add 4 teaspoons lemon juice. With machine running, add remaining canola oil and the olive oil. Season with salt and remaining lemon juice. Transfer to a bowl; refrigerate, covered, up to 2 days.

2 Season shrimp with pepper. Place a large cast-iron skillet over medium heat; lightly cover bottom with salt. Arrange half the shrimp in a single layer. Place a pan on top as a weight; cook 2 minutes. Remove top pan, and turn shrimp; cook until they are pink, about 1½ minutes. Transfer to a plate; wipe skillet with a dry paper towel. Repeat with remaining shrimp. Serve with aïoli.

from What to Have for Dinner

....

SIDE DISHES

....

baby red potatoes with cilantro

SERVES 20 TO 25

Because the potatoes are served whole, be sure to select those that are similar in size to ensure that they cook evenly.

10 pounds small red new potatoes

Coarse salt

1 cup extra-virgin olive oil

Freshly ground pepper

2 cups loosely packed fresh cilantro leaves, washed well

1 Place unpeeled potatoes in a large saucepan, and cover with cold water. Bring water to a boil over high heat, and add salt. Reduce heat to a simmer, and cook until potatoes

are tender when pierced with a fork, 15 to 20 minutes. Transfer to a colander, and drain.

2 Place the potatoes in a large serving bowl. Drizzle with the oil, and season with salt and pepper. Toss in cilantro leaves just before serving.

from Midsummer Night Dinner in Minnesota

mashed potatoes and peas

SERVES 6 | PHOTO ON PAGE 163

2 pounds medium russet and/or Yukon gold potatoes

1 tablespoon coarse salt, plus more for seasoning

5 tablespoons unsalted butter

1½ pounds fresh garden peas, shelled (1½ cups) or frozen

1 cup milk

Freshly ground pepper

1 Peel and cut potatoes crosswise into 1½-inch-thick slices. Place slices in a medium saucepan, and cover with cold water. Bring water to a boil over medium heat; add 1 tablespoon salt. Reduce to a low simmer, and cook until potatoes are tender when pierced with a paring knife, about 15 minutes. Transfer to a colander; let drain.

2 Meanwhile, melt 1 tablespoon butter in a small sauté pan over medium-low heat. Add peas, and cook until they are tender and bright green, 4 to 5 minutes. Transfer to the jar of a blender, and add milk; blend until mixture is smooth.

3 While still hot, pass potatoes through a ricer or food mill into a large heat-proof bowl. Stir with a wooden spoon until they are smooth, about 1 minute. Using a whisk, incorporate remaining 4 tablespoons butter. Whisking constantly, add puréed pea mixture, and season with salt and pepper. Serve immediately, or keep warm over a pan of simmering water.

from Peas

quick braised artichokes

SERVES 4

If you like, snip the prickly points of the leaves with scissors before you cook the artichokes. The tender leaves and hearts are delicious dipped in aïoli (page 146).

2 large artichokes

1 lemon, halved

6 sprigs thyme

1 garlic clove, smashed

2 dried bay leaves

½ teaspoon coriander seeds (optional)

2 teaspoons coarse salt

1 tablespoon extra-virgin olive oil

1 Cut each artichoke lengthwise into quarters, through the stem. Using a spoon, remove the fuzzy choke from the heart of each quarter, and immediately squeeze juice from a lemon half over all pieces to prevent them from discoloring.

2 Place all the ingredients, including the remaining lemon half, into a large saucepan; fill with enough cold water to cover artichokes. Cover pan, and bring the water to a simmer over high heat. Reduce heat to medium-low; cook just until artichoke hearts can be pierced with a fork but are not too soft, 10 to 15 minutes. Remove from heat, and let artichokes sit in cooking liquid until ready to serve, up to 10 minutes. Transfer carefully to serving plates with a slotted spoon, allowing excess liquid to drain off.

from What to Have for Dinner

swiss chard with olives

SERVES 4

Don't worry if your skillet seems overcrowded with the chard; it will quickly wilt and lose most of its volume as it cooks. Cooking the stems a bit longer than the leaves will ensure that they become perfectly tender. If you prefer, seed the jalapeño pepper before using.

2 small bunches (about 1¼ pounds) Swiss chard, trimmed and washed

1 teaspoon olive oil

1 small yellow onion, sliced ¼ inch thick

2 garlic cloves, thinly sliced

1 jalapeño pepper, finely chopped

⅓ cup pitted and roughly chopped brine-cured olives, such as Kalamata (about 16)

½ cup water

1 Separate leaves from the stems of the Swiss chard. Roughly chop leaves, and set aside. Cut stems into 1-inch pieces.

2 In a large skillet or Dutch oven, heat oil over medium heat. Add onion, garlic, and jalapeño, and sauté until onion is translucent, about 6 minutes. Add Swiss chard stems, olives, and the water; cover, and cook 3 minutes. Stir in Swiss chard leaves; cover, and continue cooking until stems and leaves are tender, about 4 minutes. Serve immediately.

PER SERVING: 101 CALORIES, 5 G FAT, 0 MG CHOLESTEROL, 13 G CARBOHYDRATE, 568 MG SODIUM, 3 G PROTEIN, 2 G FIBER

from Fit to Eat: Cooking with Olives

MUFFINS

breakfast muffins

MAKES 1 DOZEN | PHOTOS ON PAGES 153-154

You can replace some of the fruit with citrus zest, nuts, or poppy seeds (add about ¾ cup nuts or 2 tablespoons zest or poppy seeds), as long as the total amount does not exceed 1¼ cups. Try peach and pecan, blueberry and lemon zest, peach and raspberry, raspberry and walnut, strawberry and orange zest, or lemon zest and poppy seeds.

10 tablespoons (1¼ sticks) unsalted butter, melted, plus more for pan

1¾ cups all-purpose flour

1 tablespoon baking powder

1¼ teaspoons ground cinnamon

¼ teaspoon salt

½ vanilla bean, split and scraped

⅔ cup sugar

⅔ cup milk, room temperature

1 large egg, room temperature

1¼ cups fruit

Streusel or Muffin Icing (optional; page 148)

1 Preheat oven to 400°F. Butter a standard muffin tin. Combine flour, baking powder, cinnamon, and salt in a large bowl; whisk to combine.

2 In a medium bowl, combine butter, vanilla bean scrapings, sugar, milk, and egg; whisk to combine. Fold butter mixture and fruit into flour mixture; use no more than ten strokes.

3 Spoon ¼ cup batter into each prepared cup. Press 2 tablespoons streusel on top of each, if desired. Bake until tops are golden, 15 to 17 minutes. Remove from oven, and let cool in pan 15 to 20 minutes; transfer to a wire rack. Drizzle tops with icing, if desired. Serve warm or at room temperature.

from Muffins 101

streusel

MAKES ENOUGH FOR 12 STANDARD MUFFINS

- 5 tablespoons unsalted butter, melted
- ⅔ cup all-purpose flour
- ⅔ cup confectioners' sugar
- ¼ teaspoon ground cinnamon
- Pinch of salt

Combine all ingredients in a medium bowl, and mix with your fingers until mixture is moist and crumbly.

muffin icing

MAKES ENOUGH FOR 12 STANDARD MUFFINS

This icing can be used to ice any muffins, but it is especially nice over muffins with lemon zest and poppy seeds.

- 2 tablespoons freshly squeezed lemon juice
- 1 cup confectioners' sugar

Combine ingredients in a small bowl, and stir until mixture is very smooth.

cinnamon-sugar mini muffins

MAKES 2 DOZEN

You'll need a two-tablespoon-capacity mini-muffin tin for this recipe.

- 10 tablespoons (1¼ sticks) unsalted butter, melted, plus more for pan
- 1 cup sugar
- 1 tablespoon plus 1 teaspoon ground cinnamon
- 1½ cups all-purpose flour
- 2 teaspoons baking powder
- ½ teaspoon salt
- ½ cup buttermilk
- 1 large egg

1 Preheat oven to 375°F. Butter a mini-muffin tin, and set aside. In a small bowl, combine ½ cup sugar and 1 table-spoon cinnamon; set aside.

2 In a large bowl, combine flour, baking powder, salt, and remaining teaspoon cinnamon; whisk to combine. In a small bowl, combine 6 tablespoons butter, remaining ½ cup sugar, buttermilk, and egg; whisk to combine. Using a large rubber spatula, fold butter mixture into flour mixture; use no more than ten strokes. The mixture should be lumpy.

3 Spoon 1 tablespoon batter into each prepared cup, and bake until tops are nicely golden, about 8 minutes. Remove from oven; let cool in pan 10 minutes before transferring to a wire rack.

4 Dip tops of muffins in remaining 4 tablespoons melted butter, and dip in reserved cinnamon mixture. Serve warm or at room temperature.

from Muffins 101

corn muffins

MAKES 1 DOZEN | PHOTOS ON PAGES 153-154

You may add up to 1¼ cups of the following to the prepared batter: corn kernels, crumbled bacon, chopped chives, grated cheddar cheese, or diced jalapeño.

- 10 tablespoons (1¼ sticks) unsalted butter, room temperature, plus more for pan
- 1 cup yellow cornmeal
- 1 cup all-purpose flour
- ¾ teaspoon baking powder
- ¾ teaspoon baking soda
- ¾ teaspoon salt
- ¾ cup sugar
- 1 large egg
- ¾ teaspoon pure vanilla extract
- ¾ cup sour cream

1 Preheat oven to 375°F. Butter a standard muffin tin. Whisk together cornmeal, flour, baking powder, baking soda, and salt in a large bowl.

2 In the bowl of an electric mixer fitted with the paddle attachment, cream butter and sugar until mixture is light and fluffy. Add egg; beat until fully incorporated. Add vanilla. Add flour mixture and sour cream in four alternating batches, starting with the flour; beat until mixture is just combined.

3 Spoon ¼ cup batter into each prepared cup. Bake until tops are nicely golden, 15 to 17 minutes. Remove from oven; let cool in pan 15 to 20 minutes before transferring to a wire rack. Serve warm or at room temperature.

from Muffins 101

health muffins

MAKES 1 DOZEN | **PHOTOS ON PAGES 153-154**

If you prefer, you can bake these muffins in a standard muffin tin; spoon a quarter cup of batter into each cup.

- 1 cup whole-wheat flour
- 1 cup wheat bran
- 3 tablespoons flaxseed, ground, plus more for garnish
- 1¼ teaspoons baking powder
- 1¼ teaspoons baking soda
- ¾ teaspoon ground nutmeg
- ½ teaspoon salt
- 5 carrots, finely grated
- 10 ounces (about 15) dried figs, sliced into eighths
- ⅔ cup applesauce
- ⅔ cup honey
- 5 large eggs, lightly beaten
- 1 teaspoon pure vanilla extract
- Nonstick cooking spray (optional)

1 Preheat oven to 375°F. Lightly coat a ⅔-cup muffin tin with cooking spray, or line with paper cups; set aside.

2 Whisk together wheat flour, bran, flaxseed, baking powder, baking soda, nutmeg, and salt in a large bowl. Add carrots, figs, applesauce, honey, eggs, and vanilla. Using a large rubber spatula, stir until mixture is just combined.

3 Spoon ½ cup batter into each prepared cup, and bake until tops are golden, 15 to 17 minutes. Remove from oven; let cool in pan 12 to 15 minutes before transferring to a wire rack. Serve warm or at room temperature.

from Muffins 101

cherry clafoutis

SERVES 6

Made from a dense, crêpelike batter and fresh cherries (or other stone fruits), clafoutis have a delightfully moist, chewy texture that is something like cake, something like custard. As they bake, the batter forms a golden crust and the cherries burst, forming puddles of thick syrup. Topped with whipped cream, they are an ideal finish for a casual outdoor dinner.

- 3 tablespoons sliced almonds
- 3 tablespoons unsalted butter, melted
- ⅔ cup all-purpose flour
- ⅔ cup plus 2 teaspoons sugar
- ¼ teaspoon salt
- 4 large whole eggs
- 3 large egg yolks
- 1¼ cups heavy cream
- 1 vanilla bean, split lengthwise and scraped
- Finely grated zest of 1 lemon
- 1 pound fresh, ripe cherries, stemmed and pitted
- ¼ cup kirsch or brandy (optional)

1 Preheat oven to 350°F. Spread sliced almonds in a single layer on a rimmed baking sheet. Bake until toasted and fragrant, about 5 minutes. Transfer to a wire rack to cool. Use 1 tablespoon melted butter to coat six 4½-by-1¾-inch round baking dishes, and set aside.

2 Place flour, ⅔ cup sugar, salt, and almonds in the bowl of a food processor fitted with the metal blade; pulse until mixture is finely ground. Transfer to a medium bowl. Add eggs, egg yolks, ¾ cup heavy cream, vanilla scrapings, and lemon zest, and whisk to combine. Place in refrigerator 30 minutes.

3 Place cherries in a medium bowl; add kirsch, if using, and let macerate 30 minutes. Divide among prepared dishes. Whisk remaining 2 tablespoons butter into batter; pour batter over cherries, and place dishes on a rimmed baking sheet. Bake 20 minutes. Sprinkle with remaining 2 teaspoons sugar; bake until tops are golden and bubbling, 15 to 20 minutes. Transfer to a wire rack to cool.

4 Whip remaining ½ cup heavy cream until soft peaks form. Serve cherry clafoutis warm or at room temperature, topped with whipped cream.

from Dessert of the Month

cloudberry cake

MAKES 1 NINE-INCH CAKE

Cloudberries are grown primarily in Scandinavia. They are too tart to eat raw but make a wonderful jam. You could also use raspberry jam for a less traditional but equally delicious cake. If you like, pipe the whipped-cream frosting on the cake with a pastry bag fitted with an Ateco #864 star tip.

Unsalted butter, melted, for pan
¾ cup cake flour (not self-rising), plus more for pan
1 teaspoon baking powder
6 large eggs, separated
1 cup granulated sugar
½ teaspoon salt
3 cups heavy cream
4 tablespoons confectioners' sugar
2 teaspoons pure vanilla extract
3 cups cloudberry jam
Fresh edible flowers, pesticide-free, for garnish (optional)
1 pint fresh raspberries, for garnish
1 pint fresh blackberries, for garnish

1 Preheat oven to 350ºF. Line bottoms of two 9-inch round cake pans with parchment paper; brush with butter, and dust with flour. Tap out excess, and set aside.

2 In a medium bowl, combine flour with baking powder. In another medium bowl, whisk together egg yolks and ½ cup granulated sugar until thick and pale. Using a large rubber spatula, gently fold flour mixture into yolk mixture in two batches.

3 Place egg whites in the bowl of an electric mixer fitted with the whisk attachment. Beat on low speed just until frothy. With machine running on high speed, gradually add remaining ½ cup granulated sugar and the salt; continue beating until mixture is combined and stiff peaks form, about 4 minutes. Gently fold egg-white mixture into egg-yolk mixture in three batches until batter is smooth and uniform in color.

4 Divide batter between prepared pans. Bake until cake is nicely golden and springs back when touched in the center, about 20 minutes. Transfer to a wire rack; let cool 20 minutes in pan. Carefully invert cakes onto wire rack, and let cool completely before frosting.

5 Make frosting: Combine cream, confectioners' sugar, and vanilla in the bowl of an electric mixer fitted with the whisk attachment. Beat on medium speed until smooth and thick.

6 Using a serrated knife, split each cake horizontally into two layers. Set aside smoothest top layer. Spread one bottom layer with ½ cup jam and ¾ cup frosting. Repeat with remaining bottom layer and top layer, stacking each on top of the other as they are filled. Place reserved layer on top of stacked

layers; spread top with remaining 1½ cups jam and sides with remaining frosting. Garnish cake with fresh flowers, if desired. Slice into pieces; garnish slices with fresh berries.

from Midsummer Night Dinner in Minnesota

coffee ice cream affogato

SERVES 4

The word *affogato* means "drowned" in Italian; affogato al caffè is the name of a popular dessert in which hot espresso is poured over gelato just before it is eaten. The bitterness of the espresso counteracts the sweet creaminess of the ice cream. Liqueur intensifies the flavor. Although gelato is denser than ice cream and therefore melts more slowly, either one imparts equally delicious results. If you prefer, substitute very strong coffee for the espresso.

1 pint best-quality coffee ice cream or gelato
4 ounces liqueur, such as sambuca, amaretto, or Frangelico (optional)
4 demitasse cups freshly brewed espresso

Just before serving, scoop ice cream into four small bowls or large coffee cups. Divide liqueur, if using, among four small glasses; serve liqueur and espresso alongside each bowl, and let each person pour them over the ice cream.

from What to Have for Dinner

espresso granita

MAKES ABOUT ¾ QUART

¼ cup ground espresso
2 cups very hot water
1 cup Simple Syrup (recipe follows)

1 Place espresso in a medium heat-proof bowl, and pour the hot water over it. Let stand to extract as much flavor as possible without becoming bitter, about 30 minutes. The brew should be very strong; it will be diluted by the simple syrup.

2 Strain through a fine sieve into a deep-sided 9-by-12-inch metal baking pan, and discard espresso grounds. Add simple syrup, and stir until it is well combined. Place in the freezer, uncovered, until mixture is nearly set, at least 4 hours, whisking it every hour. (If necessary, the mixture can be frozen overnight without whisking; remove it from freezer in the morning, and let sit at room temperature about 10 minutes to allow it to soften before scraping.)

3 Remove mixture from freezer, and scrape surface with the tines of a fork until it is the texture of shaved ice. Serve.

from Sorbets, Sherbets, and Granitas

simple syrup

MAKES ABOUT 2 QUARTS

You can make any amount of simple syrup as long as you use equal parts sugar and water. If using additional flavorings, such as sliced ginger root, pounded lemongrass stalks, citrus peel, or fresh basil, mint, or tarragon sprigs, add them to the prepared syrup, and let them steep while the syrup cools. Discard before using or storing.

6 cups sugar

6 cups water

Prepare an ice bath; set aside. In a large saucepan, combine sugar and the water; bring to a boil over medium-high heat. Cook, stirring occasionally, until sugar has completely dissolved, about 10 minutes. Transfer to a large bowl set over the ice bath. Let stand, stirring occasionally, until syrup is well chilled. Use immediately, or transfer to an airtight container, and refrigerate up to two months.

fruit granita

MAKES ABOUT ¾ QUART

Freshly squeezed citrus juice is ideal for making granita; it is easy to extract and it freezes particularly well. We like to add three tablespoons Campari to grapefruit granita; it lends a pleasant bitterness and dash of color. To make apple granita, purée four peeled and cored apples in a food processor with one-half cup water and the juice of one lemon; strain (you should have two cups juice). For watermelon granita, purée about three cups cubed melon in a processor; strain.

2 cups fruit juice, strained

1 cup Simple Syrup (recipe above)

1 Combine ingredients in a deep-sided metal pan, and place in freezer, uncovered, until it is nearly set, at least 4 hours, whisking mixture every hour. (Mixture can be frozen overnight without whisking; remove from freezer in the morning, and let sit at room temperature about 10 minutes to allow it to slightly soften before scraping with a fork.)

2 Remove mixture from freezer, and scrape surface with the tines of a fork until it is the texture of shaved ice. Serve.

from Sorbets, Sherbets, and Granitas

fruit sherbet

MAKES ABOUT 1½ QUARTS | **PHOTO ON PAGE 171**

You can follow this basic recipe for making an enticing array of sherbets. You'll need one and a half cups purée or juice for each recipe. For citrus flavors, the following approximate quantities will produce the required amount of juice, depending on the ripeness and exact size of the fruit: six lemons; four oranges; six to seven limes; or two grapefruit. Remove sherbet from freezer about ten minutes before serving to let it soften a bit.

3 cups blackberries; 5 cups raspberries; 4 cups chopped strawberries; 2½ cups blueberries; or 2½ cups chopped pineapple

½ cup cold water

2 teaspoons unflavored gelatin

1 cup Simple Syrup (recipe above)

2 large egg whites

1 Combine berries or pineapple and ¼ cup water in the bowl of a food processor fitted with the metal blade. Process until fruit is very smooth, and pour into a fine sieve set in a deep bowl or a large glass measuring cup. Using a rubber spatula or a wooden spoon, gently press down on the mixture to extract as much liquid as possible. Don't press too hard, or some of the seeds may be forced through the sieve into the liquid. Discard any seeds or pulp that remain in the sieve. Set aside strained purée.

2 In a small bowl, stir gelatin into remaining ¼ cup cold water; let stand until gelatin dissolves, about 5 minutes. Meanwhile, in a small saucepan, heat simple syrup over medium heat just until it is warm to the touch; remove from heat. Add gelatin mixture, and stir until it has dissolved; let cool. Transfer to a large bowl or plastic storage container, and add reserved fruit purée.

3 In a mixing bowl, beat egg whites until stiff but not dry peaks form, and fold into fruit purée. Cover container, and place in refrigerator until it is well chilled before using, at least 1 hour.

4 Pour mixture into an ice-cream maker, and freeze according to manufacturer's instructions. Transfer sherbet to a large airtight container; freeze at least 2 hours or overnight.

from Sorbets, Sherbets, and Granitas

sorbets, assorted

MAKES ABOUT 1 QUART | **PHOTO ON PAGE 171**

Follow the amounts in the chart below to make the suggested flavor variations. When using only juice or liquid, you can skip step one. Citrus fruit can be squeezed by hand. For the kiwi, pineapple, and green-apple sorbet, you will need to add freshly squeezed lime or lemon juice with the water in step one. All liquids (except coconut milk) should be strained into a deep bowl or plastic container as directed in step two. If desired, add up to three tablespoons of other flavorings such as liqueur before adding the simple syrup.

Fresh fruit

Water

Simple Syrup (page 151)

1 Combine the fruit and the water in the bowl of a food processor fitted with the metal blade. Process until fruit is very smooth, and pour into a fine sieve set in a deep bowl or a large glass measuring cup. Using a rubber spatula, gently press down on the mixture to extract as much liquid as possible. Don't press too hard, or some of the seeds may be forced through the sieve into the liquid. Discard any seeds or pulp that remain in the strainer.

2 Transfer strained purée to a deep bowl or plastic storage container. Add simple syrup, and stir until it is well combined. Cover bowl or container, and place in refrigerator until completely chilled before using, at least 1 hour.

3 Pour mixture into an ice-cream maker; freeze according to manufacturer's instructions. Transfer sorbet to a large airtight container; place in freezer at least 2 hours or overnight.

from Sorbets, Sherbets, and Granitas

---

sorbet chart Because its success depends on the sugar content of the ingredients used, there is no universal formula for making flavored sorbets. You can, however, follow the master recipe to make the specific flavors in the guide below. The first two columns provide the amounts needed to make two cups of the flavor base; the last column gives the amount of simple syrup.

	type of sorbet =	fruit/other +	water →	flavor base +	syrup
berries	BLACKBERRY	4 cups (1⅛ pounds)	¼ cup	2 cups purée	2 cups
	STRAWBERRY	5 cups chopped (1⅓ pounds)	¼ cup + 2 T	2 cups purée	1¼ cups
	RASPBERRY	6 cups (1⅔ pounds)	½ cup + 4 T	2 cups purée	1¾ cups
	BLUEBERRY	5 cups (1⅔ pounds)	¼ cup + 2 T	2 cups purée	1¼ cups
citrus	LEMON	8 lemons	----------	2 cups juice	1½ cups
	ORANGE	5 oranges	----------	2 cups juice	1¼ cups
	LIME	8 limes	----------	2 cups juice	1½ cups
	GRAPEFRUIT	2½ pink or other ripe grapefruit	----------	2 cups juice	1¼ cups
tropical	MANGO	6 cups chopped (3 mangoes)	¼ to ½ cup**	2 cups purée	1¼ cups
	KIWI	4 cups chopped (16 kiwi)	½ cup + 1 T lime juice	2 cups purée	1¼ cups
	PINEAPPLE	3 cups chopped (⅔ pineapple)	¼ cup + 1 T lime juice	2 cups purée	1¼ cups
	WATERMELON	3 cups cubed (⅛ watermelon)	----------	2 cups purée	1 cup
other	COCONUT	2 cups coconut milk*	----------	2 cups liquid	1¼ cups
	GREEN TEA	3 bags or 4 tablespoons loose tea	2 cups (hot)	2 cups tea	1 cup
	ORANGE PEKOE TEA	3 bags or 4 tablespoons loose tea	2 cups (hot)	2 cups tea	1 cup
	CHOCOLATE	1½ cups cocoa powder	2 cups (hot)	2 cups liquid	2 cups
	GREEN APPLE	4 apples, peeled and cored	½ cup + 2½ T lemon juice	2 cups purée	1¼ cups
		*unsweetened; do not strain	**depending on ripeness of fruit		

ASSORTED MUFFINS | PAGE 147

MAKING MUFFINS HOW-TO

1 │ Whisk together dry ingredients in one bowl. Whisk wet ingredients, along witn vanilla scrapings, in another bowl. Make a well in center of dry ingredients; pour in wet ingredients.

2 │ With a large rubber spatula, fold wet mixture into dry one, using as few strokes as possible.

3 │ Fill buttered muffin tins about three-quarters full with batter. This leaves enough room for a crumb topping and makes muffins that are the right size for snacking.

BREAKFAST MUFFINS │ **PAGE 147**

BLUEBERRY BREAKFAST SHAKE | **PAGE 114**

CODDLED EGGS WITH FINES HERBES | **PAGE 117**

PITA-BREAD SALAD WITH CUCUMBER, MINT, AND FETA | PAGE 141

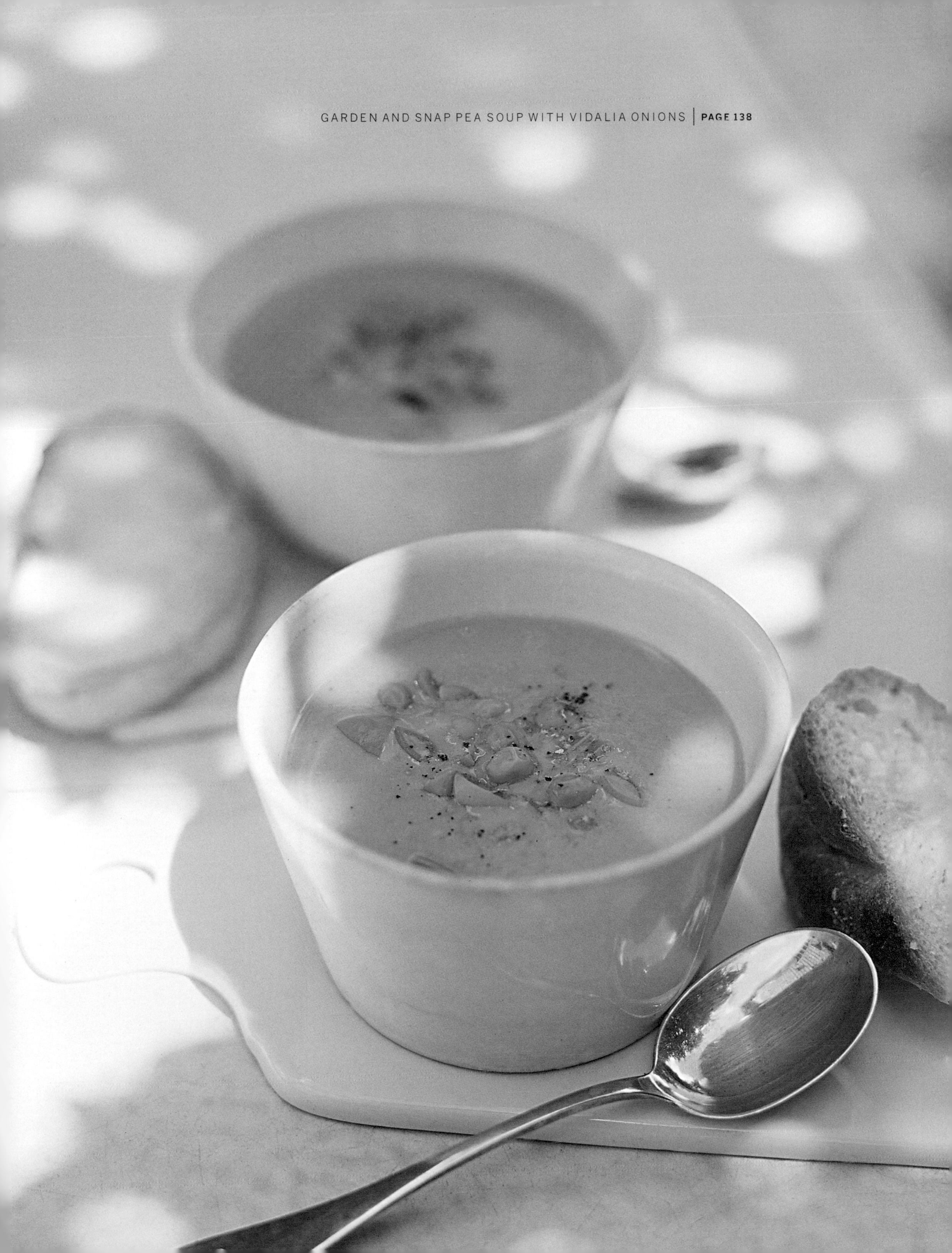

GARDEN AND SNAP PEA SOUP WITH VIDALIA ONIONS | PAGE 138

TEA SANDWICH ASSEMBLY | **PAGE 100**

ASSORTED TEA SANDWICHES | **PAGE 100**

RISOTTO WITH PEAS, MARJORAM, AND ASIAGO | **PAGE 145**

MASHED POTATOES AND PEAS | PAGE 146

WHITE ASPARAGUS WITH
HOLLANDAISE SAUCE | PAGE 107

GRILLED TROUT WITH OREGANO | PAGE 123

WARM GOAT CHEESE WITH WASABI-PFA
CRUST, PEAS, AND GREENS | PAGE 140

BROCCOLI WITH ORECCHIETTE | PAGE 98

MINT AND PISTACHIO STUFFED LEG OF LAMB | **PAGE 124**

LINGUINE WITH TWO-OLIVE TAPENADE | **PAGE 144**

TOASTED COUSCOUS TABBOULEH | **PAGE 127**

PASTA WITH PEAS, CRAB, AND BASIL | **PAGE 145**

MISO SOUP WITH TOFU AND KALE | **PAGE 96**

ROASTED CHICKEN AND JERUSALEM ARTICHOKES | PAGE 100

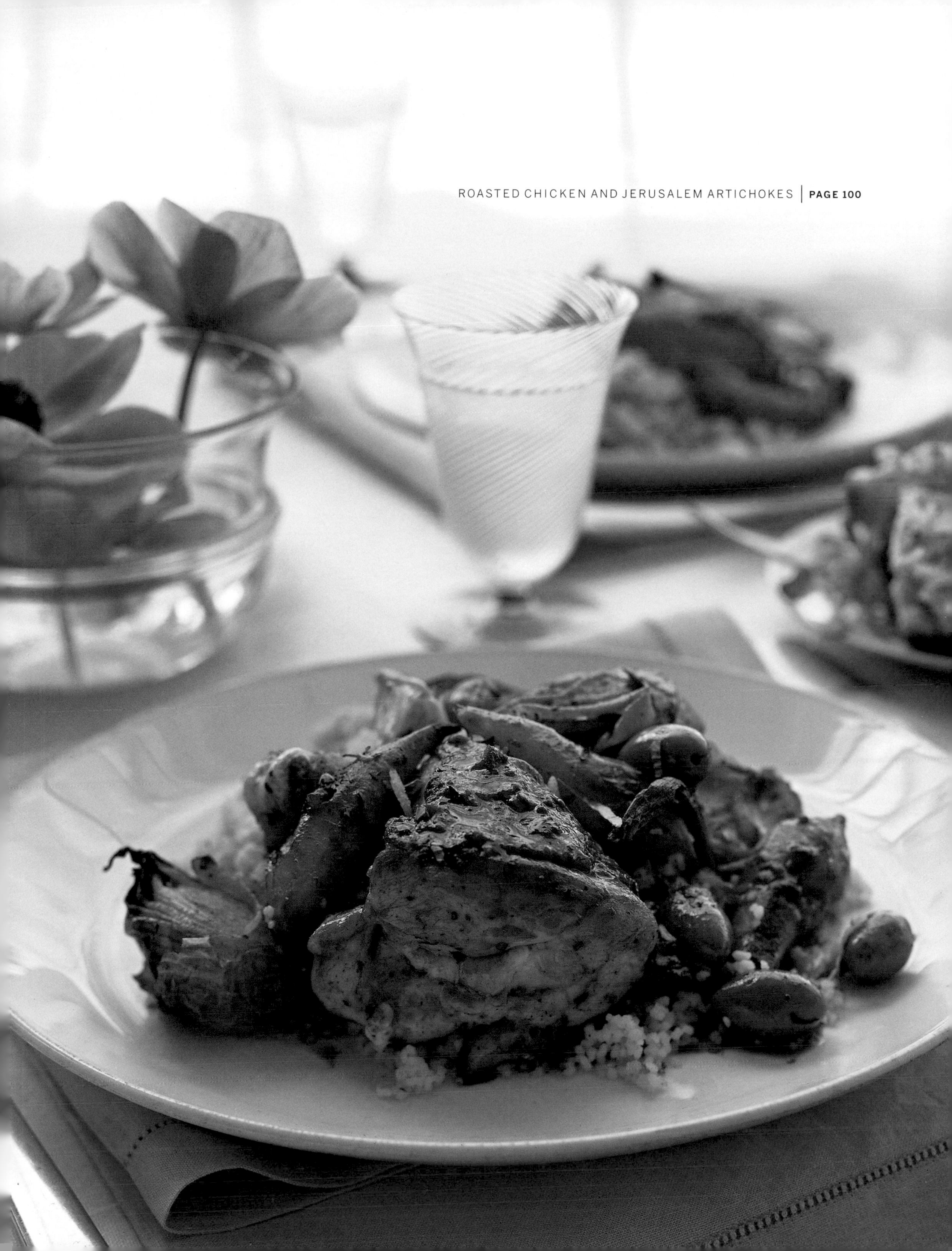

SALT-AND-PEPPER SHRIMP WITH AIOLI | PAGE 146

HERB-STUFFED CHICKEN BREASTS | **PAGE 124**

BRETON BUTTER CAKE WITH STRAWBERRY COMPOTE | **PAGE 128**

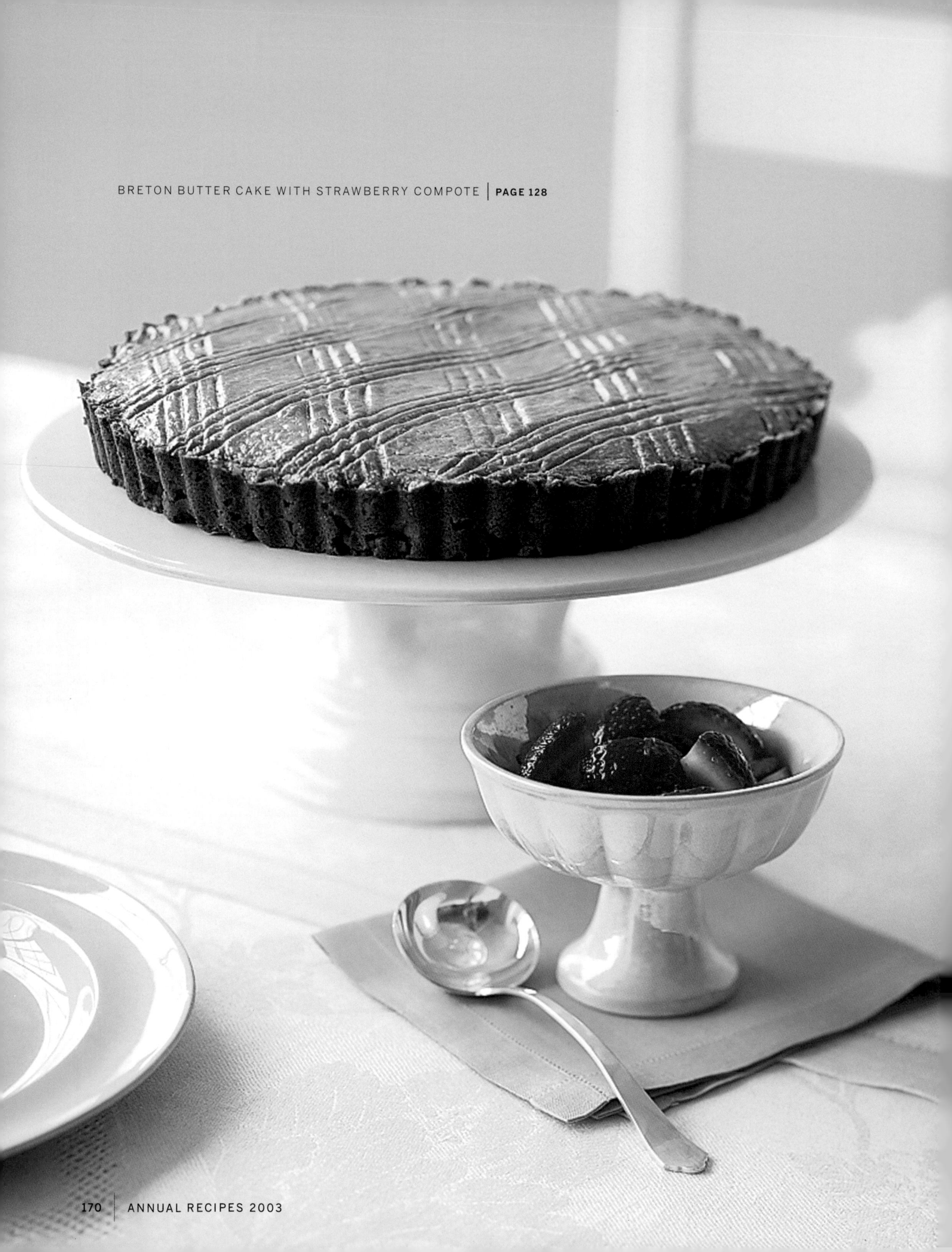

ASSORTED FRUIT SHERBETS | **PAGE 151**

RASPBERRY TART | **PAGE 133**

LAMINGTONS | **PAGE 111**

ASSORTED SORBETS | **PAGE 152**

CHOCOLATE POTS DE CREME | **PAGE 109**

FLAN | PAGE 110

GRAPEFRUIT TART | **PAGE 110**

NAPOLEON | **PAGE 131**

Summer

POTLUCK PARTY SALADS
GRILLED PEACHES WITH CHILLED SABAYON
SPICY COLD TOMATILLO SOUP
CANNING TOMATOES AT HOME

July

STARTERS

181 asian chicken soup

181 chicken liver pâté with toast points

182 cold curried buttermilk soup with corn and poblano chile

182 cucumber-coconut soup

182 cucumber summer rolls

183 le grand aïoli

183 spicy cold tomatillo soup

183 watermelon gazpacho

184 yogurt-basil soup with tomato ice

SALADS

184 chicken and shredded-cabbage salad with noodles and peanut sauce

185 chilled shrimp and chopped-tomato salad with crisp garlic croutons

185 corn and tomato salad

185 cucumber, corn, and crab salad

186 cucumber, cranberry bean, and beet salad in cucumber boats

186 farro salad with zucchini, pine nuts, and lemon zest

187 french potato salad with white wine and celery leaves

187 haricots verts and goat cheese salad with almonds

187 lentils with tarragon, shallots, and beets

188 multicolored pepper-and-bean salad with ricotta salata and herbs

188 orzo salad with roasted carrots and dill

188 shaved cucumber, fennel, and watermelon salad

MAIN COURSES

189 barbecued chicken

189 beer-battered cod in tacos

189 curried lamb chops

190 five-spice pork tenderloin

190 fried catfish sandwich

190 grilled leg of lamb

190 grilled mahimahi in tacos

191 grilled marinated strip steak with scallions

191 striped bass with cucumber broth

SIDE DISHES

191 aunt sara's cheese grits

192 green rice

192 provençal roasted tomatoes

192 roasted fingerling potatoes with seasoned salt

192 saucy black beans

193 sautéed asparagus with aged gouda cheese

193 turnip greens

193 vidalia-onion slaw

DESSERTS

193 caramel cake

194 crisp coconut and chocolate pie

194 cucumber and riesling granita

194 french flag berry tarts

195 grasshopper tarts

196 grilled peaches with chilled sabayon

196 lemon and cherry trifle

197 limeade pie

198 mango panna cotta

198 mary curll's chess pie

(continued on next page)

(continued from previous page)

198 peanut-butter-and-chocolate cups

199 skillet-baked chocolate-chip cookie

199 strawberry chiffon pie

200 tiramisu cups

201 yogurt pie

DRINKS

201 blue margaritas

201 caipirinha

201 fresh whiskey sours

202 margaritas for a crowd

202 mary brockman's favorite pimm's cup

202 passion-fruit cocktails

202 rosé melons

MISCELLANEOUS

202 black-olive relish

203 cornlight bread

203 cucumber relish

203 fried plantain chips

203 perfect hard-boiled eggs

203 pickled cucumber and cherry relish

204 pico de gallo

204 pineapple salsa

204 tropical fruit and crab salsa

204 whole grilled garlic

asian chicken soup

MAKES 1 QUART | **PHOTO ON PAGE 232**

This soup can be prepared through step two up to three days in advance; store the broth separately from all other items. Proceed with step three the day the soup will be served.

6 cups water

½ cup mixed dried mushrooms, such as porcini, shiitake, oyster, or wood ear

1 whole chicken breast (about 10 ounces)

1 carrot, roughly chopped

1 tablespoon roughly chopped jalapeño pepper

1½ tablespoons roughly chopped fresh ginger

3 garlic cloves, crushed

1 teaspoon whole black peppercorns

1 tablespoon sugar

½ cup firm tofu, cut into ¼-inch pieces

Juice of 1 lime (about 3 tablespoons)

1½ tablespoons roughly chopped fresh mint

1½ tablespoons roughly chopped fresh basil

1½ tablespoons roughly chopped fresh cilantro

1 teaspoon soy sauce

1 Bring the water to a boil in a medium saucepan. Remove from heat; add mushrooms. Cover; let sit until softened, at least 30 minutes. Strain mixture through a cheesecloth-lined sieve to remove any grit; discard mushrooms.

2 Return mushroom broth to a clean medium saucepan, and add chicken, carrot, jalapeño, ginger, garlic, and peppercorns. Bring just to a boil; reduce heat, and simmer over medium heat 20 minutes, or until broth is reduced to about 4 cups. Strain through a fine sieve back into saucepan, reserving broth and discarding everything but the chicken.

3 Remove chicken meat from the bones, and shred the meat. Return chicken meat to pan; add sugar, tofu, lime juice, herbs, and soy sauce, and stir until combined and heated through. Transfer soup to a covered container, and refrigerate until well chilled, at least 2 hours or overnight. Serve cold.

PER SERVING: 149 CALORIES, 6 G FAT, 32 MG CHOLESTEROL, 11 G CARBOHYDRATE, 188 MG SODIUM, 14 G PROTEIN, 1 G FIBER

from Fit to Eat: Cold Soups

chicken liver pâté with toast points

MAKES 2 CUPS; SERVES 6 | **PHOTO ON PAGE 231**

½ ounce mixed dried wild mushrooms, such as porcini, shiitake, or wood ear

⅔ cup boiling water

4 tablespoons unsalted butter

1 pound fresh chicken livers, tough membranes removed, rinsed, and patted dry

4 sprigs thyme, leaves roughly chopped

Coarse salt and freshly ground pepper

½ garlic clove, minced

1 tablespoon brandy

1 slice white bread, crusts removed, cut into cubes

1 tablespoon freshly squeezed lemon juice

Toast Points (recipe follows)

1 Place mushrooms in a bowl; pour the boiling water over. Cover; let steep until soft, about 15 minutes. Strain through a sieve, reserving liquid. Finely chop mushrooms.

2 Meanwhile, in a large sauté pan, melt 1 tablespoon butter over medium-high heat. Add half the chicken livers and half the thyme; season with salt and pepper. Sauté until livers are lightly browned on the outside and light pink on the inside, 6 to 7 minutes, adding half the garlic after 5 minutes. Remove from heat; stir in ½ tablespoon brandy. Transfer mixture and all juices to a large bowl. Repeat with remaining livers.

3 Melt 2 tablespoons butter in pan; add bread cubes and reserved mushroom liquid, scraping up browned bits from bottom of pan. Combine with liver mixture. Working in batches if necessary, transfer mixture to bowl of a food processor fitted with metal blade. Process until smooth, about 3 minutes. Add lemon juice; adjust seasoning. Transfer to a 2-cup dish.

4 Melt remaining butter in a small saucepan over low heat. Skim off white foam from surface; discard. Drizzle butter over pâté; refrigerate, covered, until butter is set, at least 1 hour and up to 4 days. Bring to room temperature before serving; scrape off butter, if desired. Serve with toast points.

from A Bastille Day Picnic in New Orleans

toast points

SERVES 6

12 slices good-quality white bread, such as brioche, pain de mie, or Pullman, crusts removed

Preheat oven to 375°F. Cut each bread slice diagonally into quarters. Place on a rimmed baking sheet; toast in oven until bread is golden and beginning to crisp, about 15 minutes, turning once. Transfer to a wire rack; let cool slightly.

cold curried buttermilk soup with corn and poblano chile

MAKES 1 QUART | **PHOTO ON PAGE 232**

- 1 teaspoon vegetable oil
- ½ yellow onion, finely chopped (about 1 cup)
- ½ poblano chile, seeded and finely chopped (about ½ cup)
- 1 large garlic clove, minced
- 1 teaspoon ground coriander
- ½ teaspoon ground cumin
- ⅛ teaspoon ground turmeric
- 2¼ cups corn kernels (about 4 ears)
- 3 cups nonfat buttermilk
- ¾ teaspoon coarse salt

1 Heat oil in a medium saucepan over medium heat. Add onion, poblano, and garlic; sauté until onion is translucent and chile and garlic are tender, about 5 minutes.

2 Add coriander, cumin, and turmeric, and cook until toasted and fragrant, about 2 minutes. Add corn, and sauté until kernels are lightly browned, about 5 minutes. Remove from heat, and let cool slightly.

3 Transfer 1½ cups corn mixture to bowl of a food processor fitted with metal blade, and add buttermilk and salt; purée until smooth. Transfer to a large bowl; stir in remaining corn mixture. Cover with plastic wrap, and chill in refrigerator at least 2 to 3 hours and up to 1 day. Remove from refrigerator; stir soup, ladle into bowls, and serve cold.

PER SERVING: 177 CALORIES, 4 G FAT, 7 MG CHOLESTEROL, 27 G CARBOHYDRATE, 643 MG SODIUM, 9 G PROTEIN, 5 G FIBER

from Fit to Eat: Cold Soups

cucumber-coconut soup

SERVES 6 | **PHOTO ON PAGE 233**

- 2 cups homemade or low-sodium canned chicken stock
- 1 whole skinless and boneless chicken breast
- 2 tablespoons extra-virgin olive oil
- 1 onion, finely chopped
- 1 large garlic clove, minced
- 1 jalapeño pepper, seeded and minced
- 2 pounds cucumbers, peeled, seeded, and cut into ½-inch pieces
- 1 13½-ounce can unsweetened coconut milk
- ½ cup lightly packed fresh cilantro leaves, plus more for garnish
- ¼ cup freshly squeezed lime juice
  Coarse salt and freshly ground pepper

1 Bring chicken stock to a boil in a small saucepan. Add chicken; return to a simmer, and reduce heat. Cook, covered, until chicken is cooked through, about 12 minutes. Transfer chicken to a plate, reserving stock, and let cool.

2 Heat oil in a medium sauté pan over medium heat. Add onion; cook until soft and translucent, about 4 minutes. Add garlic, jalapeño, and cucumbers; cook 1 minute. Add reserved chicken stock; bring to a simmer. Cook until cucumbers are tender, about 5 minutes. Remove from heat; let cool slightly.

3 Working in batches so as not to fill more than halfway, transfer cucumber mixture to a blender or food processor; purée until smooth. Add coconut milk and cilantro to last batch, puréeing until cilantro is very finely chopped. Transfer to a bowl. Cover with plastic; place in refrigerator until completely cool. Stir in lime juice; season with salt and pepper.

4 To serve, shred chicken into bite-size pieces. Ladle soup into bowls; top each with chicken, and garnish with cilantro.

from Cucumbers

cucumber summer rolls

MAKES 30 | **PHOTO ON PAGE 228**

- 2 Japanese, Persian, or kirby cucumbers, sliced lengthwise paper thin
- 1 teaspoon olive oil
- 30 large shrimp, peeled and deveined
- 2 tablespoons mirin (Japanese rice wine)
- 2 tablespoons rice-wine vinegar
- 4 ounces rice vermicelli
- 2 teaspoons coarse salt
- 30 basil leaves (about 1 small bunch), preferably Thai basil
  Peanut Dipping Sauce (recipe follows)

1 Heat oil in a large sauté pan over medium-high heat. Add shrimp, 1 tablespoon mirin, and 1 tablespoon vinegar; cook until shrimp are pink and opaque, and liquid is reduced.

2 Bring a medium saucepan of water to a boil over medium-high heat. Add vermicelli and salt, and cook until noodles are tender, about 3 minutes. Drain in a colander, and rinse with cold water. Transfer to a large bowl, and toss with remaining tablespoon mirin and tablespoon vinegar.

3 Lay a cucumber strip flat on a work surface. Straighten shrimp slightly by pulling the ends. Place a small bundle of noodles on top of a large basil leaf; place at one end of cucumber. Top with a shrimp, and roll cucumber around it tightly. Secure roll with a toothpick. Repeat with remaining ingredients. Serve with cucumber-peanut sauce.

from Cucumbers

peanut dipping sauce

MAKES ABOUT 1 CUP

- 1 kirby cucumber, peeled, seeded, and cut into ½-inch-thick slices
- ½ cup roasted unsalted peanuts, finely chopped
- 2 tablespoons chopped fresh cilantro leaves
- 1 teaspoon minced seeded jalapeño pepper
- 2 tablespoons freshly squeezed lime juice
- 3 tablespoons soy sauce
- 2 tablespoons honey

Place all ingredients in the bowl of a food processor fitted with the metal blade. Pulse until they are finely chopped but not puréed. Serve, or store in an airtight container in refrigerator up to 2 days.

le grand aïoli

SERVES 6; MAKES ABOUT 1 CUP AIOLI

In the Provençal tradition, we served the aïoli with an array of dipping items, such as celery sticks, lettuce hearts, fennel wedges, and pear tomatoes; boiled fingerling potatoes; steamed asparagus, zucchini, and carrots; blanched fava beans and turnips; roasted red and golden beets; Perfect Hard-Boiled Eggs (page 203); and blue-crab claws.

- 2 garlic cloves
- 3 large egg yolks
  Coarse salt
- ½ teaspoon Dijon mustard
- ¼ cup canola oil
- 3 tablespoons freshly squeezed lemon juice (1 lemon)
- ½ cup extra-virgin olive oil
- 2 teaspoons cold water

1 Mince garlic in bowl of a food processor fitted with metal blade. Add egg yolks, a pinch of salt, and mustard; process to combine. With machine running, slowly pour half the canola oil through feed tube, a few drops at a time.

2 Add 1 tablespoon lemon juice. Resume processing; slowly pour in remaining canola oil and the olive oil. Season with salt; add remaining 2 tablespoons lemon juice and the water. Process 10 seconds. Transfer to serving bowls, or store in an airtight container in the refrigerator up to 2 days.

NOTE: Raw eggs should not be used in food prepared for pregnant women, babies, young children, the elderly, or anyone whose health is compromised.

from A Bastille Day Picnic in New Orleans

spicy cold tomatillo soup

MAKES 1 QUART | PHOTO ON PAGE 232

Tomatillos, relatives of the cape gooseberry, have a papery skin that should be removed before eating or cooking.

- 1 pound tomatillos, hulled and washed
- 3 garlic cloves, unpeeled
- 1 serrano chile
- 1 cup peeled, seeded, and roughly chopped cucumber
- ¼ cup roughly chopped onion
- ¼ cup roughly chopped fresh cilantro
- ½ cup homemade or low-sodium canned chicken stock, skimmed of fat
- 1 tablespoon freshly squeezed lime juice
- ½ teaspoon coarse salt
- ½ cup plain nonfat yogurt
- ½ cup water
- 1 small avocado, peeled, pitted, and cut into 1-inch cubes

1 Heat broiler. Place tomatillos, garlic, and serrano chile in a single layer on a rimmed baking sheet; roast 5 minutes each side. Remove from heat; let cool slightly, and peel garlic.

2 In bowl of a food processor fitted with metal blade, place garlic, tomatillos, serrano, and any accumulated juices along with cucumber, onion, cilantro, stock, lime juice, and salt; blend until smooth. Add yogurt and the water; process until just combined. Transfer to a large bowl; cover with plastic wrap. Refrigerate at least 2 hours and up to 1 day. Stir soup to combine, ladle into bowls, and top with avocado; serve.

PER SERVING: 146 CALORIES, 9 G FAT, 1 MG CHOLESTEROL, 15 G CARBOHYDRATE, 372 MG SODIUM, 4 G PROTEIN, 5 G FIBER

from Fit to Eat: Cold Soups

watermelon gazpacho

MAKES 1½ QUARTS | PHOTO ON PAGE 232

- 5 cups peeled, seeded, and roughly chopped watermelon, plus 1 cup finely chopped
- ½ cup cranberry juice
- 1 cup peeled, seeded, and chopped cucumber
- 1 cup chopped celery (about 2 stalks)
- ¾ cup chopped red bell pepper (about 1 pepper)
- ¼ cup chopped red onion
- ¼ cup packed fresh mint leaves, minced
- ¼ cup packed fresh flat-leaf parsley, minced
- 3 tablespoons freshly squeezed lime juice (1 lime)
- 1½ tablespoons sherry vinegar
- 1 tablespoon jalapeño pepper, minced

1 Combine 5 cups watermelon and the cranberry juice in the jar of a blender; purée until mixture is smooth. Pass through a fine sieve into a large bowl or plastic storage container, discarding pulp. You should have 3 cups strained liquid.

2 Add cucumber, celery, bell pepper, onion, herbs, lime juice, vinegar, jalapeño, and remaining cup chopped melon to watermelon liquid; stir to combine. Cover with plastic wrap, and refrigerate until well chilled, at least 1 hour. Serve cold.

PER SERVING: 71 CALORIES, 1 G FAT, 0 MG CHOLESTEROL, 16 G CARBOHYDRATE, 35 MG SODIUM, 2 G PROTEIN, 2 G FIBER

from Fit to Eat: Cold Soups

yogurt-basil soup with tomato ice
MAKES 1 QUART

6 cups packed fresh basil leaves, rinsed

2 medium cucumbers, peeled, seeded, and roughly chopped

2 cups plain nonfat yogurt

1 cup homemade or low-sodium canned chicken stock, skimmed of fat

Tomato Ice (recipe follows)

1 Prepare an ice bath; set aside. Bring a medium saucepan of water to a boil. Add basil; blanch 1 minute. Transfer basil to ice bath. Place on paper towels; gently squeeze out water.

2 Transfer basil to the bowl of a food processor fitted with the metal blade; add cucumbers, yogurt, and stock. Process until mixture is smooth. Pass through a fine sieve into a large bowl, pressing on solids to extract liquid; discard solids.

3 Cover bowl with plastic wrap; refrigerate until soup is well chilled, at least 2 to 3 hours and up to 1 day. Stir soup, ladle into shallow bowls, and top each with a scoop of tomato ice.

PER SERVING: 124 CALORIES, 1 G FAT, 6 MG CHOLESTEROL, 22 G CARBOHYDRATE, 554 MG SODIUM, 9 G PROTEIN, 3 G FIBER

from Fit to Eat: Cold Soups

tomato ice
MAKES ABOUT 1½ CUPS

Tomato ice can be frozen in an airtight container for up to two weeks. Ice will harden when frozen; you will need to let it sit at room temperature before scooping.

1 pound ripe tomatoes, quartered (about 5 plum or 3 medium tomatoes)

Pinch of salt

Pinch of sugar

1 teaspoon freshly ground pepper

½ teaspoon balsamic vinegar

1 In the bowl of a food processor fitted with the metal blade, purée tomatoes with salt and sugar. Press through a fine sieve into a large bowl; discard solids. Stir in pepper and vinegar; transfer to a shallow metal baking pan.

2 Place pan, uncovered, in freezer; stir with a fork every 30 minutes until mixture is frozen, at least 2 to 3 hours.

SALADS   NO

chicken and shredded-cabbage salad with noodles and peanut sauce
SERVES 12

3 quarts water

2 stalks celery, cut in half lengthwise

1 two-inch piece fresh ginger, thinly sliced

2 garlic cloves

8 sprigs cilantro, including stems, roughly chopped (about ¾ cup), plus ½ cup loosely packed leaves for garnish

2 tablespoons toasted sesame oil

Coarse salt

3 boneless and skinless chicken breasts (about 3 pounds)

1 pound somen noodles or vermicelli

½ head green cabbage, halved and core removed

1 bunch carrots (about 6)

2 serrano or jalapeño chiles, seeds and ribs removed

½ cup loosely packed fresh mint leaves, chopped

1 cup Peanut Sauce (recipe follows)

½ cup roasted unsalted peanuts, for garnish

1 In a large saucepan, combine the water with celery, ginger, garlic, chopped cilantro, 1 tablespoon sesame oil, and a pinch of salt; bring to a boil over high heat. Add chicken breasts; reduce heat to medium. Simmer until cooked through, about 12 minutes. Remove from heat; let stand until cool enough to handle, about 10 minutes. Transfer chicken to a cutting board; cut into ¼-inch strips. Set aside.

2 Bring a large pot of water to a boil; add salt. Cook noodles until al dente according to package instructions, about 3 minutes. Transfer to a colander, let drain, and rinse under cold water. Place in a bowl; toss with remaining sesame oil.

3 Slice cabbage and carrots as thinly as possible; place in a bowl. Cut chiles into very thin strips; add to bowl. Add chicken and mint. Before serving, pour peanut sauce over mixture; toss to coat. Place noodles on a serving platter; pile chicken mixture on top. Sprinkle with peanuts and cilantro leaves.

from Potluck Salads

peanut sauce

MAKES 2½ CUPS

1 five-inch piece fresh ginger, minced or grated (about 3 tablespoons)

2 shallots, minced (about ⅓ cup)

¼ cup Asian fish sauce

½ cup low-sodium soy sauce

¾ cup freshly squeezed lime juice

1 cup smooth peanut butter

¼ cup toasted sesame oil

In a bowl, combine ginger, shallots, fish sauce, soy sauce, and lime juice. Whisk in peanut butter, and then sesame oil. Sauce can be refrigerated, covered, up to 4 days.

chilled shrimp and chopped-tomato salad with crisp garlic croutons

SERVES 8 TO 10 | **PHOTO ON PAGE 235**

3 quarts water

2 tablespoons coarse salt, plus more for seasoning

¼ teaspoon whole black peppercorns

1 teaspoon paprika

2 dried bay leaves

2 tablespoons freshly squeezed lemon juice

2 pounds large shrimp, peeled and deveined

5 garlic cloves

2 red bell peppers, seeds and ribs removed

4 ripe tomatoes (about 1¾ pounds) preferably beefsteak

1 medium cucumber, peeled, seeded, and cut into ¼-inch pieces

1 green bell pepper, seeds and ribs removed, cut into ¼-inch pieces

½ small red onion, finely chopped (about ¾ cup)

2 tablespoons roughly chopped fresh marjoram or oregano

2 tablespoons plus 1 teaspoon red-wine vinegar

½ cup extra-virgin olive oil, plus more for drizzling (optional)

6 slices rustic bread, crusts removed, cut into ½-inch cubes (about 2½ cups)

Freshly ground black pepper

1 Prepare an ice bath; set aside. In a 5-quart stockpot, combine the water with 2 tablespoons salt, peppercorns, paprika, bay leaves, and lemon juice; bring to a boil. Reduce heat to medium; simmer 5 minutes. Add shrimp; stir once. Cook until shrimp are pink and opaque, about 1½ minutes. With a large sieve, transfer shrimp to ice bath. Chill thoroughly, at least 2 minutes; drain in sieve. Cut shrimp in half crosswise. Place in a bowl; refrigerate, covered with plastic.

2 In a food processor fitted with the metal blade, finely chop garlic. Remove 2 teaspoons; set aside. Quarter 1 red pepper and 1 tomato; add to remaining garlic in processor. Pulse until a coarse purée forms. Pour into a large mixing bowl.

3 Cut remaining red pepper and 3 tomatoes into ¼-inch pieces; add to bowl along with cucumber, green pepper, red onion, marjoram, vinegar, and ¼ cup oil; stir to combine.

4 Meanwhile, in a large sauté pan, heat 2 tablespoons oil over medium heat; fry half the bread cubes until just beginning to turn crisp and golden brown, about 3 minutes. Add half the reserved chopped garlic and a pinch of salt; cook, stirring frequently, until garlic is fragrant and bread cubes are golden brown, about 1 minute more. Transfer to a large plate, and repeat process with remaining garlic and bread cubes. Before serving, toss shrimp and half the croutons into salad mixture; season with salt and pepper. Drizzle with more olive oil, if desired. Serve remaining croutons on the side.

from Potluck Salads

corn and tomato salad

SERVES 10 TO 12

4 ears corn, kernels sliced from cobs

2 tablespoons sugar

4 tomatoes, sliced into ⅛-inch-thick rounds

Coarse salt and freshly ground pepper

3 tablespoons extra-virgin olive oil

Bring a pot of water to a boil. Add corn and sugar; simmer 1 minute. Drain in a colander, and pat dry with paper towels. Arrange tomatoes and corn on a serving platter; season with salt and pepper. Drizzle with olive oil, and serve.

from Country Barbecue

cucumber, corn, and crab salad

SERVES 6 TO 8

1½ cucumbers, peeled, seeded, and cut into ¼-inch pieces

Coarse salt

1 pound jumbo lump crabmeat, picked over and rinsed

2 ears corn, kernels sliced from cobs

½ small red onion, finely chopped

1 avocado, peeled, pitted, and cut into ¼-inch pieces

½ cup Cucumber Vinaigrette (page 186)

Freshly ground pepper

1 Sprinkle cucumbers lightly with salt; place in a fine sieve set over a bowl. Cover with plastic wrap; place in refrigerator 30 minutes. Rinse and drain well, discarding liquid.

2 Combine cucumber, crabmeat, corn, onion, avocado, and cucumber vinaigrette in a large bowl, and stir to combine. Season with salt and pepper. Refrigerate until ready to serve.

from Cucumbers

cucumber vinaigrette

MAKES ABOUT 1 CUP

½ cucumber, peeled and seeded

2 tablespoons sherry vinegar

2 tablespoons Dijon mustard

1 tablespoon chopped fresh tarragon

Coarse salt and freshly ground pepper

½ cup grapeseed oil

Place cucumber, vinegar, mustard, and tarragon in the bowl of a food processor; process until smooth. Season with salt and pepper. With machine running, drizzle in grapeseed oil; process until emulsified.

cucumber, cranberry bean, and beet salad in cucumber boats

SERVES 6 | PHOTO ON PAGE 238

The bean mixture can be made up to one day in advance; proceed with step four just before serving.

4 garlic cloves

4 sprigs mint, plus 2 tablespoons thinly sliced leaves

½ white onion

3 one-half-inch-thick slices ginger

1 tablespoon whole black peppercorns

3 slices bacon, cut into ½-inch pieces

½ pound fresh cranberry beans, shelled

4 cups homemade or low-sodium canned chicken stock, or water

2 beets, peeled and cut into ½-inch pieces

4 teaspoons coarse salt

5 large kirby cucumbers

¼ cup plain yogurt

1 tablespoon extra-virgin olive oil

1 teaspoon curry powder

1 Place garlic, mint sprigs, onion, ginger, and peppercorns on an 8-inch square of cheesecloth. Gather into a bundle; secure with kitchen twine. Prepare an ice bath; set aside. Heat a large saucepan over medium heat; add bacon. Cook until crisp, stirring frequently, about 8 minutes. Using a slotted spoon, transfer bacon to a paper-towel–lined plate; let drain. Pour off excess fat from pan, and discard.

2 In same saucepan, combine beans, cheesecloth bundle, and stock; bring to a boil. Reduce to a simmer, and cook 5 minutes. Add beets; continue cooking until beans and beets are tender, about 15 minutes. Add 2 teaspoons salt, and remove and discard cheesecloth bundle. Transfer mixture, with the liquid, to a large bowl set over the ice bath to chill.

3 When ready to serve, drain bean mixture in a colander. Peel cucumbers, slice in half lengthwise, and remove seeds using a spoon or melon baller. Cut 2 cucumbers into ¼-inch dice. Reserve remaining cucumber halves.

4 Transfer bean mixture to a large bowl; add yogurt, oil, diced cucumbers, sliced mint, reserved bacon, curry powder, and remaining 2 teaspoons salt. Stir gently to combine. To serve, spoon mixture into reserved cucumber halves.

from Cucumbers

farro salad with zucchini, pine nuts, and lemon zest

SERVES 8 TO 10 | PHOTO ON PAGE 234

¾ pound farro or barley

Coarse salt

1 small shallot, minced

Grated zest and juice of 1½ lemons

3 tablespoons extra-virgin olive oil

½ cup pine nuts

1 pound zucchini, ends trimmed, sliced crosswise as thinly as possible

½ cup loosely packed fresh flat-leaf parsley leaves, roughly chopped

Freshly ground pepper

4 ounces Parmigiano-Reggiano cheese

1 Place farro in a large saucepan; add enough cold water to cover by about 3 inches. Bring to a boil over high heat; add salt, and stir once. Reduce heat to medium, and simmer until farro is al dente according to package instructions, 10 to 12 minutes. Drain, and let cool.

2 In a small bowl, combine shallot with lemon juice; season with salt, and let stand 15 minutes. In a small sauté pan, heat oil over medium heat; add pine nuts. Cook, stirring, until they are lightly toasted, about 5 minutes. Remove from heat; add lemon zest.

3 Place zucchini, farro, pine-nut mixture, and parsley in a large bowl; stir to combine. Stir in shallot mixture; season with salt and pepper. Transfer to a large serving bowl.

4 Using a vegetable peeler, shave half the cheese over salad; toss to combine. Salad can be stored up to 6 hours in the refrigerator, covered with plastic wrap. Just before serving, shave remaining cheese on top.

from Potluck Salads

french potato salad with white wine and celery leaves

SERVES 6

2½ pounds Yukon gold potatoes

 Coarse salt

3 tablespoons roughly chopped shallots

2 tablespoons white wine

2 tablespoons white-wine vinegar

 Freshly ground pepper

3 tablespoons extra-virgin olive oil

⅓ cup loosely packed celery leaves from inner stalks, torn in half

1 Place potatoes in a stockpot, and add enough cold water to cover by 4 inches. Bring to a boil over high heat, and add salt; reduce heat, and cook until potatoes are easily pierced with a fork, about 20 minutes. Drain; let cool slightly. Peel potatoes, and cut each into quarters or eighths.

2 In a serving bowl, combine shallots with wine and vinegar. Add potatoes to bowl; season with salt and pepper. Drizzle in oil; toss to coat. Sprinkle with celery leaves; serve.

from A Bastille Day Picnic in New Orleans

haricots verts and goat cheese salad with almonds

SERVES 6

 Coarse salt

1½ pounds haricots verts, ends trimmed

1½ teaspoons sherry vinegar

1 tablespoon extra-virgin olive oil

 Freshly ground pepper

2½ ounces fresh goat cheese, crumbled

2 ounces whole almonds, toasted (about ½ cup)

1 Bring a pot of water to a boil; add salt and haricots verts. Cook just until crisp-tender and their color brightens, about 4 minutes. Transfer to a serving bowl; let cool, 5 minutes.

2 While still warm, toss beans with vinegar and oil; season with salt and pepper. Add goat cheese, and stir to melt slightly and to coat beans. Sprinkle with almonds, and serve.

from A Bastille Day Picnic in New Orleans

lentils with tarragon, shallots, and beets

SERVES 8 TO 10 | **PHOTO ON PAGE 234**

3½ pounds beets, trimmed

2 tablespoons plus ¼ cup extra-virgin olive oil

3½ teaspoons coarse salt, plus more for seasoning

¼ cup water, plus more for cooking lentils

1 pound French green lentils, picked over

2 garlic cloves

2 dried bay leaves

1 shallot, minced

1 teaspoon Dijon mustard

2 tablespoons plus 1 teaspoon balsamic vinegar

1 tablespoon chopped fresh tarragon

 Freshly ground pepper

1 Preheat oven to 350°F. In a medium bowl, toss beets with 2 tablespoons oil and 1½ teaspoons salt. Arrange on a rimmed baking sheet; pour ¼ cup water into sheet. Cover with foil; roast until beets are easily pierced with the tip of a knife, 45 to 60 minutes. Remove from oven; let cool. Peel and cut into ½-inch cubes.

2 Combine lentils, garlic, and bay leaves in a 6-quart saucepan; add enough cold water to cover by 3 inches. Bring to a boil over medium-high heat. Reduce heat to medium-low; simmer, stirring occasionally, until lentils are tender but not mushy, 10 to 20 minutes. Stir in remaining 2 teaspoons salt; cook 5 minutes more. Drain in a colander; let cool on a baking sheet.

3 Make vinaigrette: In a small bowl, combine shallot, mustard, and vinegar; let stand 15 minutes. Slowly whisk in remaining ¼ cup oil in a steady stream.

4 Transfer lentils to a large serving bowl. Pour vinaigrette over lentils, and add tarragon; toss well to combine. Toss in beets. Season with salt and pepper, and serve, or cover with plastic wrap and place in refrigerator up to 4 hours. Bring to room temperature before serving.

from Potluck Salads

multicolored pepper-and-bean salad with ricotta salata and herbs

SERVES 10 TO 12 | PHOTO ON PAGE 235

Coarse salt

½ pound green beans, ends trimmed

½ pound yellow wax beans, ends trimmed

3 shallots, peeled and thinly sliced into half-moons (about ¾ cup)

¼ cup capers, rinsed and drained

3 tablespoons sherry vinegar

5 tablespoons extra-virgin olive oil

3 pounds assorted bell peppers, quartered, seeds and ribs removed

Freshly ground black pepper

½ cup loosely packed fresh basil leaves

½ cup loosely packed fresh mint leaves

6 to 7 ounces fresh ricotta salata or feta cheese

1 Prepare a large ice bath. Fill a stockpot with water. Bring to a boil; salt generously. Add green beans and wax beans; cook just until crisp-tender and their colors brighten, 3 to 4 minutes. Transfer beans to ice bath. Drain; pat dry with paper towels. Slice larger beans in half lengthwise. Set aside.

2 Make vinaigrette: In a small bowl, combine shallots, capers, vinegar, and a pinch of salt; let stand 15 minutes. Whisking constantly, slowly add oil.

3 Meanwhile, slice peppers as thinly as possible using a sharp knife or mandoline. Add to bowl with beans. Drizzle with vinaigrette, and toss to combine. Season with salt and pepper. Just before serving, tear basil and mint leaves into small pieces, and crumble cheese; stir into salad, and serve.

from Potluck Salads

orzo salad with roasted carrots and dill

SERVES 8 TO 10 | PHOTO ON PAGE 234

3 pounds carrots (about 4 bunches), cut diagonally into 2-inch pieces

4 garlic cloves, unpeeled

¼ cup extra-virgin olive oil

Coarse salt

1 pound orzo (Greek pasta)

Grated zest and juice of 2 lemons

4 scallions, white and light-green parts only, chopped

½ cup loosely packed fresh dill, roughly chopped

Freshly ground pepper

1 Preheat oven to 450°F with a rack in lower third. On a rimmed baking sheet, toss carrots and garlic with 2 tablespoons oil and a pinch of salt. Roast until tender and browned, about 15 minutes. Transfer sheet to a wire rack to cool. Squeeze garlic from skins; mince to a coarse paste.

2 Bring a pot of water to a boil; add salt. Stir in orzo; cook until al dente according to package instructions, about 7 minutes. Drain; while still hot, transfer to a large bowl; toss with remaining 2 tablespoons oil. Let cool slightly; add carrots.

3 Meanwhile, in a small bowl, mix together lemon zest and juice, scallions, and roasted garlic. Add dill, and pour over orzo mixture. Stir to combine; season with salt and pepper. Serve, or store, covered with plastic wrap, in refrigerator, up to 1 day; before serving, bring to room temperature.

from Potluck Salads

shaved cucumber, fennel, and watermelon salad

SERVES 6

1 fennel bulb, trimmed, plus 1 tablespoon chopped fronds

4 cucumbers, cut lengthwise into paper-thin slices

3½ pounds watermelon, cut into 1-inch cubes

2 tablespoons freshly squeezed lemon juice

2 tablespoons olive oil

Coarse salt and freshly ground pepper

4 ounces ricotta salata

Cut fennel bulb crosswise into paper-thin slices. Combine fennel and cucumbers in a large serving bowl. Add watermelon, fennel fronds, lemon juice, and oil. Season with salt and pepper; toss to combine. Using a vegetable peeler, shave ricotta salata over salad, and serve.

from Cucumbers

barbecued chicken

SERVES 10 TO 12

2 whole roaster chickens (about 3½ pounds each), each cut into 6 serving pieces, rinsed and packed dry

Tennessee Pit-Barbecue Sauce (recipe follows)

1 Place chicken in a large bowl, and toss with barbecue sauce to coat. Cover with plastic wrap; let marinate in refrigerator at least 8 hours or preferably overnight.

2 Heat grill. Remove chicken from marinade, letting excess drip off, and place on the grill, near but not directly over coals; close lid. Cook, basting with marinade every 5 minutes and rotating each time, until a meat thermometer inserted into thickest part of breasts and thighs registers 160°F, 30 to 35 minutes. The final basting should be at least 5 minutes before chicken is removed from the grill to ensure that the marinade is fully cooked. Transfer to a serving platter, and cover loosely with foil until ready to serve.

from Country Barbecue

tennessee pit-barbecue sauce

MAKES ABOUT 4 CUPS

½ cup (1 stick) unsalted butter

1 yellow onion, roughly chopped

2 garlic cloves, minced

1 tablespoon dry mustard

1 teaspoon crushed red-pepper flakes

3 tablespoons dark-brown sugar

2 cups ketchup

½ cup Worcestershire sauce

2 tablespoons hot-pepper sauce, such as Tabasco

2 tablespoons molasses

¼ cup bourbon (optional)

2 tablespoons soy sauce

1 Melt butter in a medium saucepan over medium heat. Add onion and garlic; cook, stirring, until onion is soft and translucent, about 5 minutes. Add mustard and red-pepper flakes; cook 2 minutes.

2 Stir in the remaining ingredients. Bring to a simmer, and cook 10 minutes over medium-low heat. Serve, or let cool completely; store, covered, in the refrigerator, for up to 3 days. Before using, gently reheat.

beer-battered cod in tacos

SERVES 6 TO 8

Serve tacos with Saucy Black Beans (page 192), Green Rice (page 192), Pico de Gallo (page 204), Cucumber Relish (page 203), and Pineapple Salsa (page 204).

Vegetable oil, for frying

2 large eggs

1 cup beer

1½ teaspoons coarse salt

½ teaspoon freshly ground black pepper

1 cup all-purpose flour

Pinch of cayenne pepper

1½ pounds cod fillets, cut crosswise into ½-inch-thick strips

Corn tortillas

1 Heat oil in a large cast-iron or heavy skillet until a deep-fry thermometer registers 375°F. Meanwhile, whisk together eggs, beer, ½ teaspoon salt, and ¼ teaspoon black pepper in a medium bowl; set aside.

2 In another bowl, whisk together flour, remaining teaspoon salt and ¼ teaspoon black pepper, and cayenne; add to egg mixture. Whisk until well combined; let rest 15 minutes.

3 Dip fish strips one at a time into batter, letting excess drip off. Working in batches so as not to overcrowd pan, drop carefully into hot oil; fry until fish is golden and crisp and cooked through, about 4 minutes. Remove with a slotted spoon; drain on paper towels. Wrap in corn tortillas, and serve.

from Fish-Taco Party

curried lamb chops

SERVES 6

Serve lamb chops with Cucumber, Cranberry Bean, and Beet Salad in Cucumber Boats (page 186).

¼ cup curry powder

1 tablespoon coarse salt

12 center-cut lamb chops

2 tablespoons canola oil

1 Preheat oven to 400°F. Combine curry powder and salt in a shallow bowl. Coat lamb chops on all sides. Heat a large skillet over medium-high heat; add oil. When hot, add lamb chops, working in batches; cook until well browned, 3 to 4 minutes per side. Transfer to a rimmed baking sheet.

2 Roast until chops are cooked to desired doneness, 6 to 8 minutes for medium-rare. Remove from oven; serve hot.

from Cucumbers

five-spice pork tenderloin
SERVES 6

¼ cup Chinese five-spice powder

2 teaspoons coarse salt

1 pork tenderloin (about 1¾ pounds)

3 tablespoons canola oil

1 Preheat oven to 400°F. Combine spice powder and salt on a plate; generously coat tenderloin. Heat a large oven-proof skillet over medium-high heat, and pour in oil. Brown tenderloins well on all sides, about 4 minutes per side.

2 Transfer skillet to oven, and roast until meat is cooked through, about 15 minutes or until a meat thermometer inserted in the center registers 160°F. Remove from oven; let rest 5 minutes before slicing. Serve.

from Cucumbers

fried catfish sandwich
SERVES 12

Vegetable oil, for frying

4 cups yellow cornmeal

1 teaspoon crushed red-pepper flakes

2 tablespoons coarse salt

2 teaspoons freshly ground black pepper

1 teaspoon garlic powder

12 catfish fillets (about 8 ounces each), cut in half crosswise

24 slices white bread

Mayonnaise (optional)

Pickle relish (optional)

1 Vidalia or other sweet onion, sliced into ¼-inch rounds

1 Fill a deep heavy-bottom skillet with about 2½ inches oil. Place over medium heat until oil registers 365°F on a deep-fry thermometer. Meanwhile, combine cornmeal, red-pepper flakes, 1 tablespoon salt, 1 teaspoon black pepper, and garlic powder in a shallow bowl.

2 Sprinkle fillets on both sides with remaining tablespoon salt and teaspoon black pepper; dredge in cornmeal mixture, turning to coat both sides. Working in batches, carefully submerge fillets in oil, and fry until crust is crisp and golden and fish is cooked through, about 3 minutes. Transfer to a plate.

3 To serve, spread bread slices with mayonnaise and/or relish, as desired. Place fillets on half the slices, and top with onion slices and the remaining slices of bread.

from Country Barbecue

grilled leg of lamb
SERVES 8

Serve with Black-Olive Relish (page 202), Provençal Roasted Tomatoes (page 192), and Whole Grilled Garlic (page 204).

1 leg of lamb (6 to 7 pounds), boned and butterflied

6 garlic cloves, minced

⅓ cup herbes de Provence

¼ cup plus 1 tablespoon extra-virgin olive oil

Freshly ground pepper

Coarse salt

1 Cut lamb at joint into two sections, a long, narrow piece and a wide, rounded piece. Place in a shallow bowl. In a bowl, combine garlic, herbs, and oil; season with pepper. Rub mixture over lamb to coat evenly. Cover with plastic; let marinate in refrigerator at least 1 hour and up to 6 hours. Remove from refrigerator 30 minutes before cooking.

2 Heat grill; position rack about 6 inches above flame. Season lamb with salt; grill about 9 minutes on each side, or until a meat thermometer inserted into thickest part registers 135°F (medium-rare). Transfer to a platter; cover loosely with foil. Let rest 15 minutes before slicing.

from A Bastille Day Picnic in New Orleans

grilled mahimahi in tacos
SERVES 6 TO 8

Grilled fish is a healthful alternative to the traditional fried fish in fish tacos. Serve with Saucy Black Beans (page 192), Green Rice (page 192), Pico de Gallo (page 204), Cucumber Relish (page 203), and Pineapple Salsa (page 204).

3 tablespoons extra-virgin olive oil

3 tablespoons freshly squeezed lime juice

3 garlic cloves, smashed

½ teaspoon cumin seeds

¼ teaspoon freshly ground pepper

2 to 3 sprigs thyme, oregano, or other herbs

1½ pounds mahimahi fillets

Corn tortillas

1 Combine oil, lime juice, garlic, cumin, pepper, and herbs in a large resealable plastic bag. Shake well to combine. Add fish; shake gently to coat well. Refrigerate at least 1 hour and up to 4 hours.

2 Heat grill or grill pan. Remove fish from marinade, letting excess drip off. Grill until browned on outside and cooked through, about 4 minutes per side. Wrap in tortillas; serve.

from Fish-Taco Party

grilled marinated strip steak with scallions

SERVES 4 | PHOTO ON PAGE 241

4 boneless strip steaks (about 10 ounces each)

1 bunch scallions, trimmed

¼ cup Worcestershire sauce

¼ cup soy sauce

1 teaspoon dry mustard

1 teaspoon freshly ground pepper

½ teaspoon ground cumin

Grated zest of 1 lemon

Coarse salt

1 Place steaks in a large, shallow nonreactive dish. Slice 3 scallions into thin rounds, and combine with the remaining ingredients, except the salt, in a small bowl; whisk to combine. Pour marinade over steaks. Cover with plastic wrap; set aside at room temperature 40 minutes, turning once.

2 Heat grill or grill pan. Remove steaks from marinade, letting excess drip off; pat dry with paper towels. Season both sides generously with salt. Grill until well browned on outside and cooked to desired doneness, about 6 minutes on each side for medium-rare. Transfer to a large serving platter; cover with foil, and let rest 10 minutes. Grill remaining scallions, about 1 minute on each side, and serve with the steaks.

from What to Have for Dinner

striped bass with cucumber broth

SERVES 6 | PHOTO ON PAGE 238

Ask your fishmonger to cut fillets from the center of the fish so the pieces are about one inch thick.

2½ pounds cucumbers, peeled and seeded

¼ cup heavy cream

2 tablespoons prepared horseradish

½ teaspoon coarse salt, plus more for seasoning

6 fillets striped bass (about 6 ounces each)

3 tablespoons extra-virgin olive oil

Freshly ground pepper

1 garlic clove, minced

½ teaspoon fresh thyme leaves, plus whole sprigs for garnish

1 Cut 1 cucumber into ½-inch-thick slices; set aside. Pass remaining cucumbers through a juicer; you should have about 3 cups juice. Set aside.

2 In a medium bowl, whip cream to soft peaks. Stir in horseradish and ½ teaspoon salt. Cover with plastic wrap, and place in refrigerator until ready to use.

3 Using a knife, make shallow slits in skin side of fish. Heat oil in a large ovenproof nonstick skillet over medium-high heat until very hot. Season both sides of fillets with salt and pepper; place in pan skin side down. Cook until browned, about 5 minutes; turn, and cook until fish is cooked through, about 5 minutes more. Transfer to warm shallow bowls.

4 Add garlic and reserved cucumber slices to skillet; cook over low heat until cucumber is soft. Add reserved cucumber juice and thyme leaves; cook just until hot. Season with salt and pepper. Ladle cucumber broth and slices around fish; garnish with horseradish cream and thyme sprigs.

from Cucumbers

....

SIDE DISHES

....

aunt sara's cheese grits

SERVES 8 TO 10

¾ cup (1½ sticks) unsalted butter, plus more for baking dish

3 cups water

1½ cups quick-cooking grits

1 pound sharp cheddar cheese, grated

1 teaspoon coarse salt

½ teaspoon freshly ground pepper

½ teaspoon garlic powder

½ teaspoon hot-pepper sauce, such as Tabasco (optional)

3 large eggs, lightly beaten

1 Preheat oven to 325°F. Butter an 8-inch-square baking dish. Bring the water to a boil in a medium saucepan, then stir in grits. Reduce heat; cover, and simmer about 2 minutes, stirring occasionally.

2 Add cheese, butter, salt, pepper, garlic powder, and hot-pepper sauce, if using. Stir until cheese has completely melted, and stir in eggs until well combined.

3 Pour mixture into prepared pan, and bake until creamy inside and golden on the top, about 1 hour. Transfer to a wire rack; let cool slightly before cutting into squares.

from Country Barbecue

green rice

SERVES 6 TO 8

2 tablespoons vegetable or olive oil

1 white onion, cut into ¼-inch pieces

2 garlic cloves, minced

1½ cups long-grain rice

2½ cups homemade or low-sodium canned chicken or vegetable stock, or water

½ cup finely chopped fresh cilantro

1 poblano chile, seeded and finely chopped

Coarse salt and freshly ground pepper

1 Heat oil in a large saucepan over medium heat. Add onion; cook until soft and translucent, about 8 minutes. Add garlic; cook 2 minutes. Add rice, and stir to coat. Add stock, and bring to a boil; reduce heat to a simmer. Cover, and cook until rice is tender, about 15 minutes.

2 Turn off heat; let stand, covered, until liquid is absorbed, 5 to 10 minutes. Fluff with a fork; stir in cilantro and poblano. Season with salt and pepper. Serve hot.

from Fish-Taco Party

provençal roasted tomatoes

SERVES 8 TO 10

Tomatoes will hold up very well up to two days in the refrigerator; serve as a sandwich filling or pasta topping.

12 plum tomatoes (about 3 pounds)

3 garlic cloves, minced

2 tablespoons finely chopped fresh thyme

2 tablespoons finely chopped fresh flat-leaf parsley

Coarse salt and freshly ground pepper

¼ cup extra-virgin olive oil

1 Preheat oven to 350°F. Fit a wire rack into a rimmed baking sheet. Slice each tomato lengthwise into four ½-inch slices. Place on wire rack.

2 In a small bowl, mix garlic, thyme, and parsley; season with salt and pepper. Divide mixture evenly among tomato slices, spooning about ½ teaspoon on each. Drizzle oil over tomatoes. Roast until herb mixture is lightly browned and tomato skins are wrinkled, about 1 hour. Transfer baking sheet to a wire rack; let cool. Serve.

from A Bastille Day Picnic in New Orleans

roasted fingerling potatoes with seasoned salt

SERVES 4 | PHOTO ON PAGE 241

2 teaspoons coarse salt

¼ teaspoon freshly ground pepper

¼ teaspoon finely chopped fresh thyme

¼ teaspoon finely chopped fresh rosemary

1½ pounds fingerling potatoes, scrubbed

1 tablespoon extra-virgin olive oil

1 Preheat oven to 400°F. Heat a large ovenproof gratin dish or cast-iron skillet in the oven 15 minutes. Combine salt, pepper, thyme, and rosemary in a small bowl. Set aside.

2 Slice large potatoes in half lengthwise. Toss potatoes in a medium bowl with oil. Sprinkle generously with some of the seasoned salt; arrange potatoes in a single layer in preheated dish. Roast until golden on the outside and tender when pierced with a knife, 25 to 30 minutes. Remove from oven; serve hot with additional seasoned salt on the side.

from What to Have for Dinner

saucy black beans

SERVES 6 TO 8

12 ounces dried black beans, picked over

3 tablespoons vegetable oil

1 large white onion, diced

8 cups cold water, plus more for soaking

Peel of 1 orange, pith removed (optional)

1 jalapeño pepper, sliced in half lengthwise and seeded (optional)

Coarse salt and freshly ground black pepper

Hot-pepper sauce, such as Tabasco (optional)

1 Place beans in a large bowl or stockpot; cover with cold water by 2 inches. Let stand at room temperature 4 hours or overnight. Drain, and rinse beans with cold water; set aside.

2 Heat oil in a large saucepan over medium heat. Add onion; cook until soft and translucent but not browned, about 8 minutes. Add beans, the cold water, and orange peel and/or jalapeño, if desired. Bring to a boil; reduce heat to a gentle simmer. Cover; cook, stirring occasionally, until beans are tender and most liquid has evaporated, creating a saucelike consistency, about 2 hours.

3 Remove from heat; remove orange peel and/or jalapeño, if using. Season with salt, black pepper, and hot-pepper sauce, if desired. Serve hot or at room temperature.

from Fish-Taco Party

sautéed asparagus with aged gouda cheese

SERVES 4 | PHOTO ON PAGE 241

1½ tablespoons unsalted butter

1 pound thin asparagus, trimmed

Coarse salt and freshly ground pepper

2 ounces aged Gouda cheese, shaved

Melt the butter in a large skillet over medium-high heat. Add asparagus spears, and sauté until tender and bright green, 2 to 3 minutes. Season with salt and pepper. Transfer to a large platter, and top with Gouda. Serve immediately.

from What to Have for Dinner

turnip greens

SERVES 8 TO 10

2 tablespoons unsalted butter

2 small onions, finely chopped

2 cups homemade or low-sodium canned chicken stock

1 teaspoon coarse salt

½ teaspoon freshly ground pepper

4 large bunches turnip greens, tough stems discarded and leaves roughly chopped

Hot-pepper sauce, such as Tabasco, for serving (optional)

1 Melt butter in a stockpot over medium heat. Add onions; cook until they are soft and translucent, about 6 minutes. Add stock, salt, and pepper; bring to a boil.

2 Working in batches if necessary, add turnip greens; cover, and cook until tender, 3 to 4 minutes. Transfer to a serving platter. Serve immediately with hot-pepper sauce, if desired.

from Country Barbecue

vidalia-onion slaw

SERVES 10 TO 12

2 tablespoons plus 1½ teaspoons coarse salt

4 Vidalia or other sweet onions, cut into ¼-inch pieces

1½ cups mayonnaise

¼ cup apple-cider vinegar

1 tablespoon sugar

1 teaspoon ground celery seed

½ teaspoon freshly ground pepper

1 Prepare a large ice bath; set aside. Bring a stockpot of water to a boil; add 2 tablespoons salt and the onions; simmer until onions are translucent but still firm, about 4 minutes. Transfer to ice bath to cool. Drain; pat dry with paper towels.

2 Transfer to a large bowl; mix with mayonnaise, vinegar, sugar, celery seed, remaining 1½ teaspoons salt, and pepper. Serve, or refrigerate, covered with plastic, up to 2 days.

from Country Barbecue

DESSERTS

caramel cake

MAKES 1 NINE-INCH LAYER CAKE

1¼ cups (2½ sticks) unsalted butter, softened, plus more for pan and rack

4½ cups sifted cake flour (not self-rising), plus more for pan

2 tablespoons baking powder

¾ teaspoon salt

1½ cups milk

1½ tablespoons pure vanilla extract

2¼ cups sugar

7 large egg whites

Caramel Frosting (page 194)

1 Preheat oven to 350°F. Butter two 9-by-2-inch round cake pans. Line bottoms with parchment paper; butter parchment and sides of pan; dust with flour, tapping out excess. Set aside. Sift together flour, baking powder, and salt into a medium bowl. In another bowl, combine milk and vanilla.

2 Cream butter in bowl of an electric mixer fitted with paddle attachment until smooth. With machine running, add sugar in a steady stream; beat until mixture is light and fluffy, about 3 minutes. Reduce speed to low. Add flour mixture in three batches, alternating with milk mixture and starting and ending with flour. Do not overbeat.

3 In clean mixer beat egg whites with whisk attachment until stiff peaks form. Fold a third of whites into batter to lighten; fold in remaining whites in two batches. Divide batter between prepared pans; smooth tops with an offset spatula. Bake until a cake tester inserted in center comes out clean and cake springs back when pressed lightly in enter, about 40 minutes.

4 Transfer pans to a wire rack; let cool 15 minutes. Brush rack with butter. Loosen sides of cakes with a paring knife; invert onto rack. Reinvert cakes; let cool completely.

5 Use a serrated knife to slice domed tops off cakes. Place a layer cut side up on a serving platter; spread some caramel frosting on top. Stack other layer cut side down on top; spread top and sides of both cakes with frosting. Serve, or store in airtight container at room temperature up to 3 days.

from Country Barbecue

caramel frosting

MAKES ABOUT 5 CUPS

5 cups sugar

1 cup water

2 cups heavy cream

1 teaspoon pure vanilla extract

¾ cup (1½ sticks) unsalted butter, cut into pieces

1 Bring 4 cups sugar and the water to a boil in a medium saucepan over medium heat, stirring until sugar has dissolved, about 8 minutes; wash down sides of pan with a pastry brush dipped in water to prevent crystals from forming. Raise heat to high; gently swirl pan (do not stir) until caramel is a deep amber color, about 10 minutes. Remove from heat.

2 Meanwhile, heat cream and remaining cup sugar in a small saucepan over medium heat until sugar dissolves, stirring frequently, about 5 minutes. Turn off heat; cover, and set aside.

3 As soon as caramel is desired color, add hot cream mixture in a slow, steady stream, stirring to combine. Be careful, as caramel may splatter when cream is added. Stir in vanilla, and continue stirring until mixture no longer bubbles.

4 Prepare an ice bath. Transfer mixture to bowl of an electric mixer; place in ice bath, stirring until cool. Attach bowl to mixer; using paddle attachment, beat on medium speed 5 minutes. With machine running, gradually add butter, beating to incorporate fully. Let frosting stand 20 minutes to thicken.

crisp coconut and chocolate pie

MAKES 1 EIGHT-INCH PIE │ **PHOTO ON PAGE 244**

4 tablespoons unsalted butter, softened

11 ounces sweetened shredded coconut

8 ounces semisweet or bittersweet chocolate, finely chopped

1¼ cups heavy cream

1 Preheat oven to 350°F. Place the butter and a third of the coconut in the bowl of a food processor fitted with the metal blade. Process until mixture forms a ball, 1 to 2 minutes. Transfer to a medium bowl. Sprinkle remaining coconut over mixture, and combine with your fingers.

2 Place an 8-inch tart pan with a removable bottom on a baking sheet. Press coconut mixture into bottom and up sides of pan to form a crust, leaving top edges loose and fluffy. Place a ring of aluminum foil over edge to prevent burning. Bake until center begins to brown, 10 to 15 minutes; remove foil, and cook until edges are browned, 4 to 6 minutes. Transfer to a wire rack to cool completely.

3 Place chocolate in a medium heat-proof bowl. Bring cream just to a boil in a small saucepan, and pour over chocolate. Let sit 10 minutes, and stir until chocolate is melted and combined. When cool, pour into coconut crust. Cover with plastic wrap, and transfer to refrigerator until filling is set, at least 1 hour. Cut into wedges, and serve.

from Icebox Desserts

cucumber and riesling granita

SERVES 6

Pair this refreshing granita with fresh fruit for a light dessert, or serve it as a palate cleanser, or intermezzo, between courses.

2 large cucumbers (about 1¾ pounds)

1¼ cups Riesling or other sweet white wine

2 teaspoons superfine sugar

½ teaspoon salt

Pinch of freshly ground pepper

1 Wash cucumbers, and pass through a juicer. Place juice in an 8-inch square metal baking pan, and add remaining ingredients. Stir to combine, and place in the freezer, uncovered, 1 hour; remove from freezer, and stir with a fork.

2 Return to freezer until mixture is frozen and granular, about 3 hours, stirring every 30 to 45 minutes. Serve, or cover with plastic wrap, and store in the freezer up to 2 weeks.

from Cucumbers

french flag berry tarts

MAKES 3 FOUR-BY-FOURTEEN-INCH TARTS │ **PHOTO ON PAGE 243**

You can line all three tarts with melted chocolate, if you prefer; you will need an additional two ounces of chocolate. We used golden raspberries for the white tart; red raspberries would work as well. In honor of Bastille Day, we arranged the red, white, and blue tarts to resemble the French flag.

4 ounces semisweet chocolate, for lining red- and golden-raspberry tart shells

3 prebaked Flag Berry Pâte Sucrée Tart Shells (recipe follows)

½ cup raspberry jam, for glazing red raspberries

Crème Fraîche Filling (page 195)

1 pint red raspberries

1 pint golden raspberries, picked over

Confectioners' sugar, for dusting golden raspberries

½ cup apricot jam, for lining blueberry tart shell and for glazing blueberries

1 pint blueberries, picked over

1 Make red and white tarts: In a bowl in the microwave or a bowl set over a pan of simmering water, heat chocolate until just melted, about 1½ minutes; stir until smooth. Using back of a spoon, spread half the chocolate over bottom of each of 2 tart shells; refrigerate to set, at least 5 minutes. Meanwhile, heat raspberry jam in a small saucepan with about 1 tablespoon water; strain into a bowl.

2 Remove chocolate-lined shells from refrigerator. Spread a third of crème fraîche filling over bottom of each. Arrange red raspberries in rows in a single layer in one shell; brush berries with strained jam. Arrange another layer of rows on top; brush with jam. Arrange golden raspberries in other shell, and dust with confectioners' sugar to completely coat. Set aside.

3 Make blue tart: Heat apricot jam in a small saucepan with about 1 tablespoon water; strain into a medium bowl. Using a pastry brush, thinly coat bottom of tart shell; let cool. Spread remaining crème fraîche filling on top. Toss blueberries with remaining jam; tumble into tart shell. Arrange tarts in order of French flag on a serving tray or board.

from A Bastille Day Picnic in New Orleans

flag berry pâte sucrée tart shells

MAKES ENOUGH FOR 2 FOUR-BY-FOURTEEN-INCH TARTS

Dough can be stored, wrapped well in plastic, in the refrigerator for up to three days or in the freezer for up to one month. You will need three tart shells for the French Flag Berry Tarts.

2½ cups all-purpose flour, plus more for work surface
3 tablespoons sugar
   Pinch of salt
1 cup (2 sticks) chilled unsalted butter, cut into small pieces
2 large egg yolks
¼ cup cold water

1 Place flour, sugar, and salt in a food processor fitted with the metal blade; pulse to combine. Add butter; process until mixture resembles coarse meal, about 10 seconds.

2 In a small bowl, lightly beat yolks with the water. With machine running, add yolk mixture; process just until dough holds together, no more than 20 seconds. Divide dough in half, pat into flat disks, and wrap in plastic. Chill until ready to use, at least 2 hours.

3 On a lightly floured surface, roll out one disk of pâte sucrée ⅛ inch thick to fit a 4-by-14-inch fluted tart pan with a removable bottom, allowing about an inch extra on all sides. Brush off excess flour with a pastry brush. Carefully transfer dough to tart pan, pressing it into edges and sides; trim excess by

running rolling pin over the pan. Prick the bottom of the dough all over with a fork. Cover with plastic wrap; chill in refrigerator at least 1 hour. Repeat with remaining disk.

4 Preheat oven to 375°F. Remove pans from refrigerator, and place on a rimmed baking sheet. Line each with a piece of aluminum foil that overhangs the edges by at least 2 inches. Fill foil with pie weights or dried beans; fold foil to enclose, making sure edges of tart are supported by the foil and weights.

5 Bake until edges are just starting to brown, about 25 minutes. Remove foil and weights; continue baking until crust is crisp and evenly browned, 10 to 15 minutes more. Transfer to a wire rack to cool completely before removing shells.

crème fraîche filling

MAKES ENOUGH FOR 3 FOUR-BY-FOURTEEN-INCH TARTS

2 8-ounce packages cream cheese, room temperature
1 teaspoon pure vanilla extract
8 ounces crème fraîche
1 cup confectioners' sugar

1 In the bowl of an electric mixer fitted with the paddle attachment, beat cream cheese and vanilla until soft. In a separate bowl, whisk crème fraîche until soft peaks form.

2 Whisk a third of the crème fraîche into cream-cheese mixture. Fold in remaining crème fraîche while gradually sifting confectioners' sugar over top; fold just until combined. Cover with plastic wrap; refrigerate until ready to use, up to 2 hours.

grasshopper tarts

MAKES SIX 2¾-BY-2-INCH RINGS | PHOTO ON PAGE 248

These desserts are named for the classic cocktail, which is made with crème de menthe.

¾ cup sugar
½ cup water
3½ tablespoons crème de menthe
¼ teaspoon pure spearmint extract
1 teaspoon unflavored gelatin
2½ cups heavy cream
2 cups lightly packed fresh mint leaves, plus 6 sprigs for garnish
5 large egg yolks
1 large whole egg
3 ounces semisweet chocolate, finely chopped, plus a few shavings for garnish
   Chocolate-Wafer Crust (page 196)

1   Combine sugar and the water in a small saucepan over medium-high heat; stir until sugar is dissolved. Remove from heat; let cool slightly. Stir in crème de menthe and spearmint extract. Sprinkle gelatin over; let soften, about 5 minutes.

2   Heat 1½ cups cream in another small saucepan until it is almost at a boil. Turn off heat, and add mint; cover, and let steep 10 minutes.

3   Prepare an ice bath; set aside. Whisk egg yolks and egg in a heat-proof bowl. Strain cream mixture through a fine sieve into egg mixture; place bowl over a pan of simmering water. Add gelatin mixture, and whisk constantly until mixture begins to thicken and a candy thermometer registers 160°F. Transfer bowl to ice bath; stir occasionally until mixture is cool.

4   In a medium bowl, whisk remaining cup cream to soft peaks. Gently whisk in mint mixture, and fold in chocolate pieces. Fill each crust with about ¾ cup mixture. Transfer rings to refrigerator until filling is set, at least 2 hours. To unmold, warm each ring in your hands, and shake gently until tart slides out. Serve, garnished with a sprig of mint and shaved chocolate.

from Icebox Desserts

chocolate-wafer crust

MAKES ENOUGH FOR 6 SMALL TARTS

35 chocolate wafers (about 7½ ounces)

 3 tablespoons sugar

 4 tablespoons unsalted butter, melted

1   Preheat oven to 350°F. Place chocolate wafers in the bowl of a food processor fitted with the metal blade; process until fine crumbs form. Add sugar and butter, and process until combined.

2   Place six 2¾-by-2-inch ring molds on a rimmed baking sheet. Pat 5 to 6 tablespoons crumb mixture into each, pressing in bottom and halfway up sides. Bake until crust is fragrant, about 8 minutes. Transfer to a wire rack to cool completely before filling. Store at room temperature, up to 1 day.

grilled peaches with chilled sabayon

SERVES 4

5 large egg yolks

⅓ cup plus 1 tablespoon sugar

⅓ cup Champagne or sparkling wine

2 tablespoons peach liqueur (optional)

¾ cup heavy cream, chilled

2 ripe peaches, halved and pitted

2 tablespoons unsalted butter, melted

2 tablespoons light-brown sugar

1   Heat grill or grill pan. Prepare an ice bath; set aside. Make the sabayon: Combine yolks, sugar, Champagne, and liqueur, if using, in a large metal bowl set over a pot of simmering water. Whisk until mixture is very thick and has expanded in volume, about 7 minutes. Place bowl in ice bath; let cool completely.

2   Place cream in a large bowl, and beat until stiff peaks form; fold into egg-yolk mixture. Cover with plastic wrap, and place in refrigerator at least 20 minutes.

3   Line grill or pan with heavy-duty foil. Brush peaches with butter; sprinkle with brown sugar. Grill cut side down until peaches are tender and sugar is caramelized, 6 to 7 minutes. Divide sabayon among four dishes; top each with a peach half. Serve.

from What to Have for Dinner

lemon and cherry trifle

MAKES 6 INDIVIDUAL TRIFLES | **PHOTO ON PAGE 245**

2 cups heavy cream

   Lemon-Curd Filling (recipe follows)

   Poached Cherries (recipe follows)

30 vanilla wafers

   Candied Lemon Zest (recipe follows)

6 fresh cherries, for garnish

In the bowl of an electric mixer fitted with the whisk attachment, beat cream until soft peaks form. Layer lemon curd, cherries, wafers, zest, and whipped cream in tall glasses. Cover with plastic wrap; chill in refrigerator up to 2 hours. Garnish each with a fresh cherry, and serve.

from Icebox Desserts

lemon-curd filling

MAKES ABOUT 2½ CUPS

  7 large egg yolks

  1 large whole egg

1½ cups sugar

 ¾ cup freshly squeezed lemon juice

 ¾ cup (1½ sticks) unsalted butter, cut into pieces

Prepare an ice bath; set aside. Whisking constantly, bring all ingredients to a boil in a medium saucepan over medium-high heat, 3 to 5 minutes. Transfer pan to ice bath; stir until mixture is cool. Cover with plastic wrap, pressing it onto surface to prevent a skin from forming. Refrigerate until ready to use, up to 3 days.

poached cherries

MAKES ENOUGH FOR 6 INDIVIDUAL TRIFLES

  2 pounds fresh red or yellow cherries, pitted (5 to 6 cups)

 ½ cup sugar

  1 tablespoon kirsch (optional)

  2 tablespoons freshly squeezed lemon juice

Bring all ingredients to a simmer in a saucepan over medium-low heat; cook, stirring occasionally, until cherries are tender, about 15 minutes. Transfer cherries to a large bowl. Continue cooking liquid in pan over medium heat until it is slightly thickened, about 3 minutes. Pour over cherries; let cool. Store in an airtight container in refrigerator up to 1 day.

candied lemon zest

MAKES ABOUT ½ CUP

3 lemons

1 cup sugar

½ cup water

Using a vegetable peeler, remove lemon zest in long strips; remove pith. Cut strips into fine julienne. Bring sugar and the water to a boil in a small saucepan, stirring to dissolve sugar. Add zest; boil 5 minutes. Cover, and remove from heat; let cool. Strain off syrup before using or storing. Zest can be refrigerated in an airtight container up to 2 weeks.

limeade pie

MAKES ONE 13½-BY-4½-INCH PIE | PHOTO ON PAGE 244

12 ounces cream cheese, room temperature

  1 cup granulated sugar

  2 tablespoons finely grated lime zest (about 4 limes)

 ⅓ cup freshly squeezed lime juice

   Graham-Nut Crust (recipe follows)

 ½ cup confectioners' sugar

  1 lime, washed and thinly sliced

1 Combine cream cheese and granulated sugar in the bowl of a food processor fitted with the metal blade; process until mixture is smooth. Add lime zest and juice; pulse several times to combine. Transfer filling to prepared crust; cover with plastic wrap, and refrigerate until it is set, at least 1 hour.

2 Preheat oven to 250°F. Line a baking sheet with parchment. Sprinkle confectioners' sugar on a small plate. Dredge each lime slice in sugar, turning to coat both sides. Transfer slices to prepared baking sheet. Bake until slices are just stiff but not brown, about 40 minutes. Transfer to a wire rack to cool.

3 To serve, arrange lime slices around tart, or make a slit halfway through each slice, and tuck into each pie serving.

from Icebox Desserts

graham-nut crust

MAKES ONE 13½-BY-4¼-INCH CRUST

 ¼ cup pecans

10 graham crackers (5 ounces)

  3 tablespoons sugar

 ¼ teaspoon salt

  4 tablespoons unsalted butter, melted

1 Preheat oven to 350°F. Place pecans in a single layer on a rimmed baking sheet, and toast until they are fragrant, about 8 minutes. Remove from oven; let cool.

2 Place graham crackers in the bowl of a food processor fitted with the metal blade; pulse until fine crumbs form. Add sugar, salt, and pecans; pulse to combine. Add butter; pulse until fine crumbs form.

3 Transfer to a 13½-by-4¼-inch tart pan with a removable bottom, and pat evenly into bottom and up sides. Place pan on a baking sheet; bake until crust is golden and fragrant, 8 to 10 minutes. Transfer to a wire rack to cool. Crust may be made up to 1 day ahead and stored, covered with plastic wrap, at room temperature.

mango panna cotta

SERVES 8 | PHOTO ON PAGE 244

- 5 ripe mangoes, peeled and pitted
- 2 tablespoons plus 1 cup sugar
- 1½ teaspoons unflavored gelatin
- 3 tablespoons plus ⅔ cup cold water
- 1⅓ cups heavy cream
- 2 tablespoons freshly squeezed lemon juice

1 Cut 1 mango into ¼-inch cubes; place in a small bowl. Sprinkle with 2 tablespoons sugar, and let stand 15 minutes. Meanwhile, chop remaining 4 mangoes, and place in the bowl of a food processor fitted with the metal blade; process until smooth. Strain through a sieve into a medium bowl; you should have 2½ cups. Measure out ½ cup; set aside.

2 Prepare an ice bath; set aside. In a small bowl, sprinkle 1¼ teaspoons gelatin over 3 tablespoons cold water; let soften, about 5 minutes. In a medium saucepan, combine cream and remaining 1 cup sugar; stir over medium-high heat until sugar is dissolved. Add 2 cups mango purée and the gelatin mixture; stir until gelatin is dissolved, about 2 minutes. Transfer to a large bowl set in ice bath; stir until cool.

3 Divide reserved cubed mango among eight serving glasses, and pour ½ cup chilled mango cream into each. Place in refrigerator to set, at least 2 hours.

4 Prepare an ice bath. In a small bowl, sprinkle remaining ¼ teaspoon gelatin over remaining ⅔ cup water; let soften, about 5 minutes. In a saucepan, heat reserved ½ cup purée with lemon juice. Add gelatin; stir until dissolved. Pour through a fine sieve into a bowl set in ice bath; stir until cool.

5 Pour 1½ to 2 tablespoons mixture in a thin layer over mango cream in each glass. Cover loosely with plastic wrap, and refrigerate until mixture is set, at least 5 hours or overnight. Serve.

from Icebox Desserts

mary curll's chess pie

MAKES 1 EIGHT-INCH PIE

Mary Curll and her husband, Fred, own So Smooth Soul Food, a restaurant in Franklin, Tennessee. Mary is famous for her pies.

- All-purpose flour, for work surface
- ½ recipe Pie Dough (recipe follows)
- 1½ cups sugar
- ½ cup (1 stick) unsalted butter, melted
- 3 large eggs, lightly beaten
- 1 teaspoon apple-cider vinegar
- 1 teaspoon pure vanilla extract

1 Preheat oven to 350°F. On a lightly floured work surface, roll out pie dough to ⅛ inch thick; place in an 8-inch pie plate, and press into sides. Crimp as desired. Place in refrigerator to chill.

2 Combine sugar, butter, eggs, vinegar, and vanilla in a large bowl, and whisk until smooth. Pour into lined pie plate. Bake until crust is golden brown and center is set when touched with your finger, 55 to 60 minutes. Transfer to a wire rack to cool slightly before serving.

from Country Barbecue

pie dough

MAKES ENOUGH FOR 2 EIGHT-INCH PIES

Dough can be stored in the freezer, wrapped well in plastic, up to one month.

- 2½ cups all-purpose flour, plus more for work surface
- 1 teaspoon salt
- 1 teaspoon sugar
- 1 cup (2 sticks) chilled unsalted butter, cut into pieces
- ¼ to ½ cup ice water

1 Place flour, salt, and sugar in the bowl of a food processor fitted with the metal blade; pulse to combine. Add butter, and process until mixture resembles coarse meal, about 10 seconds. With machine running, add the ice water through the feed tube in a slow, steady stream, just until mixture comes together. Do not process more than 30 seconds.

2 Turn dough out onto a lightly floured work surface. Divide into 2 equal pieces. Flatten into disks. Wrap well in plastic, and refrigerate at least 1 hour before using.

peanut-butter-and-chocolate cups

MAKES ABOUT 2½ DOZEN SMALL, PLUS 1 DOZEN LARGE

Keep the pan of simmering water nearby to rewarm the chocolate as you are working. You will need about thirty 1½-inch and twelve 2½-inch paper candy cups; they are available at most baking supply stores.

- 10 ounces semisweet or bittersweet chocolate, coarsely chopped
- 6 ounces cream cheese, room temperature
- 1 cup smooth peanut butter
- 1 cup sugar
- ½ cup heavy cream
- Chopped peanuts, for garnish

1 In a heat-proof bowl set over a pan of simmering water, melt chocolate, stirring occasionally, until smooth. Remove from heat; stir to cool slightly.

2 Working with one cup at a time, fill halfway with melted chocolate. Invert cup over bowl of chocolate; swivel to coat sides. Quickly reinvert cup; if needed, use a pastry brush to fill in any holes so that no cup is visible. Place on a baking sheet in refrigerator or freezer. Let chocolate harden before filling, 30 minutes or up to 2 days; cover with plastic once set.

3 In the bowl of an electric mixer fitted with the paddle attachment, beat cream cheese until smooth. Add peanut butter and sugar; beat until combined. In a separate bowl, whip cream until stiff peaks form; fold into peanut-butter mixture. Refrigerate 5 minutes. Transfer to a pastry bag fitted with an Ateco #863 open-star tip; pipe mixture into cups.

4 Place cups in an airtight container or baking pan; cover container or wrap pan with plastic, being careful not to touch tops of cups. Refrigerate until ready to serve, up to 4 hours. Sprinkle a few chopped peanuts over top of each cup; serve.

from Icebox Desserts

skillet-baked chocolate-chip cookie

SERVES 8

- 2 cups all-purpose flour
- 1 teaspoon baking soda
- ½ teaspoon salt
- ¾ cup (1½ sticks) unsalted butter, softened
- ½ cup sugar
- ¾ cup packed light-brown sugar
- 1 large egg
- 2 teaspoons pure vanilla extract
- 1½ cups mixed milk- and semisweet-chocolate chips (about 9 ounces)
- 2 pints vanilla ice cream
  Caramel Sauce (recipe follows)

1 Preheat oven to 350°F. In a bowl, whisk flour, baking soda, and salt. In bowl of an electric mixer fitted with paddle attachment, cream butter and sugars until light and fluffy, about 2 minutes. Add egg and vanilla; mix until fully incorporated. Add flour mixture; beat until just combined.

2 Stir in chocolate chips; transfer dough to a 10-inch oven-proof skillet; flatten to cover bottom. Bake until edges are brown and top is golden, 40 to 45 minutes. Don't overbake; it will continue to cook when taken out of oven. Transfer to a wire rack to cool 20 minutes. Cut into 8 wedges. Serve warm, topped with ice cream and caramel sauce.

from Dessert of the Month

caramel sauce

MAKES ABOUT 1 CUP

- 1 cup sugar
- ¼ teaspoon salt
- ¼ cup water
- ½ cup heavy cream
- 2 tablespoons unsalted butter
- ½ teaspoon pure vanilla extract

In a small saucepan, combine sugar, salt, and the water. Cook over medium heat until sugar is a medium amber color, about 7 minutes; wash sides of pan with a pastry brush dipped in water to prevent crystals from forming. Remove from heat. Stir in heavy cream; add butter, and stir until combined. Let cool to room temperature; stir in vanilla. Sauce can be stored in an airtight container in refrigerator up to 2 weeks. Reheat gently; serve at room temperature.

strawberry chiffon pie

MAKES 2 EIGHT-INCH PIES | **PHOTO ON PAGE 245**

If you are using pasteurized egg whites, you do not need to heat them before beating with the sugar and cream of tartar.

- 1 quart strawberries, hulled, plus 1 pint for garnish
- 1 cup plus 2 tablespoons sugar
- 1½ quarter-ounce envelopes unflavored gelatin (1 tablespoon)
- 2 large egg whites
  Pinch of cream of tartar
- 2 tablespoons freshly squeezed lemon juice
- ½ cup crème fraîche
  Almond-Shortbread Crust (page 200)

1 Combine 1 quart strawberries and ½ cup sugar in the bowl of a food processor fitted with the metal blade; process until smooth, about 3 minutes; you should have 3 cups purée. Transfer half to a large heat-proof mixing bowl. Sprinkle gelatin over the top; let soften, about 5 minutes.

2 In a heat-proof bowl of an electric mixer, combine egg whites with cream of tartar and ½ cup sugar. Place bowl over a saucepan of simmering water, and whisk until mixture is hot to the touch and sugar has dissolved, about 2 minutes. Attach bowl to mixer fitted with the whisk attachment; beat on medium-high until soft peaks form, about 2 minutes.

3 Place gelatin mixture over the pan of simmering water, stirring occasionally, until gelatin dissolves, about 5 minutes; remove from heat. Gradually whisk in the remaining purée; whisk in lemon juice.

4 In a small bowl, whisk crème fraîche until soft peaks form; whisk into purée mixture. Whisk in a third of the egg whites to lighten; fold in remaining whites just until they are combined (do not overmix). Divide among crusts; refrigerate, covered with plastic, until mixture is set, at least 4 hours or overnight.

5 Thinly slice remaining pint strawberries. Place in a small bowl, and sprinkle with remaining 2 tablespoons sugar. Let stand at room temperature until juices are running, at least 30 minutes and up to 2 hours. Serve pie cut into wedges, and garnish with sliced strawberries.

from Icebox Desserts

almond-shortbread crust
MAKES 2 EIGHT-INCH CRUSTS

40 **shortbread cookies (about 18 ounces)**
1¼ **cups blanched whole almonds, toasted**
5 **tablespoons sugar**
½ **teaspoon salt**
½ **cup (1 stick) unsalted butter, melted**

1 Preheat oven to 350°F. Place cookies in the bowl of a food processor fitted with the metal blade, and process until fine crumbs form. Add about ¾ cup almonds with the sugar and salt; process until fine crumbs form. Add butter, and process until mixture comes together.

2 Coarsely chop remaining almonds, and stir into crust mixture. Press into bottom and sides of two 8-inch pie plates to form a crust, and bake until they are just turning golden, about 10 minutes. Transfer to a wire rack to cool completely.

tiramisu cups
MAKES 10 SIX-OUNCE SERVINGS

6 **ounces store-bought ladyfingers**
1 **cup strong coffee**
  Mascarpone Filling (recipe follows)
  Mocha Filling (recipe follows)
½ **tablespoon ground espresso, for garnish**

Set aside 5 ladyfingers; break remaining ones into large pieces. To assemble, dip pieces in coffee; fit a layer into bottom of ten 6-ounce cup. Cover each layer with ¼ cup mascarpone filling. Top with another layer of ladyfingers dipped in coffee; cover with ¼ cup mocha filling. Garnish each with a dollop of mascarpone filling, half a reserved ladyfinger, and a sprinkling of espresso. Serve immediately.

from Icebox Desserts

mascarpone filling
MAKES ABOUT 5 CUPS

1 **large whole egg**
3 **large eggs, separated**
1 **cup sugar**
½ **teaspoon pure vanilla extract**
16 **ounces mascarpone, room temperature**

1 In a heat-proof bowl of an electric mixer, combine egg, egg yolks, ½ cup sugar, and vanilla. Place over a pan of simmering water; whisk until sugar is dissolved, about 3 minutes. Transfer bowl to mixer; using the whisk attachment, beat on medium-high until mixture is cool, about 5 minutes. Add mascarpone; beat on low speed to combine. Set aside.

2 Place egg whites in another heat-proof mixing bowl set over a pan of simmering water. Add remaining ½ cup sugar; whisk until dissolved, about 2 minutes. Transfer bowl to mixer; using whisk attachment, beat on medium until soft peaks form, about 5 minutes. Fold a third of egg whites into mascarpone mixture; fold in remaining whites. Refrigerate, covered, until ready to use, up to 1 day.

mocha filling
MAKES 2½ CUPS

¼ **cup plus 2 tablespoons sugar**
¼ **cup cornstarch**
  Pinch of coarse salt
1 **ounce unsweetened chocolate, chopped**
1 **cup half-and-half**
3 **large egg yolks**
1 **large whole egg**
1 **cup hot, strong coffee**
1 **tablespoon unsalted butter**

1 Prepare an ice bath; set aside. In a large heat-proof bowl set over a pan of simmering water, combine sugar, cornstarch, and salt. Add chocolate, half-and-half, egg yolks, and egg; whisk until chocolate is melted, about 3 minutes. Slowly add coffee, whisking constantly.

2 Cook, stirring with a wooden spoon, until mixture is thick enough to coat the back of the spoon, 2 to 3 minutes. Remove from heat; stir in butter. Place bowl in ice bath, stirring occasionally until mixture is cool. Store in airtight container at room temperature up to 1 day.

yogurt pie

MAKES 1 EIGHT- OR NINE-INCH PIE │ **PHOTO ON PAGE 245**

1 cup plain yogurt

8 ounces cream cheese, room temperature

3 tablespoons sugar

1 teaspoon pure vanilla extract

Granola Crust (recipe follows)

3 tablespoons granola, for garnish

½ pint blueberries, picked over, for garnish

Honey, for garnish

1 Place yogurt in a cheesecloth-lined sieve set over a medium bowl; let drain at least 30 minutes. Discard liquid.

2 Place cream cheese in the bowl of an electric mixer fitted with the paddle attachment, and beat on medium-low speed until very smooth. Add sugar and vanilla; beat until smooth. Add strained yogurt, and beat on low until smooth.

3 Pour filling into crust; refrigerate until set, at least 6 hours or overnight. Before serving, arrange granola and blueberries on top, and cut into wedges; drizzle with honey.

from Icebox Desserts

granola crust

MAKES 1 EIGHT- OR NINE-INCH CRUST

3 cups granola

3 tablespoons sugar

1 teaspoon ground cinnamon

6 tablespoons unsalted butter, melted

1 Preheat oven to 350°F. Combine 2 cups granola with sugar and cinnamon in the bowl of a food processor fitted with the metal blade; process until fine crumbs form. Drizzle in butter, and process until combined. Add remaining cup granola; process until combined but still crumbly.

2 Transfer to a pie plate, and press evenly on bottom and up sides. Bake until crust is golden and aromatic, about 10 minutes. Transfer to a wire rack to cool completely before filling.

DRINKS

blue margaritas

MAKES 6 DRINKS │ **PHOTO ON PAGE 229**

4 lime wedges

Coarse salt

Ice cubes, for serving

8 ounces tequila

8 ounces freshly squeezed lime juice

12 ounces Cointreau

5 ounces blue curaçao

½ cup sugar

Rub rims of 6 glasses with a lime wedge, and dip in salt. Fill large pitcher with ice. Add remaining ingredients, and stir well to combine. Divide among glasses.

from Tropical Cocktails

caipirinha

MAKES 1 DRINK

2 limes, washed well and dried

2 tablespoons sugar

Ice cubes

2 ounces cachaça

Slice limes in half. Using a reamer, extract juice from both limes into a tumbler. Place two lime halves in a glass; discard remaining halves. Add sugar, and fill glass with ice. Stir in cachaça, and serve.

from Tropical Cocktails

fresh whiskey sours

MAKES 4 DRINKS

1¼ cups freshly squeezed orange juice

Sanding or granulated sugar, for glasses

2 teaspoons granulated sugar

½ cup freshly squeezed lemon juice

4 ounces bourbon

Ice cubes

Orange or lemon slices, for garnish

1 Prepare 4 glasses: Place ¼ cup orange juice in a shallow dish. Fill another shallow dish ½-inch deep with sanding sugar. Dip rims of glasses into juice and then into sugar. Chill in refrigerator 10 minutes.

2 Place remaining 1 cup orange juice, granulated sugar, lemon juice, and bourbon in a blender. Fill blender to top with ice. Blend until smooth, and transfer to prepared glasses. Garnish with orange or lemon slices.

from Tropical Cocktails

margaritas for a crowd
SERVES 6 TO 8

2 cups sugar
2 cups water
Lime wedges
Coarse sea salt
2 cups freshly squeezed lime juice
2 cups tequila, preferably premium
1 cup triple sec or Grand Marnier
Cracked ice cubes

1 Make simple syrup: Bring sugar and water to a boil in a small saucepan. Simmer, stirring, until sugar has dissolved. Remove from heat; let cool. Refrigerate until ready to use.

2 Rub rims of glasses with a lime wedge; dip rims in a dish of salt. In a large pitcher, combine lime juice, tequila, and triple sec or Grand Marnier. Add chilled sugar syrup, and stir to combine. Add ice cubes, and serve in prepared glasses.

from Fish-Taco Party

mary brockman's favorite pimm's cup
SERVES 8 TO 10

½ pint (6 ounces) strawberries, hulled and quartered
1 lemon, sliced into ⅛-inch rounds
1 lime, sliced into ⅛-inch rounds
1 orange, sliced into 16 wedges
1 750-ml bottle Pimm's No. 1
  Ice cubes
4 cups ginger ale or club soda
1 cucumber, halved lengthwise, seeded, and cut into thin spears
1 bunch fresh mint, for garnish

In a large pitcher, combine fruit with the Pimm's; let stand 3 to 4 hours. Fill each glass halfway with ice. Pour about ⅓ cup fruit mixture into each, and fill with soda; stir. Place a cucumber spear in each glass; garnish with a mint sprig. Serve.

from Country Barbecue

passion-fruit cocktails
MAKES 4 DRINKS | **PHOTO ON PAGE 229**

10 ripe passion fruits, halved
2 cups freshly squeezed orange juice
1 tablespoon heavy cream
1 cup ice cubes
5 teaspoons sugar
⅓ cup white rum

Scoop flesh from 8 passion fruits (about ⅓ cup), and pass through a fine mesh sieve into a blender. Add remaining ingredients, and blend until mixture is smooth and frothy. Pour into 4 glasses. Divide the flesh from remaining 2 passion fruits among each glass. Serve immediately.

from Tropical Cocktails

rosé melons
MAKES 6 DRINKS | **PHOTO ON PAGE 229**

½ ripe cantaloupe
1 bottle rosé wine, chilled
  Fresh mint, for garnish

Using a melon baller or ice-cream scoop, scoop balls from cantaloupe, and divide them among 6 tall glasses. Fill the glasses with wine, and garnish with mint leaves.

from Tropical Cocktails

MISCELLANEOUS

black-olive relish
MAKES 1½ CUPS

1 large shallot, minced (about ¼ cup)
1 tablespoon plus 1½ teaspoons sherry vinegar
8 ounces oil-cured black olives, pitted and roughly chopped
4 sprigs thyme, leaves roughly chopped
½ cup loosely packed fresh flat-leaf parsley leaves, roughly chopped
¼ cup extra-virgin olive oil
  Freshly ground pepper

In a small bowl, combine shallot with vinegar; let stand 15 minutes. Add olives, thyme, and parsley, and stir in olive oil. Season with pepper, and serve.

from A Bastille Day Picnic in New Orleans

cornlight bread

MAKES 1 NINE-BY-FIVE-INCH LOAF

In the South, this is also called cakelike bread, which is exactly how it tastes. It is a slightly sweeter version of traditional cornbread, making it especially delicious when toasted and spread with preserves.

4 tablespoons unsalted butter, melted, plus more for pan
½ cup all-purpose flour, plus more for pan
¾ cup sugar
2 cups yellow cornmeal
¼ teaspoon salt
1 teaspoon baking soda
2 cups lowfat buttermilk

1 Preheat oven to 350°F. Butter a 9-by-5-inch loaf pan; dust with flour, and tap out excess. Sift sugar, flour, cornmeal, and salt into a large bowl. In a medium bowl, whisk baking soda into buttermilk; fold into flour mixture. Fold in the butter.

2 Pour batter into prepared pan, and bake until top is golden brown and a cake tester inserted in the center comes out clean, about 40 minutes. Transfer to a wire rack; let cool 15 minutes before inverting. Cut into slices, and serve.

from Country Barbecue

cucumber relish

MAKES ABOUT 1 QUART

1½ teaspoons cumin seeds
2 cucumbers, peeled and seeded, cut into ¼-inch pieces
2 celery stalks, finely chopped
1 bunch scallions, white and light-green parts only, thinly sliced
2 poblano chiles or green bell peppers, seeds and ribs removed, finely chopped
¼ cup finely chopped fresh cilantro
3 tablespoons freshly squeezed lemon juice
Coarse salt

Heat a small skillet over medium heat. Add cumin seeds; toast, stirring, until lightly browned. Transfer to a small bowl; let cool. Combine cucumbers, celery, scallions, poblano chiles, cilantro, lemon juice, and toasted cumin seeds in a large bowl. Season with salt; serve immediately.

from Fish-Taco Party

fried plantain chips

SERVES 4 TO 6

Select plantains that are firm and green.

8 cups vegetable oil
4 ripe plantains, peeled and sliced lengthwise
Coarse salt

In a large heavy-bottom saucepan, heat oil over medium-high heat until hot but not smoking, about 350°F on a deep-fry thermometer. Working in batches, fry plantain slices until golden and crisp, 4 to 5 minutes. Transfer to a paper-towel–lined baking sheet; sprinkle with salt. Serve hot.

from Tropical Cocktails

perfect hard-boiled eggs

MAKES 6

Adding the eggs after the water is at a boil keeps the yolks slightly soft in the center.

6 large eggs

Prepare an ice bath; set aside. Bring a large saucepan of water to a boil. Using a wire basket or sieve, gently drop eggs into water, and cook exactly 9 minutes. Transfer eggs to the ice bath until they are cool, about 5 minutes. Remove from ice bath; peel, and serve.

from A Bastille Day Picnic in New Orleans

pickled cucumber and cherry relish

SERVES 6

Serve these sweet-and-tart-pickles with Five-Spice Pork Tenderloin (page 190). The relish will keep for up to two days in an airtight container in the refrigerator.

2 cups white-wine vinegar
1 cup water
1 cup sugar
¼ cup coarse salt
1 tablespoon juniper berries
3 dried bay leaves
1 tablespoon whole black peppercorns
2 English cucumbers, peeled, seeded, and sliced ¼ inch thick on the bias
2½ cups fresh cherries, stemmed and pitted
2 small shallots, thinly sliced

1 Place vinegar, the water, sugar, salt, juniper berries, bay leaves, and peppercorns in a small saucepan; bring to a

boil. Reduce heat to medium-low, and simmer 5 minutes. Remove from heat, and let cool completely.

2 Place cucumbers, cherries, and shallots in a large bowl or storage container. Add pickling liquid, and let stand about 30 minutes at room temperature. Remove bay leaves; serve.

from Cucumbers

pico de gallo
MAKES ABOUT 1 QUART

1 medium white onion, finely chopped
4 large tomatoes, seeded and finely chopped
1 large jalapeño pepper, seeded and minced
¼ cup freshly squeezed lime juice
½ cup finely chopped fresh cilantro
   Coarse salt and freshly ground black pepper

Combine ingredients in a large bowl; let stand at least 30 minutes at room temperature to let flavors develop. Serve; or store, covered in plastic wrap, in the refrigerator up to 3 days.

from Fish-Taco Party

pineapple salsa
MAKES ABOUT 1 QUART

This sweet-and-tart salsa is a great accompaniment to grilled fish or chicken.

½ large (or 1 small) pineapple, peeled, cored, and finely chopped (about 3 cups)
1 small red onion, finely chopped
1 small yellow or orange bell pepper, seeds and ribs removed, finely chopped
½ cup finely chopped fresh cilantro
2 tablespoons finely chopped mint
   Coarse salt and freshly ground pepper

Combine first five ingredients in a large bowl; season with salt and pepper, and let stand at least 30 minutes to let flavors develop. Serve, or store, covered in plastic wrap, in the refrigerator up to 1 day.

from Fish-Taco Party

tropical fruit and crab salsa
MAKES 4½ CUPS | **PHOTO ON PAGE 229**

We served this chunky salsa in seashells as an hors d'oeuvre with cocktails, but it would also be ideal as a dip for Fried Plantain Chips (page 203).

1 small onion, finely chopped
1 ripe mango, peeled, pitted, and finely chopped
1 ripe papaya, peeled, seeded, and finely chopped
¼ pineapple, peeled, cored, and finely chopped
1 jalapeño pepper, seeds and ribs removed, finely chopped
¼ cup freshly squeezed lime juice
¼ cup fresh cilantro leaves, finely chopped
½ pound jumbo lump crabmeat, picked over and rinsed
   Coarse salt and freshly ground black pepper

Combine onion, mango, papaya, pineapple, jalapeño, lime juice, and cilantro in a large bowl. Toss well to combine. Add crabmeat, and toss gently. Season with salt and pepper. Serve immediately.

from Tropical Cocktails

whole grilled garlic
SERVES 6 TO 8

6 heads garlic, sliced in half crosswise
¼ cup extra-virgin olive oil
   Coarse salt and freshly ground pepper

1 Heat grill. Drizzle garlic with olive oil, and sprinkle with salt and pepper. Place cut side down on a large piece of aluminum foil, and place on grill. Cook until lightly browned, about 3 minutes. Turn garlic, and fold foil to enclose tightly.

2 Continue cooking until cloves are soft, 15 to 20 minutes, checking often and turning to prevent burning. Remove from grill; let cool slightly. Remove from foil, and place on a serving platter.

from A Bastille Day Picnic in New Orleans

August

BREAKFAST

207 currant scones

207 rolled omelet with ratatouille filling

207 rolled omelet with spinach and goat cheese

208 strawberry-rhubarb coffee cake

STARTERS

208 minestrone

209 tomato and ricotta bruschetta

SALADS

209 caesar salad

209 cobb salad

210 spinach salad with fennel and blood oranges

210 taco salad

210 three-bean salad with
      honey-mustard vinaigrette

MAIN COURSES

211 herbed turkey burgers

211 pizza

211 rigatoni and meatballs

SIDE DISHES

212 chopped tomato salad with toasted garlic

212 creamed fresh corn

212 stuffed eggplant

DESSERTS

213 cantaloupe granita

213 strawberry and pistachio ice-cream cake

DRINKS

214 orange lemonade

MISCELLANEOUS

214 tomato a pezzetti

214 tomato passato

currant scones

MAKES 12 TO 16 | **PHOTOS ON PAGES 225-226**

This recipe was developed by Emily Donahue for Rosey's Coffee and Tea in Hanover, New Hampshire.

4 cups all-purpose flour, plus more for work surface

2 tablespoons granulated sugar

2 tablespoons baking powder

1 teaspoon baking soda

1½ teaspoons salt

1 cup (2 sticks) chilled unsalted butter, cut into small pieces, plus more for serving

1¼ cups buttermilk

1 cup currants

1 large egg, lightly beaten

¼ cup sanding or granulated sugar

Preserves, for serving

1 Preheat oven to 350°F. Line a baking sheet with parchment paper. In a large bowl, whisk together the flour, granulated sugar, baking powder, baking soda, and salt. Using a pastry cutter or two forks, cut butter into flour mixture until it resembles coarse meal. Stir in buttermilk and currants.

2 On a lightly floured surface, roll out dough to about 1 inch thick. Using a 2½-inch biscuit cutter, cut out rounds; place on prepared baking sheet. Reroll scraps; continue cutting.

3 Lightly brush top of each scone with egg; sprinkle with sanding sugar. Bake until scones are golden, 20 to 25 minutes. Transfer to a wire rack. Serve with butter and preserves.

from Summer Breakfast Party

rolled omelet with ratatouille filling

SERVES 6 TO 8 | **PHOTOS ON PAGES 225-226**

¼ cup olive oil

1 onion, cut into ¾-inch pieces

Coarse salt and freshly ground pepper

2 small ripe tomatoes, cored and cut into 1-inch pieces

1 yellow summer squash or zucchini, cut into 1-inch pieces

1 small eggplant, cut into 1-inch pieces

¼ cup loosely packed fresh flat-leaf parsley leaves, chopped

¼ cup loosely packed fresh basil leaves, coarsely chopped

12 large eggs

2 tablespoons water

2 tablespoons unsalted butter

1 Heat 1 tablespoon oil in a 12-inch nonstick sauté pan over medium heat. Add onion, and season with salt and pepper. Cook, stirring frequently, until onion is soft and translucent, about 8 minutes. Add tomatoes, season again with salt and pepper, and cook slowly until tomatoes stop releasing juices, about 5 minutes. Transfer mixture to a large bowl; wipe pan clean.

2 Return pan to medium heat. Add 1 tablespoon oil. Add squash, and season with salt and pepper. Cook until squash is brown but still firm, about 4 minutes. Transfer mixture to bowl with tomatoes; wipe pan clean.

3 Return pan to medium heat. Add remaining 2 tablespoons oil. Add eggplant; cook until browned on all sides and completely soft, about 3 minutes. Return tomato mixture to pan. Simmer over low heat, stirring occasionally, about 10 minutes. Stir in parsley and basil, and season with salt and pepper. Return mixture to bowl, and set aside. Wipe pan clean.

4 Whisk together 6 eggs and 1 tablespoon water in a medium bowl. Season with salt and pepper. Melt 1 tablespoon butter in the sauté pan over medium heat. Add the egg mixture; as eggs begin to set, push them toward the center of the pan with a rubber spatula, letting the uncooked part run underneath to fill the void.

5 When eggs are cooked but not completely dry, slide omelet onto a baking sheet. Spoon half the filling along a long edge; with your hands, carefully roll into a neat log. Using a large metal spatula, transfer omelet to a serving platter with the seam side down. Cover with foil to keep warm.

6 Repeat process with the remaining ingredients. Cut each log on the diagonal into individual pieces, and serve.

from Summer Breakfast Party

rolled omelet with spinach and goat cheese

SERVES 6 TO 8 | **PHOTOS ON PAGES 225-226**

4 tablespoons unsalted butter

1 small onion, finely chopped

6 cups fresh spinach (about 10½ ounces), rinsed well and stems discarded

Coarse salt and freshly ground pepper

¼ teaspoon ground nutmeg

12 large eggs

2 tablespoons water

1 3-ounce log fresh goat cheese

1 Melt 2 tablespoons butter in a large sauté pan. Add onion, and cook until soft and translucent, about 8 minutes. Add spinach, one handful at a time, letting each wilt before adding more. When all spinach has been added, season generously with salt and pepper, and add the nutmeg. Remove mixture from heat, and let stand until cool enough to handle. Squeeze moisture from spinach, and coarsely chop.

2 To make omelet, proceed with step 4 of Rolled Omelets with Ratatouille Filling (recipe above). Crumble half the goat cheese onto each omelet before filling with spinach mixture.

from Summer Breakfast Party

strawberry-rhubarb coffee cake

SERVES 15 | PHOTOS ON PAGES 225, 227

This recipe was developed by Emily Donahue for Rosey's Coffee and Tea in Hanover, New Hampshire.

1¼ cups chilled unsalted butter (2½ sticks), plus more, softened, for pan

¼ cup freshly squeezed lemon juice (about 2 lemons)

⅓ cup cornstarch

2¾ cups sugar

1 pound strawberries, hulled and sliced

1½ pounds rhubarb, trimmed and cut into 1-inch pieces

3¾ cups all-purpose flour

1 teaspoon baking powder

½ teaspoon baking soda

Pinch of salt

2 large eggs

1½ cups buttermilk

1 teaspoon pure vanilla extract

1 Preheat oven to 350°F. Brush a 9-by-12-by-3-inch baking pan with butter, and set aside. Make fruit sauce: Combine lemon juice, cornstarch, and 1 cup sugar in a medium saucepan. Add strawberries and rhubarb; cook, stirring frequently, over medium heat, until rhubarb is soft and liquid has thickened, 15 to 20 minutes. Transfer to a medium bowl; let cool.

2 Make crumb topping: Combine ¾ cup sugar and ¾ cup flour in a medium bowl. Melt ¼ cup butter in a small saucepan over low heat. Drizzle butter over flour mixture; using your hands, mix until crumbly. Set aside.

3 Make cake batter: Whisk together remaining 3 cups flour and 1 cup sugar, baking powder, baking soda, and salt in a

large bowl. Using a pastry knife or two forks, cut remaining 1 cup butter into flour mixture until it resembles coarse meal. In a separate small bowl, mix eggs, buttermilk, and vanilla. Pour into flour mixture; stir to combine.

4 Spread half the cake batter evenly into the prepared pan. Top with half the fruit sauce. Carefully spread the remaining batter over the fruit, and top with the remaining fruit sauce. Sprinkle with the crumb topping.

5 Bake until cake is golden brown, about 1 hour. Transfer pan to a wire rack to cool slightly. Serve warm or at room temperature, cut into squares.

from Summer Breakfast Party

STARTERS

minestrone

MAKES 10 CUPS

7 ounces pancetta or bacon, cut into ½-inch pieces

1 leek, white and light-green parts only, roughly chopped and washed well

1 onion, cut into ¼-inch pieces

2 carrots, cut into ¼-inch pieces

1 stalk celery, cut into ¼-inch pieces

1 russet potato, peeled and cut into ½-inch pieces

1 small zucchini, quartered and sliced lengthwise

½ cup green beans, trimmed, cut into 1-inch pieces

½ cup frozen corn, thawed

6 cups water

1 pint Tomato a Pezzetti (page 214) or canned chunky tomatoes

1 15½-ounce can cannellini beans, drained and rinsed

3 ounces cooked baby shell pasta (about 1 cup)

Coarse salt and freshly ground pepper

Chopped fresh herbs, for garnish

Freshly grated Parmesan cheese, for garnish

In a medium saucepan, cook pancetta over medium heat until browned, about 8 minutes. Add leek and onion; cook until translucent, about 7 minutes. Stir in vegetables, the water, and tomatoes; simmer, uncovered, until vegetables are tender, about 30 minutes. Add cannellini and pasta; season with salt and pepper. Garnish with herbs and cheese.

from Canning Tomatoes

tomato and ricotta bruschetta

MAKES 2 DOZEN | PHOTO ON PAGE 230

- 1 baguette, cut diagonally into ¼-inch slices
- ¼ cup plus 2 tablespoons olive oil
- 1 onion, finely chopped
- 3 garlic cloves, minced
- 1 teaspoon coarse salt
- ¼ teaspoon freshly ground pepper
- 1 pint Tomato a Pezzetti (page 214) or canned chunky tomatoes
- 1 tablespoon chopped fresh flat-leaf parsley
- ½ tablespoon chopped fresh thyme, plus more leaves for garnish
- ¾ cup ricotta cheese

1 Preheat oven to 400°F. Place bread slices on a baking sheet, and brush with ¼ cup oil. Bake until golden brown, 10 to 15 minutes. Transfer to a wire rack to cool slightly.

2 In a large sauté pan, heat remaining 2 tablespoons oil over medium heat. Add onion, garlic, salt, and pepper. Cook, stirring, until onion begins to brown, about 5 minutes. Add tomatoes, parsley, and thyme; increase heat to medium-high. Cook, stirring, until tomatoes start to dry and mixture is caramelized, about 10 minutes.

3 Spread a heaping teaspoon of ricotta over each toast slice; top with a teaspoon of tomato mixture. Garnish with thyme.

from Canning Tomatoes

. . . .

SALADS

. . . .

caesar salad

SERVES 4

- 2 garlic cloves
- ⅛ teaspoon coarse salt
- ¼ pound rustic bread (half a small loaf), crusts removed, cut into ¾-inch cubes
- 1 anchovy fillet (optional)
- 1 tablespoon freshly squeezed lemon juice
- ½ teaspoon Worcestershire sauce
- ¼ teaspoon Dijon mustard
- Freshly ground pepper
- 2 tablespoons extra-virgin olive oil
- 2 heads romaine lettuce (about 10 ounces each), tough outer leaves discarded, cut into 1-inch-wide strips
- ½ ounce Parmesan cheese, shaved

1 Preheat oven to 350°F. In a bowl, mash 1 garlic clove with salt to form a smooth paste. Add bread cubes; toss to combine. Spread cubes on a rimmed baking sheet. Bake until crisp and golden brown, about 20 minutes, turning once.

2 Make the vinaigrette: In a small bowl, mince remaining garlic clove with the anchovy, if using, to form a smooth paste. Whisk in lemon juice, Worcestershire, and mustard; season with pepper. Slowly whisk in the oil until emulsified.

3 In a large serving bowl, toss lettuce with vinaigrette and reserved croutons. Serve immediately, garnished with cheese.

PER SERVING: 186 CALORIES, 10 G FAT, 4 MG CHOLESTEROL, 19 G CARBOHYDRATE, 338 MG SODIUM, 7 G PROTEIN, 3 G FIBER

from Fit to Eat: Classic Salads

cobb salad

SERVES 6

- 1 boneless and skinless chicken breast half
- 2 large hard-boiled eggs, sliced in half lengthwise
- 3 slices cooked turkey bacon, roughly chopped
- 1 head romaine lettuce, tough outer leaves discarded, sliced crosswise into ¾-inch-wide strips (about 6 cups)
- 1 cup chopped fresh watercress
- 3 tomatoes, chopped into ½-inch pieces (about 1½ cups)
- ½ small ripe Hass avocado, peeled, pitted, and cut into ½-inch pieces (about ½ cup)
- ¼ cup chopped fresh flat-leaf parsley
- ¼ cup chopped fresh chives
- 1 ounce blue cheese, crumbled
- 3 tablespoons red-wine vinegar
- 1 teaspoon Dijon mustard
- ½ teaspoon freshly ground pepper
- 1 tablespoon extra-virgin olive oil

1 Bring a saucepan of water to a boil. Add chicken; cook at a bare simmer until it is cooked through, about 15 minutes. Transfer to a plate; cut into ½-inch cubes. Discard one egg yolk; pass other through a fine sieve into a small bowl; set aside. Slice each egg white into six wedges.

2 Spread lettuce on a platter. Arrange chicken, eggs, bacon, watercress, tomatoes, avocado, parsley, and chives in rows.

3 In a bowl, whisk cheese, vinegar, and mustard. Season with pepper. Slowly whisk in the oil. Drizzle over salad; serve.

PER SERVING: 153 CALORIES, 11 G FAT, 77 MG CHOLESTEROL, 7 G CARBOHYDRATE, 210 MG SODIUM, 9 G PROTEIN, 3 G FIBER

from Fit to Eat: Classic Salads

spinach salad with fennel and blood oranges

SERVES 4

3 blood oranges

Juice of 1 lemon

2 tablespoons sherry vinegar

½ teaspoon coarse salt

Freshly ground pepper

1 bulb fennel, very thinly sliced

16 cremini mushrooms, very thinly sliced

1 red onion, very thinly sliced

6 ounces baby spinach

3 slices cooked bacon, finely crumbled

1 Use a sharp paring knife to peel 2 oranges, following curve of fruit; cut between membranes to remove whole segments. Place in a small bowl; set aside. Juice remaining orange into a separate bowl or glass measuring cup. Whisk in lemon juice and vinegar; season with salt and pepper.

2 In a large serving bowl, combine fennel, mushrooms, onion, and spinach. Add reserved orange segments and vinaigrette, and toss to combine. Divide among serving plates, and sprinkle each with crumbled bacon.

PER SERVING: 142 CALORIES, 3 G FAT, 4 MG CHOLESTEROL, 26 G CARBOHYDRATE, 468 MG SODIUM, 7 G PROTEIN, 7 G FIBER

from Fit to Eat: Classic Salads

taco salad

SERVES 6 | PHOTO ON PAGE 235

2 ears cooked corn, kernels sliced from cobs (about 1¼ cups)

3 corn tortillas, each cut into 16 wedges

¾ cup nonfat plain yogurt

2 limes

⅓ cup fresh cilantro leaves

1½ tablespoons finely chopped and seeded jalapeño pepper

½ teaspoon coarse salt

1 pound ground turkey

1 teaspoon chili powder

1 teaspoon ground cumin

½ pound iceberg lettuce, torn into 2-inch pieces (about 3 cups)

1 cup canned black beans, drained and rinsed

2 plum tomatoes, cut into ½-inch-thick wedges (about 1 cup)

½ red onion, cut into ¼-inch-thick wedges (about 1 cup)

1 small mango, peeled, seeded, and cut into ¼-inch-thick wedges (about 1½ cups)

1 Preheat oven to 350°F. Spread tortilla wedges in a single layer on a rimmed baking sheet; bake until crisp, turning once, about 10 minutes. In a medium bowl, whisk yogurt, juice from 1 lime, cilantro, jalapeño, and salt. Set dressing aside.

2 In a medium nonstick skillet, brown turkey over medium heat, stirring frequently, until no longer pink, about 7 minutes. Stir in chili powder, cumin, and juice from remaining lime.

3 Transfer mixture to a large bowl. Add lettuce, beans, tomatoes, onion, mango, corn, and tortillas. Toss to combine well. Drizzle with yogurt dressing; serve immediately.

PER SERVING: 233 CALORIES, 2 G FAT, 37 MG CHOLESTEROL, 32 G CARBOHYDRATE, 207 MG SODIUM, 25 G PROTEIN, 6 G FIBER

from Fit to Eat: Classic Salads

three-bean salad with honey-mustard vinaigrette

SERVES 4 | PHOTO ON PAGE 235

Juice of 2 limes

1½ tablespoons finely chopped fresh tarragon leaves

1½ tablespoons finely chopped fresh chives

1 tablespoon honey

1½ teaspoons Dijon mustard

¼ teaspoon coarse salt

¼ pound haricots verts or green beans, trimmed and cut into thirds

1 cup canned kidney beans, drained and rinsed

1 cup canned cannellini beans, drained and rinsed

1 ounce mâche or watercress, trimmed, rinsed, and dried

Freshly ground pepper

1 In a bowl, whisk together lime juice, tarragon, chives, honey, mustard, and salt. Set aside vinaigrette.

2 Prepare an ice bath; set aside. Bring a medium saucepan of water to a boil. Add haricots verts; simmer until bright green but still crisp, about 2 minutes. Using a slotted spoon, transfer haricots verts to ice bath, and let cool completely. Drain in a colander, and pat dry with paper towels. Place in a large serving bowl. Add kidney beans and cannellini, and drizzle with vinaigrette. Toss to coat. Gently toss in the mâche or watercress; season with pepper. Serve.

PER SERVING: 105 CALORIES, 0 G FAT, 0 MG CHOLESTEROL, 21 G CARBOHYDRATE, 164 MG SODIUM, 6 G PROTEIN, 6 G FIBER

from Fit to Eat: Classic Salads

herbed turkey burgers

SERVES 4

2 tablespoons olive oil

2 shallots, minced

1 pound ground turkey

¼ cup loosely packed fresh mint leaves, finely chopped

¼ cup loosely packed fresh parsley leaves, finely chopped

2 teaspoons Dijon mustard, plus more for serving

 Coarse salt and freshly ground pepper

4 rustic rolls, for serving

 Lettuce, for serving

 Chopped Tomato Salad with Toasted Garlic (page 212)

1 Heat 1 tablespoon oil in a sauté pan over medium heat. Add shallots; cook, stirring, until soft and translucent, about 2 minutes. Remove from heat; let cool. In a bowl, mix together turkey, shallots, mint, parsley, and 2 teaspoons mustard. Season with salt and pepper. Form meat into four patties.

2 Heat remaining tablespoon oil in a large sauté pan over medium heat. Add patties; cook until underside is brown, about 3½ minutes. Turn; continue cooking until other side is brown and center is no longer pink, about 4 minutes. Transfer to plates; serve with rolls, lettuce, mustard, and tomato salad.

from What to Have for Dinner

pizza

MAKES 2 TEN-INCH PIZZAS | PHOTO ON PAGE 237

1 envelope active dry yeast (1 scant tablespoon)

¾ cup warm water

2¼ cups all-purpose flour, plus more for work surface

1 teaspoon salt

3½ tablespoons olive oil, plus more for bowl

1 pint Tomato a Pezzetti (page 214) or canned chunky tomatoes

2 tablespoons coarse polenta or cornmeal

1 cup fresh mozzarella cheese, grated

¼ teaspoon dried oregano (optional)

¼ teaspoon red-pepper flakes (optional)

1 In a small bowl, sprinkle yeast over the water; let stand about 5 minutes until foamy. Combine flour and salt in bowl of a food processor. Add yeast mixture and 1½ tablespoons oil; process just until dough comes together. Turn out onto lightly floured surface. Knead 1 minute; shape into a ball.

Place in a lightly oiled bowl; turn to coat. Cover with plastic. Leave in warm place until doubled in bulk, about 1 hour.

2 Preheat oven to 450°F. If using a pizza stone, place on bottom rack. Pulse tomatoes in bowl of a food processor fitted with metal blade until largest pieces are ½ inch. Gently punch down dough; divide into two pieces. Sprinkle pizza peel or inverted baking sheet with polenta or cornmeal. Stretch one piece of dough on surface to an 11-inch round; rub with 1 tablespoon olive oil. Spread half the tomatoes on top, leaving a ½-inch border all around.

3 Slide onto pizza stone, or place baking sheet in oven. Bake 10 minutes; sprinkle half the cheese on top. Bake 5 minutes more, or until crust is crisp and cheese is melted. Remove from oven; sprinkle with half the oregano and red pepper, if using. Repeat with remaining ingredients. Serve hot.

from Canning Tomatoes

rigatoni and meatballs

SERVES 4 | PHOTO ON PAGE 236

½ pound ground beef

½ pound ground pork

¼ cup fresh flat-leaf parsley, finely chopped

¼ cup freshly grated Parmesan cheese

2 large eggs

6 tablespoons fresh breadcrumbs

¼ cup milk

1½ teaspoons coarse salt, plus more for seasoning

2 tablespoons olive oil, plus more as needed

½ cup dry white wine

3 pints Tomato Passato (page 214) or canned puréed tomatoes

 Freshly ground pepper

1 pound rigatoni, cooked

1 In a bowl, combine beef, pork, parsley, Parmesan, eggs, breadcrumbs, milk, and salt. Form into 1½-inch balls. Heat 1 tablespoon oil in a 6-quart saucepan over medium-high heat. Add half the meatballs; cook, turning occasionally, until brown on all sides, about 5 minutes. Transfer to a baking sheet. Repeat with remaining oil and meatballs.

2 Add wine to pan; stir up browned bits from bottom with a wooden spoon. Reduce wine by half, about 1 minute. Add tomatoes and meatballs; bring to a simmer. Reduce to medium-low; cook, uncovered, 1 hour, stirring occasionally.

3 Remove from heat; season with salt and pepper. Transfer meatballs to a serving dish. Toss pasta in sauce; serve.

from Canning Tomatoes

chopped tomato salad with toasted garlic

SERVES 4

2 tablespoons extra-virgin olive oil

2 garlic cloves, thinly sliced

3 sprigs oregano, leaves picked from stems

½ pound ripe beefsteak tomatoes, cored and cut into chunks

½ pound ripe mixed red, yellow, and orange cherry tomatoes, sliced in half

   Coarse salt and freshly ground pepper

1 tablespoon balsamic vinegar

½ cup black olives, pitted and cut into small pieces

Heat oil in a skillet over medium heat. Add garlic; cook just until golden brown. Remove from heat. Let cool slightly; add oregano. Place tomatoes in serving dish; season with salt and pepper. Pour warm garlic mixture, including oil, over top. Add vinegar and olives; toss well to combine.

from What to Have for Dinner

creamed fresh corn

SERVES 4

2 tablespoons olive oil

1 jalapeño pepper, seeded and finely chopped

8 ears fresh corn, husks and silk removed, kernels cut from cobs

¼ cup heavy cream

1¼ cups milk

   Coarse salt and freshly ground pepper

1 Heat oil in a sauté pan over medium heat. Add jalapeño; cook 1 minute. Add corn; cook, stirring, until kernels are tender, about 5 minutes. Remove from heat.

2 Transfer 1½ cups mixture to bowl of a food processor fitted with metal blade; add cream and milk. Process until smooth, about 3 minutes. Pass through a fine sieve into a bowl, pressing down on solids to extract liquid; discard solids.

3 Return strained liquid to sauté pan; stir to combine. Cook over medium heat until liquid just comes to a simmer. Remove from heat; season with salt and pepper. Serve.

from What to Have for Dinner

stuffed eggplant

SERVES 8 | **PHOTO ON PAGE 230**

4 Italian eggplants (about 1 pound)

2 teaspoons coarse salt

2 quarts water

1 tablespoon plus 1 teaspoon olive oil

2 garlic cloves, minced

2 pints Tomato a Pezzetti (page 214) or canned chunky tomatoes

1 small red bell pepper, seeds and ribs removed, cut into ¼-inch pieces

¼ cup fresh flat-leaf parsley, chopped

1 tablespoon chopped fresh oregano

1 large egg, lightly beaten

¾ cup fresh mozzarella cheese, grated

½ cup fresh breadcrumbs

1 Preheat oven to 350°F. Cut eggplants in half lengthwise; use a melon baller or small spoon to scoop out flesh, leaving a ¼-inch border around edges. Place flesh in a sieve set over a medium bowl; toss with 1 teaspoon salt. Let sit 20 minutes to drain excess moisture. Coarsely chop flesh until pieces are pea-size. Meanwhile, bring the water to a boil in a saucepan; add eggplant shells. Cook 2 minutes; transfer to drain on a baking sheet, cut side down. Let cool slightly.

2 In a medium skillet, heat 1 tablespoon oil over medium heat. Add half the garlic, the chopped eggplant, and remaining teaspoon salt; sauté, stirring occasionally, 3 to 4 minutes. Add 2 cups tomatoes; increase heat to medium-high. Continue cooking until tomatoes stop releasing juices, about 3 minutes. Add half the red pepper and the parsley and oregano. Transfer to a medium bowl; add egg, cheese, and 6 tablespoons breadcrumbs. Stir well.

3 In an 8-by-11½-inch baking dish, mix the remaining 2 cups tomatoes with the remaining garlic and red pepper. Scoop heaping amounts of the filling into eggplant shells. Arrange shells on top of the tomato mixture in baking dish. Mix remaining 2 tablespoons breadcrumbs and teaspoon oil, and sprinkle over eggplant filling. Bake until tops begin to brown, about 1 hour. Remove from oven; serve.

from Canning Tomatoes

cantaloupe granita

SERVES 4

1 ripe cantaloupe (about 3 pounds)
¼ cup sugar
2 tablespoons freshly squeezed lemon juice
2 tablespoons water

1 Using a sharp knife, cut melon in half through stem. Remove seeds with a spoon, and discard. Slice off and discard skin and pale-green flesh. Cut melon into large chunks.

2 Place in the bowl of a food processor fitted with the metal blade; purée until smooth. Transfer to a nonreactive bowl.

3 Combine sugar, lemon juice, and the water in a small saucepan. Cook over medium heat until mixture has thickened slightly. Remove from heat; let cool completely.

4 Stir sugar syrup into melon purée; place in freezer, uncovered, until chunky, about 1½ hours, whisking every 20 minutes to keep it from becoming too solid. Serve, or store in an airtight container up to 2 weeks.

from What to Have for Dinner

strawberry and pistachio ice-cream cake

SERVES 8 | **PHOTO ON PAGE 246**

Berry Syrup (recipe follows)
Yellow Génoise Cake (recipe follows)
1 pint strawberry ice cream, softened 1 hour in refrigerator
1 pint pistachio ice cream, softened 1 hour in refrigerator
½ cup heavy cream
1 tablespoon sugar
½ teaspoon pure vanilla extract

1 Line a 9½-by-5-inch loaf pan with plastic wrap, leaving a 2-inch overhang on each side. Line plastic with parchment paper, leaving a 3-inch overhang on each long side. Set aside.

2 Pour syrup into a large, shallow dish. Cut cake into three strips: two 9½ by 4¼ inches, one 9¾ by 4¾ inches; discard scraps. Soak one smaller strip in syrup 1 minute. Turn; soak 40 seconds more. Using spatulas, carefully transfer cake to pan; press into bottom. Brush with 3 tablespoons syrup.

3 In bowl of an electric mixer fitted with paddle attachment, beat strawberry ice cream on medium speed until smooth, about 30 seconds. With an offset spatula, spread over cake in

a smooth layer. Repeat soaking process with other small piece of cake; place over strawberry ice cream, gently pressing down to level layer. Brush with syrup. Freeze 30 minutes.

4 Repeat process to make a layer of pistachio ice cream and final layer of cake. Cover; place in freezer to harden completely, at least 3 hours or overnight.

5 Before serving, whip cream, sugar, and vanilla to soft peaks in a bowl. Invert pan onto a platter; pull on plastic wrap to release cake from pan. Peel off plastic and parchment. Spread whipped cream on top. Cut into slices, and serve.

from Dessert of the Month

berry syrup

MAKES 2½ CUPS

2 6-ounce containers fresh raspberries
2 6-ounce containers fresh blueberries
1 cup sugar
½ cup water
½ cup Chambord or other berry liqueur, or water

Bring berries, sugar, and the water to a boil in a small saucepan over medium heat; boil 1 minute. Strain through a fine sieve into a small bowl, pressing to extract liquid; discard pulp. Stir in liqueur, if using. Let cool completely.

yellow génoise cake

MAKES ONE 12-BY-17-INCH CAKE

3 tablespoons unsalted butter, melted, plus more for pan
¾ cup all-purpose flour, plus more for pan
½ cup sugar
3 large eggs
⅛ teaspoon salt
½ teaspoon pure vanilla extract

1 Preheat oven to 350°F with a rack in center. Butter a 12-by-17-inch jelly-roll pan or rimmed baking sheet. Line with parchment paper; butter and flour parchment. Set aside.

2 Combine sugar, eggs, and salt in a heat-proof mixing bowl set over a pan of simmering water. Whisk until sugar has dissolved and mixture is warm to the touch, 1½ to 2 minutes.

3 Attach bowl to mixer; using the whisk attachment, beat on high speed until mixture is very thick and pale, 6 to 8 minutes. Gently transfer to a large, shallow bowl. Combine butter and vanilla in a small bowl. Sift flour over sugar mixture in three batches, folding gently after each; add butter mixture in

a steady stream with the third batch. Pour into pan; smooth with an offset spatula.

4 Bake until cake is golden and springy to the touch, 10 to 12 minutes. Transfer to a wire rack to cool completely.

DRINKS

orange lemonade
MAKES 7 CUPS

¾ cup sugar

1½ cups water

4 cups freshly squeezed orange juice (about 12 oranges)

1½ cups freshly squeezed lemon juice (about 9 lemons)

   Ice, for serving

2 oranges, washed and thinly sliced

1 lemon, washed and thinly sliced

Combine sugar and the water in a small saucepan over medium heat; stir until sugar has dissolved. Remove from heat; let cool completely. Combine syrup and juices in a large pitcher or bowl. Add ice and sliced fruit; serve.

from Summer Breakfast Party

MISCELLANEOUS

tomato a pezzetti
MAKES 17½ PINTS, OR ABOUT 9 QUARTS

A pezzetti means "in pieces" in Italian. This recipe is courtesy of Maria D'Ugo. Like most Italian nonnas, she does not add lemon juice to the jars before sealing. If you want, follow USDA recommendations by adding two tablespoons lemon juice to each quart of tomatoes. Sterilize jars before filling.

25 pounds plum tomatoes

2½ tablespoons coarse salt

   Fresh large basil leaves, rinsed and dried

1 Prepare a large ice bath; set aside. Bring a large stockpot of water to a boil. Using a sharp knife, score an X in the bottom of each tomato. Working in batches, place tomatoes in boiling water a few minutes, just until skins start to split. Using a large sieve, transfer to ice bath; let cool slightly. Transfer to a paper-towel–lined baking sheet.

2 Peel tomatoes, reserving skins in a bowl; set aside. Using a paring knife, remove stem from peeled tomatoes; discard. Slice tomatoes in half crosswise; scrape seeds into bowl with peels. Cut tomatoes into ½- to 1-inch pieces; place in a separate bowl.

Pass peels and seeds through a food mill on the finest holes, and add to tomato pieces. Add salt; gently stir to combine.

3 Place a basil leaf in bottom of each jar; fill with tomato mixture. Clean and dry top rim of jars with a kitchen towel. Place lids and rings on jars; twist tightly to seal.

4 Fill a large canning pot lined with a wire rack with water; bring to a boil over high heat. (You can also fit a large stockpot with a wire rack or with a layer of extra ring lids to keep the jars from sitting directly over the heat. The stockpot should be deep enough that jars will be covered with water when they are added.)

5 When water has come to a full boil; place jars in water with tongs or a jar clamp. Boil pint jars 30 minutes and quart jars 45 minutes. Transfer jars to a baking sheet. When completely cool, check to make sure lids are sealed by pressing down on the middle. If lid pops back, it is not sealed; refrigerate unsealed jars immediately, and use within 2 weeks. Sealed jars can be stored in a cool, dark place 2 years or longer.

from Canning Tomatoes

tomato passato
MAKES 6½ QUARTS

Strained (*passato*) tomatoes are traditionally used in making meat sauces for pasta.

25 pounds plum tomatoes, quartered

2½ tablespoons coarse salt

   Fresh large basil leaves, rinsed and dried

1 Place tomatoes in a large stockpot, working in batches, if needed. Bring to a boil over medium-high heat, stirring occasionally. Add salt, and reduce heat to medium; simmer 15 minutes, uncovered. Remove from heat; let cool slightly.

2 Skim off released juices that have accumulated in pot; place in a bowl (you should have 4 to 7 cups liquid). Pass tomatoes through a food mill on finest holes into a separate large bowl. To can tomatoes, proceed with step 3 of Canned Tomatoes a Pezzetti (recipe above).

from Canning Tomatoes

September

STARTERS

217   oysters with champagne mignonette

217   tomato crostini

217   wild mushroom bruschetta

SALADS

218   endive and pear salad with oregon
blue cheese and hazelnuts

MAIN COURSES

218   chicken cassoulet with crisp breadcrumbs

219   grilled striped bass with corn and
clam chowder sauce

219   individual chicken potpies with
mushrooms and peas

220   layered eggplant and polenta casserole

220   sole rolls with spinach and lemon slices

221   yellow-pepper risotto with
shrimp and zucchini

SIDE DISHES

222   potato, zucchini, and tomato gratin

DESSERTS

222   blackberry ice cream

223   chocolate brownies

223   plum galette

223   watermelon and raspberry salad

MISCELLANEOUS

224   barbecue rub

224   oyster biscuits

oysters with champagne mignonette

MAKES ½ CUP | **PHOTO ON PAGE 230**

The addition of Champagne is not essential, but it is particularly delicious. If you are planning to serve some bubbly with your oysters, save a splash for this sauce. The recipe can be doubled or tripled for larger groups.

1 shallot, finely minced
½ cup Champagne vinegar
2 tablespoons Champagne or sparkling wine (optional)
½ teaspoon freshly ground pepper
1 dozen fresh shucked oysters

Place first four ingredients in a small bowl, and stir to combine. Cover with plastic wrap, and place in refrigerator. Serve chilled, spooned over oysters.

from Cabin Style

tomato crostini

SERVES 8 TO 10; MAKES 20

These simple canapés are designed for tomatoes at the peak of their season; select the ripest ones you can find. A combination of red, yellow, and orange tomatoes makes for a colorful presentation.

1 loaf French bread, such as ficelle or demi-baguette, thinly sliced on the diagonal
1½ tablespoons extra-virgin olive oil, plus more for brushing
1½ pounds assorted fresh garden and cherry tomatoes
Coarse salt and freshly ground pepper
½ cup loosely packed fresh basil leaves, plus small sprigs for garnish
¼ cup loosely packed fresh chervil leaves
1 tablespoon red-wine vinegar

1 Heat grill over high heat or preheat oven to 350°F. Place bread on grill or on a baking sheet in the oven; toast until golden on both sides, turning once. Transfer to a serving platter; lightly brush one side of each slice with some oil.

2 Roughly chop or slice tomatoes; place in a large bowl. Season with salt and pepper, and toss to combine. Add basil and chervil, and drizzle with the oil and vinegar. Gently toss again. To serve, spoon mixture over bread; garnish with basil sprigs.

from Cabin Style

wild mushroom bruschetta

SERVES 8 TO 10; MAKES 20 | **PHOTO ON PAGE 230**

When using different types of mushrooms, it is best to cook each one separately, as their cooking times may vary. We used three varieties in this recipe, each portion weighing a third of a pound. If you are using only one or two types, increase the amount of the other ingredients for each batch accordingly. Be careful not to overcrowd the pan or the mushrooms will steam rather than sauté to a golden brown.

1 pound assorted fresh wild mushrooms, such as chanterelle, porcini, and oyster
6 tablespoons unsalted butter
2 garlic cloves
¾ teaspoon coarse salt, plus more for seasoning
Freshly ground pepper
1 cup dry white wine
1 loaf rustic bread, such as levain, cut into thin slices
3 tablespoons olive oil

1 Heat grill over high heat or preheat oven to 350°F. Brush the mushrooms free of grit, and cut into 1-inch pieces. Melt 2 tablespoons butter in a medium sauté pan over medium heat. Mince 1 garlic clove, and add one-third to pan. Add mushrooms and ¼ teaspoon salt, and season with pepper. Cook, shaking pan, until mushrooms are golden and starting to release their juice.

2 Add ⅓ cup wine; deglaze pan, scraping up any brown bits from the bottom with a wooden spoon. The mushrooms should be tender but not mushy. Transfer to a large bowl; season with more salt and pepper, as desired. Repeat process with remaining two types of mushrooms and remaining butter, garlic, wine, and salt, seasoning each batch with pepper.

3 Place bread on grill or on a baking sheet in the oven, and toast until golden on both sides, turning once. Transfer to a serving platter. Lightly brush one side of each bread slice with oil, and rub one side with remaining garlic clove. To serve, spoon mushroom mixture over bread.

from Cabin Style

endive and pear salad with oregon blue cheese and hazelnuts

SERVES 8 TO 10

We used Oregon Caveman Blue Cheese in this salad, but any blue-veined cheese, such as Roquefort, Stilton, or Gorgonzola, would be just as delicious. Toasting hazelnuts in the oven is the easiest way to loosen their bitter, papery skins; it also brings out their rich, sweet flavor. We find that light olive oils work best in this salad, since they have a mild fruitiness that is not as overpowering as extra-virgin varieties.

1 cup hazelnuts
1 tablespoon sherry vinegar
1 tablespoon balsamic vinegar
2 tablespoons light olive oil
2 tablespoons hazelnut oil
  Coarse salt and freshly ground pepper
6 large or 8 small heads Belgian endive
4 ripe pears, such as Anjou, Bartlett, or Comice
8 ounces blue cheese

1 Preheat oven to 350°F. Spread hazelnuts on a rimmed baking sheet; toast in oven until skins begin to split and nuts are fragrant, about 10 minutes. Remove from oven. While still warm, rub nuts vigorously with a clean kitchen towel to remove skins. Discard skins, and return nuts to baking sheet; coarsely chop, and set aside.

2 Make vinaigrette: Place vinegars in a small bowl; whisk to combine. Whisking constantly, slowly pour in olive oil and then hazelnut oil in a steady stream until mixture is thick and emulsified. Season with salt and pepper.

3 Discard large outer leaves of endive, and separate interior leaves. Place in a large salad bowl. Quarter the pears, discarding core and seeds. Using a sharp knife, cut each quarter into ⅛-inch-thick slices, and add them to the bowl.

4 Drizzle endive and pears with half the vinaigrette, and gently toss to coat. Add toasted hazelnuts, half the cheese, and the remaining vinaigrette, and toss to combine. Season with salt and pepper; gently toss again. Crumble the remaining cheese on top, and serve. Alternatively, divide salad mixture among serving plates; crumble blue cheese on top of each.

from Cabin Style

chicken cassoulet with crisp breadcrumbs

SERVES 6 | PHOTO ON PAGE 238

5 garlic cloves
1 tablespoon chopped fresh rosemary
1½ teaspoons chopped fresh thyme
2 tablespoons balsamic vinegar
6 boneless and skinless chicken thighs, trimmed of fat
1 pound dried cannellini beans, soaked overnight in cold water
3 carrots, cut into ½-inch pieces
2 stalks celery, cut into ¼-inch pieces
1 onion, cut into ¼-inch pieces
1 dried bay leaf
2 tablespoons finely chopped fresh sage
1 teaspoon coarse salt
½ teaspoon extra-virgin olive oil
1 cup fresh breadcrumbs

1 Mince 3 garlic cloves; set aside. Mince remaining 2 cloves, and place in a bowl large enough to hold chicken thighs; add rosemary, ½ teaspoon thyme, and vinegar. Add chicken; toss to coat. Cover; refrigerate 1 to 2 hours.

2 Drain beans; place in a stockpot with carrots, celery, onion, reserved garlic, bay leaf, sage, and remaining teaspoon thyme. Fill with cold water to cover by 4 inches; bring to a simmer over medium-high heat. Reduce heat to medium-low; cook, stirring occasionally, until tender, 1½ to 2 hours.

3 Transfer bean mixture to a colander set over a bowl, reserving cooking liquid; let cool slightly. Purée in bowl of a food processor fitted with metal blade. With motor running, pour in about 1 cup reserved cooking liquid until thick and smooth. Return to pot. Add salt; stir to combine.

4 Preheat oven to 375°F with rack in upper third. Brush an 8-by-2½-inch baking dish with the oil. Remove chicken from marinade, and arrange in a single layer in prepared dish. Bake until chicken is cooked through, about 15 minutes.

5 Remove dish from oven. Pour bean mixture over chicken; sprinkle evenly with breadcrumbs. Set dish on a baking sheet. Return to oven; bake until breadcrumbs are golden brown and beans are bubbling, about 30 minutes. Serve hot.

PER SERVING: 446 CALORIES, 5 G FAT, 54 MG CHOLESTEROL, 68 G CARBOHYDRATE, 524 MG SODIUM, 34 G PROTEIN, 18 G FIBER

from Fit to Eat: Casseroles and Gratins

grilled striped bass with corn and clam chowder sauce

SERVES 4 | **PHOTO ON PAGE 239**

Striped bass is also sold as striper; you can substitute it with other firm, white-flesh fish such as black sea bass, trout, or grouper. We serve the fillets over Corn and Clam Chowder Sauce, but they are also delicious on their own, with just a sprinkling of lemon juice.

¼ cup extra-virgin olive oil

3 tablespoons freshly squeezed lemon juice

Several sprigs thyme or oregano

2 garlic cloves, smashed

Freshly ground pepper

4 fillets striped bass, skin on (about 6 ounces each)

Coarse salt

Corn and Clam Chowder Sauce (recipe follows)

Fresh chives, cut into ¾-inch lengths, for garnish (optional)

Lemon wedges, for garnish (optional)

1 Combine oil, lemon juice, thyme, and garlic in a large shallow bowl; season with pepper. Add fish, and turn to coat; cover with plastic wrap, refrigerate 30 minutes.

2 Heat a grill or grill pan over medium-high heat. Remove fish from marinade, letting excess drip off. Place on grill skin side down; season with salt. Grill until skin is lightly browned and starting to crisp. Carefully turn fillets; cook until well browned and cooked through (center will be opaque), 5 to 6 minutes. To serve, spoon clam sauce into 4 shallow bowls, and place fish on top; arrange clams around fish. Garnish with chives and lemon wedges, if desired.

from What to Have for Dinner

corn and clam chowder sauce

SERVES 4

4 dozen Manila or littleneck clams (about 2 pounds), scrubbed

½ cup dry white wine

1 tablespoon unsalted butter

2 shallots, thinly sliced

1 stalk celery, thinly sliced

2 Yukon gold or russet potatoes

2 cups fresh corn kernels (about 3 ears), plus scrapings from cobs

1 sprig thyme

1 fresh bay leaf

1 cup heavy cream

Freshly ground pepper

1 Place clams and wine in a large saucepan. Cover; cook over medium heat until clams open, 6 to 8 minutes. Using a slotted spoon, transfer clams to a bowl (discard any that don't open). Strain liquid into a small bowl, leaving grit and sand behind; set aside.

2 Rinse saucepan; melt butter over medium heat. Add shallots and celery; cook until they begin to soften, about 4 minutes. Cut potatoes into ¾-inch chunks; add to pan along with corn kernels and scrapings, thyme, and bay leaf. Add reserved cooking liquid and cream; stir to combine. Cover; reduce heat to medium-low, and simmer until potatoes are tender, 20 to 25 minutes. Arrange clams on top; cover, and continue cooking just until heated through, about 5 minutes. Remove from heat; season with pepper.

individual chicken potpies with mushrooms and peas

SERVES 4 | **PHOTO ON PAGE 238**

FOR THE POTATOES:

1 pound Yukon gold potatoes, peeled and cut into 1½-inch pieces

¾ pound russet potatoes, peeled and cut into 1½-inch pieces

4 garlic cloves

½ cup nonfat milk

2 tablespoons unsalted butter

Coarse salt and freshly ground pepper

FOR THE FILLING:

2 teaspoons olive oil

1 large shallot, minced (about ¼ cup)

10 ounces button mushrooms, quartered

¼ teaspoon coarse salt

2 teaspoons chopped fresh flat-leaf parsley leaves

2 teaspoons chopped fresh thyme leaves

1½ cups homemade or low-sodium canned chicken stock, skimmed of fat

2 cups plus 1 tablespoon cold water

1 dried bay leaf

4 small leeks (about 1¼ pounds), white and light-green parts only, cut into ⅛-inch rounds, washed well and drained

1 whole boneless and skinless chicken breast (about 1⅛ pounds), cut into 1-inch pieces

½ pound shelled fresh or frozen peas

1 teaspoon cornstarch

1 Make the potatoes: Place potatoes and garlic in a medium saucepan. Cover with cold water; bring to a boil over high heat. Reduce heat to a bare simmer; cook until potatoes are

easily pierced with a fork, about 15 minutes. Drain; pass through a food mill into a large bowl. In the same pan, heat milk and butter. Pour over potatoes; stir to combine. Season with salt and pepper; cover, and keep warm.

2 Make the filling: Heat broiler with rack in lowest position. In a medium sauté pan, heat the oil over medium heat, and add shallot. Cook until soft, about 3 minutes. Stir in mushrooms and salt. Cook, stirring occasionally, until mushrooms are lightly golden and beginning to soften, about 8 minutes. Add parsley and thyme; remove from heat. Divide evenly among four 2-cup ovenproof dishes.

3 Bring stock, 2 cups water, and bay leaf to a boil in a medium saucepan; add leeks and chicken. Reduce heat to medium; simmer until chicken is cooked through, about 4 minutes. Add peas; immediately turn off heat. Using a slotted spoon, divide chicken mixture evenly among baking dishes. Reserve 1 cup cooking liquid in saucepan; reserve remainder for another use.

4 In a bowl, combine cornstarch with 1 tablespoon water; whisk until smooth. Slowly whisk into reserved broth in saucepan; bring to a simmer over medium heat. Cook 1 minute; ladle into baking dishes, dividing evenly. Spoon 1 cup potato mixture on top of each dish; place under broiler until tops begin to brown, 10 to 12 minutes. Serve hot.

PER SERVING: 398 CALORIES, 10 G FAT, 82 MG CHOLESTEROL, 39 G CARBOHYDRATE, 549 MG SODIUM, 38 G PROTEIN, 10 G FIBER

from Fit to Eat: Casseroles and Gratins

layered eggplant and polenta casserole

SERVES 6

2 tablespoons extra-virgin olive oil

1 yellow onion, cut into ¼-inch pieces

4 garlic cloves, minced

2 pounds fresh or canned plum tomatoes, peeled and chopped

¼ teaspoon coarse salt

1 tablespoon balsamic vinegar

1 tablespoon roughly chopped fresh oregano

¾ cup loosely packed basil leaves, roughly chopped

Freshly ground pepper

1¼ pounds medium eggplant, sliced into ¼-inch rounds

1 16-ounce log precooked polenta, sliced into ¼-inch rounds

1 Preheat oven to 400°F with rack in upper third. In a medium saucepan, heat 1 tablespoon oil over medium heat. Add the onion and garlic, and cook, stirring, until soft and lightly golden, about 8 minutes. Add tomatoes and salt; cook, stirring occasionally, until sauce has thickened, about 30 minutes. Stir in vinegar, oregano, and basil; season with pepper. Remove sauce from heat.

2 Meanwhile, heat a large cast-iron skillet or grill pan over medium heat. Lightly brush eggplant slices with the remaining tablespoon oil. Working in batches, lay slices in skillet in a single layer; cook until browned and they begin to soften, 2 to 3 minutes per side. Transfer to a plate.

3 Spoon about ½ cup tomato sauce into a 9-inch square baking dish, spreading to coat evenly. Arrange eggplant slices snugly in a single layer. Spoon about 1 cup tomato sauce over eggplant, and arrange polenta rounds in slightly overlapping slices on top. Repeat with sauce and another layer of eggplant. Finish by dotting with remaining tomato sauce.

4 Cover with foil; bake until bubbling and juicy, about 30 minutes. Remove foil; continue baking until sauce is lightly caramelized and eggplant is tender, about 15 minutes more. Remove from oven; let cool slightly, and serve.

PER SERVING: 156 CALORIES, 3 G FAT, 0 MG CHOLESTEROL, 30 G CARBOHYDRATE, 343 MG SODIUM, 5 G PROTEIN, 7 G FIBER

from Fit to Eat: Casseroles and Gratins

sole rolls with spinach and lemon slices

SERVES 4

1 teaspoon olive oil

1 shallot, minced

¾ pound spinach, washed well, and stems removed

Pinch of coarse salt

Freshly ground pepper

1 large lemon, washed

1 tablespoon finely chopped almonds

1 tablespoon mixed finely chopped fresh herbs, such as chervil, parsley, chives, and tarragon

4 fillets (4 ounces each) gray sole, lemon sole, or flounder

¼ cup dry white wine

1 Preheat oven to 375°F with rack in center. In a large sauté pan, heat oil over low heat. Add shallot; cook, stirring frequently, until soft, about 2 minutes. Raise heat to medium;

add spinach and salt, and season with pepper. Cook, tossing frequently, until spinach is wilted and bright green, about 2 minutes. Transfer to a colander, pressing down to remove liquid. Chop finely; squeeze out remaining liquid. Divide spinach into four equal parts.

2 Slice lemon in half crosswise. Grate zest of half, and combine with almonds and herbs in a small bowl; set aside. Slice other lemon half very thinly into rounds.

3 Lay fillets flat on a work surface, most attractive side down; place one part spinach at the narrow end of each. Roll fish into a cylinder, enclosing spinach. Place in a gratin dish, with lemon rounds in between. Pour wine into dish. Sprinkle a quarter of the almond mixture on top of each roll; cover with parchment paper and then aluminum foil. Bake until fish is opaque and cooked through, 15 to 20 minutes. Remove from oven; serve immediately.

PER SERVING: 152 CALORIES, 5 G FAT, 57 MG CHOLESTEROL, 4 G CARBOHYDRATE, 236 MG SODIUM, 22 G PROTEIN, 3 G FIBER

from Fit to Eat: Casseroles and Gratins

yellow-pepper risotto with shrimp and zucchini

SERVES 8 TO 10 | PHOTO ON PAGE 240

This recipe was developed by Christopher Israel, formerly the chef and a co-owner at one of Bruce Carey's restaurants in Portland, Oregon.

4 yellow bell peppers

6 tablespoons olive oil

2 pounds medium shrimp, peeled and deveined, tails intact, shells rinsed and reserved

Coarse salt and freshly ground black pepper

10 tablespoons unsalted butter

2 large zucchini, cut into ¼-inch pieces

3 quarts homemade or low-sodium canned chicken stock

6 shallots, minced

2 cups Arborio or Carnaroli rice

1 cup dry white wine

½ cup loosely packed fresh basil, finely chopped, plus more for garnish (optional)

1 Place bell peppers directly on a gas-stove burner over high heat, turning with tongs as soon as each side is blistered and blackened. (Alternatively, roast peppers under the broiler.) Transfer to a bowl; cover with plastic wrap. Let stand until cool enough to handle. Peel peppers, discarding skins; cut in half, and discard seeds and ribs. Transfer peppers to the bowl of a food processor fitted with the metal blade. Purée until smooth; set aside.

2 Heat 2 tablespoons oil in a large skillet over medium heat. In a large bowl, season shrimp with salt and black pepper. Arrange one-third of the shrimp in a single layer in skillet. Cook until opaque and cooked through, 3 to 4 minutes, turning once. Transfer to a plate; repeat with remaining oil and shrimp, wiping out skillet with paper towels between batches, as needed. Set aside; cover loosely to keep warm.

3 In same skillet, melt 2 tablespoons butter over medium heat. Add zucchini, and season with salt and black pepper. Cook until zucchini is just tender and bright green, 3 to 4 minutes. Remove from heat; set aside.

4 Place stock in a large saucepan over medium heat. Add shrimp shells, and bring to a boil. Remove from heat, and strain through a fine sieve, discarding shells. Return stock to pan, and bring back to a boil; keep at a low simmer.

5 Meanwhile, melt 6 tablespoons butter in a large heavy-bottom saucepan over medium heat. Add shallots, and cook, stirring constantly, until soft and translucent, about 4 minutes. Add rice; cook, stirring constantly, until grains are glossy and make a sound like glass beads clicking, 3 to 4 minutes.

6 Add wine to rice mixture. Cook, stirring constantly, until wine is completely absorbed by the rice.

7 Using a ladle, add about ¾ cup hot stock to the rice along with a few tablespoons reserved pepper purée. Stir constantly with a wooden spoon at moderate speed until mixture is just thick enough to leave a clear wake behind spoon; be careful not to stir too vigorously, or mixture may become gluey.

8 Continue adding hot stock ¾ cup at a time along with some purée, stirring constantly, until rice is mostly translucent but still opaque in the center, a total of 18 to 25 minutes. As rice nears doneness, watch carefully to make sure it does not overcook. You may not need to use all of the stock and can add smaller amounts as you go along. The final mixture should be thick enough to suspend the rice in liquid that is the consistency of heavy cream.

9 Remove from heat, and stir in reserved shrimp and zucchini, remaining 2 tablespoons butter, and the basil. Season with salt and black pepper, and garnish with basil, if desired. Serve immediately.

from Risotto for a Crowd

potato, zucchini, and tomato gratin
SERVES 4

5 teaspoons extra-virgin olive oil

2 garlic cloves, minced

1 pound Yukon gold potatoes, peeled

1 medium zucchini (about 8 ounces)

2 vine-ripened or other ripe tomatoes (about ¾ pound), sliced into ¼-inch rounds

¼ teaspoon coarse salt

Freshly ground pepper

1 teaspoon finely chopped fresh thyme

2 ounces finely grated Cantal or cheddar cheese

1 Preheat oven to 375°F with rack in upper third. Coat a 9-by-13-inch gratin dish with 1 teaspoon oil, and sprinkle with garlic. Using a mandoline or a very sharp knife, slice potatoes and zucchini as thinly as possible into rounds. Arrange potatoes, zucchini, and tomatoes in overlapping layers around prepared dish; sprinkle with the salt, and season with pepper. Drizzle with remaining 4 teaspoons oil, and sprinkle with thyme and cheese.

2 Cover with aluminum foil, and bake until potatoes are tender, 35 to 45 minutes. Remove foil, and continue baking until top is golden brown, about 25 minutes more. Remove from oven, and serve.

PER SERVING: 175 CALORIES, 11 G FAT, 15 MG CHOLESTEROL, 14 G CARBOHYDRATE, 255 MG SODIUM, 8 G PROTEIN, 5 G FIBER

from Fit to Eat: Casseroles and Gratins

DESSERTS

blackberry ice cream
MAKES ABOUT 2 QUARTS | **PHOTO ON PAGE 247**

4 cups fresh blackberries

1⅓ cups sugar

½ cup water

1 vanilla bean, split lengthwise and scraped

2 cups milk

6 large egg yolks

2 cups heavy cream

1 Combine 3 cups blackberries with 1 cup sugar and the water in a medium nonreactive saucepan. Bring to a boil over medium heat. Reduce heat to a simmer; cook, stirring constantly, until sugar dissolves and berries begin to fall apart, about 4 minutes. Remove from heat.

2 Pass mixture through a fine sieve into a medium bowl, gently pressing down on solids to release as much liquid as possible. Measure out ½ cup solids, and set aside; reserve remaining solids for another use. Measure out 1⅔ cups strained purée, and return it to saucepan; reserve remaining purée for serving. (Store reserved solids and purée in separate airtight containers in the refrigerator until ready to use.)

3 Place vanilla bean and scrapings in saucepan, and add milk. Bring to a gentle boil over medium heat, and remove from heat. Discard vanilla pod.

4 Prepare an ice bath, and set aside. Combine egg yolks and the remaining ⅓ cup sugar in the bowl of an electric mixer fitted with the whisk attachment. Beat on medium-high speed until mixture is pale yellow, 3 to 5 minutes.

5 Using a measuring cup, slowly pour ½ cup hot milk mixture into egg-yolk mixture, beating constantly on low speed until blended. Continue adding milk mixture, ½ cup at a time, beating until thoroughly combined after each addition.

6 Return mixture to saucepan. Cook over medium heat, stirring constantly with a wooden spoon until thick enough to coat the back of the spoon and hold a line when drawn across the back of the spoon with your finger, 6 to 8 minutes.

7 Remove pan from heat; add reserved strained purée, and immediately stir in cream to stop the cooking. Pour through a fine sieve into a medium bowl set in the ice bath; let cool completely, stirring occasionally. Cover bowl with plastic wrap, and place in the refrigerator until thoroughly chilled, at least 30 minutes or overnight.

8 Freeze mixture in an ice-cream maker according to manufacturer's instructions; it should still be slightly soft. Transfer to an airtight container, and stir in reserved ½ cup blackberry solids and remaining 1 cup blackberries. Cover, and place in freezer until completely set, at least 4 hours and up to 1 week.

from Cabin Style

chocolate brownies

MAKES ABOUT 1 DOZEN | PHOTO ON PAGE 247

Lee Posey, baker at Portland, Oregon's Pearl Bakery, developed the recipe for these delectable brownies.

- ½ cup (1 stick) unsalted butter, plus more for pan
- 1 cup sifted all-purpose flour, plus more for pan
- 5 ounces unsweetened chocolate
- 3 large eggs
- 1½ cups sugar
- 2 teaspoons pure vanilla extract
- ½ teaspoon salt

  Blackberry Ice Cream, for serving (recipe above)

1 Preheat oven to 375°F. Brush an 8-inch square baking pan with butter. Dust with flour, and tap out excess. Set aside.

2 Place butter and chocolate in a large heat-proof bowl set over a pan of simmering water; stir until melted and combined. Remove from heat, and let cool slightly.

3 In a large bowl, whisk together eggs, sugar, vanilla, and salt until combined and sugar has dissolved. Whisk in cooled chocolate mixture, and stir in sifted flour.

4 Pour batter into prepared pan. Bake until set but still a little soft in the center, about 20 minutes. Transfer pan to a wire rack to cool completely. To serve, cut into squares, and place one on each plate; top with a scoop of ice cream.

from Cabin Style

plum galette

SERVES 8 | PHOTO ON PAGE 242

- 1 tablespoon all-purpose flour, plus more for work surface
  Pâte Brisée (recipe follows)
- ½ cup finely ground toasted hazelnuts
- 2 tablespoons light-brown sugar
- 1 tablespoon cornstarch
- ¼ teaspoon salt
- 1½ pounds ripe plums (about 5), sliced into ½-inch-thick wedges
- 3 tablespoons granulated sugar
- 1 large egg, lightly beaten
- ½ cup plum or red-currant jam

1 Preheat oven to 425°F with rack in lower third. On a lightly floured work surface, roll out pâte brisée to ⅛ inch thick. Trim edges to form an 18-by-16-inch rectangle; transfer to a parchment-lined baking sheet. In a bowl, combine flour, hazelnuts, brown sugar, cornstarch, and salt; spread to cover middle of dough, leaving a 3-inch border all around.

2 Arrange plums in rows on top, slightly overlapping the slices and alternating the direction of each row. Sprinkle plums with granulated sugar. Fold dough to enclose edges; brush dough with egg wash. Chill 30 minutes in refrigerator.

3 Bake 10 minutes. Reduce oven heat to 400°F; bake until pastry is golden brown and plums are softened, about 30 minutes. Transfer to a wire rack; let cool to room temperature. Before serving, heat jam in a saucepan over low heat, stirring until melted. Let cool a few minutes; brush evenly over fruit.

from Dessert of the Month

pâte brisée

MAKES ENOUGH FOR 1 GALETTE

- 2½ cups all-purpose flour
- 1 teaspoon salt
- 8 ounces chilled unsalted butter, cut into small pieces
- ½ cup ice water

In the bowl of a food processor fitted with the metal blade, pulse flour and salt. Add butter; pulse until mixture resembles coarse meal, about 15 seconds. With machine running, add water in a slow, steady stream; process until dough just holds together. Turn out onto a piece of plastic wrap, and flatten into a disk; wrap well. Chill at least 1 hour in refrigerator.

watermelon and raspberry salad

SERVES 4

- 1 4½-pound-piece watermelon, peeled, seeded, and cut into 1-inch cubes (about 4 cups)
- 1 pint fresh raspberries
  Juice of 1 lemon
- ¼ cup sugar
  Vanilla ice cream, for serving (optional)

Place watermelon in a large bowl. Add raspberries, lemon juice, and sugar; toss to combine. Let stand at least 30 minutes, tossing occasionally, until sugar is dissolved. Serve chilled or at room temperature with ice cream, if desired.

from What to Have for Dinner

barbecue rub

MAKES 2 CUPS

Apply rub at least one hour before cooking.

- 1 cup chili powder
- 3 tablespoons paprika
- 3 tablespoons dried thyme
- 2 tablespoons coarse salt
- 2 tablespoons garlic powder
- 1 tablespoon freshly ground black pepper
- 2 teaspoons ground cumin
- 1 teaspoon cayenne pepper

Place all ingredients in a large bowl; whisk to combine. Store in an airtight container at room temperature.

from Good Things

oyster biscuits

MAKES ABOUT 2 DOZEN | **PHOTO ON PAGE 239**

These biscuits are inspired by the oyster crackers that traditionally accompany bowls of creamy clam chowder.

- 1 cup all-purpose flour, plus more for work surface
- ¾ teaspoon coarse salt, plus more for sprinkling
- 1 teaspoon baking powder
- ½ teaspoon ground cumin or coriander
  Pinch of cayenne pepper
- 2 tablespoons unsalted butter or shortening
- ½ cup milk

1 Preheat oven to 350°F. Place the flour, salt, baking powder, cumin, and cayenne in the bowl of a food processor fitted with the metal blade, and pulse to combine. Add butter, and pulse until coarse crumbs form. With the machine running, slowly add the milk through the feed tube, just until dough comes together.

2 Turn out dough onto a lightly floured surface; knead one or two times, until smooth. Roll out to ¼ inch thick. Sprinkle with salt; press lightly with rolling pin to make it adhere. Using a 1½-inch round or octagonal cookie cutter, cut out dough; transfer to an ungreased baking sheet. Gather scraps; reroll to cut out additional biscuits, and transfer to baking sheet. Bake until golden, about 20 minutes. Transfer pan to a wire rack to cool slightly.

from What to Have for Dinner

STRAWBERRY-RHUBARB COFFEE CAKE | **PAGE 208**

CURRANT SCONES | **PAGE 207**

ROLLED OMELETS | **PAGE 207**

ROLLED OMELET WITH SPINACH AND
GOAT CHEESE | PAGE 207

ROLLED OMELET WITH RATATOUILLE
FILLING | PAGE 207

CURRANT SCONE | PAGE 207

STRAWBERRY-RHUBARB COFFEE CAKE | **PAGE 208**

CUCUMBER SUMMER ROLL WITH
PEANUT DIPPING SAUCE | **PAGE 182**

PASSION-FRUIT COCKTAILS | PAGE 202

TROPICAL FRUIT AND CRAB SALSA | PAGE 204

ROSÉ MELONS | PAGE 202

BLUE MARGARITAS | PAGE 201

WILD MUSHROOM BRUSCHETTA | **PAGE 217**

STUFFED EGGPLANT | **PAGE 212**

OYSTERS WITH CHAMPAGNE MIGNONETTE | **PAGE 217**

TOMATO AND RICOTTA BRUSCHETTA | **PAGE 209**

CHICKEN LIVER PÂTÉ WITH TOAST POINTS | **PAGE 181**

WATERMELON GAZPACHO | **PAGE 183**

ASIAN CHICKEN SOUP | **PAGE 181**

COLD CURRIED BUTTERMILK SOUP WITH
CORN AND POBLANO CHILE | **PAGE 182**

SPICY COLD TOMATILLO
SOUP | **PAGE 183**

CUCUMBER-COCONUT SOUP | PAGE 182

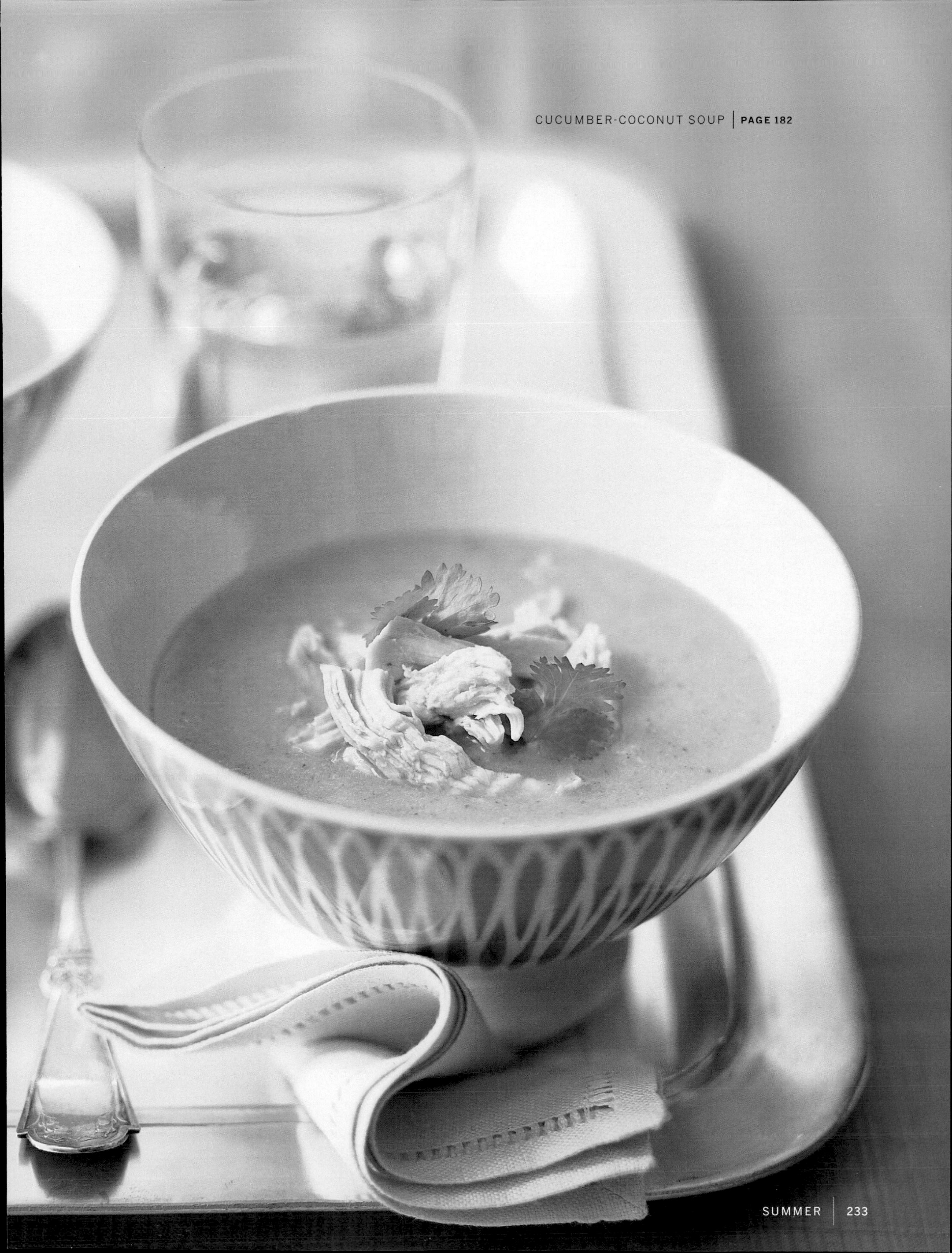

FARRO SALAD WITH ZUCCHINI, PINE
NUTS, AND LEMON ZEST | **PAGE 186**

ORZO SALAD WITH ROASTED
CARROTS AND DILL | **PAGE 188**

LENTILS WITH TARRAGON,
SHALLOTS, AND BEETS | **PAGE 187**

CHILLED SHRIMP AND CHOPPED-TOMATO SALAD
WITH CRISP GARLIC CROUTONS | **PAGE 185**

TACO SALAD | **PAGE 210**

MULTICOLORED PEPPER-AND-BEAN SALAD
WITH RICOTTA SALATA AND HERBS | **PAGE 188**

THREE-BEAN SALAD WITH HONEY-
MUSTARD VINAIGRETTE | **PAGE 210**

RIGATONI AND MEATBALLS | **PAGE 211**

PIZZA | **PAGE 211**

INDIVIDUAL CHICKEN POTPIES WITH
MUSHROOMS AND PEAS │ PAGE 219

CHICKEN CASSOULET WITH CRISP
BREADCRUMBS │ PAGE 218

CUCUMBER, CRANBERRY BEAN, AND BEET SALAD │ PAGE 186

STRIPED BASS WITH CUCUMBER BROTH │ PAGE 191

GRILLED STRIPED BASS WITH CORN
AND CLAM CHOWDER SAUCE | PAGE 219

OYSTER BISCUITS | PAGE 224

RISOTTO HOW-TO

1 Add rice to a large saucepan with cooked shallots. From this point, you will have to stir almost continuously, slowly incorporating the wine and stock, for the next half hour or so.

2 As you ladle each addition of stock into the saucepan, add a few tablespoons of pepper purée, and stir to incorporate fully.

3 When risotto has reached the perfect creamy consistency, remove the pan from the heat before adding cooked shrimp and zucchini, along with butter and herbs.

YELLOW-PEPPER RISOTTO WITH
SHRIMP AND ZUCCHINI | **PAGE 221**

GRILLED MARINATED STRIP STEAK
WITH SCALLIONS | PAGE 191

SAUTEED ASPARAGUS WITH AGED
GOUDA CHEESE | PAGE 193

ROASTED FINGERLING POTATOES
WITH SEASONED SALT | PAGE 192

PLUM GALETTE | **PAGE 223**

LIMEADE PIE | **PAGE 197**

MANGO PANNA COTTA | **PAGE 198**

CRISP COCONUT AND CHOCOLATE PIE | **PAGE 194**

LEMON AND CHERRY TRIFLE | **PAGE 196**

YOGURT PIE | **PAGE 201**

STRAWBERRY CHIFFON PIE | **PAGE 199**

STRAWBERRY AND PISTACHIO ICE-CREAM CAKE | **PAGE 213**

CHOCOLATE BROWNIE | **PAGE 223**

BLACKBERRY ICE CREAM | **PAGE 222**

GRASSHOPPER TARTS | **PAGE 195**

Autumn

HONEY-ORANGE BAKED HAM
SWEET POTATOES WITH CARAMELIZED APPLES
GRAND MARNIER TRUFFLES
PARSNIP-AND-POTATO LATKES

October

STARTERS

253 bagna cauda with broccoflower and toasted country bread

253 curried apple soup

254 miso soup with tofu, spinach, and carrots

SALADS

254 almond-coated goat cheese, frisée, and belgian endive salad

255 autumn greens with apples, radishes, and cheddar frico

MAIN COURSES

255 braised chicken tarragon

256 classic grilled cheese

256 croque monsieur

256 cornmeal-crusted pizza

258 molasses-glazed grilled pork loin with roasted italian prune plums

258 pasta with scallops, garlic, grape tomatoes, and parsley

259 sautéed mushroom, prosciutto, and taleggio panini

259 sesame-marinated tofu with vegetables

SIDE DISHES

260 cranberry-bean salad with butternut squash and broccoli rabe

260 edamame succotash

261 mashed potatoes and celeriac

261 pickled green tomatoes

261 roasted beets

261 roasted bell peppers

261 roasted carrots

262 roasted corn

262 roasted eggplant

262 roasted garlic

262 roasted onion purée

262 roasted plum tomatoes

262 roasted potatoes

263 roasted wild mushrooms

263 roasted zucchini

DESSERTS

263 baked pears with vanilla mascarpone

264 coconut chocolate patties

264 concord grape sorbet

264 cornmeal biscotti with dates and almonds

265 grandmother brinton's raisin bars

265 hermit bars with brown-sugar icing and candied ginger

266 mixed fruit-and-nut cookies

266 peanut butter surprises

267 pumpkin bread pudding

DRINKS

267 chai tea with soy milk

267 pumpkin shake

MISCELLANEOUS

268 focaccia

268 herb-infused olive oil

bagna cauda with broccoflower and toasted country bread

SERVES 4

Food editorial director Susan Spungen likes to serve steamed broccoflower whole and let guests break it into pieces. If you prefer, you can separate into florets before steaming. Broccoflower is a cross between broccoli and cauliflower. Cauliflower can be used instead.

1 head broccoflower, leaves and tough stems discarded
  Coarse salt
1 loaf country bread, sliced 1 inch thick
  Bagna Cauda (recipe follows)

1 Preheat oven to 450°F. Prepare an ice bath, and set aside. Fill a stockpot with 1 inch water, and bring to a boil. Place broccoflower in a steamer insert, and sprinkle with salt. Cover tightly; steam until just tender when pierced with a paring knife, about 10 minutes. Transfer to the ice bath until cool; drain, and pat dry.

2 Arrange bread on a baking sheet; toast until edges are brown, 10 to 12 minutes. Turn; toast until the edges of the other side are brown, about 3 minutes. Serve warm with bagna cauda and broccoflower.

from Easy Entertaining: Pasta Dinner

bagna cauda

MAKES ABOUT 1¼ CUPS

Allow this robust dip to mellow overnight in the refrigerator.

2 tablespoons unsalted butter
3 large garlic cloves, roughly chopped
½ three-ounce tin anchovy fillets, drained and
  roughly chopped
⅓ cup olive oil
1 tablespoon milk

1 Melt butter in a small sauté pan over medium-low heat. Add garlic, and cook until softened but not browned, 1 to 2 minutes. Add anchovies and oil, and reduce heat to low. Cook, stirring occasionally, until mixture is lightly browned, about 20 minutes. Remove from heat; let cool slightly.

2 Transfer the mixture to the jar of a blender, and add milk; purée until thick and smooth, about 2 minutes. Transfer to an airtight container, and store in the refrigerator until ready to serve, preferably overnight and up to 4 days. Before serving, bring to room temperature or gently reheat over low heat.

curried apple soup

SERVES 4

1 tablespoon unsalted butter
2 shallots, minced
2 teaspoons freshly grated ginger
1½ tablespoons curry powder
2 Granny Smith apples, peeled, cored,
  and cut into 1-inch pieces
1 small russet potato, peeled and cut into 1-inch pieces
1 teaspoon coarse salt, plus more for seasoning
3¾ cups homemade or low-sodium canned chicken stock
½ cup heavy cream or milk
  Freshly ground pepper
  Sour cream, for garnish

1 Melt butter in a medium saucepan over medium heat. Add shallots; cook until soft and translucent, about 2 minutes. Add ginger and curry powder; cook, stirring, 1 minute. Add apples, potato, salt, and chicken stock. Bring to a simmer over medium-high heat, and cook until potato is tender when pierced with a paring knife, about 12 minutes. Remove from heat, and let cool slightly.

2 Using an immersion blender, purée just until smooth; do not overprocess. (Alternatively, purée mixture in the jar of a blender, working in batches if necessary so as not to fill more than halfway.) Return soup to pan; stir in cream, and season with salt and pepper. Place over medium heat until soup is just heated through; do not let it boil. Divide soup among serving bowls, and garnish with sour cream.

from What to Have for Dinner

miso soup with tofu, spinach, and carrots

SERVES 4

Be sure to purchase extra-firm tofu for this soup, as it will hold up better in hot liquid than softer varieties. Because the flavor and healthful qualities of miso are affected when boiled or with prolonged exposure to high temperatures, it should only be added at the end of cooking. We used white miso in this soup, as it is lower in sodium, but you can use darker types for a stronger, more pronounced flavor.

- 3 cups homemade or low-sodium canned vegetable or chicken stock, skimmed of fat
- 2 cups water
- 2 carrots, cut into matchsticks (about 1 cup)
- ⅓ pound spinach, stems removed, cut into 1-inch strips
- 6 ounces extra-firm tofu, cut into ¾-inch cubes
- 2 tablespoons white miso
- 1 scallion, sliced crosswise into 1-inch strips

1 In a medium saucepan, bring stock and the water to a boil over high heat. Reduce heat to medium-low; add carrots. Cook until carrots are crisp-tender, about 2 minutes.

2 Add spinach and tofu, and stir to combine. Continue cooking just until spinach is wilted and tofu is heated through, about 1 minute more.

3 Meanwhile, place miso in a small bowl, and stir in ¼ cup cooking liquid until miso is dissolved. Add mixture to saucepan, stirring to combine. Do not let soup boil once miso has been added.

4 Remove from heat. Ladle soup into four serving bowls. Sprinkle each with scallions. Serve immediately.

PER SERVING: 93 CALORIES, 3 G FAT, 0 MG CHOLESTEROL, 7 G CARBOHYDRATE, 660 MG SODIUM, 6 G PROTEIN, 2 G FIBER

from Fit to Eat: Cooking with Soy Products

SALADS

almond-coated goat cheese, frisée, and belgian endive salad

SERVES 4 | **PHOTO ON PAGE 318**

The goat-cheese buttons can be made up to twelve hours ahead and kept chilled. Open the goat-cheese package with kitchen scissors to avoid squashing the cheese.

- ½ cup sliced (not slivered) almonds, lightly toasted
- ¼ cup olive oil
- 1 8-ounce log fresh goat cheese
- 1 head frisée
- 2 heads Belgian endive
- 1½ tablespoons sherry vinegar
  Coarse salt and freshly ground pepper

1 Preheat oven to 375°F. Place almonds and oil in separate shallow dishes. Using unflavored dental floss or thread, slice goat cheese into 1-inch disks.

2 Dip each disk into oil with one hand, and then into almonds with the other; press nuts to adhere. Place coated disks on a small baking sheet (if not using immediately, cover with plastic wrap, and chill in refrigerator until ready to bake). Reserve remaining oil, and discard any remaining almonds.

3 Just before serving, transfer baking sheet to oven. Bake until goat cheese is heated through and bottom edge is sizzling, about 10 minutes. Remove from oven, and let disks stand on baking sheet at least 2 minutes.

4 Meanwhile, tear frisée into bite-size pieces; cut the endive crosswise into 1-inch pieces. Place in a medium serving bowl; toss with reserved oil and the vinegar, and season with salt and pepper. Divide among four serving plates. Using a small spatula, place a warm goat-cheese disk on top of each mound of salad. Serve immediately.

from Easy Entertaining: Pasta Dinner

autumn greens with apples, radishes, and cheddar frico

SERVES 10 TO 12

2 tablespoons sherry vinegar

2 teaspoons Dijon mustard

Coarse salt and freshly ground pepper

¼ cup pumpkin-seed oil

6 tablespoons extra-virgin olive oil

2 Granny Smith apples

6 radishes, scrubbed and trimmed

9 cups mixed greens (about ¾ pound), washed and dried

Cheddar Frico (recipe follows)

1 Make the vinaigrette: In a small bowl, whisk together vinegar and mustard; season with salt and pepper. Whisking constantly, slowly add the pumpkin-seed oil and then the olive oil in a steady stream until thick and emulsified.

2 Slice apples and radishes on the thinnest setting of a mandoline or with a sharp knife. Place in a serving bowl; add mixed greens, and toss to combine.

3 Drizzle vinaigrette over salad mixture, and toss well to coat evenly. Serve immediately with cheddar frico on the side.

from An Autumn Picnic

cheddar frico

MAKES 26

Frico, or "little trifles" in Italian, are very thin and crisp wafers. When sprinkling the mixture in the skillet, don't worry if there are spaces; the cheese will melt into a lacy whole. In Italy, frico are traditionally made with Montasio cheese, but our version is made with white cheddar.

10 ounces sharp white cheddar cheese, grated (about 5 cups)

1 tablespoon all-purpose flour

1 In a bowl, toss cheese and flour. Heat a large nonstick skillet over medium-low heat. Sprinkle about 1½ tablespoons cheese mixture into skillet to form a 4-inch round.

2 Cook until cheese is starting to melt and become firm, 1½ to 2 minutes. Using a small offset spatula, flip; continue cooking until firm and slightly golden, 15 to 30 seconds.

3 Immediately drape frico over a rolling pin; let cool slightly to set the shape. Repeat with remaining cheese mixture. If skillet gets too hot and frico begin to color too quickly, remove from heat for several minutes before proceeding.

braised chicken tarragon

SERVES 4

1 whole fryer chicken (3½ to 4 pounds), quartered, rinsed, and patted dry

Coarse salt and freshly ground pepper

2 tablespoons olive oil

1 tablespoon unsalted butter

4 leeks, white and light-green parts only, halved lengthwise and then sliced into 1-inch pieces, washed well, and dried

⅓ cup chopped fresh tarragon, plus more sprigs for garnish

½ cup dry white wine

2½ cups homemade or low-sodium canned chicken stock

1 tablespoon freshly grated lemon zest

1 teaspoon freshly squeezed lemon juice

1 Season chicken with salt and pepper. Heat oil and butter in a large skillet over medium heat. Add chicken, skin side down; cook until skin is browned, about 5 minutes. Turn, and cook until other side is browned, about 3 minutes. Transfer to a plate; set aside.

2 Add leeks to the skillet, and cook until soft, about 3 minutes. Add tarragon; cook 1 minute. Add wine, and deglaze pan, scraping up any browned bits from bottom, until liquid evaporates. Add stock and zest. Cover; bring to a boil. Return chicken to the skillet, and simmer, covered, over medium-low heat until cooked through, 35 to 40 minutes.

3 Transfer the chicken to a platter, and keep warm. Place the skillet over high heat; cook until sauce thickens, 5 to 6 minutes. Stir in lemon juice. To serve, spoon sauce over chicken, and garnish with tarragon sprigs.

from What to Have for Dinner

classic grilled cheese

MAKES 2 SANDWICHES | PHOTO ON PAGE 321

For a delicious alternative to the classic sandwich, try any of the following combinations: pepper jack and roasted peppers on seeded rye (dry the peppers with a paper towel to avoid a soggy sandwich); muenster with sliced gherkins and spicy mustard on pumpernickel; white cheddar with tomato and bacon on sourdough; fresh mozzarella with avocado on whole wheat; Brie and Dijon mustard on french bread; sliced turkey and Swiss with whole-grain mustard on rye.

4 slices (½ inch thick) firm white sandwich bread
¼ pound cheddar cheese, sliced ⅓ inch thick
   Unsalted butter, room temperature

1 Heat a griddle or large cast-iron skillet over medium-low heat. Place two slices of bread on a clean work surface, and cover each with a layer of cheese; top with remaining bread slices, pressing gently to adhere. Generously butter both sides of each sandwich, spreading it to the edges.

2 Place sandwiches on griddle or in skillet. Cook until golden brown on each side and the cheese has completely melted, 3 to 4 minutes per side, turning once. Before removing from griddle, flip sandwiches to reheat first side, about 15 seconds. Cut each sandwich diagonally in half; serve immediately.

from Grilled Cheese

croque monsieur

MAKES 4 SANDWICHES | PHOTO ON PAGE 320

The croque monsieur literally means "mister crunch." An alternate version, the croque madame, has a fried egg on top, and is often made with chicken instead of ham.

2 tablespoons unsalted butter, plus more for bread, room temperature
2 tablespoons all-purpose flour
1 cup milk
½ teaspoon coarse salt
   Pinch of freshly ground nutmeg
   Pinch of cayenne pepper
   Pinch of freshly ground black pepper
8 slices rustic French or firm white sandwich bread
¼ cup Dijon or whole-grain mustard
½ pound cooked ham, thinly sliced
⅓ pound Gruyère cheese, thinly sliced, plus 1 cup freshly grated (about 2 ounces)

1 Make béchamel sauce: Melt butter in a small saucepan over medium heat until just starting to bubble. Add flour, and cook, whisking constantly, until smooth but not browned, about 3 minutes. Whisking constantly, slowly add milk; continue whisking until mixture has thickened, about 3 minutes more. Remove from heat, and add salt, nutmeg, cayenne, and black pepper. Transfer to a bowl; place plastic wrap directly on surface of sauce, and set aside.

2 Heat broiler. Heat a griddle or large cast-iron skillet over medium-low heat. Smear one side of bread slices with mustard. Layer ham and cheese over 4 bread slices; top with remaining slices, pressing gently to adhere. Generously butter outer sides of each sandwich, spreading it to the edges.

3 Place sandwiches on griddle or in skillet. Cook until golden brown and cheese has melted, 3 to 4 minutes per side, turning once. Transfer to work surface; divide béchamel sauce over tops, spreading to edges. Sprinkle with grated cheese.

4 Transfer to broiler, and cook until topping is melted and golden, 2 to 3 minutes. Serve immediately.

from Grilled Cheese

cornmeal-crusted pizza

MAKES 4 SEVEN-INCH PIZZAS | PHOTO ON PAGE 314

The dough can be made the night before and formed into rounds just before serving. You can use any combination of the toppings below. We particularly like Roasted Tomatoes with fresh mozzarella cheese. Butternut Squash Purée, Caramelized Onions, grated fontina cheese, and Toasted Pumpkin Seeds make for a delicious autumnal pie. We also made a pizza using thinly sliced baby artichokes and eggplant with grated Asiago cheese. This recipe can be doubled or tripled.

2 teaspoons active dry yeast
   Pinch of sugar
⅔ cup warm water
1⅔ cups all-purpose flour, plus more for work surface
¼ cup cornmeal, plus more for pizza peel or baking sheet
1½ teaspoons coarse salt
2 tablespoons extra-virgin olive oil, plus more for bowl
   Roasted Tomatoes (recipe follows)
   Butternut Squash Purée (recipe follows)
   Caramelized Onions (recipe follows)
   Toasted Pumpkin Seeds (page 258)

1 In a small bowl, sprinkle the yeast and sugar over the warm water. Let stand until yeast is dissolved and mixture is foamy, about 10 minutes.

2 Combine flour, cornmeal, and salt in a large bowl. Make a well in the center, and add the yeast mixture and oil. Slowly stir ingredients with a wooden spoon just until dough starts to come together. Turn out dough onto a lightly floured work surface, and knead until smooth and elastic, 7 to 10 minutes.

3 Divide dough into four 4-ounce balls. Place balls in a shallow oiled bowl, turning to coat with oil; cover with plastic wrap, and let rise 1 hour at room temperature or overnight in the refrigerator.

4 Preheat oven to 500°F with a pizza stone on lowest rack. Stretch dough into 6- or 7-inch rounds. Sprinkle cornmeal on a pizza peel or inverted baking sheet. Place dough rounds on top, and cover with toppings, as desired.

5 Slide rounds onto pizza stone, and bake until crust is crisp and golden and toppings are bubbling, 5 to 7 minutes. Remove from oven; serve immediately.

from An Autumn Picnic

roasted tomatoes

SERVES 4

We paired these tomatoes with fresh mozzarella for a delicious pizza topping. They can also be served on their own or used instead of canned tomatoes in soups and pasta sauces.

12 plum tomatoes (about 3 pounds)
½ teaspoon sugar
Coarse salt and freshly ground pepper
2 tablespoons fresh thyme leaves
3 tablespoons extra-virgin olive oil

1 Preheat oven to 275°F. Slice tomatoes in half lengthwise, and place cut side up in a single layer on a rimmed baking sheet. Sprinkle with sugar, and season with salt and pepper. Place a few thyme leaves on top of each half, and drizzle lightly with oil.

2 Roast until tomatoes have started to shrivel and caramelize, about 2½ hours. Remove from oven; let cool until ready to use. Tomatoes can be stored in the refrigerator up to 5 days.

butternut squash purée

MAKES ¾ CUP

Spread the purée on pizza dough for an unconventional sauce, or enrich it with a bit of butter and serve it as a side dish for chicken, pork, or lamb.

1 medium butternut squash (about 3 pounds), halved lengthwise, peeled, seeded, and sliced ½ inch thick
2 tablespoons extra-virgin olive oil
Coarse salt and freshly ground pepper

1 Preheat oven to 400°F. Spread squash in a single layer on a rimmed baking sheet. Toss with oil, and season with salt and pepper. Roast until golden and tender when pierced with a paring knife, about 45 minutes. Remove from oven.

2 Transfer squash to the bowl of a food processor; purée until smooth. Season with salt and pepper. Set aside at room temperature until ready to use.

caramelized onions

MAKES 2 CUPS

These slightly sweet onions are a flavorful topping for pizzas and pastas or as a condiment. To achieve a melt-in-your-mouth quality, the onions need to be cooked very slowly.

2 tablespoons unsalted butter
3 medium to large red onions, sliced ¼ inch thick
1 teaspoon sugar
Coarse salt and freshly ground pepper

Heat butter in a large skillet over medium heat. Add onions, and sprinkle with sugar. Cook, stirring frequently, until soft and golden brown, about 1 hour, reducing heat to medium-low about halfway through. If onions begin to stick to the skillet, add 1 to 2 tablespoons water. Remove from heat, and season with salt and pepper. Let cool before using.

toasted pumpkin seeds

MAKES ½ CUP

We sprinkled these seeds on pizza, but they also add crunch to salads. Eaten out of hand, they are a flavorful snack.

2 teaspoons olive oil
½ cup pumpkin seeds
Coarse salt and freshly ground pepper

Heat oil in a small nonstick skillet over medium heat. Add pumpkin seeds; cook, stirring frequently, until seeds begin to brown and pop, 3 to 4 minutes. Remove from heat; drain seeds on paper towels. Season with salt and pepper.

molasses-glazed grilled pork loin with roasted italian prune plums

SERVES 8 TO 10 | PHOTO ON PAGE 324

Leave a cool spot on the grill for cooking the roasts after they are glazed; turn them frequently to avoid burning.

1 12-ounce jar unsulphured molasses
¼ cup grainy mustard
2 teaspoons dry mustard
Coarse salt and freshly ground pepper
2 boneless pork loin roasts (3 to 4 pounds each)
Roasted Italian Prune Plums (recipe follows), for serving

1 Heat a charcoal or gas grill. In a small bowl, whisk together molasses, grainy mustard, and dry mustard, and season with salt and pepper. Set glaze aside.

2 Tie each pork loin with kitchen twine in four to five places to form a nice log shape. Season liberally with salt and pepper. Sear on hottest part of grill until well browned on all sides, 15 to 20 minutes total.

3 Brush with glaze; cook, turning and brushing with glaze frequently, 5 minutes. Move to cooler part of grill; close lid. Continue cooking, basting and turning occasionally, until an instant-read thermometer registers 160°F, 30 to 40 minutes.

4 Transfer the pork to a serving platter, and let rest 10 minutes before carving. Serve with roasted plums on the side.

from An Autumn Picnic

roasted italian prune plums

SERVES 10 TO 12

2¾ pounds Italian prune plums, halved and pitted
¼ cup sugar
2 tablespoons melted butter

Preheat oven to 400°F. Toss plums in a bowl with sugar and butter; place cut side down on a rimmed baking sheet. Roast until plums are cooked through and caramelized, 15 to 20 minutes. Remove from oven, and serve.

pasta with scallops, garlic, grape tomatoes, and parsley

SERVES 4 | PHOTO ON PAGE 318

Coarse salt
1 pound linguine or spaghetti
5 tablespoons olive oil
4 garlic cloves, thinly sliced
½ teaspoon crushed red-pepper flakes
1 pound bay or sea scallops, tough muscles removed and sea scallops cut in half
1 pint ripe grape tomatoes
Freshly ground black pepper
2 tablespoons chopped fresh flat-leaf parsley, plus more for garnish
1 tablespoon unsalted butter

1 Bring a large stockpot of water to a boil, and add salt generously. Add pasta; cook until al dente according to package instructions. Drain, reserving ¼ cup cooking water.

2 Heat oil in a large sauté pan over medium-high heat. Add garlic and red-pepper flakes; toast until lightly golden and fragrant, about 1 minute. Transfer mixture to a small bowl.

3 Add scallops to pan; sauté until opaque, about 2 minutes. Add tomatoes, and cook, stirring frequently, until the skins begin to split, 2 to 3 minutes; crush a few with the back of the spoon. Season with salt and pepper. Remove from heat.

4 Add pasta, parsley, reserved cooking water, and butter; toss to combine. Divide among bowls, and serve immediately; garnish with reserved garlic and parsley.

from Easy Entertaining: Pasta Dinner

sautéed mushroom, prosciutto, and taleggio panini

MAKES 4 SANDWICHES

Panini are Italian sandwiches that are typically made in a sandwich press. You can achieve the same result by placing a cast-iron or other heavy skillet on top of the sandwiches as they are cooking. Taleggio is a semisoft ripened cow's-milk cheese with a distinctive pungency. For a milder flavor, you can substitute either Brie or Bel Paese.

2 tablespoons extra-virgin olive oil, plus more for brushing

1 shallot, thinly sliced

1 pound fresh wild mushrooms, such as chanterelle, shiitake, or oyster, brushed clean and thinly sliced

1 teaspoon chopped fresh thyme or oregano leaves
   Coarse salt and freshly ground pepper

½ loaf Focaccia (page 268) or 1 loaf ciabatta bread, cut into quarters

2 ounces prosciutto, thinly sliced

½ pound Taleggio cheese, sliced ¼ inch thick

1 Heat oil in a large sauté pan over medium heat. Add shallot, and cook until soft and translucent, about 2 minutes. Raise heat to medium-high; add mushrooms. Cook, stirring occasionally, until they are golden brown, and most of the juices have evaporated, about 8 minutes. Add thyme or oregano; season with salt and pepper. Remove from heat.

2 Preheat oven to 200°F. Heat a griddle or large cast-iron skillet over medium-low heat. Slice bread in half horizontally. Layer each of the bottom halves with mushroom mixture, prosciutto, and cheese. Top with remaining bread halves.

3 Brush outer sides of bread with oil, spreading it to the edges. Place two sandwiches in skillet or on griddle, and weight with a sandwich press or the bottom of another skillet. Cook until golden brown on first side, 3 to 4 minutes; turn, and continue cooking until other side is golden and the cheese has completely melted, 3 to 4 minutes more. Transfer to a baking sheet, and keep warm in the oven while making remaining sandwiches. Serve immediately.

from Grilled Cheese

sesame-marinated tofu with vegetables

SERVES 4

You can substitute Chinese broccoli with broccolini or dark, leafy greens such as kale, turnip, or mustard greens. Tamari is a thicker, milder type of soy sauce. The tofu is pressed before marinating to remove excess moisture.

FOR THE TOFU:

16 ounces extra-firm tofu

1 teaspoon Dijon mustard

3 to 4 teaspoons toasted sesame seeds

1 teaspoon black sesame seeds (optional)

1 garlic clove, minced

3 tablespoons low-sodium tamari soy sauce

FOR THE STIR-FRIED VEGETABLES:

3½ teaspoons canola oil

1 tablespoon freshly minced ginger

2 garlic cloves, minced

12 shiitake mushrooms (about 4 ounces), stems removed, quartered

1 red bell pepper, ribs and seeds removed, sliced into ¼-inch strips

12 ounces Chinese broccoli (2 small bunches), cut crosswise into 2-inch pieces

4 scallions, sliced crosswise into 2-inch pieces

2 teaspoons low-sodium tamari soy sauce

½ teaspoon sesame oil
   Freshly ground black pepper

1 Press tofu: Slice tofu into 1-inch slabs, and place in a single layer on a baking sheet lined with cheesecloth or paper towels. Cover with another layer of cheesecloth or paper towels, and place another baking sheet or plate on top. Weight evenly with canned goods or other heavy items. Let stand about 30 minutes. Drain off liquid, and pat tofu dry with paper towels.

2 In a large shallow dish, combine mustard, sesame seeds, garlic, and soy sauce. Place tofu in dish, and turn once to coat evenly with marinade. Let marinate about 20 minutes at room temperature.

3 Heat a 12-inch nonstick sauté pan or a wok over medium-high heat, and add 1½ teaspoons canola oil to pan, swirling pan to coat. Add tofu; cook until lightly browned, about 1½ minutes per side. Transfer tofu to a platter; cover loosely with aluminum foil to keep warm.

4 In same pan or wok, heat remaining 2 teaspoons canola oil. Add ginger and garlic; cook, stirring constantly, until

aromatic, about 30 seconds. Add mushrooms, red pepper, Chinese broccoli, and scallions; cook, stirring constantly, until vegetables are crisp-tender and bright, about 7 minutes. Add soy sauce and sesame oil, and stir to combine. Season with pepper, and serve immediately spooned over the tofu.

PER SERVING: 191 CALORIES, 10 G FAT, 0 MG CHOLESTEROL, 13 G CARBOHYDRATE, 655 MG SODIUM, 14 G PROTEIN, 5 G FIBER

from Fit to Eat: Cooking with Soy Products

....

SIDE DISHES

....

cranberry-bean salad with butternut squash and broccoli rabe

SERVES 10 TO 12 | PHOTO ON PAGE 315

- 1 onion
- 1 dried bay leaf
- 4 to 5 whole black peppercorns
- 3 quarts water
- 2½ pounds fresh cranberry beans, shelled (about 3 cups)
- 5 tablespoons olive oil
  Coarse salt and freshly ground pepper
- 4 slices bacon (4 ounces)
- 1 small butternut squash (about 1¾ pounds), peeled, seeded, and cut into ½-inch pieces
- 4 garlic cloves, minced
- 1 bunch broccoli rabe, washed and trimmed (about 1 pound)

1 Using a sharp knife, slice off stem end of onion, and score shallow slits all over, making sure it stays intact. Place in a large saucepan with the bay leaf and the peppercorns; add the water. Bring to a boil; reduce heat, and simmer 20 minutes. Add beans; simmer until cooked through, about 15 minutes.

2 Drain beans, reserving 1 tablespoon cooking liquid. In a medium bowl, toss beans with 1 tablespoon oil and reserved cooking liquid; season with salt and pepper. Set aside.

3 Cook bacon in a large skillet over medium heat until crisp. Transfer to paper towels to drain. Crumble into pieces; set aside. Pour off all but 2 tablespoons rendered bacon fat, and return the skillet to medium heat. Working in batches if necessary, sauté squash until cooked through and golden, about 10 minutes. Season with salt and pepper, and transfer to a bowl; set aside.

4 Heat 3 tablespoons oil in the same skillet over medium heat. Add garlic, and sauté until just golden, 1 to 2 minutes.

Add broccoli rabe; sauté until wilted and heated through, about 5 minutes. Season with salt and pepper.

5 Add beans and squash to skillet, and cook just until heated through. Drizzle with remaining tablespoon oil, and season with salt and pepper. Transfer to a serving bowl. Sprinkle reserved bacon on top, and serve.

from An Autumn Picnic

edamame succotash

SERVES 6

If you can't find fresh edamame, the frozen kind works just as well. Look for it in the freezer section of your grocery store.

- 1 pound butternut squash, peeled, seeded, and cut into ½-inch pieces (about 3 cups)
- 2 ounces green beans, sliced on the bias into 1-inch pieces
- 2 teaspoons extra-virgin olive oil
- 1 small onion, finely chopped
- 1 garlic clove, minced
- ½ cup homemade or low-sodium chicken stock, skimmed of fat
- 1 cup fresh or frozen corn kernels
- 1 cup fresh or frozen shelled edamame
- 1 teaspoon roughly chopped fresh thyme
  Pinch of coarse salt
  Freshly ground pepper
- 1 tablespoon roughly chopped fresh flat-leaf parsley

1 In a steamer basket set over a pan of simmering water, steam squash until just tender enough to be easily pierced with a sharp knife, about 7 minutes. Transfer to a plate; set aside. Add green beans to basket; steam until crisp-tender, about 3 minutes. Remove from heat; set aside.

2 In a 10-inch sauté pan, heat oil over medium heat. Add onion and garlic; cook, stirring occasionally, until soft and lightly golden, about 3 minutes. Add chicken stock, and bring to a simmer. Add corn and edamame; cook, stirring occasionally, until brightly colored and crisp-tender, about 3 minutes.

3 Add thyme with steamed squash and green beans; cook until heated through, about 3 minutes, stirring to combine. Season with salt and pepper, and sprinkle with parsley. Serve.

PER SERVING: 118 CALORIES, 3 G FAT, 0 MG CHOLESTEROL, 20 G CARBOHYDRATE, 184 MG SODIUM, 5 G PROTEIN, 2 G FIBER

from Fit to Eat: Cooking with Soy Products

mashed potatoes and celeriac

SERVES 4

Celeriac is also called celery root or celery knob.

1 pound russet potatoes, peeled and sliced 1½ inches thick
1 pound celeriac, peeled and sliced 1½ inches thick
  Coarse salt
½ cup sour cream
2 tablespoons unsalted butter
¼ teaspoon freshly ground nutmeg
  Freshly ground pepper

1 Place potatoes and celeriac in a medium saucepan, and fill with enough cold water to cover by about 2 inches. Bring to a boil over high heat; add salt generously. Reduce heat to a simmer, and cook until vegetables are tender when pierced with a paring knife, 20 to 25 minutes. Drain in a colander.

2 Pass potatoes and celeriac through a ricer or food mill into a serving bowl. Add sour cream and butter, and stir until combined. Stir in nutmeg, and season with salt and pepper. Serve immediately.

from What to Have for Dinner

pickled green tomatoes

SERVES 10 TO 12

If you are unable to find green tomatoes, you can use other types. The tomatoes can be refrigerated, in brining liquid, in airtight containers for up to ten days.

¾ cup sugar
½ cup salt
1 32-ounce bottle cider vinegar
1 teaspoon whole black peppercorns
3 sprigs tarragon
3 garlic cloves
12 green tomatoes (about 3 pounds), washed and quartered

Bring all ingredients except tomatoes to a boil in a stockpot. Reduce heat, and simmer 15 minutes. Add tomatoes; cook 3 minutes. Remove from heat, and let cool completely in the brining liquid. Serve chilled or at room temperature.

from An Autumn Picnic

roasted beets

SERVES 4 TO 6 | **PHOTO ON PAGE 328**

Roasted beets taste wonderful either warm or cold. They are delightful tossed in a salad with blue cheese.

5 to 6 medium beets (about 2 pounds)
2½ tablespoons olive oil
1½ tablespoons coarse salt

Preheat oven to 450°F. Trim stems and roots from beets. Place on parchment-lined foil, drizzle with olive oil, and sprinkle with salt. Close foil into a packet. Transfer to the oven, and roast until tender, about 1 hour. Remove from oven; let cool slightly, and then slip off skins.

from Roasting Vegetables 101

roasted bell peppers

MAKES 4

Roasted peppers are flavorful right from the oven, or they can be stored in olive oil in the refrigerator, for up to two weeks.

4 large bell peppers, halved, seeds and ribs removed

Preheat oven to 500°F. Place peppers cut side down on a baking sheet, and roast until charred, about 15 minutes. Remove from oven. Place in a large bowl, and cover with plastic wrap; let cool. Slip off charred skins, and slice peppers. Peppers can be stored, covered in olive oil with herbs, if desired, in the refrigerator up to 10 days.

from Roasting Vegetables 101

roasted carrots

SERVES 4

The perfect companion to chicken or beef, roasted carrots have a sweet and earthy flavor.

8 carrots (about 1 pound)
2 tablespoons olive oil
  Coarse salt and freshly ground pepper

Preheat oven to 400°F. Peel carrots, and toss in a baking pan with olive oil, salt, and pepper. Roast, turning occasionally, until tender and caramelized to an amber brown, about 35 minutes. Remove from oven; serve hot.

from Roasting Vegetables 101

roasted corn

MAKES 6 EARS OF CORN

Roasting ears in their husks gives corn an appealing smokiness.

6 **ears corn, in husks**
Fresh herb sprigs, such as thyme, sage, and marjoram
Coarse salt
5 **tablespoons unsalted butter**

Preheat oven to 450°F. Slit husks on one side, and peel back from corn; remove corn silk. Fold husks back around corn; tuck in a few herb sprigs, a sprinkle of salt, and bits of butter. Tie with kitchen twine, and place in a baking pan. Roast until tender, about 25 minutes. Remove from oven; remove the husks, and serve.

from Roasting Vegetables 101

roasted eggplant

MAKES ABOUT 2 CUPS

Eggplant can be roasted whole or in slices, like zucchini; toss slices on a baking sheet with olive oil, salt, and pepper before roasting. The flesh can be used in recipes such as baba ghanoush and eggplant caviar.

2 **medium or 3 small eggplants (about 2 pounds)**

Preheat oven to 400°F. Pierce the skin in several places. Roast on a baking sheet until soft, 35 to 45 minutes. Remove from oven, and let cool. Slice eggplants open, and scoop out flesh.

from Roasting Vegetables 101

roasted garlic

MAKES 6 HEADS | PHOTO ON PAGE 328

Rather than the pungent flavor it has when raw, roasted garlic is mellow, sweet, and nutty. It's delicious spread on bread or mixed with cooked vegetables.

6 **heads garlic, tops trimmed by about ¼ inch**
2 **tablespoons olive oil**

Preheat oven to 425°F. Place garlic in a baking dish, drizzle with olive oil, and cover with foil. Roast until soft, about 40 minutes. Remove from oven; let cool. Squeeze cloves out of skins. Whole cloves can be stored, tightly wrapped, in the refrigerator up to 1 week.

from Roasting Vegetables 101

roasted onion purée

MAKES 2½ CUPS PUREE | PHOTO ON PAGE 328

Puréed roasted onions pep up steaks and sandwiches.

9 **medium onions (about 3 pounds)**
3 **tablespoons olive oil**
Coarse salt and freshly ground pepper

Preheat oven to 400°F. Cut onions into wedges, leaving root ends intact; peel. Toss in olive oil in a baking pan; sprinkle with salt and pepper. Roast until caramelized, about 50 minutes, turning occasionally. Transfer onions to the bowl of a food processor; purée until smooth. Refrigerate up to 1 week.

from Roasting Vegetables 101

roasted plum tomatoes

MAKES 20 HALVES | PHOTO ON PAGE 328

Roasted tomatoes are excellent alone or in salads and pastas.

10 **plum tomatoes (about 2¼ pounds)**
2 **tablespoons olive oil**
Fresh herbs, such as marjoram, thyme, and rosemary
Coarse salt and freshly ground pepper

Preheat oven to 400°F. Line a baking sheet with parchment paper, and set aside. Cut tomatoes in half; remove seeds and stems, and discard. Place on baking sheet, cut side up. Drizzle with olive oil and garnish with herbs. Sprinkle with salt and pepper. Roast 5 minutes; reduce heat to 325°F, and continue roasting 1 hour 45 minutes. Remove from oven, and let cool. If not using immediately, store the tomatoes, tightly covered, in refrigerator up to 1 week.

from Roasting Vegetables 101

roasted potatoes

SERVES 4 TO 6

With crackled skins and soft interiors, these are a welcome addition to salads and a traditional side dish for meat.

2 **pounds red or white small potatoes, scrubbed and dried**
4 **tablespoons olive oil**
Coarse salt and freshly ground pepper
Fresh herbs, such as oregano, thyme, and rosemary, finely chopped

Preheat oven to 425°F. On a baking sheet, toss potatoes with olive oil, salt, pepper, and herbs. Roast until tender, turning occasionally, about 35 minutes. Remove from oven. Serve potatoes hot or cold.

from Roasting Vegetables 101

roasted wild mushrooms

SERVES 6 | **PHOTO ON PAGE 329**

Serve these smoky mushrooms with chicken or pork.

1½ **pounds wild mushrooms, trimmed and brushed clean**
¼ **cup olive oil**
2 **tablespoons unsalted butter, melted**
Coarse salt and freshly ground pepper
1 **to 2 tablespoons fresh thyme leaves**

Preheat oven to 400°F. In a 9-by-13-inch baking dish, toss mushrooms with oil and butter. Season with salt and pepper, and sprinkle with thyme. Roast until golden and cooked through, about 40 minutes. Remove from oven; serve hot.

from An Autumn Picnic

roasted zucchini

SERVES 4

Roasting zucchini enhances their delicate flavor while giving them a slightly charred, crisp exterior.

3 **medium zucchini (about 1½ pounds)**
2 **tablespoons olive oil**
Coarse salt and freshly ground pepper

Preheat oven to 450°F. Cut zucchini into 1-inch-thick rounds. Toss in a baking pan with olive oil, salt, and pepper. Roast, turning occasionally, until caramelized, about 15 minutes. Remove from oven; serve hot.

from Roasting Vegetables 101

baked pears with vanilla mascarpone

SERVES 4

If using Bosc pears, buy only ripe ones; Anjou, which are juicier, can still be slightly firm. Avoid enamel baking dishes, as they cause the syrup to burn.

4 **Anjou or Bosc pears**
1 **tablespoon unsalted butter, softened**
2 **tablespoons granulated sugar**
1 **cup red wine**
4 **sprigs thyme (optional)**
Vanilla Mascarpone (recipe follows)
Store-bought biscotti

1 Preheat oven to 425°F. Slice off bottom end of each pear just enough so that it will stand upright. Using a melon baller or small spoon, remove seeds from the bottom. Peel upper half, leaving stem intact, and pat dry with a paper towel. Rub butter over peeled part of each pear, and arrange pears in a small baking dish (about 7 by 11 inches) so they are standing. Sprinkle with the sugar.

2 Pour wine into baking dish; add thyme sprigs, if using. Bake until pears are soft when pierced with a paring knife and well browned, about 45 minutes; using a spoon, baste pears occasionally with the wine, adding a bit of water as needed to prevent liquid from evaporating. Remove from oven.

3 To serve, spoon some of the pan juices into each serving dish, and place a pear on top. Serve with a dollop of mascarpone and several biscotti on the side.

from Easy Entertaining: Pasta Dinner

vanilla mascarpone

MAKES ABOUT 1 CUP

For the creamiest results, allow the mascarpone to stand at room temperature for fifteen minutes before serving.

½ **vanilla bean, split and scraped**
8 **ounces mascarpone cheese**
2 **tablespoons confectioners' sugar**

Combine vanilla bean scrapings, mascarpone, and sugar in a small bowl, and stir together with a wooden spoon.

coconut chocolate patties

MAKES ABOUT 20 | PHOTO ON PAGE 330

These delicious no-bake cookies can be assembled quickly and then stored in the refrigerator for up to three days.

1½ cups sweetened shredded coconut
3 drops pure almond extract
3¾ ounces semisweet chocolate, melted

1 Preheat oven to 350°F. Line a rimmed baking sheet with parchment paper, and spread coconut in a single layer on parchment. Place in oven until golden and toasted, about 10 minutes, stirring occasionally to color evenly. Remove from oven; let cool completely.

2 In a medium bowl, combine toasted coconut, almond extract, and melted chocolate. Stir gently until combined. Press about 1 tablespoon coconut mixture onto a parchment-lined baking sheet. Repeat with the remaining mixture. Place in the refrigerator until cookies are set, about 20 minutes. Store in refrigerator until ready to serve.

from What to Have for Dinner

concord grape sorbet

SERVES 10 TO 12 | PHOTO ON PAGE 331

This sorbet gets its intense purple hue from Concord grapes, which have a deep blue-black skin. The longer you process it in the ice-cream maker, the lighter and fluffier your final product will be.

1½ pounds Concord grapes (1 quart container)
¼ cup water
Simple Sorbet Syrup (recipe follows)
1½ tablespoons freshly squeezed lemon juice

1 Prepare an ice bath; set aside. Combine grapes and the water in a medium saucepan. Cook over medium-high heat until the liquid begins to bubble and grapes start releasing liquid, about 4 minutes. Reduce heat, and simmer until juices are dark purple and grapes begin to break apart, about 3 minutes more.

2 Pass the mixture through a food mill and then through a fine sieve into a large bowl set in the ice bath; discard solids. Stir frequently until completely cool. Stir in the simple syrup and the lemon juice.

3 Transfer mixture to an ice-cream maker, and freeze according to manufacturer's instructions. Place in an airtight container, and store in freezer until ready to serve, up to 2 weeks.

from An Autumn Picnic

simple sorbet syrup

MAKES ABOUT ⅔ CUP

Simple syrup can be stored in an airtight container in the refrigerator for up to two months.

⅔ cup sugar
⅔ cup water

Prepare an ice bath; set aside. In a large saucepan, combine sugar and the water; bring to a boil over medium-high heat. Cook until sugar has completely dissolved, about 10 minutes. Transfer to a medium bowl set over the ice bath. Let stand, stirring occasionally, until chilled before using or storing.

cornmeal biscotti with dates and almonds

MAKES ABOUT 2 DOZEN

These flavorful biscotti may be stored in an airtight container at room temperature for up to two weeks. Let them cool completely on the baking sheet so they get perfectly crisp and dry, ideal for dunking into espresso or dessert wine.

1¼ cups all-purpose flour
1¼ cups yellow cornmeal
½ teaspoon baking powder
½ teaspoon salt
6 tablespoons unsalted butter, room temperature
1 cup sugar
2 large eggs
2 teaspoons pure orange extract
1 tablespoon freshly grated orange zest
1 cup chopped pitted dates
1 cup chopped almonds
1 teaspoon anise seed

1 Preheat oven to 350°F with a rack in the center. Line a baking sheet with parchment paper, and set aside. Combine flour, cornmeal, baking powder, and salt in a medium bowl, and mix thoroughly with a whisk or fork; set aside.

2 In the bowl of an electric mixer fitted with the paddle attachment, cream the butter on medium speed until smooth. Add the sugar, and beat until light and fluffy. Beat in eggs one at a time until well combined; beat in orange extract.

3 Add the flour mixture all at once, and beat on low speed until just combined. Add orange zest, dates, almonds, and anise seed, and beat until combined.

4 Transfer dough to prepared baking sheet; using your hands, pat into a flattened log that is roughly 14 by 3½ inches. Bake until firm, lightly browned, and slightly cracked on top, 30 to 35 minutes. Remove from oven; let cool on baking sheet 15 minutes.

5 Transfer log to a cutting board, leaving parchment on sheet. Using a serrated knife, cut log crosswise into ½-inch-thick slices. Lay slices flat on a baking sheet. Bake until just beginning to brown at the edges, 15 to 18 minutes, rotating sheet halfway through. Remove from oven; let cool on sheet.

from Fall Cookies

grandmother brinton's raisin bars
MAKES ABOUT 3 DOZEN

This recipe comes from assistant food editor Tara Bench's family. The rustic bars can be made with dried figs instead of raisins for the filling.

FOR THE FILLING:

Unsalted butter, room temperature, for pans

2 cups raisins (about 13 ounces)

1 cup granulated sugar

1 teaspoon cornstarch

1 cup cold water

½ cup apple cider

FOR THE DOUGH:

2½ cups all-purpose flour

1¼ teaspoons baking soda

1¼ teaspoons salt

1¼ cups vegetable shortening

1¼ cups packed light-brown sugar

1 large egg

1¼ teaspoons pure vanilla extract

2½ cups old-fashioned rolled oats (not quick-cooking)

1 Preheat oven to 350°F. Butter a 10-by-15-inch baking pan; line bottom with parchment. Butter parchment.

2 Place the raisins and sugar in the bowl of a food processor fitted with the metal blade. Pulse until very finely chopped. Transfer to a small saucepan. In a bowl, whisk cornstarch into the water; whisk into pan. Stir in cider. Simmer over medium-low heat until sugar dissolves and mixture thickens, about 5 minutes. Remove from heat; let cool completely.

3 Combine flour, baking soda, and salt in a medium bowl. In the bowl of an electric mixer fitted with the paddle attachment, cream shortening on medium speed until smooth. Add brown sugar, and beat until light and fluffy. Beat in egg and vanilla. Add the flour mixture all at once; beat on low speed until combined. Beat in oats.

4 Using an offset spatula, spread half the dough in prepared pan; spread filling on top. Crumble remaining dough over top, gently pressing down to conceal filling. Bake until golden brown, about 30 minutes, rotating the pan halfway through. Remove from oven; let cool completely in pan before cutting into 2-inch squares.

from Fall Cookies

hermit bars with brown-sugar icing and candied ginger
MAKES ABOUT 3 DOZEN

These spice-laden cookies originated in colonial New England; the candied ginger is our own addition. As the name implies, the bars are best after being hidden away for a day or two, when the flavors have had a chance to deepen.

½ cup (1 stick) unsalted butter, plus more for pan, room temperature

1¾ cups all-purpose flour

¾ teaspoon baking powder

¾ teaspoon baking soda

1 tablespoon ground ginger

1 teaspoon ground cinnamon

½ teaspoon ground nutmeg

   Pinch of ground cloves

¼ teaspoon salt

¼ teaspoon freshly ground pepper

1¼ cups packed dark-brown sugar

1 large whole egg

1 large egg yolk

¼ cup molasses

1 cup (about 5 ounces) chopped candied ginger, cut into ¼-inch pieces

¾ cup raisins

   Brown-Sugar Icing (page 266)

1 Preheat oven to 350°F. Butter a 10-by-15-inch baking pan, and line the bottom with parchment paper. Butter the parchment, and set pan aside. Combine flour, baking powder, baking soda, ginger, cinnamon, nutmeg, cloves, salt, and pepper in a medium bowl; set aside.

2 In bowl of an electric mixer fitted with paddle attachment, cream butter on medium speed until smooth. Add sugar; beat until light and fluffy. Beat in egg, egg yolk, and molasses.

3 Add flour mixture; beat on low speed until combined. Add ½ cup candied ginger and the raisins; beat until combined.

4 Spread dough into the prepared pan in an even layer, and bake until firm to the touch, 18 to 22 minutes, rotating pan halfway through. Remove from oven; let cool completely in pan before icing.

5 Drizzle with icing, and then sprinkle with remaining ½ cup candied ginger. Let stand until icing has set, about 15 minutes. Cut into 2-inch squares, and serve.

from Fall Cookies

brown-sugar icing
MAKES ¾ CUP

¼ cup packed light-brown sugar

2 tablespoons milk, plus more as needed

2 tablespoons unsalted butter

1 teaspoon pure vanilla extract

1 cup sifted confectioners' sugar, plus more as needed

Combine brown sugar, milk, and butter in a medium saucepan. Stir over medium heat until the butter has melted and sugar has dissolved. Remove from heat, and whisk in vanilla and confectioners' sugar. If the icing is too thick to drizzle, stir in a little more milk. If it is too thin, add a little more confectioners' sugar. Let cool slightly before using.

mixed fruit-and-nut cookies
MAKES ABOUT 3 DOZEN | PHOTO ON PAGE 332

2¼ cups all-purpose flour

1 teaspoon baking soda

1 teaspoon salt

1 cup (2 sticks) unsalted butter, room temperature

1 cup packed light-brown sugar

½ cup granulated sugar

2 large eggs

1 teaspoon pure vanilla extract

1½ cups sweetened shredded coconut

1½ cups chopped dried apricots

1½ cups dried cherries

1½ cups sliced blanched almonds

1½ cups chopped unsalted pistachios

1 Preheat oven to 375°F. Line two baking sheets with parchment paper, and set aside. Combine flour, baking soda, and salt in a medium bowl; set aside.

2 In the bowl of an electric mixer fitted with the paddle attachment, cream butter on medium speed until smooth. Add the sugars, and beat until light and fluffy, about 3 minutes. Beat in eggs one at a time until combined; beat in vanilla.

3 Add the flour mixture all at once, and beat on low speed until combined. Add coconut, apricots, cherries, almonds, and pistachios; beat until combined.

4 Drop batter 2 heaping tablespoons at a time onto prepared baking sheets, about 2 inches apart. Bake until golden brown, 12 to 15 minutes, rotating sheets halfway through. Remove from oven, and transfer cookies on parchment-paper lining to a wire rack to cool completely.

from Fall Cookies

peanut butter surprises
MAKES ABOUT 2 DOZEN | PHOTO ON PAGE 332

These chewy cookies are best eaten when they are fresh from the oven, while the chocolate center is still warm.

1½ cups all-purpose flour

1 teaspoon baking soda

¼ teaspoon salt

½ cup (1 stick) unsalted butter, room temperature

1 cup packed light-brown sugar

1 large egg

1 teaspoon pure vanilla extract

1 cup smooth peanut butter

1 cup roughly chopped, roasted salted peanuts, plus about 48 halves for pressing into tops

10 ounces semisweet chocolate, cut into 1-inch chunks

1 Combine flour, baking soda, and salt in a medium bowl, and set aside. In the bowl of an electric mixer fitted with the paddle attachment, cream butter and sugar on medium speed until light and fluffy. Add egg and vanilla; beat until well combined. Add peanut butter, and beat until combined.

2 Add the flour mixture all at once, and beat on low speed until just combined. Add chopped peanuts, and beat until combined. Wrap dough in plastic wrap, and chill in refrigerator at least 2 hours or overnight.

3 Preheat oven to 350°F. Line two baking sheets with parchment paper. Remove dough from refrigerator; pinch off about 2 tablespoons of dough, and make a well in your hand with the dough. Place one chunk of chocolate in center, and enclose with dough to cover completely. Roll dough into about a 1¾-inch ball with your hands.

4 Place ball of dough on a baking sheet; repeat with the remaining dough and chocolate, placing cookies about 2 inches apart. Press 2 peanut halves into the top of each cookie.

5 Bake until cookies are golden, 16 to 18 minutes, rotating the sheets halfway through. Remove from the oven; transfer cookies to a wire rack to cool slightly before serving.

from Fall Cookies

pumpkin bread pudding

SERVES 6 | PHOTO ON PAGE 332

If you omit the bourbon, double the amount of hot water.

Unsalted butter, room temperature, for ramekins
6 tablespoons dark-brown sugar
1 cup raisins
⅓ cup bourbon (optional)
⅓ cup hot water
1 15-ounce can pumpkin purée
4 large eggs
1 cup granulated sugar
1½ cups milk
2 teaspoons pure vanilla extract
1 teaspoon ground cinnamon
1 teaspoon ground ginger
¼ teaspoon ground allspice
Pinch of salt
1 12-ounce day-old loaf brioche or challah bread, cut into ¾-inch cubes
Confectioners' sugar, for dusting

1 Preheat oven to 350°F. Butter six 10-ounce ramekins or custard cups. Sprinkle each with 1 tablespoon brown sugar; set aside on a baking sheet. Place raisins in a small bowl, and cover with bourbon, if using, and the hot water; let soak until plump, about 20 minutes. Drain; set aside.

2 In a large bowl, whisk together pumpkin, eggs, granulated sugar, milk, vanilla, spices, and salt. Toss in the bread cubes, and stir gently to coat evenly; let stand a few minutes. Fold in the raisins. Divide among prepared dishes, pressing down slightly to make level.

3 Bake until custards are set in center and tops are golden, about 40 minutes. If bread browns too quickly, cover loosely with aluminum foil. Remove from oven; let cool slightly. To serve, unmold onto plates; dust with confectioners' sugar.

from Dessert of the Month

DRINKS

chai tea with soy milk

SERVES 4

Chai tea has been a favorite refreshment in India for centuries. Essentially a blend of tea, ground spices, honey, and milk, it can be enjoyed hot or cold. Our version, which replaces cow's milk with soy milk, is served hot.

3 cups water
10 whole green cardamom pods, lightly crushed
5 whole cloves
2 cinnamon sticks
1 2-inch piece fresh ginger, peeled and quartered
½ vanilla bean, split lengthwise and scraped
⅓ cup honey
4 black tea bags, such as English Breakfast
1½ cups soy milk

1 Place the water in a small saucepan, and add cardamom, cloves, cinnamon, ginger, and vanilla bean and scrapings. Bring to a boil over high heat. Reduce heat to low, and simmer until mixture is aromatic, about 15 minutes. Whisk in honey; drop tea bags in pan. Turn off heat; steep 3 minutes.

2 Strain tea through a fine strainer or a coffee filter into a warmed serving pot. Heat soy milk in same saucepan over medium-high heat, about 3 minutes; do not let it come to a boil, or it will separate. Pour into serving pot with the tea, and stir well to combine. Serve immediately.

PER SERVING: 82 CALORIES, 1 G FAT, 0 MG CHOLESTEROL, 18 G CARBOHYDRATE, 12 MG SODIUM, 2 G PROTEIN, 1 G FIBER

from Fit to Eat: Cooking with Soy Products

pumpkin shake

SERVES 1

½ cup pumpkin purée
1 cup vanilla ice cream
½ cup milk
Pinch of cinnamon

Mix together purée, ice cream, milk, and cinnamon in a tall glass. Serve cold.

from Good Things

focaccia

MAKES 1 ELEVEN-BY-SEVENTEEN-INCH LOAF

This Italian flatbread is best eaten the day it is made but will stay fresh for up to four days when wrapped well in plastic and stored in the refrigerator.

1 envelope dry yeast (¼ ounce)

Pinch of sugar

2½ cups warm water

4 tablespoons olive oil, plus more for bowl and baking sheet

6 to 7 cups all-purpose flour

1 tablespoon coarse salt

1 Sprinkle yeast and sugar over ½ cup warm water in a large bowl. Stir to dissolve; let stand 10 minutes, until the mixture is foamy. Add remaining 2 cups warm water, 2 tablespoons oil, 2 cups flour, and salt; stir with a wooden spoon until smooth. Gradually add 4 cups flour, using your hands once mixture becomes too thick to stir. If dough is still too wet, add just enough of the remaining cup flour until it is no longer sticky.

2 Turn out dough onto a clean work surface; knead until smooth and elastic, about 10 minutes, using any remaining flour, if needed. Place dough in a lightly oiled bowl; cover with plastic wrap. Let rise in a warm place until doubled in bulk, about 1½ hours.

3 Preheat oven to 425°F. Transfer dough to an oiled 11-by-17-inch rimmed baking sheet; stretch to fill sheet, and press to form an even thickness. If dough shrinks back, cover with a damp towel, and let rest 10 minutes before proceeding. Once dough fills sheet, cover with a damp kitchen towel; let rise again until doubled in bulk, about 30 minutes.

4 Using your fingers, make dimplelike indentations all over surface of dough. Drizzle with remaining 2 tablespoons oil; spread with your hands to coat evenly.

5 Place baking sheet in oven. Toss a cupful of ice cubes into bottom of oven to create steam (if using a gas oven, place a small baking dish of ice water on oven floor). Bake until golden brown, about 30 minutes, rotating pan half-way through; avoid opening oven any more than necessary or the steam will escape. Transfer focaccia to a wire rack to cool.

from Grilled Cheese

herb-infused olive oil

MAKES 2 CUPS

Almost any herb can be used to flavor olive oil. Drizzle over pasta, fish, roasted vegetables, or use to make vinaigrettes.

Herbs, such as rosemary, thyme, tarragon, or chives

2 **cups olive oil**

Preheat oven to 400°F. Place herbs in a baking dish, and pour olive oil over top. Cover dish with foil, and roast until oil is sizzling and slightly colored, about 15 minutes. Cool; store up to 2 weeks in an airtight container in the refrigerator.

from Roasting Vegetables 101

November

STARTERS

271 elwood's ham chowder

271 low country steamed carolina cup oysters
with melted butter

272 roasted red pepper and walnut dip

272 steamed littleneck clams

SALADS

272 green salad with toasted walnuts,
walnut oil, and green beans

MAIN COURSES

273 cedar-plank roasted salmon

273 herb-roasted turkey with pan gravy

274 pork loin braised in milk

275 spinach linguine with walnut-arugula pesto

SIDE DISHES

275 best whipped sweet potatoes with
caramelized apples

275 butternut squash with brown butter

276 church street squash

276 cornbread dressing

277 cranberry chutney

277 cream biscuits

277 maple-glazed sweet potatoes

278 mashed potatoes with bacon and cheddar

278 sautéed brussels sprouts with raisins

278 savory twice-baked sweet potatoes

279 scalloped mushrooms

279 southern green beans

279 spicy sweet potatoes with lime

280 stuffing

280 sweet-potato rolls

DESSERTS

281 amaretti crisps

281 cecilia's sweet potato pie

282 pear pandowdy

283 pear pavlova

284 pumpkin-pecan pie

284 warm cream-cheese brownies

285 yogurt drizzled with honey and walnuts

MISCELLANEOUS

285 bread-and-butter pickles

285 breakfast butter

285 buttermilk and blue cheese dressing

286 pickled beets

286 pickled green beans

286 pickled watermelon rind

elwood's ham chowder

MAKES ABOUT 5 QUARTS

This recipe is courtesy of chef Donald Barickman; it was created with and named for his father, Elwood.

1 tablespoon vegetable oil

1 pound Virginia ham, cut into ½-inch pieces

2 large onions, cut into ½-inch pieces (about 3 cups)

4 garlic cloves, thinly sliced

2 bunches collard greens (about 1 pound), stems discarded, washed, and roughly chopped

1 28-ounce can whole tomatoes with juice, roughly chopped

7 cups homemade or low-sodium canned chicken stock

2 cups homemade or low-sodium canned beef stock

8 medium red potatoes, cut into ½-inch cubes (about 6 cups)

1½ tablespoons chopped fresh thyme leaves

1½ tablespoons chopped fresh flat-leaf parsley

Coarse salt and freshly ground pepper

Hot-pepper sauce, such as Tabasco (optional)

1 Heat the oil in a large stockpot over medium-low heat. Add ham, and cook until it starts to release juices, about 2 minutes; do not brown. Add onions and garlic; cook, stirring occasionally, until soft, about 10 minutes.

2 Working in batches, if necessary, so as not to overcrowd pot, add collard greens, tossing with tongs until wilted. Add tomatoes, chicken and beef stocks, potatoes, thyme, and parsley. Bring to a boil, and reduce to a gentle simmer; cook, stirring occasionally and skimming any foam from surface, until potatoes are easily pierced with a paring knife, 30 to 40 minutes. Remove from heat; season with salt, pepper, and hot-pepper sauce, as desired. Serve hot.

from Thanksgiving: An All-Day Affair

low country steamed carolina cup oysters with melted butter

SERVES 8 TO 10

This recipe is courtesy of Donald Barickman, a longtime chef and backyard barbecuer. To prevent the burlap bags from scorching during cooking, soak them in water for several hours. Donald uses a galvanized tub to hold the large bags. You can also roast the oysters over a large gas or charcoal grill; place them in a roasting pan, and cover with aluminum foil. Another way to steam oysters is to cook them in a large stockpot filled with about one inch of water over high heat for about ten minutes.

Seasoned oak or hickory chips, for fire

Bricks, large stones, or cinder blocks, to support sheet metal

1 piece sheet metal (at least 3 by 3 feet and 3/16 inch thick)

10 to 20 pounds oysters, rinsed

2 to 3 large burlap sacks, soaked in water

2 cups butter (4 sticks), melted, for serving

2 cups cocktail sauce, for serving

3 to 4 lemons, cut into wedges, for serving

1 Build a hot fire with wood chips. Stack bricks or stones around fire so that the sheet metal sits securely on top.

2 Once metal is very hot, place oysters on top, and cover completely with wet burlap. Steam until shells begin to open, checking frequently, 12 to 18 minutes.

3 Shovel oysters onto a serving platter, discarding any that do not open, and serve immediately with melted butter, cocktail sauce, and lemon wedges.

from Thanksgiving: An All-Day Affair

roasted red pepper and walnut dip

MAKES 2¼ CUPS; SERVES 10 TO 12

This chunky, robust dip is based on muhammara, a Middle Eastern specialty whose name describes its brick-red color. For best results, make the dip a day ahead to let the flavors mellow and blend. Serve with toasted pita bread or crackers.

- 3 red bell peppers (about 1 pound)
- 1 6-inch pita bread (2 ounces)
- 1 small garlic clove
- 4 ounces walnut pieces (about 1 cup), toasted, plus more for garnish
- 1½ teaspoons ground paprika, plus more for garnish
- ¾ teaspoon ground cumin
- 1 tablespoon balsamic vinegar
- 1 tablespoon freshly squeezed lemon juice
- 2 teaspoons extra-virgin olive oil, plus more for drizzling
- ¾ teaspoon coarse salt
  Freshly ground black pepper

1 Roast peppers over a gas burner until blackened all over, turning with tongs as each side is blistered. (Alternatively, place under a broiler.) Transfer to a bowl, and cover with plastic wrap; let cool, about 15 minutes. Peel, and remove stems and seeds. Set peppers aside.

2 Toast pita until crisp and golden. Break into 2-inch pieces; place in a bowl, and cover with water. Soak until soft, about 10 minutes. Drain in a sieve, pressing out excess water.

3 Combine garlic and walnuts in the bowl of a food processor; process until fine crumbs form, about 10 seconds. Add paprika, cumin, peppers, and pita; process until smooth, about 10 seconds. Add vinegar, juice, oil, and salt; season with black pepper. Pulse to combine.

4 Transfer to a serving bowl; cover with plastic wrap. Refrigerate at least 1 hour or overnight. Before serving, bring to room temperature. Drizzle with oil; sprinkle with paprika and more walnuts, as desired.

PER SERVING: 100 CALORIES, 7 G FAT, 0 MG CHOLESTEROL, 8 G CARBOHYDRATE, 160 MG SODIUM, 3 G PROTEIN, 2 G FIBER

from Fit to Eat: Walnuts

steamed littleneck clams

SERVES 8 TO 10

Serve these clams with melted butter and lemon wedges.

- 100 littleneck clams (3 to 4 pounds), rinsed and scrubbed
- 3 to 4 sprigs thyme
- 3 tablespoons unsalted butter
- 2 cups beer or water

Bring all ingredients to a boil in a large stockpot; reduce heat to a simmer. Cover tightly, and steam 3 to 5 minutes. Carefully remove lid; stir with a wooden spoon until clams open, discarding any that do not open. Serve immediately.

from Thanksgiving: An All-Day Affair

SALADS

green salad with toasted walnuts, walnut oil, and green beans

SERVES 4 | **PHOTO ON PAGE 318**

Walnut oil can be found at most gourmet markets. Once it has been opened, walnut oil should be stored in the refrigerator, as it spoils more quickly than other types of oils.

- 6 ounces green beans, each trimmed, halved crosswise
- ¼ teaspoon coarse salt
- ½ teaspoon plus 1 tablespoon walnut oil
- 2 ounces walnut halves (about ½ cup), toasted and roughly chopped
- ½ shallot, minced (about 1 tablespoon)
- 2 teaspoons white-wine vinegar
- 4 ounces mixed salad greens
  Freshly ground pepper

1 Bring a medium saucepan of water to a boil. Add beans, and cook until bright green and crisp-tender, about 2 minutes. Using a slotted spoon or tongs, transfer to a medium serving bowl. Immediately toss with the salt and ½ teaspoon walnut oil. Toss in walnuts, and transfer mixture to a plate to cool. Reserve bowl for serving.

2 In a small bowl, combine shallot with vinegar. Whisk in remaining tablespoon walnut oil until thick and emulsified.

3 Place salad greens in reserved bowl; add dressing. Toss well to combine; season with pepper. Divide greens among four plates, pile green beans and walnuts on top, and serve.

PER SERVING: 141 CALORIES, 6 G FAT, 0 MG CHOLESTEROL, 6 G CARBOHYDRATE, 123 MG SODIUM, 5 G PROTEIN, 3 G FIBER

from Fit to Eat: Walnuts

cedar-plank roasted salmon

SERVES 8 TO 10

Chef Donald Barickman, who developed this recipe, cooks the salmon over a homemade barbecue pit, but you can use a large gas or charcoal grill. Stack fire-resistant supports, such as bricks, stones, or cinder blocks, on each side of the grill so that the cedar plank will rest at least fifteen inches above the hot coals. The longer the salmon cooks, the more pronounced the wood-roasted flavor, so you want to avoid cooking it too close to the heat. If at any time the fish or plank begins to smolder, spritz it with water.

1 cedar plank, untreated (at least 8 by 5 inches and 1 inch thick)

2 fire-resistant supports, such as cinder blocks, for cedar plank

⅓ cup coarse sea salt

1 bunch fresh thyme

1 bunch fresh rosemary

1 3-pound whole side of salmon, skin on, boned and trimmed of excess fat

2 small nails or screws, for cedar plank

1 tablespoon freshly ground pepper

Picture wire (at least 15 feet)

1   Build a hot fire. Prepare cedar plank by placing it over hot coals until it begins to blacken slightly on one side; remove from heat, and let cool completely.

2   Place board, charred side up, with both ends resting on supports. Sprinkle with one-third of the salt and a few sprigs each thyme and rosemary. Place salmon on plank, skin side down. About 2 inches from each end, tap one nail horizontally into side of plank, leaving head protruding for the wire. Sprinkle salmon with remaining salt and the pepper, and arrange remaining herbs across the top.

3   Starting at the larger end of fish, twist wire around the nail several times to secure. Wrap wire entirely around salmon and plank at 2-inch intervals, making sure that it is tight enough to hold fish in place without slicing through the tender flesh. When you reach the other end of the plank, twist the wire several times around the other nail, and trim any excess wire with wire cutters.

4   Arrange plank supports near the fire, and rest the plank, fish side down, on top, 15 to 20 inches above the coals. Cook until thicker part of fish is firm to the touch, 25 to 35 minutes, depending on the heat of the fire, the distance from the heat during cooking, and the thickness of the fish. Check fish several times during cooking for doneness.

5   Remove plank from heat, and let fish cool slightly. Remove wire and herbs, and discard. Cut fish on the diagonal, or flake the flesh into large pieces with a fork, and serve hot, warm, or at room temperature, directly from the plank.

from Thanksgiving: An All-Day Affair

herb-roasted turkey with pan gravy

SERVES 8 TO 10 | PHOTO ON PAGE 325

An instant-read thermometer is more accurate than the pop-up timers that sometimes come with frozen turkeys. The thighs should be cooked to an internal temperature of 180 degrees; to avoid overcooking, remove turkey from the oven once it reaches 175 degrees, as it will continue to cook out of the oven. Check again after about twenty minutes, and return to oven if it hasn't reached 180 degrees.

1 18- to 21-pound fresh turkey (thawed if frozen), giblets and neck removed from cavity and reserved for gravy

6 tablespoons unsalted butter, room temperature

Grated zest of 1 lemon

3 tablespoons finely chopped fresh flat-leaf parsley

3 tablespoons finely chopped fresh thyme leaves

3 teaspoons coarse salt, plus more for gravy

1½ teaspoons freshly ground pepper, plus more for gravy

3 to 4 lemons, each cut into quarters

2 to 3 onions, each cut into 6 wedges

1 cup dry white wine or water, for gravy

3 cups Giblet Stock (page 274) or homemade or low-sodium canned chicken stock, for gravy

1   Rinse turkey with cool water, and pat dry with paper towels. Let stand, uncovered, 2 hours at room temperature.

2   Combine butter, lemon zest, parsley, thyme, 1 teaspoon salt, and ¼ teaspoon pepper in a small bowl. Using your fingers, gently loosen turkey skin from over the breast meat, and smear half the butter mixture under skin.

3   Preheat oven to 450°F with rack on lowest level. Place turkey, breast side up, on a roasting rack set in a heavy roasting pan. Tuck wing tips under. Sprinkle ½ teaspoon each salt and pepper inside cavity. Fill cavity loosely with as many lemon and onion wedges as will fit comfortably.

4   Tie legs together loosely with kitchen twine. Fold neck flap under, and secure with toothpicks. Rub entire turkey with remaining herb butter, and sprinkle with remaining 1½ teaspoons salt and ¾ teaspoon pepper, pressing to adhere.

5 Cook 30 minutes, rotating pan halfway through. Using a pastry brush, baste turkey with pan drippings. Reduce oven heat to 350°F; continue cooking 2 hours more, basting turkey and rotating pan every 30 minutes. If pan gets too full, spoon out some of the juices, reserving them for gravy.

6 Insert an instant-read thermometer into thickest part of thigh, avoiding bone. The temperature should register 175°F, and the turkey should be golden brown. If thighs are not yet fully cooked, baste turkey again, and continue cooking.

7 When fully cooked, transfer turkey to a serving platter, and let rest, about 30 minutes. Meanwhile, make the gravy; pour the pan juices into a large glass measuring cup or heatproof container; let stand until fat rises to the surface, about 10 minutes, then skim off fat with a large spoon, and discard.

8 Meanwhile, place roasting pan over medium-high heat. Add the wine or water, and bring to a boil; deglaze pan by scraping up any browned bits from the bottom with a wooden spoon. Add stock; stir well, and return to a boil. Cook until reduced by half, about 5 minutes. Add the defatted pan juices, and cook 5 minutes more; you will have about 2 cups gravy. Remove from heat, and season with salt and pepper. Strain into a warm gravy boat, and serve with turkey.

from Thanksgiving: An All-Day Affair

giblet stock

MAKES ABOUT 3 CUPS

Giblets, which are the heart, gizzard, and liver of turkeys and other fowl, along with the neck, can be used to make a rich stock for homemade gravy. The liver should be cooked separately before being added to the stock, or it will make it too bitter. You can make this stock while your turkey is roasting.

Giblets (heart, gizzard, and liver) and neck, reserved from turkey

4 tablespoons unsalted butter

1 onion, cut into ¼-inch pieces

1 stalk celery with leaves, stalk cut into ¼-inch pieces, leaves roughly chopped

1 small leek, white and pale-green parts only, halved lengthwise, cut into ¼-inch pieces, washed well and drained

Coarse salt and freshly ground pepper

4 cups water

1 dried bay leaf

1 Trim any fat or membrane from giblets. The liver should not have the gallbladder (a small green sac) attached. If it is attached, trim it off carefully, removing part of the liver if necessary. Do not pierce the sac; the liquid it contains is very bitter. Rinse giblets and neck, and pat dry.

2 In a medium saucepan, melt 3 tablespoons butter over medium heat. Add onion, celery, and leek. Cook, stirring occasionally, until onions are translucent, about 8 minutes. Season with salt and pepper, and cook 1 minute more.

3 Add the water, bay leaf, gizzard, heart, and neck (do not add liver yet). Bring to a boil over medium-high heat, and reduce to a full simmer. Cook until gizzard is tender when pierced with a paring knife, about 45 minutes. Transfer gizzard, heart, and neck to a plate; set aside. You should have about 3 cups liquid; if you have more, raise heat, and cook until liquid is reduced, 10 to 15 minutes more.

4 Meanwhile, finely chop liver. Melt remaining tablespoon butter in a small skillet over medium-low heat. Add liver, and cook, stirring constantly, until it no longer releases any blood, 3 to 4 minutes. Transfer to a plate, and cover with plastic wrap. Refrigerate until ready to use.

5 Strain stock through a fine sieve into a heatproof, airtight container, discarding the bay leaf; let stand until grease rises to the top, and skim off with a large spoon. Finely chop gizzard and heart, and pull meat from neck; add to the stock along with the reserved liver. Cover, and store in the refrigerator until ready to use.

pork loin braised in milk

SERVES 4 | **PHOTO ON PAGE 323**

2 tablespoons olive oil

8 boneless pork loin chops (about 1¼ pounds)

Coarse salt and freshly ground pepper

2 cups milk

5 to 6 sprigs thyme, plus 1 teaspoon fresh thyme leaves

1 tablespoon cornstarch

1 tablespoon water

1 Heat oil in a large skillet over medium heat. Season pork chops on both sides with salt and pepper. Working in batches if necessary, so as not to overcrowd skillet, sear until brown on both sides, about 3 minutes per side. Transfer pork to a large plate.

2 Pour off fat from skillet, and place over low heat. Return pork and any accumulated juices to skillet; add milk and thyme sprigs. Bring to a boil over high heat; cover, and reduce heat to low. Simmer until pork is cooked through and tender, turning once, about 45 minutes.

3 Transfer pork to a serving platter, and cover with aluminum foil to keep warm. Return skillet to medium-high heat, and bring remaining liquid to a boil. Whisk together cornstarch and the water in a small bowl; whisk into liquid in skillet, and boil 1 minute. Transfer mixture to a blender or food processor. Add thyme leaves, and purée until smooth. Pour sauce over pork, and serve immediately.

from What to Have for Dinner

spinach linguine with walnut-arugula pesto

SERVES 6 | **PHOTO ON PAGE 318**

The pesto can be made up to one hour before serving without losing its freshness; store it at room temperature.

2 small garlic cloves

3 ounces toasted walnut pieces (about ¾ cup)

4 ounces arugula, trimmed and roughly chopped

½ teaspoon coarse salt

1 ounce Parmesan cheese, finely grated (about ⅓ cup)

1 pound spinach linguine

3 teaspoons extra-virgin olive oil

Freshly ground pepper

1 In the bowl of a food processor fitted with the metal blade, chop garlic as finely as possible. Add walnuts and arugula; process to form a coarse paste, about 5 seconds. Transfer to a serving bowl. Stir in salt and cheese, and set aside.

2 Bring a large pot of water to a boil. Add linguine; cook until al dente according to package instructions, about 8 minutes. Drain in a colander; immediately add to bowl with walnut-arugula mixture. Drizzle with oil, and season with pepper. Toss thoroughly to coat evenly, and serve.

PER SERVING: 415 CALORIES, 13 G FAT, 4 MG CHOLESTEROL, 59 G CARBOHYDRATE, 826 MG SODIUM, 16 G PROTEIN, 9 G FIBER

from Fit to Eat: Walnuts

best whipped sweet potatoes with caramelized apples

SERVES 6 | **PHOTO ON PAGE 327**

4 large sweet potatoes (about 3 pounds)

3 tablespoons unsalted butter, room temperature

2 tablespoons heavy cream

½ cup applesauce, preferably homemade

2 teaspoons grated fresh ginger

Coarse salt and freshly ground pepper

2 apples, peeled and cored

3 tablespoons sugar

1 Preheat oven to 375°F. Place sweet potatoes on a parchment-lined baking sheet; pierce each several times with a fork. Bake until very tender when pierced with a knife, about 50 minutes. Remove from oven; let cool slightly.

2 Cut open potatoes; scoop flesh into the bowl of an electric mixer fitted with the paddle attachment. Add 2 tablespoons butter and the cream, and beat until smooth. Add applesauce and ginger; beat to combine. Season with salt and pepper.

3 Transfer sweet-potato mixture to an ovenproof serving dish. Place in oven until heated through, 10 minutes.

4 Meanwhile, cut apples into 1-inch pieces. Melt remaining tablespoon butter in a nonstick skillet over medium-high heat. Add apples and sugar; sauté until golden and nicely caramelized, about 8 minutes. Remove from heat.

5 Remove serving dish from oven, and top with apples. Serve immediately.

from Sweet Potatoes

butternut squash with brown butter

SERVES 4 | **PHOTO ON PAGE 323**

The easiest way to peel butternut squash is with a vegetable peeler; the harp-shaped variety works particularly well.

2 tablespoons unsalted butter

1 butternut squash (about 1¾ pounds), peeled, seeded, and cut into ¾-inch cubes

½ cup low-sodium canned chicken broth

¼ cup water

1 tablespoon dark-brown sugar

Coarse salt and freshly ground pepper

1 Heat butter in a large skillet over medium-high heat until golden brown. Add squash; sauté, stirring occasionally, until golden brown and tender when pierced with a fork, about 16 minutes.

2 Add chicken broth, the water, and brown sugar; cook until liquid has evaporated and squash is nicely caramelized, about 6 minutes. Remove from heat, and season with salt and pepper. Serve immediately.

from What to Have for Dinner

church street squash

SERVES 8 TO 10

This savory dish is named for one of the streets in historic Charleston, South Carolina. Crookneck squash is a summer squash that is available year-round in certain regions. You can substitute zucchini or a winter squash, such as butternut or acorn, depending on what's in season in your area.

3 tablespoons unsalted butter

2 pounds yellow crookneck squash, cut into ½-inch pieces

1 large onion, finely chopped

¾ cup grated cheddar cheese (3 ounces)

1 cup sour cream

1 teaspoon coarse salt

½ teaspoon freshly ground pepper

1 large egg, lightly beaten

½ teaspoon paprika

1 Preheat oven to 350°F. Melt 2 tablespoons butter in a large skillet. Add squash, and cook over medium-low heat until tender. Transfer to a medium bowl, and mash lightly with a fork or a wooden spoon.

2 Melt remaining tablespoon butter in same skillet. Add onion; sauté until tender. Add to bowl with squash. Stir in cheese, sour cream, salt, pepper, and egg. Transfer to a 2-quart baking dish; sprinkle with paprika. Bake until golden and bubbling, 30 to 35 minutes. Serve hot.

from Thanksgiving: An All-Day Affair

cornbread dressing

SERVES 8 TO 10 | **PHOTO ON PAGE 325**

Stuffing is commonly known as dressing in the South, where it is frequently made with buttermilk cornbread, another regional specialty.

4 tablespoons unsalted butter, plus more for baking dish

2 onions, finely chopped

4 garlic cloves, minced

4 stalks celery, finely chopped

   Buttermilk Cornbread (recipe follows)

½ cup finely chopped fresh flat-leaf parsley

2 tablespoons finely chopped fresh thyme leaves

2 tablespoons finely chopped fresh oregano

4 large eggs, lightly beaten

2 cups homemade or low-sodium canned chicken stock

1½ teaspoons coarse salt

½ teaspoon freshly ground pepper

1 Preheat oven to 375°F. Melt butter in a large sauté pan. Add onions, garlic, and celery; cook over medium heat until just tender, about 8 minutes.

2 Crumble cornbread into a bowl; add onion mixture, parsley, thyme, oregano, eggs, chicken stock, salt, and pepper. Stir well until combined.

3 Transfer mixture to a buttered 2-quart casserole or large ovenproof skillet, and bake until golden on top and cooked through, about 45 minutes. Remove from oven; serve hot.

from Thanksgiving: An All-Day Affair

buttermilk cornbread

MAKES 1 EIGHT-INCH SQUARE

This cornbread has a sturdy texture that holds up well in stuffings; it is also delicious when eaten on its own.

4 tablespoons unsalted butter, melted and cooled, plus more for pan

2½ cups yellow cornmeal

1¼ teaspoons salt

1 teaspoon sugar

4 teaspoons baking powder

3 large eggs

1¼ cups buttermilk, room temperature

1 Preheat oven to 425°F. Butter an 8-inch square baking pan; set aside. Whisk together cornmeal, salt, sugar, and baking powder in a medium bowl.

2 In a separate bowl, whisk eggs, buttermilk, and melted butter. Add to cornmeal mixture; stir until well combined.

3 Pour into prepared pan. Bake until golden and a cake tester inserted in the center comes out clean, about 25 minutes. Transfer pan to a wire rack to cool slightly before removing cornbread from pan.

cranberry chutney

MAKES 5 CUPS

You can use frozen cranberries in this recipe, but fresh ones make a more flavorful dish.

- 2 tablespoons unsalted butter
- 1 small onion, finely chopped
- 1 12-ounce bag fresh cranberries
- 1 cup raisins
- 1½ cups honey
- 1 tablespoon ground cinnamon
- 1½ teaspoons ground ginger
- ¼ teaspoon ground cloves
- ¼ cup apple-cider vinegar
- ¾ cup water
- 1 red or green apple, peeled, cored, and chopped into ¼-inch pieces
- 1 stalk celery, thinly sliced (about ½ cup)

1 In a medium saucepan, melt butter over medium heat. Add onion; cook until softened, about 3 minutes. Add cranberries, raisins, honey, cinnamon, ginger, cloves, vinegar, and the water. Bring to a boil over medium-high heat; reduce heat to low, and simmer until cranberries begin to soften, about 15 minutes.

2 Remove from heat, and stir in apple and celery; let cool completely. Pour into jars or airtight containers, and store, covered, in the refrigerator, up to 1 week.

from Thanksgiving: An All-Day Affair

cream biscuits

MAKES ABOUT 30

White Lily flour is widely used throughout the South. Made with only soft winter wheat, it is finer, lighter, and whiter than other types of flour and can be used to make everything from these biscuits to flaky piecrusts.

- 2½ cups White Lily all-purpose flour, plus more for work surface
- 1 tablespoon plus 1 teaspoon baking powder
- ½ teaspoon salt
- 2 cups heavy cream
- 3 tablespoons unsalted butter, melted

1 Preheat oven to 450°F. Whisk together flour, baking powder, and salt in a medium bowl. Pour in cream, and stir with a wooden spoon until combined but still wet and tacky. Use your hands if mixture becomes too hard to stir.

2 Turn out dough onto a well-floured work surface, and use your fingers to pat into a square about ½ inch thick. Let rest about 5 minutes.

3 Using a 2-inch-round biscuit cutter, cut out 24 rounds. Gather together scraps; pat into a square, and cut out more rounds. Place on a baking sheet, and bake until golden on the tops, 12 to 14 minutes. Remove from oven, and immediately brush tops with butter. Transfer to a wire rack to cool slightly. Serve warm or at room temperature.

from Thanksgiving: An All-Day Affair

maple-glazed sweet potatoes

SERVES 6

- 3 medium sweet potatoes (1 to 2 pounds), scrubbed well
- 4 tablespoons unsalted butter
- ¾ cup pure maple syrup
- Coarse salt and freshly ground pepper

1 Preheat oven to 400°F. Using a sharp knife, slice sweet potatoes in half lengthwise; cut each half crosswise into 1-inch-thick slices.

2 Melt butter in a large cast-iron or ovenproof skillet over medium heat. Add the sweet potatoes, and toss to coat evenly. Add the maple syrup, and bring to a boil. Transfer the skillet to the oven, and cook, stirring occasionally, until potatoes are golden, well glazed, and tender when pierced with a paring knife, about 20 minutes. Remove from oven, and season with salt and pepper. Serve hot.

from Sweet Potatoes

mashed potatoes with bacon and cheddar

SERVES 8 TO 10

You can prepare this dish through step three the night before, and save the final baking for Thanksgiving day.

- 5 pounds russet or Yukon gold potatoes
- 8 ounces bacon (about 10 slices)
- 1 8-ounce package cream cheese, room temperature
- ½ cup (1 stick) unsalted butter, melted, plus more for baking dish
- 1 cup sour cream
- 1 small onion, grated on the large holes of a box grater, juice reserved
- ½ bunch fresh chives, finely chopped (about ¼ cup)
- 2½ cups grated cheddar cheese (about 10 ounces)
- 2 teaspoons coarse salt
- ½ teaspoon freshly ground pepper

1 Preheat oven to 350°F. Peel potatoes, and cut into 1-inch chunks. Place in a large saucepan, and add enough cold water to cover by about 2 inches. Bring to a boil over medium-high heat, and reduce to a simmer. Cook until easily pierced with a paring knife, about 20 minutes. Transfer to a colander to drain; return to pan, cover, and set aside.

2 Meanwhile, heat a large skillet over medium heat. Add bacon, and cook until crisp and browned, turning once. Transfer to paper towels; let cool, and crumble.

3 Using a fork, mash potatoes in pan until light and fluffy; add cream cheese, butter, and sour cream, and stir until combined and smooth. Add the onion and any onion juice, chives, 2 cups cheese, half the bacon, salt, and pepper. Stir until well combined.

4 Transfer to a buttered 3-quart baking dish. Top with remaining ½ cup cheese. Bake until top is slightly golden and potatoes are heated through, about 30 minutes. Remove from oven; garnish with remaining bacon. Serve immediately.

from Thanksgiving: An All-Day Affair

sautéed brussels sprouts with raisins

SERVES 4 | PHOTO ON PAGE 323

Brussels sprouts are members of the cabbage family. They are in season from late August through March.

- 1 tablespoon extra-virgin olive oil
- 10 ounces brussels sprouts (about 25), trimmed and thinly sliced
- 2 carrots, cut into ¼-inch pieces (about ½ cup)
- ¼ cup golden raisins
- 1 cup low-sodium canned chicken broth
  Coarse salt and freshly ground pepper

Heat oil in a skillet over medium heat. Add brussels sprouts and carrots; sauté until sprouts start to turn golden brown, about 3 minutes. Add raisins and chicken broth; cook, stirring occasionally, until sprouts are tender when pierced with a knife, about 12 minutes. (If skillet becomes too dry before sprouts are tender, add up to 3 tablespoons water.) Remove from heat; season with salt and pepper. Serve.

from What to Have for Dinner

savory twice-baked sweet potatoes

SERVES 6 | PHOTO ON PAGE 327

For a less formal but equally appealing presentation, you can spoon rather than pipe the filling into the shells.

- 3 medium sweet potatoes (1 to 2 pounds), scrubbed well
- 4 ounces smoked bacon, about 5 slices
- 2 tablespoons dark-brown sugar
- 3 tablespoons unsalted butter, room temperature
- 2 small shallots, finely minced
- 1 teaspoon minced fresh rosemary, plus more for garnish
- 1 large egg
- 2 tablespoons heavy cream
- 2 ounces Gruyère cheese, finely grated, plus more for garnish
  Coarse salt and freshly ground pepper

1 Preheat oven to 400°F. Place sweet potatoes on a parchment-lined baking sheet, and bake until tender when pierced with a paring knife, about 45 minutes. Remove from oven; let cool slightly.

2 Line a rimmed baking sheet with aluminum foil; fit with a wire rack. Arrange bacon strips on rack, and sprinkle with brown sugar. Cook until well glazed and crisp, 12 to 15 minutes. Remove from oven; let cool slightly, and roughly chop.

3 Melt 1 tablespoon butter in a small skillet over medium heat. Add shallots; sauté until soft and fragrant, about 2 minutes. Add rosemary; cook 1 minute more. Remove from heat.

4 When sweet potatoes are cool enough to handle, slice each in half lengthwise. Carefully scoop out flesh, leaving about a ¼-inch border all around halves; set halves aside on a baking sheet. Place flesh in the bowl of an electric mixer fitted with the paddle attachment. Add remaining 2 tablespoons butter, reserved shallot mixture, egg, cream, and Gruyère. Mix well until combined. Season with salt and pepper.

5 Transfer mixture to a pastry bag fitted with a star tip. Pipe mixture into reserved sweet-potato shells. Bake until golden, about 20 minutes. Remove from oven; garnish with Gruyère, rosemary, and reserved bacon.

from Sweet Potatoes

scalloped mushrooms

SERVES 8 TO 10

We used frozen pearl onions, but you could use fresh instead. To peel, place them in boiling water for one minute, and then let them cool slightly before slipping off their papery skins.

9 tablespoons unsalted butter

1 1-pound bag frozen pearl onions, thawed and drained

3 pounds assorted mushrooms, such as button, cremini, or shiitake, trimmed and cut in half (large ones should be quartered)

¾ cup heavy cream

1 cup freshly grated Parmesan cheese (4 ounces)

1 teaspoon coarse salt

¼ teaspoon freshly ground pepper

1 cup plain coarse breadcrumbs, preferably homemade

1 Preheat oven to 350°F. Heat 1 tablespoon butter in a large cast-iron or ovenproof skillet over medium-high heat. Add onions, and cook until soft and just starting to brown, about 5 minutes. Transfer to a large mixing bowl.

2 Working in four batches, melt 2 tablespoons butter in same skillet; add one-fourth of the mushrooms, tossing to coat evenly with butter. Cook until mushrooms have released their juices and most of the juices have evaporated, about 5 minutes. Transfer to bowl with onions. Repeat with remaining butter and mushrooms.

3 Add cream, ½ cup Parmesan, salt, and pepper to bowl, and stir until combined. Return mixture to skillet or a baking dish. Sprinkle breadcrumbs and remaining ½ cup Parmesan over the top, and bake until bubbling and golden, about 25 minutes. Remove from oven. Serve hot.

from Thanksgiving: An All-Day Affair

southern green beans

SERVES 8 TO 10

1 large or 2 small ham hocks

1 large onion, cut into quarters

1 small dried red pepper (optional)

8 cups water

1 tablespoon sugar

2 pounds green beans, ends trimmed

Coarse salt and freshly ground black pepper

1 Place ham hock, onion, and dried pepper, if using, in a medium saucepan, and add the water. Bring to a boil over medium-high heat; reduce heat, cover, and gently simmer 2 hours. Using a slotted spoon, transfer ham and onion to a plate, and set aside; discard dried pepper. Return liquid to a boil over medium-high heat, and cook, stirring occasionally, until reduced to 2 cups, about 45 minutes.

2 Shred any meat from hocks with a fork, and return to pan. Add sugar; stir until dissolved. Reduce heat to medium; add beans. Simmer, stirring occasionally, until cooked through and most of the liquid has evaporated, about 8 minutes. Remove from heat. Season with salt and black pepper. Serve.

from Thanksgiving: An All-Day Affair

spicy sweet potatoes with lime

SERVES 6 | PHOTO ON PAGE 327

4 medium sweet potatoes (about 2½ pounds), scrubbed well

2 tablespoons extra-virgin olive oil

2 teaspoons ground cumin

1 teaspoon hot paprika

1 teaspoon ground ginger

Coarse salt and freshly ground white pepper

Lime wedges, for serving

Yogurt Dipping Sauce, for serving (page 280)

1 Preheat oven to 400°F. Place a baking sheet in the oven until hot, about 15 minutes. Meanwhile, slice sweet potatoes in half lengthwise; slice each half into three wedges. Place in a medium bowl, and toss with oil, cumin, paprika, and ginger. Season with salt and pepper.

2 Remove baking sheet from oven. Arrange sweet potatoes in a single layer on sheet. Return to oven; cook until potatoes are crisp and golden on the bottom, about 15 minutes. Turn; continue cooking until golden all over, about 15 minutes more. Remove from oven; season with salt and pepper. Serve with lime wedges and yogurt sauce.

from Sweet Potatoes

yogurt dipping sauce

MAKES ABOUT 1 CUP

- 1 cup plain yogurt
- 3 tablespoons roughly chopped fresh cilantro
- 2 tablespoons chopped toasted walnuts
- 1 tablespoon freshly squeezed lime juice
- ½ teaspoon ground cumin

  Coarse salt

Combine all ingredients in a small bowl. Cover with plastic wrap, and refrigerate until ready to serve, up to 1 day.

stuffing

MAKES 12 CUPS (6 CUPS IF USING CORNBREAD) | **PHOTO ON PAGE 326**

This recipe gives suggested ingredients to mix and match any way you please. Combine complementary flavors, such as citrus rind and fruit juice, or those that contrast, like pecans and dried cherries. Use a variety of colors and textures, too. For best results, include plenty of vegetables, herbs, and spices. For a fluffy texture, add up to three eggs, lightly beaten; measure eggs in a liquid measuring cup, and reduce liquid by that amount. The stuffing can be prepared up to one day ahead and stored, covered, in the refrigerator.

- 1 loaf bread (1 pound) set out overnight
  (or 1½ pounds cornbread)
- 1 pound meat, such as sausage, ground pork, ground beef, or cured ham

  Unsalted butter or olive oil, if desired
- 4 cups assorted vegetables, such as onion, celery, carrots, fennel, mushrooms, or leeks, cut into ¼-inch pieces
- 4 cups or less assorted fruit and nuts, such as apples, pears, oranges, dried apricots, cranberries, raisins, chestnuts, pine nuts, walnuts, or hazelnuts, finely chopped
- 1 cup assorted fresh herbs, such as parsley, sage, and thyme, finely chopped
- 3 tablespoons assorted seasoning, such as coarse salt, freshly ground pepper, cumin, cayenne, fennel seeds, turmeric, paprika, and cinnamon
- 2 cups or less liquid, such as chicken stock, fruit juice, red wine, or maple syrup

1 If using white bread, cut it into ¼- to ½-inch-thick slices, and set out overnight to dry. Break bread into ¼-inch pieces. If using cornbread, break ½-inch-thick slices into 1-inch pieces.

2 In a large skillet, sauté meat (unless using cured ham) until cooked through. Using a slotted spoon, transfer meat to a large bowl. In the same skillet, sauté the chopped vegetables in the rendered fat until they are softened. (Alternatively, cook the vegetables in a clean skillet with butter or olive oil.)

3 Add the sautéed vegetables, cured ham, if using, fruit, nuts, and bread to the bowl of cooked meat; toss to combine. Add the herbs and seasoning, and toss again. Add the liquid, and adjust the seasoning. (If using eggs, decrease other liquid accordingly.) Toss just until combined; do not overmix, or the stuffing will become gummy in texture.

4 Stuff turkey just before roasting it. Use ½ to ¾ cup stuffing for each pound of turkey. Don't pack tightly; stuffing expands as it cooks. Use a thermometer to ensure that stuffing reaches 165°F; remove stuffing as soon as turkey comes out of oven. Bake extra stuffing in a covered buttered baking dish at 375°F until heated through and top is golden, 30 to 40 minutes.

from Stuffing 101

sweet-potato rolls

MAKES 20 | **PHOTO ON PAGE 327**

You will need to cook about two medium sweet potatoes to obtain two cups cooked flesh. We like the flavor of roasted potatoes best, but you could also use boiled or steamed ones. Before using, peel and discard skins.

- ¼ cup warm water
- 1 envelope active dry yeast (1 scant tablespoon)
- 1 cup milk
- ⅓ cup unsalted butter
- ½ cup sugar
- 1½ tablespoons coarse salt
- 1 teaspoon ground cardamom
- 2 cups cooked sweet potatoes (about 2 medium)
- 1 teaspoon freshly squeezed lemon juice
- 1 large egg, lightly beaten
- 7 cups sifted all-purpose flour

  Vegetable oil, for bowl

  Melted butter, for brushing

1 Place the warm water in a small bowl, and sprinkle with yeast. Let stand until yeast is dissolved and mixture is foamy, about 7 minutes.

2 In a small saucepan, heat milk over medium heat just until it begins to steam and bubble around the sides. Remove from heat; add the butter, and stir until melted and combined. Stir in sugar, salt, and cardamom. Let cool slightly.

3 Combine sweet potatoes and lemon juice in the bowl of an electric mixer fitted with the paddle attachment; beat until smooth, 2 to 3 minutes. Beat in egg and the milk and yeast mixtures until smooth.

4 Switch to the dough-hook attachment. Add flour, 1 cup at a time, beating until a stiff dough forms. Continue kneading dough on medium speed until smooth, about 8 minutes. The dough will still be slightly sticky.

5 Transfer dough to a large oiled bowl. Cover with a clean kitchen towel, and let rise in a warm place until doubled in bulk, about 1 hour.

6 Preheat oven to 400°F. Line a baking sheet with parchment paper; set aside. Punch down dough, and turn out onto a clean work surface. Knead again with your hands, just until smooth. Using a bench scraper or sharp knife, cut dough into 20 equal pieces, and shape into round rolls.

7 Place rolls on prepared baking sheet, about 2 inches apart; cover with a clean kitchen towel, and let rise again in a warm place until doubled in bulk, about 40 minutes.

8 Using kitchen scissors or a sharp paring knife, snip an X in the top of each roll. Brush tops with melted butter. Bake until tops of rolls are golden, about 20 minutes, rotating pan halfway through. Transfer to a wire rack to cool slightly.

from Sweet Potatoes

....

DESSERTS

....

amaretti crisps

MAKES 20

To achieve the most volume, whisk egg whites in a metal bowl set over a pot of simmering water until just warm to the touch.

1¾ cups sliced almonds (about 7 ounces)
1 cup confectioners' sugar
2 large egg whites
½ teaspoon pure almond extract

1 Preheat oven to 350°F. Spread almonds in a single layer on a rimmed baking sheet; toast until lightly browned and fragrant, 7 to 9 minutes. Remove from oven; let cool.

2 Combine almonds and sugar in the bowl of a food processor fitted with the metal blade, and grind to a fine powder. Transfer to a medium bowl. In a separate bowl, beat egg whites until stiff peaks form. Fold egg whites into almond mixture; fold in almond extract.

3 Line a baking sheet with parchment paper. Transfer almond mixture to a pastry bag fitted with a ½-inch plain tip. Pipe twenty 2-inch rings onto sheet, about 1 inch apart. Bake until golden brown and firm to the touch, about 25 minutes. Remove from oven; transfer to a wire rack to cool.

from What to Have for Dinner

cecilia's sweet potato pie

SERVES 8

All-purpose flour, for work surface
½ recipe Pâte Brisée (page 282)
2 medium sweet potatoes (about 1½ pounds), cooked and peeled
2 tablespoons unsalted butter, room temperature
½ cup plus 3 tablespoons light-brown sugar
2 tablespoons pure maple syrup
1 tablespoon bourbon (optional)
1 teaspoon pure vanilla extract
½ teaspoon ground cinnamon
¼ teaspoon salt
Pinch of freshly grated nutmeg
1 cup half-and-half
2 large whole eggs
1 large egg yolk
½ cup plus 1 tablespoon pecans, toasted and roughly chopped
1 tablespoon heavy cream
Bourbon Whipped Cream, for serving (page 282)

1 On a lightly floured surface, roll out dough to a 13-inch round about ⅛ inch thick. Brush off excess flour. Wrap the dough around the rolling pin, and lift it over a 9-inch pie plate. Line the plate with the dough, pressing it into the sides. Trim dough, leaving about ¼-inch overhang all around; fold dough under to form a rim. Crimp edge with a fork. Cover with plastic wrap, and chill in refrigerator at least 30 minutes or up to 1 day.

2 Preheat oven to 375°F with rack in center. Remove pie plate from refrigerator, and prick bottom of dough all over with a fork. Line with parchment paper, pressing into corners, and fill with pie weights or dried beans. Bake until edges begin to turn brown, 15 to 20 minutes. Transfer to a wire rack to cool, removing paper and weights.

3 Combine sweet potatoes and butter in the bowl of an electric mixer fitted with the paddle attachment. Beat on medium speed until smooth. Add ½ cup brown sugar, the maple syrup, bourbon, if using, vanilla, cinnamon, salt, and nutmeg. Mix until well combined. Add half-and-half, 1 egg, and the egg yolk; mix until smooth.

4 Sprinkle remaining 3 tablespoons brown sugar and chopped pecans evenly over bottom of prepared crust. Pour in filling. In a small bowl, whisk remaining egg and cream; brush egg wash evenly over edge of crust. Transfer to oven; bake until set, 30 to 40 minutes. Transfer to a wire rack to cool. Serve with whipped cream.

from Sweet Potatoes

pâte brisée

MAKES 2 EIGHT- TO TEN-INCH SINGLE-CRUST PIES OR
1 EIGHT- TO TEN-INCH DOUBLE-CRUST PIE

The pie dough may be made one week ahead and refrigerated, wrapped in plastic, or frozen for up to one month.

2½ cups all-purpose flour

1 teaspoon salt

1 teaspoon sugar

1 cup (2 sticks) chilled unsalted butter, cut into pieces

¼ to ½ cup ice water

1 Combine flour, salt, and sugar in the bowl of a food processor fitted with the metal blade, and pulse a few times until combined. Add the butter, and process until mixture resembles coarse meal, about 10 seconds. With the machine running, add the ice water in a slow, steady stream through the feed tube, just until dough holds together. Do not process more than 30 seconds.

2 Turn dough out onto a work surface. Divide into 2 pieces, and flatten into disks. Wrap well in plastic, and refrigerate at least 1 hour before using.

bourbon whipped cream

MAKES 2½ CUPS

Crème fraîche imparts a tangy flavor and a velvety texture.

1 cup heavy cream, chilled

1 vanilla bean, split lengthwise and scraped

½ cup crème fraîche

2 tablespoons pure maple syrup

2 teaspoons bourbon

In the bowl of an electric mixer fitted with the whisk attachment, beat the cream and vanilla scrapings until mixture is thick, about 5 minutes. Add crème fraîche, maple syrup, and bourbon; continue beating until stiff peaks form, about 2 minutes. Serve immediately, or transfer to a bowl and refrigerate, covered, until ready to serve, up to 1 hour.

pear pandowdy

SERVES 8 TO 10 | PHOTO ON PAGE 333

In pandowdy, a spiced fruit filling is topped with mounds of biscuit dough and then baked, similar to cobblers. Traditionally made with apples, this version of the dessert features pears; dried cranberries add a tart note. The name is believed to refer to its rather old-fashioned appearance.

FOR THE CRUST:

¾ cup cake flour (not self-rising)

½ cup all-purpose flour, plus more for work surface

½ teaspoon salt

1 teaspoon baking powder

10 tablespoons (1¼ sticks) unsalted butter

¼ cup sugar

Grated zest of 1 lemon

½ teaspoon pure vanilla extract

1 large whole egg

1 large egg yolk

FOR THE FILLING:

4 large ripe Bartlett pears (about 2½ pounds)

1½ cups fresh cranberries

½ cup packed dark-brown sugar

¼ teaspoon salt

¾ cup shelled unsalted pistachios, coarsely chopped

¾ cup sweetened shredded coconut

2 tablespoons brandy or cider

¼ teaspoon ground cloves

2 tablespoons unsalted butter, cut into pieces

1 large egg, lightly beaten, for glaze

1 tablespoon heavy cream

1 tablespoon granulated sugar

1 Sift together flours, salt, and baking powder into a medium bowl, and set aside. In the bowl of an electric mixer fitted with the paddle attachment, cream butter, sugar, lemon zest, and vanilla on medium speed until light and fluffy.

2 Add egg and yolk, one at a time, beating until well incorporated after each addition. Add flour mixture; beat on low speed until just combined. Turn out onto a piece of plastic wrap, and flatten into a square about 1 inch thick. Wrap well in plastic; chill in the refrigerator until firm, at least 2 hours.

3 Transfer dough to a lightly floured work surface, and roll out to ¼ inch thick. Cut into 2-inch squares with a paring knife. Using a spatula, transfer squares to a parchment-lined baking sheet. Cover with plastic wrap, and chill again in the refrigerator until firm, at least 30 minutes.

4 Preheat oven to 375°F. Make the filling: Peel and core pears, and chop into ½-inch pieces. Place in a large bowl, and add cranberries, brown sugar, salt, pistachios, coconut, brandy or cider, and cloves; toss until well combined. Transfer to a 2-quart ceramic or Pyrex baking dish. Dot top of filling with butter.

5 Remove dough squares from refrigerator, and place on top of filling so that they are slightly overlapping, leaving some of the filling uncovered. In a small bowl, whisk together egg and cream; brush over dough. Sprinkle with granulated sugar.

6 Bake until crust is golden and filling is bubbling, 30 to 35 minutes. Remove from oven, and push crust partly down into fruit mixture. Serve warm.

from Thanksgiving: An All-Day Affair

pear pavlova

SERVES 6 | **PHOTO ON PAGE 332**

FOR PEARS:

1 750-ml bottle dry red wine, such as Cabernet or Zinfandel
3 cups water
1 cup sugar
1 teaspoon whole black peppercorns
3 dried bay leaves
2 cinnamon sticks
3 to 6 ripe Bosc pears

FOR MERINGUE BASE:

4 large egg whites
Pinch of salt
¾ cup packed light-brown sugar
¼ cup superfine sugar
1 teaspoon distilled white vinegar
1 teaspoon pure vanilla extract

FOR TOPPING:

1 cup heavy cream
2 tablespoons superfine sugar

1 Poach pears: Combine wine, the water, sugar, peppercorns, bay leaves, and cinnamon sticks in a large saucepan. Bring to a boil, and stir until sugar has dissolved. Reduce heat to a gentle simmer.

2 Carefully peel pears, leaving stems attached. Place in pan; cover, and cook, rotating occasionally, until base of pears are easily pierced with a paring knife, 20 to 25 minutes depending on the ripeness of the fruit. Prepare an ice bath; set aside.

3 Using a large slotted spoon, carefully transfer pears to a large metal bowl set in the ice bath. Pour poaching liquid

through a fine sieve into bowl with pears; let cool completely. Cover with plastic wrap; refrigerate overnight to let pears absorb the poaching liquid.

4 Preheat oven to 300°F with rack in center. Using an overturned bowl or cake pan as a guide, trace an 8-inch circle onto a sheet of parchment paper. Line a baking sheet with parchment, marking side down.

5 Make meringue base: Place egg whites, salt, and brown sugar in the bowl of an electric mixer fitted with the whisk attachment. Beat on low speed until well combined and no lumps of sugar remain. Increase speed to medium; beat until soft peaks form, about 9 minutes. With mixer running, gradually add ¼ cup superfine sugar. Beat until peaks are stiff and glossy, about 2 minutes more. Beat in vinegar and vanilla.

6 Using a large rubber spatula, spread egg-white mixture into an 8-inch round on prepared baking sheet, using the marked circle as a guide; form peaks around the edge and a well in the center.

7 Bake meringue until crisp around the edge and just set in the center, about 1¼ hours. Transfer baking sheet to a wire rack until meringue is cool enough to handle. Carefully peel off parchment; let meringue cool completely on rack.

8 In a small bowl, whip cream with 2 tablespoons superfine sugar until stiff peaks form. Cover with plastic wrap; refrigerate until ready to use.

9 Remove pears from the refrigerator. Slice pears in half lengthwise; remove seeds and stem with a melon baller, and discard. Cut pears into ¾-inch pieces, and place in a bowl; cover with plastic wrap, and set aside.

10 Prepare an ice bath, and set aside. Bring 3 cups poaching liquid to a boil in a medium saucepan; reduce heat, and simmer until syrupy and reduced to about 1 cup, 20 to 25 minutes. Pour into a clean bowl set in the ice bath; stir frequently until cool and thickened.

11 To assemble, carefully place meringue on serving platter. Spoon whipped cream on top, and then add pears. Serve, sliced into wedges and drizzled with syrup.

from Dessert of the Month

pumpkin-pecan pie

MAKES 1 NINE-INCH PIE | **PHOTO ON PAGE 333**

½ recipe Pâte Brisée (page 282)

1 15½-ounce can pumpkin purée

¾ cup granulated sugar

½ teaspoon salt

1 teaspoon ground ginger

½ teaspoon ground nutmeg

3 large eggs

¾ cup plus 1 tablespoon heavy cream

½ cup milk

¼ cup bourbon

⅔ cup packed dark-brown sugar

3 tablespoons unsalted butter, melted

1 cup coarsely chopped pecans,
plus halves for garnish

Whipped cream or vanilla ice cream,
for serving (optional)

1 Preheat oven to 425°F. Place pâte brisée between two pieces of plastic wrap, and roll out to a 12-inch round. Remove and discard plastic, and fit dough into a 9-inch Pyrex or ceramic pie plate; trim dough evenly along edge, leaving about a ½-inch overhang all around. Crimp edge, as desired. Prick the bottom of the dough all over with a fork. Place in the freezer until firm, about 15 minutes.

2 Remove from freezer, and line with parchment paper. Fill with pie weights or dried beans, and bake until edges are starting to turn golden, about 15 minutes. Remove paper and weights, and continue baking until center is lightly browned, about 5 minutes more. Remove from oven. Reduce oven temperature to 350°F.

3 Meanwhile, in a large bowl, whisk together pumpkin purée, granulated sugar, salt, ginger, nutmeg, eggs, ¾ cup heavy cream, milk, and bourbon until combined; set aside.

4 Fill pie shell with pumpkin mixture, and return to oven. Bake until filling is set around the edges but still slightly soft in the center, about 55 minutes. Remove from oven; let cool. The filling will continue to firm as it cools.

5 Heat broiler. In a small bowl, combine brown sugar, melted butter, remaining tablespoon cream, and chopped pecans. Sprinkle evenly over pie. Arrange pecan halves around the top, in a circle near the edge. Place pie under broiler just until topping begins to bubble, being careful not to let nuts burn. Transfer to a wire rack to cool slightly. Serve with whipped cream or ice cream, if desired.

from Thanksgiving: An All-Day Affair

warm cream-cheese brownies

MAKES 1 NINE-BY-THIRTEEN-INCH PAN | **PHOTO ON PAGE 333**

FOR THE CREAM CHEESE BATTER:

4 tablespoons unsalted butter, room temperature,
plus more for pan

6 ounces cream cheese, room temperature

½ cup sugar

2 large eggs

1 teaspoon pure vanilla extract

2 tablespoons all-purpose flour

½ cup semisweet chocolate chips (3½ ounces)

FOR THE CHOCOLATE BATTER:

4 ounces unsweetened chocolate

4 ounces semisweet chocolate

6 tablespoons unsalted butter

4 large eggs

1½ cups sugar

2 teaspoons pure vanilla extract

1 cup all-purpose flour

1 teaspoon baking powder

1 teaspoon salt

1 cup semisweet chocolate chips (7 ounces)

1 Preheat oven to 325°F. Butter a 9-by-13-inch baking pan; set aside. Make cream cheese batter: Beat cream cheese, butter, and sugar in the bowl of an electric mixer fitted with the paddle attachment until well blended. Add eggs, one at a time, beating well and scraping down sides of bowl at least once. Beat in vanilla. Fold in flour and chips; set aside.

2 Make chocolate batter: Melt chocolates and butter in a heatproof bowl set over a pan of simmering water. Remove from heat; let cool completely. In a separate bowl, beat eggs with a whisk, gradually adding sugar, until thick and pale. Whisk in chocolate mixture. Add vanilla; combine well.

3 Combine flour, baking powder, and salt in a medium bowl, and fold into the chocolate mixture. Fold in chocolate chips. Reserve about ½ cup chocolate batter. Spoon the rest into prepared baking pan, and spread with the cream cheese batter. Dollop reserved chocolate batter on top. Run a knife or offset spatula through batters to lightly swirl.

4 Bake until a cake tester inserted near edges comes out clean, about 35 minutes. The center will be fairly soft, but will continue to firm once removed from oven. Transfer to wire rack; let brownies cool in pan before cutting into squares.

from Thanksgiving: An All-Day Affair

yogurt drizzled with honey and walnuts

SERVES 6

You may want to try using low-fat Greek-style yogurt, which is thicker and richer in flavor than other varieties. Once combined, walnuts and honey can be stored in an airtight container up to two weeks at room temperature.

3 ounces walnut halves (about ¾ cup)
1 cup good-quality honey, such as clover or wildflower
24 ounces plain low-fat yogurt

1 Preheat oven to 350°F. Spread walnuts in a single layer on a rimmed baking sheet; toast until fragrant and browned, 7 to 8 minutes. Transfer to a plate. Rub with a damp kitchen towel to remove as much loose skin as possible.

2 While still warm, place walnuts in a small bowl, pour honey over, and stir to coat evenly. Let cool, about 2 minutes. Divide yogurt among six dessert bowls, and spoon honey mixture over each. Serve immediately.

PER SERVING: 321 CALORIES, 10 G FAT, 10 MG CHOLESTEROL, 56 G CARBOHYDRATE, 95 MG SODIUM, 9 G PROTEIN, 1 G FIBER

from Fit to Eat: Walnuts

. . . .

MISCELLANEOUS

. . . .

bread-and-butter pickles

MAKES 3 QUARTS

These are the familiar pickles that are a staple at delis. For best results, use only kirby cucumbers; they are firmer and have fewer seeds than other types.

4 pounds kirby cucumbers, washed well
1½ pounds onions, thinly sliced
½ cup coarse salt
3 cups cider vinegar
2 cups sugar
2½ teaspoons mustard seed
1½ teaspoons turmeric
2 teaspoons ground celery seed

1 Cut away any bruises or blemishes from cucumbers, and cut into ¼-inch slices. Place in a large bowl, and add onions and salt; toss well to combine, and add enough cold water to cover by about 1 inch. Let stand, covered, 2 hours.

2 Transfer mixture to a colander to drain, discarding liquid; rinse cucumbers and onions with cold running water, and drain again. Set aside.

3 Combine vinegar, sugar, and spices in a large saucepan; bring to a boil over high heat. Add cucumbers and onions, and return to a boil. Cook 1 minute.

4 Transfer mixture to jars or airtight containers, and store, covered, in the refrigerator up to 2 weeks.

from Relish Trays

breakfast butter

MAKES 1 CUP

Serve this tart, jamlike topping with biscuits or scones.

½ cup (1 stick) unsalted butter, softened
½ cup cranberry sauce

Stir the butter in a bowl until smooth, and fold in the cranberry sauce. Serve immediately or store, covered, in the refrigerator up to 5 days.

from Good Things

buttermilk and blue cheese dressing

MAKES ABOUT 2 CUPS

We tossed this dressing with well-chilled chopped romaine lettuce and thinly sliced red onions.

¼ cup mayonnaise
¼ cup sour cream
¾ cup buttermilk
1 small garlic clove, minced
¼ teaspoon coarse salt, plus more for seasoning
2 tablespoons honey
2 tablespoons cider vinegar
2 tablespoons thinly sliced fresh basil leaves
1 cup crumbled blue cheese, such as Danish Blue or Roquefort (4 ounces)
Freshly ground pepper

In a medium bowl, whisk together mayonnaise, sour cream, buttermilk, garlic, salt, honey, and vinegar until smooth. Fold in basil and blue cheese. Season with pepper and more salt, as desired. Cover with plastic wrap, and store in the refrigerator until ready to use.

from Thanksgiving: An All-Day Affair

pickled beets

MAKES 2 QUARTS

8 to 10 small to medium beets, washed well

2 cups cider vinegar

1 cup sugar

2 teaspoons coarse salt

2 tablespoons mustard seed

1   Place beets in a large nonreactive saucepan; add enough cold water to cover by about 2 inches. Bring to a boil over high heat; reduce heat to medium, and cook until easily pierced with a paring knife, about 45 minutes.

2   Transfer to a colander, and let drain, reserving 1 cup cooking liquid. Let beets cool slightly, and then peel. The beets will be easier to peel when still warm. Cut into quarters.

3   Combine vinegar, reserved cooking liquid, sugar, salt, and mustard seed in the same saucepan. Bring to a boil over high heat, and continue boiling 2 minutes. Remove from heat, and add beets; let stand overnight, covered, at room temperature. Transfer mixture to jars or airtight containers, and store in the refrigerator, covered, up to 2 weeks.

from Relish Trays

pickled green beans

MAKES 2 QUARTS

2 pounds green beans, ends trimmed

2 cups white-wine vinegar

2¼ cups water, plus more for green beans

3 tablespoons coarse salt

1 teaspoon whole black peppercorns

¾ teaspoon cayenne pepper

2 garlic cloves, peeled

¼ cup fresh dill

1   Bring a large pot of water to a boil over high heat. Add the beans, and cook until crisp-tender, about 5 minutes. Drain beans in a colander. Transfer to a heat-proof bowl or storage container, and set aside.

2   Combine vinegar, the water, salt, peppercorns, and cayenne in a medium saucepan. Bring to a boil over high heat. Add garlic and dill, and remove from heat. While still hot, pour vinegar mixture over green beans; let cool. Cover tightly, and store in the refrigerator up to 2 weeks.

from Relish Trays

pickled watermelon rind

MAKES 7 PINTS

This sweet-tart relish is a staple of the American South; it is particularly good with barbecued chicken or pork. Instead of watermelon, you can substitute three cantaloupes, two medium pumpkins, or two pounds of pearl onions (begin with step three). Before pickling, peel the items, and cut into slightly larger than one-inch chunks; pearl onions can be left whole. To peel pearl onions, drop them in boiling water for one minute, and then drain in a colander. When cool enough to handle, slip off the papery skins.

1 watermelon (about 20 pounds)

1 gallon water

½ cup coarse salt

3 cups sugar

2 cups cider vinegar

2 teaspoons whole cloves

2 teaspoons allspice

1 cinnamon stick

1 half-inch piece fresh ginger, peeled

1 lemon, thinly sliced

1   Using a sharp knife, slice watermelon in half lengthwise; scoop out flesh and seeds, and reserve for another use. Using a large metal spoon, scrape rind to remove all traces of pink. Cut rind crosswise into 1-inch-wide strips. Using a sharp knife, peel green skin from rind, and discard. Cut away any bruises or bad spots. Cut rind into 2-inch lengths.

2   In a large nonreactive bowl, combine the water and salt. Add watermelon rind; let soak overnight at room temperature. Rinse rind 2 or 3 times in fresh cold water; drain well.

3   Heat sugar and vinegar in a large nonreactive pot over medium-high heat until sugar has dissolved. Add remaining ingredients and watermelon rind, and bring to a boil over medium-high heat. Reduce heat; simmer, covered, 30 minutes. Remove from heat, and let stand, covered, overnight at room temperature. Place in jars or airtight containers, and store in the refrigerator, covered, up to 2 weeks.

from Relish Trays

December

STARTERS

289 brie and walnut cake

289 cheese fondue

290 eggplant-pomegranate relish

290 focaccia cake

291 smoked salmon cake

291 sushi cake

SALADS

292 endive and radish salad

292 honey tangerines and kumquats with
     shaved celery and walnuts

292 mixed lettuces with grapefruit, goat cheese,
     and black pepper

293 oranges with olives, parsley, and paprika

293 pomegranate, fennel, and green bean salad

294 thinly sliced beets with blood oranges
     and watercress

MAIN COURSES

294 honey-orange baked ham

295 miso-glazed cod

295 roasted cornish hens with
     pomegranate-molasses glaze

296 walnut chicken strips with pomegranate
     dipping sauce

SIDE DISHES

296 basic potato latkes

297 carrot and beet latkes

297 ginger-peanut somen noodles

298 green beans and spaetzle

298 orange spiral rolls

299 parsnip latkes

299 pomegranate pilaf

299 potato rösti

300 sesame steamed spinach

300 spinach and currant latkes

301 sweet-potato latkes

301 vanilla applesauce

DESSERTS

301 almond shortbread cookies

302 bratselies

302 broiled persimmons with mascarpone

303 chocolate butterscotch-chip cookies

303 chocolate-hazelnut torte

303 chocolate-pecan fudge

304 dobos torte

305 gingerbread cookies

305 individual no-bake cheesecakes

306 linzertorte

307 mile-high apple pie

307 peanut brittle

308 peppermint semifreddo

308 poppy-seed torte

309 three-nut torte

(continued on next page)

(continued from previous page)

TRUFFLES

310 classic truffles

310 candy cane truffles

311 champagne truffles

311 coconut truffles

311 grand marnier truffles

311 hazelnut truffles

311 mocha truffles

311 orange-ginger truffles

312 praline truffles

312 sambuca truffles

DRINKS

312 pomegranate punch

312 pomegranate tea

brie and walnut cake

SERVES 10 TO 12 | **PHOTO ON PAGE 316**

This savory cake is delicious at room temperature. If making it the night before, remove cake from refrigerator at least two hours before serving.

15 ounces fresh goat cheese

 4 ounces mild blue cheese, such as Gorgonzola dolce

 1 9-inch wheel Brie, chilled

 1 cup walnut halves, toasted and chopped, plus more for garnish

 1 cup ruby port

¼ cup honey

  Fresh thyme

 4 cups red seedless grapes, sliced into ¼-inch pieces

1 In the bowl of an electric mixer fitted with the paddle attachment, beat goat cheese and blue cheese until mixture is softened and smooth. Set aside.

2 Using a sharp serrated knife, carefully slice Brie in half horizontally, gently easing the two halves apart. Spread ¾ cup goat-cheese mixture on one half; sprinkle with walnuts. Place other Brie half, cut side down, on top of walnuts.

3 Using an offset spatula, spread remaining goat-cheese mixture over top half of Brie. Chill 2 hours or overnight.

4 Up to 1 hour before serving, combine port, honey, and 2 sprigs thyme in a medium saucepan. Bring to a boil over medium-high heat; cook until reduced by half, about 6 minutes. Add grapes; cook 30 seconds more. Using a slotted spoon, transfer grapes to a bowl; let cool. Reduce remaining liquid until thickened, about 6 minutes. Remove from heat.

5 Just before serving, place cake on a platter, and arrange grapes on top of goat-cheese mixture. Drizzle with port syrup. Garnish the platter with walnut halves and thyme sprigs.

Easy Entertaining: Party Fare

cheese fondue

SERVES 8 TO 10

If your fondue is too thick, thin it with more warmed cider or wine; if it is too thin, stir in a bit of cornstarch. If the fondue separates and becomes lumpy, return the pot to the stove, and gently whisk over moderate heat; mix some cornstarch with cider or wine, and stir into the fondue.

 1 garlic clove, halved horizontally

1½ cups apple cider or dry white wine

 8 ounces grated Gruyère cheese (about 3 cups)

 8 ounces grated Emmental cheese (about 3 cups)

 8 ounces grated raclette cheese (about 3 cups)

 2 tablespoons freshly squeezed lemon juice

 2 tablespoons cornstarch

  Freshly grated nutmeg

  Freshly ground white pepper

 1 loaf French bread, cut into 1-inch cubes

  Assorted pickled vegetables, such as cornichons, pearl onions, cauliflower florets, baby carrots, and mushrooms (optional)

1 Rub the inside of a fondue pot with the cut garlic clove, then discard garlic. Pour apple cider or wine into pot, and heat slowly over low heat. When it begins to bubble, start adding cheeses by the handful, stirring until melted.

2 When all of the cheese has melted, whisk together lemon juice and cornstarch in a small bowl until cornstarch has dissolved; stir into cheese mixture. Continue stirring until mixture is smooth and bubbling slightly, about 5 minutes. Season with nutmeg and pepper.

3 Transfer fondue pot to table, and keep warm over a burner. Serve with bread and pickled vegetables, if desired.

from Rocky Mountain Christmas

eggplant-pomegranate relish

MAKES ABOUT 2 ⅓ CUPS | PHOTO ON PAGE 313

Serve with toasted pita bread or lavash.

1 large eggplant (about 1½ pounds)
2 tablespoons plain yogurt
1 tablespoon pomegranate molasses
1 tablespoon freshly squeezed lemon juice
  Coarse salt and freshly ground pepper
½ red onion, cut into ¼-inch pieces
1 garlic clove, minced
½ cup chopped toasted walnuts (about 2 ounces)
½ cup pomegranate seeds (about ½ pomegranate)
2 tablespoons finely chopped fresh flat-leaf parsley

1 Heat broiler. Place eggplant on a rimmed baking sheet, and pierce a few times with a fork. Cook, turning occasionally as skin blackens, until very tender, about 35 minutes. Remove from oven; let cool.

2 Scrape flesh of eggplant into the bowl of a food processor fitted with the metal blade. Add yogurt, pomegranate molasses, and lemon juice, and season with salt and pepper; pulse a few times until almost smooth, but with some chunks remaining. Transfer to a serving bowl, and stir in onion, garlic, walnuts, pomegranate seeds, and parsley. Cover with plastic wrap, and chill until ready to serve.

from Pomegranates

focaccia cake

SERVES 6 TO 8 | PHOTO ON PAGE 316

Using store-bought ingredients makes this cake a cinch to prepare. You can substitute more basil pesto for the artichoke-lemon pesto, if desired.

1 8-inch round loaf focaccia
¼ cup prepared artichoke-lemon pesto
2 whole roasted red peppers, patted dry (8-ounce jar)
¼ cup prepared basil pesto
¼ cup prepared black-olive tapenade
4 ounces prosciutto, plus more for garnish
½ cup fresh basil leaves, plus more for garnish
1 pound mascarpone cheese
  Coarse salt and freshly ground black pepper
  Grape or cherry tomatoes, for garnish
  Marinated artichoke hearts, drained, for garnish
  Assorted olives, for garnish

1 Slice focaccia horizontally into three even layers. Using an offset spatula, spread artichoke-lemon pesto evenly over bottom layer. Top with peppers, 3 tablespoons basil pesto, and middle bread layer; spread with an even layer of tapenade. Top with prosciutto, basil, and final bread layer.

2 In the bowl of an electric mixer fitted with the paddle attachment, beat mascarpone and remaining basil pesto until smooth. Season with salt and pepper.

3 Using an offset spatula, spread mascarpone mixture evenly over cake. Transfer to a serving platter. Place in the refrigerator to chill until very firm, at least 1 hour or overnight. Remove from refrigerator, and garnish with prosciutto, tomatoes, artichoke hearts, olives, and basil.

Easy Entertaining: Party Fare

smoked salmon cake

SERVES 8 TO 10 | **PHOTO ON PAGE 316**

3 8-ounce packages cream cheese, softened

½ cup finely chopped red onion

2 tablespoons capers, drained and chopped

2 tablespoons fresh dill, finely chopped,
plus more for garnish

1 teaspoon freshly squeezed lemon juice

Coarse salt and freshly ground pepper

2 loaves pumpernickel bread, cut into 16
half-inch slices, with crusts

1 pound smoked salmon, thinly sliced

1½ seedless cucumbers, thinly sliced into ⅛-inch slices,
patted dry, plus more slices for decorating cake

½ cup crème fraîche

2½ ounces salmon roe

1 ounce black caviar

Lemon wedges, for garnish

1 In a small bowl, combine 8 ounces cream cheese, red onion, capers, dill, and lemon juice; season with salt and pepper, and stir until smooth. Lay 4 bread slices on a clean work surface; trim ¼ inch from all sides of slices. Spread 1 tablespoon cream-cheese mixture on top of 1 slice, and layer with smoked salmon and cucumber (try not to overlap cucumber slices). Spread another thin layer of the cream-cheese mixture on top. Repeat with 2 more bread slices.

2 Neatly stack prepared slices, filling side up, squaring the sides with your hands; top with the fourth bread slice. Repeat with remaining bread and filling to create three more stacks.

3 Transfer stacks to a serving platter with their long sides touching. In a small bowl, combine remaining 16 ounces cream cheese and crème fraîche until smooth. Using an off-set spatula, spread mixture evenly over assembled cake. Refrigerate, covered, at least 2 hours or overnight.

4 Before serving, arrange overlapping cucumber slices around the base of the cake; spoon salmon roe and caviar down the center of the cake, and sprinkle with dill. Garnish the platter with lemon wedges.

Easy Entertaining: Party Fare

sushi cake

SERVES 8 TO 10 | **PHOTO ON PAGE 316**

Wasabi, nori, pickled ginger, and sushi rice can be found in the Asian-food section of some supermarkets.

½ cup rice-wine vinegar

1 tablespoon coarse salt

2 tablespoons sugar

3¾ cups water

3 cups sushi rice

2 tablespoons mayonnaise

2 teaspoons fresh chives, finely chopped

2 tablespoons powdered wasabi,
mixed with 2 tablespoons water

1 teaspoon freshly squeezed lemon juice

Coarse salt and freshly ground pepper

4 ounces jumbo lump crabmeat, picked over

4 ounces cooked large shrimp, peeled, deveined, and roughly chopped, plus several more whole for garnish

2 tablespoons pickled ginger, finely shredded,
plus more for garnish

3 sheets nori (paper-thin dried seaweed)

Radish sprouts, for garnish

1 teaspoon toasted sesame seeds, for garnish

Wasabi Mayonnaise, for serving (page 292)

1 In a small bowl, whisk together vinegar, salt, and sugar; set aside. Place the water and rice in a large saucepan; bring to a boil over high heat. Reduce heat to low; simmer, covered, until rice has absorbed all water, about 15 minutes.

2 Transfer rice to a large bowl. Stirring constantly, slowly add reserved vinegar mixture until fully incorporated. Let cool completely, stirring occasionally.

3 In a medium bowl, whisk together mayonnaise, chives, 2 teaspoons wasabi mixture, and lemon juice; season with salt and pepper. Let stand 10 minutes at room temperature. Transfer to a nonreactive bowl, and add crab, shrimp, and 1 tablespoon ginger. Mix well to combine.

4 Toast nori sheets to enhance their flavor: Using tongs, wave each sheet over a gas burner or Sterno flame, flipping and turning until crisp and darkened in color, 30 to 60 seconds; both changes are subtle, so watch carefully.

5 Assemble cake: Place a nori sheet, shiny side down, on a dry work surface. Cover, using moistened fingers, with 2½ cups rice. Cover with plastic wrap; level with rolling pin. Remove plastic wrap, and brush with wasabi mixture. Place a nori sheet on top; spread with 1 cup rice. Cover with plastic; level with a rolling pin; brush rice with wasabi mixture.

Arrange crab mixture evenly on top; sprinkle with remaining tablespoon ginger. Spread with 1 cup rice. Place remaining nori sheet on top; cover with 2½ cups rice. Cover with plastic; level cake with rolling pin. Trim edges, using a wet, sharp knife; transfer cake to a plate. Cover with plastic wrap; refrigerate at least 2 hours or overnight.

6 To serve, slice the cake crosswise into three equal pieces. Place on a platter, and garnish with pickled ginger, radish sprouts, shrimp, and toasted sesame seeds. Serve with wasabi mayonnaise.

Easy Entertaining: Party Fare

wasabi mayonnaise
MAKES ½ CUP

Wasabi, also known as Japanese horseradish, is a traditional condiment for sushi and sashimi. This pungent mayonnaise can be made up to one day ahead.

- **1 teaspoon powdered wasabi mixed with 1 teaspoon water**
- **1 teaspoon freshly squeezed lemon juice**
- **½ cup mayonnaise**

Combine the wasabi mixture, lemon juice, and mayonnaise in a small bowl; stir well to combine. Store, covered with plastic wrap, in the refrigerator until ready to serve.

....

SALADS
....

endive and radish salad
SERVES 8 TO 10

- **2 heads Bibb or Boston lettuce**
- **1 small bunch radishes, trimmed and thinly sliced**
- **6 heads Belgian endive, each halved lengthwise and sliced crosswise into 1-inch pieces**
- **1 bunch scallions, white and light-green parts only, thinly sliced**
- **2 tablespoons freshly squeezed lemon juice**
- **2 tablespoons extra-virgin olive oil**
- **Coarse salt and freshly ground pepper**

Tear lettuce into bite-size pieces, and place in a large serving bowl. Add radishes, endive, and scallions. Drizzle with lemon juice and oil, and toss to combine. Season with salt and pepper. Serve immediately.

from Rocky Mountain Christmas

honey tangerines and kumquats with shaved celery and walnuts
SERVES 4

The combination of walnuts, Pecorino Romano cheese, and palate-cleansing citrus makes this a fine after-dinner salad. We used honey tangerines, but clementines, which are also members of the mandarin-orange family, work just as well.

- **3 honey tangerines, clementines, or mandarin oranges**
- **6 kumquats (about 2 ounces)**
- **4 stalks celery**
- **1½ ounces walnut halves (about ½ cup)**
- **1 tablespoon plus 1 teaspoon freshly squeezed lemon juice**
- **2 teaspoons extra-virgin olive oil**
- **Freshly ground pepper**
- **1 ounce Pecorino Romano cheese (optional)**

1 Using your hands, peel tangerines, and separate fruit into segments; pop out seeds. Slice kumquats into very thin rounds, and remove seeds. Combine tangerines and kumquats in a medium bowl.

2 Using a mandoline or sharp knife, slice celery thinly on the bias. Add to bowl with fruit. Toss in walnuts.

3 In a small bowl, whisk together lemon juice and oil; season with pepper. Drizzle dressing over citrus mixture, and toss to combine. Divide among four salad plates. Shave cheese over each salad, if desired, and serve immediately.

PER SERVING: 161 CALORIES 11 G FAT 7 MG CHOLESTEROL
13 G CARBOHYDRATE 122 MG SODIUM 5 G PROTEIN 9 G FIBER

from Fit to Eat: Citrus Salads

mixed lettuces with grapefruit, goat cheese, and black pepper
SERVES 4

- **1 ruby-red grapefruit**
- **2 teaspoons white-wine vinegar**
- **Pinch of coarse salt (optional)**
- **1 tablespoon plus 1 teaspoon extra-virgin olive oil**
- **1 head Belgian endive**
- **6 ounces mixed baby lettuces, such as frisée, mizuna, arugula, and tatsoi**
- **1 3-ounce log fresh goat cheese, cut in half crosswise**
- **Freshly ground pepper**

1 Before peeling, zest one-quarter of the grapefruit with a grater or zester (you should have about 1 teaspoon zest). Set aside in a small bowl. Peel grapefruit: Using a sharp knife, slice off both ends. Carefully slice downward, following the curve of the fruit, to remove large strips of rind. Be sure to remove all white pith, as it is bitter. Slice grapefruit in half through the stem; place cut side down on a cutting board. Slice each half into six semicircles, and set aside.

2 Add vinegar and salt, if using, to the grated zest. Whisk in the oil, and set aside.

3 Slice endive in half lengthwise, and remove core with a small knife. Slice each half lengthwise into ¼-inch-wide strips. Place in a medium bowl along with the salad greens; drizzle with dressing, and crumble half of the goat cheese into the salad. Toss thoroughly to coat. Divide among four salad plates, and arrange three grapefruit slices on top of each serving. Slice remaining goat cheese into four rounds, and place one on each salad. Season with pepper, and serve.

PER SERVING: 155 CALORIES 10 G FAT 10 MG CHOLESTEROL
12 G CARBOHYDRATE 258 MG SODIUM 7 G PROTEIN 5 G FIBER

from Fit to Eat: Citrus Salads

oranges with olives, parsley, and paprika

SERVES 4

4 navel oranges
¼ cup Niçoise olives, pitted and halved
½ teaspoon paprika
2 tablespoons freshly squeezed lemon juice
1 tablespoon extra-virgin olive oil
1½ tablespoons finely chopped fresh flat-leaf parsley, plus more leaves for garnish

1 Peel oranges: Using a sharp knife, slice off both ends. Carefully slice downward, following the curve of the fruit to remove wide strips of rind. Be sure to remove all of the white pith, as it is bitter. Slice each orange crosswise into about six rounds, and arrange them in slightly overlapping rows on a serving plate. Scatter olives over oranges.

2 In a small bowl, combine paprika and lemon juice; whisk in oil. Add parsley, and whisk to combine. Drizzle dressing over oranges and olives, then serve immediately.

PER SERVING: 143 CALORIES 9 G FAT 0 MG CHOLESTEROL
17 G CARBOHYDRATE 177 MG SODIUM 2 G PROTEIN 3 G FIBER

from Fit to Eat: Citrus Salads

pomegranate, fennel, and green bean salad

SERVES 4 TO 6 | PHOTO ON PAGE 317

1 small bulb fennel, trimmed
Juice of 1 lemon
Coarse salt
6 ounces green beans, ends trimmed, cut into 2-inch pieces
2 tablespoons Dijon mustard
2 tablespoons pomegranate molasses
1 tablespoon honey
Freshly ground pepper
½ cup extra-virgin olive oil
1 bunch watercress, trimmed and rinsed
2 ounces crumbled feta or goat cheese
½ cup pomegranate seeds (from about ½ pomegranate)

1 Cut fennel bulb in half through the root. Thinly slice each half crosswise, and place in a small bowl. Toss with lemon juice to prevent discoloration, and set aside.

2 Prepare an ice bath; set aside. Bring a small saucepan of water to a boil; add salt. Add beans; cook until bright green, about 1 minute. Using a slotted spoon, transfer beans to ice bath to stop the cooking. Drain; pat dry with paper towels.

3 In a bowl, whisk together mustard, molasses, and honey; season with salt and pepper. Gradually whisk in oil until emulsified.

4 Arrange watercress on a serving platter, and place fennel and green beans on top. Sprinkle with cheese and pomegranate seeds. Drizzle some of the dressing over, and serve immediately with remaining dressing on the side.

from Pomegranates

thinly sliced beets with blood oranges and watercress

SERVES 4

5 medium beets (about ¾ pound), trimmed and scrubbed

2 tablespoons extra-virgin olive oil

2 pinches of coarse salt

¼ cup water

4 blood oranges

1 small shallot, minced (about 1 tablespoon)

1 teaspoon red-wine vinegar

Freshly ground pepper

2 ounces fresh watercress

1 Preheat oven to 375°F. Place beets in a baking pan; drizzle with ½ tablespoon oil. Sprinkle with a pinch of salt. Toss to combine. Pour the water into pan; cover tightly with aluminum foil. Cook until beets are easily pierced with the tip of a paring knife, about 45 minutes. Remove from oven; remove foil, and let cool. Peel beets; slice into thin rounds using a mandoline or a sharp knife. Divide among four salad plates, arranging slices in a circular pattern over entire surface of plate.

2 Peel blood oranges: Using a sharp paring knife, slice off both ends. Working over a bowl to catch the juices, carefully slice downward, following the curve of the fruit to remove wide strips of rind. Be sure to remove all white pith, as it is bitter. Cut between membranes to remove whole segments.

3 Make the dressing: Measure out 2 tablespoons blood orange juice, and pour into a small bowl. Add shallot, vinegar, pepper, and remaining pinch of salt. Gradually whisk in remaining 1½ tablespoons oil.

4 Mound watercress and blood orange segments in center of each plate, over beets. Drizzle with dressing, and serve.

PER SERVING: 194 CALORIES 7 G FAT 0 MG CHOLESTEROL 32 G CARBOHYDRATE 438 MG SODIUM 4 G PROTEIN 7 G FIBER

from Fit to Eat: Citrus Salads

honey-orange baked ham

SERVES 10 WITH LEFTOVERS

To carve the ham, begin by cutting out a small V-shaped piece of meat from the top near the hock end. From that point, cut ham at a 45-degree angle into thin slices.

1 whole smoked ham (14 to 18 pounds), bone in and rind on

½ cup honey

⅓ cup freshly squeezed orange juice

3 tablespoons balsamic vinegar

1 tablespoon Dijon mustard

1 large onion, peeled cut into 6 wedges

1 large orange, peeled and cut into 6 wedges

4 sprigs rosemary

½ cup cider vinegar

3½ cups homemade or low-sodium canned chicken stock (two 14½-ounce cans)

3 tablespoons all-purpose flour

Coarse salt and freshly ground pepper

1 Rinse ham with cool water, and dry with paper towels. Let ham stand at room temperature, uncovered, 1 hour. Meanwhile, whisk together honey, orange juice, balsamic vinegar, and mustard. Set marinade aside.

2 Preheat oven to 300°F, with rack in lower third. Fit a roasting pan with a rack. Transfer ham, with the thicker rind on top, to rack. Scatter onion and orange wedges and rosemary around pan. Cook 1 hour.

3 Remove ham from oven; let cool slightly. Raise oven temperature to 350°F. Trim fat to a ¼-inch layer all around ham (it does not need to be perfectly even, since the bottom will have less fat and more skin). Turn ham bottom side down. Score the remaining fat on top of ham in a diamond pattern, each 1 to 2 inches, cutting about ¼ inch into meat. Baste with some of the honey marinade. Add enough water to the roasting pan to cover the bottom by about ¼ inch.

4 Return ham to oven; cook 1 hour more, basting often with remaining marinade. (Do not baste with pan juices. If necessary, add additional water to roasting pan to keep pan juices from burning.) Remove from oven; let cool slightly. Transfer to a serving platter, and let stand 30 minutes before carving.

5 While ham is resting, make the gravy: Strain liquid from roasting pan into a liquid measuring cup or bowl; skim off fat that rises to the surface with a large spoon. Place roasting pan over medium-high heat. Add cider vinegar, and simmer until most of the liquid has evaporated. Return defatted juices to pan along with 2 cups chicken stock. Bring to a boil, then keep at a simmer. In a small bowl, whisk together remaining 1½ cups stock with the flour until well combined. Whisk into sauce; continue simmering until liquid is reduced by half and somewhat thickened. Season with salt and pepper; transfer to a gravy boat, and serve hot with slices of ham.

from Rocky Mountain Christmas

miso-glazed cod

SERVES 4 | **PHOTO ON PAGE 319**

Miso is a fermented soybean paste. The lighter, or "white," version is milder and less salty than brown miso, and is sometimes referred to as sweet miso. It can be found in the Asian section of some supermarkets and health-food stores.

¼ cup mirin (Japanese sweet rice wine)

¼ cup white miso paste

¼ cup sugar

   Olive oil, for baking sheet

4 skinless cod fillets (6 ounces each)

1 In a small saucepan, combine mirin, miso, and sugar. Whisking constantly, cook over medium heat until sugar has dissolved. Remove from heat, and let cool completely.

2 Heat broiler, with rack 6 inches from heat. Coat a baking sheet with oil. Place fish on baking sheet, and brush liberally with miso mixture. Broil until fillets are browned on top and opaque in the center, 6 to 8 minutes. If tops brown before fish is cooked through, cover loosely with aluminum foil. Remove from oven; serve immediately.

from What to Have for Dinner

roasted cornish hens with pomegranate-molasses glaze

SERVES 4 | **PHOTO ON PAGE 322**

⅓ cup pomegranate molasses

⅓ cup extra-virgin olive oil

¼ teaspoon freshly ground pepper

2 cornish hens (each 1 to 1½ pounds), rinsed and patted dry

2 onions, 1 thinly sliced and the other cut into 8 wedges

4 garlic cloves, smashed

1 lemon, cut into 8 wedges

2 tablespoons unsalted butter, melted

   Coarse salt and freshly ground pepper

   Cooking spray, for roasting rack

1 In a small bowl, whisk together pomegranate molasses, oil, and pepper; set aside. Place each hen in a large resealable plastic bag. Pour half of the marinade into each bag, and divide sliced onion and garlic between bags. Seal bags, and and turn to coat hens with marinade. Refrigerate at least 4 hours or overnight, turning occasionally.

2 Preheat oven to 350°F, with rack in lower third. Line a shallow roasting pan or rimmed baking sheet with a roasting rack, and coat rack with cooking spray; set aside.

3 Remove hens from plastic bags, letting excess marinade drip off. Place hens on rack, breast side up, and tuck wing tips under body. Fill each cavity with 4 onion wedges and 4 lemon wedges; tie legs together with kitchen twine. Brush hens with melted butter, and sprinkle with salt and pepper. Roast until golden and cooked through, about 1½ hours, rotating pan every half hour. If hens start to get too dark, cover loosely with foil. Remove from oven, and let rest about 5 minutes before serving.

from Pomegranates

walnut chicken strips with pomegranate dipping sauce

MAKES ABOUT 4 DOZEN PIECES AND 2 CUPS SAUCE

FOR THE CHICKEN STRIPS:

1½ cups coarsely chopped walnuts (about 6 ounces)

¾ cup all-purpose flour

½ teaspoon ground cinnamon

1½ teaspoons coarse salt

¼ teaspoon freshly ground pepper

 1 cup heavy cream

 4 boneless and skinless chicken breasts (about 2 pounds)

½ to ¾ cup vegetable oil

FOR THE SAUCE:

 2 tablespoons unsalted butter

 2 small shallots, finely chopped

½ cup finely chopped walnuts (about 2 ounces)

½ cup dry white wine

1½ cups homemade or low-sodium canned chicken stock

½ cup freshly squeezed pomegranate juice
    (about ½ pomegranate)

 2 tablespoons pomegranate molasses

 2 tablespoons all-purpose flour

 1 cup pomegranate seeds (1 large pomegranate)
    Coarse salt and freshly ground pepper

1 Preheat oven to 350°F. Make the chicken strips: Place walnuts, flour, cinnamon, salt, and pepper in the bowl of a food processor fitted with the metal blade. Process until finely chopped and well combined; transfer to a shallow bowl. Pour heavy cream into another shallow bowl.

2 On a clean work surface, place chicken between two pieces of plastic wrap or wax paper. Using a meat pounder, flatten to an even thickness, about ½ inch. Cut chicken into ½-by-3-inch strips. Dip strips in heavy cream with one hand, letting excess drip off; using your other hand, dredge in flour mixture, turning to coat both sides and tapping off excess. Place on an ungreased baking sheet.

3 Heat 2 tablespoons vegetable oil in a large skillet over medium-high heat. Working in batches, add chicken strips; cook, turning occasionally, until golden brown all over, about 3 minutes. Transfer to a wire rack set over a baking sheet. Wipe out skillet; repeat with remaining chicken, adding 2 tablespoons oil with each batch. Transfer baking sheet with chicken to oven, and bake until chicken is cooked through, about 10 minutes.

4 Meanwhile, make the sauce: Melt butter in a clean skillet over medium heat. Add shallots and walnuts, and cook until shallots are tender and nuts are golden, about 2 minutes.

5 Add wine; cook until most of the liquid has evaporated. Add 1¼ cups chicken stock, pomegranate juice, and molasses. Raise heat to medium-high; cook until liquid is reduced by half, about 10 minutes. Whisk remaining ¼ cup chicken stock with flour in a bowl until well combined. Stir into sauce; simmer until thickened, about 1 minute. Stir in pomegranate seeds; season with salt and pepper. Serve hot.

from Pomegranates

SIDE DISHES

basic potato latkes

MAKES ABOUT 2 DOZEN

When making latkes, you don't have to squeeze the moisture out of the potato mixture. Instead, stir it right before forming it into pancakes, incorporating the liquid from the bottom of the bowl. There may be as much as one-third cup liquid left over after pancakes have been formed. To prevent the potatoes from discoloring, peel and grate them just before using.

 1 yellow onion, grated on the large holes of a box grater

1½ teaspoons coarse salt

¼ teaspoon freshly ground pepper

 2 large eggs, lightly beaten

¼ cup matzo meal

 2 pounds (4 large) russet potatoes, peeled and grated
    on the large holes of a box grater
    Peanut oil, for frying
    Pink Applesauce, for serving (optional; recipe follows)
    Sour cream, for serving (optional)

1 In a large bowl, combine onion, salt, and pepper. Add eggs, and stir until incorporated. Stir in matzo meal until mixture is smooth. Add potatoes; toss until evenly coated.

2 Fill a large, heavy-bottom skillet with about ½ inch oil. Place over medium heat until oil is almost smoking. (To test, drop a bit of batter into skillet; oil should sizzle upon contact.)

3 Working in batches so as not to overcrowd the skillet, carefully spoon about 2 tablespoons batter into oil for each pancake. Lightly tamp down to flatten. Cook until golden on each side, 2 to 3 minutes, turning once. Using a slotted spatula, transfer to a paper-towel–lined wire rack to drain, and repeat with remaining batter. Serve immediately with applesauce and sour cream, if desired.

from Celebrating Hanukkah

pink applesauce

MAKES ABOUT 1 QUART

You can omit the sugar from this recipe for an unsweetened but equally delicious sauce. Applesauce can be stored in an airtight container for up to three days in the refrigerator.

9 ripe, firm apples (about 3 pounds), such as McIntosh, cored and quartered
½ cup apple cider
1 large cinnamon stick
½ teaspoon ground ginger, plus more for seasoning
Pinch of freshly grated nutmeg, plus more for seasoning
¼ cup sugar, plus more for seasoning
1 tablespoon freshly squeezed lemon juice

Combine all ingredients in a large, wide, heavy-bottom saucepan set over medium heat. Cook, covered, stirring occasionally with a wooden spoon to prevent scorching, until apples have broken down and are saucy, 50 to 60 minutes. Mash any large pieces of apple with spoon. Adjust seasoning with more sugar and spices, as desired. Remove from heat; let cool before serving, and discard cinnamon stick.

carrot and beet latkes

MAKES ABOUT 2 DOZEN

The beets turn these latkes a festive shade of red, while carrots add a note of sweetness. Because beets are high in sugar, these latkes brown very quickly.

1 small white onion, grated on the large holes of a box grater
1 teaspoon freshly squeezed lemon juice
2 large eggs, lightly beaten
3 tablespoons all-purpose flour
1 teaspoon coarse salt
¼ teaspoon freshly ground pepper
½ pound (about 4) carrots, grated on the large holes of a box grater
¼ pound (about 2) beets, peeled and grated on the large holes of a box grater
¼ pound (about 1 small or ½ medium) russet potato, peeled and grated on the large holes of a box grater
Peanut oil, for frying
Pink Applesauce, for serving (optional; recipe above)
Sour cream, for serving (optional)

1 In a medium bowl, combine onion, lemon juice, and eggs. Add flour, salt, and pepper, and stir until incorporated. Add carrots, beets, and potato; toss until evenly coated.

2 Fill a large, heavy-bottom skillet with about ½ inch oil. Place over medium heat until almost smoking. (To test, drop a bit of batter into skillet; the oil should sizzle upon contact.)

3 Working in batches so as not to overcrowd skillet, carefully spoon about 2 tablespoons batter into oil for each pancake. Lightly tamp down to flatten. Cook until golden on each side, 2 to 3 minutes, turning once. Using a slotted spatula, transfer to a paper-towel–lined rack to drain; repeat with remaining batter. Serve immediately with applesauce and sour cream, if desired.

from Celebrating Hanukkah

ginger-peanut somen noodles

SERVES 4 | PHOTO ON PAGE 319

Somen are thin Japanese noodles made from wheat flour; they're available in the Asian section of many grocery stores. Vermicelli or thin spaghetti can be used instead.

3 tablespoons freshly grated ginger
Grated zest of 1 lime
3 tablespoons freshly squeezed lime juice
3 tablespoons rice-wine vinegar
½ teaspoon coarse salt
¼ teaspoon freshly ground pepper
½ cup extra-virgin olive oil
2 8-ounce packages somen noodles
½ cup thinly sliced scallions, plus more for garnish
½ cup chopped roasted peanuts, plus more for garnish

1 Make the dressing: In a medium bowl, whisk together ginger, lime zest, lime juice, vinegar, salt, and pepper. Whisking constantly, gradually add oil in a steady stream until mixture is emulsified; set aside.

2 Bring a large saucepan of water to a boil. Add noodles, and cook until al dente according to package instructions, about 6 minutes. Drain in a colander; transfer to a serving bowl.

3 Add dressing, scallions, and peanuts to noodles; toss to combine. Serve warm, at room temperature, or chilled, and garnish with additional scallions and peanuts.

from What to Have for Dinner

green beans and spaetzle

SERVES 8 TO 10

Spaetzle, a type of pasta, is usually made by forcing dough through the large holes of colander; we used a potato ricer.

2½ cups all-purpose flour

½ teaspoon freshly grated nutmeg

¼ cup minced fresh flat-leaf parsley leaves, plus more for garnish

Coarse salt and freshly ground pepper

⅔ cup milk

5 large eggs

7 tablespoons extra-virgin olive oil

6 quarts water

2 pounds green beans, trimmed and cut into 1½-inch pieces

1 Whisk together flour, nutmeg, and parsley in a large bowl; season with salt and pepper. In another bowl, whisk together the milk, eggs, and 5 tablespoons oil until combined. Whisk milk mixture into flour mixture until smooth.

2 In a large stockpot, bring the water to a boil, and add salt. Working in batches, pass batter through a potato ricer fitted with a ⅛-inch-hole attachment into the boiling water. Cook until the dumplings float to the top, about 30 seconds. Using a slotted spoon, transfer the dumplings to a colander to drain. Repeat until all of the batter is used.

3 Heat remaining 2 tablespoons oil in a large nonstick skillet over medium-high heat. Add beans, and sauté until just tender and bright green. Add spaetzle, season with salt and pepper, and cook until heated through. Serve immediately, garnished with minced parsley.

from Rocky Mountain Christmas

orange spiral rolls

MAKES 3 DOZEN

1¼ cups warm water

2 envelopes active dry yeast (each 1 scant tablespoon)

½ cup vegetable shortening, melted

1 cup sugar

2 teaspoons salt

3 large eggs

Finely grated zest of 2 oranges

5 cups all-purpose flour, plus more for work surface

Vegetable oil, for bowl

Juice of 1 orange (about ⅓ cup)

6 tablespoons unsalted butter, melted

Cooking spray

1 Place warm water in the bowl of an electric mixer, and sprinkle with yeast. Let stand until foamy, about 5 minutes.

2 Add shortening, ½ cup sugar, and salt to yeast mixture. Attach bowl to mixer fitted with the paddle attachment, and beat until smooth and combined. Add eggs and half the orange zest; beat until thoroughly combined.

3 With the mixer on low speed, add flour, ½ cup at a time, beating after each addition until incorporated. Transfer to a floured work surface, and knead slightly to form a ball. Transfer to an oiled bowl, cover loosely with plastic wrap, and let rise in a warm place until doubled in bulk, about 1 hour.

4 Punch down dough with your hands, and cover again with plastic wrap. Refrigerate overnight. About 4 hours before proceeding with recipe, remove dough from refrigerator, and let stand at room temperature.

5 Coat three 12-cup muffin tins with cooking spray. In a medium bowl, whisk together remaining ½ cup sugar and orange zest with the orange juice and butter; set aside.

6 Divide dough into three equal pieces, and cover with plastic wrap or a damp kitchen towel. On a lightly floured work surface, roll out one piece into an 8-by-14-inch rectangle. Let rest a few minutes if dough resists. Brush top of dough with orange mixture; starting at one long side, roll into a tight cylinder. Cut crosswise into 12 slices, about 1 inch thick. Repeat with remaining two pieces of dough. Place slices in prepared muffin tins. Cover loosely with plastic wrap sprayed with cooking spray. Let dough rise until it fills cups, about 45 minutes.

7 Meanwhile, preheat oven to 375°F. Remove plastic wrap, and gently brush tops of rolls with remaining orange mixture. Bake until rolls are golden brown, 10 to 12 minutes. Remove from oven, and let cool slightly. Serve warm.

from Rocky Mountain Christmas

parsnip latkes

MAKES ABOUT 2 DOZEN

Parsnips add a tinge of sweetness to these latkes; for a delicious twist, serve them with pear sauce. (To make, substitute peeled pears for the apples in Pink Applesauce.)

1 yellow onion, grated on the large holes of a box grater, or minced

Finely grated zest of 1 orange

1½ teaspoons coarse salt

½ teaspoon cayenne pepper

¼ teaspoon freshly ground black pepper

2 large eggs, lightly beaten

⅓ cup all-purpose flour

1½ pounds (about 5 medium) parsnips, peeled and grated on the large holes of a box grater

½ pound (about 1 medium) russet potato, peeled and grated on the large holes of a box grater

Peanut oil, for frying

Pink Applesauce, for serving (optional; page 297)

Sour cream, for serving (optional)

1 In a large bowl, combine onion, orange zest, salt, cayenne, and black pepper. Add eggs, and stir until incorporated. Stir in flour until mixture is smooth. Add parsnips and potato, and toss until evenly coated.

2 Fill a large, heavy-bottom skillet with about ½ inch oil. Place over medium heat until almost smoking. (To test, drop a bit of batter into skillet; the oil should sizzle upon contact.)

3 Working in batches so as not to overcrowd the skillet, carefully spoon about 2 tablespoons batter into oil for each pancake. Lightly tamp down to flatten. Cook until golden on each side, 2 to 3 minutes, turning once. Using a slotted spatula, transfer to a paper-towel–lined wire rack to drain, and repeat with remaining batter. Serve immediately with applesauce and sour cream, if desired.

from Celebrating Hanukkah

pomegranate pilaf

SERVES 4 TO 6 | **PHOTO ON PAGE 322**

2 tablespoons unsalted butter

1 small red onion, cut into ¼-inch pieces

1 cup basmati or jasmine rice

1½ cups homemade or low-sodium canned chicken stock

½ cup chopped dried apricots

½ cup chopped unsalted pistachios or almonds

½ cup pomegranate seeds (about ½ pomegranate)

1 tablespoon chopped fresh thyme leaves

Coarse salt and freshly ground pepper

1 Melt butter in a medium saucepan over medium-low heat. Add onion, and cook until softened, about 4 minutes. Add rice; cook, stirring 1 minute to coat with butter. Add chicken stock, and bring to a boil; cover, and reduce heat to low. Cook until all liquid has been absorbed, 15 to 20 minutes.

2 Remove from heat, and fluff with a fork. Stir in apricots, nuts, pomegranate seeds, and thyme. Season with salt and pepper, and serve immediately.

from Pomegranates

potato rösti

SERVES 8 TO 10

Rösti is a Swiss term for "crisp and golden." Potato rösti is usually fried in a skillet; we baked ours for a leaner version.

¼ cup extra-virgin olive oil, plus more for baking sheet

2 large onions, grated on the large holes of a box grater

5 pounds (about 10 medium) Yukon gold or russet potatoes

1 tablespoon coarse salt, plus more for seasoning

¾ teaspoon freshly ground pepper, plus more for seasoning

8 ounces freshly grated Swiss cheese (about 2 cups)

1 Preheat oven to 375°F, with rack in lower third. Brush a 16½-by-11½-inch rimmed baking sheet generously with oil.

2 Place onions in a large bowl. Peel potatoes, and grate on the large holes of a box grater, adding them to the bowl and stirring into onions as you work, to prevent discoloration. Squeeze handfuls of grated potato and onion to release excess water, and transfer to another bowl. Add salt, pepper, cheese, and oil; toss to combine. Sprinkle potato mixture over prepared baking sheet, and press lightly to form an even layer.

3 Bake until golden, about 1 hour. Remove from oven, and cut into squares. Serve immediately.

from Rocky Mountain Christmas

ok

sesame steamed spinach

SERVES 4 | **PHOTO ON PAGE 319**

Although three pounds may seem like too much spinach, the leaves wilt quickly when heated. For best results, toast the sesame seeds in a dry skillet over medium-high heat until fragrant and starting to turn golden, shaking pan to color evenly.

½ cup water

3 pounds (3 to 4 large bunches) spinach, tough stems discarded, rinsed well and drained

4 teaspoons sesame oil

4 teaspoons rice-wine vinegar

2 tablespoons toasted sesame seeds

Coarse salt and freshly ground pepper

1 Bring the water to a boil in a large saucepan. Add spinach one bunch at a time, covering pan after each addition and adding more spinach once the prior batch has wilted. When all spinach is in the pan, let steam, covered, until completely wilted, about 30 seconds.

2 Drain spinach in a colander, pressing down with a wooden spoon to extract as much liquid as possible; let cool slightly.

3 Transfer spinach to a serving bowl; drizzle with sesame oil, vinegar, and half the toasted sesame seeds. Toss well to combine. Season with salt and pepper. Serve warm, at room temperature, or chilled; garnish with remaining sesame seeds.

from What to Have for Dinner

spinach and currant latkes

MAKES ABOUT 2 DOZEN

1 tablespoon unsalted butter

1 10-ounce package prewashed spinach, tough stems discarded, finely chopped

8 ounces (about 1 medium) zucchini, grated on the large holes of a box grater

1 small onion, grated on the large holes of a box grater

1 tablespoon freshly squeezed lemon juice

½ pound (about 1 medium) russet potato, peeled and grated on the large holes of a box grater

½ cup currants

3 large eggs, lightly beaten

½ cup all-purpose flour

¾ teaspoon ground cumin

¾ teaspoon ground coriander

¾ teaspoon coarse salt

¼ teaspoon freshly ground pepper

Peanut oil, for frying

Pink Applesauce, for serving (optional; page 297)

Sour cream, for serving (optional)

1 Melt butter in a large sauté pan over medium heat. Add spinach, and gently cook until wilted, about 2 minutes. Transfer to a clean kitchen towel or paper towels, and ring out as much liquid as possible. Transfer to a medium bowl. Add remaining ingredients through the pepper; stir to combine.

2 Fill a large, heavy-bottom skillet with about ½ inch oil. Place over medium heat until oil is almost smoking. (To test, drop a bit of batter into the skillet; the oil should sizzle upon contact.)

3 Working in batches so as not to overcrowd the skillet, carefully spoon about 2 tablespoons batter into oil for each pancake. Lightly tamp down to flatten. Cook until golden on each side, 2 to 3 minutes, turning once. Using a slotted spatula, transfer to drain on paper-towel–lined rack, and repeat with remaining batter. Serve immediately with applesauce and sour cream, if desired.

from Celebrating Hanukkah

sweet-potato latkes

MAKES ABOUT 2 DOZEN

Keep a close eye on these latkes while they are frying; the sugar in the sweet potatoes causes them to brown quickly.

3 scallions, white and light-green parts only, thinly sliced

2 large eggs, lightly beaten

⅓ cup all-purpose flour

1½ teaspoons coarse salt

½ teaspoon ground ginger

¼ teaspoon ground cardamom

¼ teaspoon freshly ground pepper

1½ pounds (about 3 medium) sweet potatoes, peeled and grated on the large holes of a box grater

1½ pounds (about 3 small) Yukon gold potatoes, peeled and grated on the large holes of a box grater

Peanut oil, for frying

Pink Applesauce, for serving (optional; page 297)

Sour cream, for serving (optional)

1 In a large bowl, combine scallions and eggs. Add flour, salt, ginger, cardamom, and pepper, and stir until mixture is smooth. Add potatoes, and toss until evenly coated.

2 Fill a large, heavy-bottom skillet with about ½ inch oil. Place over medium heat until almost smoking. (To test, drop a bit of batter into skillet; the oil should sizzle upon contact.)

3 Working in batches so as not to overcrowd the skillet, carefully spoon about 2 tablespoons batter into oil for each pancake. Lightly tamp down to flatten. Cook until golden on each side, 2 to 3 minutes, turning once. Using a slotted spatula, transfer to drain on a paper-towel–lined wire rack, and repeat with remaining batter. Serve immediately with applesauce and sour cream, if desired.

from Celebrating Hanukkah

vanilla applesauce

MAKES ABOUT 6 CUPS

14 Gala apples (about 6 pounds), peeled, cored, and quartered

1 cup apple cider

¼ cup sugar, plus more as needed

1 large cinnamon stick

1 teaspoon ground ginger, plus more for seasoning

½ teaspoon ground nutmeg, plus more for seasoning

2 tablespoons freshly squeezed lemon juice

1 vanilla bean, split lengthwise and scraped

Combine all ingredients in a large, wide, heavy-bottom saucepan over medium heat. Cook, covered, stirring occasionally with a wooden spoon to prevent scorching, until apples have broken down and are saucy, 50 to 60 minutes. Discard cinnamon stick and vanilla pod. Mash any large pieces of apple with the spoon. Add more sugar and spices, as desired. Remove from heat, and let cool completely before serving. Refrigerate in an airtight container up to 3 days.

from Rocky Mountain Christmas

DESSERTS

almond shortbread cookies

MAKES ABOUT 3 DOZEN | **PHOTO ON PAGE 336**

1 cup all-purpose flour

1 cup cornstarch

½ teaspoon salt

¾ teaspoon ground cardamom

1 teaspoon freshly ground white pepper

1 cup (2 sticks) unsalted butter, room temperature

2½ cups confectioners' sugar, sifted

1 teaspoon pure almond extract

1 large egg white

3 ounces whole blanched almonds

1 In a medium bowl, whisk together flour, cornstarch, salt, cardamom, and pepper; set aside.

2 In the bowl of an electric mixer fitted with the paddle attachment, cream butter and 1 cup confectioners' sugar until light and fluffy. Add almond extract, and beat to combine. With mixer on low speed, gradually add flour mixture until a dough forms, scraping down sides of bowl as needed.

3 Turn out dough onto a clean work surface; pinch off tablespoons of dough, and roll into 1½-inch balls. Place on two

baking sheets, 2 inches apart. Flatten each ball slightly with your fingertips. Cover with plastic wrap, and chill 30 minutes.

4 Preheat oven to 325°F. Whisk egg white in a small bowl. Add blanched almonds, and toss to coat. Remove dough from refrigerator; press 2 almonds on top of each ball of dough.

5 Bake until slightly golden, about 18 minutes. Remove from oven, and immediately transfer cookies to a wire rack.

6 Place the remaining 1½ cups confectioners' sugar in a medium bowl. While cookies are still warm, roll them in the sugar, reserving any remaining sugar. Return cookies to baking sheets, and let cool 15 minutes more, then roll again in sugar. Store cookies in an airtight container at room temperature up to 1 week.

from Rocky Mountain Christmas

bratselies

MAKES ABOUT 6 DOZEN

This is a family recipe passed down from Vera Carlson, great aunt of Brooke Hellewell Reynolds, senior art director at MARTHA STEWART LIVING. We used a special bratselies iron, which makes four cookies at a time, but you can also use a pizzelle iron. These wafer-thin cookies can be stored in an airtight container in the refrigerator for up to two weeks.

- 7 **to 9 cups all-purpose flour, sifted**
- ¼ **teaspoon salt**
- 1 **tablespoon ground cinnamon**
- 1 **cup (2 sticks) unsalted butter, room temperature**
- 1½ **cups sugar**
- 1 **tablespoon pure vanilla extract**
- 1 **tablespoon pure lemon extract**
  Finely grated zest of 1 lemon (optional)
- 2 **large eggs, lightly beaten, room temperature**
- 1 **cup heavy cream, room temperature**
  Cooking spray

1 In a medium bowl, whisk together 3 cups flour, the salt, and cinnamon, and set aside. In the bowl of an electric mixer fitted with the paddle attachment, cream butter and sugar until light and fluffy. Add vanilla and lemon extracts and lemon zest, if using, and beat until combined. Add eggs, and beat until combined.

2 In a separate bowl, whisk the cream until just slightly thickened, then add to butter mixture. Add flour mixture to butter mixture, and beat until combined. Add remaining 4

to 6 cups flour, 1 cup at a time, beating until incorporated after each addition, until dough is soft enough to handle but still slightly sticky. Pinch off ½-teaspoon pieces of dough, and roll into balls; place on baking sheets.

3 Coat a bratselie iron with cooking spray, and heat. Place one ball of dough in each grid, and press handle down tightly. Cook until golden, 20 to 25 seconds. Using a spatula, transfer cookies to a cutting board; cut into four wedges with sharp knife. Let cool completely. Store, refrigerated, in an airtight container up to 2 weeks.

from Rocky Mountain Christmas

broiled persimmons with mascarpone

SERVES 4

When fully ripe, persimmons have a glossy red-orange skin, similar to tomatoes', and a tangy-sweet flavor. They are available at most markets from October through February; choose fruit that is plump and slightly soft but not at all mushy.

- 4 **ripe persimmons**
- 3 **tablespoons honey**
- 2 **tablespoons freshly squeezed lime juice**
- 9 **ounces mascarpone cheese**
- 1 **teaspoon pure vanilla extract**
  Crystallized ginger or turbinado sugar, for garnish (optional)

1 Heat broiler with rack 6 inches from heat. Slice persimmons in half crosswise. Place halves cut side up in a baking dish; drizzle each half with honey. Broil until tops are golden brown and caramelized, 6 to 8 minutes. Remove from oven; immediately drizzle 1 tablespoon lime juice over the tops.

2 While persimmons are broiling, whisk together mascarpone, vanilla, and remaining tablespoon lime juice in a medium bowl. Serve persimmons hot, each half topped with a dollop of mascarpone mixture and sprinkled with ginger or sugar, if desired.

from What to Have for Dinner

chocolate butterscotch-chip cookies

MAKES ABOUT 4 DOZEN | PHOTO ON PAGE 336

- 2 cups all-purpose flour
- 1 teaspoon baking soda
- ¼ teaspoon salt
- 1¼ cups (2½ sticks) butter, room temperature
- 1 cup sugar
- ¾ cup packed dark-brown sugar
- 2 large eggs
- 1 teaspoon pure vanilla extract
- 1 cup butterscotch chips
- 1 cup semisweet chocolate chips

1 Preheat oven to 350°F. Line two baking sheets with parchment paper, and set aside.

2 In a medium bowl, whisk together flour, baking soda, and salt; set aside. In the bowl of an electric mixer fitted with the paddle attachment, cream butter and sugars until light and fluffy, about 3 minutes. Add eggs and vanilla, and beat until well combined. Add flour mixture, and beat until just combined. Stir in butterscotch and chocolate chips.

3 Working in batches, drop batter by the tablespoon onto prepared baking sheets, 2 inches apart. Bake until golden brown, about 12 minutes. Transfer to wire rack to cool on baking sheets 1 minute before transferring cookies to rack. Repeat with the remaining batter.

from Rocky Mountain Christmas

chocolate-hazelnut torte

MAKES ONE 8½-INCH TORTE

- ¾ cup unsalted butter, plus more for pan
  Unsweetened cocoa powder, for pan and dusting
- 1 cup currants
- ½ cup whiskey or hot water
- 1⅓ cups heavy cream
- 1 pound bittersweet chocolate, chopped
- 6 large eggs
- 1 cup sugar
- ¼ teaspoon salt
- 1½ cups finely chopped toasted hazelnuts (6½ ounces)

1 Preheat oven to 225°F. Butter an 8½-inch springform pan; sprinkle with cocoa, and tap out excess. In a small bowl, combine currants and whiskey. Let macerate at least 10 minutes and up to 30 minutes. Strain currants in a fine sieve, and discard whiskey.

2 In a small saucepan over medium heat, bring cream and butter almost to a boil, making sure all butter is melted. Place chocolate in a medium heatproof bowl, and pour cream over, completely covering chocolate. Whisk gently until chocolate is melted and mixture is combined.

3 In a medium bowl, whisk together eggs, sugar, and salt. Whisk into chocolate mixture, and stir in nuts and currants. Pour mixture into prepared pan.

4 Bake until edges are set and center is still a little soft to the touch, about 2 hours. Transfer pan to a wire rack to cool completely. Cover with plastic wrap, and chill overnight in the refrigerator. When ready to serve, remove from refrigerator, and remove sides of pan. Dust with cocoa powder.

from Favorite Tortes

chocolate-pecan fudge

MAKES ABOUT 3 POUNDS

This fudge is even better the day after it is made. You will need to pull the fudge on a clean work surface; we like to use a marble slab or a lightly buttered baking sheet. The pecans can be replaced with other nuts, such as almonds, if desired.

- 4½ cups sugar
- ½ cup Dutch-process cocoa powder
- 1½ cups heavy cream
- ½ cup (1 stick) unsalted butter, plus more for fingertips
- 3 tablespoons light corn syrup
- 1½ teaspoons pure vanilla extract
- 1½ cups chopped pecans

1 Line an 8-inch square baking pan with wax paper; set aside. In a heavy, medium saucepan, combine the sugar and cocoa; stir to mix. Add the cream, butter, and corn syrup; cook over medium-high heat, stirring constantly, just until mixture begins to bubble around the edges, about 5 minutes. Continue cooking, without stirring, until mixture reaches the soft-ball stage on a candy thermometer (238°F to 240°F), 12 to 15 minutes, washing down sides of pan with a pastry brush dipped in water to prevent crystals from forming. Immediately remove from heat; let cool in pan until temperature has cooled to 160°F, about 40 minutes. Do not stir until the mixture has cooled, as stirring will cause crystals to form.

2 When temperature reaches 160°F, quickly pour fudge onto clean work surface, using a rubber spatula to gently empty pan while holding it very close to surface to prevent splattering. Spoon vanilla extract over fudge, and let cool until it is almost at room temperature, about 15 minutes more.

3 Using a long offset spatula, begin pulling fudge in a figure-eight motion, moving from the bottom right up and over to the top left, then back down to the right. Repeat, from bottom left, up and over to the top right and back down, pushing fudge onto itself. Continue this process until you see a sudden change in appearance, from glossy to flat, 12 to 15 minutes. Sprinkle with nuts, and stir to combine.

4 Spread onto prepared baking sheet, and flatten with lightly buttered fingertips. Cover with wax paper, and let stand until set, at least 4 hours or overnight. To prevent fudge from drying out, cut into squares just before serving.

from Rocky Mountain Christmas

dobos torte
SERVES 12

The original Dobos recipe was created in 1887 by the Hungarian chef whose name it bears.

- 6 tablespoons unsalted butter, melted, plus more for sheets
- 1½ cups all-purpose flour, plus more for sheets
- 1 cup sugar
- 6 large eggs
- ¼ teaspoon salt
- ½ teaspoon pure vanilla extract
- ½ teaspoon pure almond extract
- Hazelnut Simple Syrup (recipe follows)
- Caramel Buttercream (recipe follows)
- Caramel, for garnish (recipe follows)

1 Preheat oven to 350°F, with rack in center. Butter two 12-by-17-inch rimmed baking sheets. Line sheets with parchment paper. Butter the parchment, and sprinkle with flour, tapping out excess. Set aside.

2 Set the heatproof bowl of an electric mixer over a pot of simmering water. Combine sugar, eggs, and salt in the bowl, and whisk until mixture is warm to the touch and sugar has dissolved, about 2 minutes.

3 Attach bowl to the mixer fitted with the whisk attachment, and beat on high speed until mixture is very thick and pale, 6 to 8 minutes. Using a rubber spatula, gently transfer the mixture to a large, wide bowl.

4 Sift in two-thirds of the flour in two batches, folding gently after each addition. In a small bowl, combine melted butter and vanilla and almond extracts, and add to the bowl in a steady stream as you sift in the remaining one-third flour; fold gently, and divide batter between prepared pans, smoothing the tops with an offset spatula.

5 Bake until cakes are springy to the touch and lightly golden brown, 10 to 12 minutes. Transfer pans to a wire rack to cool completely. Invert cakes onto rack; remove parchment paper. Cut each cake into three 5¼-by-11¼-inch rectangles (you will use only five; reserve the last piece for another use).

6 Lay one rectangle on a clean work surface. Using a pastry brush, soak with a little less than ¼ cup simple syrup. Using an offset spatula, spread 1 cup buttercream evenly over the top. Place another rectangle on top, and continue until you have five layers of cake soaked with simple syrup and topped with buttercream. Coat sides of cake with remaining buttercream. Smooth top and sides to form a neat block. Refrigerate until firm, at least 30 minutes. Sprinkle chopped caramel on top of cake, and serve cut into slices.

from Favorite Tortes

hazelnut simple syrup
MAKES 1⅛ CUPS

- ½ cup sugar
- ½ cup water
- ½ cup hazelnut liqueur, such as Frangelico

In a small saucepan set over medium heat, bring sugar and the water to a boil, swirling to dissolve the sugar. Remove from heat; cover, and let cool completely. Stir in the liqueur. Use immediately, or store in an airtight container in the refrigerator up to 2 weeks.

caramel buttercream
MAKES ABOUT 8 CUPS

- 2¼ cups sugar
- ½ cup water
- ½ cup heavy cream
- 3 cups (6 sticks) unsalted butter, room temperature
- 9 large egg whites
- 1½ teaspoons pure vanilla extract

1 Combine 1¼ cups sugar and the water in a medium heavy saucepan; bring to a boil over medium-high heat, washing down sides of pan with a pastry brush dipped in water to prevent crystals from forming. Continue cooking, without stirring, until dark amber in color, swirling pan to color evenly. Remove from heat; slowly stir in cream with a wooden spoon until completely smooth; set aside until cool to the touch.

2 In the bowl of an electric mixer fitted with the paddle attachment, cream the butter on medium speed until fluffy and pale; set aside.

3 In a heatproof bowl of an electric mixer set over a pan of simmering water, gently whisk together remaining cup sugar and the egg whites until mixture is warm to the touch and sugar has dissolved, about 3 minutes.

4 Attach bowl with egg-white mixture to mixer fitted with the whisk attachment, and beat on medium speed until mixture is fluffy and cooled, about 10 minutes. Increase speed to high, and whisk until stiff peaks form. Reduce speed to medium-low, and add butter, ¼ cup at a time, beating well after each addition. Beat in vanilla.

5 Switch to the paddle attachment. Add caramel; beat on lowest speed until very smooth, 3 to 5 minutes. If using the same day, set aside at room temperature, covered with plastic wrap. Otherwise, refrigerate in an airtight container up to 3 days. Before using, bring to room temperature; beat until smooth with the paddle attachment.

caramel

MAKES ABOUT 1 CUP

Unsalted butter, for baking sheet (optional)
½ **cup sugar**
3 **tablespoons water**

Butter a baking sheet or line with a Silpat baking mat. In a small saucepan, bring sugar and the water to a boil, washing down sides of pan with a pastry brush dipped in water to prevent crystals from forming. Continue cooking until dark amber in color, swirling pan to color evenly. Immediately pour onto prepared baking sheet, and let cool completely, until hardened. Coarsely chop, and store in an airtight container at room temperature until ready to use.

gingerbread cookies

MAKES ABOUT 5 DOZEN

1 **cup sugar**
½ **cup unsulphured molasses**
½ **cup (1 stick) unsalted butter**
1 **tablespoon ground cinnamon**
1 **tablespoon ground ginger**
1 **teaspoon ground cloves**
1 **teaspoon ground cardamom**
1 **cup milk**
5½ **cups all-purpose flour, plus more for work surface**
1 **tablespoon baking powder**

1 Combine sugar, molasses, butter, and spices in a small saucepan set over medium heat. Cook, stirring occasionally, until butter has melted. Stir in milk until combined, and remove from heat. Let stand until cool, about 30 minutes.

2 In a medium bowl, combine flour and baking powder, and stir into milk mixture to form a soft dough. Turn out dough onto a piece of plastic wrap, and cover tightly. Refrigerate at least 5 hours or overnight.

3 Preheat oven to 400°F. Place dough on a lightly floured work surface, and divide into four equal pieces. Roll out each piece to ⅛ inch thick. Cut out desired shapes with cookie cutters. Working in batches, place shapes on parchment-lined baking sheets, 1 inch apart. Bake until just brown on edges, about 12 minutes, rotating sheets halfway through. Transfer to a wire rack to cool. Repeat with remaining dough.

from Rocky Mountain Christmas

individual no-bake cheesecakes

MAKES 6 | **PHOTO ON PAGE 334**

We used homemade pomegranate jelly as a simple topping for this creamy cheesecake, and we garnished the dish with jewel-like pomegranate seeds, but you can use your favorite jam or fresh fruit instead.

3 **tablespoons granulated sugar**
7 **ounces graham crackers (about 13)**
½ **cup (1 stick) unsalted butter, melted and cooled**
10 **ounces cream cheese, room temperature**
6 **ounces crème fraîche**
⅔ **cup sifted confectioners' sugar**
1 **cup heavy cream**
1 **cup Mrs. Gubler's Pomegranate Jelly, for serving (page 306)**
   Pomegranate seeds, for garnish

1 Line six (8-ounce) cups of a large muffin tin with plastic wrap; set aside. Combine sugar and graham crackers in the bowl of a food processor fitted with the metal blade; pulse until very finely chopped. Transfer to a small bowl, and stir in melted butter. Press evenly into prepared muffin tin. Place in freezer while preparing the filling.

2 In the bowl of an electric mixer fitted with the paddle attachment, beat cream cheese, crème fraîche, and confectioners' sugar until well combined. In another mixing bowl, beat heavy cream just until stiff peaks form, and fold into cream-cheese mixture. Spoon into prepared crusts, and freeze until firm, about 30 minutes.

3 Prepare topping: Heat jelly in a small saucepan over low heat, stirring until just melted and smooth. Remove from heat; let stand until cool but still pourable. Remove muffin tin from freezer. Remove cheesecakes by gently pulling up on the plastic wrap. Carefully remove plastic wrap from crusts; set cheesecakes on serving plates. Drizzle each with jelly, garnish with pomegranate seeds, and serve. Unglazed cakes can be refrigerated up to 3 days or frozen up to 1 week.

from Pomegranates

mrs. gubler's pomegranate jelly
MAKES 3 PINTS

This recipe was provided by Julie Gubler, the mother of Angela Gubler, senior art director for MARTHA STEWART LIVING. To obtain pomegranate juice, purée seeds in a food processor until smooth, then strain in a sieve, discarding pulp.

1 package (1¾ ounces) pectin

5 cups sugar

5 cups fresh pomegranate juice
(from about 10 pomegranates)

1 Sterilize canning or jelly jars, and let dry without touching insides or rim. Place lids in a saucepan, cover with boiling water, and let stand while preparing jelly.

2 In a small bowl, mix pectin with ¼ cup sugar. Place juice in a large saucepan, and stir in pectin mixture. Bring to a boil, and add remaining 4¾ cups sugar. Stir until dissolved, while returning mixture to a boil; continue cooking 2 minutes.

3 Remove from heat; ladle into sterilized jars. Carefully place lids on jars, and twist shut. Invert jars; let stand 30 minutes.

4 Reinvert jars, and check seals by pressing middle of lids with finger. They should not spring back; if lid springs up when finger is released, jar is not sealed. Store sealed jars in a cool, dry, dark place up to 1 year. Unsealed or opened jars should be refrigerated and will keep up to 3 weeks.

linzertorte
MAKES 1 NINE-INCH TORTE

1½ cups all-purpose flour, plus more for work surface

½ cup finely ground toasted almonds (2 ounces)

½ teaspoon ground cinnamon

½ teaspoon baking powder

½ teaspoon salt

½ cup (1 stick) unsalted butter

⅔ cup packed light-brown sugar

1 large egg

1¼ cups seedless raspberry jam
Confectioners' sugar, for dusting

1 In a small bowl, combine flour, almonds, cinnamon, baking powder, and salt; set aside.

2 In the bowl of an electric mixer fitted with the paddle attachment, cream butter and brown sugar until smooth. Beat in egg. Gradually add flour mixture, beating on low speed just until mixture comes together to form a dough.

3 Turn out dough onto a lightly floured work surface. Remove one-third of the dough, and set aside. Roll out remaining dough to ⅛ inch thick, and fit into a 9-inch square or round tart pan, pressing into corners and up sides. Using a paring knife, trim dough flush with edges of pan, and patch any holes or tears with extra dough.

4 Roll out the reserved dough into a rectangle at least 13 inches long and ⅛ inch thick. Cut lengthwise into ½-inch-wide strips. Transfer to a baking sheet, and refrigerate, along with shell in pan, 30 minutes.

5 Preheat oven to 350°F. Melt the raspberry jam in a small saucepan over medium heat, stirring occasionally until smooth. Remove from heat, strain through a fine sieve into a small dish, and let jam cool slightly.

6 Remove tart pan from refrigerator; pour jam into shell. Remove dough strips from refrigerator; arrange over the top in a lattice pattern. Trim excess dough; press ends onto edge of shell to adhere. Bake until pastry is golden brown and jam is bubbling, 30 to 35 minutes. Transfer to a wire rack to cool completely. Dust top with confectioners' sugar, and serve.

from Favorite Tortes

mile-high apple pie

MAKES 1 NINE-INCH PIE | **PHOTO ON PAGE 336**

Resist the urge to cut this pie before it is completely cool so the juices have time to thicken. We love this pie even more the day after it has been made.

Deep-Dish Pâte Brisée (recipe follows)

6 tablespoons all-purpose flour, plus more for work surface

5½ pounds firm, tart apples, such as empire or Granny Smith

Juice of 2 lemons

1 cup granulated sugar

2 teaspoons ground cinnamon

3 tablespoons chilled unsalted butter, cut into small pieces

1 large egg yolk

2 tablespoons water

Sanding sugar, for sprinkling

1 Remove pâte brisée from refrigerator. On a lightly floured work surface, roll out one piece to an 11-inch round, about ⅛ inch thick, dusting work surface with flour to prevent sticking as necessary. Brush off excess flour with a dry pastry brush. Roll dough around rolling pin, and lift it over a deep-dish 9-inch pie pan. Line the pan with the dough, pressing it into the corners. Trim dough so that it hangs over pie plate by about ¼ inch. Roll out another piece of dough to an 11-inch round. Transfer dough round to a parchment-lined baking sheet, and refrigerate along with dough in pan, 30 minutes.

2 Preheat oven to 450°F. Peel and core apples, and cut into ¼-inch-thick slices. As you cut, place slices in a large bowl, and sprinkle with lemon juice to prevent discoloration. In a small bowl, combine flour, granulated sugar, and cinnamon; toss with apple slices.

3 Remove dough from refrigerator. Place apples in prepared pan, mounding them in a tall pile. Dot apples with butter. In a small dish, whisk egg yolk with the water to make a glaze; brush glaze on edge of dough in pan. Center and place other dough round over apples. Tuck edges of top crust under bottom dough, on top of rim of pan. Using your fingers, gently press crusts together along edge to seal; crimp as desired.

4 Roll out remaining piece of dough, if desired, and cut out apple or leaf shapes with cookie cutters. Brush bottom with glaze, and press to adhere to top edge of shell.

5 Using a sharp paring knife, cut several vents in top of dough to let steam escape. Brush surface with egg glaze; sprinkle with sanding sugar. Bake until golden brown on top, about 15 minutes. Reduce oven temperature to 350°F; continue baking until crust is golden brown and juices are bubbling, 45 to 50 minutes. Remove from oven; let cool completely before serving.

from Rocky Mountain Christmas

deep-dish pâte brisée

MAKES ENOUGH FOR 1 NINE-INCH DOUBLE-CRUST PIE

3¾ cups all-purpose flour

1½ teaspoons salt

1½ teaspoons sugar

1½ cups (3 sticks) unsalted butter, cut into small pieces

½ to ¾ cup ice water

1 Place flour, salt, and sugar in the bowl of a food processor fitted with the metal blade; process until combined. Add butter, and process until mixture resembles coarse meal, about 10 seconds. With the machine running, add the ice water in a slow, steady stream through the feed tube, just until the dough holds together. Do not process for more than 30 seconds. Test dough by pinching a small amount; if it is still crumbly, add a bit more water.

2 Turn out dough onto a clean work surface, and divide into three equal pieces. Place each piece on plastic wrap, and flatten into a disk; wrap tightly. Refrigerate at least 1 hour before using. Dough can be frozen up to 1 month.

peanut brittle

MAKES ONE 9-BY-13-INCH SQUARE

Although peanut brittle may be the most common variety, you can also use other whole nuts, such as cashews, hazelnuts, almonds, or pecans, as well as toasted pumpkin seeds.

Unsalted butter, room temperature, for baking sheet

1½ cups sugar

½ cup light corn syrup

¾ cup cold water

Pinch of salt

2½ cups dry-roasted peanuts

1 teaspoon pure vanilla extract

1 teaspoon baking soda

Vegetable oil, for spatula

1 Brush a 9-by-13-inch rimmed baking sheet with butter; set aside. Combine the sugar, corn syrup, water, and salt in a medium saucepan. Bring to a boil over medium-high heat, stirring until sugar has dissolved. Cook, swirling pan occasionally (do not stir), until mixture reaches the soft-ball

stage on a candy thermometer (238°F to 240°F), washing down sides of pan with a pastry brush dipped in water to prevent crystals from forming. Stir in nuts; continue cooking, stirring frequently with a wooden spoon to prevent nuts from burning, until the mixture is light amber in color.

2 Remove from heat. Carefully stir in vanilla and baking soda (the mixture will foam up in the pan). Pour the mixture onto the prepared baking sheet, and quickly spread into a ½-inch-thick layer with an oiled metal spatula. Let cool completely.

3 Break brittle into large pieces; store in an airtight container at room temperature up to 1 month.

from Rocky Mountain Christmas

peppermint semifreddo
SERVES 6 | **PHOTO ON PAGE 335**

8 tablespoons peppermint candies (about 4 ounces)
1½ cups heavy cream
3 large eggs, separated
9 tablespoons sugar
6 tablespoons peppermint liqueur
Chocolate sauce, for serving (recipe follows)
Peppermint sticks, for serving

1 Using a rolling pin, finely crush 5 tablespoons candies between parchment paper. Place cream in a medium bowl; whisk in crushed candy, and whip until stiff peaks form. Chill until ready to use. Roughly crush remaining 3 tablespoons candy, and set aside.

2 Prepare an ice bath. In a large heatproof bowl set over a pan of simmering water, whisk egg yolks and 3 tablespoons sugar until pale. Add liqueur; whisk vigorously until mixture is thick, 3 to 4 minutes. Transfer to ice bath; whisk until cool.

3 In the heatproof bowl of an electric mixer set over a pan of simmering water, whisk egg whites and remaining 6 tablespoons sugar until sugar dissolves and mixture is warm to the touch, about 2 minutes. Attach bowl to mixer fitted with the whisk attachment; beat until stiff and glossy peaks form.

4 Fold one-third of the egg-white mixture into the egg-yolk mixture. Add remaining egg whites, one-third at a time. Fold in whipped-cream mixture. Spoon mixture into six individual serving dishes, layering it with reserved crushed candies. Freeze until firm, about 1½ hours. Serve semifreddo with chocolate sauce and peppermint sticks.

from Dessert of the Month

chocolate sauce
MAKES 2 CUPS

8 ounces bittersweet chocolate, finely chopped
1¼ cups heavy cream

Place chocolate in a medium heatproof metal bowl. Bring cream to a boil; pour over chocolate. Let stand 15 minutes; stir until smooth and combined. Store in an airtight container in the refrigerator up to 1 week. Before using, reheat gently in a heatproof bowl set over a pan of simmering water.

poppy-seed torte
MAKES 1 SEVEN-INCH TORTE

Unsalted butter, for pan
3 tablespoons all-purpose flour, plus more for pan
½ cup poppy seeds
3 tablespoons finely ground toasted walnuts (¾ ounce)
½ teaspoon pure almond extract
¼ teaspoon salt
2 large eggs, separated
½ cup granulated sugar
Confectioners' sugar, for dusting

1 Preheat oven to 350°F. Butter a 7-inch springform pan. Line the bottom with parchment paper; butter parchment, and dust with flour, tapping out excess. In a small bowl, combine poppy seeds, walnuts, flour, almond extract, and salt.

2 In the bowl of an electric mixer fitted with the whisk attachment, beat egg yolks and ¼ cup sugar on medium-high speed until pale and thick, about 3 minutes. Transfer to a large mixing bowl. Add poppy-seed mixture, but do not stir in.

3 Place egg whites in the heatproof bowl of an electric mixer set over a pan of simmering water until warm to the touch. Attach bowl to mixer fitted with a clean, dry whisk attachment, and beat on high speed until soft peaks form. Beat in remaining ¼ cup sugar until stiff and glossy peaks form. Fold egg whites into egg-yolk mixture in three batches.

4 Spread batter evenly in prepared pan, and bake until lightly golden and firm on top, about 30 minutes. Transfer to a wire rack to cool completely. Carefully remove sides of pan, and transfer torte to a serving plate. Dust with confectioners' sugar, and serve in wedges.

from Favorite Tortes

three-nut torte

MAKES 1 EIGHT-INCH TORTE

Unsalted butter, for pans

All-purpose flour, for pans

6 large eggs, separated

¼ cup plus 3 tablespoons sugar

½ cup finely ground toasted hazelnuts

½ cup finely ground toasted blanched almonds

¾ cup finely ground toasted walnuts

3 ounces bittersweet chocolate, finely chopped or grated

1 tablespoon finely grated orange zest

½ teaspoon baking powder

¼ teaspoon salt

Praline Buttercream (recipe follows)

Chocolate Ganache (page 310)

1 Preheat oven to 300°F. Butter three 8-inch round cake pans. Line bottoms with parchment; butter parchment, and sprinkle with flour, tapping out excess.

2 In the bowl of an electric mixer fitted with the whisk attachment, beat yolks and ¼ cup sugar until thick and pale, about 3 minutes. In a separate bowl, toss together nuts, chocolate, orange zest, baking powder, and salt. Pour over yolks; do not mix in.

3 Whisk egg whites in the clean heatproof bowl of an electric mixer set over a pan of simmering water until warm to the touch. Attach bowl to mixer fitted with a clean, dry whisk attachment, and beat on high speed until soft peaks form. Beat in remaining 3 tablespoons sugar until stiff and glossy peaks form.

4 Fold egg whites into egg-yolk mixture one-third at a time. Divide batter evenly among prepared pans, and spread with an offset spatula to smooth the tops. Bake until springy to the touch, about 20 minutes. Transfer to a wire rack to cool 10 minutes. Run a knife around the edge of each cake to loosen, and invert cakes onto wire racks, removing parchment paper. Let cool completely before assembling.

5 Place one cake layer on a turntable or flat work surface. Using an offset spatula, spread 1¼ cups buttercream evenly over the top. Place second cake layer on buttercream, and evenly spread 1¼ cups buttercream over the top. Place final cake layer on top, and evenly spread the remaining ½ cup buttercream on top to create a smooth surface. Refrigerate at least 30 minutes while you make the ganache.

6 Transfer cake to a wire rack set over a rimmed baking sheet. Pour ganache over top of cake; use an offset spatula to smooth top and sides. Transfer cake to the refrigerator to let ganache set, at least 30 minutes, before serving.

from Favorite Tortes

praline buttercream

MAKES 3 CUPS

Buttercream can be refrigerated up to 3 days; before using, bring to room temperature, and beat with the paddle attachment on low speed until smooth, about 5 minutes.

1 cup (2 sticks) unsalted butter, room temperature, cut into small pieces, plus more for baking sheet

1½ cups sugar

¼ cup water

¾ cup chopped toasted blanched almonds

4 large egg whites

1 Butter a baking sheet, or line it with a Silpat baking mat; set aside. In a small saucepan, bring 1 cup sugar and the water to a boil over medium heat, washing down sides of pan with a pastry brush dipped in water to prevent crystals from forming. Continue cooking until dark amber in color, swirling pan to color evenly. Stir in nuts, distributing evenly, and immediately pour caramel onto prepared baking sheet. Let cool until praline has hardened.

2 Break praline into pieces, and place in the bowl of a food processor fitted with the metal blade. Process to a fine powder. Measure out 1½ cups powder, and set aside. Reserve any remaining praline for another use.

3 In the bowl of an electric mixer set over a pan of simmering water, whisk together egg whites and remaining ½ cup sugar until mixture is warm to the touch and sugar has dissolved. Attach bowl to the mixer fitted with the whisk attachment, and beat on high speed until thick and cool, about 5 minutes. Add butter all at once, and beat until mixture has a smooth, spreadable consistency, about 5 minutes. Don't worry if the buttercream separates and appears curdled; it will come back together with continued beating. Add reserved praline powder, and beat to combine. If using the same day, set aside, covered with plastic wrap, at room temperature.

chocolate ganache

MAKES ABOUT 1 CUP

⅔ cup heavy cream

6 ounces semisweet chocolate, finely chopped

1 teaspoon light corn syrup

Place chocolate in a small heatproof bowl. In a small saucepan, bring heavy cream just to a boil; pour over chocolate. Whisk gently until smooth. Whisk in corn syrup. Let thicken slightly, about 10 minutes, before using.

....

TRUFFLES

....

classic truffles

MAKES ABOUT 4 DOZEN

When working with chocolate, be sure to work in a cool room. Since chocolate is the primary ingredient in truffles, use the best-quality chocolate you can find. We like to use Valrhona, Callebaut, or Scharffen Berger. Butter melts at a lower temperature than chocolate and helps to give truffles their luscious quality and richness; corn syrup imparts smoothness. If you like, roll the coated truffles in finely chopped pistachios instead of cocoa powder; you will need about two cups for this recipe.

1 cup heavy cream

4 tablespoons unsalted butter

2 teaspoons light corn syrup

1 pound finely chopped semisweet chocolate,
  plus 12 ouncesmore for dipping

1 cup Dutch-process cocoa powder, sifted

1 Make ganache: In a small saucepan, bring cream, butter, and corn syrup to a full boil. Turn off heat; add 1 pound chopped chocolate; do not stir. Gently swirl pan to cover chocolate completely with cream. Let stand, undisturbed, 5 minutes; slowly whisk until chocolate is melted and combined.

2 Transfer mixture to a large bowl; place in the refrigerator, stirring every 15 minutes. After 45 minutes, the mixture will begin to thicken very quickly, so begin stirring every 3 to 5 minutes until thick enough to scoop with the spoon, 10 to 20 minutes more; the consistency should be similar to pudding.

3 Using two spoons or a 1¼-inch ice-cream scoop, form ganache into 1-inch balls, and transfer to a parchment-lined baking sheet. Refrigerate until firm, but not hard, about 10 minutes. Remove from refrigerator, and squeeze pieces with your fingers to soften slightly and form into roughly shaped

balls. Return to refrigerator until ready to dip. The truffle centers can be refrigerated, covered, up to 1 week before finishing.

4 Bring a medium saucepan, one-quarter full of water, to a boil. Reduce heat to a gentle simmer. Place the remaining 12 ounces chocolate in a medium heatproof bowl. Place over the simmering water, and stir occasionally until chocolate is completely melted. Remove from heat, and cool slightly.

5 Place cocoa powder in a small bowl. Line another baking sheet with parchment paper. Remove truffle centers from refrigerator. Using one hand for melted chocolate and the other hand for the cocoa, dip a truffle into the melted chocolate and roll around in your hand to evenly coat. Let excess drip back into bowl. Drop the coated truffle into the bowl of cocoa powder and, using your other hand, turn to coat. Let set in bowl, about 20 seconds, then pick up the truffle and roll around in your hand to evenly coat. Set on prepared baking sheet. Repeat with remaining truffles. If the kitchen is not cool enough for the truffles to set immediately, place them in the refrigerator 5 minutes. Store up to 1 week in an airtight container in a cool place or in the refrigerator.

from Truffles 101

candy cane truffles

MAKES 5½ DOZEN

18 candy canes or 8 ounces round peppermint candy

Ingredients for Classic Truffles (recipe above), omitting cocoa powder

1 tablespoon pure peppermint extract

Working in two batches, place candy canes or peppermint candy in the bowl of a food processor fitted with the metal blade; pulse several times until finely chopped. (Alternatively, place on a large cutting board, cover with plastic wrap, and crush with a kitchen mallet.) Using a sieve, sift out and discard powdery residue. Measure out 1 cup chopped candy; reserve the rest for rolling. Follow recipe for Classic Truffles. Once the cream and chocolate have been fully combined at the end of step 1, stir in peppermint extract. When the ganache has been chilled to a pudding consistency at the end of step 2, stir in 1 cup candy cane pieces. Proceed with recipe. Finish dipped truffles by rolling in reserved chopped candy.

champagne truffles

MAKES 5½ DOZEN

This classic truffle does not contain any Champagne. Instead, the name refers to "Fine Champagne," which is a grade of cognac. They are typically rolled in confectioners' sugar.

Ingredients for Classic Truffles (page 310), increasing chocolate for ganache to 1 pound 2 ounces and omitting cocoa powder

6 tablespoons cognac

1 cup sifted confectioners' sugar

Follow the recipe for Classic Truffles. Once the cream mixture and chocolate have been fully combined at the end of step 1, stir in cognac. Proceed with recipe. To finish the dipped truffles, roll in confectioners' sugar.

coconut truffles

MAKES ABOUT 4 DOZEN

4 cups (11 ounces) sweetened shredded coconut

Ingredients for Classic Truffles (page 310), omitting cocoa powder

4 teaspoons coconut oil

Preheat oven to 300°F. Spread coconut on a rimmed baking sheet, and transfer to oven. Heat about 15 minutes, stirring occasionally. Coconut should be dry, but without any color. Remove from oven; let cool completely, and very finely chop. Set aside. Follow the recipe for Classic Truffles. Once the cream mixture and chocolate have been fully combined at the end of step 1, stir in coconut oil. Proceed with recipe. Finish dipped truffles by rolling in toasted coconut.

grand marnier truffles

MAKES 5 DOZEN

Ingredients for Classic Truffles (page 310), increasing the chocolate for ganache to 1 pound 2 ounces and omitting cocoa powder

6 tablespoons Grand Marnier or other orange-flavored liqueur

12 ounces semisweet chocolate, very finely chopped and sifted to remove powdery residue

Follow the recipe for Classic Truffles. Once the cream mixture and chocolate have been fully combined at the end of step 1, stir in liqueur. Proceed with recipe. Finish dipped truffles by rolling in chopped semisweet chocolate.

hazelnut truffles

MAKES 5½ DOZEN

2½ cups (11 ounces) shelled hazelnuts

Ingredients for Classic Truffles (page 310), increasing chocolate for ganache to 1 pound 2 ounces and omitting cocoa powder

¼ cup Nutella (a chocolate-hazelnut spread)

Preheat oven to 375°F. Spread hazelnuts on a rimmed baking sheet; toast in oven until lightly browned and skin cracks, 5 to 7 minutes. Rub hazelnuts vigorously in a kitchen towel until most skins are removed. Let cool, and chop very finely. Follow the recipe for Classic Truffles. Once cream and chocolate have been fully combined at the end of step 1, stir in Nutella. To finish dipped truffles, roll in chopped nuts.

mocha truffles

MAKES 4 DOZEN

2 cups heavy cream

2 tablespoons high-quality ground coffee

Ingredients for Classic Truffles (page 310), omitting cream

In a small saucepan, bring heavy cream and ground coffee to a boil. Cover, and let steep 20 minutes. Strain the mixture through a fine sieve into a clean bowl, discarding solids. Measure out 1 cup liquid, and use in place of cream in the Classic Truffles recipe.

orange-ginger truffles

MAKES 4½ DOZEN

Ingredients for Classic Truffles (page 310), omitting cocoa powder

4 teaspoons finely grated orange zest (about 3 oranges)

1 cup confectioners' sugar

1 tablespoon ground ginger

Follow the recipe for Classic Truffles. Once the cream mixture and chocolate have been fully combined at the end of step 1, stir in grated orange zest. Proceed with recipe. Sift together sugar and ginger into a small bowl. To finish dipped truffles, roll in confectioners' sugar mixture.

praline truffles

MAKES 5 DOZEN

5 cups (about 1 pound) sliced blanched almonds
2½ cups sugar
½ cup water
   Ingredients for Classic Truffles (page 310),
   omitting cocoa powder

1 Preheat oven to 400°F. To make praline, spread almonds on a rimmed baking sheet; toast in oven until lightly browned, about 10 minutes, stirring halfway through. Set aside. Line a baking sheet with parchment paper or a Silpat baking mat. In a medium saucepan, bring sugar and the water to a boil over medium heat, washing down sides of pan with a pastry brush dipped in water to prevent crystals from forming. Once sugar has dissolved, increase heat to medium-high; continue cooking until syrup is light amber in color. Remove from heat. Stir in almonds with a wooden spoon.

2 Working quickly, pour mixture onto prepared baking sheet, and spread with the back of a large spoon. Let cool completely. Break into pieces, and finely chop into ⅛-inch pieces. Using a sieve, sift out and discard powdery residue. Set praline aside. Follow the recipe for Classic Truffles. Once the ganache has been chilled to a pudding consistency at the end of step 2, stir in 1½ cups praline pieces. Proceed with recipe. Very finely chop the remaining praline pieces in the bowl of a food processor. Do not let praline become powdery. Finish dipped truffles by rolling in the ground praline.

sambuca truffles

MAKES 5 DOZEN

   Ingredients for Classic Truffles (page 310), increasing the chocolate for ganache to 1 pound 2 ounces and omitting cream and cocoa powder
1½ cups heavy cream
1 tablespoon anise seed
6 tablespoons sambuca
1 cup sifted confectioners' sugar

Follow the recipe for Classic Truffles. In a small saucepan, bring cream and anise seed to a boil. Turn off heat; cover, and let steep 20 minutes. Strain mixture through a fine sieve into a clean bowl; discard solids. Measure out 1 cup liquid, and use in place of the cream in the recipe. Once the cream mixture and chocolate have been fully combined at the end of step 1, stir in sambuca. Proceed with recipe. Finish dipped truffles by rolling in confectioners' sugar.

pomegranate punch

MAKES 2 QUARTS

For a pretty presentation, serve punch with ice made by freezing pomegranate seeds and water in ice-cube trays.

8 cups pomegranate seeds (about 5 pomegranates)
2 cups water
¾ cup sugar
1 bunch fresh mint, trimmed and rinsed
¼ cup freshly squeezed lemon juice

1 Place pomegranate seeds in the bowl of a food processor fitted with the metal blade, and process until smooth. Strain liquid through a fine sieve, and discard seeds and pulp. You should have about 3⅓ cups juice.

2 Place the water and sugar in a small saucepan, and bring to a boil. Reduce to a simmer, and stir until sugar has dissolved. Add pomegranate juice, mint, and lemon juice. Cover; let steep 30 minutes to allow the flavors to blend. Remove mint, and let cool completely. Transfer to an airtight container, and chill until ready to serve, up to 2 days.

from Pomegranates

pomegranate tea

MAKES 3 CUPS

This tea is one of Martha's favorites.

1 large pomegranate, rinsed well and quartered
4 cups cold water
   Few tablespoons honey (optional)
   Few sprigs mint (optional)

Place pomegranate quarters in a small saucepan. Cover with the water; bring to a boil. Reduce heat, add mint, if desired, and simmer until very fragrant and colorful, about 15 minutes. Stir in honey, if desired; strain tea, and serve hot.

from Pomegranates

CORNMEAL-CRUSTED PIZZAS WITH
ASSORTED TOPPINGS | **PAGE 256**

CRANBERRY-BEAN SALAD WITH BUTTERNUT SQUASH AND BROCCOLI RABE | PAGE 260

BRIE AND WALNUT CAKE | **PAGE 289**

FOCACCIA CAKE | **PAGE 290**

SMOKED SALMON CAKE | **PAGE 291**

SUSHI CAKE | **PAGE 291**

POMEGRANATE, FENNEL, AND GREEN
BEAN SALAD | **PAGE 293**

SPINACH LINGUINE WITH WALNUT-ARUGULA PESTO | **PAGE 275**

GREEN SALAD WITH TOASTED WALNUTS, WALNUT OIL, AND GREEN BEANS | **PAGE 272**

ALMOND-COATED GOAT CHEESE, FRISEE, AND BELGIAN ENDIVE SALAD | **PAGE 254**

PASTA WITH SCALLOPS, GARLIC, GRAPE TOMATOES, AND PARSLEY | **PAGE 258**

MISO-GLAZED COD | **PAGE 295**

GINGER-PEANUT SOMEN NOODLES | **PAGE 297**

SESAME STEAMED SPINACH | **PAGE 300**

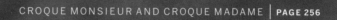
CROQUE MONSIEUR AND CROQUE MADAME | **PAGE 256**

ASSORTED GRILLED CHEESE SANDWICHES | PAGE 256

ROASTED CORNISH HENS WITH
POMEGRANATE-MOLASSES GLAZE | **PAGE 295**

POMEGRANATE PILAF | **PAGE 299**

PORK LOIN BRAISED IN MILK | **PAGE 274**

SAUTEED BRUSSELS SPROUTS WITH RAISINS | **PAGE 278**

BUTTERNUT SQUASH WITH BROWN BUTTER | **PAGE 275**

MOLASSES-GLAZED GRILLED PORK LOIN WITH
ROASTED ITALIAN PRUNE PLUMS | **PAGE 258**

HERB-ROASTED TURKEY WITH PAN GRAVY | **PAGE 273**

CORNBREAD DRESSING | **PAGE 276**

STUFFING HOW-TO

1 In a large bowl, combine cubes of day-old bread with desired chopped vegetables, fruit, nuts, and cooked meat (or cured meat such as ham), and toss to combine.

2 Add chopped fresh herbs and seasoning, and toss again.

3 Add liquid until desired consistency is reached. Adjust the seasoning, and toss just until combined. Do not overmix, or the stuffing will become gummy in texture.

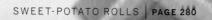

SWEET-POTATO ROLLS | **PAGE 280**

BEST WHIPPED SWEET POTATOES WITH
CARAMELIZED APPLES | **PAGE 275**

SPICY SWEET POTATOES
WITH LIME | **PAGE 279**

SAVORY TWICE-BAKED SWEET POTATOES | **PAGE 278**

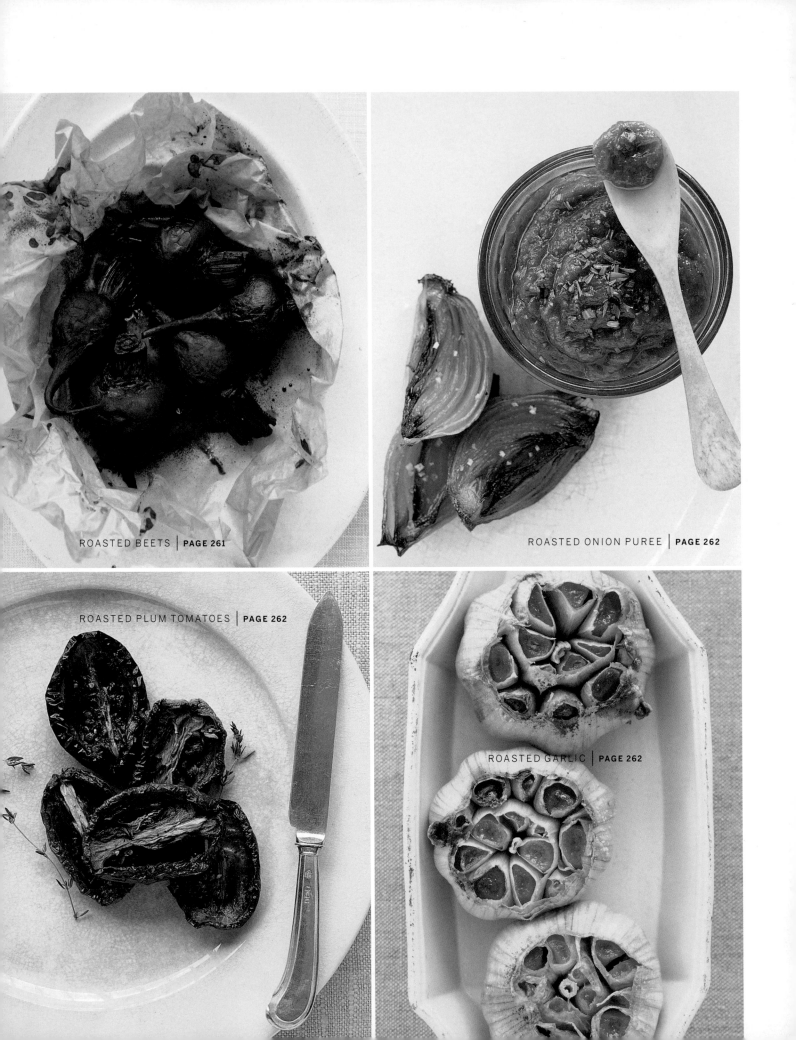

ROASTED BEETS | **PAGE 261**

ROASTED ONION PUREE | **PAGE 262**

ROASTED PLUM TOMATOES | **PAGE 262**

ROASTED GARLIC | **PAGE 262**

COCONUT CHOCOLATE
PATTIES | PAGE 264

CONCORD GRAPE SORBET | **PAGE 264**

PEANUT BUTTER SURPRISES | PAGE 266

PEAR PAVLOVA | PAGE 283

MIXED FRUIT-AND-NUT COOKIES | PAGE 266

PUMPKIN BREAD PUDDING | PAGE 267

PUMPKIN-PECAN PIE | **PAGE 284**

WARM CREAM-CHEESE BROWNIES | **PAGE 284**

PEAR PANDOWDY | **PAGE 282**

INDIVIDUAL NO-BAKE CHEESECAKES WITH
MRS. GUBLER'S POMEGRANATE JELLY | PAGE 305

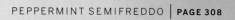

PEPPERMINT SEMIFREDDO | **PAGE 308**

ALMOND SHORTBREAD COOKIES | PAGE 301

CHOCOLATE BUTTERSCOTCH-CHIP COOKIES | PAGE 303

MILE-HIGH APPLE PIE | PAGE 307

Menus

JANUARY

CHILI FOR A CROWD

Greens with Orange Vinaigrette
and Toasted Sesame Seeds 19

Chili con Carne 22

Chunky Guacamole 22

Brown-Sugar Cornbread 25

A WINTER DINNER PARTY
WITH FRIENDS

Cream of Belgian Endive Soup 15

Eggplant Kuku 16

Fresh-Herb Kuku 16

Moules Poulette (Broiled
Mussels with Mushrooms,
Lemon, and Cream) 17

Pommes Frites 17

Braised Lamb Stew
(Fresh-Herb Khoresh) 19

Baked Saffron Rice 24

Belgian Chocolate Birthday Cake 25

Chocolate Mousse with Banana
Purée and Grated Coconut 27

WHAT TO HAVE FOR DINNER

Green and White Salad 19

Striped Sea Bass with
Blood Oranges and Olives 23

Baked Potato Slices 24

Chocolate Whole-Wheat
Biscuit Cake 27

FEBRUARY

WHAT TO HAVE FOR DINNER

Crisp Mustard-Glazed
Chicken Breasts 38

Braised Potatoes 40

Winter Greens and Bacon 40

Vanilla Pudding 50

MARCH

FROM THE GARDEN
TO THE TABLE

Pan-Fried Scallops on
Caramelized Fennel 53

Pistou Soup 54

Roasted Cherry Tomatoes,
Baked Buffalo Mozzarella,
and Eggplant 55

Tomato Essence and Timbales
of Pressed Tomatoes 55

Confit of Wild Salmon on Cucumber
Salad with Horseradish Sauce 58

Roast Best End of Highgrove
Lamb and Fava Beans with Mint
and Marjoram 60

Fricassée of Wild Mushrooms 61

Melon and Berries Steeped
in Red Wine, Sauternes, Basil,
and Mint 62

Peach Tartes Tatin 62

WHAT TO HAVE FOR DINNER

Artichoke Bruschetta 53

Spaghetti with Clams 60

Sautéed Chicory 61

Grapefruit in Moscato 62

APRIL

SPRING HARVEST LUNCH

Fluke Sashimi with Baby Greens 95

Spring Pea Soup with
Smoked Bacon 96

Long Island Duckling Two Ways 99

Glazed Baby Turnips and
Cipollini Onions 106

Soft Polenta with Fresh Herbs 106

White Asparagus with
Hollandaise Sauce 107

Chocolate and Mint Parfaits 108

WHAT TO HAVE FOR DINNER

Radish Butter On
Toasted Baguette 96

Roasted Chicken and
Jerusalem Artichokes 100

Herbed Couscous 106

Baked Camembert with
Fresh Fruit 107

MAY

A MOTHER'S DAY ALBUM

Peach Tea Punch 134

Chilled Fennel and Leek Soup 119

Mini Corn Cakes with Goat
Cheese and Pepper Jelly 120

Arugula Risotto 122

Seared Shrimp with
Lemon and Garlic 126

Mango and Tomato Salsa 126

Simple Steamed Thick
Asparagus 127

Lemon Semifreddo Cake 130

WHAT TO HAVE FOR DINNER

Rice Salad with Lemon, Dill,
and Red Onion 121

Seared Salmon with Creamy
Leek Sauce 125

Sugar Snap Peas with
Toasted Almonds 127

Fresh-Raspberry Gelatin
and Whipped Cream 130

JUNE

MIDSUMMER NIGHT DINNER
IN MINNESOTA

Lingonberry Punch 137

Blinis with Caviar and
Cucumber-Dill Dressing 137

Karjalan Potato Pies with
Egg Butter 138

Pickled Herring Canapes 139

Rye Sourdough Bread 140

Cucumber Salad 141

Garden Tomato Salad 141

Finnish Fish Chowder 142

Hot-Smoked Salmon
Steaks with Morel Sauce 144

Baby Red Potatoes with
Cilantro 146

Cloudberry Cake 150

WHAT TO HAVE FOR DINNER

Pita-Bread Salad with Cucumber,
Mint, and Feta 141

Salt-and-Pepper Shrimp
with Aïoli 146

Quick Braised Artichokes 147

Coffee Ice Cream Affogato 150

JULY

FISH-TACO PARTY

Margaritas for a Crowd 202

Beer-Battered Cod in Tacos 189

Grilled Mahimahi in Tacos 190

Green Rice 192

Saucy Black Beans 192

Cucumber Relish 203

Pico de Gallo 204

Pineapple Salsa 204

COUNTRY BARBECUE

Mary Brockman's Favorite
Pimm's Cup 202

Corn and Tomato Salad 185

Barbecued Chicken 189

Fried Catfish Sandwich 190

Aunt Sara's Cheese Grits 191

Turnip Greens 193

Vidalia-Onion Slaw 193

Cornlight Bread 203

Caramel Cake 193

Mary Curll's Chess Pie 198

A BASTILLE DAY PICNIC
IN NEW ORLEANS

Chicken Liver Pâté
with Toast Points 181

Le Grand Aïoli 183

Haricots Verts and Goat
Cheese Salad with Almonds 187

French Potato Salad with
White Wine and Celery Leaves 187

Grilled Leg of Lamb 190

Provençal Roasted Tomatoes 192

Black-Olive Relish 202

Perfect Hard-Boiled Eggs 203

Whole Grilled Garlic 204

French Flag Berry Tarts 194

WHAT TO HAVE FOR DINNER

Grilled Marinated Strip
Steak with Scallions 191

Roasted Fingerling Potatoes
with Seasoned Salt 192

Sautéed Asparagus
with Aged Gouda 193

Grilled Peaches with
Chilled Sabayon 196

AUGUST

SUMMER BREAKFAST PARTY

Currant Scones 207

Rolled Omelet with
Ratatouille Filling 207

Rolled Omelet with Spinach
and Goat Cheese 207

Strawberry-Rhubarb
Coffee Cake 208

WHAT TO HAVE FOR DINNER

Herbed Turkey Burgers 211

Chopped Tomato Salad
with Toasted Garlic 212

Creamed Fresh Corn 212

Cantaloupe Granita 213

SEPTEMBER

CABIN STYLE

Oysters with Champagne Mignonette 217

Tomato Crostini 217

Wild Mushroom Bruschetta 217

Endive and Pear Salad with Oregon Blue Cheese and Hazelnuts 218

Yellow-Pepper Risotto with Shrimp and Zucchini 221

Blackberry Ice Cream 222

Chocolate Brownies 223

WHAT TO HAVE FOR DINNER

Grilled Striped Bass 219

Corn and Clam Chowder Sauce 219

Oyster Biscuits 224

Watermelon and Raspberry Salad 223

OCTOBER

PASTA DINNER

Bagna Cauda with Broccoflower and Toasted Country Bread 253

Almond-Coated Goat Cheese, Frisée, and Belgian Endive Salad 254

Pasta with Scallops, Garlic, Grape Tomatoes, and Parsley 258

Baked Pears with Vanilla Mascarpone 263

AN AUTUMN PICNIC

Autumn Greens with Apples, Radishes, and Cheddar Frico 255

Cornmeal-Crusted Pizza 256

Molasses-Glazed Grilled Pork Loin with Roasted Italian Prune Plums 258

Cranberry-Bean Salad with Butternut Squash and Broccoli Rabe 260

Pickled Green Tomatoes 261

Roasted Wild Mushrooms 263

Concord Grape Sorbet 264

WHAT TO HAVE FOR DINNER

Curried Apple Soup 253

Braised Chicken Tarragon 255

Mashed Potatoes and Celeriac 261

Coconut Chocolate Patties 264

NOVEMBER

THANKSGIVING: AN ALL-DAY AFFAIR

Elwood's Ham Chowder 271

Low Country Steamed Carolina Cup Oysters with Melted Butter 271

Steamed Littleneck Clams 272

Herb-Roasted Turkey with Pan Gravy 273

Cedar-Plank Roasted Salmon 273

Church Street Squash 276

Cornbread Dressing 276

Cranberry Chutney 277

Cream Biscuits 277

Mashed Potatoes with Bacon and Cheddar 278

Scalloped Mushrooms 279

Southern Green Beans 279

Green Salad with Buttermilk and Blue Cheese Dressing 285

Pear Pandowdy 282

Pumpkin-Pecan Pie 284

Warm Cream-Cheese Brownies 284

WHAT TO HAVE FOR DINNER

Pork Loin Braised in Milk 274

Butternut Squash with Brown Butter 275

Sautéed Brussels Sprouts with Raisins 278

Amaretti Crisps 281

DECEMBER

ROCKY MOUNTAIN CHRISTMAS

Cheese Fondue 289

Endive and Radish Salad 292

Honey-Orange Baked Ham 294

Green Beans and Spaetzle 298

Orange Spiral Rolls 298

Potato Rösti 299

Vanilla Applesauce 301

Almond Shortbread Cookies 301

Bratselies 302

Chocolate Butterscotch-Chip Cookies 303

Chocolate-Pecan Fudge 303

Gingerbread Cookies 305

Mile-High Apple Pie 307

Peanut Brittle 307

WHAT TO HAVE FOR DINNER

Miso-Glazed Cod 295

Ginger-Peanut Somen Noodles 297

Sesame Steamed Spinach 300

Broiled Persimmons with Mascarpone 302

Sources

Addresses and telephone numbers of sources may change prior to or following publication, as may availability of any item.

ANCHO CHILES *Kitchen Market*

APPLE WOOD CHIPS *The Barbecue Store*

ARTICHOKE-LEMON PESTO *Dean & DeLuca*

ARUGULA *The Herb Lady*

AVOCADO SLICER *Martha Stewart: The Catalog for Living*

BAKER'S PIN, PROFESSIONAL *Martha Stewart: The Catalog for Living*

BAKING DISH, 8-INCH ROUND PORCELAIN *Bridge Kitchenware*

BAKING DISH, 9¾-INCH SQUARE *Broadway Panhandler*

BAKING DISH, WHITE 9-BY-13-INCH OVAL PORCELAIN *Cooking.com*

BAKING SHEETS *Martha Stewart: The Catalog for Living*

BAKING SHEETS, RIMMED *Broadway Panhandler; Kitchen Etc.*

BARBECUE SAUCE, SANKATY *Martha Stewart: The Catalog for Living*

BASIL FLOWERS *Indian Rock Produce*

BEECHWOOD SERVING BOARDS *Martha Stewart: The Catalog for Living*

BISCUIT CUTTERS, COPPER *Martha Stewart: The Catalog for Living*

BLACK OLIVE TAPENADE *Dean & DeLuca*

BOUQUET OF PROVENCE *Oliviers & Company*

BREAD KNIFE, WUSTHOF SERRATED *Martha Stewart: The Catalog for Living*

BRIOCHE MOLD, 8-INCH TINNED-STEEL *Bridge Kitchenware*

BROCCOFLOWER *Indian Rock Produce*

BUFFALO MOZZARELLA *Murray's Cheese*

BUTTER WARMERS *Martha Stewart: The Catalog for Living*

CAKE DECORATING KIT *Martha Stewart: The Catalog for Living*

CAKE RING, NONSTICK 2¾-INCH DIAMETER-BY-2⅜-INCH DEEP *Bowery Kitchen Supply*

CAKE STANDS *Martha Stewart: The Catalog for Living*

CHEESE VARIETIES *The Better Cheddar*

CHERRY PITTER *Sur La Table*

CLOUDBERRY JAM *Taste of Scandinavia*

COCONUT MILK *Pacific Rim Gourmet*

COOKIE-CUTTER SET *Sweet Celebrations*

CREAM HORN MOLDS *Bridge Kitchenware*

CREOLE CREAM CHEESE *Mauthe's Dairy*

CRYSTALLIZED GINGER *Adriana's Caravan*

DELONGLU GELATO SUPREME *Martha Stewart: The Catalog for Living*

EMPELTRE OLIVES *Balducci's*

FARRO *Whole Foods Market*

FENNEL FLOWERS *Indian Rock Produce*

FENUGREEK *Penzeys Spices*

FLAX SEEDS *Whole Foods Market*

FLOUR, WHITE LILY *White Lily*

FOOD MILL, DELUXE *Martha Stewart: The Catalog for Living*

FRENCH ROLLING PIN *Martha Stewart: The Catalog for Living*

FRENCH ROSE WATER *Adriana's Caravan*

FRESH MINT FLOWERS *Indian Rock Produce*

GARLIC-CHIVE BLOSSOMS *Indian Rock Produce*

GOAT-CHEESE BUTTONS *Dean & DeLuca*

GREAT GRATER *Martha Stewart: The Catalog for Living*

GREEN CARDAMOM PODS *Adriana's Caravan*

GREEN PEAS, KASUGAI WASABI-ROASTED *Asia Foods*

GRUYERE CHEESE *Pars Foods International*

HALF SHEET PAN, 17-BY-12-INCH *Broadway Panhandler*

HAM *The Honeybaked Ham Company*

HYSSOP FLOWERS *Indian Rock Produce*

ICE CREAM MACHINE *Martha Stewart: The Catalog for Living*

ICE CREAM MAKER *Williams-Sonoma*

ICE CREAM SCOOP, 1¼-INCH *Bridge Kitchenware*

ICE CREAM SCOOP, EXPERT *Martha Stewart: The Catalog for Living*

JUMBO LUMP CRAB MEAT *Wild Edibles*

KALAMATA OLIVES *Balducci's*

KUMQUATS *Indian Rock Produce*

LAVENDER, WHOLE DRIED *Adriana's Caravan*

LINGONBERRY CONCENTRATE *Wikstrom's Gourmet Foods*

LITTLENECK CLAMS *Wild Edibles*

LOAF PAN *Bridge Kitchenware*

LONG ISLAND DUCKLINGS
Dean & DeLuca

MANDOLINE, JAPANESE
Martha Stewart: The Catalog for Living

MEASURING CUPS *Martha Stewart:
The Catalog for Living*

METAL RING MOLDS *Kerekes Bakery &
Restaurant Equipment*

MIRIN *Adriana's Caravan*

MIXING BOWLS, STAINLESS STEEL
Martha Stewart: The Catalog for Living

MULATO CHILES *Kitchen Market*

NIÇOISE OLIVES *Balducci's*

NORI *Adriana's Caravan*

PANCAKE WARMER *Crate & Barrel*

PANCETTA, WHOLE OR SLICED
Zingerman's Delicatessen

PASTRY BAG SET *Martha Stewart:
The Catalog for Living*

PASTRY BRUSH *Martha Stewart:
The Catalog for Living*

PASTRY TIPS *Sweet Celebrations*

PEPPER JELLY *Foster's Market*

PERSIAN LIME POWDER
Pars Foods International

PERSIAN LIMES *Pars Foods International*

PERSIMMONS *Indian Rock Produce*

PICHOLINE OLIVES *Balducci's*

PICKLED GINGER *Adriana's Caravan*

PICKLED HERRING *Taste of Scandinavia*

PIZZA KIT *Martha Stewart:
The Catalog for Living*

PIZZELLE IRON *Martha Stewart:
The Catalog for Living*

PLUGRA EUROPEAN-STYLE BUTTER
Keller's Creamery

POMEGRANATE MOLASSES
Pars Foods International

POMEGRANATES *Indian Rock Produce*

PURE VANILLA SET (VANILLA
BEANS, VANILLA POWDER, AND
VANILLA EXTRACT)
Martha Stewart: The Catalog for Living

RAMEKINS
Martha Stewart: The Catalog for Living

RAMEKINS, 4-OUNCE
Kitchen Conservatory

RAMEKINS, OVAL *Sur La Table*

RICE COOKER *Williams-Sonoma*

RICOTTA SALATA *Murray's Cheese*

ROTATING CAKE STAND
Martha Stewart: The Catalog for Living

RUBBER SPATULA, HEATPROOF
Bridge Kitchenware

SAFFRON *Pars Foods International*

SALMON ROE *Petrossian Paris;
Wild Edibles*

SANDING SUGAR *Martha Stewart:
The Catalog for Living*

SESAME OIL *Island Market Foods /
Vashon Thriftway*

SEVRUGA CAVIAR *Wild Edibles*

SILPAT BAKING MAT *Martha Stewart:
The Catalog for Living*

SMOKED MAGRET DUCK BREAST
D'Artagnan

SOUFFLE DISH, 8-OUNCE
Bridge Kitchenware

SOUFFLE DISH, 1-CUP
Bridge Kitchenware

SOUFFLE DISHES *Cooking.com*

SPATULA SET, SILICONE
Martha Stewart: The Catalog for Living

SPRINGFORM PAN, 7-INCH
Bridge Kitchenware

SPRINGFORM PAN, 8.5-INCH
Dorothy McNett's Place

STOCKPOT WITH LID,
STAINLESS STEEL *Kmart*

STRAINER *Martha Stewart:
The Catalog for Living*

SWEET ONIONS *Greenleaf Produce*

TART PANS *Bridge Kitchenware*

TATSOI *Indian Rock Produce*

THYME *The Herb Lady*

THYME FLOWERS *Indian Rock Produce*

TURMERIC *Adriana's Caravan*

UDON NOODLES *Katagiri*

UNSWEETENED CORNFLAKES
Lifethyme Natural Market

VALENTINE TREAT STENCILS
Martha Stewart: The Catalog for Living

VOL-AU-VENT CUTTERS *Dean & DeLuca*

WALNUT OIL *Balducci's*

WASABI POWDER *Adriana's Caravan*

WILD MUSHROOMS *Urbani Truffles
and Caviar*

WILD THYME HONEY *Adriana's Caravan*

Directory

ADRIANA'S CARAVAN
78 Grand Central Terminal
New York, NY 10017
212-972-8804
800-316-0820
www.adrianascaravan.com

ASIA FOODS
28 Damrell Street
South Boston, MA 02128
877-902-0841
www.asiafoods.com

BALDUCCI'S
424 Avenue of the Americas
New York, NY 10011
212-673-2600

THE BARBECUE STORE
14601 Bellaire, Suite 260
Houston, TX 77083
888-789-0650
www.barbecue-store.com

THE BETTER CHEDDAR
604 West 48th Street
Kansas City, MO 64112
888-561-8204

BOWERY KITCHEN SUPPLY
The Chelsea Market
460 West 16th Street
New York, NY 10011
212-376-4982
www.bowerykitchens.com

BRIDGE KITCHENWARE
214 East 52nd Street
New York, NY 10022
800-274-3435
www.bridgekitchenware.com

BROADWAY PANHANDLER
477 Broome Street
New York, NY 10011
866-266-5927
212-966-3434
www.broadwaypanhandler.com

COOKING.COM
2850 Ocean Park Blvd., Suite 310
Santa Monica, CA 90405
800-663-8810
www.cooking.com

CRATE & BARREL
800-323-5461
www.crateandbarrel.com

D'ARTAGNAN
280 Wilson Avenue
Newark, NJ 07105
800-327-8246
www.dartagnan.com

DEAN & DELUCA
560 Broadway
New York, NY 10012
212-226-6800
www.deananddeluca.com

DOROTHY MCNETT'S PLACE
800 San Benito Street
Hollister, CA 95023
831-637-6444
www.happycookers.com

FOSTER'S MARKET
2694 Durham Chapel Hill Blvd.
Durham, NC 27707
877-455-3944
www.fostersmarket.com

GREENLEAF PRODUCE
1955 Jerrold Avenue
San Francisco, CA 94112
415-647-2991

THE HERB LADY
52792 42nd Avenue
Lawrence, MI 49064
616-674-3879

THE HONEYBAKED HAM COMPANY
1550 New State Highway
Route 44
Raynham, MA 02767
800-343-4267
www.honeybaked.com

INDIAN ROCK PRODUCE
530 California Road
Quakertown, PA 18951
800-882-0512
www.indianrockproduce.com

**ISLAND MARKET FOODS/
VASHON THRIFTWAY**
P.O. Box 307
9740 Southwest Bank Road
Vashon Island, WA 98070
206-463-2446
www.islandmarketfoods.com

KATAGIRI
224 East 59th Street
New York, NY 10022
212-755-3566
www.katagiri.com

KELLER'S CREAMERY
832 Harleysville Pike
Harleysville, PA 19438
800-582-4382
www.butter1.com

**KEREKES BAKERY &
RESTAURANT EQUIPMENT**
6103 Fifteenth Avenue
Brooklyn, NY 11219
800-525-5556
www.kerekesequip.com

KITCHEN CONSERVATORY
8021 Clayton Road
St. Louis, MO 63117
866-862-2433
www.kitchenconservatory.com

KITCHEN ETC.
800-232-4070
www.kitchenetc.com

KITCHEN MARKET
218 Eighth Avenue
New York, NY 10011
888-468-4433
www.kitchenmarket.com

KMART
800-866-0086
www.bluelight.com

LIFETHYME NATURAL MARKET
410 Avenue of the Americas
New York, NY 10011
212-420-9099

**MARTHA STEWART:
THE CATALOG FOR LIVING**
800-950-7130
www.marthastewart.com

MAUTHE'S DAIRY
Highway 25
Folsom, LA 70437
601-542-3471

MURRAY'S CHEESE
257 Bleecker Street
New York, NY 10014
888-692-4339
www.murrayscheese.com

OLIVIERS & COMPANY
412 Grand Central Terminal
New York, NY 10017
877-828-6620
www.oliviers-co.com

PACIFIC RIM GOURMET
4905 Morena Boulevard
Suite 1313
San Diego, CA 92117
800-910-9657
www.pacificrim-gourmet.com

PARS FOODS INTERNATIONAL
145 West 30th Street
New York, NY 10001
212-760-7277
www.parsfoods.com

PENZEYS SPICES
www.penzeys.com
800-741-7787

PETROSSIAN PARIS
911 Seventh Avenue
New York, NY 10019
212-245-2217
800-828-9241
www.petrossian.com

SUR LA TABLE
800-243-0852
www.surlatable.com

SWEET CELEBRATIONS
P.O. Box 39426
Edina, MN 55439
800-328-6722
www.sweetc.com

TASTE OF SCANDINAVIA
845 Village Center Drive
North Oaks, MN 55127
651-482-8876
www.tasteofscandinavia.com

URBANI TRUFFLES AND CAVIAR
29-24 40th Avenue
Long Island City, NY 11101
800-281-2330
www.urbani.com

WHITE LILY
218 East Depot Street
Knoxville, TN 37917
800-264-5459
www.whitelily.com

WHOLE FOODS MARKET
250 Seventh Avenue
New York, NY 10001
212-924-5969
www.wholefoods.com

WIKSTROM'S GOURMET FOODS
5247 North Clark Street
Chicago, IL 60640
773-275-6100
www.wikstromsgourmet.com

WILD EDIBLES
Grand Central Market
89 East 42nd street
New York, NY 10017
212-687-4255

WILLIAMS-SONOMA
800-541-2233
www.williams-sonoma.com

ZINGERMAN'S DELICATESSEN
422 Detroit Street
Ann Arbor, MI 48104
734-663-3354
www.zingermans.com

Index

A

Aïoli, Le Grand, 183
Aïoli, Salt-and-Pepper Shrimp with, 146, *168**
Almond(s)
  -Coated Goat Cheese, Frisée, and Belgian Endive Salad, 254, *318*
  -Crusted Curry Chicken Salad Tea Sandwiches, 100, *160-61*
  -Shortbread Crust, 200
  Amaretti Crisps, 281
  Brittle, Persian, 28
  Cornmeal Biscotti with Dates and, 264–65
  Linzertorte, 306
  Mixed Fruit-and-Nut Cookies, 266, *332*
  Pithiviers, 133
  Praline Buttercream, 309–10
  Praline Truffles, 312
  Shortbread Cookies, 301–2, *336*
  Three-Nut Torte, 309
  Toasted, Sugar Snap Peas with, 127
Amaretti Crisps, 281
Appetizers. See Starters
Apple(s)
  Baked Camembert with Fresh Fruit, 107
  and Brie Custard Tart, 94
  Caramelized, Best Whipped Sweet Potatoes with, 275, *327*
  Pie, Mile-High, 307, *336*
  Pink Applesauce, 297
  Radishes, and Cheddar Frico, Autumn Greens with, 255
  Soup, Curried, 253
  Tarte Tatin, 134
  Vanilla Applesauce, 301

Applesauce, Pink, 297
Applesauce, Vanilla, 301
Artichoke Bruschetta, 53, *78*
Artichokes, Quick Braised, 147
Arugula
  -Walnut Pesto, Spinach Linguine with, 275, *318*
  and Cannellini Salad with Olive Vinaigrette, 141
  Risotto, 122
  Salad with French Lentils, Smoked Chicken, and Roasted Peppers, 37
Asiago, Risotto with Peas, Marjoram, and, 145, *162*
Asian Chicken Soup, 181, *232*
Asian Steak Salad with Spicy Vinaigrette, 97, *158*
Asparagus
  Crisp Squid, and Tangerines, Salad of, 57, *73*
  and Egg-Yolk Butter Tea Sandwiches, 101–2, *160-61*
  Sautéed, with Aged Gouda Cheese, 193, *241*
  Thick, Simple Steamed, 127
  Timbale, 93
  White, with Hollandaise Sauce, 107, *163*
Avocado(s)
  Chunky Guacamole, 22, *77*
  with Grapefruit and Sweet-Onion Salsa, 93

B

Bacon
  -and-Egg Salad Tea Sandwiches, 101, *160-61*
  and Cheddar, Mashed Potatoes with, 278

and Sautéed-Mushroom Butter Tea Sandwiches, 103–4, *160-61*
Bagna Cauda, 253
Bagna Cauda with Broccoflower and Toasted Country Bread, 253
Banana Purée and Grated Coconut, Chocolate Mousse with, 27
Bananas Foster, 40–41
Barbecue Rub, 224
Barbecue Sauce, Tennessee Pit, 189
Barbecued Chicken, 189
Bars
  Chocolate Brownies, 223, *247*
  Hermit, with Brown-Sugar Icing and Candied Ginger, 265–66
  Raisin, Grandmother Brinton's, 265
  Warm Cream-Cheese Brownies, 284, *333*
Basil
  -Yogurt Soup with Tomato Ice, 184
  Flowers, Cold Soba Noodles with, 53, *72*
  Garden Tomato Salad, 141
  Mozzarella, Prosciutto, and Pesto Butter Tea Sandwiches, 103, *160-61*
  Pistou Soup, 54–55, *75*
Bean(s). See also Black Beans; Chickpeas; Green Beans; Lentils
  -and-Pepper Salad, Multicolored, with Ricotta Salata and Herbs, 188, *235*
  Arugula and Cannellini Salad with Olive Vinaigrette, 141
  Black-Eyed Peas with Escarole, Potatoes, and Turkey Sausage, 38, *80*
  Chicken Cassoulet with Crisp Breadcrumbs, 218, *238*
  Chili con Carne, 22, *76*

*Page numbers in italics indicate color photographs.

Cranberry, Cucumber, and Beet Salad
in Cucumber Boats, 186, *238*
Cranberry-, Salad with Butternut
Squash and Broccoli Rabe,
260, *315*
Edamame Succotash, 260
Fava, Roast Best End of Highgrove
Lamb and, with Mint and Marjoram,
60, *74*
Flageolets, 126
Minestrone, 209
Taco Salad, 210, *235*
Three-, Salad with Honey-Mustard
Vinaigrette, 210, *235*
Beef
Asian Steak Salad with Spicy
Vinaigrette, 97, *158*
Chili con Carne, 22, *76*
Grilled Marinated Strip Steak with
Scallions, 191, *241*
Pot Roast, 39, *80*
Pot Roast Ragu, 39–40, *81*
Rigatoni and Meatballs, 211, *236*
Roast, and Caramelized Onion Tea
Sandwiches, 101, *160-61*
Beer-Battered Cod in Tacos, 189
Beet(s)
and Carrot Latkes, 297
Lentils with Tarragon, Shallots, and,
187, *234*
Pickled, 286
Roasted, 261, *328*
Thinly Sliced, with Blood Oranges and
Watercress, 294
Belgian Chocolate Birthday Cake,
25–26, *87*
Belgian Endive
Almond-Coated Goat Cheese, and
Frisée Salad, 254, *318*
Green and White Salad, 19
and Pear Salad with Oregon Blue
Cheese and Hazelnuts, 218
and Radish Salad, 292
Soup, Cream of, 15, *70*
Berry(ies). See also Raspberry(ies);
Strawberry(ies)
Blackberry Ice Cream, 222, *247*
Breakfast Shake, 114, *155*

Cloudberry Cake, 150
Cranberry Chutney, 277
Lingonberry Punch, 137
and Melon Steeped in Red Wine,
Sauternes, Basil, and Mint, 62, *86*
Syrup, 213
Tarts, French Flag, 194–95, *243*
Beverages. See Drinks
Biscotti, Cornmeal, with Dates and
Almonds, 264–65
Biscuits, Cream, 277
Biscuits, Oyster, 224, *239*
Black Bean(s)
Saucy, 192
Smoked Turkey, and Avocado Tea
Sandwiches, Southwest, 104–5,
160-61
Taco Salad, 210, *235*
Black-Eyed Peas with Escarole,
Potatoes, and Turkey Sausage, 38, *80*
Blackberry(ies)
Ice Cream, 222, *247*
Melon and Berries Steeped in Red
Wine, Sauternes, Basil, and Mint,
62, *86*
Blinis with Caviar and Cucumber-Dill
Dressing, 137
Blue Cheese
and Buttermilk Dressing, 285
Oregon, and Hazelnuts, Endive and
Pear Salad with, 218
Roquefort Butter and Red Pear Tea
Sandwiches, 103, *160-61*
Blueberry(ies)
Berry Syrup, 213
Breakfast Shake, 114, *155*
French Flag Berry Tarts, 194–95, *243*
Bouchées, 117
Bratselies, 302
Bread(s). See also Cornbread
Cream Biscuits, 277
Currant Scones, 207, *225, 226*
Focaccia, 268
Orange Spiral Rolls, 298
Oyster Biscuits, 224, *239*
Pita-, Salad with Cucumber, Mint,
and Feta, 141, *157*
Pudding, Pumpkin, 267, *332*

Rye Sourdough, 140
Rye Sourdough Starter, 137
Stuffing, 280, *326*
Sweet-Potato Rolls, 280–81, *327*
Toast Points, 181, *231*
Breakfast
Breakfast Butter, 285
Breakfast Muffins, 147, *153-54*
Coddled Eggs with Fines Herbes,
117, *156*
Currant Scones, 207, *225, 226*
Rolled Omelets with Ratatouille
Filling, 207, *225, 226*
Rolled Omelets with Spinach and
Goat Cheese, 207–8, *225, 226*
Strawberry-Rhubarb Coffee Cake,
208, *225, 227*
Breton Butter Cake, 128, *170*
Brie and Apple Custard Tart, 94
Bric and Walnut Cake, 289, *316*
Brioche Pain Perdu, Thyme-Roasted
Figs over, 64, *67*
Brittle, Peanut, 307–8
Brittle, Persian Almond, 28
Broccoflower and Toasted Country
Bread, Bagna Cauda with, 253
Broccoli Rabe, Cranberry-Bean Salad
with Butternut Squash and, 260, *315*
Broccoli with Orecchiette, 98, *164*
Brown-Sugar Cornbread, 25, *76-77*
Brown-Sugar Icing, 266
Brownies, Chocolate, 223, *247*
Brownies, Cream-Cheese, Warm,
284, *333*
Bruschetta, Artichoke, 53, *78*
Bruschetta, Ricotta and Tomato,
208, *230*
Bruschetta, Wild Mushroom, 217, *230*
Brussels Sprouts, Sautéed, with
Raisins, 278, *323*
Burgers, Herbed Turkey, 211
Butter
Breakfast, 285
Chutney, 104
Egg, 139
Egg-Yolk, 101-2
Lemon-Caper, 102

Pesto, 103
Radish, 96
Roquefort, 103
Sautéed-Mushroom, 103–4
Buttercream, Caramel, 304–5
Buttercream, Praline, 309–10
Butterflies, 128
Buttermilk
    and Blue Cheese Dressing, 285
    Cornbread, 276–77
    Soup, Cold Curried, with Corn and
        Poblano Chile, 182, *232*
Butternut Squash
    and Broccoli Rabe, Cranberry-Bean
        Salad with, 260, *315*
    with Brown Butter, 275–76, *323*
    Edamame Succotash, 260
    Purée, 257
Butterscotch-Chip Cookies, Chocolate,
    303, *336*

C

Cabbage
    Asian Steak Salad with Spicy
        Vinaigrette, 97, *158*
    Red, Slaw and Rutabaga Potatoes,
        Cornflake-Crusted Chicken with,
        59, *78*
    Shredded-, and Chicken Salad with
        Noodles and Peanut Sauce, 184
Caesar Salad, 209
Caipirinha, 201
Cake(s), savory
    Brie and Walnut, 289
    Focaccia, 290
    Smoked Salmon, 291
    Sushi, 291
Cake(s), sweet
    Belgian Chocolate, 25–26, *87*
    Breton Butter, 128, *170*
    Caramel, 193
    Chocolate Hazelnut Torte, 303–4
    Chocolate Spice, 44–45, *82*
    Chocolate Whole-Wheat Biscuit, 27
    Cloudberry, 150
    Coffee, Strawberry-Rhubarb, 208,
        225, 227

Dobos Torte, 304
Ice-Cream, Strawberry and Pistachio,
    213, *246*
Inside-Out German Chocolate, 28
Lamingtons, 111, *171*
Lemon Semifreddo, 130–31
Linzertorte, 306
Molten Chocolate, with Earl Grey Ice
    Cream, 48, *82*
Poppy-Seed Torte, 308
Raspberry-Filled Layer, 29
Three-Nut Torte, 309
Vanilla Sheet, 131
White Sheet, 31–32
Yellow Génoise, 213–14
Camembert, Baked, with Fresh Fruit, 107
Canapes, Pickled Herring, 139
Candied Lemon Zest, 197
Candy. See also Truffles
    Caramel, 305
    Caramel-Dipped Pecans, 42
    Chocolate Fudge, 43, 303
    Peanut Brittle, 307–8
    Persian Almond Brittle, 28
Cantaloupe Granita, 213
Caramel, 305
    -Dipped Pecans, 42
    Buttercream, 304–5
    Cake, 193
    Frosting, 194
    Sauce, 199
Carrot(s)
    and Beet Latkes, 297
    Health Muffins, 149
    Miso Soup with Tofu, Spinach, and, 254
    Roasted, 261
    Roasted, and Dill, Orzo Salad with,
        188, *234*
Cassoulet, Chicken, with Crisp
    Breadcrumbs, 218, *238*
Catfish, Fried, Sandwich, 190
Caviar and Cucumber-Dill Dressing,
    Blinis with, 137
Cedar-Plank Roasted Salmon, 273
Celeriac and Potatoes, Mashed, 261
Cereal-Cube Castle, 27
Chai Tea with Soy Milk, 267

Champagne
    Beurre Blanc, Baked Oysters with
        Spinach and, 15
    Mignonette, Oysters with, 217, *230*
    Truffles, 311
Cheddar
    Aunt Sara's Cheese Grits, 191
    Classic Grilled Cheese, 256, *321*
    Frico, 255
    Mashed Potatoes with Bacon
        and, 278
Cheese. See also Cheddar; Goat
    Cheese; Gouda Cheese; Mascarpone;
    Mozzarella
    Arugula Risotto, 122
    Baked Camembert with Fresh
        Fruit, 107
    Baked Stuffed Sweet Onions, 105
    Blue, and Buttermilk Dressing, 285
    Brie and Apple Custard Tart, 94
    Brie and Walnut Cake, 289, *316*
    Bruschetta, 208, *230*
    Croque Madame (var.), 256, *320*
    Croque Monsieur, 256, *320*
    Focaccia Cake, 290, *316*
    Fondue, 289
    Gougères, 35
    Multicolored Pepper-and-Bean Salad
        with Ricotta Salata and Herbs,
        188, *235*
    Oregon Blue, and Hazelnuts, Endive
        and Pear Salad with, 218
    Pita-Bread Salad with Cucumber,
        Mint, and Feta, 141, *157*
    Potato Rösti, 299
    Risotto with Peas, Marjoram,
        and Asiago, 145, *162*
    Roquefort Butter and Red Pear Tea
        Sandwiches, 103, *160–61*
    Sautéed Mushroom, Prosciutto,
        and Taleggio Panini, 259
    Straws, 119
Cheesecakes, Individual No-Bake,
    305–6, *334*
Cherry(ies)
    Clafoutis, 149
    and Lemon Trifle, 196, *245*

Mixed Fruit-and-Nut Cookies, 266, *332*

and Pickled Cucumber Relish, 203–4

Poached, 197

Chess Pie, Mary Curll's, 198

Chicken

Barbecued, 189

Braised, with Olives, Carrots, and Chickpeas, 142

Breasts, Crisp Mustard-Glazed, 38, *80*

Breasts, Herb-Stuffed, 124, *169*

Breasts, Soy-Lime, Grilled, 23

Cacciatore, 20–21

Cassoulet with Crisp Breadcrumbs, 218, *238*

Cobb Salad, 209

Cock-a-Leekie, 23

Cornflake-Crusted, with Red Cabbage Slaw and Rutabaga Potatoes, 59, *78*

Cucumber-Coconut Soup, 182, *233*

and Dumplings, 20

Liver Pâté with Toast Points, 181, *231*

Pot Pies, Individual, with Mushrooms and Peas, 219–20, *238*

Roasted, and Jerusalem Artichokes, 100, *167*

Salad Tea Sandwiches, Almond-Crusted Curry, 100, *160-61*

and Shredded-Cabbage Salad with Noodles and Peanut Sauce, 184

Smoked, French Lentils, and Roasted Peppers, Arugula Salad with, 37

Soup, Asian, 181, *232*

Stew, Winter Vegetable, 24

Strips, Walnut, with Pomegranate Sauce, 296

Tarragon, Braised, 255

Tortilla Soup, 21, *70*

Chickpeas

Braised Chicken with Olives, Carrots, and, 142

Roasted-Garlic Hummus, 36

Chicory, Sautéed, 61–62

Chile, Poblano, Cold Curried Buttermilk Soup with Corn and, 182, *232*

Chili con Carne, 22, *76*

Chocolate

-and-Peanut-Butter Cups, 198–99

-Chip Cookie, Skillet-Baked, 199

-Wafer Crust, 196

Belgian, Birthday Cake, 25–26, *87*

Bowls, 43–44

Brownies, 223, *247*

Butterscotch-Chip Cookies, 303, *336*

Cakes, Molten, with Earl Grey Ice Cream, 48, *82*

Candy Cane Truffles, 310

Caramel Tart, 41, *88*

Champagne Truffles, 311

Classic Truffles, 310

and Coconut Pie, Crisp, 194, *244*

Coconut Truffles, 311

Cream Pie, 42

Crêpes (var.), 30, 66

Curls, Candied Hazelnuts and, 26, *87*

Fudge, 43, 303

Fudge Frosting, 45

Ganache, 310

Ganache Glaze, 26

Gelato, 43

German, Torte, Inside-Out, 28

Grand Marnier Truffles, 311

Grasshopper Tarts, 195–96, *248*

Hazelnut Torte, 303–4

Hazelnut Truffles, 311

Hot Fudge Sauce, 30

Icing, 112

Malted, Frozen, 47

and Mint Parfaits, 108

Mocha Filling, 200

Mocha Steamed Puddings, 47, *83*

Mocha Truffles, 311

Mousse with Banana Purée and Grated Coconut, 27

Napoleon, 131–32, *176*

Orange-Ginger Truffles, 311

Pâte Sucrée, 41

Patties, Coconut, 264, *330*

Peanut Butter Surprises, 266–67, *332*

Pots de Crème, 109, *172*

Praline Truffles, 312

Profiteroles, 49, *82*

Sambuca Truffles, 312

Sandwich Cookies, 44, *82*

Sauce, 108, 308

Spice Cake, 44–45, *82*

Three-Nut Torte, 309

Tiramisu Cups, 200

Truffles, 49

Turnovers, 129

Warm Cream-Cheese Brownies, 284, *333*

Whole-Wheat Biscuit Cake, 27

Chowder, Elwood's Ham, 271

Chowder, Finnish Fish, 142

Chutney, Cranberry, 277

Chutney Butter and Smoked Duck Tea Sandwiches, 104, *160-61*

Cilantro

Baby Red Potatoes with, 146

Fresh-Herb Kuku, 16, *69*

Green Rice, 192

Mango and Tomato Salsa, 126

and Roasted Tomatillo Pesto, Mexican Fiesta Soup with, 120

Cinnamon-Sugar Mini Muffins, 148

Citrus-Cumin Vinaigrette, 98

Clafoutis, Cherry, 149

Clam(s)

and Corn Chowder Sauce, 219, *239*

Fish Stew, 143

Littleneck, Steamed, 272

Spaghetti with, 60

Cloudberry Cake, 150

Cobb Salad, 209

Cock-a-Leekie, 23

Cocktails

Blue Margaritas, 201, *229*

Caipirinha, 201

Fresh Whiskey Sours, 201–2

Margaritas for a Crowd, 202

Mary Brockman's Favorite Pimm's Cup, 202

Passion-Fruit, 202, *229*

Rosé Melons, 202, *229*

Coconut

-Pecan Filling, 28

Chocolate Patties, 264, *330*

and Chocolate Pie, Crisp, 194, *244*

Lamingtons, 111, *171*

Mixed Fruit-and-Nut Cookies, 266, *332*

Pear Pandowdy, 282–83, *333*
Truffles, 311
Cod, Beer-Battered, in Tacos, 189
Cod, Miso-Glazed, 295, *319*
Coffee
　Espresso Crème Anglaise, 48
　Espresso Granita, 150
　Ice Cream Affogato, 150
　Mocha Filling, 200
　Mocha Steamed Puddings, 47, *83*
　Mocha Truffles, 311
　Tiramisu Cups, 200
Coffee Cake, Strawberry-Rhubarb, 208,
　225, 227
Concord Grape Sorbet, 264, *330*
Condiments
　Barbecue Rub, 224
　Berry Syrup, 213
　Black-Olive Relish, 202
　Bread-and-Butter Pickles, 285
　Breakfast Butter, 285
　Caramelized Onions, 257
　Caramelized Sweet Onions, 114
　Chutney Butter, 104
　Cranberry Chutney, 277
　Cucumber Relish, 203
　Egg Butter, 139
　Egg-Yolk Butter, 101–2
　Eggplant-Pomegranate Relish,
　　290, *313*
　Flower Sugar, 64
　Hazelnut Simple Syrup, 304
　Herb-Infused Olive Oil, 268
　Homemade Mayonnaise, 17, *69*
　Lemon-Caper Butter, 102
　Lemon Curd, 30
　Mango and Tomato Salsa, 126
　Mint Jelly, 125
　Mrs. Gubler's Pomegranate Jelly,
　　306, *333*
　Pesto Butter, 103
　Pickled Beets, 286
　Pickled Cucumber and Cherry
　　Relish, 203–4
　Pickled Garlic, 64
　Pickled Green Beans, 286
　Pickled Watermelon Rind, 286
　Pico de Gallo, 204

Pineapple Salsa, 204
Radish Butter, 96
Roasted Garlic, 262, *328*
Roasted Onion Purée, 262, *328*
Roasted Plum Tomatoes, 262, *328*
Roquefort Butter, 103
Rose Petal Jelly, 64
Sautéed-Mushroom Butter, 103–4
Simple Sorbet Syrup, 264
Simple Syrup, 151
Tennessee Pit Barbecue Sauce, 189
Tropical Fruit and Crab Salsa,
　204, *229*
Whole Grilled Garlic, 204
Cookie, Chocolate-Chip, Skillet-
　Baked, 199
Cookies. See also Bars; Biscotti
　Almond Shortbread, 301–2, *336*
　Amaretti Crisps, 281
　Bratselies, 302
　Chocolate Butterscotch-Chip,
　　303, *336*
　Chocolate Sandwich, 44, *82*
　Coconut Chocolate Patties, 264, *330*
　Gingerbread Cookies, 305
　Mixed Fruit-and-Nut, 266, *332*
　Peanut Butter Surprises, 266–67, *332*
　Walnut Shortbread, 113–14
Corn
　Cakes, Mini, with Goat Cheese and
　　Pepper Jelly, 120
　and Clam Chowder Sauce, 219, *239*
　Cucumber, and Crab Salad, 185–86
　Edamame Succotash, 260
　Fresh, Creamed, 212
　Mexican Fiesta Soup with Roasted
　　Tomatillo and Cilantro Pesto, 120
　Muffins, 148
　and Poblano Chile, Cold Curried
　　Buttermilk Soup with, 182, *232*
　Roasted, 262
　Taco Salad, 210, *235*
　and Tomato Salad, 185
Cornbread
　Brown-Sugar, 25, *76-77*
　Buttermilk, 276–77
　Cornlight Bread, 203
　Dressing, 276, *325*

Cornflake-Crusted Chicken with
　Red Cabbage Slaw and Rutabaga
　Potatoes, 59, *78*
Cornish Hens, Roasted, with
　Pomegranate-Molasses Glaze,
　295, *322*
Cornmeal
　-Crusted Pizza, 256–57, *314*
　Biscotti with Dates and Almonds,
　　264–65
　Brown-Sugar Cornbread, 25, *76-77*
　Buttermilk Cornbread, 276–77
　Cornbread Dressing, 276, *325*
　Cornlight Bread, 203
　Layered Eggplant and Polenta
　　Casserole, 220
　Polenta, 127
　Soft Polenta with Fresh Herbs, 106
Couscous, Herbed, 106
Couscous, Toasted, Tabbouleh,
　127–28, *166*
Crab(meat)
　Cucumber, and Corn Salad, 185–86
　Peas, and Basil, Pasta with, 145, *166*
　Sushi Cake, 291–92, *316*
　and Tropical Fruit Salsa, 204, *229*
Cranberry Bean, Cucumber, and Beet
　Salad in Cucumber Boats, 186, *238*
Cranberry-Bean Salad with Butternut
　Squash and Broccoli Rabe, 260, *315*
Cranberry Chutney, 277
Cream, Pastry, 132
Cream Biscuits, 277
Cream Cheese
　Brownies, Warm, 284, *333*
　Herb, with Grated Vegetables Tea
　　Sandwiches, 102, *160-61*
　Individual No-Bake Cheesecakes,
　　305–6, *334*
Cream Filling, Pastry, 46
Cream Horns, 129
Cream Puffs, 45–46
Crème Anglaise, 113, *173*
Crème Anglaise, Espresso, 48
Crème Brûlée, 109
Crème Fraîche Filling, 195
Crêpe Filling, Ricotta-Mascarpone, 31
Crêpe Filling, Sautéed Pineapple, 31

Crêpes, Chocolate (var.), 30, 66
Crêpes, Vanilla, 30, *65-66*
Croque Madame (var.), 256, *320*
Croque Monsieur, 256, *320*
Crostini, Tomato, 217
Crust
    Almond-Shortbread, 200
    Chocolate-Wafer, 196
    Graham-Nut, 197
    Granola, 201
Cucumber(s)
    -Coconut Soup, 182, *233*
    -Dill Dressing, 137
    -Peanut Sauce, 183, *228*
    Bread-and-Butter Pickles, 285
    Broth, Striped Bass with, 191, *238*
    Corn, and Crab Salad, 185–86
    Cranberry Bean, and Beet Salad in
      Cucumber Boats, 186, *238*
    Mint, and Feta, Pita-Bread Salad with,
      141, *157*
    Pickled, and Cherry Relish, 203–4
    Relish, 203
    and Riesling Granita, 194
    Salad, 141
    Shaved, Fennel, and Watermelon
      Salad, 188
    Summer Rolls, 182, *228*
    Vinaigrette, 186
    Yogurt-Basil Soup with Tomato Ice, 184
Cumin-Citrus Vinaigrette, 98
Curd, Lemon, 30
Currant(s)
    Chocolate Hazelnut Torte, 303–4
    Scones, 207, *225, 226*
    and Spinach Latkes, 300
Curried Apple Soup, 253
Curried Buttermilk Soup, Cold, with
    Corn and Poblano Chile, 182, *232*
Curried Lamb Chops, 189, *238*
Curry Chicken Salad Tea Sandwiches,
    Almond-Crusted, 100, *160-61*
Custard(s)
    Asparagus Timbale, 93
    Chocolate Pots de Crème, 109, *172*
    Crème Anglaise, 113, *173*
    Crème Brûlée, 109
    Flan, 110, *174*

Grapefruit Tart, 110, *175*
Maple Pudding, 112
Raspberry Floating Island, 113, *173*
Roasted-Garlic, Fried, 95–96
Tart, Brie and Apple, 94

D

Dal, Warm Red-Lentil, with Pita Chips, 37
Dates and Almonds, Cornmeal Biscotti
    with, 264–65
Desserts. See also Bars; Cake(s);
    Candy; Cookies; Ice Cream; Pastries;
    Pie(s); Tarts, dessert
    Baked Camembert with Fresh Fruit, 107
    Baked Pears with Vanilla
      Mascarpone, 263
    Bananas Foster, 40–41
    Broiled Persimmons with
      Mascarpone, 302
    Cantaloupe Granita, 213
    Cereal-Cube Castle, 27
    Cherry Clafoutis, 149
    Chocolate and Mint Parfaits, 108
    Chocolate Crêpes (var.), 30, 66
    Chocolate Gelato, 43
    Chocolate Mousse with Banana Purée
      and Grated Coconut, 27
    Chocolate Pots de Crème, 109, *172*
    Concord Grape Sorbet, 264, *330*
    Crème Anglaise, 113, *173*
    Crème Brûlée, 109
    Cucumber and Riesling Granita, 194
    Espresso Crème Anglaise, 48
    Espresso Granita, 150
    Flan, 110, *174*
    Fresh-Raspberry Gelatin and
      Whipped Cream, 130
    Frozen Chocolate Malted, 47
    Fruit Granita, 151
    Fruit Sherbet, 151, *171*
    Grapefruit in Moscato, 62
    Grilled Peaches with Chilled
      Sabayon, 196
    Individual No-Bake Cheesecakes,
      305–6, *334*
    Lemon and Cherry Trifle, 196, *245*
    Mango-Lime Granita, 112
    Mango Panna Cotta, 198, *244*

Maple Pudding, 112
Melon and Berries Steeped in Red
    Wine, Sauternes, Basil, and Mint,
    62, *86*
Mocha Steamed Puddings, 47, *83*
Pear Pandowdy, 282–83, *333*
Pear Pavlova, 283, *332*
Peppermint Semifreddo, 308
Pumpkin Bread Pudding, 267, *332*
Pumpkin Shake, 267
Raspberry Floating Island, 113, *173*
Skillet-Baked Chocolate-Chip
    Cookie, 199
Sorbets, Assorted, 152, *171*
Strawberry Compote, 128, *170*
Thyme-Roasted Figs over Brioche
    Pain Perdu, 64, *67*
Tiramisu Cups, 200
Vanilla Crêpes, 30, *65-66*
Vanilla Pudding, 50, *85*
Watermelon and Raspberry Salad, 223
Yogurt Drizzled with Honey and
    Walnuts, 285
Dill
    Cucumber Salad, 141
    Fresh-Herb Kuku, 16, *69*
    Orzo Salad with Roasted Carrots and,
      188, *234*
Dips
    Bagna Cauda, 253
    Cheese Fondue, 289
    Chunky Guacamole, 22, *77*
    Eggplant-Pomegranate Relish,
      290, *313*
    Le Grand Aïoli, 183
    Pico de Gallo, 204
    Pineapple Salsa, 204
    Roasted-Garlic Hummus, 36
    Roasted Red Pepper and Walnut, 272
    Tropical Fruit and Crab Salsa,
      204, *229*
    Warm Red-Lentil Dal with Pita
      Chips, 37
Dobos Torte, 304
Dough. See Pastry Dough
Dressing
    Cornbread, 276, *325*
    Stuffing, 280, *326*

Dressing, salad. See Salad Dressing
Drinks
    Blue Margaritas, 201, *229*
    Blueberry Breakfast Shake, 114, *155*
    Caipirinha, 201
    Chai Tea with Soy Milk, 267
    Fresh Whiskey Sours, 201–2
    Frozen Chocolate Malted, 47
    Lingonberry Punch, 137
    Margaritas for a Crowd, 202
    Mary Brockman's Favorite Pimm's
        Cup, 202
    Orange Lemonade, 214
    Passion-Fruit Cocktails, 202, *229*
    Peach Tea Punch, 134
    Pomegranate Punch, 312
    Pomegranate Tea, 312
    Pumpkin Shake, 267
    Rosé Melons, 202, *229*
    Spiced Lemonade, 32
    Spiced Rose Lassi, 50
Duck, Smoked, and Chutney Butter Tea
    Sandwiches, 104, *160-61*
Duckling, Long Island, Two Ways, 99
Dumplings, Chicken and, 20

E

Earl Grey Ice Cream, 49, *82*
Eclairs, 46–47
Edamame Succotash, 260
Egg(s). See also Custard(s)
    -and-Bacon Salad Tea Sandwiches,
        101, *160-61*
    -Yolk Butter and Asparagus Tea
        Sandwiches, 101–2, *160-61*
    Butter, 139
    Coddled, with Fines Herbes, 117, *156*
    Hard-Boiled, Perfect, 203
    Rolled Omelets with Ratatouille
        Filling, 207, *225, 226*
    Rolled Omelets with Spinach and
        Goat Cheese, 207–8, *225, 226*
Eggplant
    -Pomegranate Relish, 290, *313*
    Kuku, 16, *69*
    and Polenta Casserole, Layered, 220

Roasted, 262
Roasted Cherry Tomatoes, Baked
    Buffalo Mozzarella, and, 55, *75*
Rolled Omelets with Ratatouille
    Filling, 207, *225, 226*
Stuffed, 212, *230*
Endive. See Belgian Endive
Escarole, Potatoes, and Turkey Sausage,
    Black-Eyed Peas with, 38, *80*
Espresso Crème Anglaise, 48
Espresso Granita, 150

F

Farro Salad with Zucchini, Pine Nuts,
    and Lemon Zest, 186–87, *234*
Fennel
    and Blood Oranges, Spinach Salad
        with, 210
    Braised Lamb Shanks with Tomato
        and, 122–23
    Caramelized, Pan-Fried Scallops on,
        53–54
    and Leek Soup, Chilled, 119
    Pomegranate, and Green Bean Salad,
        293, *317*
    Shaved Cucumber, and Watermelon
        Salad, 188
Feta, Pita-Bread Salad with Cucumber,
    Mint, and, 141, *157*
Figs
    Health Muffins, 149
    Thyme-Roasted, over Brioche Pain
        Perdu, 64, *67*
Filling
    Caramel Buttercream, 304–5
    Coconut-Pecan, 28
    Crème Fraîche, 195
    Crêpe, Ricotta-Mascarpone, 31
    Crêpe, Sautéed Pineapple, 31
    Lemon Curd, 30
    Lemon-Curd, 197
    Mascarpone, 200
    Mocha, 200
    Pastry Cream, 46, 132
    Praline Buttercream, 309–10
Finnish Fish Chowder, 142
Fish
    Beer-Battered Cod in Tacos, 189

Blinis with Caviar and Cucumber-Dill
    Dressing, 137
Cedar-Plank Roasted Salmon, 273
and Chips, 59–60
Chowder, Finnish, 142
Confit of Wild Salmon on Cucumber
    Salad with Horseradish Sauce,
    58–59, *75*
Fluke Sashimi with Baby Greens, 95
Fried Catfish Sandwich, 190
Grilled Mahimahi in Tacos, 190
Grilled Striped Bass with Corn and
    Clam Chowder Sauce, 219, *239*
Grilled Trout with Oregano, 123, *163*
Hot-Smoked Salmon Steaks with
    Morel Sauce, 144
Lemon-Caper Butter and Smoked
    Salmon Tea Sandwiches, 102,
    160-61
Miso-Glazed Cod, 295, *319*
Pickled Herring Canapes, 139
Salmon Cake, 291, *316*
Seared Salmon with Creamy Leek
    Sauce, 125–26
Sole Rolls with Spinach and Lemon
    Slices, 220–21
Stew, 143
Stock, 143
Striped Bass with Cucumber Broth,
    191, *238*
Striped Sea Bass with Blood Oranges
    and Olives, 23–24, *71*
Five-Spice Pork Tenderloin, 190
Flageolets, 126
Flan, 110, *174*
Flower Sugar, 64
Fluke Sashimi with Baby Greens, 95
Focaccia, 268
Focaccia Cake, 290, *316*
Fondue, Cheese, 289
Frosting. See also Icing
    Caramel, 194
    Chocolate Fudge, 45
    Seven Minute, 29
Fruit. See also specific fruits
    -and-Nut Cookies, Mixed, 266, *332*
    Breakfast Muffins, 147, *153-54*
    Granita, 151

Sherbet, 151, *171*
Sorbets, Assorted, 152, *171*
Stuffing, 280, *326*
Tropical, and Crab Salsa, 204, *229*
Fudge, Chocolate, 43, 303

G

Galette, Plum, 223, *242*
Ganache, Chocolate, 310
Ganache Glaze, 26
Garlic
    Pickled, 64
    Roasted, 262, *328*
    Roasted, Hummus, 36
    Roasted-, Custard, Fried, 95–96
    Whole Grilled, 204
Garlic-Chive Blossoms, Tomato and
    Bean Salad with, 57
Gazpacho, Watermelon, 183–84, *232*
Gelatin, Fresh-Raspberry, and Whipped
    Cream, 130
Gelato, Chocolate, 43
German Chocolate Torte, Inside-Out, 28
Ginger, Candied, Hermit Bars with
    Brown-Sugar Icing and, 265–66
Ginger-Peanut Somen Noodles, 297, *319*
Gingerbread Cookies, 305
Glaze. See Icing
Goat Cheese
    Almond-Coated, Frisée, and Belgian
        Endive Salad, 254, *318*
    Brie and Walnut Cake, 289, *316*
    Grapefruit, and Black Pepper, Mixed
        Lettuces with, 292–93
    and Haricots Verts Salad with
        Almonds, 187
    Marinated, with Oregano, 53
    and Pepper Jelly, Mini Corn Cakes
        with, 120
    Rolled Omelets with Spinach and,
        207–8, *225, 226*
    Warm, with Wasabi-Pea Crust, Peas,
        and Greens, 140, *163*
Gouda Cheese
    Aged, Sautéed Asparagus with,
        193, *241*
    Sweet Onion Sandwiches, 105

Gougères, 35
Graham-Nut Crust, 197
Grains. See also Cornmeal; Rice
    Aunt Sara's Cheese Grits, 191
    Farro Salad with Zucchini, Pine Nuts,
        and Lemon Zest, 186–87, *234*
Grand Marnier Truffles, 311
Granita
    Cantaloupe, 213
    Cucumber and Riesling, 194
    Espresso, 150
    Fruit, 151
    Mango-Lime, 112
Granola Crust, 201
Grape, Concord, Sorbet, 264, *330*
Grapefruit
    with Avocado and Sweet-Onion
        Salsa, 93
    Goat Cheese, and Black Pepper,
        Mixed Lettuces with, 292–93
    in Moscato, 62
    Tart, 110, *175*
Grasshopper Tarts, 195–96, *248*
Gratin, Potato, Zucchini, and Tomato, 222
Green Bean(s)
    Green Salad with Toasted Walnuts,
        Walnut Oil, and, 272, *318*
    Haricots Verts and Goat Cheese
        Salad with Almonds, 187
    Multicolored Pepper-and-Bean
        Salad with Ricotta Salata and
        Herbs, 188, *235*
    Pickled, 286
    Pomegranate, and Fennel Salad,
        293, *317*
    Southern, 279
    and Spaetzle, 298
    Three-Bean Salad with Honey-
        Mustard Vinaigrette, 210, *235*
    Tomato and Bean Salad with Garlic-
        Chive Blossoms, 57
Greens. See also Arugula; Belgian
    Endive; Spinach
    Almond-Coated Goat Cheese, Frisée,
        and Belgian Endive, 254, *318*
    Asian Steak Salad with Spicy
        Vinaigrette, 97, *158*

    Autumn, with Apples, Radishes, and
        Cheddar Frico, 255
    Baby, Fluke Sashimi with, 95
    Black-Eyed Peas with Escarole,
        Potatoes, and Turkey Sausage,
        38, *80*
    Caesar Salad, 209
    Chicken and Shredded-Cabbage
        Salad with Noodles and Peanut
        Sauce, 184
    Cornflake-Crusted Chicken with Red
        Cabbage Slaw and Rutabaga
        Potatoes, 59, *78*
    Elwood's Ham Chowder, 271
    Endive and Radish Salad, 292
    Green and White Salad, 19
    Green Salad with Toasted Walnuts,
        Walnut Oil, and Green Beans,
        272, *318*
    Miso Soup with Tofu and Kale,
        96, *166*
    Mixed Lettuces with Grapefruit, Goat
        Cheese, and Black Pepper, 292–93
    with Orange Vinaigrette and Toasted
        Sesame Seeds, 19, *76-77*
    Sautéed Chicory, 61–62
    Swiss Chard with Olives, 147
    Turnip, 193
    Winter, and Bacon, 40
Grits, Cheese, Aunt Sara's, 191
Gruyère
    Baked Stuffed Sweet Onions, 105
    Cheese Fondue, 289
    Croque Madame (var.), 256, *320*
    Croque Monsieur, 256, *320*
    Gougères, 35
Guacamole, Chunky, 22, *77*

H

Ham
    Baked Stuffed Sweet Onions, 105
    Chowder, Elwood's, 271
    Croque Monsieur, 256, *320*
    Honey-Orange Baked, 294–95
    Mozzarella, Prosciutto, and Pesto
        Butter Tea Sandwiches, 103,
        160-61
    Sautéed Mushroom, Prosciutto, and
        Taleggio Panini, 259

Haricots Verts and Goat Cheese Salad
   with Almonds, 187
Hazelnut(s)
   Candied, and Chocolate Curls, 26, *87*
   Chocolate Torte, 303–4
   Endive and Pear Salad with Oregon
      Blue Cheese and, 218
   Simple Syrup, 304
   Three-Nut Torte, 309
   Truffles, 311
Health Muffins, 149
Herb(s). See also Basil; Cilantro; Dill;
   Mint; Parsley
   -Infused Olive Oil, 268
   -Roasted Turkey with Pan Gravy,
      273–74, *326*
   -Stuffed Chicken Breasts, 124, *169*
   Braised Chicken Tarragon, 255
   Coddled Eggs with Fines Herbes,
      117, *156*
   Flower Sugar, 64
   Fresh, Khoresh (Braised Lamb Stew),
      19–20
   Fresh, Kuku, 16, *69*
   Fresh, Rub, Roasted Whole Leg of
      Lamb with, 125
   Fresh, Soft Polenta with, 106
   Grilled Trout with Oregano, 123, *163*
   Herbed Couscous, 106
   Marinated Goat Cheese with
      Oregano, 53
   Thyme-Roasted Figs over Brioche
      Pain Perdu, 64, *67*
   Tomato and Bean Salad with Garlic-
      Chive Blossoms, 57
Hermit Bars with Brown-Sugar Icing
   and Candied Ginger, 265–66
Herring, Pickled, Canapes, 139
Hollandaise Sauce, 107, *163*
Honey and Walnuts, Yogurt Drizzled
   with, 285
Honey-Mustard Vinaigrette, Three-Bean
   Salad with, 210, *235*
Honey-Orange Baked Ham, 294–95
Honey Tangerines and Kumquats with
   Shaved Celery and Walnuts, 292
Horns, Cream, 129
Hummus, Roasted-Garlic, 36

I

Ice Cream
   Blackberry, 222, *247*
   Cake, Strawberry and Pistachio,
      213, *246*
   Coffee, Affogato, 150
   Earl Grey, 49, *82*
Icing
   Brown-Sugar, 266
   Chocolate, 112
   Chocolate Ganache, 310
   Ganache Glaze, 26
   Muffin, 148
   White Confectioners' Sugar, 32

J

Jelly
   Mint, 125
   Pomegranate, Mrs. Gubler's, 306, *333*
   Rose Petal, 64
Jerusalem Artichokes, Roasted Chicken
   and, 100, *167*
Jícama and Orange Salad with Citrus-
   Cumin Vinaigrette, 98

K

Kale
   Miso Soup with Tofu and, 96, *166*
   Winter Greens and Bacon, 40
Karjalan Potato Pies with Egg
   Butter, 138
Khoresh, Fresh-Herb (Braised Lamb
   Stew), 19–20
Kuku
   Eggplant, 16, *69*
   Fresh-Herb, 16, *69*
Kumquats and Honey Tangerines with
   Shaved Celery and Walnuts, 292

L

Lamb
   Braised, Stew (Fresh-Herb Khoresh),
      19–20, *70*
   Butterflied Leg of, with Lemon and
      Garlic Marinade, 123
   Chops, Curried, 189, *238*

Grilled Leg of, 190
Highgrove, Roast Best End of, and
   Fava Beans with Mint and
   Marjoram, 60, *74*
Leg of, Mint and Pistachio Stuffed,
   124, *165*
Roasted Whole Leg of, with Fresh
   Herb Rub, 125
Shanks, Braised, with Tomato and
   Fennel, 122–23
Lamingtons, 111, *171*
Lassi, Spiced Rose, 50
Latkes
   Basic Potato, 296–97
   Carrot and Beet, 297
   Parsnip, 299
   Spinach and Currant, 300
   Sweet-Potato, 301
Leek and Fennel Soup, Chilled, 119
Leek Sauce, Creamy, Seared Salmon
   with, 125–26
Lemon(s)
   -Caper Butter and Smoked Salmon
      Tea Sandwiches, 102, *160-61*
   -Curd Filling, 197
   and Cherry Trifle, 196, *245*
   Curd, 30
   Orange Lemonade, 214
   Semifreddo Cake, 130–31
   Spiced Lemonade, 32
   Zest, Candied, 197
Lemonade, Orange, 214
Lemonade, Spiced, 32
Lentils
   French, Smoked Chicken, and
      Roasted Peppers, Arugula Salad
      with, 37
   Tarragon, Shallots, and Beets with,
      187, *234*
   Warm Red-, Dal with Pita Chips
      with, 37
Limeade Pie, 197, *244*
Lingonberry Punch, 137
Linguine, Spinach, with Walnut-Arugula
   Pesto, 275, *318*
Linguine with Two-Olive Tapenade,
   144–45, *166*

Linzertorte, 306

Liver, Chicken, Pâté with Toast Points, 181, *231*

Long Island Duckling Two Ways, 99

M

Mahimahi, Grilled, in Tacos, 190

Main courses

meat

Boneless Pork Chops and Roasted Yam Fries, 58, *78*

Braised Lamb Shanks with Tomato and Fennel, 122–23

Braised Lamb Stew (Fresh-Herb Khoresh), 19–20, *70*

Butterflied Leg of Lamb with Lemon and Garlic Marinade, 123

Chili con Carne, 22, *76*

Curried Lamb Chops, 189, *238*

Five-Spice Pork Tenderloin, 190

Grilled Leg of Lamb, 190

Grilled Marinated Strip Steak with Scallions, 191, *241*

Honey-Orange Baked Ham, 294–95

Mint and Pistachio Stuffed Leg of Lamb, 124, *165*

Molasses-Glazed Grilled Pork Loin with Roasted Italian Prune Plums, 258, *324*

Pork Loin Braised in Milk, 274–75, *323*

Pot Roast, 39, *80*

Pot Roast Ragu, 39–40, *81*

Rigatoni and Meatballs, 211, *236*

Roast Best End of Highgrove Lamb and Fava Beans with Mint and Marjoram, 60, *74*

Roasted Whole Leg of Lamb with Fresh Herb Rub, 125

Veal Scallopini Milanese, 61, *78*

meatless

Arugula Risotto, 122

Broccoli with Orecchiette, 98, *164*

Classic Grilled Cheese, 256, *321*

Cornmeal-Crusted Pizza, 256–57, *314*

Croque Madame (var.), 256, *320*

Croque Monsieur, 256, *320*

Layered Eggplant and Polenta Casserole, 220

Linguine with Two-Olive Tapenade, 144–45, *166*

Pizza, 211, *237*

Risotto with Peas, Marjoram, and Asiago, 145, *162*

Sautéed Mushroom, Prosciutto, and Taleggio Panini, 259

Sesame-Marinated Tofu with Vegetables, 259–60

Spinach Linguine with Walnut-Arugula Pesto, 275, *318*

poultry

Barbecued Chicken, 189

Black-Eyed Peas with Escarole, Potatoes, and Turkey Sausage, 38, *80*

Braised Chicken Tarragon, 255

Braised Chicken with Olives, Carrots, and Chickpeas, 142

Chicken and Dumplings, 20

Chicken Cacciatore, 20–21

Chicken Cassoulet with Crisp Breadcrumbs, 218, *238*

Chicken Tortilla Soup, 21, *70*

Cock-a-Leekie, 23

Cornflake-Crusted Chicken with Red Cabbage Slaw and Rutabaga Potatoes, 59, *78*

Crisp Mustard-Glazed Chicken Breasts, 38, *80*

Grilled Soy-Lime Chicken Breasts, 23

Herb-Roasted Turkey with Pan Gravy, 273–74, *326*

Herb-Stuffed Chicken Breasts, 124, *169*

Herbed Turkey Burgers, 211

Individual Chicken Pot Pies with Mushrooms and Peas, 219–20, *238*

Long Island Duckling Two Ways, 99

Roasted Chicken and Jerusalem Artichokes, 100, *167*

Roasted Cornish Hens with Pomegranate-Molasses Glaze, 295, *322*

Walnut Chicken Strips with Pomegranate Sauce, 296

Winter Vegetable Chicken Stew, 24

seafood

Beer-Battered Cod in Tacos, 189

Cedar-Plank Roasted Salmon, 273

Confit of Wild Salmon on Cucumber Salad with Horseradish Sauce, 58–59, *75*

Finnish Fish Chowder, 142

Fish and Chips, 59–60

Fish Stew, 143

Fried Catfish Sandwich, 190

Grilled Mahimahi in Tacos, 190

Grilled Striped Bass with Corn and Clam Chowder Sauce, 219, *239*

Grilled Trout with Oregano, 123, *163*

Hot-Smoked Salmon Steaks with Morel Sauce, 144

Miso-Glazed Cod, 295, *319*

Pasta with Peas, Crab, and Basil, 145, *166*

Pasta with Scallops, Garlic, Grape Tomatoes, and Parsley, 258, *318*

Salt-and-Pepper Shrimp with Aïoli, 146, *168*

Seared Salmon with Creamy Leek Sauce, 125–26

Seared Shrimp with Lemon and Garlic, 126

Sole Rolls with Spinach and Lemon Slices, 220–21

Spaghetti with Clams, 60, *79*

Striped Bass with Cucumber Broth, 191, *238*

Striped Sea Bass with Blood Oranges and Olives, 23–24, *71*

Yellow-Pepper Risotto with Shrimp and Zucchini, 221, *240*

Mango(es)

-Lime Granita, 112

Panna Cotta, 198, *244*

and Tomato Salsa, 126

Tropical Fruit and Crab Salsa, 204, *229*

Maple-Glazed Sweet Potatoes, 277

Maple Pudding, 112

Margaritas, Blue, 201, *229*

Margaritas for a Crowd, 202

Mascarpone

-Ricotta Crêpe Filling, 31

Broiled Persimmons with, 302

Filling, 200
Focaccia Cake, 290, *316*
Tiramisu Cups, 200
Vanilla, 263
Mayonnaise, Homemade, 17, *69*
Meat. See also Beef; Lamb; Pork; Veal
Stuffing, 280, *326*
Meatballs, Rigatoni and, 211, *236*
Melon(s)
and Berries Steeped in Red Wine,
Sauternes, Basil, and Mint, 62, *86*
Cantaloupe Granita, 213
Pickled Watermelon Rind, 286
Rosé, 202, *229*
Shaved Cucumber, Fennel, and
Watermelon Salad, 188
Watermelon and Raspberry Salad, 223
Watermelon Gazpacho, 183–84, *232*
Mexican Fiesta Soup with Roasted
Tomatillo and Cilantro Pesto, 120
Minestrone, 209
Mint
and Chocolate Parfaits, 108
Cucumber, and Feta, Pita-Bread
Salad with, 141, *157*
Grasshopper Tarts, 195–96, *248*
Jelly, 125
and Pistachio Stuffed Leg of Lamb,
124, *165*
Toasted Couscous Tabbouleh,
127–28, *166*
Miso-Glazed Cod, 295, *319*
Miso Soup with Tofu, Spinach, and
Carrots, 254
Miso Soup with Tofu and Kale, 96, *166*
Mocha Filling, 200
Mocha Steamed Puddings, 47, *83*
Mocha Truffles, 311
Molasses-Glazed Grilled Pork Loin with
Roasted Italian Prune Plums, 258, *324*
Morel Sauce, 144
Moules Poulette (Broiled Mussels
with Mushrooms, Lemon, and Cream),
17, *68-69*
Mousse, Chocolate, with Banana Purée
and Grated Coconut, 27

Mozzarella
Baked Buffalo, Roasted Cherry
Tomatoes, and Eggplant, 55, *75*
Pizza, 211, *237*
Prosciutto, and Pesto Butter Tea
Sandwiches, 103, *160-61*
Stuffed Eggplant, 212, *230*
Muffins
Breakfast, 147, *153-54*
Corn, 148
Health, 149
Icing for, 148
Mini, Cinnamon-Sugar, 148
Streusel for, 148
Mushroom(s)
Baked Stuffed Sweet Onions, 105
Lemon, and Cream, Broiled Mussels
with (Moules Poulette), 17, *68-69*
Morel Sauce, 144
Sautéed, Prosciutto, and Taleggio
Panini, 259
Sautéed-, Butter and Bacon Tea
Sandwiches, 103–4, *160-61*
Scalloped, 279
Wild, Bruschetta, 217, *230*
Wild, Fricassée of, 61
Wild, Roasted, 262, *329*
Mussels, Broiled, with Mushrooms,
Lemon, and Cream (Moules Poulette),
17, *68-69*
Mustard-Glazed Chicken Breasts, Crisp,
38, *80*

N

Napoleon, 131–32, *176*
Noodle(s)
Cold Soba, with Basil Flowers, 53, *72*
Green Beans and Spaetzle, 298
and Peanut Sauce, Chicken and
Shredded-Cabbage Salad with, 184
Salad, Cold Sesame, 18
Somen, Ginger-Peanut, 297, *319*
Nut(s). See also Almond(s); Hazelnut(s);
Walnut(s)
-and-Fruit Cookies, Mixed, 266, *332*
Caramel-Dipped Pecans, 42
Chocolate Caramel Tart, 41, *88*

Coconut Chocolate Patties, 264, *330*
Coconut-Pecan Filling, 28
Crisp Coconut and Chocolate Pie,
194, *244*
Cucumber-Peanut Sauce, 183, *228*
Ginger-Peanut Somen Noodles,
297, *319*
Lamingtons, 111, *171*
Mint and Pistachio Stuffed Leg of
Lamb, 124, *165*
Peanut Brittle, 307–8
Peanut-Butter-and-Chocolate Cups,
198–99
Peanut Butter Surprises, 266–67, *332*
Peanut Sauce, 185
Pear Pandowdy, 282–83, *333*
Pomegranate Pilaf, 299, *322*
Pumpkin-Pecan Pie, 284, *333*
Strawberry and Pistachio Ice-Cream
Cake, 213, *246*
Stuffing, 280, *326*
Three, Torte, 309

O

Olive Oil, Herb-Infused, 268
Olive(s)
Black-, Relish, 202
Carrots, and Chickpeas, Braised
Chicken with, 142
Fish Stew, 143
Parsley, and Paprika, Oranges
with, 293
Swiss Chard with, 147
Two-, Tapenade, Linguine with,
144–45, *166*
Vinaigrette, Arugula and Cannellini
Salad with, 141
Omelets
Rolled, with Ratatouille Filling, 207,
225, 226
Rolled, with Spinach and Goat
Cheese, 207–8, *225, 226*
Onion(s)
Caramelized, 257
Caramelized, and Roast Beef Tea
Sandwiches, 101, *160-61*
Cipollini, and Baby Turnips,
Glazed, 106

Roasted, Purée, 262, *328*

Scalloped Mushrooms, 279

Sweet, Baked Stuffed, 105

Sweet, Braised, 105

Sweet, Caramelized, 114

Sweet, Sandwiches, 105

Sweet-, Salsa, Avocado with Grapefruit and, 93

Vidalia-, Slaw, 193

Orange(s)

-Ginger Truffles, 311

Blood, and Olives, Striped Sea Bass with, 23–24, *71*

Blood, and Watercress, Thinly Sliced Beets with, 294

Blood, Rice Pudding Tarts with, 63, *84*

Blood, Spinach Salad with Fennel and, 210

Citrus-Cumin Vinaigrette, 98

Honey Tangerines and Kumquats with Shaved Celery and Walnuts, 292

and Jícama Salad with Citrus-Cumin Vinaigrette, 98

Lemonade, 214

with Olives, Parsley, and Paprika, 293

Spiral Rolls, 298

Vinaigrette and Toasted Sesame Seeds, Greens with, 19, *76–77*

Orecchiette, Broccoli with, 98, *164*

Oregano, Grilled Trout with, 123, *163*

Oregano, Marinated Goat Cheese with, 53

Orzo Salad with Roasted Carrots and Dill, 188, *234*

Oysters

Baked, with Spinach and Champagne Beurre Blanc, 15

with Champagne Mignonette, 217, *230*

Low Country Steamed Carolina Cup, with Melted Butter, 271

P

Palmiers, 132

Pancakes, Pea, with Sour Cream and Bacon, 139

Pandowdy, Pear, 282–83, *333*

Panini, Sautéed Mushroom, Prosciutto, and Taleggio, 259

Panna Cotta, Mango, 198, *244*

Parfaits, Chocolate and Mint, 108

Parmesan

Arugula Risotto, 122

Cheese Straws, 119

Parsley

Braised Lamb Stew (Fresh-Herb Khoresh), 19–20, *70*

Egg Butter, 139

Fresh-Herb Kuku, 16, *69*

Toasted Couscous Tabbouleh, 127–28, *166*

Parsnip Latkes, 299

Passion-Fruit Cocktails, 202, *229*

Pasta

Broccoli with Orecchiette, 98, *164*

Chicken and Shredded-Cabbage Salad with Noodles and Peanut Sauce, 184

Cold Sesame Noodle Salad, 18

Cold Soba Noodles with Basil Flowers, 53, *72*

Ginger-Peanut Somen Noodles, 297, *319*

Green Beans and Spaetzle, 298

Linguine with Two-Olive Tapenade, 144–45, *166*

Orzo Salad with Roasted Carrots and Dill, 188, *234*

with Peas, Crab, and Basil, 145, *166*

Rigatoni and Meatballs, 211, *236*

with Scallops, Garlic, Grape Tomatoes, and Parsley, 258, *318*

Spaghetti with Clams, 60, *79*

Spinach Linguine with Walnut-Arugula Pesto, 275, *318*

Pastries

Butterflies, 128

Chocolate Turnovers, 129

Cream Horns, 129

Cream Puffs, 45–46

Eclairs, 46–47

Napoleon, 131–32, *176*

Palmiers, 132

Profiteroles, 49, *82*

Sacristains, 134

Pastry Cream, 132

Pastry Cream Filling, 46

Pastry dough

Chocolate Pâte Sucrée, 41

Deep-Dish Pâte Brisée, 307

French Flag Berry Pâte Sucrée Tart Shells, 195

Pâte à Choux, 35

Pâte Brisée, 223, 282

Pâte Brisée Tart Shells, 94

Pâte Sucrée, 63

Pâte Sucrée Tart Shells, 111

Pie Dough, 198

Puff Pastry, 118

Pâté, Chicken Liver, with Toast Points, 181, *231*

Pâte à Choux, 35

Cream Puffs, 45–46

Eclairs, 46–47

Profiteroles, 49, *82*

Pâte Brisée, 223, 282

Deep-Dish, 307

Tart Shells, 94

Pâte Sucrée, 63

Chocolate, 41

Tart Shells, 111

Tart Shells, French Flag Berry, 195

Pavlova, Pear, 283, *332*

Pea(s)

Bisque with Shrimp and Tarragon, 36, *80*

Black-Eyed, with Escarole, Potatoes, and Turkey Sausage, 38, *80*

Crab, and Basil, Pasta with, 145, *166*

Garden and Snap Pea Soup with Vidalia Onions, 138, *159*

Marjoram, and Asiago, Risotto with, 145, *162*

Mashed Potatoes and, 146, *163*

Pancakes with Sour Cream and Bacon, 139

Soup, Spring, with Smoked Bacon, 96–97

Sugar Snap, with Toasted Almonds, 127

Warm Goat Cheese with Wasabi-Pea Crust, Greens, and, 140, *163*

Peach(es)

Grilled, with Chilled Sabayon, 196

Tartes Tatin, 62–63

Tea Punch, 134

Peanut(s)
-Cucumber Sauce, 183, *228*
-Ginger Somen Noodles, 297, *319*
Brittle, 307–8
Peanut Butter Surprises, 266–67, *332*
Sauce, 185
Peanut Butter
-and-Chocolate Cups, 198–99
Cold Sesame Noodle Salad, 18
Surprises, 266–67, *332*
Pear(s)
Baked, with Vanilla Mascarpone, 263
Baked Camembert with Fresh Fruit, 107
and Endive Salad with Oregon Blue
Cheese and Hazelnuts, 218
Pandowdy, 282–83, *333*
Pavlova, 283, *332*
Red, and Roquefort Butter Tea
Sandwiches, 103, *160-61*
Pecan(s)
-Coconut Filling, 28
-Pumpkin Pie, 284, *333*
Caramel-Dipped, 42
Chocolate Caramel Tart, 41, *88*
Pepper(s)
-and-Bean Salad, Multicolored, with
Ricotta Salata and Herbs, 188, *235*
Bell, Roasted, 261
Chili con Carne, 22, *76*
Cold Curried Buttermilk Soup with
Corn and Poblano Chile, 182, *232*
Red, Roasted, and Walnut Dip, 272
Yellow-, Risotto with Shrimp and
Zucchini, 221, *240*
Peppermint
Candy Cane Truffles, 310
Semifreddo, 308
Persian Almond Brittle, 28
Persimmons, Broiled, with
Mascarpone, 302
Pesto, Roasted Tomatillo and Cilantro,
Mexican Fiesta Soup with, 120
Pesto, Walnut-Arugula, Spinach
Linguine with, 275, *318*
Pesto Butter, Mozzarella, and Prosciutto
Tea Sandwiches, 103, *160-61*
Pickled Beets, 286

Pickled Garlic, 64
Pickled Green Beans, 286
Pickled Green Tomatoes, 261
Pickled Watermelon Rind, 286
Pickles, Bread-and-Butter, 285
Pico de Gallo, 204
Pie(s)
Apple, Mile-High, 307, *336*
Chess, Mary Curll's, 198
Chocolate Cream, 42
Crisp Coconut and Chocolate, 194, *244*
Limeade, 197, *244*
Pumpkin-Pecan, 284, *333*
Strawberry Chiffon, 199–200, *245*
Sweet Potato, Cecilia's, 281
Yogurt, 201, *245*
Pie crust. See Crust; Pastry Dough
Pilaf, Pomegranate, 299, *322*
Pimm's Cup, Mary Brockman's
Favorite, 202
Pineapple
Salsa, 204
Sautéed, Crêpe Filling, 31
Tropical Fruit and Crab Salsa, 204, *229*
Pistachio(s)
and Mint Stuffed Leg of Lamb, 124, *165*
Mixed Fruit-and-Nut Cookies, 266, *332*
Pear Pandowdy, 282–83, *333*
Pomegranate Pilaf, 299, *322*
and Strawberry Ice-Cream Cake,
213, *246*
Pistou Soup, 54–55, *75*
Pita-Bread Salad with Cucumber, Mint,
and Feta, 141, *157*
Pithiviers, 133
Pizza, 211, *237*
Pizza, Cornmeal-Crusted, 256–57, *314*
Plantain Chips, Fried, 203
Plum Galette, 223, *242*
Polenta, 127
Polenta, Soft, with Fresh Herbs, 106
Polenta and Eggplant Casserole,
Layered, 220
Pomegranate
-Eggplant Relish, 290, *313*
-Molasses Glaze, Roasted Cornish
Hens with, 295, *322*
Fennel, and Green Bean Salad,
293, *317*

Jelly, Mrs. Gubler's, 306, *333*
Pilaf, 299, *322*
Punch, 312
Sauce, Walnut Chicken Strips
with, 296
Tea, 312
Pommes Frites, 17, *69*
Poppy-Seed Torte, 308
Pork. See also Bacon; Ham
Chops, Boneless, and Roasted Yam
Fries, 58, *78*
Loin, Molasses-Glazed Grilled,
with Roasted Italian Prune Plums,
258, *324*
Loin Braised in Milk, 274–75, *323*
Rigatoni and Meatballs, 211, *236*
Tenderloin, Five-Spice, 190
Pot Pies, Individual Chicken, with
Mushrooms and Peas, 219–20, *238*
Potato(es). See also Sweet Potato(es)
Baby Red, with Cilantro, 146
Braised, 40
and Celeriac, Mashed, 261
Escarole, and Turkey Sausage, Black-
Eyed Peas with, 38, *80*
Fish and Chips, 59–60
Individual Chicken Pot Pies with
Mushrooms and Peas, 219–20, *238*
Latkes, Basic, 296–97
Mashed, and Peas, 146, *163*
Mashed, with Bacon and Cheddar, 278
Pies, Karjalan, with Egg Butter, 138
Pommes Frites, 17, *69*
Roasted, 262–63
Roasted Fingerling, with Seasoned
Salt, 192, *241*
Rösti, 299
Rutabaga, Cornflake-Crusted Chicken
with Red Cabbage Slaw and, 59, *78*
Salad, French, with White Wine and
Celery Leaves, 187
Slices, Baked, 24, *70*
Sweet-Potato Latkes, 301
Zucchini, and Tomato Gratin, 222
Pots de Crème, Chocolate, 109, *172*
Poultry. See also Chicken; Turkey
Long Island Duckling Two Ways, 99

Roasted Cornish Hens with Pomegranate-Molasses Glaze, 295, *322*

Smoked Duck and Chutney Butter Tea Sandwiches, 104, *160-61*

Praline Buttercream, 309-10

Praline Truffles, 312

Profiteroles, 49, *82*

Prosciutto, Mozzarella, and Pesto Butter Tea Sandwiches, 103, *160-61*

Prosciutto, Sautéed Mushroom, and Taleggio Panini, 259

Provençal Roasted Tomatoes, 192

Prune Plums, Italian, Roasted, 258, *324*

Pudding, Bread, Pumpkin, 267, *332*

Pudding, Maple, 112

Pudding, Vanilla, 50, *85*

Puddings, Mocha Steamed, 47, *83*

Puff Pastry, 118

Bouchées, 117

Butterflies, 128

Cheese Straws, 119

Chocolate Turnovers, 129

Cream Horns, 129

Napoleon, 131–32, *176*

Palmiers, 132

Pithiviers, 133

Raspberry Tart, 133, *171*

Sacristains, 134

Tarte Tatin, 134

Vol-au-Vents, 121

Pumpkin Bread Pudding, 267, *332*

Pumpkin-Pecan Pie, 284, *333*

Pumpkin Seeds, Toasted, 258

Pumpkin Shake, 267

Punch, Lingonberry, 137

Punch, Peach Tea, 134

Punch, Pomegranate, 312

R

Radish and Endive Salad, 292

Radish Butter on Toasted Baguette, 96

Radishes, Apples, and Cheddar Frico, Autumn Greens with, 255

Ragu, Pot Roast, 39–40, *81*

Raisin Bars, Grandmother Brinton's, 265

Raspberry(ies)

-Filled Layer Cake, 29

Berry Syrup, 213

Floating Island, 113, *173*

French Flag Berry Tarts, 194–95, *243*

Fresh-, Gelatin and Whipped Cream, 130

Linzertorte, 306

Melon and Berries Steeped in Red Wine, Sauternes, Basil, and Mint, 62, *86*

Tart, 133, *171*

and Watermelon Salad, 223

Ratatouille Filling, Rolled Omelets with, 207, *225*, *226*

Relish

Black-Olive, 202

Cucumber, 203

Eggplant-Pomegranate, 290, *313*

Pickled Cucumber and Cherry, 203–4

Rhubarb-Strawberry Coffee Cake, 208, *225, 227*

Rice. See also Risotto

Green, 192

Pomegranate Pilaf, 299, *322*

Pudding Tarts with Blood Oranges, 63, *84*

Saffron, Baked, 24–25, *70*

Salad with Lemon, Dill, and Red Onion, 121

Sushi Cake, 291–92, *316*

Ricotta

-Mascarpone Crêpe Filling, 31

Bruschetta, 208, *230*

Ricotta Salata and Herbs, Multicolored Pepper-and-Bean Salad with, 188, *235*

Rigatoni and Meatballs, 211, *236*

Risotto

Arugula, 122

with Peas, Marjoram, and Asiago, 145, *162*

Yellow-Pepper, with Shrimp and Zucchini, 221, *240*

Rolls, Orange Spiral, 298

Rolls, Sweet-Potato, 280–81, *327*

Roquefort Butter and Red Pear Tea Sandwiches, 103, *160-61*

Rosé Melons, 202, *229*

Rose Petal Jelly, 64

Rösti, Potato, 299

Rub, Barbecue, 224

Rutabaga Potatoes, Cornflake-Crusted Chicken with Red Cabbage Slaw and, 59, *78*

Rye Sourdough Bread, 140

Rye Sourdough Starter, 137

S

Sabayon Sauce, 196

Sacristains, 134

Saffron Rice, Baked, 24–25, *70*

Salad

Almond-Coated Goat Cheese, Frisée, and Belgian Endive, 254, *318*

Arugula, with French Lentils, Smoked Chicken, and Roasted Peppers, 37

Arugula and Cannellini, with Olive Vinaigrette, 141

Asian Steak, with Spicy Vinaigrette, 97, *158*

Autumn Greens with Apples, Radishes, and Cheddar Frico, 255

Caesar, 209

Chicken and Shredded-Cabbage, with Noodles and Peanut Sauce, 184

Cobb, 209

Corn and Tomato, 185

Cranberry-Bean, with Butternut Squash and Broccoli Rabe, 260, *315*

of Crisp Squid, Asparagus, and Tangerines, 57, *73*

Cucumber, 141

Cucumber, Corn, and Crab, 185–86

Cucumber, Cranberry Bean, and Beet, in Cucumber Boats, 186, *238*

Cucumber, Shaved, Fennel, and Watermelon, 188

Endive and Pear, with Oregon Blue Cheese and Hazelnuts, 218

Endive and Radish, 292

Farro, with Zucchini, Pine Nuts, and Lemon Zest, 186–87, *234*

Green, with Toasted Walnuts, Walnut Oil, and Green Beans, 272, *318*

Green and White, 19

Greens with Orange Vinaigrette and Toasted Sesame Seeds, 19, *76-77*

Haricots Verts and Goat Cheese, with Almonds, 187

Honey Tangerines and Kumquats with Shaved Celery and Walnuts, 292

Jícama and Orange, with Citrus-Cumin Vinaigrette, 98

Lentils with Tarragon, Shallots, and Beets, 187, *234*

Mixed Lettuces with Grapefruit, Goat Cheese, and Black Pepper, 292–93

Oranges with Olives, Parsley, and Paprika, 293

Orzo, with Roasted Carrots and Dill, 188, *234*

Pepper-and-Bean, Multicolored, with Ricotta Salata and Herbs, 188, *235*

Pita-Bread, with Cucumber, Mint, and Feta, 141, *157*

Pomegranate, Fennel, and Green Bean, 293, *317*

Potato, French, with White Wine and Celery Leaves, 187

Rice, with Lemon, Dill, and Red Onion, 121

Sesame Noodle, Cold, 18

Shrimp and Chopped-Tomato, Chilled, with Crisp Garlic Croutons, 185, *235*

Soba Noodles, Cold, with Basil Flowers, 53, *72*

Spinach, with Fennel and Blood Oranges, 210

Taco, 210, *235*

Thinly Sliced Beets with Blood Oranges and Watercress, 294

Three-Bean, with Honey-Mustard Vinaigrette, 210, *235*

Tomato, Chopped, with Toasted Garlic, 212

Tomato, Garden, 141

Tomato and Bean, with Garlic-Chive Blossoms, 57

Vidalia-Onion Slaw, 193

Watermelon and Raspberry, 223

Salad Dressing

Buttermilk and Blue Cheese, 285

Citrus-Cumin Vinaigrette, 98

Cucumber-Dill, 137

Cucumber Vinaigrette, 186

Honey-Mustard Vinaigrette, 210

Olive Vinaigrette, Arugula and Cannellini Salad with, 141

Orange Vinaigrette, Greens with Toasted Sesame Seeds, with 19, *76-77*

Spicy Vinaigrette, 97

Salmon

Cedar-Plank Roasted, 273

Seared, with Creamy Leek Sauce, 125–26

Smoked, and Lemon-Caper Butter Tea Sandwiches, 102, *160-61*

Smoked, Cake, 291, *316*

Steaks, Hot-Smoked, with Morel Sauce, 144

Wild, Confit of, on Cucumber Salad with Horseradish Sauce, 58–59, *75*

Salsa

Mango and Tomato, 126

Pico de Gallo, 204

Pineapple, 204

Tropical Fruit and Crab, 204, *229*

Sambuca Truffles, 312

Sandwiches. See also Sandwiches, Tea

Classic Grilled Cheese, 256, *321*

Croque Madame (var.), 256, *320*

Croque Monsieur, 256, *320*

Fried Catfish, 190

Herbed Turkey Burgers, 211

Sautéed Mushroom, Prosciutto, and Taleggio Panini, 259

Sweet Onion, 105

Sandwiches, Tea

Almond-Crusted Curry Chicken Salad, 100, *160-61*

Bacon-and-Egg Salad, 101, *160-61*

Caramelized Onion and Roast Beef, 101, *160-61*

Egg-Yolk Butter and Asparagus, 101–2, *160-61*

Grated Vegetables with Herb Cream Cheese, 102, *160-61*

Lemon-Caper Butter and Smoked Salmon, 102, *160-61*

Mozzarella, Prosciutto, and Pesto Butter, 103, *160-61*

Roquefort Butter and Red Pear, 103, *160-61*

Sautéed-Mushroom Butter and Bacon, 103–4, *160-61*

Shrimp Salad, 104, *160-61*

Smoked Duck and Chutney Butter, 104, *160-61*

Southwest Black Bean, Smoked Turkey, and Avocado, 104–5, *160-61*

Sashimi, Fluke, with Baby Greens, 95

Sauce

Barbecue, Tennessee Pit, 189

Caramel, 199

Chocolate, 108, 308

Corn and Clam Chowder, 219, *239*

Cucumber-Peanut, 183, *228*

Dipping, Soy, 18

Dipping, Yogurt, 280

Espresso Crème Anglaise, 48

Hollandaise, 107, *163*

Homemade Mayonnaise, 17, *69*

Hot Fudge, 30

Mango and Tomato Salsa, 126

Morel, 144

Peanut, 185

Pico de Gallo, 204

Pineapple Salsa, 204

Pink Applesauce, 297

Sabayon, 196

Tomato Passato, 214

Tropical Fruit and Crab Salsa, 204, *229*

Vanilla Applesauce, 301

Wasabi, 292

Sausage, Turkey, Black-Eyed Peas with Escarole, Potatoes, and, 38, *80*

Scallions, Grilled Marinated Strip Steak with, 191, *241*

Scallops

Fish Stew, 143

Garlic, Grape Tomatoes, and Parsley, Pasta with, 258, *318*

Pan-Fried, on Caramelized Fennel, 53–54, *75*

Scones, Currant, 207, *225, 226*
Semifreddo.
　Cake, Lemon, 130-31
　Peppermint, 308
Sesame-Marinated Tofu with
　Vegetables, 259-60
Sesame Noodle Salad, Cold, 18
Sesame Steamed Spinach, 300, *319*
Seven Minute Frosting, 29
Shake, Blueberry Breakfast, 114, *155*
Shake, Pumpkin, 267
Shellfish. See also Shrimp
　Baked Oysters with Spinach and
　　Champagne Beurre Blanc, 15
　Corn and Clam Chowder Sauce,
　　219, *239*
　Cucumber Corn, and Crab Salad,
　　185-86
　Fish Stew, 143
　Low Country Steamed Carolina Cup
　　Oysters with Melted Butter, 271
　Moules Poulette (Broiled Mussels
　　with Mushrooms, Lemon, and
　　Cream), 17, *68-69*
　Oysters with Champagne Mignonette,
　　217, *230*
　Pan-Fried Scallops on Caramelized
　　Fennel, 53-54, *75*
　Pasta with Peas, Crab, and Basil,
　　145, *166*
　Pasta with Scallops, Garlic, Grape
　　Tomatoes, and Parsley, 258, *318*
　Salad of Crisp Squid, Asparagus, and
　　Tangerines, 57, *73*
　Spaghetti with Clams, 60, *79*
　Steamed Littleneck Clams, 272
　Sushi Cake, 291-92, *316*
　Tropical Fruit and Crab Salsa,
　　, 204, *229*
Sherbet, Fruit, 151, *171*
Shortbread, Walnut, 113-14
Shortbread-Almond Crust, 200
Shortbread Cookies, Almond, 301-2, *336*
Shrimp
　and Chopped-Tomato Salad, Chilled,
　　with Crisp Garlic Croutons, 185, *235*
　Cucumber Summer Rolls, 182, *228*
　Salad Tea Sandwiches, 104, *160-61*

Salt-and-Pepper, with Aïoli, 146, *168*
Seared, with Lemon and Garlic, 126
Summer Rolls, 18
Sushi Cake, 291-92, *316*
and Tarragon, Pea Bisque with, 36, *80*
and Zucchini, Yellow-Pepper Risotto
　with, 221, *240*
Side dishes
　grains, breads, and pasta
　　Aunt Sara's Cheese Grits, 191
　　Baked Saffron Rice, 24-25, *70*
　　Brown-Sugar Cornbread, 25, *76-77*
　　Buttermilk Cornbread, 276-77
　　Cornbread Dressing, 276, *325*
　　Cream Biscuits, 277
　　Focaccia, 268
　　Ginger-Peanut Somen Noodles,
　　　297, *319*
　　Green Rice, 192
　　Herbed Couscous, 106
　　Orange Spiral Rolls, 298
　　Polenta, 127
　　Pomegranate Pilaf, 299, *322*
　　Soft Polenta with Fresh Herbs, 106
　　Stuffing, 280, *326*
　　Sweet-Potato Rolls, 280-81, *327*
　　Toasted Couscous Tabbouleh,
　　　127-28, *166*
　vegetables and fruits
　　Baby Red Potatoes with Cilantro, 146
　　Baked Potato Slices, 24, *70*
　　Baked Stuffed Sweet Onions, 105
　　Basic Potato Latkes, 296-97
　　Best Whipped Sweet Potatoes with
　　　Caramelized Apples, 275, *327*
　　Braised Potatoes, 40
　　Braised Sweet Onions, 105
　　Butternut Squash Purée, 257
　　Butternut Squash with Brown
　　　Butter, 275-76, *323*
　　Caramelized Onions, 257
　　Carrot and Beet Latkes, 297
　　Chopped Tomato Salad with Toasted
　　　Garlic, 212
　　Church Street Squash, 276
　　Cranberry-Bean Salad with
　　　Butternut Squash and Broccoli
　　　Rabe, 260, *315*
　　Cranberry Chutney, 277

Creamed Fresh Corn, 212
Edamame Succotash, 260
Flageolets, 126
Fricassée of Wild Mushrooms, 61
Glazed Baby Turnips and Cipollini
　Onions, 106
Green Beans and Spaetzle, 298
Mango and Tomato Salsa, 126
Maple-Glazed Sweet Potatoes, 277
Mashed Potatoes and Celeriac, 261
Mashed Potatoes and Peas, 146, *163*
Mashed Potatoes with Bacon and
　Cheddar, 278
Parsnip Latkes, 299
Pickled Green Tomatoes, 261
Pink Applesauce, 297
Potato, Zucchini, and Tomato
　Gratin, 222
Potato Rösti, 299
Provençal Roasted Tomatoes, 192
Quick Braised Artichokes, 147
Roasted Beets, 261, *328*
Roasted Bell Peppers, 261
Roasted Carrots, 261
Roasted Corn, 262
Roasted Eggplant, 262
Roasted Fingerling Potatoes with
　Seasoned Salt, 192, *241*
Roasted Garlic, 262, *328*
Roasted Onion Purée, 262, *328*
Roasted Plum Tomatoes, 262, *328*
Roasted Potatoes, 262-63
Roasted Tomatoes, 257
Roasted Wild Mushrooms, 262, *329*
Roasted Zucchini, 263
Saucy Black Beans, 192
Sautéed Asparagus with Aged
　Gouda Cheese, 193, *241*
Sautéed Brussels Sprouts with
　Raisins, 278, *323*
Sautéed Chicory, 61-62
Savory Twice-Baked Sweet
　Potatoes, 278-79, *327*
Scalloped Mushrooms, 279
Sesame Steamed Spinach, 300, *319*
Simple Steamed Thick
　Asparagus, 127
Southern Green Beans, 279

Spicy Sweet Potatoes with Lime, 279, *327*

Spinach and Currant Latkes, 300

Stuffed Eggplant, 212, *230*

Sugar Snap Peas with Toasted Almonds, 127

Sweet-Potato Latkes, 301

Swiss Chard with Olives, 147

Turnip Greens, 193

Vanilla Applesauce, 301

Vidalia-Onion Slaw, 193

Warm Red-Lentil Dal with Pita Chips, 37

White Asparagus with Hollandaise Sauce, 107, *163*

Winter Greens and Bacon, 40

Smoked Duck and Chutney Butter Tea Sandwiches, 104, *160-61*

Smoked Salmon and Lemon-Caper Butter Tea Sandwiches, 102, *160-61*

Smoked-Salmon Cake, 291, *316*

Soba Noodles, Cold, with Basil Flowers, 53, *72*

Sole Rolls with Spinach and Lemon Slices, 220–21

Somen Noodles, Ginger-Peanut, 297, *319*

Sorbet, Concord Grape, 264, *330*

Sorbet, Tomato, 56

Sorbet Syrup, Simple, 264

Sorbets, Assorted, 152, *171*

Soup, first course

    Belgian Endive, Cream of, 15, *70*

    Chicken, Asian, 181, *232*

    Cucumber-Coconut, 182, *233*

    Curried Apple, 253

    Curried Buttermilk, Cold, with Corn and Poblano Chile, 182, *232*

    Elwood's Ham Chowder, 271

    Fennel and Leek, Chilled, 119

    Garden and Snap Pea, with Vidalia Onions, 138, *159*

    Mexican Fiesta, with Roasted Tomatillo and Cilantro Pesto, 120

    Minestrone, 209

    Miso, with Tofu, Spinach, and Carrots, 254

    Miso, with Tofu and Kale, 96, *166*

Pea Bisque with Shrimp and Tarragon, 36, *80*

Pistou, 54–55, *75*

Spring Pea, with Smoked Bacon, 96–97

Tomatillo, Spicy Cold, 183, *232*

Watermelon Gazpacho, 183–84, *232*

Yogurt-Basil, with Tomato Ice, 184

Soup, main course. See also Soup, main course; Stew; Stock

    Chicken Tortilla, 21, *70*

    Cock-a-Leekie, 23

    Finnish Fish Chowder, 142

Sourdough Bread, Rye, 140

Sourdough Starter, Rye, 137

Southwest Black Bean, Smoked Turkey, and Avocado Tea Sandwiches, 104–5, *160-61*

Soy Dipping Sauce, 18

Soy Milk, Chai Tea with, 267

Soybeans. See Edamame

Spaetzle, Green Beans and, 298

Spaghetti with Clams, 60, *79*

Spinach

    and Champagne Beurre Blanc, Baked Oysters with, 15

    and Currant Latkes, 300

    and Goat Cheese, Rolled Omelets with, 207–8, *225*, *226*

    and Lemon Slices, Sole Rolls with, 220–21

    Linguine with Walnut-Arugula Pesto, 275, *318*

    Salad with Fennel and Blood Oranges, 210

    Sesame Steamed, 300, *319*

    Tofu, and Carrots, Miso Soup with, 254

Squash. See also Zucchini

    Butternut, and Broccoli Rabe, Cranberry-Bean Salad with, 260, *315*

    Butternut, Purée, 257

    Butternut, with Brown Butter, 275–76, *323*

    Church Street, 276

    Edamame Succotash, 260

    Pumpkin Bread Pudding, 267, *332*

Pumpkin-Pecan Pie, 284, *333*

Pumpkin Shake, 267

Rolled Omelets with Ratatouille Filling, 207, *225*, *226*

Toasted Pumpkin Seeds, 258

Veal Scallopini Milanese, 61, *78*

Squid, Crisp, Asparagus, and Tangerines, Salad of, 57, *73*

Starter, Rye Sourdough, 137

Starters. See also Dips; Soup; first course

    Artichoke Bruschetta, 53, *78*

    Asparagus Timbale, 93

    Avocado with Grapefruit and Sweet-Onion Salsa, 93

    Bagna Cauda with Broccoflower and Toasted Country Bread, 253

    Baked Oysters with Spinach and Champagne Beurre Blanc, 15

    Blinis with Caviar and Cucumber-Dill Dressing, 137

    Bouchées, 117

    Brie and Apple Custard Tart, 94

    Brie and Walnut Cake, 289, *316*

    Bruschetta, Tomato and Ricotta, 208, *230*

    Cheese Straws, 119

    Chicken Liver Pâté with Toast Points, 181, *231*

    Cold Soba Noodles with Basil Flowers, 53, *72*

    Cucumber Summer Rolls, 182, *228*

    Eggplant Kuku, 16, *69*

    Fluke Sashimi with Baby Greens, 95

    Focaccia Cake, 290, *316*

    Fresh-Herb Kuku, 16, *69*

    Fried Plantain Chips, 203

    Fried Roasted-Garlic Custard, 95–96

    Gougères, 35

    Karjalan Potato Pies with Egg Butter, 138

    Low Country Steamed Carolina Cup Oysters with Melted Butter, 271

    Marinated Goat Cheese with Oregano, 53

    Mini Corn Cakes with Goat Cheese and Pepper Jelly, 120

Moules Poulette (Broiled Mussels with Mushrooms, Lemon, and Cream), 17, *68-69*

Oysters with Champagne Mignonette, 217, *230*

Pan-Fried Scallops on Caramelized Fennel, 53–54, *75*

Pea Pancakes with Sour Cream and Bacon, 139

Pickled Herring Canapes, 139

Pommes Frites, 17, *69*

Radish Butter on Toasted Baguette, 96

Roasted Cherry Tomatoes, Baked Buffalo Mozzarella, and Eggplant, 55, *75*

Rye Sourdough Bread, 140

Shrimp Summer Rolls, 18

Smoked-Salmon Cake, 291, *316*

Steamed Littleneck Clams, 272

Sushi Cake, 291–92, *316*

Tomato Crostini, 217

Tomato Essence and Timbales of Pressed Tomatoes, 55–56

Vol-au-Vents, 121

Warm Goat Cheese with Wasabi-Pea Crust, Peas, and Greens, 140, *163*

Wild Mushroom Bruschetta, 217, *230*

Stew

Braised Lamb (Fresh-Herb Khoresh), 19–20, *70*

Chicken and Dumplings, 20

Chicken Cacciatore, 20–21

Chili con Carne, 22, *76*

Fish, 143

Pot Roast Ragu, 39–40, *81*

Winter Vegetable Chicken, 24

Stock, Fish, 143

Stock, Giblet, 274

Strawberry(ies)

-Rhubarb Coffee Cake, 208, *225, 227*

Chiffon Pies, 199–200, *245*

Compote, 128, *170*

Melon and Berries Steeped in Red Wine, Sauternes, Basil, and Mint, 62, *86*

and Pistachio Ice-Cream Cake, 213, *246*

Streusel, 148

Striped Bass, Grilled, with Corn and Clam Chowder Sauce, 219, *239*

Striped Bass with Cucumber Broth, 191, *238*

Striped Sea Bass with Blood Oranges and Olives, 23–24, *71*

Stuffing, 280, *326*

Cornbread Dressing, 276, *325*

Succotash, Edamame, 260

Sugar, Flower, 64

Summer squash. See Zucchini

Sushi Cake, 291–92, *316*

Sweet Potato(es)

Best Whipped, with Caramelized Apples, 275, *327*

Latkes, 301

Maple-Glazed, 277

Pie, Cecilia's, 281

Rolls, 280–81, *327*

Savory Twice-Baked, 278–79, *327*

Spicy, with Lime, 279, *327*

Swiss Chard

with Olives, 147

Winter Greens and Bacon, 40

Swiss cheese

Baked Stuffed Sweet Onions, 105

Cheese Fondue, 289

Croque Madame (var.), 256, *320*

Croque Monsieur, 256, *320*

Gougères, 35

Potato Rösti, 299

Syrup, Berry, 213

Syrup, Hazelnut Simple, 304

Syrup, Simple, 151

Syrup, Simple Sorbet, 264

T

Tabbouleh, Toasted Couscous, 127–28, *166*

Taco Salad, 210, *235*

Tacos, Beer-Battered Cod in, 189

Tacos, Grilled Mahimahi in, 190

Taleggio, Sautéed Mushroom, and Prosciutto Panini, 259

Tangerines, Honey, and Kumquats with Shaved Celery and Walnuts, 292

Tapenade, Two-Olive, Linguine with, 144–45, *166*

Tarragon, Braised Chicken, 255

Tart, Brie and Apple Custard, 94

Tart Shells

French Flag Berry Pâte Sucrée, 195

Pâte Brisée, 94

Pâte Sucrée, 111

Tarts, dessert

Chocolate Caramel Tart, 41, *88*

French Flag Berry Tarts, 194–95, *243*

Grapefruit Tart, 110, *175*

Grasshopper Tarts, 195–96, *248*

Peach Tartes Tatin, 62–63

Pithiviers, 133

Plum Galette, 223, *242*

Raspberry Tart, 133, *171*

Rice Pudding Tart with Blood Oranges, 63, *84*

Tarte Tatin, 134

Tea, Chai, with Soy Milk, 267

Tea, Pomegranate, 312

Tea Punch, Peach, 134

Tea sandwiches. See Sandwiches; Tea

Tennessee Pit Barbecue Sauce, 189

Thyme-Roasted Figs over Brioche Pain Perdu, 64, *67*

Tiramisu Cups, 200

Toast Points, 181, *231*

Tofu

and Kale, Miso Soup with, 96, *166*

Sesame-Marinated, with Vegetables, 259–60

Spinach, and Carrots, Miso Soup with, 254

Tomatillo, Roasted, and Cilantro Pesto, Mexican Fiesta Soup with, 120

Tomatillo Soup, Spicy Cold, 183, *232*

Tomato(es)

Arugula and Cannellini Salad with Olive Vinaigrette, 141

and Bean Salad with Garlic-Chive Blossoms, 57

Bruschetta, and Ricotta, 208, *230*

Cherry, Roasted, Baked Buffalo Mozzarella, and Eggplant, 55, *75*

Chopped, Salad with Toasted Garlic, 212

Chopped-, and Shrimp Salad,
Chilled, with Crisp Garlic Croutons,
185, *235*
and Corn Salad, 185
Crostini, 217
Essence and Timbales of Pressed
Tomatoes, 55–56
and Fennel, Braised Lamb Shanks
with, 122–23
Green, Pickled, 261
Ice, 184
and Mango Salsa, 126
Mexican Fiesta Soup with Roasted
Tomatillo and Cilantro Pesto, 120
Minestrone, 209
Passato, 214
a Pezzetti, 214
Pico de Gallo, 204
Pizza, 211, *237*
Plum, Roasted, 262, *328*
Potato, and Zucchini Gratin, 222
Rigatoni and Meatballs, 211, *236*
Roasted, 257
Roasted, Provençal, 192
Rolled Omelets with Ratatouille
Filling, 207, *225*, *226*
Salad, Garden, 141
Sorbet, 56
Stuffed Eggplant, 212, *230*
Torte
Chocolate Hazelnut, 303–4
Dobos, 304
Linzer, 306
Poppy-Seed, 308
Three-Nut, 309
Trifle, Lemon and Cherry, 196, *245*
Trout, Grilled, with Oregano, 123, *163*
Truffles
Candy Cane, 310
Champagne, 311
Chocolate, 49
Classic, 310
Coconut, 311
Grand Marnier, 311
Hazelnut, 311
Mocha, 311

Orange-Ginger, 311
Praline, 312
Sambuca, 312
Turkey
Burgers, Herbed, 211
Herb-Roasted, with Pan Gravy,
273–74, *326*
Sausage, Black-Eyed Peas with
Escarole, Potatoes, and, 38, *80*
Smoked, Black Bean, and Avocado
Tea Sandwiches, Southwest, 104–5,
160-61
Taco Salad, 210, *235*
Turnip Greens, 193
Turnips, Baby, and Cipollini Onions,
Glazed, 106

V

Vanilla
Applesauce, 301
Crêpes, 30, *65-66*
Mascarpone, 263
Pudding, 50, *85*
Sheet Cake, 131
Veal Scallopini Milanese, 61, *78*
Vegetable(s). See also specific
vegetables
Grated, with Herb Cream Cheese Tea
Sandwiches, 102, *160-61*
Minestrone, 209
Pistou Soup, 54–55, *75*
Sesame-Marinated Tofu with, 259–60
Stuffing, 280, *326*
Winter, Chicken Stew, 24
Vinaigrette
Citrus-Cumin, 98
Cucumber, 186
Honey-Mustard, 210
Olive, Arugula and Cannellini Salad
with, 141
Orange, and Toasted Sesame Seeds,
Greens with, 19, *76-77*
Spicy, 97
Vol-au-Vents, 121

W

Walnut(s)
-Arugula Pesto, Spinach Linguine
with, 275, *318*
and Brie Cake, 289, *316*
Chicken Strips with Pomegranate
Sauce, 296
and Honey, Yogurt Drizzled with, 285
Honey Tangerines and Kumquats with
Shaved Celery and, 292
and Roasted Red Pepper Dip, 272
Shortbread, 113–14
Three-Nut Torte, 309
Toasted, Walnut Oil, and Green
Beans, Green Salad with, 272, *318*
Wasabi Sauce, 292
Watermelon
Gazpacho, 183–84, *232*
and Raspberry Salad, 223
Rind, Pickled, 286
Shaved Cucumber, and Fennel
Salad, 188
Whipped Cream, Bourbon, 282
Whipped Cream, Fresh-Raspberry
Gelatin and, 130
Whiskey Sours, Fresh, 201–2

Y

Yam Fries, Roasted, Boneless Pork
Chops and, 58, *78*
Yogurt
-Basil Soup with Tomato Ice, 184
Blueberry Breakfast Shake, 114, *155*
Dipping Sauce, 280
Drizzled with Honey and Walnuts, 285
Pie, 201, *245*
Spiced Rose Lassi, 50

Z

Zest, Candied Lemon, 197
Zucchini
Pine Nuts, and Lemon Zest, Farro
Salad with, 186–87, *234*
Potato, and Tomato Gratin, 222
Roasted, 263
Yellow-Pepper Risotto with Shrimp
and, 221, *240*

Photography Credits

SANG AN *pages 80 (bottom left), 85, 228, 232, 233, 238 (bottom left, bottom right), 326, 332 (top right, bottom left)*

QUENTIN BACON *pages 70 (bottom right), 235 (top right, bottom right), 239, 318 (top left, top right), 325, 333*

JAMES BAIGRIE *pages 157, 168, 241, 242, 246, 332 (top left)*

CHRISTOPHER BAKER *page 163 (top right)*

CHUCK BAKER *page 229*

EARL CARTER *pages 68, 69, 70 (top left, top right), 80 (top left, bottom right), 87, 230 (top left, bottom left), 240, 247, 318 (bottom left, bottom right), 323, 336*

BEATRIZ DA COSTA *pages 76, 77, 319*

REED DAVIS *page 84*

ROB FIOCCA *page 171 (bottom left)*

FORMULA Z/S *pages 156, 163 (bottom left), 166 (top right), 169*

DANA GALLAGHER *pages 67, 72, 320, 321, 327, 328*

GENTL & HYERS *pages 172-175, 231, 243-245, 248*

HANS GISSINGER *pages 171 (top right), 176*

LISA HUBBARD *pages 65, 66, 78 (top left), 79, 249*

RICHARD GERHARD JUNG *pages 70 (bottom left), 71, 82 (bottom left), 155, 158, 164, 166 (bottom right)*

VANESSA LENZ *pages 11, 89, 177*

DAVID LOFTUS *pages 74, 75, 86*

JONATHAN LOVEKIN *page 171 (top left, bottom right)*

ERICKA MCCONNELL *page 165*

MAURA MCEVOY *pages 332 (bottom right), 335*

ALISON MIKSCH *pages 153, 154*

AMY NEUNSINGER *pages 225-227*

VICTORIA PEARSON *pages 159, 162, 163 (top left, bottom right), 166 (bottom left)*

MARIA ROBLEDO *pages 82 (top left, top right, bottom right), 83, 88, 230 (top right, bottom right), 236, 237, 313, 317, 322, 334*

CHARLES SCHILLER *pages 73, 78 (top right, bottom left, bottom right), 80 (top right), 81, 160, 161, 170*

MIKKEL VANG *page 238 (top left, top right)*

LISA CHARLES WATSON *page 166 (top left)*

ANNA WILLIAMS *pages 167, 234, 235 (top left, bottom left), 314-316, 324, 329-331*

FRONT COVER EARL CARTER

BACK COVER
EARL CARTER *(top right, bottom right)*
VICTORIA PEARSON *(top left)*
ANNA WILLIAMS *(bottom left)*

CONVERSION CHART *Equivalent Imperial and Metric Measurements*

American cooks use standard containers, the 8-ounce cup and a tablespoon that takes exactly 16 level fillings to fill that cup level. Measuring by cup makes it very difficult to give weight equivalents, as a cup of densely packed butter will weigh considerably more than a cup of flour. The easiest way, therefore, to deal with cup measurements in recipes is to take the amount by volume rather than by weight. Thus the equation reads: 1 cup = 225 ml = 8 fl. oz.; ½ cup = 110 ml = 4 fl. oz. It is possible to buy a set of American cup measures in major stores around the world. In the States, butter is often measured in sticks. One stick is the equivalent of 8 tablespoons. One tablespoon of butter is therefore the equivalent to ½ ounce/15 grams.

SOLID MEASURES

U.S./IMPERIAL MEASURES		METRIC MEASURES	
ounces	pounds	grams	kilos
1		28	
2		56	
3½		100	
4	¼	112	
5		140	
6		168	
8	½	225	
9		150	¼
12	¾	340	
16	1	450	
18		500	½
20	1¼	560	
24	1½	675	
27		750	¾
28	1¾	780	
32	2	900	
36	2¼	1000	1
40	2½	1100	
48	3	1350	
54		1500	1½
64	4	1800	
72	4½	2000	2

LIQUID MEASURES

FLUID OUNCES	U.S.	IMPERIAL	MILLILITERS
	1 teaspoon	1 teaspoon	5
¼	2 teaspoons	1 dessert spoon	7
½	1 tablespoon	1 tablespoon	15
1	2 tablespoons	2 tablespoons	28
2	¼ cup	4 tablespoons	56
4	½ cup or ¼ pint		110
5		¼ pint or 1 gill	140
6	¾ cup		170
8	1 cup or ½ pint		225
9			250, ¼ liter
10	1¼ cups	½ pint	280
12	1½ cups	¾ pint	340
15	¾ pint		420
16	2 cups or 1 pint		450
18	2¼ cups		500, ½ liter
20	2½ cups	1 pint	560
24	3 cups or 1½ pints		675
25		1¼ pints	700
27	3½ cups		750, ¾ liter
30	3¾ cups	1½ pints	840
32	4 cups or 2 pints or 1 quart		900

OVEN TEMPERATURE EQUIVALENTS

FAHRENHEIT	CELSIUS	GAS MARK	DESCRIPTION
225	110	¼	cool
250	130	½	
275	140	1	very slow
300	150	2	
325	170	3	slow
350	180	4	moderate
375	190	5	
400	200	6	moderately hot
425	220	7	fairly hot
450	230	8	hot
475	240	9	very hot
500	250	10	extremely hot

EQUIVALENTS FOR INGREDIENTS

all-purpose flour	plain flour
arugula	rocket
buttermilk	ordinary milk
confectioners' sugar	icing sugar
cornstarch	cornflour
eggplant	aubergine
granulated sugar	caster sugar
half-and-half	12% fat milk
heavy cream	double cream
light cream	single cream
lima beans	broad beans
scallion	spring onion
squash	courgettes or marrow
unbleached flour	strong, white flour
zest	rind
zucchini	courgettes

LINEAR AND AREA MEASURES

1 inch	2.54 centimeters